Holism and the Cultivation of Excellence in Sports and Performance

Skillful Striving

Skillful Striving is a multi-methodological and cross-cultural examination of how we flourish holistically through performative endeavors, e.g., sports, martial, and performing arts. Relying primarily on sport philosophy, value theory, phenomenology, philosophy of mind, pragmatism, and East Asian philosophies (Japanese and Chinese), it espouses thick holism. Concerned with an integrative *bodymind* gradually achieved through performance that aims at excellence, the process of self-cultivation proper of thick holism relies on an ecologically rich epistemic landscape where skills are coupled to virtues in pragmatic contexts. Ultimately, this process results in admirable performances and exemplary character. Japanese *dō* (practices of self-cultivation) are prominent modes and models of such flourishing. A holistic and radically enactive approach that advances contentless capacities in lieu of representations transparently accounts for the kind of action that characterizes such expert performances. Importantly, these performer-centered endeavors unfold within communities that foster the cultivation of our abilities as lifelong quests for human excellence. Each chapter can be read independently but still forms part of a continuous argumentative and narrative thread. This book was previously published as a special issue of *Sport, Ethics and Philosophy*.

Jesús Ilundáin-Agurruza is Professor and Chair of the Department of Philosophy at Linfield College, USA. In 2013–2015, he served as the President of the International Association for the Philosophy of Sport (IAPS). His research and publications focus on and integrate sport philosophy, East Asian philosophy (especially Japanese), phenomenology, and philosophy of mind. He has also edited (with Mike Austin) *Cycling—Philosophy for Everyone: A Philosophical Tour de Force* (2010).

Ethics and Sport

Edited by
Mike McNamee, *University of Wales Swansea, UK*
Jim Parry, *University of Leeds, UK*

The Ethics and Sport series aims to encourage critical reflection on the practice of sport, and to stimulate professional evaluation and development. Each volume explores new work relating to philosophical ethics and the social and cultural study of ethical issues. Each is different in scope, appeal, focus, and treatment, but a balance is sought between local and international focus, perennial and contemporary issues, level of audience, teaching and research application, and variety of practical concerns.

Sport and Art
An essay in the hermeneutics of sport
Andrew Edgar

Dispute Resolution in Sport
Athletes, law and arbitration
David McArdle

Philosophy and the Martial Arts
Engagement
Edited by Graham Priest and Damon Young

Talent Development, Existential Philosophy and Sport
On becoming an elite athlete
Kenneth Aggerholm

On Sport and the Philosophy of Sport
A Wittgensteinian approach
Graham McFee

Phenomenology and Pedagogy in Physical Education
Øyvind Førland Standal

Gender Testing in Sport
Ethics, cases and controversies
Edited by Sandy Montañola and Aurélie Olivesi

Holism and the Cultivation of Excellence in Sports and Performance
Skillful striving
Jesús Ilundáin-Agurruza

Holism and the Cultivation of Excellence in Sports and Performance

Skillful striving

Jesús Ilundáin-Agurruza

LONDON AND NEW YORK

First published 2016
by Routledge
2 Park Square, Milton Park, Abingdon, Oxon, OX14 4RN, UK

and by Routledge
711 Third Avenue, New York, NY 10017, USA

Routledge is an imprint of the Taylor & Francis Group, an informa business

© 2016 Taylor & Francis

All rights reserved. No part of this book may be reprinted or reproduced or utilised in any form or by any electronic, mechanical, or other means, now known or hereafter invented, including photocopying and recording, or in any information storage or retrieval system, without permission in writing from the publishers.

Trademark notice: Product or corporate names may be trademarks or registered trademarks, and are used only for identification and explanation without intent to infringe.

British Library Cataloguing in Publication Data
A catalogue record for this book is available from the British Library

ISBN 13: 978-1-138-67162-1

Typeset in MyriadPro
by diacriTech, Chennai

Publisher's Note
The publisher accepts responsibility for any inconsistencies that may have arisen during the conversion of this book from journal articles to book chapters, namely the possible inclusion of journal terminology.

Disclaimer
Every effort has been made to contact copyright holders for their permission to reprint material in this book. The publishers would be grateful to hear from any copyright holder who is not here acknowledged and will undertake to rectify any errors or omissions in future editions of this book.

Contents

Citation Information	vii
Preface	ix
Introduction—Holism and the Cultivation of Excellence in Sports and Performance: Skillful Striving	1

SECTION I
Holism and the Quest for Excellence

1. Nothing New Under the Sun: Holism and the Pursuit of Excellence	9

SECTION II
Pragmatic Dark Horses: Dewey, James, Ortega y Gasset, and Zhuanzgi

2. William James—Pragmatic Pioneer	37
3. John Dewey—Experiential Maverick	49
4. José Ortega y Gasset: Exuberant Steed	63
5. Zhuangzi—Playful wanderer	93

SECTION III
Holistic Bridges: The Mind Sciences, Phenomenology, and Our Skills

6. Waking Up From the Cognitivist Dream—the Computational View of the Mind and High Performance	122
7. Riding the Wind—Consummate Performance, Phenomenology, and Skillful Fluency	152
8. Fractured Action—Choking in Sport and its Lessons for Excellence	198

CONTENTS

SECTION IV
East and West Teamwork: A Comparative Analysis of Skillful Performance

9. Reflections on a Katana—The Japanese Pursuit of
    Performative Mastery   233

10. Everything Mysterious Under the Moon—Social Practices
    and Situated Holism   281

    Epilogue   345

    Appendix—Much Ado About Nothing   351

    Index   363

Citation Information

The following chapters were originally published in *Sport, Ethics and Philosophy*, volume 8, issue 3 (August 2014). When citing this material, please use the original page numbering for each article, as follows:

Preface
Jesús Ilundáin-Agurruza
Sport, Ethics and Philosophy, volume 8, issue 3 (August 2014) pp. 221–222

Introduction
Holism and the Cultivation of Excellence in Sports and Performance: Skillful Striving
Jesús Ilundáin-Agurruza
Sport, Ethics and Philosophy, volume 8, issue 3 (August 2014) pp. 223–229

Chapter 1
Nothing New Under the Sun: Holism and the Pursuit of Excellence
Jesús Ilundáin-Agurruza
Sport, Ethics and Philosophy, volume 8, issue 3 (August 2014) pp. 230–257

Chapter 2
William James—Pragmatic Pioneer
Jesús Ilundáin-Agurruza
Sport, Ethics and Philosophy, volume 8, issue 3 (August 2014) pp. 258–270

Chapter 3
John Dewey—Experiential Maverick
Jesús Ilundáin-Agurruza
Sport, Ethics and Philosophy, volume 8, issue 3 (August 2014) pp. 271–284

Chapter 4
José Ortega y Gasset: Exuberant Steed
Jesús Ilundáin-Agurruza
Sport, Ethics and Philosophy, volume 8, issue 3 (August 2014), pp. 285–314

Chapter 5
Zhuangzi—Playful wanderer
Jesús Ilundáin-Agurruza
Sport, Ethics and Philosophy, volume 8, issue 3 (August 2014) pp. 315–342

CITATION INFORMATION

The following chapters were originally published in *Sport, Ethics and Philosophy*, volume 8, issue 4 (December 2014). When citing this material, please use the original page numbering for each article, as follows:

Chapter 6
Waking Up From the Cognitivist Dream—the Computational View of the Mind and High Performance
Jesús Ilundáin-Agurruza
Sport, Ethics and Philosophy, volume 8, issue 4 (December 2014) pp. 344–373

Chapter 7
Riding the Wind—Consummate Performance, Phenomenology, and Skillful Fluency
Jesús Ilundáin-Agurruza
Sport, Ethics and Philosophy, volume 8, issue 4 (December 2014) pp. 374–419

Chapter 8
Fractured Action—Choking in Sport and its Lessons for Excellence
Jesús Ilundáin-Agurruza
Sport, Ethics and Philosophy, volume 8, issue 4 (December 2014) pp. 420–453

Chapter 9
Reflections on a Katana—The Japanese Pursuit of Performative Mastery
Jesús Ilundáin-Agurruza
Sport, Ethics and Philosophy, volume 8, issue 4 (December 2014) pp. 455–502

Chapter 10
Everything Mysterious Under the Moon—Social Practices and Situated Holism
Jesús Ilundáin-Agurruza
Sport, Ethics and Philosophy, volume 8, issue 4 (December 2014) pp. 503–566

Appendix
Much Ado About Nothing
Jesús Ilundáin-Agurruza
Sport, Ethics and Philosophy, volume 8, issue 4 (December 2014) pp. 573–584

For any permission-related enquiries please visit:
http://www.tandfonline.com/page/help/permissions

HOLISM AND THE CULTIVATION OF EXCELLENCE IN SPORTS AND PERFORMANCE: SKILLFUL STRIVING

Jesús Ilundáin-Agurruza

Skillful Striving *investigates the nature of the cultivation of excellence, the conditions that render it possible, and its potential for inspiration from the perspective of enactive wisdom—one that by enacting lays down a way or path. Performative endeavors whose* telos *centrally involves physical performance—sports, martial and performing arts, crafts-—are the focus of this inquiry. These are privileged ways for a holistic cultivation of our talents and limitations. The main philosophical thrust can be summarized as a "thick holism" where naturalism and normativity combine.* Skillful Striving *is concerned with an integrative* bodymind *and its ways of knowing and experiencing that issue forth from active engagements with the world, and whose goal is defined by certain standards of qualitative performance that ultimately aim at excellence. The process of cultivation relies on a rich epistemic landscape where skills are coupled to virtues in pragmatic contexts. These contexts are ecologically broad in the sense that our environment, broadly construed, constitutes these. Ultimately, this process results in admirable performances by, and exemplary character for, the enactors. Endowed with unique gifts, it is argued that they should become exemplary in the full sense of their lives. Laudable character is built on discipline, responsibility, and a social framework that provides personal paradigms and standards of excellence. A key element is that this cultivation happens in and through our moving and acting as holistic, integrative bodyminds. Eastern ways or paths, and especially Japanese* do, *are modes of self-cultivation that are prominent in this regard. They enable working within the framework of this* bodymind *where its unity is gradually achieved through performance. Importantly for this study, these active endeavors are performer-centered yet deeply communitarian practices. In the end,* Skillful Striving *is an exploration of how we may flourish as members of practice communities that encourage open, responsible exploration, and the cultivation of our abilities as lifelong quests for human excellence.*

Introduction

In the elder days of Art
Builders wrought with the greatest care
Each minute and unseen part;
For the gods see everywhere. Longfellow[1]—(1849)

Longfellow's words capture an ethos that embodies unwavering commitment to excellence, even if no one might possibly notice—except perhaps the unforgiving gods of one's conscience. They speak of persons who strive not simply to do their best, but to continually raise the bar. They become individuals whose mastery within a practice makes them admirable, even exemplary. Their superb performances and wise judgment establish them as masters we rightly refer to as models of excellence. Moreover, these enactors—persons who craft new ways of being and doing—are inspiring paragons of what may be possible on a deeper existential sense that plays a key role in human communities. *Skillful Striving* investigates the nature of this cultivation of excellence, the conditions that render it possible, and its potential for inspiration from the perspective of enactive wisdom—one that by enacting lays down a way or path. Performative endeavors whose *telos* centrally involves physical performance—sports, martial and performing arts, crafts––are privileged ways for a holistic cultivation of our talents *and* limitations.

This essay is written in the sense of Montaigne's *essayer*: writing to test one's ideas on a topic. Its main philosophical thrust can be summarized as a 'thick holism' in pursuit of a normative 'gnoseology'; a term more familiar to continental philosophers.[2] Normative gnoseology is concerned with an integrative *bodymind* and its ways of knowing and experiencing that issue forth from active engagements with the world, and whose goal is defined by certain standards of qualitative performance that ultimately aim at excellence. This approach is underpinned by a broadly construed virtue theoretical account in two senses: in terms of the underlying normative framework, and also because it often seeks to find the sweet spot between competing philosophical accounts that attempt to explain our ways of knowing both ourselves and the world. In terms of our cognition, the approach set out here seeks gnostic wisdom, rather than epistemological intelligence. The former keeps close to its heart the revelatory; the latter, as engaged in modern philosophical discourse, is concerned with rational ways, scientific know-that, and truth-functionality (Peters 1968). Gnostic truths are resonantly felt in our bodymind, they are holistic, integrating reason, emotion, movement (as cognitive, meaningful, and expressive), sociohistorical facets, and the larger environment. *Phronesis*, sound and practical judgment, lies behind it. And behind this lies an existential soteriology, a way to salvation (understood here as an engaged and meaningful life in *this* world). This richer epistemic landscape brings it closer to *animate* wisdom: one accrued through our peripatetic, moving ways. It denotes a broader palette of requisite skills coupled to virtues in pragmatic contexts. These contexts are ecologically extensive, in the sense that our environment, broadly construed, constitutes it.

Ultimately, this process results in admirable performances by, and exemplary character for, the enactors. Readers may already be thinking that this places the essay in supererogatory terrain; being an athlete, a dancer, or *aikidōka* need not entail becoming morally exemplary. And this is correct. Moreover, many a gifted performer, whether artist or athlete, has created a vicious character. Yet, claims for normative neutrality give an anemic version of our values. They impartially stick to the facts when they should also be reflexively normative (as this evaluative statement): those with unique gifts *should* become exemplary in the full sense of their lives. This will be argued overtly, but mostly implicitly, via a kaleidoscopic narrative that gradually insinuates its accruing case. Laudable character is built on discipline, responsibility, and a social framework that provides personal paradigms and standards of excellence. In the case of performance in the worlds of athletics, martial and performing arts, latent skills flourish and weaknesses can be made assets by nurturing intellectual, physical, emotional, and social abilities through disciplined movement, purposeful reflection, and emotional control. A key element is that this cultivation happens in and through our moving and acting as holistic, integrative bodyminds. Eastern ways or paths, and especially Japanese *dō*, are modes of self-cultivation that are prominent in this regard. They enable working within the framework of this *bodymind,* where its unity is gradually achieved through performance. Importantly for this study, these active endeavors are performer-centered yet deeply communitarian practices. Truly, the activities under consideration are best considered from the perspective of practitioners with degrees of refinement and expertise within a shared social background.

Methodologically, the essay is pragmatic through and through, relying on conceptual analysis, phenomenology, empirical evidence—whether scientific or historical— and pragmatism itself. In terms of sources, and specifically figures of renown that have written on many of the topics covered (e.g. Aristotle, Heidegger, Husserl, Merleau-Ponty), their views deeply inform this essay, but are not often directly cited. One of the goals of this project is to bring to the fore the work of other thinkers, their equal in terms of originality and depth, but who are not part of the orthodox philosophical discourse (whether in sport philosophy or philosophy generally), such as Ortega y Gasset (Ortega hereafter in this work), Zhuangzi, and in the case of James and Dewey, ideas of theirs not often referenced. Accordingly, the length of treatment of each author is proportional to their 'dark horse' status within the field; the less the attention paid by mainstream views, the longer the discussion and examination. In the case of contemporary philosophy and philosophers, the modus operandi adopted is analogous to this accentuation. Instead of extensively relying on mainstream intellectuals, for instance, Hubert Dreyfus on expertise, other thinkers who ably incorporate and critique his views are given center stage, e.g. the phenomenologist Shaun Gallagher or, in the case of Husserl, Maxine Sheets-Johnstone. These 'alternative' sources are fitted into the rich framework that contemporary sport philosophy affords. Certain themes arise in connection with a particular philosopher, for example, William James on self-cultivation and perfection, and then are considered again from other less well-known perspectives and with different methodologies, such as Ortega and Zhuangzi. One thread that unites these and other primary sources, many from the ranks of contemporary sport philosophy, is that they are philosophers who lead by example, with an existential authenticity where life and work interweave, as their words and the context show. Pontification from the sidelines will not do for this kind of enterprise. Authority is earned at the expense of a life lived in active effort at the frontlines. Observing life as spectators is requisite to obtaining a perspective, but when performance is the subject, performers who reflectively engage their experience shine.

Four sections and ten chapters comprise this holistic, radically enactive *bodymind* thesis and its role in the cultivation of performing excellence.

Section one addresses questions such as: How are performative endeavors— sports, martial and performing arts—suited to the development of human excellence? How should we understand holism in this context? What are skills, and how do they connect with the normative and excellence? *Nothing New Under the Sun: Holism and the Pursuit of Excellence,* the first essay, lays out the conceptual map, briefly discussing the notion of performance and relevance of sports, martial and performing arts, and crafts. Presently referred to as active pursuits or performative endeavors, these provide a 'real life' alternative and a complementary paradigm to purely intellectual cogitations or laboratory data and hypotheses. It proceeds to explain the thick holism that scaffolds this project, and argues for the primacy of the performer's perspective and experience over that of the spectator's. It closes with a discussion of excellence, perfectionism, and skills, where normativity arises from a naturalistic stance.

The second section relies on pragmatic thinkers and incorporates what I call 'philosophical dark horses': thinkers with much to contribute but often ignored by modern academia. This section comprises four essays and further addresses two questions: What can we learn about self-cultivation from these dark horses? What is the best way to develop the requisite skills? It offers historical roots that inform thick holism and many of our ideas about self-cultivation and excellence.

Essay two, *William James—Pragmatic Pioneer,* discusses James' views concerning habit as a source of character building, looking at his very life as it intertwines with his intellectual views. It centers particularly on his psychology and philosophy of mind, and highlights the remarkably insightful role of James' ideas, especially his 'background,' or 'fringe of consciousness.' This phenomenologically validated phenomenon acts as functional bridge between reflective and conscious processes, and subpersonal or unconscious ones, and is incorporated at various key points over the length of *Skillful Striving.*

The third essay, *John Dewey—Experiential Maverick,* presents the pragmatist's views on habit and its crucial role in cultivating our talents as both limiting and enabling factor. The second section segues from his views on habit, and critically examines Deweyan ideas on self-cultivation and another recurrent theme, perfectionism. Finally, the inquiry turns to Dewey's deeply holistic commitments, which thoroughly inform this project. He coined the term *body-mind,* and stresses time and again throughout his works, firmly opposing both dualism and the already reductionist tendencies of his coetaneous science, the validity of the psychophysical, and the primacy of function over mechanism or even process. This leads to a discussion of his notion of 'continuity of experience,' which again, underscores the holistic theme of the monograph.

Essay four, *José Ortega y Gasset—Exuberant Steed,* offers an extended discussion of the Spaniard's views. It begins with an overview of his philosophy, particularly its relevance for sport philosophy. It then delves into Ortega's quest for an active, engaged, and reflective excellence that perfects our character. Hence, Ortega further hones perfectionism as a personal perfection where the effort's quality prevails over the result. Other salient themes are his vital philosophy, where sportspersons' superfluous effort stimulates grander existential endeavors, his integrative mind-body stance that extends into the environment, very amenable to Dewey's psychophysical unity and James's naturalistic stance, and his strong emphasis on the positive emotions as key to a virtuous life.

The fifth essay, *Zhuangzi—Playful Wanderer,* initiates the point of contact with Asian philosophy with a detailed exposition of the Chinese sage. First comes an exposition of basic concepts in Daoism and Zhuangzi's philosophy that are pertinent to the main themes of this inquiry. Subsequently, we explore a truly holistic model of skill development where the bodymind flourishes and form and function entwine. Analyzing the developmental growth from inferior to superior stages that mark achievement, the essay exhibits the ever-refining levels of expertise from virtuoso performances by cooks to the intellectual and emotional achievement of 'sages.' Moreover, his ideas are also fruitful in rethinking disability and disability sport, here seen as a manifestation of power.

Together, these dark horses comprise a formidable team that helps diagnose the genesis and development of excellences, bypass dualism with their bodymind (countering reductive views), and act as inspirational models. They set up the next section, devoted to contemporary work.

Section three intends to bridge the sciences of the mind with value theory. To put it briefly, it considers the question: 'How do we integrate the mind sciences with the normative?'. It supplements the normative discourse on excellence with empirical and theoretical new work in cognitive science, neuroscience, philosophy of mind, and skillful coping. Work by contemporary sport philosophers proves crucial in critiquing and developing an alternative. Three essays comprise this section.

Essay six, *Waking Up from the Cognitivist Dream: The Computational View of the Mind and High Performance*, develops the 'negative' or critical facet of the examination of skillfulness as it conducts a critique of traditional views on cognition. This is important because of the strong influence these notions have on both popular and academic views on skilled movement and its cultivation. It critically appraises cognitivist, representational, and reductionist views of mind, action, and movement. Besides inherent conceptual problems, these approaches prove inadequate for the explanation of the skillful deeds of elite performers and risk sportswomen and men. This leads to a second section on embodied cognition, which discusses salient conceptualizations from its burgeoning program, advances a phenomenologically responsive radical enactivism and sets up a subsequent challenge to two dogmatic tenets of skillful coping the literature relies on, 'mindless coping' and the 'automatization of skill'.

Riding the Wind: Consummate Performance, Phenomenology, and Skillful Fluency is the seventh essay. At length, it lays out the positive case to complement and fill in the space opened by the previous chapter's critique. The first section develops a phenomenology of skillful movement. Reframing the *bodymind* theme, it abandons ontology for description, and examines and describes the invariant structure of the skillful experience in terms of proprioceptive and kinesthetic dynamics central to active pursuits. These dynamics act as experiential doors toward superb performance. The second section presents the idea of 'exemplar execution' under the rubric of skillful fluency, discussing its normative facets, specifically, aesthetic and moral, which conflate under the Greek concept of *kalon*—the noble and beautiful deed. Normative valuations arise from our kinetic possibilities, the kind of movements we can do, which the rules of sports especially, and other practices exploit. Further, the limits and applications of said fluency are analyzed, and it is argued that the experience of masterly performers is qualitatively different from that of non-experts on account of better perceptual discrimination and enhanced kinesthetic and proprioceptive dynamics.

Closing this section, the eighth essay, *Fractured Action: Choking in Sport and its Lessons for Excellence* looks at the flip side of the skillful coin, failure. In particular, it takes up the enigmatic phenomenon of 'choking' in sport, which baffles critics because it concerns failure by those who *already* possess the requisite skills. It discusses and analyzes philosophical views as well as empirical research and theories from cognitive science and sport psychology, which are amended by way of a thorough holistic and ecological battery of arguments that stay close to the actual ways sportspersons and performers train, compete, and feel. 'Slumps,' 'choking patterns,' and 'choking' in team sports are considered next, while the closing section outlines a phenomenological model of the experience of 'choking,' and closes with some lessons applicable to the cultivation of excellence. A recent work of fiction, Chad Harbach's *The Art of Fielding: A Novel* helps give substance to the choking phenomenon. This chapter reinforces previous arguments and lays the ground to engage the ensuing analysis of Japanese practices of self-cultivation and philosophy.

Section Four looks beyond the West, into East Asia, specifically Japan, and expands its scope to consider the sociohistorical facet. It asks: What framework is best suited to cultivate the endorsed model of excellence? What connects the individual, the social context, and the ethos of excellence?

Essay nine, *Reflections on a Katana: Japanese Thought and the Pursuit of Mastery*, takes the enquiry to Japan, where *dō*—contemplative, active paths toward human excellence—integrate theory and practice and show an inspiring and refined way to cultivate human excellence. These practices focus on the experience of the performer, unlike the West's emphasis in both the arts and athletics on the audience and spectator. This means delving into the ideal of *shugyo*, the endeavor to excel in a lifelong commitment. Nishida Kitarō and contemporary interpreters conceptualize this philosophically, while Zen Buddhism, bushido, and *kenjutsu* (swordsmanship) manuals offer insights and concretely exemplify the process. In addition, the different ethos and philosophical underpinnings of sports and martial arts are contrasted, then pursuit of excellence lies a strong community-centered ethos that segues into the last chapter.

Everything Mysterious Under the Moon: Social Practices and Situated Holism, essay ten, voices the underlying condition that makes possible the personal growth that this project articulates: the fertile ground that practice-specific communities provide. This shows how these communities provide standards of excellence, the means to develop our skills, and social and material support. Flourishing is tied to a cooperative spirit and a shared body of knowledge and values. As the lessons from Japan take root, this chapter re-envisions the means/ends and process/results relations. A caring attitude of *attendance* (devotion of aesthetic temperament) properly accompanies this shift. The relevance of the geo-historical circumstances is sketched from a phenomenological perspective. In turn, situatedness and intersubjectivity come to the forefront, and a radically enactive analysis of the meaning of movement brings matters to where we began—only that, with a deeper understanding.

In the end, *Skillful Striving* is an exploration of how we may flourish as members of practice communities that encourage open exploration and the cultivation of our abilities as lifelong quests for human excellence.

NOTES

1. Longfellow, 1992, 108.
2. See Ilundáin-Agurruza (Forthcoming) for the theme of gnostic knowledge in the context of risk sports.

REFERENCES

ILUNDÁIN-AGURRUZA, J. Forthcoming. The eye of the hurricane: Philosophical reflections on risky sports, self-knowledge, and flourishing. *Journal of the Philosophy of Sport*.

LONGFELLOW, H.W. 1992. *Complete poetical works*. Boston, MA: Houghton.

PETERS, F.E. 1968. *Greek philosophical terms: A historical lexicon*. New York, NY: New York University Press.

SECTION I. HOLISM AND THE QUEST FOR EXCELLENCE

This section discusses the cultivation of excellence in the context of performative endeavors, those that denote activity and where movement plays a key role to how they accomplish their ends. It centers on and argues for the primacy of the experience of the performer rather than the observer. This leads to a consideration of 'thick holism', which advances a functional, flexible, and ecological model that emphasizes the continuities, fluidities, and connections that permeate our bodymind. It holds that we are richly complex, dynamic, animate organisms whose bodily, psychic, emotional, affective, sensory, kinetic, energetic, socio-historical, and environmental facets form a unity that is consummated to various degrees of competence and integration. Perfecting our skills achieves this integration, which is requisite for the kind of excellence proper of these endeavors. Our skills, which are practice-specific, are capacities to do proficiently certain actions in consonance with our endowments. Moreover, said skills are imbued with normative value (aesthetic *and* ethical). These ideas are argued for and developed more fully as applicable throughout *Skillful Striving*.

1—NOTHING NEW UNDER THE SUN: HOLISM AND THE PURSUIT OF EXCELLENCE

Jesús Ilundáin-Agurruza

What has been is what will be,
and what has been done is what
will be done;
and there is nothing new under the
sun

Ecclesiastes 1:9

We
keep on
adding sides
to the equation
conflating its complexion
with everything under the sun
until it is in fact everything under the sun

(Mutchslecner 2012)

The context for the citation from Ecclesiastes (1971) discusses nature, the coming and going of the sun, and our limited lifetimes in order to render poetically the feeling of *plus ça change plus c'est la même chose*, the more things change, the more they remain the same. Even if all is the same, our perspective on things can change, including the received wisdom of that very view. We can bring new ways of looking at the old. One advantage of our finite lives is that we can only experience so much. For us, there is always something new under the sun, some new side we can add to the equation. Which adds up to a whole, everything under the sun.

Holism is not new either. It has been around in one way or another far too long to surprise anyone. It is also not very common a topic these days among philosophers. To many, it smacks of the esoteric. And not only because phonetically it may be much too close to holier than thou attitudes. Its ontological and conceptual contours are too vague and fluid for those who prefer their metaphysics clear and demarcated, and their concepts exact. But as James, Dewey, and the rest of philosophers with holistic temperaments show here, we can espouse holism and also have a robust metaphysics and precise conceptualizations.

As the words begin to flow, three 'foundational' tenets by way of caveats to keep on the fringe of our attention ensue. One, this inquiry is about excellence, where the *quality* of the movement is central. Excellence here is meant in the customary but rich sense of Aristotle's aretē, and which connotes not just excellence, virtue, but also skill honed through disciplined effort.[1] The qualitative aspect refers to how the movement *feels* in itself, its different kinesthetic tonalities and dynamics (see *Riding the Wind*). This segues into the *inherent* normativity to such discriminations or valuations: some movements feel better than others; some are superior and excellent, while others are, well, inferior and subpar. We use this to gage the intensity and kind of effort, and when coupled to standards and rules within a practice, say fencing, to determine its athletic, aesthetic, and ethical worth. Kinesthetic feel and normative judgment are but two sides of the same coin even as each side bears different icons and different meanings. Two, function takes primacy over mechanism (see *John Dewey—Experiential Maverick*); process and result, means and ends are complex and 'bidirectional'. The crucial 'thing' to avoid is the reification of functions we perform and their qualitative dynamics, as is wont of much work in the mind sciences. These often turn the fluid continuities of our functions into ontologically distinct substances, into things (see *Waking Up from the Cognitivist Dream*). When it comes to sports and active endeavors, it is not a matter of favoring results over process or ends before means. Rather, it is a matter of embracing both, the trick being in making this conceptually feasible (see *Everything Mysterious Under the Moon*). Three, writes phenomenologist Gallagher, 'we understand our own actions on the highest pragmatic level possible. [We] tend to understand [our] actions at just that pragmatic, intentional (goal oriented) level, ignoring possible subpersonal or lower level descriptions, and also ignoring ideational or mentalistic interpretations' (2005, 229). Even if this describes how we actually come to make sense of our actions, it can also do double duty as a principle to keep in mind when evaluating issues, particularly empirical evidence from the mind sciences to avert those reifying tendencies or the ideation of disembodied entities.

The first section discusses the notion of active pursuits or performative endeavors, and their role in the cultivation of excellence. It also argues for the primacy of the performer's perspective and experience over that of the spectator as it compares art and sport. Section two explains holism, which scaffolds the project. The third section examines skills and excellence, and discusses how skills are normative.

1. Performative Endeavors and the Performer's Perspective

Sports, martial and performing arts, and crafts constitute what here is referred to as performative endeavors, active pursuits or practices, and similar locutions that denote *activity*. In particular, these are activities that require us to *move*. Movement here implies intentionality at some point in the motion (distinguishing it from reflex limb movements). Surely, movement is common to them all and they pursue excellence, but is this sufficient to group and intend to study them together? Indeed, we can find relevant similarities and marked differences among these endeavors. The latter advise against such a grouping. They all have very different goals and methods of achieving this. Crafts are the outlier. They create or produce actual objects, compared to performers' dancing, acting, singing, or playing,[2] and particularly the athlete's performance. As five-time Tour de France winner Miguel Induráin ruefully said, whereas a farmer reaps his harvest, at the end of the day, after going up and down mountain after mountain, what did he have to show for all his efforts?[3]

Ortega's revaluation of sport's gratuitousness would go a long way to assuage these concerns (see *José Ortega y Gasset—Exuberant Philosophical Steed*). Crafts such as woodworking or swordsmithing either seek to develop new techniques or to emulate

HOLISM AND THE CULTIVATION OF EXCELLENCE IN SPORTS AND PERFORMANCE

past masters as they attempt to recreate forgotten techniques. There are also differences between sport and the performing arts. Edgar (2013) formulates an interesting difference, namely that 'failure in sport is of a different order to that of performance art' (3). Whereas in the case of art, if unsuccessful, the artist merely turns out a spoiled artwork (133), when an athlete fails, the competition is not suspended, e.g. a runner's fall does not make it less of a race. He discusses the ambiguous case of Philippe Petit's 1874 high-wire act across the twin towers: if we suppose a failed attempt, this does not invalidate its status as art, but as sport, he would have failed much like a mountaineer can fail to summit a peak. Edgar revisits this again in the context of modernist aesthetics and Kant's purposiveness without a purpose (which ties to Induráin and Ortega), stating that, 'in sport, unlike any other practices, vulnerability to defeat is unavoidable.' (2013, 132) There are no guarantees in sport, much less in elite sport, where degrading abilities over time ensure failure at some point (similar ideas resonate throughout this project). Moreover, dance, theater, and music focus on exploring movement itself, a particular character's personality, or our vocal and instrumental abilities, respectively. Martial arts' relation to sport is more complex, and the full treatment is left for *Reflections on a Katana*. Suffice it mention that sports paradigmatically focus on results, winning, and testing one's athletic abilities, whereas *traditional* martial arts choose process and quality of the moves themselves. However, turning the matter inside out, and echoing Ortega's view of the sportsman as heir to the warrior, today, risk sports bring an element of danger missing from traditional martial arts.[4] This is related to Edgar's point insofar as the lack of guarantees in risk sports means not just losing a contest and thereby metaphorically facing death, but quite concretely beholding a terminal encounter with the grim reaper. In spite of these differences (for brevity's sake these suffice), much of the subsequent analysis *does* apply across all these practices in very meaningful ways. When there are pertinent differences, these will be pointed out, but *ceteris paribus*, what goes for sport applies to the rest of performative endeavors.

Accordingly, *all* these activities nurture excellence, abilities, and character by way of cultivated movement. In the best cases, they strive for perfected movement; they are a skillful striving. As such, they are exemplary ways to delve into this cultivation process that requires endless dedication and refinement. Additionally, they require a creative modus operandi and the exercise of skill to handle their inherently practical challenges. They are privileged ways of pursuing excellence with much to offer across the full philosophical spectrum, aesthetically, epistemologically, ethically, existentially, and ontologically.

To begin with, they are simply a source of joy—even when suffering is part of the bargain whether in training, competition, or practice. As sportspeople, musicians, dancers, martial artists know, there is a sheer enjoyment that accompanies these, which now is often theorized in terms of flow (Csikszentmihalyi 2008). There is joy, perceived effortlessness, a distorted sense of time when we find our bodymind in complete absorption in the task. (An absorption that is anything but mindless, see essay *Riding the Wind*). But if there is flow, there is also pain. Which is not necessarily bad. Sportspeople in particular know the value of a good hurt. In fact, it is this very suffering that brings a number of benefits.

Similar to how suffering in the existential sense was a source of insight for Dostoevsky, in sport and active endeavors, it gives us the possibility for self-knowledge as it also discloses the world to us in unforeseen ways. Sport philosopher Rich Lally, citing runner and author George Sheehan, writes:

> On those early weekend mornings we runners, 'are as it were, introduced into a world beyond this world which is nevertheless the deeper reality of the world in which we live in our ordinary experience. We are carried out beyond ourselves to find ourselves.' It is our practice of running, and the suffering we welcome on those mornings, that makes this possible. These two components are vital to the cultivating process undergone by the athlete. Each is also a tenet of pragmatism and needs further explication within a philosophy of sport. (2012, 196)

Certain things we learn about ourselves, that lie at the very core of our being, can only be revealed through committed and engaged action. As Lally points out, it is the practice of running itself and the suffering that make possible that carrying beyond ourselves to find ourselves. Self-knowledge already entails there is a non-self against which we define the self. But even as we draw the difference, we come to realize that there is no sharp line or solid border. Rather, it is a porous, fluid, and dynamic process where runner, running, and trail co-create each other (much as art is created also). The tendency is to look for differences and divisions that separate us into a seemingly autonomous entity where our skin marks and embodies the metaphysical frontier. We know better; our skin, so vulnerable, is but a permeable membrane in constant exchange with 'the outside'; we are colonized by innumerable bacteria, many in our stomach and intestinal tract that strongly influence our hunger patterns, even our cravings for chocolate; our breathing is perhaps our most intimate, essential, and taken-for-granted connection to the world. The world and us are part of a larger whole. Of course, this line of reasoning does not intend to do away with discrimination and distinction. In fact, it is because of these that we can raise as a bas-relief from the sea of moments those events, experiences, and phenomena that matter to us. But we need to be reminded sometimes that such differences can only happen against a background that contains them. This larger background begs exploration.

Exploring this world in wonder is an existential duty. It also entails risks. Freedom is not free; the toll is paid in the currency of risk. As Maxine Sheets-Johnstone writes, 'Where there is no felt risk, there is no personal involvement, and where there is no personal involvement, there is no freedom.' (2011, 292) Performative pursuits entail taking risks. Sometimes, we risk health and life, as many sporting activities require if they are to be done at all. We cannot ski a slope without the risk of slipping and subsequent harm. In fact, this risk so proper of active practices, as I argue below, is also crucial to skill acquisition. At other times, it is the risk of failure, of being found wanting by others, but above all, by ourselves. Competition, contests, and tests are valuable means to find our mettle. Athletic contests are the paradigm here, where we seek that 'sweet tension' that Kretchmar (1972) so incisively theorized after Fraleigh's genial coinage (1984).[5] This sweet tension balances on the uncertainty of the outcome, which depends on our ability to meet the challenge of the test or contest through requisite skills, e.g. getting to the top of the mountain via helicopter[6] would not amount to meeting the challenge of climbing. These contests, if we are invested in the activity, reveal to us the level of our expertise and skill development, and also how we react during (do we cheat?) and afterward (we take stock of our athletic worth). Related but different, we can encounter risk as an Orteguian sportive ethos. We expend ourselves in a task with all our heart, and since there is no assurance in sport as per Edgar, there can be deep disappointment or joy (and attendant emotional and existential ramifications too extensive to follow for now) when we fail or succeed after preparing for a competition or event for months or even years. In a way, we display and bet our abilities and our sum worth on a given moment, on a given performance. How we meet victory or defeat is as telling as anything.

This is of import not only for participants but audiences also, as they learn from the display of virtue and vice in the athletic arena. McNamee (2008) has argued that contemporary sport acts as medieval morality plays did, educating spectators about virtues and vices in ways that we can integrate into the narratives of our lives. Mumford (2012) writes of contests of virtue, following Reid (2010), who pioneered analysis of sports as public displays and tests of our athletic and moral strengths and weaknesses. This is based on her earlier examination of sport as a quest for knowledge (2009). There she identifies three characteristics of philosophical sport, uncertainty and authentic questioning, open and impartial testing, and public display of evidence. The idea is that these scenarios subject our performance to rational and impartial tests before everyone's eyes, where 'the public's interest in accurate results requires that popular opinion defer to demonstrable evidence' (Reid 2009, 43–44). Nonetheless, we should note that this need not be a strictly public process. We can athletically and otherwise test our skills, courage, determination, and other variables on our own. For instance, a climber can attempt to send (climbers' term for successful ascents) a difficult and novel route on her own with no witnesses. She can find out about her climbing abilities vis à vis test, and much more about herself. Much as in golf, certain bouldering problems and routes can be claimed on the honor system. If she failed by nary a hair of margin, will she be tempted to lie or interpret the event in a way not fitting the facts? She may honestly think she had succeeded when in fact she had not. Philosopher and climber Stephen Downes (Schmid 2010) contends how climbers' self-assessments can be unreliable, given the facility with which our feelings and expectations can be manipulated or misinterpreted, either by others or by our own doing, intentional or not. Regardless, failure *and* success can be complex events to handle, above all in terms of our affects; we may not be emotionally capable of dealing with the truth.

Something missing from some of these perceptive analyses is a deeper look at our emotions and their role in virtuous and vicious actions. Many actions are deeply motivated by little understood emotional undercurrents. The knowledge to be gained through performance is not merely a matter of episteme but gnosein, as adumbrated in the introduction, the former, characterized by its truth-functional value and propositional content, 'this sentence has eight words and 35 letters,' (its truth value to be verified by readers so disposed). This is often seen as the proper and particularly unique philosopher's and scientist's lair and aim. But, gnostic insight can not only include the former, but expand the scope, such that it integrates our felt realities as well, whether fully articulated or not. Much as Collingwood (1958) argued that art was about the clarification of emotion, sport and related practices can help illuminate truths about ourselves that would remain hidden in our innermost recesses. In fact, these truths are not waiting to be discovered. Rather, we enact them; we generate them from the often turbulent waters where our talents, character, and circumstances meet. This forms part of a larger issue: the advisability of expanding the scope of our inquiry ecologically, encompassing a broader range of phenomena and variables that go beyond self-knowledge and virtue.

Breivik bemoans the disappearance of excellence as a focal point in sport philosophy, writing that, 'There is no discussion of performance and of sport as an important part of a whole life' (2010, 89). He mentions the work of a number of seminal sport philosophers—Hyland, Wertz, and Reid— as fine examples where sport is discussed in the context of self-discovery, responsibility, or aesthetic dimensions. But, he contends, 'These are important phenomena but not intrinsically related to sport. We need discussions that (a) include the subjective view of the athlete, the view from within; (b) have a focus on sport performance as such; (c) view athletic excellence as a human good; and (d) clarify sport as an integral part of life as a whole.' (Breivik, ibid.) His aim is to do so in the context of perfectionism. This very inquiry is partially a kindred project, and the theme of perfectionism is a theme considered in depth later. But, now is the time to divert into a related but different subject, namely the performer's perspective.

Sport philosophy has often priced the experience of the observer and spectator over the performer's, and in aesthetics, the metaphysical disquisition that compares art and sport prevailed for a number of years (Best 1979; Cordner 1988; Roberts 1986, 1992). The fields of aesthetics, art criticism, and philosophy of art parallel this in the West: they have favored the perspective of the observer focusing on discussions of aesthetic properties and categories, interpretation, or the aesthetic point of view.[7] The focus presently falls on the performers, on the athletes, the martial artists, dancers, or singers, and their experience. Experience is meant in a broad sense to include also the pertinent intersubjective background that makes it rigorously meaningful in the first place. It also goes beyond the narrow and unreflective 'experiences,' perhaps 'happenings' is the more apt word, where the sportsperson or performer expends herself on the court or stage, but fails to reflectively engage it. In contrast, in the East, particularly in Japan, the practices themselves and criticism emphasize predominantly the perspective of the performers, the actors, the warriors, and the athletes. These practices are first and foremost intended for self-cultivation. Examples are any of the traditional martial arts, as well as *chanoyu* (茶の湯) or *sadō, or chadō* (茶道), all of which refer to the way of tea, *Ikebana* (生け花 or *kadō* (華道), which is the art of flower arrangement, and *Nō* (能) acting (which, genially, derives from the word for 'skill'). But even sumo (相撲) or kendō (剣道) contests, which are spectator-affairs, have an overt facet where sumōtori or *kendōka*, as part of their training, reflect on their performance and activity. No doubt, this is much encouraged by being embedded in deep traditions that assiduously and deliberately nurture values, such as those encoded in *bushidō* (武士道) and inherited from a larger sociohistorical context (see *Reflections on a Katana* and *Everything Mysterious Under the Moon*).

There are a number of historical reasons partially responsible. In the West, since the Enlightenment and after the Romantic Movement, creative efforts by the artist have been seen as the stuff of genius, and hence beyond the reach of mere mortals. One need only consider Kant's view on genius in his *Critique of Judgment*, which makes genius unexplainable (1951).[8] But in the East, artists, performers, and martial artists are *meant* to be imitated. Their inward (not private) processes are the object of exacting analysis by themselves and others. Moreover, their training, instruction, and critical manuals, whether for martial arts or acting, are to be used in conjunction with direct transmission from their master, and encourage the readers continually to vet the ideas with their own experience. It is a soteriological approach that seeks students to experience things themselves as they throw themselves into active and enacted practice and reflection. There is much to be gained from adopting and inquiring into the perspective of the performer. Philosopher Schacht (1998) presented *Sport? Nietzschean Appreciation* for a televized roundtable with Warren Fraleigh, Joseph Gilbert, and Paul Weiss, where he argued that, 'Sport, like dance and music, in the first instance is something to be <u>done</u> or engaged in rather than watched or listened to. Spectator sports are spectacles rather than sports for those who merely watch them, however fanatical the spectators may be in their enthusiasm for their teams or favored stars.' (1998, his emphasis)[9] Agreeably with the aesthetic line of argumentation developed next, he draws heavily from the kinship between sport and art. Very much with the Japanese understanding regarding their arts of self-cultivation, Schacht writes,

> The basic premise of the interpretation offered here is that, in the case of sport as (for Nietzsche) in the case of art, the primary modality at issue is that of <u>participation</u> rather than mere observation. There is nothing wrong with being a sport spectator, just as there is nothing wrong with being an art spectator. But one gets both sport and art wrong, from a Nietzschean point of view, if one takes them to be fundamentally spectator affairs rather than <u>activities</u>. [...] for Nietzsche it is crucial to grasp the centrality and priority of <u>active engagement</u> in these and all other such forms of human life. (ibid., his emphasis)

Schacht enumerates a number of qualified similarities (he is too savvy a philosopher, sportsman, and musician to simply elide them), of which the most salient ones for our purpose show that he takes 'sport like art, to be a loose and open-ended profusion of psychosomatic activities' (1998), and that it involves the cultivation of skills that 'can be taught and learned but cannot be reduced to mechanical formulas and rules' (ibid.). We will return to Schacht's perceptive assessment in *Everything Mysterious Under the Moon*. Nevertheless, we must face the fact that many in the West eye with reticence inquiry into this participatory aspect of sport and performance.

Graham McFee, who has written so excellently on sport and art, favors the perspective of the spectator, as his writings and presentations seem to indicate (2004, 2013). Drawing an analogy from the arts, he considers the 'experience of the athlete' philosophically uninteresting (September 9, 2013, personal conversation). For him, just as artists' intentions and experiences are not strictly pertinent to the meaning or interpretation of a work of art, neither are performers' experiences or intentions. In the wake of David Best (1979), he focuses his attention on the purposive and aesthetic sports, and shares with him the common Wittgensteinian commitment that makes the former suspicious of phenomenological claims (for a discussion of this refer to *Riding the Wind*). McFee is correct that *actual* artists' intentions are not pertinent to the status, interpretation, and meaning of the artwork. With their influential writings on the subject, William Wimsatt and Monroe Beardsley (in Margolis 1987) and Hospers (1969) cogently argued, among other things, (1) that the intentions were not only 'untraceable' because for many artists, we do not have the means to ascertain what they meant to paint or write, but (2) that there is no room for them in a cogent theory of aesthetics, as the simple case of authors, who do not know what work expresses shows (Hospers 1969). The nail in the coffin was hammered by Frenchmen confreres Barthes (1977) and Foucault

(1984), when they confined the author to the trash heap of oblivion. Nonetheless, intention as a concept is not out of the equation, there is room under the sun for it. As I argue elsewhere (Ilundáin-Agurruza 2000), to guide our interpretation of artworks, we only need to assume an intentional stance *without* content that is analogous to a logical operator, it can stand for any value but is bound by its historical context (there are ontologically and phenomenological reasons for this, which I cannot pursue here). Now, there are a number of ways in which intentions and experiences (which intertwine in various ways) can be relevant or extraneous.

Historical and biographical facts are crucial to *which* artwork we end up with, as Danto's ingenious examples of indiscernibles show (1973, 1981). For example, Danto has a brilliant exposition on Argentine writer Jorge Luis Borges's *Pierre Menard Author of the Don Quixote* (1974), a story that tells how Menard manages to recreate, *not* copy, some chapters of *Don Quixote* word for word. In the process, Menard makes it *his* own *Quixote*; it is perceptually identical yet utterly different. Danto, citing Borges, observes that Pierre Menard's work is 'infinitely more subtle than that of Cervantes, while that of Cervantes is immeasurably more coarse than its counterpart even though every word contained in the Menard version can be found in Cervantes' and in the corresponding position' (1981, 35). In the end, 'The upshot of this is that in this case knowledge of the origin of the piece, of who and how it was created is crucial for its being a creative and created work of art instead of a forgery made by a counterfeiter' (Ilundáin-Agurruza 2000, 56). In sport, history and biography can be just as crucial, less outlandish, and more common. For instance, first summits, circumnavigations, or athletic world or national records are all historically indexed: only one person can get the credit (obviating cases where teams or groups are involved, in which case recognition goes to the set of people).

Just as many kinds of 'intentions'—desires, hopes, fears, expectations, and other thoughts, 'what to have for lunch'—that artists have in connection to their work are completely irrelevant, what the 'intentions' of the sportspersons matter not either. For instance, what they wanted to do at the race, or what they expected to accomplish, how they felt after being defeated or coming victorious, are only pertinent for bland interviews or their therapist; they are not suitable for philosophical inquiry. On the other side, there is a more philosophical sense of intention, captured by the locution -intent to act- and related to agency, which is *very* relevant for both art and sport. It comes with moral and legal obligations. As the Menard case shows, if he had intended to copy the Quixote, he would be guilty of plagiarism; and athlete that intends to bite his opponent or take a banned substance is blameworthy.

There are two deeper reasons, unique to sport now, in which the experiences and intentions of athletes (and performers) are quite relevant philosophically. One, Lally's keen observations as he expounds on Deweyan self-cultivation help make the case,

> The incredible power of sport to cultivate the self is derived from the impulsions the athlete lives with each day. Unlike the *passive spectator* who may shy away from cultivating experience, the athlete often rushes toward the encounter, welcoming the struggle and its power to create aesthetic meaning. When the runner accepts the challenge of the hill, or the cyclist fights the headwind, the cultivating power of the impulsion is at work. (Lally 2013, 195, my emphasis)

Unlike in the 'fine' arts,[10] where audience members can cultivate themselves quite richly in museums, galleries, studios, and through conversation and observation, in sport, observers can be very cultivated but there is no self-cultivation. Watching an Ironman on TV, no matter how well our mirror neurons fire, is not the same as doing it. (The same goes for performing arts to some extent.) Again, taking the helicopter to the top of the mountain will not count, this time because it is impossible to cultivate our character by taking the easy way to the top. We may gain a deep appreciation for the landscape, but no insight into our mettle (except perhaps that we do not have what it takes to be a mountaineer). But that is a pale trophy compared to the athlete or performer who has given her all. Of course, more is needed than the actual performance; we need to reflect, but these are issues to be refined as we move ahead. There are truths, gnostic ones, that to be understood have to be lived. We cannot be spectators. If Borges had a regret, it was, 'Not to leave my library. To be Alonso Quijano and not dare to be Don Quijote.' (Borges 2005, 97) He was a timid soul that never got to act or live any of the fabulous adventures he wrote about. Philosophy can be sportive also (see *José Ortega y Gasset—Exuberant Philosophical Steed*). Much as Pierre Hadot (1995) argues that the ancient tradition cultivated philosophy as *a way of life*, a sportive philosophy takes risks, both intellectual and existential. It jumps into the arena and gets covered in sand, sweat, and bruises.

As to the second reason, ever since Ryle's seminal *The Concept of Mind* (1949) articulated the difference between know-that and know-how, philosophers have been busy with their complex differences and similarities. Basically, the former is akin to the already mentioned episteme, being truth-functional, propositional, and favoring rationality over other cognitive modes. The latter is practical, non-discursive, and takes a broader palette of faculties that can integrate emotional intelligence and more. Probably not without a modicum of self-interest, philosophers favor the former, with *theoria* prevailing over techné and praxis. Yet, as Philosopher Robert Crease writes, 'Conflating the senses of knowing—and giving priority to the theoretical sense over the practical—simply reflects our adherence to the ancient myth that *true* knowledge is theoretical.' (2012, 19) This prejudice is long due a revaluation. Dewey begins the process,

> More specifically, play and work correspond, point for point, with the traits of the initial stage of knowing, which consists [...] in learning how to do things and in acquaintance with things and processes gained in the doing. It is suggestive that among the Greeks, till the rise of conscious philosophy, the same word, techné, was used for art and science. Plato gave his account of knowledge on the basis of an analysis of the knowledge of cobblers, carpenters, players of musical instruments, etc., pointing out that their art (so far as it was not mere routine) involved an end, mastery of material or stuff worked upon, control of appliances, and a definite order of procedure—all of which had to be known in order that there be intelligent skill or art. (1922, 229)

A return to an appreciation for the skill, art, and know-how of *techné* would be advantageous. It is not meant to supplant rational deliberation. But it can do better in many realms, where rationality runs into a wall too tall for it to clear. *Techné* comes with the requisite skills. The realm of excellence is one such realm, as is ethics, as the next section will discuss.

Breivik (2014) discusses the relevance of knowing-how for sport and its relative absence from contemporary sport philosophy discourse. Very much in line with the holistic and ecologically broad stance of this project, he considers the athlete's knowing-how, whose analysis he extends with phenomenology and a Heideggerian analysis that appeals to the value of practical knowledge and emphasizes how 'knowing how is, from an existential point of view, more important than knowing that.' (Breivik 2014, 152–153) He amends Ryle's views by appealing to a cognitive grasp that goes beyond propositional knowledge, and highlights 'Heidegger's interactive and holistic approach [that] draws the environing world into the discussion' (ibid., 153). The role of the environment, which can be rendered in terms of a situated cognition, is another theme that will reverberate much in these pages with Dewey, Ortega, and when phenomenology takes center stage. Breivik deftly makes patent the relevance of the social and environmental aspects of our experience with the example of football, 'a complex and interactive pattern of players and environment,' where we must take into account the flat turf and physical elements and dimensions as well as the other players, who, he cites his 2008 paper, 'get their meaning and place as part of the practice of playing football' (ibid., 154). The key idea is that our very 'being-in-the-world,' to use Heidegger's coinage, is intimately connected with our knowing-how and our practical and sportive ways. Such situated and expansive ways are not only found in the German's oeuvre. Ortega, in a 1931 essay, echoing themes from his earlier work, writes that 'to live is to find oneself in the world' (2008, 501). Here he discusses how to live is first to become reflectively aware of being alive, 'To live, is for now, to see oneself' (ibid.). This entails the gnostic existential realization that gives us a new perspective. As I indicate earlier, we do this against the background of the world. Ortega goes on to say, in a clear jab at Heidegger, 'Someone in Germany has recently insisted on this formula, which by the way, is found already in my first books.' Polemics aside, the genesis of the point is not critical for the present project. Both give the idea their personal *imprimatur*: Ortega, an optimistic hue; Heidegger, a darker one. The issue is the fact that phenomenologically, we are *already*, from the moment we first see ourselves, situated and connected with the world. This is holistic terrain.

2. Thick Holism—A Brief Manifesto

For the last decade, I have pondered on how to designate the inherent unity of our animate and corporeal existence that Descartes so brilliantly and vexingly managed to split asunder. Finding a way to bring them together is peremptory. Dewey states that in contrast to the wholeness among philosophy, the arts and sciences,

> the very problem of mind and body suggests the disastrous effect of the divisions that may have since grown up. I do not know of anything so disastrously affected by the tradition of separation and isolation as this particular theme of body-mind. In its discussion is reflected the splitting off from each other of religion, morals and science; the divorce of philosophy from science and of both from the arts of conduct. (1963, 301–302)

And Sigmund Loland aptly explains the problematic situation from the perspective of sport and contemporary science,

> The fact that sport is a bodily practice has exerted significant impact on the way it is analysed and understood. The predominant scientific approach is that of the natural sciences [...] The body is seen as a mechanistic object and as part of the deterministic nature in movements can be quantitatively described and explained in causal relationships. The basic premise is a dualistic worldview in which body and mind are considered to belong to two different spheres of reality. (2011, 16)

The problem in the West begins with what to call or how to describe this, so that its unity is articulated meaningfully. Having tinkered with all kinds of appalling locutions that used various Greek, Latin, and other language's roots, such as 'nousomatic' and worse (from 'nous' organizing principle and 'soma' body), I have decided the best way to capture the quality of our experience and nature of our being is with the old terms, holism and bodymind (Dewey hyphenated it as body-mind, but this slight 'separation' still and already suggests a lessening of the required seamlessness). The latter adequately, if not optimally, denotes what other languages, such as Chinese and Japanese, render so effectively and poetically as one: *xin* (ch.) and *shin* (jp.) 心 literally translate as heart-mind (the character evokes the heart pumping blood). The traditional understanding stresses the unity of our functions and processes. We cannot just think with our mind/head/brain; our emotions color our every thought (James makes this clear). The bodymind, while one, achieves different degrees of higher or lesser integration, depending on the person and their level of cultivation. Unique to some Asian traditions, and most clearly seen in Japanese *dō*, this progressive refinement is gradually achieved through performance (see *Reflections on a Katana*). In other words, our holistically connected (to varying degrees) bodyminds give us a range of possible experiences, affordances in a Gibsonian framework (1979), or 'I Cans' (Husserl 1989) that allow us experience the world in a way commensurate with our abilities. And this integrative bodymind is not a purely individual or personal phenomenon, but deeply social. It is with and through others that we set on the road.

It is preferable to speak of *thick* holism to emphasize that it must be radical and uncompromising in its thorough emphasis of continuities, fluidities, and connections. Thick holism advances a functional, flexible, and ecological model. We are richly complex, dynamic, animate organisms, whose bodily, psychic, emotional, affective, sensory, kinetic, energetic, sociohistorical, and environmental facets form a unity that is consummate to various degrees of competence and integration. Paragons of performance, when at their best, exhibit a holistic dynamics; schizophrenia, where the person has a sense of ownership for her actions but not of agency, that is she feels actions and thoughts happening to her, shows dramatically a complete breakdown of this bodymind. Choking in sport is the counterpart in performance (an analysis carried out in *Fractured Action*). A convention I adopt to maintain the mutually constitutive unity of the bodymind yet be able to capture its fluid dynamics, is to parenthetically bracket the one aspect that is de-emphasized or is less integrated. Accordingly, we would parenthetically bracket 'mind,' as in body(mind) if bodily phenomena prevail, or we would or bracket 'body,' as (body)mind, if psychic elements are pre-eminent, with the understanding that one does not happen without the other, and that these are in a constant state of flux. To use two 'caricaturesque stereotypes,' for clarity of purpose, an unreflective bloke who cannot write his name with a stick on the mud would be a case of body(mind); a bookworm unable to tie his shoes demonstrates (body)mind. This seeks to bypass 'dualistic' renderings that speak of embodiment, holistic minds, or bodies that think.

Thick holism is functional, in the sense, to say it with Dewey, that the body is 'the mechanism, the instrumentality of behavior, and the mind is the *function* or its fruit and consummation' (1963, 302, my italics). James' fringe of consciousness gives a clear and multivalent manifestation of said functionality (essay 2). Further, thick holism advocates naturalism and embraces empirical accounts so long as these are true to the facts of the matter, both as observed empirically and phenomenologically felt and validated. Current naturalist accounts tend to posit physiological structures at various length scales (brain, specific cerebral areas, neural networks, neurons, and even neuronal subcomponents and electrochemical processes), and they habitually hypothesize mechanisms or processes. Surely, anatomical processes and components are necessary as constituents of our restless ways of engaging the world. But they lack sufficient explanatory power to account for the complex phenomena they purportedly give rise to, particularly the complexities of high-performance kinematics, the kinesthetic and proprioceptive dimensions of our experience, and the attendant pragmatic semantics underlying our phenomenological articulations and existential narratives. Similarly, hypothetical mechanisms advance empirically uncorroborated and overly complex and theoretically dubious models. The emphasis lies on keeping front and center the qualities of actions and functions as ongoing dynamics that unfold heterochronically: they happen at varying rates, synchronically, as Sheets-Johnstone (2009) adduces with regard to our kinesthetic, tactile and kinetic dynamics, and diachronically, as Gallagher (2005) proposes in his rejoinder to Sheets-Johnstone (*Riding the Wind*).

Thick holism is also flexible, favoring neither top-down theoretical constructs nor bottom-up physiological structures. It relies on thick phenomenological descriptions of our experience and the explanatory virtue that pragmatic and, broadly, ecological contexts afford. Both top-down and bottom-up views shed light from opposite ends; the trick is to ensure they properly line up. This fluidity takes place as a 'both/and stance' that courts a Zhuangzian spontaneous mastery of our abilities (essay 5). Moreover, cognitive processes and our knowing ways are not circumscribed to higher order intellectual and rational capacities *alone*. As the above discussion on knowing-how suggests and subsequent sections in this inquiry will bolster, praxis is superior and more prevalent not only in everyday life, but also in expert performance (where radically enactive contentless bodyminds prevail, see *Waking Up from the Cognitivist Dream*). Moreover, higher faculties work best when subtended by and properly fitted to our affects, bodily processes, and Orteguian *circumstantial* interactions under an 'egalitarian ontology,' where all functions and skills are necessary, and hierarchy is fluid, and situated, that is, context and the 'needs of the moment' dictate primacy, e.g. the ability to solve quadratic equations rises to the top when being tested at school, whereas survival know-how is king in the Amazon jungle, and consummate coordination is pre-eminent on the balance beam at the Olympics.

The ecological facet of holism understands us as organic beings for whom cognition, movement, and the environment are closely intertwined, and who flourish through reflective habits. Environmental variables inform this process, with agent and environment mutually and causally influencing each other. The ecological facet of holism is not solely a matter of biological and evolutionary import, but also, and primarily for us, social and cultural. While normativity permeates and issues forth from biological conditions (section C), it is sublimated into standards of excellence in the case of human beings and the practices they develop. Among these practices, those that can be categorized as performative are paramount. These allow for the cultivation of our skills to skillful levels in arduous pursuit of an ever-elusive perfection. The phenomenon of choking in sports, which entails failure in deploying *already* mastered skills, helps elucidate the commitments of thick holism further, since understanding and treating it engages the full theoretical spectrum just described.

Thick holism is aligned with so-called cognitively embodied stances, although it takes an even more 'radical' turn toward vigorous qualitative, process-oriented, contentless bodyminds and functional conceptualizations and phenomenological descriptions (essays 6 and 7). It still embraces philosophical naturalism, not positing any sort of mysterious entity to account for the ontology of minds or consciousness (McGinn 1999), but is open to developmental and cultural histories. Rather than being antagonistic, thick holism complements embodied cognition, expanding or limiting some of its claims. Such holism, instead of dispensing with the cognitive stance wholesale, incorporates empirical evidence from the mind sciences, but avoids reductionist traps, bypasses ontological dualism or materialism, and integrates a thicker cognition that is truly dynamic and phenomenologically true to our experience. Thus, it circumvents Western post-Cartesian ontological quagmires about the mind-body problem because the dynamic processes it deals with avoid both reduction and reification of our so-called 'mental processes.' It also avoids attitudinal stances, behavioral consequences, and misguided pragmatic strategies typical of such metaphysical commitments, e.g. instrumentalized and reified bodies, overvaluing of rational over practical intelligences, or curricular imbalances, as Kretchmar (2005) charges and tries to redress in his pedagogical signature work.

In fact, sport philosophy has been more welcoming of holistic advances than other areas of philosophical investigation. Scott Kretchmar is clearly its paladin and most able defender (2005, 2013), and his work will be duly echoed. Breivik's work (2014), on account of its Heideggerian influences, as we have just seen, is also deeply amenable. And Russell (2007) exhibits a holistic temperament from an ethical stance, when he develops a friendly amendment to Robert Simon's broad internalism (2000). Russell endorses the continuity thesis, which claims that the most distinctive values in sport 'are expressions or reflections of more basic moral values found outside of sport.' (2007, 52) Such continuity naturally aligns with thick holism. But as Russell draws out its implications and defends the internal principle, this becomes genuinely holistic. The internal principle promotes sports' distinctive excellences, and is derived 'from a general moral ideal of promoting human flourishing.' (ibid., 57) This crescendoes until it surges with the following analysis Russell makes:

> Virtually all moral theories recognize either direct or indirect duties to promote such human flourishing. For example, Kantian deontology, utilitarianism, and Aristotelian perfectionist theories all recognize the moral importance of developing human talents and capacities. Sporting games institutionalize the production and development of excellences that contribute to such human flourishing by promoting *certain physical, emotional, and intellectual excellences*. (ibid., my emphasis)

Had he extended the excellences into a sociohistorical context, this would be holistic through and through. In fact, such an extension can be assumed, given the institutionalization he appeals to, and the implicit background that these excellences regulate social life to, for we flourish in the company of others, ethics regulating such interactions. Discoursing on the development of talents and capacities in this context comes next.

3. Excellence, Perfection, and Skills

In life, either we flourish or perish. Far from a fallacious false alternative, our lived experience is constant change. We are either improving or worsening, like an athlete's fitness. There may be a veneer of stability, of stasis, but whether we realize it or not, fluctuations are happening at the subpersonal level, an undercurrent of affects that work in ways we become aware afterwards, when the impulse is a fait accompli. Gallagher explains:

> As a reader in this situation, I am not at first conscious of my posture, or of my eyes as they scan the pages. Rather, totally absorbed in my project, I begin to experience eyestrain as a series of changes in the things and states of affairs around me. Gradually the perceived environment begins to revise itself; the text seems more difficult, the lighting seems too dim, the body shifts itself closer to the desk, etc. In the end I discover the true problem—the fatigue, the headache. The eyes that have been reading have been anonymous eyes [...] I was not conscious of my eyes at all. Now, however, my attention is directed to my eyes. (2005, 34)

It seems that if the eye cannot see itself, it can feel itself: it can feel its worsening focus and the increasing strain. More to the purpose, three lessons follow. First, a pragmatic bit of advice, should readers find themselves losing patience with *this* text, perhaps they should 'see' whether the text or something else is the cause. Secondly, still minding practicality, with this explicit knowledge, we can develop a habit of scanning our states: runners, dancers, judokas are all familiar with the feeling that practice is not going well, to find out later a poor fit with the shoe–foot interface, a strained calf, or the uncomfortable fabric of the new judogi were the culprits. Elite athletes, as *Riding the Wind* details excel at monitoring sensory input, its complex intermodal dynamics, and correlating them efficiently and effectively to the task at hand (or foot). Being aware of this process does not mean complete transparency or even monitoring of most sensations. But it does afford us a bigger perceptual window, and a bit more control. Of course, we cannot do this *all* the time; we must choose what is important to us. Concerning perceptual discrimination, our attentional ability to select is arguably even more crucial than being aware of a rich field of sensations. Sportspeople and performers excel at discriminating within their domains of expertise. Third, Gallagher's phrasing reveals a limitation language imposes and which means we fail to do justice to the complexity of the phenomena: we discover the eyes, but it is not just the eyes that we discover. Should we couple a bit of anatomical and physiological knowledge with careful attention of our sensations, it is a whole lot of elements that make up even as simple an experience as eyestrain. It is the muscles surrounding the eye, medial and lateral rectus muscles, and the suspensory ligament, that control its movement; it is the internal dynamics between lens, cornea, and aqueous humor trapped in between; it is the enveloping cornea and sclera, the optic nerve and other nerve endings that relay

HOLISM AND THE CULTIVATION OF EXCELLENCE IN SPORTS AND PERFORMANCE

sensations of and around the eyeball; it is the drying eyelids that in turn cause an increase in lacrimal production and the consequent blurriness that means more eye strain. All of this leads to very intricate anatomical-kinesthetic-tactile sensations that become perceptions of strain. We are conscious of the eyes, and yet so much more is possible with a bit of attention. And yet, this still leaves out the bigger picture the eye cannot see unless we think it: we are *forcing* ourselves to read, thus straining, because, with an impending deadline for a manuscript, we are determined to see it through— blurry and bleary-eyed or not. This naturalistic basis does not reduce eyestrain or any other process to its physiology. If anything, this underscores the need for a holistically situated account, where we also take into account the social context that places burdens and opportunities to flourish or perish.

The road to flourishing is strewn with many opportunities (and setbacks) to exercise our abilities to discern, move, and act. The problem becomes how to walk this path: with careful short steps as the above piecemeal analysis of eyestrain? With confident long strides that go for the bigger picture? Perhaps daringly running to cover more terrain? Or, maybe playfully skipping around, infusing our explorations with spontaneity? A combination considerate of our needs, talents, and means is best. To take a bigger leap for now, the question arises: what conception of flourishing should we take?

For starters, there is a choice to be made between two incommensurable models aimed at the good life. One eyes well-being, while the other has its heart set on excellence. Well-being opts for the more sedate path, and might appeal to those of an epicurean temperament. They will sensibly prefer the charms of well-being, much like Tolkien's hobbits favor the predicable quiet of the pastoral. As Tolkien's Frodo remarks to Pippin, citing a 'lesson' born out of Bilbo's original outing, 'It's a dangerous business, Frodo, going out of your door.' (1981, 107) On the other side, the road to excellence promises arduous work, sacrifice, and no guarantee of success. Their disposition is more like Dwarf Gimli who, as they are about to set out to attack the Black Gate of Mordor exclaims, 'Certainty of death, small chance of success … What are we waiting for?' (Jackson 2003). Tom Hurka (1993) argues for the latter. Breivik (2010) finds that it is a 'good antidote to the focus in present society on pleasure and well-being. Perfectionism contrasts thus with both hedonism and desire satisfaction accounts of the human good' (100). James could not agree more. After only a week at a quiet resort, he was hyperbolically eulogizing war, as we will see in the next essay. Since the premise of this essay is the pursuit of excellence, the answer to which one to pick is a foregone conclusion. But, do we have to be perfectionists to achieve it? The answer depends on the kind of perfectionism we opt for.

Perfectionism goes back to Aristotle, and comes in various shapes and colors. Breivik's assessment that the Aristotelian notion of a static human nature has been surpassed in many ways by more dynamic and integrated views is appropriate. It seems wiser to use broad perfectionism and a wider set of human capabilities as a basis to develop philosophical perfectionism (2010, 91). The common and central focus among them is the development of human talents, which we have a moral *obligation* to develop. The strongest version of the theory implies that this is a moral duty for all of us. The weaker version considers perfection to be an option (Breivik 2010, 89). To perfect or not to perfect—obligation or choice— that is the question here.

Breivik opts for choice. He concludes that 'it is difficult to uphold the idea of human nature and human essences as defined by Aristotle and Hurka. Instead I favour a concept of sets of human faculties and capacities based on biological and cultural influences that can be further developed and perfected.' (2010, 102) In agreement with Breivik, prescribing a moral obligation to a particular and narrowly defined notion of perfection, as Aristotle's life of the intellect, seems mistaken. On this ground, we cannot establish universal and all-binding obligation. Even if virtue ethics and theory is a core element in this account, and the Aristotelian view of virtues as the means between two extremes is a good principle to orient us, we must leave the thinker from Stagira behind on this issue. We will return to this issue and critically engage Breivik and Hurka with Ortega y Gasset (Essay 4).

Philosopher James Wallace helps to explain why we are better off looking for a broader more flexible model than Aristotle's *linear* account, 'The Aristotelian account of deliberation, taken to cover all deliberations, implies that we are equipped at the outset with clearly and concretely articulated purposes, goals, or ends that will provide us with our starting point of deliberation.' (2009, 22) Deliberation here is taken in the Deweyan sense of unifying or harmonizing competing tendencies (ibid., 21). The linear account is true for certain deliberative processes, as Wallace explains, a householder figures out how to deal with a clogged drain or a golfer knows what her goal is, to put the ball in the hole in as few strokes as possible. It is not at all clear that his use of the golfing case does the work he thinks it does. The goal is clear in a prelusory manner in Bernard Suits' sense (1990): one must put the ball in the hole. But not any way of achieving this counts; she must do so according to certain freely embraced constitutive rules, which entails the possibility or temptation of cheating. It is not solely a matter of the goal but of *how* to achieve it, which itself is a second-order type of goal she must deliberate. It seems closer to those 'many challenging practical circumstances [for which], however, we are not guided at the outset by a concrete conception of the outcome we want.' (Wallace 2009, 22) For instance, we may want to be fair to everyone, 'But what is that in this particular situation?' (ibid., 22–23) This is determined by deliberating, starting without a clear conception.

This points to the alternative. Wallace sides with Dewey's view of a deliberative process, where we often begin with incommensurate or conflicting considerations, such as our current dilemma of well-being or perfection (2009, 22). We then reason our way guided by practical reason aided by *phronesis,* sound judgment. We discover the good and articulate it as a result of deliberation, much as physicians diagnose. And this must be particularized. Wallace cites Dewey:

> We cannot seek or attain health, wealth, learning, justice, or kindness in general. Action is always specific, concrete, individualized, unique. And consequently judgments as to acts to be performed must be similarly specific … How to live healthily or justly is a matter which differs with every person. It varies with his past experience, his opportunities, his temperamental and acquired weaknesses and abilities. (2009, 23–24)

This sets up Ortega's view, which slips between the horns and permits to find the middle between two extremes; it sees excellence as perfection, but a *personal* perfection. On this ground, we can establish an obligation for self-cultivation that is concordant with Breivik's broader palette then. In this case, the onus lies not in following an external criterion of perfection, but that *personal* perfection. Before looking at this with Ortega's essay, we will learn about perfectionism, self-cultivation, and excellence with James and Dewey.

Three more elucidations before we consider how to pursue perfection. First, for those who choose the perfectionist path, however, what would be supererogatory demands become but 'business as usual,' meaning that they *should* take on, within their means, what for others entails going beyond any moral expectations. Italian cyclist Marco Pantani crashed during a mountain stage in his debut 1995 Tour de France. Miguel Induráin, in the yellow jersey and about to win his fifth consecutive and last tour, as the established *patron*, by force of will ensured the whole *pelotón* slowed down so that a distraught Pantani could catch up. Lesser riders would have attacked to get rid of someone who was proving quite pestering on the climbs. Induráin, confident of his abilities, wanted Pantani in the race because he made it a better race (besides sympathizing for the then Tour rookie). His prowess allowed him, but his character enabled him. He was not obliged to do it from the standpoint of a non-perfectionist morality. But he *did* have to do it if he was to deserve the mantle of greatness. Subsequent elucidations on *kalon*, the noble and beautiful deed, will further refine this. In the case of paragons of excellence, they should not be mere role models but moral exemplars. They are gifted, indeed: they were given a gift in the lottery of life; this may have led to many rewards, from prestige to material means for many. Someone as gifted *and* rewarded as Michael Jordan, whom so many have looked up to over the years, on account of his better talents and means, has a larger obligation to lead by example. As Luke writes, 'For unto whomsoever much is given, of him shall be much required' (12:48, Online). These are preparatory statements to set the tone (see *Reflections on a Katana* for a fuller discussion). Secondly, we should not confuse excellence, which is attainable, with perfection, which is best seen as a goal that we lucidly see as unattainable yet desirable. In other words, perfectionism is best conceived processually, rather than as a terminus. In fact, imperfection itself is a way to perfect ourselves: failure and losing can be wonderful teachers, sources of self-reliance, and help refine our skills (also discussed in essays 8 and 9) Thirdly, the *pursuit* of excellence—not excellence itself—can be pathological when taken to an extreme. A relentless drive to excel can be dangerous, setting us for failure if overly ambitious or confident. The less-known Delphic command for moderation in all things, and Buddha's analogous Middle Path, are reminders of such dangers. The common bridge between the pursuit of excellence and harm is risk. In both, it plays a central role. We fail or lose because we took the risk in the first place, and this may be a matter of excessive zeal in the pursuit of excellence. The other Delphic command, 'know thyself,' comes to the rescue, as we need to know our limits in order to handle risk, success, and failure. Partially, this entails a wise development and management of our skills, such that we may know what to take on.

Being in the business of excellence is challenging. We meet challenges through our skills. Performance-centered pursuits, particularly sports, offer creative and exceptional ways to enhance our lives' experiential possibilities. We call these ways skills. Following Wallace (1978), a skill is a capacity to do something well in the sense of doing it '*proficiently*.' (44, his italics) For Wallace, proficiency is not mere competence, as some might assume: 'Proficiency involves the *mastery* of a technique, the mastery of something that is technically difficult.' (ibid., my italics) Expertise is required. Skills are capacities that take on their true meaning when acted. Else, as with any practice, e.g. speaking non-native languages, painting, knitting, as sport makes literally and painfully clear, they get rusty and deteriorate. Flourish or perish. Skills are ways of purposeful acting that, pragmatically oriented, help us meet challenges. They are not haphazard efforts but targeted functions. If of sound judgment, we choose the *best* way within our means to handle the problem at hand: those who exhibit athletic or martial virtue and *phronesis* choose the 'best' movement (which may be most effective or efficient depending on circumstances) from their repertoire of possible movements. The repertoire is derived from the exploration of possibilities.

The relation between skills and excellence is complex. Wallace's skillful analysis provides an excellent map. Relying on Aristotle's example of the eye of *Nicomachean Ethics* II 6 (unstrained now, we may suppose), Wallace determines that human excellences are tendencies or capacities to act in ways that constitute living and doing well the sorts of things characteristic of human life. For Wallace, 'the notion of an action's being fully characteristic of an excellence is a crucial one,' and keenly discerns that, 'Not every action that is characteristic of an excellence, however, is also *fully* characteristic of it.' (1978, 42) Fulfilling this "fullness," the action 'must be *strictly speaking* the sort of action that the excellence is the tendency or capacity to perform.' (ibid.) Shooting an arrow and hitting the target characterizes archery skill, but if the individual did so through accidental or random discharge, this fails to hit the conceptual mark. The more important point is that such a fully characteristic act be good so as to reflect credit upon the agent (ibid.). This brings virtues and skills together. Both must reflect credit upon the agent: 'the fact that his action is characteristic of a skill or a virtue is sufficient grounds for praising *him*, if one is so inclined' (ibid., 44, his italics). In the case of skills now, this praiseworthiness must be because the person has the pertinent skill and her act satisfies the criteria of a good performance of that kind *because* of that person's skill, not due to accident or someone else's doing (49). Essential to skills is that the difficulty is inherent in the doing of the action itself, as we see in hitting baseballs, performing eye surgery, riding bicycles, or typing fast (ibid., 45). These difficulties are overcome through skills, common to which capacities is that they can be improved through instruction and learning; with practice these lead to proficiency (ibid.) The technique is an action inherently difficult in a way peculiar to itself, and the skill the mastery of said technique, which is generally acquired through learning and improved through training (ibid., 46).

Given that proficient skill reflects credit on the person because she possesses the requisite skill, one 'consequence of this […] is that one cannot gradually acquire a certain level of skill by performing a number of acts *fully* characteristic of that level of skill' (ibid., 52) We can still learn, of course, but 'it is impossible gradually to acquire a certain level of skill by repeatedly doing well at *that* level.' (ibid., my italics) Again, experienced performers know well the truth of this; they must up the challenge if they are to improve. Continually swimming slow will make us 'good' slow swimmers; to become faster will take more complex coordination (the faster the arm-swing rate, the easier one becomes sloppy) and aerobic capacities. One last, related, point concerning skills concerns its relationship to risk. As philosopher and white water rafter Marv Henberg puts it, 'the element of controlling risk (but it has to be real risk, not ersatz) lies at the heart of authentic skill acquisition.' (Personal correspondence, 4/25/2014) To refine and develop our skills, we need to take real risks that test them. Else, we simply perform

HOLISM AND THE CULTIVATION OF EXCELLENCE IN SPORTS AND PERFORMANCE

what we *already* master, and such timidity as Wallace points out does not lead to improvement. We must risk failure, as mentioned earlier. Sometimes we must risk life and limb. This truly sharpens our wits about us.

Given the centrality of skill for this enterprise, it is prudent to consider a challenge to the relevance of skill in the first place. In his polemic piece on phenomenology and sport, Henning Eichberg (2013) finds that,

> 'Sport skill' is, however, a poor concept, as thin as the reduction used by quantifying and measuring positivism. Furthermore, it is—if remaining uncommented— narrowly linked to elite sport or competitive sport.

> At the same time, the word 'skill' may be too broad. Some of the 'phenomenological' reflections about sport skill may also be true for the artisan's skill. (274)

First, there is much to connect the elite sportsperson's skill with that of the consummate craftsperson's. And this should not count against one or the other, phenomenologically or otherwise. Phenomenologically, they are both guided by kinesthetic and tactile dynamics; they are also guided by a tradition that has refined those skills—and their ability to discriminate and recognize the right dynamics—in consonance with the very objects the craftsman creates or the performances the athlete, dancer, or martial artist carries to fruition. This is applicable not just to elite sportspersons. Within our means, we can *approximate* their experience and performance. Much as other expert performers, skill is there for the taking, to be cultivated as best as we can. It is argued later (*Riding the Wind*) that experts' dynamics are qualitatively different, but this is so along a continuum. This line of reasoning does not entail that we elide the athlete's and the craftsperson's. That is precisely the task of phenomenology: find the invariants of the experience, then compare and contrast meaningfully. Secondly, skill, as contextualized by Eichberg, *can* be too broad and narrow. *This* is precisely what lends it flexibility to be meaningful in various contexts without being overly vague. When looked at narrowly, they allow us to match them to the specificity proper of practices. Even as similar an event as the shot put and the hammer throw show very different skills and attendant dynamics. The broad and abstract view allows finding the common facet to understand skills generally; the narrow and concrete perspective permits to make relevant and insightful discriminations. On the subject of discrimination, we should be wary of conflating skills and virtues.

Both virtues and skills have normative value, but whereas the former can put on a moral cloak, the latter are not so invested, arguably. MacIntyre (1984) argues that skills are specific to a particular type of situation, whereas virtues are applicable variously,

> What are spoken of as the virtues of a good committee man or of a good administrator or of a gambler or a good pool hustler are professional skills professionally deployed in those situations where they can be effective, not virtues. Someone who genuinely possesses a virtue can be expected to manifest it in very different types of situations where the practice of a virtue cannot be expected to be in the way a professional skill to be. (205)

Echoing him, Heather Reid explains, 'Virtues may be associated with sport, but they are something different from athletic skills. Unlike technical abilities needed for success with a sport—things like leg speed in cycling or batting skill in cricket—virtues are dispositions that can be expressed in a variety of actions and activities.' (2012, 63) Moreover, Wallace also points out how we do not call a virtue so unless it is thought worth having, unlike skills, given that some are not worth having (1978, 43). Further, whereas virtues have opposites, namely vices, not all excellences, skills among these, have such an opposite (ibid., 50). What is the counterpart to a lack of skill? There is no corresponding vice to not being able to play the violin, just the absence of the skill. Nevertheless, there is a sense in which once we begin to develop a skill, there are performative criteria, and we can then perform better or worse in a similar way to how we may be more or less generous. Our skill level may be limiting us, in which case we are simply not proficient enough. But we can also *choose* not to perform well, for example, we are capable of playing much better tennis or guitar than we are doing. In this case, we are blameworthy (the implications of this and its connections to a personal perfectionism unfold below and in later essays). This brings the functional equivalent of a vice. Finally, virtues are not masteries of techniques (ibid., 46).

Our skills are capacities to do proficiently certain actions, and these are practice-specific. But just as virtues manifest across a wide range of situations, skills can also do the same *qua* skills. Throwing the hammer, the discus, or putting the shot are different skills. The conditions of satisfaction for each event are distinctive. But this specificity is malleable, and adaptable, even if it requires more or less extensive retraining or improvisation. Our baseball throwing ability can be used on a number of practical scenarios, from throwing back a ball back over the fence to some young children who have misplaced it, to lobbing a grenade, or striking out an opponent in baseball. Of course, this is still throwing a ball or similar object, but the situations are very different and require different implementation. The professional pitcher had better not throw the ball back at the kids at 90 mph! Additionally, skills often come in 'families,' much as languages can be grouped and relate more or less closely. And analogously as some languages are easier to learn when they share more grammatical, syntactical, and etymological structures, some skills are easier to pick up when these share basic dynamics and movements. All three 'throwing events' use the power of rotation, the hips, and a sense of balance and timing to release the pertinent object. Just as we must watch for false cognates in languages, in skills the hindrance is that already automatized skills may act as bad habits that get in the way of learning the new skill. Hammer thrower and Linfield College record-woman Anna LaBeaume speaks to this when learning the hammer after many years of doing the shot put. The rotation is similar, but unlike the shotput, the hammer acts as a counterweight against which she can 'throw' herself, aided by heel-toe dynamics also inexistent in the shot put. This took some adjusting to, but compared to a novice she had the advantage of being able to eye the release point without getting dizzy (personal conversation, 5/12/2014). This does not argue against specificity per se; it simply shows that while skills are specific they also have a broader range of application than MacIntyre or Reid credit them with. Practically this makes transfer and learning easier; theoretically this shows the continuities among many of them and a fluid applicability. It may seem that this has little to do with normative concerns. But it does.

From the moment we can speak of being more or less skilled we are making a normative claim. Being or doing something better or worse necessarily entails qualitative comparisons of a normative nature. This is hardly contentious. What is more controversial is that some skillful actions can be imbued with moral content. As explained above, both skill and virtue must reflect credit upon the agent and be fully characteristic of the excellence. This credit entails a normative judgment. As adumbrated above, this credit can consider the actual skill level, is it novice-like, proficient, or expert? It can also reflect the *quality* of the effort itself, is the performer trying her or his best? Moreover, there is also a deeper connection to this moral facet of skillful action: such actions, as performed, embody and happen through a fully characterized excellence, as the next paragraph explains.

Throughout, *Skillful Striving* intends to reclaim a thick and vigorous normativity for skills. It does not to argue that skills *are* virtuous in the narrow moral sense. Rather, they can partake of virtuous tendencies in such intricate ways that in their most refined expression, they are coterminous with their attendant virtue: the skill makes the virtue realizable and the virtue displays the skill in its best light. And in keeping with holistic commitments, they are one *whole* we differentiate but conceptually. This is particularly the case when those skills are worth having as part of a flourishing human life. Within a holistically thick framework, there is a continuity and congruence between aesthetics and ethics. When a midfielder in football ably manages to dribble the ball around opponents playing dirty without stooping to similar tactics solely building on his skill, this is an action both beautiful and morally good (Ilundáin-Agurruza and Torres 2010). Skills then, can be normatively imbued with aesthetic and ethic value in the sense that *kalon* had for the Ancient Greeks (See essay 7 for *kalon;* other essays gradually fill in the argument in other ways). Moreover, McNamee's perceptive analysis, following Pincoffs, advances what could be called a pluralist view of virtues (2008, 58 ff.). McNamee seeks to expand on MacIntyre's reductive tripartite model of justice, courage, and honesty (what Pincoffs classifies as 'non-instrumental') with a broader suite of instrumental virtues such as alertness, cool-headedness, tenacity, and energy, to mention some that are more pertinent to sport and active pursuits. These are more readily connected with skills in the way just discussed. Alertness and energy readily tie with elite performance in dire and limit situations. As we will see in *Reflections on a Katana*, these *naturally* integrate into a holistically thick framework where skills, virtue, performer, and situation form part of an excellent 'wholeness.'

We can look at virtues separate from their *function*, the way we look at a specimen in formaldehyde. We will capture just as much of their animate dynamics and what they are like when alive or performed. Our very skills *are* fruitful loci of normativity when studied *as* they take place, in the doing. They are functions, not mechanisms or objects. As functions, they are expressed in the actions of living beings. As such they are richly endowed with animate dynamics. Quality fully permeates them: kinesthetic, proprioceptive, and perceptual dynamics for agents and observers, and the very quality of the action as better or worse in a practical, aesthetic, and moral sense. In the thick of the action, these are one. A deployed skill is not simply an action with a particular 'truth value' of either successful or not, but a totality with kinesthetic, tactile, and other dynamics that give the action its unique quality as compared to others of its kind. No two tennis serves are ever identical. In addition, we must incorporate the agent's attendant thoughts, the way others may react to her action (her surprised opponent as she drops the ball next to the net), environmental surroundings, and sociohistorical variables.[11] All constitute the *skillful action*, or rather, skillful acting, as the gerund stresses it is a happening and not an object (in a jar perhaps). And those most refined skillful 'actings' display true *virtuosity*. This virtuosity reflects the performer's character as much as her performance.

Speaking of character, it is pertinent to consider its development. When looking at character training Mike McNamee judiciously argues that it,

> helps our evolving moral agent to reliably (re)produce the right acts at the right times while coming to feel appropriately about them. It is a mistake, however, to think of this habituation as mere rote learning in the way that early skill-psychologists believed. It is as if we need to replace this arcane way of thinking with a more open-ended framework to understand and explain action. *One learns the generalised responses and then one must refine them, becoming even more sensible to the particularities of the situation.* (2008, 84, my emphasis)

This open-ended framework that bespeaks of generalization, refinement, and sensibility to particularities of the situation is congruent with a situated and holistic view of ethics, where know-how is exhibited across a range of capacities, skillful and virtuous, that work together to produce the desired results. It does no good to know what to do virtuously without the requisite skills to pull it off, and the skills need to be guided so they are suitably deployed. To adapt Kant's famous dictum: virtues without skills are powerless, and skills without virtues are lost. We refine our virtuous responses in tandem, jointly, and concurrently with the development of our skills. This applies in terms of implementation, i.e. the more skillful the person, the more can that person handle complex challenges. A corollary is that this endows her with the greater ability to assess the response to situations where deliberation may not be possible because of urgency, or for less burdened deliberation.[12] Of course, as we learn from superhero comics or the tales of heroes of yore, extraordinary skills can also be used viciously. A *kungfu* expert can be a virtuous paladin of justice, a veritable master or sensei, or a murderous thug for hire, a mere technician. This is a misuse of skill; and a skill not worth developing to flourish as a human being. The answer this effectively requires more stage setting than is possible now (see the last two essays).

Assuming we have skills and are virtuous enough, the next question is a practical one, *how* do we develop excellence? This is a long story better left for later. But the upshot can be nicely summarized in advance of a fuller treatment via Will Durant's not-so-long *The Story of Philosophy*. When discussing Dewey's views on excellence, he writes:

> Excellence is an art won by training and habituation: we do not act rightly because we have virtue or excellence, but we rather have these because we have acted rightly; 'these virtues are formed in man by his doing the actions'; we are what we repeatedly do. *Excellence, then, is not an act but a habit.* (Durant 1991, 76, my italics)

We cultivate excellence in the very doing. Skills, in this view, are 'actings' not potentialities, and as such it is in the very enactment of skills that we develop them. A favorite poet of my youth, Antonio Machado once wrote, 'Wayfarer, you lay the path in walking'

(My translation of 'Caminante, se hace camino al andar'). In doing so, and as far as our experience in concerned a new sun rises in the morning for us. As the way is long, it is necessary to enlist the help of some horses; some audacious and capable dark horses that we ride in the next section.

NOTES

1. Holowchak and Reid (2011) develop a very congenial line of argumentation, where, what they call *Aretism,* tackles many of the challenges from which the modern sports world suffers. They focus on aretē, as their coinage evinces, to draw a balance between an inflexible instrumentalism of a martial and commercial model of competitive sport, and recreational and playful models. There are many similarities with the thesis developed here, though it is worth nothing that their approach is explicitly Aristotelian, whereas *Skillful Striving* draws deliberately on a more eclectic range of authors and is therefore more heterogeneous.

2. Taking the live performance as primary and the recording as a posterior and convenient artifact with a complex ontology.

3. I have been unable to find the original source, as it was in a local newspaper, *Diario de Navarra,* which has resisted all attempts at finding it. In personal conversation, Induráin confirmed this view (July 10, 1996).

4. Contemporary fighting martial arts, such as boxing, wrestling, or MMA are closer to their origins in terms of risk, if much further with regard to their philosophy.

5. For a phenomenological analysis of Kretchmar's development of sweet tension, see Standal and Moe 2011; Torres and McLaughlin 2011.

6. This example comes from Stephen Davies (1997) illuminating discussion of why sad music makes us sad; and essay with an interesting application to sport philosophy if we wish to explain why suffer in sport if it hurts.

7. There is another issue, large and controversial enough not to tackle it fully here, so the following perhaps 'inflammatory' remarks are offered at face value. First, there is a patent difference between the philosophical writings of aestheticians and philosophers of art who are also artists. Even when they limit their discussion to the most arcane and abstract issues, their 'alternate trade' shows, pace Arthur Danto, philosopher by day and printmaker and painter by night (or perhaps the reverse) (in addition to those works cited already see 1986, 1992, 1994); or consider philosopher-musicians Levinson (1990), Davies (2003), and Kivy (2002). Similarly, sport philosophers who are or have practiced sport bring an authenticity to their work that informs their argument much in the same way as Longfellow's craftsmen put details only the gods see: there are subtleties that show their colors. (Given the many examples, I simply cite some whose works I reference in this monograph already and refer readers to them: Gunnar Breivik, Scott Kretchmar, Sigmund Loland, Mike McNamee, and Heather Reid). This does not mean that those who prefer to spectate should be discounted as charlatans. Far from being the case, their 'removed' perspective is necessary. However, to this day in the West, just as in the arts, the performer's experience—in a rich and wholesome sense—is seen as less genuine. Second, we should not forget that even the most sedate of philosophers have to deal with the world in innumerable pragmatic ways, relying on processes long ago mastered but now forgotten (e.g. the very fine motor skills that writing or walking

took them to learn). Hence, they can postulate intuition pumps about brains in vats (see Sheets-Johnstone for a critique of this 2011, and *Riding the Wind*).

8. See Ilundáin-Agurruza (2000) for a very extensive analysis and critique of genius in the arts.

9. It took place at the Center for Philosophic Exchange of the College at Brockport, State University of New York on February 10, 1972, under the title 'Records and the Man.' For a reference to the event and photographs see Cesar Torres 2014, 8–9. Citations are from a personal correspondence with Schacht.

10. The inherited distinction into fine arts and the 'rest' (crafts, performing arts) is very problematic for historical and conceptual reasons. I use the term here for convenience, as that will be clearest to readers. I do not endorse the distinction.

11. The environmental surroundings are those that are *alive* for us, those with which we directly interact, as Ortega would say. These include the landscape (urban, rural), and even elements such as weather. The sociohistorical facet covers both a personal sphere where we create our own personal narratives that interweave our story with those of others and our times, and the broader canvas of the historical conditions in which we live, which in turn are embedded in the larger context of our lifeworld. Ortega refers to these as our *circumstances*.

12. Deliberation often informs spontaneous responses heuristically; a previous generalized pattern that we apply to the particularities of the situation.

REFERENCES

BARTHES, R. 1977. The death of the Author. In *Image, music, text*. Translated by S. HEATH. New York, NY: Fontanal Press: 142–8.

BEST, D. 1979. *Philosophy and human movement*. London: George Allen & Unwin.

BORGES, J.L. 1974. *Pierre Menard, autor del Quijote* [Pierre Menard, Author of Don Quixote] in Jorge Luis Borges, Obras Completas Emecé Editores. Buenos Aires.

———. 2005. Otros Textos [Other texts]. In *Cervantes y el Quijote*, edited by S.L. DEL CARRIL and M.R. DE ZOCCHI. Buenos Aires: Emecé: 95–157.

BREIVIK, G. 2010. Philosophical perfectionism—Consequences and implications for sport. *Sport, Ethics and Philosophy* 4 (1): 87–105.

———. 2014. Sporting knowledge and the problem of knowing how. *Journal of the Philosophy of Sport* 41 (2): 143–62.

COLLINGWOOD, R.G. 1958. *The principles of art*. Oxford: Oxford University Press.

CORDNER, C. 1988. Differences between sport and art. *Journal of the Philosophy of Sport* 15: 31–47.

CREASE, R.P. 2012. Critical point: Sporting knowledge. *Physics World* 25 (7) July: 19.

CSIKSZENTMIHALYI, M. 2008. *Flow: The psychology of optimal experience*. New York, NY: Harper Perennial.

DANTO, A. 1973. Artworks and real things. *Theoria* 39: 1–17.

———. 1981. *The transfiguration of the commonplace: A philosophy of art*. Cambridge, MA: Harvard University Press.

———. 1986. *The philosophical disenfranchisement of art*. New York, NY: Columbia University Press.

———. 1992. *Beyond the Brillo Box: The visual arts in post-historical perspective*. New York, NY: The Noonday Press.

———. 1994. *Embodied meanings: Critical essays and aesthetic meditations*. New York, NY: Farrar, Strauss, Giroux.

DAVIES, S. 1997. Why listen to sad music if it makes one feel sad? In *Music and meaning*, edited by J. ROBINSON. Ithaca, NY: Cornell University Press: 242–54.

———. 2003. *Themes in the philosophy of music*. Oxford: Oxford University Press.

DEWEY, J. 1922. *Democracy and Education: An introduction to the philosophy of education*. New York, NY: The MacMillan.

———. 1963. *Philosophy and civilization*. New York, NY: Capricorn Books.

DOWNES, S.M. 2010. Are you experienced? What you don't know about your climbing experience. In *Climbing—Philosophy for everyone. Because it's there*, edited by S. SCHMID. Malden, MA: Blackwell: 195–205.

DURANT, W. 1991. *The story of philosophy: The lives and opinions of the world's greatest philosophers*. New York, NY: Simon & Schuster.

ECCLESIATES. 1971. *The Holy Bible*. Grand Rapids, MI: Zondervan Bible Publishers.

EDGAR, A. 2013. Sport and art: An essay in the hermeneutics of sport. *Sport, Ethics and Philosophy*. 7 (1): 1–9.

EICHBERG, H. 2013. Back to the phenomena (of sport)—or back to the phenomenologists? Towards a phenomenology of (sports) phenomenology. *Sport, Ethics and Philosophy* 7 (2): 271–82.

FOUCAULT, M. 1984. What is an Author. In *The Foucault reader*, edited by P. RABINOW. New York, NY: Pantheon Books: 101–20.

FRALEIGH, W.P. 1984. *Right actions in sport. Ethics of contestants*. Champaign, IL: Human Kinetics.

GALLAGHER, S. 2005. *How the body shapes the mind*. Oxford: Oxford University Press.

GIBSON, J.J. 1979. *The ecological approach to visual perception*. Boston, MA: Houghton-Mifflin.

HADOT, P. 1995. *Philosophy as a way of life*. London: Blackwell.

HOCHSTETLER, D., and P.M. HOPSICKER. 2012. The heights of humanity: Endurance sport and the Strenuous Mood. *Journal of the Philosophy of Sport* 39 (1): 117–35.

HOLOWCHAK, M.A., and H.L. REID. 2011. *Aretism: An ancient sports philosophy for the modern sports world*. London: Lexington Books.

HOSPERS, J. 1969. The concept of artistic expression. In *Introductory readings in aesthetics*, edited by J. HOSPERS. New York, NY: The Free Press: 143–67.

HURKA, T. 1993. *Perfectionism*. New York, NY: Oxford University Press.

HUSSERL, E. 1989. *Ideas pertaining to a pure phenomenology and to a phenomenological philosophy*. Dordrecht: Kluwer Academic Publishers.

ILUNDÁIN-AGURRUZA, J.M. 2000. … In the realms of art: A conceptual inquiry of the genesis of the work of art. Ph.D. thesis, University of Illinois at Urbana-Champaign.

ILUNDÁIN-AGURRUZA, J. and C. TORRES. 2010. Embellishing the ugly side of the beautiful game. In *Beautiful thoughts on the beautiful game*, edited by T. RICHARDS. Chicago, IL: Open Court: 185–96.

JACKSON, P. 2003. *The lord of the rings: The return of the king*. Los Angeles (CA): [DVD] New Line Home Video.

KANT, I. 1951. *Critique of judgement*. Translated by J.H. BERNARD. New York, NY: Hafner Press.

KIVY, P. 2002. *Introduction to a philosophy of music*. Oxford: Clarendon Press.

KRETCHMAR, S. 1972. From test to contest: An analysis of two kinds of counterpoint in sport. *Journal of the Philosophy of Sport* 2: 23–30.

———. 2005. *Practical philosophy of sport and physical activity*. Champaign, IL: Human Kinetics.

———. 2013. Mind-bodyholism, paradigm shifts, and education. *Fair Play. Revista de Filosofía, Ética y Derecho del Deporte* 1 (1): 28–43.

LALLY, R., D. ANDERSON, and J. KAAG. 2013. *Pragmatism and the philosophy of sport.* London: Lexington Books.

LEVINSON, J. 1990. *Music, art, and metaphysics: Essays in philosophical aesthetics.* Ithaca, NY: Cornell University Press.

LOLAND, S. 2011. The normative aims of coaching. In *The ethics of sports coaching*, edited by A. HARDMAN and C. JONES. London: Routledge: 14–22.

MACINTYRE, A. 1984. *After virtue: A study in moral virtue.* 2nd ed. Notre Dame, IN: University of Notre Dame.

MCFEE, G. 2004. *Sport, rules and values: Philosophical investigations into the nature of sport.* London: Routledge.

———. 2013. Making sense of the philosophy of sport. *Journal of the Philosophy of Sport* 7 (4): 412–29.

MCGINN, C. 1999. *The mysterious flame: Conscious minds in a material world.* New York, NY: Basic Books.

MCNAMEE, M. 2008. *Sports, virtues and vices: Morality plays.* London: Routledge.

MUMFORD, S. 2012. *Watching sport: Aesthetics, ethics and emotions.* London: Routledge.

MUTCHSLECNER, D. 2012. *Enigma and light.* Boise, ID: Ahsahta Press, Boise State University: 20.

ORTEGA Y GASSET, J. 2008. Hombre y circumstancia [Man and circumstance]. *Obras Completas.* VIII: 499–511.

REID, H.L. 2009. Sport, philosophy, and the quest for knowledge. *Journal of the Philosophy of Sport* 36 (1): 40–9.

———. 2010. Special issue: Athletics and philosophy in ancient Greece and Rome: Contests and virtue. *Sport, Ethics and Philosophy* 4 (2): 109–234.

———. 2012. *Introduction to the philosophy of sport.* Plymouth: Rowan & Littlefield.

ROBERTS, T. 1986. Sport, art and particularity: The best equivocation. *Journal of the Philosophy of Sport* 13: 49–63.

———. 1992. The making and remaking of sport actions. *Journal of the Philosophy of Sport* 19: 15–29.

RUSSELL, J.S. 2007. Broad internalism and the moral foundations of sport. In *Ethics in sport*. 2nd ed, edited by W.J. MORGAN. Champaign, IL: Human Kinetics: 51–66.

RYLE, G. 1949. *The concept of mind.* New York, NY: Barnes & Noble.

SCHACHT, R. 1998. Nietzsche and sport. *International Studies in Philosophy* 30 (3): 123–30.

SHEETS-JOHNSTONE, M. 2009. *The corporeal turn: An interdisciplinary reader.* Exeter: Imprint Academic.

———. 2011. *The primacy of movement.* 2nd ed. Amsterdam: John Benjamins.

SIMON, R. 2000. Internalism and internal values in sport. *Journal of the Philosophy of Sport* 27 (1): 1–16.

STANDAL, O., and V. MOE. 2011. Merleau-Ponty meets Kretchmar: Sweet tensions of embodied learning. *Sport, Ethics and Philosophy* 5 (3): 256–69.

SUITS, B. 1990. *The grasshopper: Life, games and Utopia.* Boston, MA: David R. Godine Publisher.

TOLKIEN, J.R.R. 1981. *The lord of the rings: The fellowship of the ring.* London: Unwin Paperbacks.

TORRES, C., ed. 2014. Introduction. In *The Bloomsbury companion to the philosophy of sport*, edited by C. Torres. London: Bloomsbury Publishing: 1–14.

TORRES, C., and D. MCLAUGHLIN. 2011. Sweet tension and its phenomenological description: Sport, intersubjectivity, and horizon. *Sports, Ethics and Philosophy*. 5 (3): 270–84.

WALLACE, J. 1978. *Virtues and vices*. Ithaca, NY: Cornell University Press.

———. 2009. *Norms and practices*. Ithaca, NY: Cornell University Press.

WIMSATT, W.K. and M.C. BEARDSLEY. 1987. The intentional fallacy. In *Philosophy looks at the arts: Contemporary readings in aesthetics*, edited by J. MARGOLIS. Philadelphia, PA: Temple University Press: 367–80.

SECTION II. *PRAGMATIC DARK HORSES: DEWEY, JAMES, ORTEGA Y GASSET, AND ZHUANZGI*

This quartet of dark horses, whose seminal contributions do not nowadays command center stage as compared to their halcyon days (despite their remarkable relevance), is united by four main factors: One, by their inherent pragmatic temperament, whether professed on their sleeve as James and Dewey's, veiled as Ortega's, or *avant la lettre* as Zhuangzi's. After all James writes, "Of whatever temperament a professional philosopher is, he tries, when philosophizing, to sink the fact of his temperament," and a practical mien indeed underwrites their philosophies (2000, 8); this segues into the second one, as all four *live* their philosophical views, that is, their lives exemplify their philosophical commitments and writings. The opening citation is demonstrative of an underlying attitude to life where adventurousness and decisive action is central, and where each achieved fulfillment in his own way; three, by their thick phenomenological descriptions and keen observations, firmly rooted in experience and a "rational intuition"; and four, by a sophisticated, uncharacteristic, and illuminating thinking where the body took centre stage. Their views prove indispensable for Thick Holism and its emphasis on animation and a mindful corporeality. Together they form a formidable group to help diagnose the genesis and development of excellences, integrate body and mind (countering mainstream reductive views of the mind), and act as inspirational models of thinkers and persons after which we may model ourselves. Four essays, one devoted to each philosopher, comprise this section. These provide an overview of key themes pertinent to this inquiry, thus being largely foundational of ideas that percolate into subsequent discussion. Those dedicated to Ortega and Zhuangzi are substantially longer. The reason is that their "dark horse" status is more pronounced in sport philosophy, and this redresses matters to some extent. Subsequent essays in the monograph build on their ideas, and integrate new ones when appropriate.

REFERENCE

JAMES, W. 2000. *Pragmatism and other writings*. New York and London: Penguin Books.

2—WILLIAM JAMES—PRAGMATIC PIONEER

Jesús Ilundáin-Agurruza

It is not the critic who counts: not the man who points out how the strong man stumbles or where the doer of deeds could have done better. The credit belongs to the man who is actually in the arena, whose face is marred by dust and sweat and blood, who strives valiantly, who errs and comes up short again and again, because there is no effort without error or shortcoming, but who knows the great enthusiasms, the great devotions, who spends himself for a worthy cause; who, at the best, knows, in the end, the triumph of high achievement, and who, at the worst, if he fails, at least he fails while daring greatly, so that his place shall never be with those cold and timid souls who knew neither victory nor defeat. (Roosevelt 1910)[1]

The opus of William James (1842–1910) is revolutionary, forward looking, and particularly suited for a holistic conception of enactive performance and cognition. Of particular interest in terms of self-cultivation are James' views on asceticism and risk, and those regarding cognition and action: his notions of the fringe and pure experience. The pivotal role of the body in this exposition partially redresses the academic ignorance that, as philosopher Shusterman (2008) remarks, exists regarding the body's importance in James thinking. Additionally, this examination validates James's dynamic view of the brain where localized processes richly interact with one another. As Bruce Mangan explains this guides his phenomenology of consciousness not as a series of discrete elements but a continuous process (2007, 673). While James' introspective methodology and phenomenology are still viewed with suspicion (ibid., 674), this essay further validates the Jamesian legacy while underwriting many of the ideas in the third section of *Skillful Striving*.

1. James on Habit as Character Building

Habit has long played a key role in character building and ethical behavior, mostly, but not exclusively, in virtue ethics. Precisely, how to develop and how to instill habit is less clear a matter. Auspiciously for our purposes, James' theory of habit brings mind and body together. In this view, our physiology anchors our character. This applies readily to self-cultivation within the framework of active pursuits and excellence-seeking performance. As Shusterman explains, the idea is to shape our embodied selves into habits of mind and action, premised on an automaticity that replaces previous conscious thought, time, and effort (2008, 140)[2]. Shusterman cites James' *Principles of Psychology*, 'this requires a good measure of asceticism to push our nervous system further into the right directions it may not be prone to take' (ibid.). Ignoring the ill-phrased reductionism that Shusterman is elsewhere careful to avoid, sports and performative endeavors, when engaged autotelically, are the sorts of activities in which we willfully push ourselves into ascetic pursuits where pain is the price to develop our character and integrate our bodily processes.

Elsewhere, the Jamesian analysis of asceticism reads like an analysis of athletic forays (2002). Thus, he speaks of asceticism in terms of an organic hardiness (resolve) that shuns too much ease, a dietary temperance and non-pampering of the body, one that beckons a sacrifice for a god highlights the obsession with a challenge to overcome (2002, 325, 326). He pointedly notes how this leads to 'exercises' prompted by genuine perversions where pain is felt as pleasure (ibid.). If we exchange the 'higher being' for the notion of a 'calling,' we have a list of prerequisites to truly engage in the aforementioned pursuits and a way to explain for that perversion that Nike's 'No Pain, No Gain' so pithily embodies. The intrinsic enjoyment that many of us *habit*ually find on the slopes, waters, turfs, courts, roads, gymnasiums, dojos, dance studios, and workshops is predicated on nurturing a toughness that battens the hatches against the lure of sedate, painless, and oftentimes mind-numbing hedonistic leisure outlets the likes of which TV consumption or endless hours of online 'activity' illustrate. An ascetic disposition—not at odds with enjoyment of a refined kind—lies at the heart of successful habit. And this happens in and through engaged and living bodies.

It may be argued that a disposition toward asceticism is actually built on habit, and thus its role in shoring up habit itself is a case of putting the horse before the cart. Looking for a simple single cause–effect relationship here misses the wood for the trees. The search for a linear causal origin leads to the impasse of attempting to decide whether the disposition to ascetic endeavors comes first or the habit required for these precedes the resolve needed for asceticism. Rather, it is a dynamic relation where both asceticism and habit coevally grow together: a Spartan character only becomes solidified as tendencies grow into habit while the latter results from the capacity to endure and repeat. When it comes to active pursuits, we get started through a serendipitous mix of exposure and opportunity that our temperamental affinities spur, nurture, and augment. These affinities or dispositions are not reducible to one reason. Nor should they be limited on account of a misplaced hunger for theoretical parsimony. People engage and cultivate these active pursuits (indeed activities generally) for *many* reasons whose value changes in asynchronous fashion. For example, consider a chance encounter with *parkour* or freerunning. It revives movements, sensations, and a playfulness one may have thought were long and irredeemably lost. We embark on a new course where initial if rusty skills are slowly, painfully, and joyfully pried from the embers of emotional and corporeal memory while a sense of community within and with which we practice further reaffirms our commitment. Our involvement with freerunning will undergo periods of unquestioned devotion with others where injury perhaps, or other activities jostle for our attention and limited energies. Discipline, but another name for Jamesian asceticism, and habit are the sine qua non to becoming a freerunner. And yet, the land of asceticism and habit is not all roses' velvety petals, there are thorns too. While James extols the value of danger and effort, he also perceptively notes the vice of excess to which asceticism is prone to in religious matters (2002, 372), and finds that saner channels for its underlying heroism can be found, for example, in athletics, militarism, and adventure (ibid., 399).

One aspect why active endeavors are philosophically and existentially appealing is the promise of an adventurous life that may chisel our character. Indeed, James acknowledges that 'in moderate degrees it is natural or even usual to court the arduous' (2002, 327); only extreme manifestations prove paradoxical for him. His recipe for an admirable character centers on a strenuous and vigorous life that courts effort and danger as he proclaims throughout his writings.[3] He writes, 'Some austerity and wintry negativity, some roughness, danger, stringency, some effort, some "no! no!" must be mixed in, to produce the sense of an existence with character and texture and power' (ibid., 328). This endorsement of risk is something to which James is very partial. There are momentous lessons and an inspiring life to be found when one leaves the safe shoals of too comfortable a life. His experience in the 'idyllic' and quiet life of Chautauqua is clear, for after a week of its pastoral pleasures he writes, perhaps with a bit of hyperbole, 'Ouf! What a relief! Now for something primordial and savage, even though it were as bad as an Armenian massacre to set the balance straight again' (2000, 288). By means of a via *negativa*, he meditates on what was lacking in that Sabbatical city and realizes that he 'soon recognized that it was the element that gives the wicked outer world all its moral style, expressiveness and picturesqueness—the element of precipitousness, so to call it, of strength and strenuousness, intensity and danger' (James 2000, 289). And he practiced more than what he preached, going to extremes when he jumped into the arena of the strenuous life. He undertook such vigorous hikes that, Shusterman argues, these may have played a role in his demise. He also adds that James overplayed the strenuous and active, however, at the expense of the reflective, instructing us to trust spontaneity (2008, 169). This spontaneity, borne from habit, sometimes may reinforce bad habits (ibid.).

Some of these habits, Shusterman suggests, would undo James or shorten his overstrenuous life. Led by a 'heroic ideal that was martial and dynamic', he would have been better served by a strong and striving life that more effectively combined effort and restful calm (2008, 175–178). Nonetheless, athletics can temper excess, not the least because extreme practice often leads to injury or poorer performance; these are not in themselves a solution to intemperance—the failure to contain excesses. There are always those sportspersons, martial artists, and performers whose *métier* becomes a vicious, all-consuming affair that goes beyond the single-minded focus of elite sport. In the end, for most, we need temperance as Aristotle's virtue theory or Buddha's Middle Way proposed. This moderating virtue does not require that we should become timid observers, only that we nurture the requisite skills and good judgment before we jump into the arena. Thus, more positively, for Richard Lally sport adopts a Jamesian attitude in so far as it tests our limits, and more to the point, 'with the acceptance of risk and a wholehearted approach to living comes the possibility of excellence' (2013, 13). On the safe side lays mediocrity, on the risky one the possibility of both tragedy and triumph —something to be expounded upon with Ortega presently. Moreover, this is the path to self-knowledge. As Lally states, James radical empiricism espoused two kinds of knowledge: knowledge about and knowledge by acquaintance. The latter is particularly pertinent for athletics because it 'generates living personal truths' that allow us to make claims about the world and 'form an intimate catalogue of knowledge' to act as our guide (ibid., 2–3). Sports and performative endeavors place us in situations where we cannot hide, and act as moral laboratories (McFee 2004), or truth-seeking enterprises (Reid 2009, 2012). They are paths for skillful striving. But simple risk taking will not suffice; character and self-knowledge are to be tempered in the crucible of measured self-cultivation.

Indomitable lives whose faces are marred by dust and sweat and blood are predicated on a willingness to jump into the fray and not become mere spectators, let alone critics. Just as the other dark horses presently to be engaged, James lived his philosophy on his sleeve so to speak. He was an inveterate 'self-experimenter' who tirelessly worked on himself as he battled his inner demons and ailments, whether it was through various medical and alternative healing methods or using oft-denigrated introspection as central methodology for his psychological investigations. 'Self-cultivation' is a core concept that permeates the Jamesian ethos. Yet, as Shusterman avows, James does not 'develop his insights into practical ways of deploying [...] heightened awareness for enhancing our performance in the wider world of action' (2008, 164). This somewhat ironic lapse when it comes to being practical and detailing how to actually bring about self-development can be partially redressed if we consider the world of sport and, also ironically, the lair of 'removed-from-this-word' sainthood.

To begin with the latter, writing about saintliness, James says, 'Speaking generally, our moral and practical attitude [...] is always the resultant of two sets of forces within us, impulses pushing us one way and obstructions and inhibitions holding us back' (2002, 287). For him, this explains the differences in character among people, and moreover sets a framework to walk toward the side of risk, effort, and possible excellence. It is tied to emotional processes, which can be conflicted, that channel such inhibitions or impulses. Anger, fear, and bravery, understood as a feeling of resoluteness to overcome or resist the former, set the stage for an embarkation to an inspiring life full of challenges and precipitousness. The idea is that developing our talents rides on emotional processes that channel our impulses and inhibitions (which in turn shape our affinities). This we must learn to bridle.

How to harness emotion suitably is a more complicated story than merely willing whatever it is that we wish to bring about—as if will power itself were sufficient. But we can get a glimpse from James' discussion of the transformation of character in the context of religious conversion (2002, 215). This transformation also bridges to the cognitive facet of his views, for character transformations must rein in the emotions. For James, there are two forms of mental occurrence applicable to this process of conversion and character transformation: volitional and self-surrendering, or, we could say, voluntary and unconscious or 'subconscious,' using James' preferred term.[4] The voluntary route is explicit and laid out in the open; we openly decide on a certain course of action and set out to realize it. The latter is more interesting, pertinent for high performance, and mysterious as well. In this context, James approvingly and opportunely bringing up sport, cites Starback, 'An athlete ... sometimes awakens suddenly to an understanding of the fine points of a game and to a real enjoyment of it [...] if he keeps on engaging in the sport, there may come a day when all at once the game plays itself through him—when he loses himself in the contest' (ibid., 228). The crucial idea here is the disappearance of the explicit route and a transformation grounded in our self; there is a surrendering and evanescence of the self that is replaced, for James, by subconscious processes. With this, we arrive at his views on consciousness and cognition readily pertinent to active pursuits and exemplar performances, namely the fringe and pure consciousness.

2. James Psychology and Philosophy of Mind

As noted above, James' original and keen observations in his *Principles of Psychology* (1918) are still largely relevant and correct. His views are particularly apposite for sport philosophy because they afford phenomenologically thick analyses of our experience that reveal their underlying dynamics. In particular, his views on the continuity and flowing aspect of our experience, in which our very thinking *is* corporeal, and his views on the background or fringe of consciousness illuminate phenomena that often remain in the shadows no matter what newfangled gadgets are fit to someone's head (a tendency that is assessed in the sixth essay).

For James, consciousness is not as a discrete phenomenon but a continuous one (something more fully developed with Dewey next). Mark Johnson highlights this continuity in James' thinking in relation to concepts that are not discrete or radically different in nature from percepts: 'rather, [they are] two aspects of a continuous flow of feeling-thinking' (2007, 87). For him, instead of 'concept,' we should speak of the act of conceptualizing (Johnson 2007, 88).[5] Johnson persuasively argues relying on this that even logic itself is incarnate not only in origin but also in how it manifests itself in our lives (2007, 94 ff.), for ultimately, in observance of James' pragmatic rule of meaning, it finds its meaning 'if not in some sensible particular [...] in some particular difference in the course of human experience which its being true will make' (2007, 92). The aptness of the analysis with regard to that quality of continuity standing, we should also realize that in some contexts emphasizing concept rather than act of conceptualizing may be the best thing to do, as per the pragmatic rule of meaning itself. In fact, we often allow this 'concepts' to work in tandem with the act of conceptualizing, very much like the two wheels of a cart: a certain concept is given shape by the act as it unfolds it, and the unfolding, similar to how Michelangelo liberated the statues in the marble reveals the act what to do or where to go. In sporting practice we do this often, e.g. when we try to figure out a new movement or technique. We feel our way with the hand or foot or body led by a certain conceptual understanding (which can be an image, but not necessarily, as it is usually a conglomerate of kinesthetic and proprioceptive sense along with visualizations, rules, and more). But there is more to this.

In reference to James' idea that when thinking we often 'feel' our way, Johnson cheekily writes, using the preposition as an indicator of indecision, that we are 'to feel James' 'but,' for to do so, to think disjunctively, is to feel the quality of a situation as a kind of hesitancy or qualification of something asserted or proposed' (2007, 95). 'I would play ball, but my knee will get sore' expresses hesitation and the unsavory anticipated result if indulgence leads to a game. Moreover, Johnson helps extract the radical implications of James thought, which are predicated on his notion of fulsome experience. For James 'every thought implicates a certain bodily awareness [...] in all thinking, we are in some degree aware,' however vaguely, of our bodily states as they result from our interactions with the world' (2007, 94). For James, phrases such as 'either one or the other,' 'a is *b*, but' are '*signs of direction* in thought, of which direction we nevertheless have an acutely discriminative sense, though no definite sensorial image plays a part in it whatsoever' (1918, 253, his italics). How we feel and discriminate this sense of direction without tying it to sensations becomes clearer momentarily with the discussion of feelings of relations.

41

For now, we can say that prepositions are not simply those propositional elements the kind of which logicians formalize into mere syntactical connectors where 'but' and 'and' become equivalent. Yet, he also advocated a principle of parsimony in consciousness for *ordinary life* whereby we leave to habit or automatism as much as possible because 'it would distract us from the ends of our practical enterprises rather than aiding their realization' (Shusterman 2008, 164). This is generally correct, but in section three we will see that expert action is the exception that proves the rule—in the original sense that it tests it, not confirms it.[6] For now, it is worth emphasizing that the Jamesian feeling of relations is no mere garnish but a key and rich ingredient of experience.

It is necessary to say a little more about these experiences of relations. For James, consciousness is characterized by relational experiences—a much overlooked aspect of his phenomenology as Mangan observes (2007, 674). James divides the contents of consciousness into two kinds, those that attention can inspect, percepts and sensory contents he calls 'the nucleus' (ibid., 676), and those outside its purview, feelings of relations he calls the 'fringe of consciousness' (ibid., 675). The moment we try to attend to the latter, these disappear under a layer of sensory information. The fringe, much like glial cells in the brain are much more prevalent than neurons and act as a supporting substrate, also acts as a dynamic substrate that binds the explicit contents of consciousness into larger and meaningful wholes. It acts as an invisible background on which sensory experiences are highlighted, as if one were to put paint on a clear film should the film change dynamically with our comings and goings. In a way it is also much like the eye that cannot see itself. James' genially ascertains its presence and operations indirectly, through memory and analysis of scenarios we are all familiar with:

> What is that, shadowy scheme of the 'form' of an opera, play, or book, which remains in our mind and on which we pass judgment when the actual thing is gone? What is our notion of a scientific or philosophical system? Great thinkers have vast premonitory glimpses of schemes of relation between terms, which hardly even as verbal images enter the mind, so rapid is the whole process. We all of us have this permanent consciousness of whither our thought is going. It is a feeling like any other, a feeling of what thoughts are next to arise, before they have arisen. (James 1918, 255)

This is also applicable to patterns of movement typical of active pursuits. The concatenation of the dancer's pirouettes or the karateka's kata, the drilled-in patternings of gymnast or swimmer, the master woodworker's precise incisions with the carving tools, these all issue forth from the tenuous epistemological nether-world where spontaneity arises from both unconscious levels *and* the fringe. As something that gives us intimations of what is to arise, the fringe is neither unconscious nor fully within the scope of our focal attention.[7] Hence, after we read a book, watch a film, or recall a marathon we do not have a discrete moment-by-moment or play-by-play sensory reexperience, but rather that ghost-like aura from which we issue forth our words or movements. This is most pronounced in tip-of-the-tongue occasions, as Mangan explains (2007, 677). The forgotten name encounters 'a gap therein; [...] a sort of wraith of the name [...] beckoning us in a given direction, making us [...] tingle with the sense of closeness [...] If the wrong names are proposed to us, this singularly definite gap acts immediately to negate them' (James 1918, 251). In this sense, and importantly, the fringe of consciousness allows for valuations of right and wrong by providing that sense of direction that we may punctuate with a 'but' soaked in hesitancy or the skier's confident leaning into the turns as she speeds down the slope. From the fringe, as we feel our way, arise our conscious experiences (this should not be read causally), those overt sensations that make up the nuclei, and which constantly change as they ride on the river's waters, to echo James' fecund image (1918, 255).

An important function of the fringe is to provide that sense of flow and continuity that Mangan explains gives us our sense of time, as it 'rests on the ability of the fringe to evoke, dimly, past and future in the present' (2007, 677). Arguably, a more important function for the fringe is its role in complementing consciousness, whose capacity to process phenomena or compute, as cognitive theorists are wont to say, is very limited. In spite of claims to the contrary by many who claim they can multitask, research conclusively shows that trying to do two things concurrently impairs our cognitive system (Gorlick 2009; Ophir, Nass, and Wagner 2009). Nonetheless, there is a way in which we can do more than one thing at once, and here is where cultivated active pursuits shine. As psychologist Art Markman says, 'if the exercises you're doing feel habitual. "You can easily complete a task that you don't need to think about, like walking or brushing your teeth, while also having a conversation".' (Megroz 2014) Walking, cycling, running, or swimming are the kind of activities that lend themselves to this reflective and subpersonal double-dipping where attentional resources are ably toggled between explicit and implicity systems, as cognitive science mechanistically theorizes it, or reflective and supersonal, as phenomenology would describe it. This attentional-sharing at the fringe level is sport and situation specific: it will work for some sports and activities for experts or those with a minimum proficiency that allows them to move and think in some contexts. A demanding competitive situation or a hard anaerobic spring workout will not allow for such sharing, nor will it work in the context of a heatedly contested football or tennis match. Nonetheless, Aristotle was on to something with his peripatetic ways. Regardless, the fact that we can do so still needs explaining. Mangan highlights how, '[t [he fringe is designed to deflect direct acts of attention because this allows the transformation of imminent to explicit information in consciousness' (2007, 680). Further, it binds reflective, conscious and subconscious or subpersonal processes into an integrated cognitive system.

This fusion or interpenetration between the different levels is of importance for our understanding of skillful performances. It allows for a more refined analysis, in my view, than conventional and prevalent views in cognitive science (Bruya 2010; Jeannerod 1997, 2008), philosophy (Dreyfus and Dreyfus 1986; Searle 1983, 1992), and sport philosophy (Breivik 2007, 2013; Eriksen 2010; Moe 2004, 2007), many of which are discussed in further detail in the third section of this monograph. These take the ideas of 'consciousness' and 'unconsciousness' as sufficient to account for skillful coping, attributing to the unconscious most of the cognitive load when performing expertly (or simply beyond the level of novice).[8] The fringe acts as a hinge between those two levels of awareness, articulating experience and, I argue, also action. After all for James (and pragmatists generally) thinking *is* doing, as Johnson stresses (2007, 92). Mangan argues how this works: '[t]hough completely conscious the fringe stands between non-conscious and focal conscious processing, using a few wisps of experience to radically *condense and summarize* non-conscious information of extreme complexity' (2007, 682, his italics). This is imcumbent on the fact that the fringe does not overtly calculate

HOLISM AND THE CULTIVATION OF EXCELLENCE IN SPORTS AND PERFORMANCE

(ibid.), and that it remains non-descript and vague (ibid., 681). Unburdened by the need to monitor closely sensorial information, this reduces load on attentional focus and conscious processing. Crucial to this process is that sense of something fitting or not fitting the mold, two fringe experiences Mangan calls 'rightness' or 'wrongness' (2007, 682). These do not compute anything specific in the cognitivist sense of relying on explicit symbol manipulation, but they do signal to consciousness the degree to which nonconscious processing fits (ibid.). Moreover, this constitutes a dynamic meaning for James: something is meaningful or not to the extent that this sense of right or wrong fit transforms what would be mere background noise into something understood (ibid.; see also James 1918, 265f).

This capacity to evaluate and guide consciousness is crucial to expert performances. Automatization, spontaneity, flexibility, effectiveness, and efficiency characterize mastered skills and actions. This frees consciousness to deal with what is novel and more pertinent in any given situation. While this is customarily attributed to subpersonal processes, as I will argue in the next essay, careful phenomenological analysis reveals that this fails to capture the complexity of expert performance in the practices under discussion. The pole-vaulter does not need to monitor each step as she sprints down the runway or coordinate explicitly running steps with arm swinging as she holds the pole and aims for the point of contact to propel her skyward. And yet she *is* aware of where the tip of the pole is in relation to where she is and where it needs to go (Polanyi and Prosch (1975), inspired by Gestalt psychology would speak of focal knowledge and tacit knowledge here). This does not take place inside a black box, or else how could she succeed time and time again? Rather, this coordination takes place largely at the level of the fringe, where the tenuous layering allows meaningful nuclei or data to come forth in real time, as it is vetted efficiently by what I call the fringe's *sense of fit*. While far from ensuring success, it does allow to make the decision on when to plant the pole timely and without overburdening conscious attention.

The virtue of James' analysis is that it allows for a transparent connection between the reflective, conscious and explicit level of processing and the subpersonal, unconscious and implicit one. Anne Dietrich and Oliver Stoll, discussing the interaction of the implicit and explicit systems in connection with high performance, point out how '[f[or implicit knowledge to reach consciousness, it must first be explicated, which cannot proceed, due to its concrete-operational organization, through a bottom-up process,' and hence this is achieved at the implicit level that allows the explicit system to pick the needed components (2010, 161). However, it is unclear at what level the interface takes place and precisely how the explicit system reads off needed input given that implicit system precludes metarepresentations. There is a gap here that is problematic for, as Dietrich and Stoll state earlier in their discussion, 'the explicit system, or any other functional system in the brain, does not know about knowledge imprinted in the implicit system, making it unavailable for representation in [...] consciousness' (ibid.). The explicit, conscious system brings in flexibility given its ability to deliberate, but it is slow, the unconscious, implicit system brings in efficiency and speed, but it lacks imaginative possibilities. This has a certain ad hoc element to it that still does not clarify the mystery behind our skillful movements and actions.

Indeed, just how these interact is not clear. The tendency in the mind sciences is to attribute some level of representational processing at a metalevel for the explicit system and lower subpersonal processes for the implicit one, with the need to

44

down-regulate the higher order elements. This notion is criticized in section three alongside the ideas of 'expertise' and 'failure.' For now, suffice it to point out that the fringe actually brings in the requisite layer. Being validated experientially, it enriches and further current attempts to explain skillfulness without the need to attribute representational content of any kind to unconscious processing.

A last and pertinent piece of the Jamesian analysis of consciousness, renowned for its 'stream of thought, of consciousness, or of subjective life' (1918, 239), is what he called 'pure experience.'[9] For James pure experience 'is plain, unqualified activity or existence, a simple *that,*' our actions being based upon it (1976, 13). It is a raw, non- or pre-conceptual experience that, analogous to the fringe, subtends, or underlies our actions. Bower and Gallagher argue similarly that such experience influences our actions and behavior: subconsciously but unerringly (2013).[10] John Kaag illuminatingly applies the concept of 'pure experience' to rowing: sport, remaining close to pure experience in the sharp aches and pains of hard practice, permits the seasoned rower to disappear in a 'willingness to be as nothing' (2013, 59). During intense practice as well as when engaging others, active pursuits' capacity to 'create experience' elicits or makes possible a subject/object unity where our consciousness blends with the activity or the other—something to be explored with Nishida Kitarō, who developed James' insight more deeply and broadly (essay 9).

From a different but related angle, and for a French audience, James once explained the concept thus, 'within this full experience, concrete and undivided, such as it is, a given, the objective physical world and the interior and personal world of each of us meet and fuse the way lines fuse at their intersection' (1976, 115, my translation). This foregrounds an element that Dewey develops more fully, namely how our subjective experience becomes intersubjective in that meeting and fusing of lines where they intersect (a theme further developed below, in essays 4 and 10).[11] The point to take home and to stress is that pragmatist thought stresses the continuity of cognition across the board: from percepts to concepts, from the individual organism to its surrounding social environment, from the emotions to rational thinking, from unconsciousness and the fringe to consciousness. All these are not different in kind but contiguous and continuous. Moreover, they extend to the environment: 'Mental facts cannot be properly studied apart from the physical environment in which they take cognizance' (Johnson 2007, 121), something both Dewey and Ortega took pains to emphasize and integrate into their philosophies more than James. Much of this, from a developmental and genetic stance, has social ramifications that Dewey helps us explore below.

NOTES

1. 'Citizenship in a Republic,' or 'The Man in the Arena,' at the Sorbonne in Paris.
2. This automaticity is challenged and refined in essays 6–9.
3. For other writings evoking this idea see James' 'The Moral Philosopher and the Moral Life' (James 2000, 242–263) and 'What Makes a Life Significant' (ibid., 286–303), and Shusterman's analysis of this (2008, 169–179).
4. Terminology about our mental processes and level of awareness is a complex matter, with different disciplines and methodologies preferring divergent terms. Consciousness is often qualified as 'reflective consciousness' in the phenomenological tradition, which

prefers to use pre-reflective, subpersonal, and pre-noetic to refer to what psychologists refer to as subconscious and unconscious. Presently, there is a preference for the phenomenological terminology as it captures better our experience in ways that, theoretically, are important. Discussion of these issues in detail goes beyond the scope of this inquiry. When discussing the views of a particular author, I will use his terminology, sometimes alongside the phenomenological one.

5. Johnson points out that the problem James faces is 'how to explain perception and conceptualization without resorting to a homunculus within the mind that does the perceiving and conceptualizing' (2007, 89). He solves this impasse by appealing to an organism-environment transaction that appeals to J. J. Gibson's notion of affordance (1979), and to Dewey's view of an ongoing flow of experience within which conceptualization unfolds (ibid.).

6. Nowadays 'an exception that proves the rule' is used to indicate that the rule is confirmed, the exception noted. But originally, the saying meant that the exception actually tested it, and proved it wrong.

7. Some readers may be reminded of Polanyi and Prosch's views (1975). Pete Hopsicker has been his strongest and clearest advocate in sport philosophy (2009). Since this chapter is strictly focused on James, I bypass this interesting connection. In *Fractured Action*, I briefly consider one particularly insightful line of argumentation that Hopsicker develops around the idea of the value of inexact (2013).

8. Breivik is a clear exception as he attributes a bigger role to consciousness in skillful performance than others (2013). However, this also still reduces the pertinent elements to the two usual suspects of conscious or reflective and unconscious or subpersonal systems. While more parsimonious, it presents the problem of interaction between them. Eastern views will supplement the present account (See essays 4, 7, and 9).

9. For a more in depth analysis of James's pure experience and Dewey's bodymind in relation to Japanese philosophy see Ilundáin-Agurruza, Fukawsawa, and Takemura 2014.

10. See Bower and Gallagher (2013).

11. Lally opts to emphasize the Jamesian facet of individual exploration against a background of communal institutions (2013). While much of this inquiry discourses on individual experience, said experience originates ontogenetically, phylogenetically, and conceptually within a community— *Riding the Wind* delves into this.

REFERENCES

BOWER, M., and S. GALLAGHER. 2013. Bodily affects as prenoetic elements in enactive perception. *Phenomenology and Mind* 4 (1): 78–93.

BREIVIK, G. 2007. Skillful coping in everyday life and in sport: A critical examination of the views of Heidegger and Dreyfus. *Journal of the Philosophy of Sport* 34 (2): 116–34.

———. 2013. Zombie-like or superconscious? A phenomenological and conceptual analysis of consciousness in elite sport. *Journal of the Philosophy of Sport* 40 (1): 85–106.

BRUYA, B. 2010. *Effortless attention: A New Perspective in the Cognitive Science of Attention and Action*. Cambridge, MA: MIT University Press.

DIETRICH, A., and O. STOLL. 2010. Effortless attention, hypofrontality, and perfectionism. In *Effortless attention: A new perspective in the cognitive science of attention and action*, edited by B. BRUYA. Cambridge, MA: MIT University Press: 159–78.

DREYFUS, H.L., and S.E. DREYFUS. 1986. *Mind over machine*. New York, NY: Free Press.

ERIKSEN, J. 2010. Mindless coping in competitive sport: Some implications and consequences. *Sport, Ethics and Philosophy* 4: 66–86.

GIBSON, J.J. 1979. *The ecological approach to visual perception*. Boston, MA: Houghton-Mifflin.

GOLRICK, A. 2009. Media multitaskers pay mental price, Stanford study shows. *Stanford Report*. Available at http://news.stanford.edu/news/2009/august24/multitask-research-study-082409.html (accessed 25 July 2014).

HOPSICKER, P. 2009. Polanyi's 'from-to' knowing and his contribution to the phenomenology of skilled motor behavior. *Journal of the Philosophy of Sport* 36: 76–87.

———. 2013. 'The value of the inexact': An apology for inaccurate motor performance. *Journal of the Philosophy of Sport* 40 (1): 65–83.

ILUNDÁIN-AGURRUZA, J., K. FUKASAWA, and M. TAKEMURA. 2014. The philosophy of sport in relation to japanese philosophy and pragmatism. In *A companion for the philosophy of sport*, edited by C. TORRES. London: Bloomsbury Editions: 66–79.

JAMES, W. 1918. *Principles of psychology*. New York, NY: Dover Publications.

———. 1976. La Notion de Conscience [The idea of consciousness]. In *The works of William James: Essays in radical empiricism*, edited by F. Bowwers. Cambridge, MA: Harvard University Press: 105–17.

———. 2002. *The varieties of religious experience: A study in human nature*. New York, NY: The Modern Library.

JEANNEROD, M. 1997. *The cognitive neuroscience of action*. Oxford: Blackwell.

———. 2008. *Motor Cognition: What Actions Tell the Self*. New York, NY: Oxford University Press.

JOHNSON, M. 2007. *The meaning of the body*. Chicago, IL: University of Chicago Press.

KAAG, J. 2013. Paddling in the stream of consciousness: Describing the movement of Jamesian inquiry. In *Pragmatism and the philosophy of sport*, edited by R. LALLY, D. ANDERSON, and J. KAAG. London: Lexington Books: 47–61.

LALLY, R. 2013. Introduction. In *Pragmatism and the philosophy of sport*, edited by R. LALLY, D. ANDERSON, and J. KAAG. London: Lexington Books: 1–16.

MANGAN, B. 2007. Cognition, fringe consciousness, and the legacy of William James. In *Blackwell companion to consciousness*, edited by M. VELMANS and S. SCHNEIDER. Malden, MA: Blackwell: 673–85.

MCFEE, G. 2004. *Sport, rules and values*. London: Routledge.

MEGROZ, G. 2014. Advice from our fittest real Athletes. *Outside Magazine*. Available at http://www.outsideonline.com/fitness/fittest-real-athletes/How-to-Do-More-With-Your-Life-Advice-from-Our-Fittest-Real-Athletes.html (accessed 28 July 2014).

MOE, V.F. 2004. How to understand the 'magic' of skill acquisition in sport. *Bulletin of Science, Technology & Society* 24: 1–12.

———. 2007. Understanding the background conditions of skilled movement in sport: A study of Searle's 'background capacities'. *Sport, Ethics and Philosophy* 1: 299–324.

OPHIR, E., C. NASS, and A. WAGNER. 2009. Cognitive control in media multitaskers. *Proceedings of the National Academy of Sciences*. 106 (37). Available at http://www.pnas.org/content/106/37/15583.full.pdf+html?sid=70ad8886-cfb6-4c2d-b551-f3560953681f (accessed 25 July 2014).

POLANYI, M., and H. PROSCH. 1975. *Meaning*. Chicago, IL: University of Chicago Press.

REID, H. 2009. Sport, philosophy, and the quest for knowledge. *Journal of the Philosophy of Sport* 36 (1): 40–9.

———. 2012. *Introduction to the philosophy of sport*. Lanham, MD: Rowman & Littlefield.

ROOSEVELT, T. 1910. *Man in the Arena*. Available at http://www.theodore-roosevelt.com/trsorbonnespeech.html (accessed 16 December 2013).

SEARLE, J. 1983. *Intentionality*. Cambridge: Cambridge University Press.

SHUSTERMAN, R. 2008. *Body consciousness: Philosophy of mindfulness & Somaesthetics*. Cambridge: Cambridge University Press.

3—JOHN DEWEY—EXPERIENTIAL MAVERICK

Jesús Ilundáin-Agurruza

Be careful
about the blank slate
because it is never really blank

the beginning not inchoate,
but full of proclivities
swept out in registers of fire,

a fundament whose filament
is subtle beyond idea
Beyond the dreamed

beginning, the breathed
beginning, the ignition
of primordial equation. (Mutchslecner 2012)

John Dewey (1859–1952) is another seminal thinker who, for all the preeminence in his heyday, is often ignored today by mainstream research in the mind sciences and analytic philosophical circles. Sport philosophy and the philosophy of education mind his work better, but he is not central to mainstream discourse. A recent volume edited by Lally, Anderson, and Kaag, aptly titled *Pragmatism and the Philosophy of Sport* (2013), and Hochstetler and Hopsicker's article 'The Heights of Humanity' (2012) partially address this neglect. Presently, this essay highlights Dewey's holistic view of human nature, bodily cultivation, and their contribution to excellence. Much as Hume awoke Kant from his dogmatic slumber, so James influenced Dewey. Shusterman shows how James' *Principles of Psychology* (1918) was exceptional for Dewey, who normally eschewed academic works in order to vet his ideas with life's experience (2008, 181). Of his plethora of ideas, those of 'habit', 'body-mind', the 'continuity of experience', and 'self-cultivation' are critically discussed here.

1. Dewey on Habit and Experience

Dewey's work on habit and conduct is of particular relevance for our purposes. It acts as bridge to the bodymind, informs experience's continuity, and is the wellspring that feeds self-cultivation. In *Human Nature and Conduct,* Dewey uses the example of the seemingly simple case of changing one's physical posture, which most people assume is as easy as understanding what needs to be done and willing it to happen; a Cartesian understanding of action and how the mind 'directs' the body. For both Dewey and F. M. Alexander, the founder of the Alexander Technique method (AT henceforth), the idea that merely willing to implement a change suffices once a desire or need is identified is a grave conceptual error and bound to fail practically. Relying on Alexander's methods and ideas, Dewey argues that willing is not sufficient to bring about such transformations, whether physical, mental, or moral (separable but conceptually in our active lives); rather, we need habit to intervene between wish and execution of our ideas or bodily acts (1988, 23–25). Those who *can* stand do so, and only a man who can does, Dewey says (ibid., 24). In other words, we carry out those actions and changes that we are *able* to do. This ability is gained on the anvil of habit. A corollary is that we are not free to merely will, but must adapt ourselves to habit's strictures. That is, we can will as we please, but we are verily bound by those habits we have cultivated. If we shape our life like a sword's blade, its shape and quality are dependent on our work on that anvil. Being a sword, it will not do the job of an ax or spear point.

Habits act as conditions of intellectual efficiency that restrict the intellect (Dewey 1988, 121). When learning a foreign language, proficiency is both afforded and restricted by habit. Repeated exposure and repetitive practice are requisite, and their cumulative effect leading to proficiency in *that* language and its specific phonetic, syntactical, grammatical, and semantic patterns. Surely, there are 'families' of languages, movements, disciplines, crafts, sports, and martial arts that share basic moves and complement one another. These shared affordances facilitate learning or performing across *some* boundaries. But these also limit us with 'false cognates' and acquired kinetic habits that get in the way of the new skill acquisition, as we saw in *Nothing New Under the Sun* with LaBeaume's challenges when transferring from the shot put to the hammer throw. To sum up, habits are limitations that we develop in our quest to do more or better. Yet such restrictions are also the door to possibilities: 'Habits become negative limits because they are first positive agencies' that allow for the sailor to be 'intellectually at home on the sea' (ibid., 123). Constraints are the door to a modicum of freedom and spontaneity, paradoxically. It is through the restrictions of rules that freedom and creativity arise. Kant's image beautifully explains this: for the dove, the resistance it encounters is a precondition of flight and not an obstacle to it (Kant 2003).[1]

As we *voluntarily* embrace them, in virtue of the very limits they pose, we must creatively engage our abilities to solve problems. In the case of sports and other performance-oriented practices, we can see this voluntary adoption of restrictive rules just because they make the activity possible (this is considered again in essay 4). And this leads to creative exploration of possibilities that must be sharpened on the whetstone of habit. To cast this in terms of sailing then, since Dewey above sets the stage with the sailor, 'The discipline and rigor needed to develop our abilities allow us to sail in more challenging conditions *and* to perform beautifully. The economy of movement and elegance of accomplished sailors' movements are honed by the constraints of training. Here the ethos of discipline and aesthetics blend into a liberating performance in whose wake we divine the traces of restrained autonomy. Freedom by way of constraint, if you will' (Ilundáin-Agurruza, Gagliardini, and Jáuregui 2012, 120). We are hindered by the wind, the currents, the very hull of the boat that must part the waters, and if racing in a regatta, the rules of that particular event. And yet, these very limitations are themselves the conditions that enable us to sail even upwind by adjusting the sails and 'tacking' (crisscrossing) to our intended destination. The power of habit is that it gives significance to our actions: it allows for spontaneity and freedom; it also makes actions meaningful. We get intentional action rather than mere reflex acts, in today's parlance. That is, thought without habit is rendered ineffectual and powerless, as contrasting habit with mere repetitive, thoughtless acts shows (Dewey 1988, 49).

Crucial to habitual processes is the ability to deliberate, which Dewey casts as 'a dramatic rehearsal (in imagination) of various competing possible lines of action' that holds overt action and checks established habits (1988, 132). Amid an excess of preferences, when we are pulled in different ways by incompatible wants or needs, 'all deliberation is a search for *a way* to act, not for a final terminus' (ibid., 134, Dewey's italics). And apt deliberation depends on balancing and harmonizing all reasonable possibilities rather than allowing one to overpower all others, or succumb to paralysis by an excess of them. These possibilities are not merely executive functions, but *all* possibilities. Refining our abilities is both wise and necessary. To do this ably we must be able to discriminate judiciously, which is not simply a matter of lucky or inborn good judgment, but is rather traceable to a process of cultivation of skill:

> To be able to single out a definitive sensory element in any field is evidence of a high degree of previous training, that is, of well-formed habits. A moderate amount of observation of a child will suffice to reveal that even such gross discrimination as black, white, red, green are the result of some years of active dealings in the course of which habits have been set up. It is not such a simple matter to have a clear-cut sensation. The latter is a sign of training, skill, habit. (Dewey 1988, 25)

The fine discriminations of experienced sportspersons and performers result from an analogous process. But a key difference is that whereas the child learns unreflectively, unbidden, the former makes of this process a very deliberate process that pays attention to the proprioceptive qualities of movement, tactics, competitors, and so on, as performers refine their abilities.

Not recognizing the role of habit in the execution, formation, and quality of ideas results in the mind and body split that encourages people to think of 'mental' mechanisms as different to bodily operations. When it comes to rectifying conduct, this results in a disciplinary dualism where for one 'scientific' camp the mental suffices to effect desired changes, and for the other it is all a purely physiological matter. Both ignore 'the whole complex of organic habits' (Dewey 1988, 27). This whole complex is what Dewey called 'body-mind,' an integrated psychophysical unity that, while conceptually separable, is holistically and organically a unity de facto: 'body-mind simply designates what actually takes place when a living body is implicated in situations of discourse, communication and participation' (1929, 285). The whole import of this will progressively unfold below, and in subsequent chapters, particularly the externalist tendencies that constitutively connect the body-mind with its biological and social environment, and its deep and congruent connections with Eastern notions. For now, this body-mind dodges dualism, which for him is an 'intellectual reflex of the social divorce of routine habit from thought, of means from ends, practice from theory' (1988, 52). Dewey goes on to clarify that 'In the hyphenated phrase body-mind, body' designates the continued and conserved, the registered and cumulative operation of factors continuous with the rest of nature, inanimate as well as animate; while 'mind' designates the characters and consequences which are differential, indicative of features which emerge when 'body' is engaged in a wider, more complex and interdependent situation (ibid.). For Dewey,

'[...] the "solution" of the problem of mind-body is to be found in a revision of the pre-liminary assumptions about existence which generate the problem' (1929, 263). These assumptions attribute metaphysical existence to the objects of knowledge that must correspond to an external reality. In this case, immediate qualities that nowadays we classify as qualia are placed in a psychic realm distinct from material objects that science deals with. However,

> Change the metaphysical premise; restore, that is to say, immediate qualities to their rightful position as qualities of inclusive situations, and the problems in question cease to be epistemological problems. They become specifiable scientific problems: questions, that is to say, of how such and such an event having such and such qualities actually occurs. (Dewey 1929, 265)

For Dewey, this allows to classify mental phenomena like other events of empirical reality while avoiding a fall back on dualistic foundations. For organisms that feel roughness or smoothness, see blue and green, or taste sweet or bitter, the differences are felt in the sense that they are individuated and come to exist in themselves. Thus, feelings are actualized qualities that occur first at the physical level that then intertwine into more complex and nuanced relationships (ibid., 267). These nuanced relationships give rise to psychophysical processes. There is never a blank slate; rather the very beginning of our inter*actions* with the world full of proclivities that sweep out in registers of fire, of red, of green, and their complex and nuanced relations. These relations are incarnate, fundaments whose filaments go beyond mere ideal or dualist metaphysical dreams. Our very nature grounds them as a holistic Deweyan body-mind.

As a proponent of empirical naturalism there is for Dewey no mind/body problem; neither is there one regarding how to account for psychic events and their relation to the physical. In *Experience and Nature,* he writes that

> 'psycho-physical' denotes the conjunctive presence in activity of need demand-satisfaction, in the sense in which these terms have been defined. In the compound word, the prefix 'psycho' denotes that physical activity has acquired additional properties, those of ability to procure a peculiar kind of interactive support of needs from surrounding media. Psycho-physical does not denote an abrogation of the physico-chemical; nor a peculiar mixture of something physical and something psychical (as a centaur is half man and half horse); it denotes the possession of certain qualities and efficacies not displayed by the inanimate [...] Thus conceived there is no problem of the relation of physical and psychic. There are specifiable empirical events marked by *distinctive qualities and efficacies.* (1929, 254–255, my italics)

We will encounter centaurs soon enough with Ortega; similarly, we will delve into those distinctive qualities and efficacies, and how they connect with our skills in *Riding the Wind*. Presently, the point to emphasize is that the psychical concerns physical abilities that respond to an environment, whether it is plants photosynthesizing nutrients, or a jockey and horse attuned to each other as they race in the Kentucky Derby. Dewey's holistic body-mind is a patent thoroughbred, as his discussion of instincts shows, where basic instincts such as sex, hunger, fear, or more complex ones, he argues, are neither purely psychic as was the wont of many psychologists of his time (and that still linger

HOLISM AND THE CULTIVATION OF EXCELLENCE IN SPORTS AND PERFORMANCE

in popular notions of the mind), nor physical (as the mind sciences hold today). Rather, 'The whole organism is concerned in every act to some extent and in some fashion, internal organs as well as muscular, those of circulation, secretion, etc.' (Dewey 1988, 105) The import of this is that experience is not atomistic but rather marked by a continuity of thought, perception, and feeling rooted in the body (Johnson 2007, 122). It is the foundation of what Dewey called a 'situation': 'the whole complex of physical, biological, social, and cultural conditions that constitute any given experience' (ibid., 72). And this situation Dewey writes is 'dominated and characterized throughout by a single quality' (cited in Johnson 2007, 72). We do not feel a number of discrete steps as we run a 10 k charity race, but rather there is a flowing quality to the event that makes for the run itself, marked by surges, slowing downs, and the myriad nuanced relationships that give the unique qualities and efficacies of our psychophysical processes: the wind on the face, the pain in the thighs, the other runners and our interactions with them, the very fact that it is a *race* for a charity (two very different sociocultural constructs), and for a common *cause*, and not simply discrete runners on the street at the same time.

Many of Dewey's previous ideas mature and coalesce in *Art as Experience*, originally published in 1934, and thus postdating the others books presently referenced. Therein, we find the clearest exposition of what *an* experience amounts to for the American pragmatist. Dewey explains, 'Experience in this vital sense is defined by those situations and episodes that we spontaneously refer to as being "real experiences"; those things of which we say in recalling them, "that *was* an experience"' (1980, 36). This sense of intensely lived moments makes sports a ripe ground for experiences accented by exclamation marks.[2] Surfer extraordinaire Garrett McNamara describes how he and Hawaiian surfer Keali'I Mamal surfed a day in Antarctica in waves caused by gargantuan ice fragments falling from a calving glacier. The massive and violent waves these set off, which required tow-in and careful monitoring by the jet skiers should a rescue, be needed were so difficult to ride that he describes the rides as 'the most horrifying, closest to death, heaviest rush that I have ever experienced' (Wade 2012, 6). McNamara, it should be noted, is legendary for his prowess and ability to surf some of the largest waves in the world, including a world-record setting 80 + footer (25 m) in Nazaré, Portugal in 2013.[3] Surfing in Antarctica for McNamara definitely was *an* experience 'complete in itself, standing out because marked out from what went before and what came after' (Dewey 1980, 36). So much so that McNamara goes on to say 'I can't get a rush like that anymore in the ocean' (ibid.). But when asked whether he would do it again, McNamara vehemently says: 'Never again. It was as extreme as it gets. Definitely not.' (Wade 2012, 6) This tells us at least two pertinent things about McNamara, sport, and Deweyan experience. First, some experiences are not worth repeating; we are best never to attempt to repeat them, but we need not regret them either. Secondly, McNamara, like most practitioners of risk sports is prudent if brave. He prepared conscientiously for it beforehand, and in his reflective analysis he wisely opts to leave it as is even if he will never have such a 'rush' again.

This underscores the point that for risk sportspersons, it is not simply or even about the adrenaline 'rush' but the overall quality of the experience and our ability to test our skills. In the case of gifted performers, and uniquely risk sportspeople, this testing sometimes requires life-endangering challenges (this is revisited in the next essay, Section D). More broadly, Lally makes the point with runner extraordinaire

George Sheehan, and Dewey too, that our experiences are unified 'wholes' complete in themselves: 'the meaning generated by *real* experiences is never something that is bestowed on us; it is a problem worked out, a solution sought, and a vitality generated through active participation' (2013, 192). Finally, such risky business can help us grow. Hochstetler and Hopsicker write, 'The requirements for growth involve significant effort and risk, commitment and immersion.' (2012, 124) They cite Dewey, 'We become uneasy at the idea of initiating new courses; we are repelled by the difficulties … In this way, we withdraw from actual conditions and their requirements and opportunities; we contract and harden the self. (1988, 353),' on their way to conclude that, 'to avoid challenging opportunities leads to a life of stasis rather than growth.' (Hochstetler and Hopsicker 2012, 124) This is the wrong side of the primordial equation to be in.

Of course, experiences in Dewey's sense need not be about exploits. But *an* experience, to mark a 'before' and an 'after', to become complete and mature, must also include an element of suffering because 'otherwise there would be no taking in of what preceded' (ibid., 41). It could be as benign and placid as an easy sculling practice on the crystalline waters of a summer day at sunset, when the feathering of the oars caresses the water as our rowing dips into suffering's water upon realizing that this perfect moment will not return. When it comes to experience, Dewey is much in agreement with James. For Dewey, the emphasis is on quality. Following him, we can say that experience's heart pumps an aesthetic quality all its own (1980, 38). It also implies a consummation, as it is 'a whole and carries with its own individualizing quality and self-sufficiency' (ibid., 35). Indeed, Dewey's complex conception of experience as fulfilled, holistic, complete, and unified, dovetails with James' and Nishida's thick notions of experience. Only that he is closer to the Eastern ideal, as he emphasizes development in terms of continuous refinement of skills where the body-mind is central.

However, unless we philosophically court a myopic holism, our habits, body-mind, and experiences must incorporate the environment. For Dewey, habits are adjustments *of*, not *to*, our environment, which, moreover, is multifaceted (1988, 38). He strongly emphasized the codependence between organism and the environment. He expands, 'The world is subject-matter for knowledge, because mind has developed in that world; a body-mind, whose structures have developed according to the structures of the world in which it exists, will naturally find some of its structures to be concordant and congenial with nature, and some phases of nature with itself' (Dewey 1929, 279). The role of these 'environments' resonates loudly in other thinkers who also developed similar ideas, and is something we will consider in more detail with Ortega. But Dewey is clear when it comes to making a case for the importance of this thick, wholesome holism of our performing bodies within their natural context. Our habits, expressed through action and performance are a pervasive function where biological, physiological, environmental, and social facets coalesce. Opportunely for the aims of this study, he explains in *Democracy and Education* that,

> a habit is a form of executive skill, of efficiency in doing. A habit means an ability to use natural conditions as means to ends. It is an active control of the environment through control of the organs of action. We are perhaps *apt to emphasize the control of the body at the expense of control of the environment*. We think of walking, talking, playing the piano, the specialized skills characteristic of the etcher, the surgeon, the bridge-builder, as if they were simply ease, deftness, and accuracy on the part of the

organism. They are that, of course; *but the measure of the value of these qualities lies in the economical and effective control of the environment which they secure.* To be able to walk is to have certain properties of nature at our disposal—and so with all other habits. (Dewey 1922, 55, my italics)

While we are apt to stress the role of bodily cultivation, this is done in relation to the environment and the constraints that arise at the contact surface, as well as the possibilities these create. As Lally explains, 'Within the pragmatic conception, all human action involved a transaction with the environment, and thus caused a remaking of the momentarily established self' (2013, 177). Much like the consummate sportsperson's kinetic signature is an economy of movement to the goals of the task, our habit-honed skills are efficient adaptations to the environment. Aesthetic and artistic considerations may seem to flout such economical calculations, but within the artistic-aesthetic and sporting environments, what may seem profligacies to outsiders of the practices actually evolve toward efficiently developed habits and skills. Moreover, this efficiency does not mean a utilitarian adherence to calculated maximum return on our investment. As Ortega makes clear, these efficiencies are borne from exuberant spillovers, exploratory and risky undertakings with no guaranteed success. Finally, if the value for Dewey is cashed out in terms of environmental expediency, this takes place *originally* through *deliberate cultivation* of that ease and deftness that habit makes possible in the first place.

2. Deweyan Self-cultivation and Perfectionism

Dewey lived life and his philosophy unapologetically and with verve. In spite of the monumental size of his writings, he was far from being ensconced in the ivory tower of academia. Extremely active politically and institutionally, he founded his Laboratory School, several labor unions, The National Association for the Advancement of Colored People, and the New School of Social Research (Shusterman 2012, 186). And similarly to James but more resolute, he also was willing to adopt life-cultivating practices. After years of debilitating neck and back pain, he met Alexander, and began following the AT method. Relieved of ailments through a retraining of postural habits, Dewey became a staunch advocate of the AT. In fact, Dewey wrote lengthy prefaces to several of Alexander's works, and incorporated Alexander's ideas into his own work. Dewey gets in the arena decidedly, but prepared, having gone through a rigorous program to habituate himself to the challenges he foresees.

Dewey emphasizes the potential for shared experience in James' intimate catalog of knowledge (Lally 2013, 3). This makes matters public, testable, and brings into the equation the larger community, a perspective with which Heather Reid's views of sport as truth-seeking (2009, 2012) and this present study align. Sports, genuinely engaging discipline and cultivation, imply an exquisite attunement to the body that coheres with Dewey's and James' ethos. As explained above, for Dewey, revealing and fulsome experience is tied to suffering, something that is unavoidable in sport. And yet, lest one fall into mere masochism, it begs for justificatory explanation. This suffering is not merely bodily: as sportspeople we also suffer in defeat, having been tested and found wanting, or when we cave in to pain and self-doubt and cheat to regret it later (a pain that we cannot but *feel* psycho-somatically in Dewey's sense). Lally, in his essay 'Deweyan

Pragmatism and Self-Cultivation,' applies Dewey's interest in human self-cultivation to endurance sports highlighting the import of faith in the experimental method, risk, and will power (2013, 16–23). These three elements coalesce into present moments that define our character through those 'moments of present choice [that] are significant for just this reason: they make the world other than it is, or would have been had we acted otherwise … This moral choice is an effective agent in the world, and it is this fact which gives meaning and zest to life. Indeed this is Dewey's call to the heroic life.' (Murphey, cited in Lally 2013, 193) We can suffer and be able to affirm life as we take risks; we can suffer and have regrets. The latter are meaningful too, in themselves and as opportunities to develop habits to act otherwise. This is a privileged route toward those goings and undergoings that may become *an* experience. For Dewey, the cultivation of the self means 'the development of the individual's personality to its fullest potential and energies,' but he eschews specific instructions for description of catalytic conditions that would not lead us by the hand (Lally 2013, 175). Something quite agreeable to Japanese pedagogical mores as embodied in their *dō*'s, their arts of self-cultivation. Lally, relying on James and Dewey, emphasizes how this cultivating process does not happen at the purely individual level, rather it needs a community: We 'live in a community in virtue of the things which they have in common' (2013, 12).[4] Before considering the issue of perfectionism, there are a couple of small, provisional steppingstones we must consider: emotion and skills.

We cannot ignore the role that emotion plays in self-cultivation. For Dewey (1988), the one positive way to deal with emotions and impulses is by way of sublimated habit. Max Scheler (1961) would also appeal to the powers of sublimation when considering man's unique place in nature, through which we liberate ourselves from our drives' shackles. Dewey, more concretely grounded, praises, 'the humanizing capabilities of sport in its varied forms, drama, fiction, [which for him] have been neglected' (1988, 111). For him, an emotion combines both cognitive and bodily elements that only become distinct and identified when behavior becomes problematic, as when fear arises from the distinct emotion of fear and the object of our fear (Shusterman 2008, 186). One sport where training and habit overcome one of our strongest instincts and fears (survival) and urges (breathing) is freediving. Common wisdom has it that no person can willfully drown herself because the fear of drowning and death are powerful, and the urge to breathe proves too strong for anyone over a sufficient time. However, it is not rare for freedivers, who train themselves to withstand diaphragmatic pain, to actually hold their breath underwater long enough to pass out, which is long past the point where others give into the urge to breathe. Should a freediver blackout, attendant divers ready at hand during competition close airways and bring them back to the surface. Of course, a freedivers' goal is not to drown. The point is that whether in training or competition, habit and the framework of competition and/or self-improvement have sublimated the survival drive and its attendant emotional undertone of fear for one's life. This demonstrates the formidable ways habits sublimate our emotions and how deeply transformative they can be. But this transformation, while it may flourish best when exuberantly pursued does not happen quite the same was as a plant flowers, in spite of itself. It must be deliberately pursued. Moreover, and echoing two other pragmatist themes Lally expounds upon (2013, 180): (1) we must relentlessly test for validity of our beliefs in this regard (am I really as fast or strong as I believe?) (2) with enough hardiness to handle setbacks and failure (how do I handle the emotional pain

HOLISM AND THE CULTIVATION OF EXCELLENCE IN SPORTS AND PERFORMANCE

of failure? Can we sublimate such pain into motivation?). Keen perception of emotional and sensuous feelings is crucial to organize our experience as meaningful (Lally 2013, 189). Learning to work with these strictures and regimen leads to more refined skills and character.

In terms of our skills and their relation to habit, Dewey observes how all habit involves mechanization, which sets up the physiologically ingrained, spontaneous or automatic, mechanism for action (1988, 50). Importantly, mechanization is not mere unintelligent automatism and aimless splurge, as many suppose. He makes this point in a manner quite suitable for the present project, 'How delicate, prompt, sure and varied are the movements of a violin player or an engraver!! How unerringly they phrase every shade of emotion and every turn of idea! Mechanism is indispensable. If each act has to be consciously searched for at the moment of being intentionally performed, execution is painful and the product is clumsy and halting' (1988, 51). A number of issues arise in this citation. Contemporary research on sport psychology validates Dewey's assessment of the role consciousness plays in (under)performance, and Eastern views and Japanese practices have traditionally and explicitly engaged it theoretically and practically, as will be seen in *Riding the Wind* and *Reflections on a Katana*, respectively. More to the point, outstanding performers, whether in sports or the performing and martial arts, unerringly embody and express rich shades of emotions and ideas. And sublimated emotion, as with Scheler and this reading of Dewey, provides the necessary fuel for the enthusiasm that dedication to these active pursuits demands. The serious athlete preparing for a tri-athlon, as Lally recounts, centers her life around the varied and daily workouts in the three disciplines, nutrition, and rest, and 'it is through this habits that we can come to know her' (Lally, Anderson, and Kaag 2012, 179). Yet, even in cases where skills have been learned to the level of expertise, not all those we might consider experts or professionals, are the same. Dewey elaborates,

> The difference between the artist and the mere technician is unmistakable. The artist is a masterful technician. The technique or mechanism is fused with thought and feeling. The 'mechanical' performer permits the mechanism to dictate the performance. [...] We are confronted with two kinds of habit, intelligent and routine. (1988, 51).

Both may have mechanization in the requisite sense, but only one reaches a level of virtuosity deserving the ascription of excellence. The masterful technician most likely specializes in and delves deeply into one endeavor, as Breivik argues (2010, 97), in contrast to the thinly spread or more superficial dilettante, or even the multifaceted yet well-rounded person favored by Hurka (1993), who argues for a perfectionism across a wide range of abilities to the exclusion of single-minded focus. Nonetheless, those who become excellent exemplars should develop strategies and abilities that have wider repercussion in their lives generally for there are dangers associated with unbridled skill. Verily, elite sportspersons, artists, masterful technicians' display a dynamic attunement to changing conditions, and habit makes this ease possible through its efficiency. Yet, all too commonly, this ease devolves into a misguided pursuit of a static perfection whose attainment becomes the goal (Dewey 1988, 122). The danger is that the dynamic and creative becomes stultified and barren. The very prowess can lead to complacency and mechanicism. Our strengths can become our weaknesses. Mechanical performers and regular experts focus on results; their performances become routine. Paladins of excellence stay alive in the process, and recycle ends as means. They are resolute and brave with how the live their lives, like Charlemagne's Peers, known as Paladins, always first to lead into battle. *Growing* athletes, perennially challenging themselves to meet their potential as well as to reestablish equilibrium, do not have a static life, Lally argues (2013, 186–187). Which model we choose, whether that of the masterful technician or the 'artist,' has radical consequences for sports and performative endeavors. Ortega, Zhuangzi, and the Japanese arts of self-cultivation will help us delve into this. All of them see this dynamic excellence as radically embodied.

3. Dewey's Body-mind and Philosophy of Mind

Dewey coined the term 'body-mind' to emphasize the creative coupling of our organic self with the environment, which so loudly resonates through his writings. Johnson elucidates that, 'Dewey attempts to explain "mind" and all its operations and activities non-dualistically, as grounded in bodily operations of living human creatures' (2010, 126). Complete experiences are the result of a whole organism, a body-mind, fully engaged with the challenges of its unerringly insecure environment as what Dewey calls impulsions; these transform the body-mind's instinctive tendencies into meaningful, continued undertakings (1988, 58–59; cited in Lally 2013, 194). Further, Shusterman explains that in Dewey's 'body-mind' 'Rather than an interaction between a body and a mind, we have a transactional whole of body-mind' (2008, 184). More pointedly, he clarifies that this ontological union does not mean there will be a harmonious unity in our behavior. These two aspects make Dewey's notion uncannily reminiscent of Eastern views on the matter, which also conceptualize us as an integrative *bodymind* that is in varying stages of development and amalgamation.[5]

Dewey writes in his essay 'Body and Mind' that the erstwhile wholeness of philosophy, art, and science is bygone, and that the problem of the mind and body is the most disastrous development among all the various divisions since arisen (1963). Dewey finds the solution in a unity of body-mind through action. When he speaks of 'wholeness of operation,' Dewey is intimating a solution where act, action, and behavior are the solution if made central (1963, 302). In fact, for Dewey, 'the question of the integration of mind-body *in action* is the most practical of all questions we can ask our civilization' (ibid., 304, my italics). This integration entails bringing together intellectual pursuits and physical achievement. Some may worry about a dumbing down of our abilities or a messy blending of disparate phenomena, and worry that the apex of our faculties, our rationality, has somehow been shortchanged. We need to carry out a much finer thinking, one that can discriminate 'between action that is routine and action alive with purpose and desire.' (ibid., 305). Even the highest cogitations on mathematics or philosophy, no matter how removed, are connected to our *mindful* bodily functions. Dennett (1991) is arguably one ivory tower thinker much happier in lofty platonic realms, even as he decries dualism and ponders the nature of the existence of brains in vats. His (in)famous intuition pumps (1988), however, if they carry any force, pump our intuition precisely through a mélange of bodily, emotional, and intellectual elements.

Dewey also made much of James' fringe of consciousness, though for him it is a more subconscious phenomenon. In functional terms, however, it plays an analogous role: 'Even our most highly intellectualized operations depend upon them as a "fringe" by which to guide our inferential movements. They give us our sense of rightness and wrongness, of what to select and emphasize and follow up, and what to drop, slur over and ignore, among the multitude of inchoate meanings that are presenting themselves' (Dewey 1963, 299–300). For him, as for James, we could not even make sense of these words on the page if we sharply separated them from those that precede them; we need to have a sense of what he have already read. But he parts ways with James because of a concern that the terminology fails to do justice to the richness of the phenomenon: 'Indeed, the use of such words as context and background, fringe, etc., suggests something too external to meet the facts of the case. The larger system of meaning suffuses, interpenetrates, colors what is now and here uppermost; it gives them sense, feeling, as distinct from signification' (Dewey 1963, 305–306).

And yet we *must* speak of the phenomenon. The danger of nomenclature lies in reification, in turning a process into a product, in theorizing functions into substances or entities. One strategy I will rely upon is the use of the gerund to indicate a process or a function-in-happening. When the phrasing may be so cumbersome that any apparent conceptual gains are counterproductive, I suggest alternatively to keep in mind that such the phenomenon is not a structure, concept (unless in the Jamesian sense of conceptualizing), or even a process if we think of it as an entity or, say, fully distributed among various neural networks. Rather, it is a *dynamic layering* of our awareness. Minding Dewey again, we should not conceive of 'bodymind' cognition and action as substances, nor even processes, but rather as functions and qualities of action (1963, 302). Thus, the body is 'the mechanism [recall Dewey's creative sense], the instrumentality of behavior, and the mind is the function or its fruit and consummation' (ibid.). The former can be described in terms of physico-chemical interactions, which is indispensable for him, but not the whole story. 'The remainder of the story is that the chemicophysical processes go on in way and by interactions which have reference to the need of the organism as a whole and thus take on psychical quality, and in human beings at least are in such connection with the social environment as confers upon them intellectual quality' (ibid., 307).

Freedivers' ability to push past certain, perhaps prudent, points is not just a matter of physiology and biomechanics, although it happens *through* such mechanisms. (Interestingly, physiologists and neuroscientists cannot yet explain how the freedivers' bodies adapt nor the mechanism for the irrepressible urge to breath when we *still* have sufficient oxygen; it is not merely a matter of 'toughing it out.') Rather there is a complex working of said body-mind whereby what we might call 'bodily' functions have been honed by habit, as have the accompanying valuations, discriminations, emotions, and thoughts, all of which are separable conceptually but coalesce as the nuanced relationships and psycho-physical processes we call 'freediving.' There is more to the story of body-mind, for reductionist accounts cut off the environment from behavior by treating it merely as an external occasion. By now we know that Dewey holds a rich view of the environment, which 'in reality is just as much comprised within behaviour as are organic processes' (ibid., 311). For him this is nowhere clearer than with the social environment, 'for it is the incorporation of this environment in action which is most intimately and extensively connected with the intellectual and emotional quality of behavior' (ibid., 313). In freediving, the complexities of said functions, which we describe as abilities (to dive) belie a very complex learning process, from proper alignment of head, neck, back, and legs, to how to breathe in the minutes before the dive, to the complex training regimes, compensation techniques, and myriad other elements that happen through the practices that human culture and civilization make possible.

I wish to emphasize that the 'body-mind' is an unfolding function that takes place in the doing itself. Dewey (1963) rightly explains that speaking of body or mind is a matter of emphasis. Hence, a fertile way to interpret Dewey is to see acts and actions as unfolding totalities. An ultramarathoner's or cyclist's act of eating or 'fueling' during training, before, or during a race, is not simply a physiological matter of putting calories in the gut. We also find the elation and optimism that renewed vigor brings to the challenge. Alternatively, failure to fuel properly can result in a depletion of energy that results in nausea, disorientation, confusion, and distress. Elation and optimism, confusion and distress *are* that being in action. The resulting rejoicing at successfully deployed expertise or disappointment in failing is one wholesome 'action-ing.' This actioning ignites the primordial equation of our skillful strivings.

Ever the pedagog, Dewey takes his body-mind views in the direction of education, pointing how the mind and body split has resulted in a separation of theory and practice, of thought and action, and concludes, 'The full realization of the integration of mind and body in action waits upon the reunion of philosophy and science, in art, above all in the supreme art, the art of education' (1963, 316)). Self-cultivation begins for us through our education, and this is something at which Eastern practices excel, as we will see. Elsewhere, I have minded this charge by Dewey, arguing for an active education where our 'body-mind', educated through sport and movement redresses many of the ills Dewey diagnoses, and moreover constitutes the key to a meaningful existence (Ilundáin-Agurruza 2014). This appreciation of education leads us to another philosophical pedagog, a roughly contemporary of Dewey who hailed from Spain. Ortega's philosophical views help deepen the inquiry of central themes, for the cultivation of excellence in and through meaningful movement, such as perfectionism, the role of the environment, and the body-mind dynamics.

NOTES

1. My appreciation to Mike McNamee for reminding me of this analogy.
2. See Elcombe (2012), for an insightful discussion of art, sport, and their aesthetic dimension.
3. The wave height has been calculated in the range between 80 and 100 feet. For stunning images, see http://www.youtube.com/watch?v=74pnrYPozcU The clip includes a short interview that belies ideas defended here and elsewhere (Ilundáin-Agurruza 2007, 2008, Forthcoming; Krein 2007; Russell 2005) regarding risk sports, namely that they take as extreme preparation as the extreme risks over many years.
4. This communitarian facet is the focus of *Everything Mysterious Under the Moon*.
5. For an examination of Dewey's body-mind and Japanese philosophy, see Ilundáin-Agurruza, Fukasawa, and Takemura 2014.

REFERENCES

BREIVIK, G. 2010. Philosophical perfectionism—Consequences and implications for sport. *Sport, Ethics and Philosophy* 4 (1): 87–105.

HOLISM AND THE CULTIVATION OF EXCELLENCE IN SPORTS AND PERFORMANCE

DENNETT, D. 1988. Quining qualia. In *Philosophy of mind: Classical and contemporary readings*, edited by D. Dennett. New York, NY: Oxford University Press: 226–46.

———. 1991. *Consciousness explained*. Boston, MA: Little, Brown, and Co.

DEWEY, J. 1922. *Democracy and education*. New York, NY: The Macmillan.

———. 1929. *Experience and nature*. Chicago, IL: Open Court.

———. 1963. *Philosophy and civilization*. New York, NY: Capricorn Books.

———. 1980. *Art as experience*. New York, NY: Perigee Books.

———. 1988. *Human nature and conduct; an introduction to social psychology*. New York, NY: Holt.

ELCOMBE, T. 2012. Sport, aesthetic experience, and art as the ideal embodied metaphor. *Journal of the Philosophy of Sport* 39 (2): 201–17.

HOCHSTETLER, D., and P.M. HOPSICKER. 2012. The heights of humanity: Endurance sport and the Strenuous Mood. *Journal of the Philosophy of Sport* 39 (1): 117–35.

HURKA, T. 1993. *Perfectionism*. New York, NY: Oxford University Press.

ILUNDÁIN-AGURRUZA, J. 2007. Kant goes skydiving: Understanding the extreme by way of the sublime. In *Philosophy, risk and adventure sports*, edited by M. McNamee. London: Routledge: 149–67.

———. 2008. Between the Horns: A dilemma in the interpretation of the running of the bulls —Part 2: The Evasion. *Sport, Ethics, and Philosophy* 2: 18–38.

———. 2014. The quest for meaningful and lifelong learning. In *philosophy, sport and education: International perspectives*, edited by M. Isidori, F. J. López Frías, and A. Müller. Roma: Sette Cità: 43–70.

———. Forthcoming. The eye of the hurricane: Philosophical reflections on risky sports, self-knowledge and flourishing. *Journal of the Philosophy of Sport*.

ILUNDÁIN-AGURRUZA, J., L. GAGLIARDINI, and J.A. JÁUREGUI. 2012. On the crest of the wave: The sublime, tempestuous, graceful and existential facets of sailing. *Sailing–philosophy for everyone. Catching the drift of why we sail*, edited by P. Goold. Chichester: Wiley & Blackwell: 109–21.

ILUNDÁIN-AGURRUZA, J., K. FUKASAWA, and M. TAKEMURA. 2014. The philosophy of sport in relation to Japanese philosophy and pragmatism. In *A companion for the philosophy of sport*, edited by C. Torres. London: Bloomsbury Editions: 66–79.

JAMES, W. 1918. *Principles of psychology*. New York, NY: Dover Publications.

JOHNSON, M. 2007. *The meaning of the body*. Chicago, IL: University of Chicago Press.

———. 2010. Cognitive science and Dewey's theory of mind, thought, and language. In *The Cambridge companion to Dewey*, edited by M. Cochran. Cambridge: Cambridge University Press: 123–44.

KANT, I. 2003. *Critique of pure reason*. Translated by N. Kemp Smith. London: Palgrave McMillan.

KREIN, K. 2007. Risk and adventure sports. In *Philosophy, risk, and adventure sports*, edited by M. McNamee. London: Routledge: 80–93.

LALLY, R. 2013. Introduction. In *Pragmatism and the philosophy of sport*, edited by R. Lally, D. Anderson, and J. Kaag. London: Lexington Books: 1–16.

———. 2013. Deweyan pragmatism and self-cultivation. In *Pragmatism and the philosophy of sport*, edited by R. Lally, D. Anderson, and J. Kaag. London: Lexington Books: 175–98.

MUTCHSLECNER, D. 2012. *Enigma and light*. Boise, ID: Ahsahta Press, Boise State University: 10.

REID, H. 2009. Sport, philosophy, and the quest for knowledge. *Journal of the Philosophy of Sport*. 36 (1): 40–9.

———. 2012. *Introduction to the philosophy of sport*. Lanham, MD: Rowman & Littlefield.

RUSSELL, J.S. 2005. The value of dangerous sport. *Journal of the Philosophy of Sport*. 32 (1): 1–19.

SCHELER, M. 1961. *Man's place in nature*. New York, NY: The Noonday Press.

SHUSTERMAN, R. 2008. *Body consciousness: Philosophy of mindfulness & somaesthetics*. Cambridge: CUP.

———. 2012. *Thinking through the body*. Cambridge: Cambridge University Press.

WADE, A. 2012. *Amazing surfing stories*. West Sussex: Wiley Nautical.

4—JOSÉ ORTEGA Y GASSET: EXUBERANT STEED

Jesús Ilundáin-Agurruza

Indeed a skittish horse, with its nervous head and fiery eye, is a splendid image of stirring life. (Ortega y Gasset)

José Ortega y Gasset (1883–1955) was a relentless 'missionary' for philosophical thinking, writing for and editing newspapers, academic journals, books, delivering conferences to large audiences, and even founding political organizations. Interestingly, for the philosophy of sport community, as editor of *Revista de Occidente* and *El espectador*, he published and introduced to his fellow Spaniards the work of many contemporary luminaries, among them Johan Huizinga, Max Scheler, or Jacob Von Uexküll. Nowadays, his work does not garner the broad attention it once enjoyed, at one point, the Spaniard being as much a celebrity in the US, Europe, South America, and Asia as intellectuals might hope for. There are a number of reasons that account for this (Ilundáin-Agurruza 2013a), but one of the more interesting ones is that many of his ideas have become familiar in one way or another, as Philip Silver notes in his introduction to a compilation of Ortega's signature phenomenological works (Ortega y Gasset 1975, 7). Sport philosophy in English echoes the academic silence. There are few references to his work, much less dedicated focus, excepting David Inglis' splendidly thorough *Meditations on Sport* (2004), Klaus Meier's signal *An Affair of Flutes*, (1980), Orringer's erudite *Ortega y Gasset's Sportive Vision of Plato* (1973), and my work (2008, 2010, 2011, 2012, 2013). Inglis harangues us: 'we must seriously attend to Ortega's ideas and rescue his shade from the penumbra into which it has in part been cast' (2004, 94). As further endorsement and spur for readers, I add that long before academia seriously considered sport, Ortega enthusiastically and fearlessly jumped into the arena of sport and made it a pivotal element of cultural and philosophical significance. Indeed, he built a genuine and thoroughly sportive philosophy.

Much like James, Ortega enjoyed vigorous walking in the countryside, and was a keen observer of the intersection of the natural and human worlds as his 'meditations' (his word for phenomenological analyses) demonstrate. Nominally a phenomenologist, Ortega had much more in common with James and Dewey than is readily apparent. As I suggested earlier, there is a pragmatist strain in Ortega that for various reasons he tried to hide, even though he paid skewed tribute to pragmatism's 'audacious ingenuousness' (1960, 44). At times, he was patently adversarial, as Orteguian scholar Eduardo Armenteros Cuartango documents (2006, 162–164). Yet, John Graham's monumental work compellingly traces James', Dewey's, and other pragmatist influences, titling one volume of his trilogy on the Spaniard *A Pragmatist Philosophy of Life in Ortega y Gasset*

(1994). Ortega would acknowledge his debt to James' radical empiricism late in his career, but Graham painstakingly draws out the influence of the American pragmatists' through the books that Ortega owned, read, and wrote. Armenteros corroborates and connects these pragmatist imprints to Ortega's overall and core philosophical tenets by arguing that the recalcitrant Spaniard subjected it to a 'centrifugal process' (2006, 165–166). Regardless of such somewhat arcane academic disputes, the Orteguian themes discussed here readily fit the tenor set by the two Americans (and the praxis-oriented ethos pursued in this monograph) albeit with Ortega's idiosyncratic imprimatur. A preliminary overview to his thought opens matters to segue into his philosophy of life, which issues forth into the sportive as ideal, then perfectionism and risk. His views on mind and body integration close this essay.

1. Philosophical Landscape

Ortega arguably was the first philosopher of international renown to engage sport not sporadically but truly philosophically throughout his writings. José Lasaga Medina points out that 'sportive effort' (and satellite ideas) became prominent in the Orteguian discourse with the 1919 essay, *El Quijote en la escuela. Biología y pedagogía* (2006, 109). These ideas, fitting a thoroughbred philosopher of Ortega's mien, ranged over an expansive philosophical landscape, concurrently entwining metaphysics, ethics, epistemology, and aesthetics, and in turn, being intimately connected to his life and his calling as educator. Among the plethora of concepts that spread over the three main phases of his philosophical career, four are crucial to understanding his thinking: circumstance, historical reason, love, and existential possibility. These are set in a framework that perspectivism and ratio-vitalism (a term specific to his philosophy) scaffold.

Epistemologically, Ortega's main concern was to avoid the subjectivism and relativism that certain pragmatist readings courted (Armenteros 2006 168; Graham 1994, 178). Accordingly, he developed a view of truth that was perspectival, vitalist, and historical. His particular take on perspectivism, related to but different from Nietzsche's perspectivism and James' 'point of view,' posits that perspectives are complementary yet there is no single overarching perspective or Godhead stance that unites them. Ortega develops a ratio-vitalist perspective, according to which reason, but not narrow rationality as exemplified by Kant, is necessary but needs to be complemented by an emotion fully invested in life, hence his vitalism. His mature philosophy centers around historical reason which, with emblematic Orteguian exaggeration, intended to rebalance argumentative extremes, states that we do not have a nature, but rather, a history: our lives make sense in terms of narratives. The starting point is the radical fact of our life. 'Circumstance' is the first key element. It refers to all those things, ideas, and events in our existential and topographical landscape that are relevant for *us*. As he memorably puts it, 'I am I am and my circumstance, and if I do not save it I do not save myself' (2004c: 757, vol. II).[1] Salvation for him refers to finding meaning in things. This is connected to his views on the environment as a totalizing and enveloping horizon (see section 5). Living in relation to and within this personal conglomerate of 'things,' we cannot overcome them because they act as limits that also inexorably prune our possibilities. This strongly constrains our ethical options. Love, the third element, shows how to find salvation through these very circumstances.

His inveterate optimism and the centrality he accords to love sets him apart from the darker musings of fellow phenomenologists and existentialists Jean Paul Sartre or Martin Heidegger. As Antonio Rodríguez Huéscar puts it, 'Ortega did exercise his ironical wit at the expense of the 'lovers of anxiety' of those days. As opposed to their characteristic somber disposition of mind, he adopted an attitude [of serenity, that mental bent corresponding to] ataraxia or halcyonism' (1995, xxvii).[2] This plays a key role in his mature views regarding our self-development. Finally, there is the role that possibilities play in our lives and our attitude toward them. These tenets inform and constitute his philosophy of life.

2. A Philosophy of Life

Life is a problem for Ortega (Ortega y Gasset 2004a, 2006b). We neither ask nor are asked to be born into it. Living, as such an imposition, is an unavoidable necessity (Ortega 2006a, 555). And then, we have to figure out what to do with our life; we need to invent our life and work to that end. This is why life is a problem for humans but not animals; 'the bull exists being bull,' but for humans, being human is merely the possibility of being and the effort to become such (2006b, 573, my translation). This results in two practical outcomes. First, this is the origin of technology, into which his 1939 meditation on technology delves (Ortega 2006a). For him, the essence of our lives lies in our occupations (2006b). Interestingly, technological development is not due to life's needs and our work to meet them, but rather, to a suspension of our primitive repertoire to meet said necessities (Ortega 2006a, 556). Animals' existence is bound by their needs, but our lifeworld is vastly larger; most of our endeavors go well beyond the narrow confine of our needs. Technology allows us to efficiently meet our needs beyond what nature provides, thus creating the capacity to adapt the environment to our needs *and* our wishes (Ortega 2006b). This very efficiency introduces another problem: it gives us free time. What to do with our leisure? Technology is a liberating yet problematic process because it creates responsibility alongside that freedom.

The second outcome, developed in his 1942 *Meditations on Hunting*, is more foundational in scope (1995). For us, 'existence becomes a poetic task,' such that we must invent a plot for our existence 'that will make it both appealing and interesting' (ibid., 123). Hence, we meet the challenge of existence through both a technological praxis and a narrative-based philosophical attitude. Extrapolating the second argument to the first one gives us an idea of what the good life is then and provides technology with direction. Invention and imagination for our existence suffuse technology with the requisite ingenuity. Using hyperbole methodologically to address conceptual imbalances, he states that 'human,' 'technology,' and 'wellbeing' are synonymous (2006b, 562).[3] Well-being is tied to our conception of the good life. Now the question is, how do we *spend* our free time so it amounts to a well-lived life?

Dramatically, but as we will see integral to a noble conception of life, Ortega writes that, 'Man is an animal for whom only the superfluous is necessary' (2006b, 561, my translation). Because not all ways of spending our leisure time are worth the same, we feel the nudge of unfolding normativity: a set of constraints and the resulting lifestyles issuing from these. Ortega presents two basic ways of life, utilitarian and sportive, each tied to its own lifeworld, which he calls a landscape (2004a; 2004d). Each displays its own attitude to and conception of the good life. The utilitarian attitude is valuable on its own and as guiding principle. After all it is what produces goods, and more importantly frees up our time. Entrenched in that protestant ethic that Max Weber so perceptively theorized (1992) and connected to the Christian Neo-platonic distaste for bodily affairs, it has resulted in a skewed understanding and use of sport. Seen as child's pastime when played for its own sake, it is mainly appreciated instrumentally in terms of what it can produce: health benefits or revenues. And the educational milieu, where one might expect a more enlightened attitude, mirrors societal values. Academically, Reid details, sport does not command respect either, whether it be as subject matter, or those who practice it, student athletes, those who teach it, coaches and staff, or those who study it (2012, 147–154). Equally, Joe Humphreys reflects how many academics approach the subject, 'Sport has largely been left in the hands of [...] fanatics. Intellectuals are loath to debate the subject [...] if they criticize sport they leave themselves open to the change of elitism [...] if they praise it they are almost sure to attract scorn from their bookish peers. To professional philosophers [...] sport is not serious; it is a matter to be addressed only in a detached, mocking tone' (2008, 9).

Ortega challenges directly the very foundation of such a viewpoint. The utilitarian attitude is a sign of weakness, living life at its minimum (Ortega 2004c, 708; 1961, 19). For all its advantages, this ethos entails a narrow vital horizon (Ortega 2004a, 426). In line with him, I contend that a strictly instrumental attitude to sport and life is a mistake because it outsources the meaning of the activity itself to the terminus, forsaking the value of the process *and* its functional role. Stinginess never was conducive to magnanimity, fiscally, morally, or existentially. Ortega in fact considers that philosophy and science are best undertaken in the spirit of a game, rather than in earnest and seriousness, that is with *gravitas* (which is not the same as taking a game seriously). The latter is resistant to change, whereas the former is amenable to reason and evidence: 'do not seek to be convinced by what you are going to hear and what you are told to think; do not treat this so seriously, but treat it like a game in which you are invited to observe the rules' (Ortega 2001, 96; 1960, 115, my translation). What is more, the Spaniard finds inspiration in Plato's encouragement to find our sense in playing games, joking, and dancing (Plato 2002, 1398), which is at the heart of his foundation for a cultivated life (Ortega 2001, 99; 1960, 118). Ortega asserts that culture and philosophy spring from joviality, that is the state of mind of Jove (Jupiter): 'in cultivating joviality we do it in imitation of Olympic Jove' (Ibid., 100, my translation). Molinuevo explains how Ortega, taking the Platonic definition of philosophy as the 'science of athletes,' posits the image of the sportsperson and the archer as symbol of a full life, a life in tension, in form because 'life is a planned adventure of uncertain ending' (2002, 163, my translation). This is what philosophy is for Ortega, an adventure that appreciates the problem. The gratuitous activity of the philosopher is assimilated into the athlete's luxurious and sportive attitude (Molinuevo 2002). This does not imply that it is any less thoughtful or contemplative, but that it is done with the same ethos of superfluity. For Ortega, the sportive ethos does not seek to escape life aesthetically, rather what we should value is the way it rigorously and decidedly confronts life's problems (Molinuevo 2002).

To foreshadow the next waypoint in this philosophical trek, an inspiring life is founded on the splendid sportive spirit. Ortega builds his philosophy of life on Sport. Phenomenologically, he uses sport to reveal the structure of life and how we experience it.

3. The Sportive as Ideal

The sportive ethos exerts its energy superfluously, generously, without reservations. It favors an aesthetic and festival sense of life where life is personified at its maximum. Ortega states that, 'Sportive activity seems to us the foremost and creative, the most exalted, serious, and important part of life' (2004c, 707; 1961, 18). Persons endowed with this sportive character embrace risk resolutely, as their devoted efforts may come to naught. While contemporary thinker Frenchman Roger Callois would write that play is pure waste of time, energy, ingenuity, and skill even as he also highlighted its benefits (2001, 5–6), the Iberian actually saw this purported 'waste' as the sunnier side of the issue, as veritable gain. Suitably paradoxical, the sportive effort and a playful attitude actually result in creative windfalls in contrast to utilitarian labor, which 'ranks second as its [sport's] derivative and precipitate (2004c, 707; 1961, 18). In a little-known work entitled 'Letter to a young Argentinian who studies philosophy,' Ortega expounds on this: 'solid and stable wealth is, in the end, the outcome of energetic souls and clear minds. These energy and clarity are only acquired through purely sporting exercises of a superfluous aspect' (Ortega 2004b, 468, my translation). In short, Ortega celebrates a life that spills over with exuberance, and which is spurned by a playful, 'cares to the wind' attitude. In his essay 'The sportive sense of vitality,' he explains how even as simple an animal as a single-celled paramecium chooses its useful movements from myriad exploratory, superfluous, and spontaneous ones fruit of an irrepressible vitality that affords the animal a rich repertoire (Ortega 2007, my translation of the title). That is, life grows out of spontaneous and energetic expressions and explorations. This vitality is sportive in character in the way captured by this analysis. Ortega and Huizinga see play eye to eye as the source of culture (Huizinga 1955), the former writing that culture is the daughter not of work but sport (Ortega 2004a, 427), as are scientific endeavors, art, and morality (2004c, 467–471).[4] To poignantly illustrate this, Ortega claims that calculus was not invented as a matter of obligation and at a fixed time (2004c, 470). In a way, sports are the inverse of technological efficiency. They expend our time and energy unproductively, and in doing so, endow our activities with meaning. Thus we become fulfilled. In this way, sports markedly differ from performative activities that result in products, cultural (performing arts that create artworks) or manufacturing ones (craftspeople and artisans).[5]

A writer of unforgettable images, Ortega gifts us with his account of a clown's inexhaustible supply of flutes and enthusiasm for playing music as the ringmaster keeps on breaking them. Ortega concludes, 'life is an affair of flutes. It is overflow that it needs most' (Ortega 2004c, 709; 1961, 21). 'Success in life depends on amplitude of possibilities' (ibid.; 1961, 20), because of life's fatal and relentless pruning knife (2004c, 708; 1961, 19). Accordingly, a sportive attitude to life is such that, 'Every blow we receive must serve as another impulse toward new attempts' (2004, 708; 1961, 19). In other words, setbacks and blows are but springs to new opportunities then. This ethos embraces challenges that demand suffering and discipline. It also values activities non-instrumentally, for what they are, focusing on the process not the result. Inimitable, Ortega compares the impulse a billiard ball receives when hit by another, where there is equivalence of cause and effect, with the out-of-proportion reaction of a skittish horse which, ever so lightly spurred, obeys no outer impulse but the 'release of exuberant inner energies' (Ortega 2004, 709; 1961, 22). These enthused, inspiring exertions are vital to a flourishing life where its ebullient overflow brings creative undertakings. This is Ortega's vitalism, which redressed the excesses of narrow rationalism. But before excitedly jumping ahead, this exuberance needs to be bridled.

This restrain arises from normative facets resulting from the interplay between limitations imposed by the formal structure of sports, games, and performative endeavors, and our species' morphokinetic endowments and limitations—those movements we can physically perform. That is, these activities are defined by rules devised around our physical capabilities. Our hands' fingers can grasp certain-sized spheres but not others, they can catch them at some speeds but not others, so different games and sports devise specific rules and devise and allow for the use of various tools: we get European handball played with a leather ball, American handball played with gloves and a small rubber ball, and Basque handball's varieties (*pelota a mano, jai alai, pala corta,* and *larga*), where a much harder and compact ball is hit or caught with and without tools. The willingly accepted rules limit efficient means. In so doing, we open creative spaces that engage our abilities variously. As argued in the first essay, what is to count as excellent (already a normatively laden judgment) is set by the repertoire of possible movements. This formal restriction creates normative and experiential spaces. By further restricting the types of movements and actions possible in a given context, rules create realms of excellence and creativity. They force participants to imaginatively solve athletic and creative problems that rules and games pose, leading in the best cases to a sweet tension between challenge and abilities, as Kretchmar argues (1972).[6] Richard Fosbury's revolutionary high-jump technique inventively accomplished this. Paradoxically, inefficiency—elsewhere connected with lack of skill—becomes actually the precondition for skillful performances (when rule-limited and willingly embraced). Notably, Ortega phenomenologically extends this examination of rules and efficiency to life. He tethers it to the previous existential analysis of life as sportive affair, placing as keystone the voluntary and inefficient means of expending surplus energy gratuitously.

Play, as primeval and spontaneous ludic activity, is common to humans and other animals. Sheets-Johnstone's phenomenological analysis views play as marked by a spontaneity of movement where 'the sheer exuberance of movement dominates and in which a certain freedom of movement obtains' (2009, 323). But games, when viewed as formalized by explicit rules are a human affair. As mentioned, both games and sports are characterized by rules that prescribe inexpedient means of achieving an activity's goal—something *first* adumbrated by Ortega, as Inglis points out when he contrasts the Spaniard's views with Bernard Suits' (2004, 85). Inglis (2004) singles out four similarities: both see sports as willingly undertaken yokes; the free adoption of handicaps characterizes humans; their forms of life are more or less like elaborate games (thus Ortega also precedes Wittgenstein); games and sports are played with a particular autotelic spirit (ibid). But there are differences. Most notably, Suits (2005) is more focused on the formal aspects of games and rules, and advances an utopian view, whereas Ortega's interest lies in the existential role of games and sports in our lives, is not so concerned with rules, and is a realist that considers what is (Ibid., 95). Until now, the sportive spirit has joyfully mingled with play and playful attitude, but we need to distinguish between them.

Where sport –competitive or recreational– differs from games and play is in its *willing* cultivation of suffering, discipline, and danger through habit-developing training. There is an asceticism, which as Ortega explains monks took from the Greek athletes' vocabulary (2004d, 713; 1961, 29). *Ascesis*, meaning 'training exercise,' 'was the regime of the life of an athlete, and it was crammed with exercises and privations' (2004d, 714; 1961, 30.) He explains, 'For adults a game is not effort but leisure and fun. They stop where the toilsome begins which is precisely where sport starts. It is lacking all the attributes of the latter: training, discipline, risk—in sum, seriousness and earnestness' (2007a, 833, my translation). This does not mean there is no enjoyment or that the ludic attitude is lost, only that one must learn to value and enjoy suffering; the kind of meaningful suffering at which sports and some active pursuits such as martial arts excel. Moreover, such disciplined movement shapes sportspeople's bodies, gives sport its deeper significance, and leads to refined abilities (Ilundáin-Agurruza 2013b). The highest exponent is the athlete in top form, whose absolute devotion means that she never lets herself go in anything for any reason, as Ortega asserts (2004d, 20, 2005d, 1039, 2009, 11). Formal and physical restrictions, as we saw with Dewey, afford us space for a modicum of freedom and creativity (without devolving into a Jamesian dualism to preserve such choice). Privations here fuel the stirring inner energies of the steed and Orteguian enthusiasm and vigor. Scheler, who influenced Ortega's theory of values, helps explain the origin of this energy: asceticism is precisely the source of energetic surplus by repressing basic animal instincts through a process he calls sublimation, which transforms lower level impulses into higher ones (1979). Moreover, David Sansone details how the squandering of energy as the common element among rituals, games, and sports entails two outcomes when we consider what we can characterize as a transactional equation where we must give energy to receive energy: it is unimportant how energy is spent, and the tendency is toward repetition and exaggeration (1992). The multiplicity of sports, games, artistic, and ritualistic performances attests to this.

The contingency and historical nature of these practices, as well as their kinship in terms of praxis, means that they sometimes intertwine, as when a ritual takes on sportive characteristics. Allen Guttmann traced the different historical phases from ritual to record-focused sports—even if some claims and causal continuities can be questioned, the ethnographic value of his examples is not lessened (1978). The facet of repetition is explained by the intersection of two elements. Normatively, there is a confluence between conceptions of excellence and worship where sacrifice of what is most precious to us, our life-sustaining energy, becomes the gift of choice when done in the proper way (as per standards of excellence) whether it be expressed through contests, rituals, or artwork. Empirically, repetition is simply the way we may refine best many of our skills. In this way, we can perform at the requisite level to satisfy the normative requirements. Exaggeration underlies the 'Baroque-like' tendency of more is better exemplified by the unsustainable quest for records (Loland 2001), and the propensity in many to ignore prudence and choose instead to indulge in extremes. Finally, recall that for James asceticism was also a profound way of dealing with life itself, and that he singled out sports also as a healthy ascetic practice that leads to a superior affirmation. Ortega goes beyond this instrumentalism by *additionally* embracing sports and the requisite attitude for their own sake. The athletic training regimen thus entails an ascetic regime where privations and exertion result in squandered energy. But it is that generous gift of energy that precisely makes it meaningful and marks the risky but creative enterprises of admirable individuals.

4. Self-Development as Personal Perfectionism

'The best of people have spent their lives in pure sportive frenzy' (Ortega 2007a, 832–833, my translation). The Iberian builds his pedagogy of self-cultivation around such sporting aspirations; the preceding permits us to see through the Orteguian hyperbole and realize what this sportive frenzy entails: a generous, fearless pursuit of life's possibilities when uncertainty is the only given. And nothing is riskier than lucidly chasing after an ever-elusive perfection. He endorses a particular version of what Socrates saw as the good life, pragmatists thought of as amelioration if we look at James and Dewey's tenor, and today is called philosophical perfectionism—how to develop ourselves so as to live good lives. His ethical views are partial to a virtue theoretic account (Ilundáin-Agurruza 2013a). Much as virtue ethics thinks that we should conceive of ethics is in terms of character and rethink what is a good action as how would a virtuous person act, Ortega looks at this in terms of 'heroes.' His heroes are dramatic, they are not necessarily tragic, given an inherent tension in life whose measure is not so much victory but how we fight the battle. Life is a drama because it is always a frenetic fight to be able to realize who we are as a project (Ortega 2004e, 308). With Ortega, we should speak of an ethos as a way of life, being what we *are to be*, rather than an ethics, which applies to what one should be (Molinuevo 2002, 212). A number of concepts help us navigate the Orteguian waters we are about to embark upon (even if invariably we all end shipwrecked). Among these, perfection is paramount, but the measure of what this cultivation is like and to what extent it is achievable is taken when discussing plenitude and vocation, love, individuals of excellence, and risk.

There are many different views regarding what perfection amounts to: Aristotle's *eudaimonia*, various versions of self-realization or flourishing, e.g., Martha Nussbaum's (2000) or Wallace's (1978), and those who settle for a more wide-ranging and stringent perfectionism such as Thomas Hurka (1993). We have seen that James focuses on emotional temperance by way of asceticism and a resolute, adventurous life, while Dewey adopts a meliorist version wherein individuals are to realize their fullest potential within the context of a democratic community. Breivik enters the fray looking at philosophical views of perfectionism, specifically Hurka's, as he centers on sport (2010). Next, the focus falls on Ortega, Hurka, and Breivik.

St. Frances de Sales said, 'Do not try to be anything but what you are, and try to be that perfectly' (quotationsbook n.d.). This sums up the Orteguian ethos of self-cultivation and acts as North Star for our inquiry. Ortega's self-cultivation is about perfecting oneself. On the one side, he differs from Aristotle and like-minded thinkers, who see a specific *telos* built around our highest intellectual capacities first, then (perhaps) the cultivation of physical and practical ones. Breivik asserts that views that apply to most people are less applicable when we consider elite sport: 'I think to be realistic the international elite athlete pursuing perfection has very limited possibilities of being involved in various other activities than sport. A certain single-mindedness is needed. Specialised perfection has a prize. Too much well-roundedness detracts from the possibility of a successful career' (2010, 99). Ortega's perfectionism cuts into this issue at a right angle. The Spaniard does not think there is a specific highest perfection universal to humans; we each have our perfection to seek. On the other side, he does not side with the alternative camp that propounds a moderate, well-rounded development of our talents. His view, while applicable to any and all humans, does not determine the content of self-fulfillment. Ortega's ethos seeks perfection, rather than duty, and is motivated by Pindar's 'Learn and become who you are,' whom he often cites (online, Pythian 2, Epode 3, 70). This is about personal perfection; one not set by external or others' standards. Reflective individuals have the opportunity to find out much about themselves when pitted in competition against others, as in athletic contests, but these are particulars to be considered later. In essence, it is a call to arms to rally behind what he calls our *vocation*, an existential project for our life. Lasaga cites Ortega to show how vocation and sportive ethos come together: 'happy occupations, mind you, are not merely pleasures; they are efforts, and effort is what true sports are about' (2006, 199, my translation). Now, Sartre's existential project is reminiscent and posterior to Ortega's, but differs significantly. In contrast to the Frenchman's radical freedom, for the Iberian, it is the case that we do not choose our vocation, rather it precedes us in the sense that it does not depend on decisions made by the will. Our choice is either to embrace it and be authentic, or not to embrace it and be inauthentic (2006c, 124). Ortega puts it thus,

> Each one of us then is one's own determined vital project, which is realized or not, but with which we compress circumstance and we compress fatality, to see which proportion of it can be realized. Well then, the two foundations for falsification of life are these: either we do not accept in all its rigor and clarity the circumstances that surround us, so that we live in imaginary circumstances, deceptions, or the vital project with which we press destiny is not sincere, not authentically our own, that it not be our own vocation [...] The project needs to be authentic. (Ortega 2008, 510, my translation)

Hence our task is not to invent ourselves, but to realize our pre-given vocation, that to which we are suited for. This is the source of the drama or tragedy for those heroic ones who embrace their projects with sportive vigor. 'The hero's tragedy does not consist in being thus, but in wanting to be thus' (Molinuevo 2002, 76, my translation). If we consider the extreme specialization required of elite sportspersons, martial artists, dancers, etc., Ortega's framework endorses such single-minded pursuit for *some* individuals: those whose vital project calls for that and have the requisite talents. This is consistent with Breivik's keen critique of Hurka when he remarks that 'in addition to common properties individual differences should be important' (2010, 92). The Orteguian stance speaks precisely to this nurturing of what we share with others, but above all our personal talents, since these make our vocation.

Obviously, besides having the resolve to follow our project, the biggest challenge is to find out the contours of our vocation. In other words, there is the problem of determining what our vital project is; others cannot tell us, for being our personal project it is for us to find. Are we 'destined' to be an Olympic athlete? Does that define us afterwards also? If so, How? Does our vocation change as we change '*métier*,' or is there an underlying structure that is kept as we cycle through life's stages? Sport philosopher Heather Reid recounts her own bid for a 1988 Olympic berth when she was one of the best US track cyclists (Reid 2010). She writes, 'I had ridden a good race—maybe the perfect race. I knew my strengths and weaknesses and played my cards as well as they could be played—my opponent was simply faster. And so my question was answered: I was not an Olympian' (ibid., 152). After so many years of privations and dedication, the

Olympic dream evanesced with a rude awakening. Had Reid misread her vocation? How could she have found out unless she tried? Were all those efforts and sufferings for nothing?

This personal gnostic dilemma, rather than a problem with the Orteguian stance illustrates the kind of thinking it behooves us to do. It requires careful reflection, which as Lasaga explains for Ortega implies solitude, time to look within us in a self-absorbed way ('*ensimismación*') (2006, 205). As epistemological stance, and not a moral one, it has nothing to do with being self-centered or selfish. Instead, it has everything to do with lucid, fearless inquiry into the core of our self. If action and vitalism are essential for his conception of (the good) life, reflection or contemplation is the way to make our endeavors meaningful. Ortega's decades long series of essays called *The Spectator* and his occupation as philosopher evince this. There are two sides to this, first, we are to embrace our vocation and *act* alongside others, to then seek *solitude* and *reflection*, that is what the Orteguian ethos prescribes for life (Lasaga 2006, 248). Suitably, this is a type of contemplative thinking that his phenomenological meditations model. Breivik writes that high levels of performance in sport (and certainly we can extend this to other performative endeavors) make use not only of physical prowess, but also equally of practical *and* theoretical rationality (strategic and scientific knowledge) (2011, 92–93). He also rightly chastises Hurka and others for underestimating the role of the latter (ibid.). Breivik goes even so far as to emphatically recommend that sprinters and those in non-tactical sports study philosophy (ibid., 96, 102). The Iberian would look very favorably upon this. Nonetheless, I deem that Ortega's ideas allow, perhaps require, us to combine the theoretical and practical rationality with an engaged contemplation of existential contours. Our involvement with the practice should be deeper: through it, we are to learn about ourselves such that it sets us on the road toward our plenitude. Sports themselves are to be methods, ways, to our fulfillment through their very sportive ethos. This seems to me, if not more correct, more inspiring—which is a kind of correctness when existential considerations are at stake. While Breivik would need to include all sportspersons not just to athletes in non-tactical sports, I do not see any reason why he cannot recommend that. Ortega, with good philosophical sense but not overly helpful, refrains from specifics. Talents and abilities are part of the equation, as are our circumstances. If this is not sufficient to chart our path, he does provide an indirect method and an answer to Reid's quandary. The method revolves around love, and the answer spins around the effort's quality.

Ortega's vitalism emphasized the positive emotions, particularly love, as central to a virtuous life where action is enhanced by contemplation. However, his idea of love, while inclusive of romantic love, is much more complex. We should understand love under the rubric first expounded in his maiden book *Meditations on Quixote* (Ortega 2001, 1963). There he states that we should think of love after Spinoza's *amor intellectualis* (ibid.; ibid.; Spinoza and Andrew 1948). It is about a Spinozistic and Platonic ideal of knowledge and understanding. It seeks salvation form our circumstances in taking something to its own plenitude and fulfillment from a critical distance (Marías 1970, 76). Accordingly, for him, contemplation and thinking is an erotic art in Plato's sense, whom he follows when he states: 'in my opinion, philosophy, which searches for the meaning of things, is driven by '*eros*" (Ortega 2004a, 782; 1963, 89). This also highlights the cognitive facet of the sportive and festival sense of life. As his writings on art evince (2005c, 1948), aesthetics and also the aesthetic of the well-lived life must be conducted under the clarity and rigor of our intellect, with careful contemplation. The importance of concepts as means to endow our thinking with luminosity is crucial (Ortega 2001, 783–785, 787–789; 1963 91–93, 97–9). The third phase of his thinking focused on a historicist narrativism that *History as a System* conceptually shores (2006d, 1961), and his biographical studies such as Goethe's make this patent (2006c). As living projects, we unfold historically and make sense of our life through either original or plagiarized narrative. Just as with Suits' ideas, this precedes accounts of narrative lives such as McIntyre's (1981), fruitfully echoed in sport philosophy by McNamee, 'One key point is such a scheme is the notion of a virtue conceived not as an isolated act but as part of a narrative that is my life' (2011, 33). Speaking of a historically located life, being a man of his time, some of Ortega's ideas are expressed in sexist language or from a preeminently masculine perspective, as when he analyzes love in terms of romantic love and the role women play as muses for men. This point noted, what we should take is that any person of whichever gender can aspire to these ideals.

To reiterate, through this kind of love, we seek salvation from our circumstances—a meaningful life—by taking something to its own fulfillment. We flourish by giving the best of us. But rather than being about ourselves in a narrow sense, it is about others (which includes by extension our vocation and activities in life). It entails that we seek the best in and for others in two ways. First, it is a *devotional* attitude that recognizes that 'there is inside of each thing an indication of a possible plenitude,' which we make our life's center as we endeavor to perfect it (2004a, 747; 1963, 32). This means that we should seek the perfection of those people, things, practices that we love, for what they are and not what we want them to be. Those who identify themselves as rock climbers, in making it the center of their lives, soon realize it is not about merely going up mountain faces or being the first to the top. Climbing the learning curve to become a de facto member of the community is more challenging than practicing knots, belaying, rappelling, and learning to use pitons and carabiners. From etiquette on rock faces, respecting first ascenders, to learning about redpointing, climbing in style, or entering the debate on whether to bolt or not to bolt, climbers who truly love the activity exert themselves to better the practice; it is not simply about their enjoyment.

Learning to love something or someone is about making the other the center of our life. In keeping with thick holism, I conceive this as a perspectival shift that entails the union of lover and loved. It is about unity, about bringing together what was asunder before. We cannot live without the loved object—we consider it part of ourselves—and through concatenation of those things about which the loved one cares and so on, we ultimately are led into a Spinozistic 'pan-holism' where all is united. Ortega's and Spinoza's holism correlate, for different reasons, with Eastern views that endorse egolessness, emotionally and ontologically. This bypasses the perennial problem of the one and the many and the subject/object dichotomy, if for a time: 'Love [...] binds us to things, eve if only temporarily' (Ortega 2004a, 749; 1963, 33). One who acts thus becomes a noble exemplar for Ortega and is willing to take risks most others skirt around.

We find the core of Ortega's analysis of the noble individual in his 1930 *The Revolt of the Masses* (2005c, 1932). While politically read when excised from its overall context in his oeuvre, it is rather an ethical work. Orteguian excellent individuals, adhering to the sportive ethos, are demanding with themselves. Taking on their project as a duty, they see their liberty as inherently tied to their responsibilities, which they emphatically embrace. Far from a universal Kantian duty, this is all about their personal imperative, a freely adopted vocation that indefatigably strives after an ever-elusive perfection without losing heart. As he explains, both history and life are a *perpetual effort*, the only thing we are gifted with being possibilities out of which to *make* this or that (2005a, 1991). This contrasts with "mass individuals" who, satisfied and even delighted with who they are, loudly proclaim and demand their rights and entitlement. Moreover, this is also intimately connected to the community in Ortega's case. He favored virtues that reverted to it, such as magnanimity, in contrast to smaller ones like honesty or chastity, which he saw as small virtues for the masses (2005d).

Tellingly, Molinuevo explains how philosophers can be like sportspersons,

> Ortega is speaking of [...] the elite sportsperson or athlete, the high-performance one. Her level is defined by herself, by what she demands of herself, not for what she asks for: she only has, like the noble person, obligations not rights (2002, 164, my translation).

It is not coincidental that Molinuevo speaks of the elite sportsperson, for there, we find the requisite will for sacrifice. There are three thorny issues to address in this respect. One pertains to the unhealthy extremes, literally and ethically, to which elite sportspeople are prone. The other is a possible social elitism in Ortega's views. The last one regards the putative obligation to excel. As to the first, contemporary rampant performance enhancement shows that the pursuit of perfection, when seen as obtaining specific goals, e.g. victory in competition, can lead to ethically murky or downright censurable practices such as doping and cheating. Regarding the second, some passages in his work and the general tone lend themselves to be read as endorsing a social elitism whereby superior individuals are identified with aristocratic classes and the mass individuals with those of middle class or lower "stock." This seems the case even when, it is clear, these are neither ontologically, historically, or sociopolitically predetermined. Another possible ramification of elitism is by way of prioritarian views. By putting extra weight on the more valuable forms of perfection, this "means that we should value perfection of each and every human being, but in aggregating we should count the greater perfections more, by some multiplier, than lesser perfections. Greater perfections count for more" (Breivik 2010, 101). Finally, Breivik argues that while aiming for perfection is laudable, it is not obligatory but "one of the plausible deep life goals" that may be attractive to some talented young people (2011, 102).

The answer to all three is found in one standard already mentioned and one word that sums up the whole of Ortega's ethos, *quality*. First, as Ortega writes, "Each person must be measured against himself, his own ideal of perfection, not an outside standard" (2004, 181, my translation). Hence, it is a personal standard determined by our possibilities, abilities, and circumstances. This partially takes off the pressure to perform against others, even in athletic competition, to some extent. This is developed further below. It also means that the elitism is not internal to the project and the qualities of the noble person, but rather, an external valuation. Moreover, it is important that such perfectionism be open to a number of ways of approaching the issue depending on the particular person's talents and her circumstances. The obligation is not external but self-imposed. It cannot be obligatory in the sense that worries Breivik. We willingly choose this, just as we choose sports. But there are consequences for not doing so: we fail ourselves. This is something some people are willing to "endure," as slothful non-flourishing individuals demonstrate.

But this means they cannot complain later on but only regret. Second, Ortega's perfectionism is qualitative to the core. In the letter to the Argentinian philosophy student, Ortega makes a crucial statement, "Those endeavors that matter most are but games where the most important thing is that we play them as well as may be possible" (2004c, 469, my translation). What matters is not the end result, for there is much we do not control in life, but the kind of effort we put, its quality (2007a, 832). Is it our best? Well, then, even losing we need not worry about being last. This is so from an ethos-ethical point of view of course. Were we a professional and our salary depended on this, it might be a different matter. But still, the latter measures our worth in a utilitarian and economic sense, not a sportive one. There can be a different yardstick that even professional athletes, thoughtful ones, adhere to. American 1988 Giro d'Italia winner Andy Hampsten liked to say that in cycling, while there is always a winner there are no losers, because 129 out of 130 cannot be considered losers (Abt 1993, 142). Speaking of losers misrepresents the achievement of 130 finishers who, after three grueling weeks, are separated by mere seconds or minutes. It fails to capture the prowess and ability each of them is capable of *and* the quality of the effort they put to make it to the finish. To say it with Ortega, what *is* valuable is the "tone, its perfection, its gentle impetus" (2007a, 832–833, my translation). This is readily applicable to other sports and activities.

To delve some more, noble individuals see life as a "quehacer," a word Ortega often used, and which is not translatable in a literal manner. It refers to a willful "doing-what-is-to-be-done" that entails working to actualize our possibilities then executing them by putting one's nose to the grind. This can be done in two ways, with quality effort and "pundonor," where we give our best, or with *"chabacanería"*— another pair of Spanish untranslatable and idiosyncratic words. American Novelist James Michener writes at length on *pundonor* (1968). After discussing the sense of the word in France, Germany, US, and even Japanese samurai culture, he writes

> It has been left to Spain to cultivate not only the world's most austere definition of honor but also to invent a special word to cover that definition. Of course, Spanish has the word honor, which means roughly what it does in French, but also the word *pundonor*, which is a contraction of *punta de honor* (point of honor). (Michener 1968, 72)

Michener finds that coming to this "acute or even preposterous sense of honor" helps explain some Spaniards' actions, whose paladin, fittingly, is no other than Don Quixote (1968, 72). Thus, an exceptional individual has a high sense of *pundonor*, a deep sense of honor and honorability that, out of principle, will not let him take dubious shortcuts, legal or not. She would rather come last than skip over the fence to take a shortcut even if all are doing it. This is admirable in just the sense Lally describes a competitor in his first training race with a particular triathlete group in California when all but the last among the top six finishers took a shortcut to the finish: 'His simple choice to honor the racecourse told me all I needed to know about his character. I have never seen the man again, but I could testify to this day to his extraordinary excellence' (2013, 184).

Chabacanería, Ortega sees as designating one of Spain's vices (and explains a lot of the country's former and current woes). To put it bluntly, it refers to something done in poor taste or lacking worth or merit. It is a way of "cultivating" mediocrity branded by sloppy work of shoddy quality. Slovenliness might be a way to render it (Ortega 2009, 9), if the English term were "slightly milder". Athletes, martial artists, craftspeople, performers who act like this, even if greatly talented, do not shine. While Orteguian qualitative emphasis is about *how* the task is undertaken, rather than the result, this does not mean that the latter is an afterthought. Talented people who do not put the effort may be lucky for a while, but invariably lackluster effort will result in poor quality and outcomes. Those untalented ones who do not put the effort will stridently fail—no sympathy points from Ortega. It is those who are talented but unlucky in spite of effort, those who mismatch their gifts with the task, or those who simply lack talent but try regardless of what Lady Luck decides that see the quality of their effort validated. On the subject of fortune, Ortega often cited from Cervantes' *Don Quixote,* whose lonesome knight defiantly declared, *"Enchanters may deprive me of good fortune, but of spirit and courage, never!"* (Cervantes 1994, 565; 2003, 518)

Interestingly for us, Ortega finds that

> the contrary of *chabacanería* is *being in top form*. Well known is the fabulous difference there is between a player when he is in top form, and the same player when he is not in shape. One would say they are not the same person: such a difference we notice between what he is capable of doing in one and the other case

(2005d 1039–40; 2009, 11, his italics my translation). It proves instructive how Ortega explains the mechanics to achieving admirable fitness (athletic and existential):

> But form has to be conquered: to obtain it means that the individual has withdrawn and concentrated upon himself [let's remember *ensimismación* and reflective cultivation], that he has conducted training, that he has renounced to many things, that he lives focused, alert, in tension, elastic. Nothing is indifferent to him, because each thing is either favorable to that form or makes it worse, and with this in mind, it is either sought or avoided. In sum, being in form is not to abandon oneself in nothing, ever. (2005d 1039–40; 2009,11, his italics, my translation)[7]

In contrast to someone who acts with *pundonor* and conquers form, Ortega further explains, that 'Well then, this abandoning oneself, this "in whichever way,' this 'it is all the same', this 'a bit more or less,' this 'What does it matter!' this is *chabacanería*' (ibid,). Some might liken this to a 'bullshit attitude.' But as Henry Frankfurt makes clear in his brilliant little book *On Bullshit*, if we obviate the difference that one has to do with enacted actions not just verbal utterances, the English concept shows a 'lack of concern with truth—this indifference to how things really are—that I regard as the essence of bullshit' (2005, 33–34). The latter is an in your face matter, the former may or may not try to hide the sloppiness. Sometimes they can happily coexist.

Lance Armstrong, and many others, have done all the hardcore training and seemed to check all the requirements for being in top form. They definitely could not be accused of not conquering their form and status. Except that by now we know better. What is their standing in this ethos? We should remember that for Ortega this is tied to the issue of quality. This is not given by the results but by *how* we go about them. Knowingly trying to sidestep what in principle one has willfully agreed to—in this case, freely agreeing to abide by the rules of the sport—means that the effort's quality is tainted. In other words, it is about the process, rather than the result; and when results matter, these must be according to certain standards. Or rather, the quality of the process marks the excellence of the result (or lack thereof). Armstrong and others like him sidestep this crucial fact. Moreover, cheating and breaking rules is not something that the excellent person will do, not the least, because she has an obligation to her community, whether it be the cycling or cancer communities. As a preview of Eastern ways to be pursued in *Reflections of a Katana*, Karate master Miyagi Gojun said something that many a sportsperson would do well to mind: 'The true victory is defeat of your base nature. That triumph is far superior to conquering any foe. The ultimate strategy is to win through virtue and perseverance, not by battle' (Stevens 2001, 106). Last, known for their boundless 'self-confidence' and arrogance, these individuals actually do not know how to face defeat. Their strength is built on weakness in the end, idols with clay feet. Excellence is not tantamount nor builds on a *boundless and purported self-confidence.* [8]

For Ortega, excessive self-confidence is likely to turn against oneself. This, he illustrates with the World War I German loss. They lost because they were fully committed in mind and heart to winning and not simply to combatting. Ortega explains that when fighting, one has to be ready for anything, even defeat and failure, 'which are, no less than victory, faces that life takes on. Each day, the conviction imposes itself on me that an excess in self-confidence demoralizes people more than anything' (2005d 1034; 2009, 4, my translation.). When the going gets tough, the overconfident resort to tricks or come crashing down. To return to the charge of elitism now, the noble attitude is something *all* can embrace, no matter their social station. It also means that the right kind of pride, *pundonor*, in doing things, well forestalls temptations to find shortcuts. Unsure of victory, the person of noble qualities is willing to take risks, to put out the best effort and have it come down to nothing, or to harm herself in the attempt, morally or physically, much like how Don Quixote charges against 'giants' no matter the odds.

Ortega proposes a 'risky perfectionism.' It should not be surprising. Much as Nietzsche's call to live dangerously, he was partial to a life where we *joyfully* confront peril. Throughout his career, Ortega relied on several metaphors to embody this: the first two were the warrior and then the sportsperson (the latter being symbol of an aesthetic life). With the latter, Ortega wants to 'to introduce the element of risk, of danger in the affair of one's own life, transforming life not into a game […] but into a sporting affair. The sportsman is the heir of the warrior who has disappeared' (Molinuevo 1995, 26, my translation). Lasaga cites Ortega, 'The sportsperson, instead of fleeing danger, goes to meet it, and that is why she is a sportsperson' (2006, 249, my translation). Ortega's last metaphor was the archer as a hybrid and heir of warrior and sportsperson. I surmise he was thinking of Aristotle ethics, for he wrote 'At the beginning of his ethics Aristotle says beautifully: the archer seeks a target for his arrows, and won't we seek one for our lives?' (Ortega 2007c, 690, my translation) For Ortega, there is a cultivation of the self that needs 'a constant adventure and attempt to widen our limits' (2007d, 317, my translation). What the archer adds to the sportive and risky life when releasing the arrow is the aim toward truth and wisdom that widens our limits as we come to know ourselves better. Ortega understood this as *aletheia*, that is revelation, already in 1914, well before Heidegger. This connects the playful spirit and rigorous discipline of sport to philosophy and truth, which has been echoed independently and for different reasons by among others, Reid (2009, 2012).

There is a tension between the carefree sportive ethos and the one of authenticity, to be sure, but this does not result in a contradiction. It is a philosophical problem, and for Ortega, these are solved in a higher level, like a paradox. The sportive facet brings this willingness to take chances, while the vocational aspect directs the direction of this risk-taking, fully aware of the consequences. Moreover, risk is a prerequisite to enjoy a modicum of freedom. Lasaga connects this with Ortega's overall ethos for us: 'As a task, life is effort; but as free, [it is] preference and choice. To go on with life or not to go on with life: this is the dilemma. 'But to go on with life is to freely accept the hard task it is. And this is the definition of sportive effort" (2006, 249, my translation). This resolutely courts danger.

There is a rich literature in sport philosophy that explores risk and sports from various angles, and which wisely avoids superficial and mistaken subjectivist valuations that reduce risk sports to adrenaline rushes. Leslie Howe considers remote sports where aid is too far for comfort as venues for self-knowledge. For his part, Kevin Krein looks at alternative sports in terms of their non-competitive ethos (2007), and the potential for world making of said activities (2008). Mike McNamee's edited book on risk sports offers the broadest philosophical analysis of the phenomenon from conceptual and phenomenological stances (2007). And John Russell's articles have become points of reference where he argues for risk sports as source of self-affirmation (2005), or makes room for dangerous activities during childhood (2007). I have explored risk and sport with regard to the Kantian sublime (2007a), also, as as the interplay of death and joy and the corresponding emotional attunement in the running of the bulls[9] (2007b, 2008), and as conducive to existential self-knowledge within an East/West comparative framework (Forthcoming). Regardless of whether danger is instrument for self-affirmation, self-knowledge, or joy, there is a common element for its role in risk sports and activities where it may be present, such as the *traditional* martial arts of yore or contemporary fighting martial sports.

This takes place within an underlying structure common to dangerous experiences where phenomenological description, sport and martial rules, and our morphological and kinetic endowments meet. Those who excel in dangerous situations and seek them with Orteguian sportive spirit do so at the interface of the enjoyment of an activity they *already* love, whose artificial challenges they meet through skills they have honed over years. And a primary reason is that continued improvement means taking on bigger risks. The rush is a great perk, but not why it is done. To highlight a point that basically all references mentioned agree upon, it is not the danger per se, as it can be found more easily in many other ways that do not require so much toil. Most people who embrace the utilitarian ethos (and criticize 'risk takers') crave security (as if life were ever safe!). But as Molinuevo writes, the want for security Ortega counters with a courtship of insecurity that should begin by assuming one's own death as the currency of life (1995, 26). What commentators often downplay is the fact that courting danger is done joyfully, finding

HOLISM AND THE CULTIVATION OF EXCELLENCE IN SPORTS AND PERFORMANCE

pleasure in the activity for the reasons elucidated above. The paradoxical trick is to put life on the line precisely because it is the most precious thing we have.

To come back to Reid and her failed Olympic bid, she undertook risks not only on the roads and tracks, but also used her life as the currency for risk when she opted to spend so much time and energy on her Olympic dream. Given her talents, she would not have found out unless she had tried. Beautifully embodying the combination of Orteguian vitalism with contemplation, she concludes,

> But in all those years of trying to become an Olympic athlete, I had been cultivating a kind of Olympic soul. Cycling was the medium through which I learned about myself and pursued lofty ideals. It was my path toward wisdom and excellence. It was a lived philosophy. And now that I am a professor of philosophy, immersed in books and lectures and conferences, I still ride my bike in the pursuit of wisdom. The difference is that now I understand that cycling for me is philosophy, back then I only knew that I could be satisfied. (2010, 152)

Such wise development takes place through a vital body and mind as we shall discover.

5. Mind and Body integration, and the Role of the Environment

While Dewey speaks of centaurs, it is Ortega who philosophically rides astride them and realizes their significance for us. But before becoming familiar with the mythological animals, it is advisable to consider Ortega's 1925 essay entitled 'Vitality, Soul, and Spirit,' *Vitalidad, alma y* espíritu (2004i, my translation). This seminal article, not available in English to my knowledge, lays out a sophisticated description of bodymind dynamics that predates much contemporary thinking in philosophy of mind and allows us to further delve phenomenologically into the bodymind, making it well worth discussing in detail. It presents a tripartite analysis of our holistic being: (1) a vital core he called 'vitality,' (2) an intellectual and volitional facet he termed 'spirit,' and (3) an emotional facet he referred to as' soul.' (2004i). It is critical to emphasize that these are separable experientially but not metaphysically.

Ortega's holistic credentials are impeccable. He is emphatic, 'It is false, it is unacceptable to even intend to divide the human whole into mind and body [...] because it is impossible to determine where our body begins and our soul begins' (2004i, 568, my translation). Molinuevo stresses the underlying holism, 'We need to highlight the revalorization that Ortega gives to the role of the body in considering the totality of the human' (2002, 140, my translation). Ortega's tripartite analysis may seem redolent of Platonic or even Freudian views. But beyond the triadic analysis and a few perfunctory similarities, the resemblance stops there. His peculiar and overtly religious terminology contrasts with contemporary philosophy of mind's technical jargon. It is not used religiously *strictu sensu,* however, the choice of words is geared toward a non-philosophical public reading him in a very Catholic Spain. Ever the pedagogue, he crafted the message such that it would best resonate with its intended readers. He also took advantage of the terms' poetic nuances to evoke fluidity among the three phenomena. His method is strictly phenomenological, mapping the topography of our animate, corporeal consciousness in its fullest sense. Of note is that twice he reminds readers that the three names 'denominate but what are clear differences describing phenomena that we find in our intimate events; they are *descriptive* concepts, not *metaphysical* hypothesis' (Ortega 2004i, 579, my italics, my translation). Any of us can analyze these alongside him; it does not posit any ontological entities. The substratum is a complex holistic and fluid relationship among the three. This is crucial, given that Western metaphysics goes astray when it looks for substances when it should be considering functions, as Dewey and James emphasize (even processes *can* be suspect). What is interesting is how Ortega rearranges the 'usual' phenomena functionally, avoiding pre-packaged mental–corporeal or conscious–unconscious categorizations.

The first phenomenon, 'vitality,' refers to a *'carnal* soul' that blends psychosomatic phenomena, the corporeal and the spiritual, which arise out of and derive nourishment from said vitality (Ortega 2004i, 570). 'Soul' here is not to be conceived in the usual sense as an immaterial and immortal essence. Current terminology would rephrase vitality as 'embodied awareness,' or 'animate dynamics,' and classify it as 'interoceptive,' that is inward looking. It forms part of what he calls the *intracuerpo,* which can be rendered as 'inward-body.' It is opposed to a visually observable *extracuerpo,* 'outward-body' that is exteroceptive. The inward body 'is constituted by movement and tactile sensations of viscera and muscles, by the impression of the dilations and contractions of conduits, by the minute perceptions of the passage of blood through veins and arteries, by the sensations of pain and pleasure, etc.' (ibid., 571, my translation). Ortega offers a first glimpse of the relevance of such phenomena and gives them theoretical import. Nowadays, this is spoken of in terms of proprioceptive, kinesthetic, vestibular, nociceptive (pain), and related dynamics. *Riding the Wind* focuses on these aspects of our experience, which Gallagher (2005, 2007) and Sheets-Johnstone (2009, 2011) deftly use to differentiate between body schema and body image, and argue for the primacy of movement respectively. This vitality unfolds at the pre-reflective and reflective levels of consciousness. Vitality is, for Ortega, 'in a sense subconscious, dark and latent, [and] extends to the depths of our persona like a landscape on the background of a painting' (Ortega 2004i, 576, my translation). Nevertheless, it is clear that we can learn to discriminate these latent and dark phenomena: dancers, martial artists, and athletes do so to a high degree. Their skills are refined largely in correlation with their discriminatory capacities. Working on her swing, the golfer pays close attention to her kinesthetic and proprioceptive dynamics, and to the extent that she is able to discern the subtler elements of that landscape or background—that Dreyfus and Dreyfus (1986) and Searle (1983) theorize *sui generis*—the better chance she has of refining it, all things being equal. From this vitality, and apposite for active endeavors, our energetic mien with its tidal ebbs and flows issues forth. Ortega points out that there are two kinds of beings, those with energetic overabundance, whose disposition is positively contagious, and those deficiently so, and who bring us down (ibid., 573).

The second aspect is the 'spirit,' which refers to the mind, specifically its cognitive abilities and volition. Ortega explains that he calls spirit to 'the group of intimate acts of which each of us feels as true author and protagonist. The clearest example being volition. That internal fact we express with the phrase 'I want' [...] that emanates from a central point [...] that is what strictly should be called 'I'' (2004i, 575, my translation). When we do something under obligation, there is a sense in which we do so against ourselves. This is profitably related how Gallagher conceives of the relation between embodied cognition and action (2007). Gallagher makes a distinction between two mechanisms that usually are almost indistinguishable in everyday life, the sense of ownership and the sense of agency. The former refers to how we feel our body and its movement being ours, the latter to the feeling that we causally and intentionally effect our actions, e.g. being pushed from behind clearly shows that we feel it is *us* moving *unintentionally* (Gallagher and Zahavi 2008, 40). Likewise, Ortega's spirit or cognitive volition affords us our sense of agency for our actions: it is *I* who wills and acts. In contrast, the sense that it is our body clearly belongs to vitality and its corporeal soul with its proprioceptive sensitivity. This does not entail treating the body as an object nor does it bring dualism through the back door. These two mechanisms work in unison in normal subjects and conditions, and it is in pathological conditions that we see the effects of the mismatch (See *Fractured Action*). The fencer *is* her bodymind in action as she parries and launches a counterattack in tierce, for example, feeling the agent every bit. But if she trips, for example, her agency is taken from her. It is not movement, as intentionally willed, but motion of her body out of control— now objectified and felt as foreign. A reminder is in order before explaining the third phenomenon, for it is easy to misread these: these are experiential discriminations, descriptions of how we experience said phenomena, not ontological distinctions.

For those who sharply distinguish between executive functions (will) and theoretical ones (reasoning), it may be perplexing that Ortega joins cognition and volition, but he does so for sound reasons. From the perspective of how we actually experience reasoning and volition, as Ortega explains (2004i, 575–579), both are characterized by the fact that acts of understanding and decision are: 1) executed from that central 'I'; the sense of agency is primary. 2) When we understand or will something, there is no space between our thought and us; we immediately know when we understand or are confused (and thinking takes place in tension not somnolent states). In other words, they are also 'instantaneous,' in the sense that 'spiritual or mental phenomena do not last. We understand $2 + 2 = 4$ immediately. We can think at length about something, but each thought-moment takes place in a moment, as does the realization of understanding. Moreover, this feature of being instantaneous means that 'I cannot think one thing with one part of my mind and a contrary one or merely different with another part, nor can I have at once two divergent volitions' (Ortega 2004i, 579 my translation). And 3) these are impersonal and abstract acts. The conceptual understanding of a specific tactical sequence by two players is the same *qua* thought, just as the understanding of the principle of the excluded middle is the same for all those who get it. This concerns the content strictly. The same goes for deliberation and willful decision. For our purposes, in antagonistic sports and endeavors with athletes or performers in tactical situations, this can help explain the immediacy where understanding, movement, and action are one. For example, when in a basketball game, the shooting guard dribbles past two opponents and *sees* the center poised under the basket, his hands and arms pass the ball with no delay; the seeing and the passing are one. Nishida's thought will enable us to delve into the nature of this unity later (essay 9). But this is not sufficient to capture the totality of the action as executed and *felt*. The emotional facet is missing.

Ortega contrasts and complements vitality with the 'soul,' which is 'the region of our feelings and emotions, desires impulses and appetites.' (Ortega 2004i, 576, my translation) Rather than punctual and sequential as thoughts and volitions, it is extended and dynamic. He writes, 'love is not a series of discontinuous points that take place in us, but a continuous current in which, without interruption, feeling acts' (ibid.).

HOLISM AND THE CULTIVATION OF EXCELLENCE IN SPORTS AND PERFORMANCE

Another characteristic of Orteguian emotive and sentimental life is that oftentimes it surges spontaneously, as when we feel antipathy or fondness for someone. Moreover, "My' impulses, inclinations, loves, hatreds, desires belong to me [...] but are not 'me.' The 'I' attends to them as a spectator, intervenes on them like a police chief, sentences on them like the judge, disciplines them like a captain' (Ortega 2004i, 577, my translation). The import of this is that the emotional part of our life is not something we willfully, freely, and positively 'create.' At best, most of us control it some of the time. Zhuangzi, whom we encounter in the next essay, offers a way to expand on our 'executive abilities.' Finally, in contrast to the universality of our thoughts and acts of will, which as explained are universal as abstractions, emotions and kindred sensations that populate our soul are fully private and individual. My joy or sadness are strictly mine and yours are yours *as* felt, while Euclid's theorem as thought by you or me is the same should both of us know it. In modern terms, the *qualia* of these experiences are unique to us. This does not have to mean that they are private as an inner life that only we can access. Ortega's adamant and pervasive argumentation for the coupled relation between us and the environment, couched as externalist or situated nowadays (see below), belie any solipsistic charges. The nature of this 'privacy' concerning our sensations, ideas, qualia, etc. is considered in more depth in *Everything Mysterious Under the Moon*. Finally, analogous to James' fringe of consciousness and Dewey's reworking of it, Ortega writes that, 'there is an intermediate sphere clearer than vitality but less illuminated than spirit that has a strange atmospheric character' (20,041, 576, my translation). In short, our emotional undertone sits between our vitality or proprioceptive and kinesthetic bodily dynamics, being less 'obscure' or unconscious, and our explicit cognitive and volitional faculties. They are functionally different, however: the fringe involved judgment and a sense of right or wrong, whereas the Orteguian soul is concerned with an emotional tonality. And yet, they also operate in between the conscious and reflective consciousness and the pre-reflective and subpersonal one. Because neither construct posits an entity or part of the brain, both are strictly functional and both capture a relevant aspect of our experience, James' and Ortega's are complementary and not competing accounts. This will become clearer when we discuss expert and failed action in *Fractured Action*.

For now, and to bring this to a close, a few words about the holistic aspect in these Orteguian ideas. His explanation shows that while there are three 'I's', each belonging to one of the three facets discussed, and while we can distinguish them conceptually and phenomenologically, there is an inherent continuity among all three. As he says with regard to bodily awareness and emotional life, 'this spherical volume of the soul ends in a periphery that is the corporeal 'I,' of larger extension, but which does not constitute as the soul does, an enclosed and filled enclosure, but rather a film of varied thickness, adhered on the one side to the soul and on the other to the shape of the material body' (Ortega, 2004i, 579, my translation). But, it is best not to make the fabulous and restless creatures wait.

Ortega was fond of centaurs.[10] In fact, the centaur is one of Ortega's tropes to illustrate, among other things, his views on the mind/body relation. The horse part stands for body and emotion, the human part for mind and intellect. Among centaurs, Chiron, the fabled mentor to many a mythical Greek hero, was a favorite of the Spaniard. His name, also spelled 'Kheiron,' is derived from the Greek word for hand (*kheir*), which also means 'skilled with the hands' (Theoi Greek Mythology, n.d.). This tactile patronymic 'connection' is more than apt, given that exploratory movements with our hands are some of the most basic ways we spatially interact with and learn from the world. Indeed, counting and spatiality are predicated on our corporeal worldly engagements (Lakoff and Nuñez 2000). The name is also related to *kheirourgos* or surgeon (Theoi Greek Mythology, n.d.). The refined skills requisite for surgery bespeak of a long and arduous process of learning that combines extreme dexterity with both experiential and conceptual knowledge. It is a most apposite combination of interwoven intellectual and physical skill and emotional control, for the thinking takes place as and with the controlled movements of hands, arms, and supporting bodily structures and processes. Chiron is then *the* learned centaur, famous as educator and healer. Moreover, tradition also places under his aegis writing and divination (Graves 1990, 151). As a centaur, he acts as a metaphor that underpins the theme of a holistic bodymind not yet fully integrated.

Centaurs and Chiron's hybrid nature, as both horses and men, illustrate how two radically blended bodies *can* act functionally as a *singular* being bypassing the ontological issue of whether it is half horse or half man. This is similar to how Derek Parfit (1991), echoing Gilbert Ryle's category mistake arguments, asks with regard to split-brain patients what the critical percentage is to assume one or two streams of consciousness and identities existing in a body. Here, asking a parallel question about whether they are horse or man misses the point, or at least obfuscates it. However, even if the ontology is sidestepped, and although by all appearances, they act and move as one, Ortega's analysis reveals a schism in the centaurian lived experience.

> To his human torso belonged a world of human visions; to his horseback an equine universe. The man's nerves and the steed's joined at the same junctures, and the robust veins spilled onto the same heart the theology of the European and the bellowing of the stallion. Poor heart always vacillating between a mare and a bacchant! What was true for one half of himself was false for the other half [...] But this duality is impossible: centaurs had to decide for a third world neither human nor equestrian, result of the compromise of their two natures. (2004f, 38, my translation)

Chiron and his kin are never at ease being horse and man yet fully neither. Our very lives echo the centaurs' predicament... only worse. We are heirs to a Western dualistic metaphysics where the two halves are irreconcilable. At least the centaurs can opt for a third way, with hopes of achieving a better amalgamation. We have become disconnected from the organic unity that our childhood's unreflective bodies, for all their unrefined mechanics, afforded us. When Eugen Herrigel's master is at pains to teach him how to hold the string firmly to then release it spontaneously, he speaks of the way a little child holds a finger (Herrigel 1989, 30). Our dualistic tradition has riddled us with an analogous tension between body and mind, and *we* have solved the equation for a third term, an ontologically irreducible and unsatisfying compromise. Indeed, Western thought in particular has proved quite deft in advancing the experience of a discomfiting interaction between body and mind by way of emotional disturbance, psychophysical ailment, or uncoordinated movement, with only the rarest people truly experiencing and exhibiting a *lived* and graceful unity.[11] The alternative, which one imagines is Chiron's dream, posits a holistic bodymind where reason, will, and emotion, subjectivity and objectivity, social milieu and surroundings form part of a flowing *toto*.

That is, an ontologically *singular* entity that harmonically moves and responds to its environment, much as a dancer's improvised dance is a matter of the movements being the meaningful thoughts themselves (Sheets-Johnstone 2009). The centaur becomes liberated when embracing itself as one, as a third possible way of being-in-the-body. This echoes phenomenology, which argues that our *lived* experience is not one of mind and or body, neither subjective nor objective, but rather both/and: a third way through which we *are*. Thus, Chiron ably illustrates metaphorically Ortega's sophisticated, integrative mind-body stance redolent of Dewey and as a work in progress, part of reaching our plenitude.

To close this essay, a brief presentation of three radical views that have been 'discovered' recently. First, in relation with vitality, Ortega makes a contribution that long precedes contemporary views. Gallagher (often in collaboration with other researchers) has long used pathological cases in conjunction with phenomenology to understand how our body shapes our cognition and experience. Thus, Gallagher and Zahavi state that, 'Pathological cases can function heuristically to make manifest what is normally or simply taken for granted' to gain distance from the familiar (2008, 140).[12] Gallagher, relying on this approach, goes on to phenomenologically diagnose cases of schizophrenia as those where, among other things, hyperreflection hijacks the sense of ownership for our actions (2007). Schizophrenics find themselves as agents, that is, performing actions tied to their self, but feel that these are caused externally, and thus, do not feel as if they own them. Ortega uses pathology, in particular that of neurasthenia, something from which James was supposed to suffer, to also gain insight into the illness and concurrently understand the phenomenon of vitality and its role for humans.[13] Basically, he argues that neurasthenics reflect overly on their inner proprioceptive sensations (Gallagher's analysis parallels this): 'when these astounding sensations take place, attention begins to withdraw from the external world and focuses with abnormal frequency and insistence on our body's interiority' (Ortega 2004i, 572, my translation). James' introspective skills, which provided such great insight into the inner workings of our psyche, also proved his bane in this respect. Ortega puts it in a way that is quite amenable, and worded in rabidly contemporary fashion, to Gallagher's philosophical commitments and his analysis of our experience in terms of body image and schema: 'This goes as just an example of the fecund consequences that an investigation of the image of the body affords us' (2004i, 572, my translation). Moreover, and in another first, he points out how this intensified introspection gives rises and produces itself that inversion of our attention toward ourselves, for in full health, our attention would be outwardly oriented (ibid).

Second, clearer than the high noon sun on a cloudless day, the notion of metaphor is crucial for Ortega. He used many to great effect, as we have seen so far (e.g. besides centaurs, and archers, he wrote of Janus bifrontis, and scores of 'minor' but memorable ones like the steed or the flute). An in-depth look at Ortega's theory of metaphor is outside of our purview, but a swift look is pertinent because of two reasons. [14] One, this gives a rich sense of the vital role the body plays in Ortega's thinking. Second, his basic insight predates the influential and much-lauded work of George Lakoff and Mark Johnson on metaphor and embodied cognition (1999). Ortega writes,

> Elemental and inveterate metaphors are as true as Newton's laws: if it were not inopportune I would attempt to convince you that they are, in a rigorous sense, even more truthful. In these venerable metaphors that have become already words in our language [...] are kept perfect intuitions of the most fundamental phenomena. Thus, we speak often that we are downcast,[15] that we find ourselves in a 'grave' situation. Being downcast [*Pesadumbre*] and gravity are metaphorically transposed from physical weight, from pondering a body on ours and weighing ourselves, to the most intimate order. (2008, 505, my translation)

The origin of many of our metaphors that anchor our thinking and expressions in our bodies and their dynamic sensations and interactions with the environment is *the* deeply rooted insight found in cognitively embodied views of metaphor.

Third, Ortega also precedes what today in analytic circles is known as externalist and extended views of the mind (Clark 2008; Menary 2010), in phenomenological ones as enactive cognition (Varela, Thompson, and Rosch 1991), and in both circles as situated cognition (Gallagher, 2009). The common idea underpinning the three versions is that our environment and us are intimately and mutually connected, even if their emphasis is somewhat different: the first is concerned with the extent of cognitive offloading into the environment, the second one fully integrates perception and thinking with motor action, and the latter takes a more holistic and radical approach, congruent with Ortega and Dewey, that makes the environment constitutive of our cognition. Ortega developed these ideas before he read if not earlier than Jacob von Uexküll, a biologist who has become a point of reference for many in this camp. Incidentally, the important role the landscape plays, literally and as Uexküllian *umwelt*, also predates Watsuji's Tetsuro's criticism of Heidegger from the perspective of spatiality as climate and landscape (1996). The extensive presence of these views in his work, spanning several decades, testifies to the centrality of this in Ortega's thought (2004a, 2004i, 2005d, 2006a, 2006b, 2007b). To have Ortega present his version of this environment and human interaction while reflecting his views on mind and body,

> I am not my body; I am not my soul. My body and soul are either perfect mechanisms or sickly and insufficient with which I find myself when I meet my landscape. I am, if you will, the things of the world that are nearest me, those that I have to handle most immediately to live. I have a sick body and disabled or I have a soul without memory and without will, and yet, I have to use those instruments to live my life, to solve the problem of my existence. I am neither my body nor my soul; I find myself with them as with the landscape, they are elements in the landscape. That is why, from the landscape we receive so many and constant influences (2008, 509).

Let's recall that a landscape is Ortega's notion for a surrounding environment that becomes our circumstance, all those things with which we come in contact pertinent and present to us (ideas included, even if they are of centaurs).[16] They form an environment that is not the world, but 'only that group of objects or portions of this world that exist in a vital way for the animal' (Ortega 2004a, 425). This is an *umwelt* for Ortega, in Uexküll's sense, where organism and environment mutually shape each other (Uexküll 2010). For both, this landscape is species specific and entails a mutual adaptation of human or animal to landscape-environment and *vice versa*. Both thinkers also make our relationship with the environment an organic one. Ortega compares animals and humans, and finds both just as effective to handle the environment according to the finality of sustaining their organism in the world. Organic life is an adaptation of the subject to the environment, while the good life implies adaptation of the environment to the subject (Ortega 2006a, 562). For example, the mutual color adaptation between bees and certain flowers whereby the insects see specific ultraviolet frequencies that the plants project such that they may be pollinated. There is a communion between the environments we live in and us. These are our landscapes; our lives unfold in them. Humans' complex sociocultural environments, which act as both pre-reflective and reflective lifeworlds, shape their experiences as they are shaped by their actions. Remember also that love gives us a sense of union with the other. This makes possible a union with said personal environment to the extent that we attend to it.

Kretchmar's holistic views concerning the relations between practitioners and their sport fit this model like a custom glove. Notice the mutual relationship between player and playground when he writes,

> For holists, would be players and would be playgrounds are not independent. As strange as it sounds, the playground is expected to infiltrate the player and the player will infiltrate the playground. Like two sides of a single coin, *the two develop together*, seamlessly, as one *whole*. In terms of Husserl's intentionality, intending consciousness, on the one hand, and the object intended, on the other, are correlates and not independent phenomena. The act of playing presents the world-as-played. The world-as-played, in turn, affects future acts of playing—back and forth, each side of the *equation* affecting the other (2013, 34, my italics).

Thus, for him, there is a gradual progression in a continuum from total ignorance of an activity to a fusion with it. To echo his main idea while broadening the applicable scope for our purposes, sportspersons and performers go from people who begin to throw a ball, pedal a bicycle, take a few dance steps, or learn an Aikido kata to people who love the game, bicycling, dance, or aikido until at the highest level, they become 'baseballers,' cyclists, dancers, and aikidokas (Kretchmar 2013, 40). That is, they do not simply learn to love the activity, but in true Orteguian fashion, they become one with the activity: their identity *is* now defined through the practice. Thus, after falling in love with an activity, in this case table tennis, Kretchmar explains, 'They became playgrounded. In this case, they were literally table-tenissed. The game had invaded their persons (ibid., 36). This also goes the other way around, of course, for the environment of the game is also affected. As Kretchmar unforgettably renders it, we also define the activity through our actions, 'In turn, they had invaded the game. Their shots, the quality of their game, had become Williamed, Franciscoed, Sallyed, and Mariaed—shaped by them, their unique talent, genders, handedness, their personalities, the things they alone wanted to say about this game' (ibid). The brilliance of this is how clearly it sets off the background of how we define the activities also through our actions. In playing a golf game when we resort to trickery, we in effect define how the game should be and is played. What kind of game it becomes depends on us as much as this game helps us define who we are as golfers. In the last essay, we will discuss more fully how sportive and performative endeavors and their skills fit into a communitarian framework.

There is great affinity between Ortega's ideas and those of James', and specially Dewey's, for whom the environment was part and parcel of the human condition. Dewey and Ortega profoundly agree. The former explains how human behavior is longitudinal, not just cross-sectional, 'It forms a history, an autobiography, not indeed written but enacted' (Dewey 1963, 308–309). Ortega takes this at the pragmatic and existential level of how we narratively make sense of them. Dewey expands Ortega's conceptual space, however, in taking his insight as battering ram to burst the gate of reductive neuropsychology. Holistically he argues how simple events, such as reflexes, are neither primitive nor original, but the opposite if we pay attention to phylogeny, species development, and ontogeny, our development: 'the beginning is with action in which the entire organism is involved, and the specialized differentiation within an inclusive whole of behavior' (Dewey 1963, 309). The Orteguian example of the paramecium's exuberant explorations illustrates this. Organisms choose from a rich repertoire of explorations, and in accord with Uexküll's insight, in narrow connivance with their environments. Both perspectives serve us well, however, in these reductionist times where everything is lessened to its minimal physiological expression (brain, neurons, or computational renditions thereof).

This reductionism is analyzed in section three of *Skillful Striving* after a stroll through Ancient China in the company of Daoist, Zhuangzi. Ortega himself mentions Zhuangzi with an apposite story about the Lord of the North Sea who wonders how he could talk to the frog about the ocean if it has never left its well, to the summer birds about ice if it lives ensconced in its season, and to the wise man if he lives prisoner of his doctrine (2005b, 2009). Uexküll discusses how one subject, in his case an oak tree, can be a number of environments for all the creatures that interact with it—forester, young girl, fox, owl, beetle, and more—which is never known by all the subjects of said environments nor knowable for each of them (2010). Let these closing ideas be a call by these three thinkers to keep as philosophical compass and openness to broader views than we may be used to swimming in, even if, or particularly if these come from an eccentric Daoist.

NOTES

1. Much of the material cited and referenced in this essay has not been translated. I rely on the latest edition of his collected works for these sources. If possible, I also cite alternate editions that are more readily obtainable. When possible, I cite from and/or refer to available English translations or reference these alongside the Spanish edition. Occasionally, when I deem a certain Orteguian subtlety is compromised, I provide my own translation even if there is already an English version. The referencing here is also more extensive that would be expected for two reasons. One, to underscore how Ortega's thought on the matter was integral to his philosophical views throughout his life. Two, to provide alternative sources that may be less familiar to readers. These have been chosen as emblematic of his thought.
2. As the translator explains, 'Halcyonism' derives from 'halcyon,' a mythical bird that supposedly calmed the seas during the winter solstice, when it hatched its young and set them afloat. The expression 'halcyon days,' much loved by Ortega, means then 'days of tranquility.' It is also connected to ataraxia, tranquility or peace of mind for Democritus, the Greek Epicureans, Stoics, and Skeptics (Rodriguez 1995, 159 fn. 3). This can also be connected to Eastern quietist views that espouse desirelessness.

HOLISM AND THE CULTIVATION OF EXCELLENCE IN SPORTS AND PERFORMANCE

3. Contrary to Heidegger's negative stance (1977), Ortega has a generally positive view of technology. Anything but naïve, he unwaveringly admonishes those who would be blinded by it. Ortega says that it only takes for us to change our conception of the good life to have traditional, established technology come crashing down (2006a, 565).

4. Huizinga (1955) makes of play the original engine for civilization, spurring into motion the arts, sciences, and philosophy. For his seminal set of characteristics unique to play, see 8–13.

5. The ontological status of performance in the arts is beyond the scope of this inquiry. There are many parallels between artistic ones and performances in sport or martial arts. Historical and practice-specific elements entail that these various performances be interpreted differently. This results in different metaphysical status for the given actions involved as accorded by different interpretive frameworks (Ilundáin-Agurruza 2000).

6. For a phenomenological discussion of sweet tension, see McLaughlin and Torres (2011).

7. A recent translation of the same passage renders it thus: "In order to achieve it [form], the individual must first go off by himself and concentrate on his own development: he has to go into training and give up many things, in the determination to surpass himself, to be more alert, tense, supple. There is nothing tha tis indifferent to him, for every little thing either is favorable to his form, or else pulls it down, and with this in mind he goes out for one thing and avoids the other. Briefly, to be in form means never indulging in any dissipation whatever." (Ortega 2009, 11) In this instance I opt for my rendering because it captures underlying Orteguian themes that this translation, while "smoother", leaves out.

8. Verily, the truly confident person has no need to be arrogant, whereas conceit, haughtiness, and condescendence mark a lack of confidence that often expresses itself in abusive, demeaning, and bullying behavior.

9. I argue that Heidegger's and Sartre's respective views on death handle the anticipation of death and our attitude toward it, whereas with Nietzsche, the *encierro* becomes transformative, the ordinary becomes extraordinary, and with Ortega, the very risking of life turns out to be the strongest affirmation of its importance and enjoyment.

10. For a discussion of the holistic views of Ortega, Dewey, and other intellectuals in the context of education, sport, and movement, see Ilundáin-Agurruza (2014).

11. Consummate sportspeople, meditators, and children engrossed in a game are exceptions to this when they experience those moments that some describe as flow, *mushin*, or simply being lost in play. Subsequent essays discuss this.

12. See Ilundáin-Agurruza (2013b) for a critique of this that seeks to expand the scope beyond pathology and to the exceptional.

13. Nowadays, neurasthenia is discredited. However, there is mounting evidence for physical causation for similar illnesses regarding phantom pains that were written off as 'imaginary' by the medical establishment, and which corroborates Ortega's views.

14. See Ortega (2004i) for a discussion of the relevance of analogies and images in philosophy and science.

15. Ortega writes, 'we suffer from a *'pesadumbre,'* a sadness; *pesadumbre* in Spanish brings the connotation of 'pesar' to weigh.

16. Ortega wrote a phenomenological essay on consciousness, concepts, and reality, where he discusses the reality of centaurs as objects of consciousness, in contrast to roses, and other elements. It is available in English as 'Consciousness, the Object, and the Three Distances' (Ortega 1975, 116–124).

REFERENCES

ABT, S. 1993. *Champion: Bicycle racing in the age of Indurain*. Mill Valley, CA: Bicycle Books.

BREIVIK, G. 2010. Consequences and implications for sport. *Sport, Ethics and Philosophy* 4 (1): 87–105.

———. 2011. Dangerous play with the elements: Towards a phenomenology of risk sports. *Sport, Ethics and Philosophy* 5 (3): 314–30.

CALLOIS, R. 2001. *Man, play and games*. Urbana: University of Illinois Press.

CERVANTES, M. 1994. *El Ingenioso Hidalgo Don Quijote de la Mancha*. Madrid: Espasa-Calpe.

CLARK, A. 2008. *Supersizing the mind*. Oxford: Oxford UP.

DEWEY, J. 1963. *Philosophy and civilization*. New York, NY: Capricorn Books.

DREYFUS, HUBERT L., and STUART E. DREYFUS. 1986. *Mind over machine*. New York, NY: Free Press.

FRANKFURT, H.G. 2005. *On bullshit*. Princeton, NJ: Princeton University Press.

GALLAGHER, S. 2005. Dynamic models of body schematic processes. In *Body image and body schema*, edited by H. De Preester and V. Knockaert. Amsterdam: John Benjamins: 233–50.

———. 2007. *How the body shapes the mind*. Oxford: Oxford University Press.

———. 2009. Philosophical antecedents of situated cognition. In *The Cambridge handbook of situated cognition*, edited by P. Robbins and M. Aydede. London: Cambridge University Press: 35–52.

GRAHAM, J.T. 1994. *A pragmatist philosophy of life in Ortega y Gasset*. Columbia, SC: University of Missouri Press.

GRAVES, R. 1990. *The Greek myths I*. Middlesex: Penguin.

GUTTMANN, A. 1978. *From ritual to record*. New York, NY: Columbia University Press.

HEIDEGGER, M. 1977. *The question concerning technology*. New York, NY: Harper & Row.

HERRIGEL, EUGEN. 1989. *Zen in the art of archery*. New York, NY: Vintage Books.

HUIZINGA, J. 1955. *Homo Ludens; A study of the play-element in culture*. Boston, MA: Beacon Press.

HUMPHREYS, J. 2008. *Foul play: What's wrong with sport*. Thriplow: Icon Books.

HURKA, T. 1993. *Perfectionism*. Oxford: Oxford University Press.

ILUNDÁIN-AGURRUZA, J. 2000. *In the realms of art: A conceptual inquiry of the genesis of the work of art*. PhD diss., University of Illinois at Urbana-Champaign.

———. 2007a. Kant goes skydiving: Understanding the extreme by way of the sublime. In *Philosophy, risk and adventure sports*, edited by M. McNamee. London: Routledge: 149–67.

———. 2007b. Between the horns. Part I: A dilemma in the interpretation of the running of the bulls—Part 1: The confrontation. *Sport, Ethics, and Philosophy*. 1 (3): 325–45.

———. 2008. Between the Horns: A dilemma in the interpretation of the running of the bulls–Part 2: The evasion. *Sport, Ethics, and Philosophy*. 2 (1): 18–38.

———. 2010. Taking a shot. In *Hunting—Philosophy for everyone*, edited by N. Kowalski. Wiley & Blackwell: 11–22.

———. 2011. Weaving the magic: Philosophy, sports and literature. In *Philosophy of sport: International perspectives*, edited by A. Hardman and C. Jones. Cambridge Scholars Publishing: 50–71.

———. 2012. Go tell the spartans: Honor, courage, and excellence. In *The Olympics and Philosophy*, edited by H. Reid and M. Austin. Kentucky University Press: 68–85.

———. 2013a. Ortega y Gasset, José. In *International encyclopedia of ethics*. Wiley & Blackwell.

———. 2013b. Moving wisdom: Explaining cognition through movement. *Fair Play: Journal of Philosophy, Ethics and Law*. 1 (1): 58–87. Barcelona: Pompeu Fabra.

———. 2014. The quest for meaningful and lifelong. In *Philosophy, sport and education: international perspectives*, edited by M. Isidori, A. Müller and F.J. Frías. Roma: Sette Citá: 43–70.

———. Forthcoming. The eye of the hurricane: Philosophical reflections on risky sports, self-knowledge and flourishing. *Journal of the Philosophy of Sport*.

INGLIS, D. 2004. Meditations on sport: On the trail of Ortega y Gasset's philosophy of sportive existence. *Journal of the Philosophy of Sport* 31: 78–96.

KREIN, K. 2008. Sport, nature and worldmaking. *Sport, Ethics and Philosophy* 2 (3): 285–301.

KRETCHMAR, S. 1972. From test to contest: An analysis of two kinds of counterpoint in sport. *Journal of the Philosophy of Sport* 2: 23–30.

———. 2013. Mind-body Holism, paradigm shifts, and education. *Fair Play. Revista de Filosofía, Ética y Derecho del Deporte*. 1 (1): 28–43.

LAKOFF, G., and M. JOHNSON. 1999. *Philosophy in the flesh*. New York, NY: Basic Books.

LAKOFF, G., and R.E. NÚÑEZ. 2000. *Where mathematics comes from: How the embodied mind brings mathematics into being*. New York, NY: Basic Books.

LALLY, R. 2013. Deweyan pragmatism and self-cultivation. In *Pragmatism and the philosophy of sport*, edited by R. Lally, D. Anderson and J. Kaag. London: Lexington Books: 175–98.

LASAGA MEDINA, J. 2006. *Figuras de la vida buena* [Figures of the good life]. Madrid: Enigma Editores.

LOLAND, S. 2001. Record sports: An ecological critique and a reconstruction. *Journal of the Philosophy of Sport* 28 (2): 127–39.

MARÍAS, J. 1970. *José Ortega y Gasset. Circumstance and Vocation*. Norman, OK: University of Oklahoma Press.

MCLAUGHLIN, D., and C. TORRES. 2011. Sweet tension and its phenomenological description: Sport, inter subjectivity and horizon. *Sport, Ethics and Philosophy*. 5 (3): 270–84.

MCNAMEE, M.J. 2007. *Philosophy, risk and adventure sports*. London: Routledge.

———. 2011. Celebrating trust: Virtues and rules in the ethical conduct of sports coaches. In *The ethics of sports coaching*, edited by A. Hardman and C. Jones. London and New York: Routledge: 23–40.

MEIER, K.V. 1980. An affair of flutes. *Journal of the Philosophy of Sport* 7 (1): 24–45.

MENARY, RICHARD. 2010. *The extended mind*. Cambridge, MA: MIT Press.

MICHENER, J.A. 1968. *Iberia: Spanish travels and reflections*. New York, NY: Random House.

MOLINUEVO, J.L. 2002. *Para leer a Ortega* [In order to read Ortega]. Madrid: Alianza Editorial S. A.

NUSSBAUM, M.C. 2000. *Women and human development*. Cambridge: Cambridge University Press.

ORRINGER, N.R. 1973. Ortega y Gasset's sportive vision of plato. *MLN—Hispanid Issue* 88 (2): 24–280.

ORTEGA Y GASSET, J.. 1948. *The dehumanization of art*. Garden City, NY: Double Day and Co.

———. 1960. *What is philosophy?* New York, NY: W.W. Norton & Co.

———. 1961. *History as a system and other essays toward a philosophy of history*. New York & London: Norton.

———. 1963. *Meditations on Quixote*. New York, NY: W.W. Norton & Co.

———. 1975. *Phenomenology and art*. New York, NY: W.W. Norton & Co.

———. 1995. *Meditations on hunting*. Belgrade, MT: Wilderness Adventures Press.

———. 1995. In *El sentimiento estético de la vida (Antología)* [The Aesthetic Sentiment of Life], edited by J.L. Molinuevo. Madrid: Editorial Tecnos S.A.

———. 2001. *Qué es filosofía?* [What is philosophy?]. Madrid: Alianza Editorial.

———. 2004a. Meditaciones del Quijote [Meditations on Quixote]. In *Obras completas* [Complete works]. Vol. I. Madrid: Taurus: 747–828.

———. 2004b. El Quijote en la Escuela [The Don Quixote in school]. In *Obras completas* [Complete works]. Vol. II. Madrid: Taurus: 401–30.

———. 2004c. Carta a un jóven argentino que estudia filosofía [Letter to a young Argentinian who studies philosophy]. In *Obras completas* [Complete works]. Vol. II. Madrid: Taurus: 467–71.

———. 2004d. El Origen Deportivo del Estado [The sportive origin of the state]. In *Obras completas* [Complete works]. Vol. II. Madrid: Taurus: 707–19.

———. 2004e. Qué es un Paisaje? [What is a landscape?]. In *Misión de la Universidad y Otros Ensayos Sobre Educación Pedagogía* [Mission of the university and other essays on education and pedagogy]. Madrid: Alianza Editorial: 139–54.

———. 2004f. Meditación de Renan [Meditation on renan]. In *Obras completas* [Complete works]. Vol. II. Madrid: Taurus: 31–52.

———. 2004g. Las Dos Grandes Metáforas [The two great metaphors]. In *Obras completas* [Complete works]. Vol. II. Madrid: Taurus: 505–18.

———. 2004i. Vitalidad, alma y espíritu [Vitality, soul, and spirit]. In *Obras completas* [Complete works]. Vol. II. Madrid: Taurus: 566–92.

———. 2005a. La Rebelión de Las Masas [The rebellion of the masses]. In *Obras completas* [Complete works]. Vol. IV. Madrid: Taurus: 349–530.

———. 2005b. Misión de la Universidad [Mission of the university]. In *Obras completas* [Complete works]. Vol. IV. Madrid: Taurus: 529–68.

———. 2005c. La Deshumanización del Arte e Ideas Sobre la Novela [The dehumanization of art and ideas on the novel]. Vol. V. Madrid: Taurus: 847–916.

———. 2005d. Temple Para la Reforma [Fortitude for reform]. In *Obras completas* [Complete works]. Vol. IV. Madrid: Taurus: 1034–41.

———. 2006a. Prólogo a Veinte Años de Caza Mayor [Prologue to twenty years of big game hunting]. In *Obras completas* [Complete works]. Vol. IV. Madrid: Taurus: 269–333.

———. 2006b. Meditación de la Técnica [Meditation on technology]. In *Obras completas* [Complete works]. Vol. V. Madrid: Taurus: 551–605.

———. 2006c. Goethe Desde Dentro [Goethe from the inside]. In *Obras completas* [Complete works]. Vol. V. Madrid: Taurus: 109–247.

———. 2006d. Historia como Sistema y del Imperio Romano [History as a system and on the Roman Empire]. In *Obras completas* [Complete works]. Vol. VI. Madrid: Taurus: 47–132.

———. 2007a. El Sentido Deportivo de la Vitalidad [The sportive sense of vitality]. In *Obras completas* [Complete works]. Vol. VII. Madrid: Taurus: 818–34.

———. 2007b. Temas del Escorial [Themes on the Escorial]. In *Obras completas* [Complete works]. Vol. VII. Madrid: Taurus: 405–21.

———. 2007c. Pedagogía de la contaminación [Pedagogy of contamination]. Vol. VII. Madrid: Taurus: 685–91.

———. 2007d. La voluntad del Barroco [The will of the Baroque]. Vol. VII. Madrid: Taurus: 307–21.

———. 2008. Hombre y Circunstancia [Man and circumstance]. In *Obras completas* [Complete works]. Vol. VIII. Madrid: Taurus: 499–511.

———. 2009. *Mission of the University*. New Bunswick & London: Transaction Publishers.

PARFIT, D. 1991. *Reasons and persons*. Oxford: Clarendon Press.

PINDAR. *Pythian 2*. Epode 3, 70. Available at http://www.clas.ufl.edu/users/kapparis/AOC/Pindar.html (accessed 21 September 2011).

REID, H.L. 2010. My life as two-wheeled philosopher. In *Cycling—Philosophy for everyone*, edited by J. Ilundáin-Agurruza and M.W. Austin. Malden, MA: Wiley & Blackwell: 151–61.

———. 2012. *Introduction to the Philosophy of Sport*. Rowman & Littlefield.

RODRÍGUEZ HUÉSCAR, A. 1995. *Jose Ortega Y Gasset's Metaphysical Innovation: A Critique and Overcoming of Idealism*. Buffalo, NY: State University of New York Press.

RUSSELL, J.S. 2005. The value of dangerous sport. *Journal of the Philosophy of Sport* 32 (1): 1–19.

———. 2007. Children and Dangerous Sport and Recreation. *Journal of the Philosophy of Sport* 34 (2): 176–93.

DE SALES, ST. FRANCIS. *Quotations book*. Available at http://quotationsbook.com/quote/20746/ (accessed 1 January 2014).

SANSONE, D. 1992. *Greek athletics and the genesis of sport*. Berkeley: University of California Press.

SCHELER, M. 1979. *Man's place in nature*. New York, NY: The Noonday Press.

SEARLE, J. 1983. *Intentionality*. Cambridge: Cambridge University Press.

SHEETS-JOHNSTONE, M. 2009. *The corporeal turn: An interdisciplinary reader*. Exeter: Imprint Academic.

———. 2011. *The primacy of movement*. 2nd ed. Amsterdam & Philadelphia: John Benjamins Publishing Co.

SPINOZA, B., and B. ANDREW. 1948. *Ethics of Spinoza*. London: J.M. Dent and Sons.

STEVENS, J. 2001. *Budo secrets: Teachings of the martial arts masters*. Boston, MA: Shambhala.

SUITS, BERNARD. 2005. *The grasshopper: Games, life and Utopia*. Peterborough: Broadview Press.

TETSURO, WATSUJI, and ROBERT EDGAR CARTER. 1996. *Watsuji Tetsuro's Rinrigaku*. Albany, NY: State University of New York Press.

THEOI GREEK MYTHOLOGY. Available at http://www.theoi.com/Georgikos/KentaurosKheiron.html (accessed 12 November 2012).

UEXKÜLL, J.V. 2010. *A foray into the worlds of animals and humans: With A theory of meaning*. Minneapolis, MN: University of Minnesota Press.

VARELA, F., E. THOMPSON, and E. ROSCH. 1991. *The embodied mind*. Cambridge, MA: MIT Press.

WALLACE, JAMES D. 1978. *Virtues and vices*. Ithaca, NY: Cornell University Press.

WEBER, M. 1992. *The protestant ethic and the spirit of capitalism*. London: Routledge.

5—ZHUANGZI—PLAYFUL WANDERER

Jesús Ilundáin-Agurruza

His batting stance was pure Skrimmer, the easy sink of the knees, the sense of prevailing silence, the dart of the hands to the ball. Good players tended to be good mimics: old footage of Aparicio, if you were as familiar as Schwartz with Henry's movements and mannerisms, was downright eerie to watch. And now, in a similar way, it was eerie to watch Izzy. The lineage was clear. (The Art of Fielding: A Novel —Chad Harbach)

Embrace joyfully your limitations and weaknesses
Suffer gratefully your talents and strengths. (Jesús Ilundáin-Agurruza)

Let the following describe Zhuangzi, 莊子 (c.369–286 BCE): playful and earnest, irreverent yet respectful, deep while seemingly superficial, sceptical but wise, pragmatic yet unconcerned with this world, sensible and coarse, serious while mocking and mockingly serious, one and many, most unassuming and yet a philosophical firework! When embodied *in* him, these pairs are 'complementary pairs,' not contraries, just in the sense that J. Scott Kelso and David Engstrøm mean when they argue, based on coordination dynamics and in accord with Niels Bohr's maxim *Contraria sunt complementa,* for a dynamic view of complementarity rather than opposition (2008). This also sets the tone as to how to approach the many paradoxical stances his views adopt. Trying to pin down the Daoist is like trying to catch a fish with your bare hands. Zhuangzi endorses a position of non-position: he opposes opposition when he often confronts his friend Huizi, 惠子, a logician from the School of Names (the Ancient Chinese equivalent of contemporary analytic philosophy of language) (Wu and Zhuangzi 1990). For example, in their famous encounter over the river Hao, the former comments on how happy the fish are, while the latter argues that Zhuangzi, not being a fish, cannot know how they feel. The denouement to this story will come much later, in the last essay's discussion on intersubjectivity and private mental lives that closes this project. First, some background concerning the Daoist and those views of his relevant for this study.

Zhuangzi lived during a very tumultuous time in China: the Warring States Period—the epithet says it all. He was a small-time officer who refused higher posts, being too aware that this would likely involve him in political intrigues sure to cut his life short (Socrates, of different temperament, was put to death because he involved himself too much with Athenian politics). He often employed humour and sarcasm to make his points, and to this end used, to great effect, images of events and things that were most sacred to his contemporaries (e.g. mocking burial rites), while revaluing positively members of society

HOLISM AND THE CULTIVATION OF EXCELLENCE IN SPORTS AND PERFORMANCE

that were looked upon in the worst light (cripples and robbers). Of a highly pragmatic bent, he sits comfortably with the other three dark horses, James, Dewey and particularly Ortega. The eponymous text we read nowadays was compiled after his death. The *Zhuangzi* contains 33 chapters. There is scholarly agreement that Zhuangzi wrote the first seven, called 'the inner chapters.' The rest are apocryphal, but inspired by him. While I speak of Zhuangzi and *his* views for convenience, it should be understood that the name represents more of a school of philosophical thought within Daoism. Nevertheless, I rely on the inner chapters as much as feasible. The book is a compendium of anecdotes, dialogues, parables, stories, poems, aphorisms, unforgettable characters and other literary pearls that are designed to evoke and resonate with the reader rather than have one particular meaning. The very lushness of Zhuangzi's writing, which scholar Kuang-Ming Wu characterizes as 'goblet', 'doublet' and 'lodge' words in an attempt to capture the variety of meanings they contain, is a reader's delight: a colourful wordplay to be read in numerous ways depending on the connotations the words take in different contexts (1990). The peculiarities of Chinese language abet philosophical puns. Chinese is evocative, poetic, highly metaphorical, as it relies on concrete nouns rather than abstract ones, and the many layers of this phonetically tonal language, with homonyms that take on different meanings depending on which tone is used, multiply resonances and encourage thoughtful badinage. The strategy I follow is to present a few canonical, poignant or fitting 'goblet stories' to help illustrate main points, concretely ground ideas in the text, and advance our understanding. But readers should be aware that this barely gives a flavour of the Daoist's wide-ranging views. An overview of Daoist key concepts and Zhuangzi's philosophy is followed by specific discussions of bodymind and self-cultivation, and a section on how his views recast the issue of (dis)ability closes this essay. We may wonder, what a Chinese quirky philosopher who lived 24 centuries ago has to contribute to contemporary sport philosophy? Much, as it turns out. This is the first thorough engagement of Zhuangzi in relation to sport philosophy in English to my knowledge, and the expectation is that his ideas will find a broader echo in the discipline.

1. Overview—Dao and The Dream of the Butterfly

Dao, 道, for obvious reasons, sits at the center of Daoism. Yet it neither originates with it nor is it its sole purview. Confucianism and other indigenous philosophical schools made ample use of it, and it deeply affected Chinese Buddhism.[1] Yet, for these *dao* had mostly ethical signification, while for Daoism its connotations are metaphysical. In spite of its centrality, ascertaining its conceptual contours is almost self-defeating: Laozi says in the opening words of the *Daodejing*, as translated by Red Pine, 'The way that becomes a way is not the immortal way/ the name that becomes a name is not the Immortal Name' (1996, 2).[2] Paradoxically, Laozi presents many sides of this enigmatic *dao*: we come to see the *dao* as nameless, eternal, spontaneous, at once the beginning of everything as well as the path in which all things unfold. But its ineffability means that equating it, as many Westerners do when coming to grips with it, with ultimate reality, absolute truth, Being itself, or perhaps more accurately, even Non-being, falls short. Unlike calling a dog a 'dog,' which brings to mind certain attributes, for the Chinese, calling the *dao* '*dao*,' is like giving it an empty designation, a way to refer to

HOLISM AND THE CULTIVATION OF EXCELLENCE IN SPORTS AND PERFORMANCE

something that has no *actual* attributes ultimately but about which we want to some-how think or speak without pinning down its essence. I suggest thinking of it not as 'indescribable,' because we would be describing it, but rather as 'non-describable.' This limits the range of the adjective from its actually describing the *dao*, to its merely specifying the conditions under which one can talk (or not talk) about it. In this way we *can* speak about it without ascribing to it any attributes de facto.[3] The notion of dao and the Hindu conception of *Brahman* are very similar, since both are about an ultimate reality that cannot be 'named.'

To 'non-describably' speak of it then, we may say that—in a sense—*dao* is tran-scendent. It remains outside of all phenomena, yet immanent since all things originate and partake of it. To court paradox, *dao* is that through which all things are but it itself is not a thing: if it were one then it could not be a part of all things. When the *dao* is embodied in concrete things it is called *de*, 德—which can be translated as virtue, power or character (these fall short of its broad and wider nuances as well). Another 'non-feature' of the *dao* sees it as a creative and fecund duality made up of *yin*, 陰, female principle, and *yang*, 陽, male principle. Through their interactions, these create Heaven and Earth—the two reference points in human life, the former a creative princi-ple and the latter where fulfilment takes place. Among other reasons, Daoism—seeking harmony—favours *yin* to redress the emphasis on *yang* and male nepotism in Chinese culture. A prolific and lush concept for Daoism, *yin* is equated with water, the moon, darkness, the mother, femaleness and more. Laozi's chapter eight says, 'The highest excellence is like (that of) water. The excellence of water appears in its benefiting all things, and in its occupying, without striving (to the contrary), the low place which all men dislike. Hence (its way) is near to (that of) the Tao' (Legge 1981b).[4] The Daoist goal is harmony with *dao* and, by extension as the milieu within which our lives unfold, nat-ure. In fact, the good life for Daoists lies in attuning our inner being (our desires, thoughts and inclinations) with the outer world of nature (*dao*'s manifestation). Ideally this results in a holistic integration where we find happiness, and which sages embody. Loland's arguments for an ecosophy of sport based on gestalts, self-realization for all, and joy—as inspired by Arne Naess—are consistent within this Daoist framework (2001, 2006). Gracefulness best displays *yin* and this attunement in the sporting and performa-tive context: even when jumping as high and far as the ballet dancer is able during a *grand Jeté*, he epitomizes this ease; even when the weightlifter does a clean and jerk with maximum weight she looks supple and flowing. Of course, this requires consider-able effort. But, when embodying Daoist *yin* effort's travails are, paradoxically, less so at the highest intensities of exceptional performance.

Wuwei, 為, embodies this effortlessness that gets things done without trying (too) hard. *Wu*, 無, literally a negative, can be translated as 'without', 'no', 'void', 'nothingness' or 'emptiness,' among others, whereas *Wei*, 為, means 'action.' Accordingly, 'effortless action' or 'taking no action' are apt translations. This principle is also rendered as *weiwuwei*, 為無為, that is, 'action without action' or 'doing without doing.' There are different ways of implementing this. Far from quietism or apoplectic passivity, one idea is to match oneself to the rhythms of nature and the *dao*, allowing things to take their natural course. Practically, for athletes and performers, this means listening to the bodymind and its proprioceptive and kinesthetic dynamics, our mood, e.g. being aware of fatigue, for example, or the cause for our downtrodden or overen-thusiastic mood, all of which could lead to inauspicious results. Another method is to act spontaneously and naturally, that is not forcing ourselves either by overly harsh training or actually straining with our body. The idea is to act softly even when we are trying our hardest. As many an athlete and martial artist can attest, actually relaxing the body in situations of maximal efforts *does* improve the performance. The trick is to wilfully relax, which is achieved through indirect means, e.g. relax the grip, focus on breathing and the like. Obviously, developing this takes discipline and extended commitment during which time one builds slowly. Yet, another way is to conceive of this as a process where we begin with the opposite of what we seek. To explain, if we want to nurture or preserve a certain skill, we admit that there is something of its opposite in it: to improve our shooting we begin by admitting that we are weak when it comes to aiming. Were we to think ourselves accurate sharpshooters already, why bother?

There are two underlying ideas here, nurturing and preservation. The issue of nurturing ourselves is developed in section 2 below. As to preservation, this connects with the idea of slow progress. As my maternal grandfather used to say to inculcate quality and avoid sapping frustration, 'Slowly and with good penmanship.'[5] The idea is to take sufficient time to complete tasks, as well as to avoid trying too hard. In terms of bodily action, hurried movement, forcing too much too soon and overly straining often enough not only lead to failure, but worse, overtraining and injury. When Laozi and Zhuangzi speak of doing nothing, what they have in mind is 'doing less' in this context. Acting thusly we achieve our goals without undue exertion. Again this takes work, but the emphasis is on the 'undue.'

A hallmark of great athletes, martial artists and performers is the economy of movement they display. They push themselves further than even very competent performers when it comes to enduring pain, but their prowess is premised on economical movement honed over years of practice (which entails talent, reflection and luck at least). They do not waste their greater effort, or rather, their efforts are more successful in the task at hand. There are some sports in which this is more evident if we consider the exertion required for locomotion. Swimming, on account of water's higher density than air, readily shows inefficiencies. If we compare the stroke of elite swimmers to that of average swimmers, it is easy to see in just the recovery portion of the stroke significant differences in how hands enter the water and how they exit it, the streamlined position of head and hips, or the side-to-side gliding. Of course, the 'magic' happens under the water, as with icebergs, where minute adjustments terribly difficult to implement make the biggest difference, where less means more displacement for a comparable exertion. These finely tuned movements result in their kinetic signatures, their personal imprint. To continue in the water, and to use one of Daoism's favourite analogies, *wuwei* is like water, since it is most yielding yet it can break the hardest rock. These are some of the ways through which *wuwei* begins to take root as better judgement, *phronesis,* by performers, coaches and mentors—a judgement that eventually should become spontaneous and intuitive.

Before focusing on Zhuangzi, let's look at the issue of society under the guise of government and Daoist political theory, as this affects the view of sport as social practice. Both Confucians, the clearest exponent of communitarian views in the East, and Daoists place sages at the forefront of government. However, whereas the former want them to be rulers with active agendas, the latter think rulers should not do 'anything' in the sense that they should act without being noticed. For Laozi enacting too many laws, having too many prohibitions and rules, devising many weapons, not only means more trouble but is actually the cause of the very issues it wants to avoid ultimately; for Zhuangzi, 'the ruler in his efforts to rectify, will draw a cloud over his own virtue, and his virtue will no longer extend over all things (Chuang Tzu and Watson 1968, 171).[6] This creates divisions, desires and tensions. Both Daoists have in mind the Confucian penchant to place at the centre of society *li* (禮), which are institutionalized rites, rituals and the observance of tradition, as vehicles toward self-cultivation and a harmonious society. Some would charge the Daoists with being overly individualistic at the expense of community. While there is some truth to this, theirs is a reaction to balance the very intrusive role that government and its regulations took at the time. Moreover, Zhuangzi himself criticized hermits and recluses, favoring a vigorous involvement with everyday life in one's community, though this does not entail partaking in political intrigue as noted above.

To bring these views to doping policy as a practical application, the causes of this malady, while complex, cannot be addressed by punitive measures for Daoists. Such coercive measures treat the symptoms but not the origin of the illness. Worse, these criminalize athletes and create a two-speed system, one for those who observe the rules and another for those who manage to flout them. Besides, it devolves into a self-replicating cat and mouse system. The Daoist solution means a radical rethinking of sport (largely aligned with what unfolds in subsequent sections). It begins by looking at the root cause of doping, not just as the athletes' immediate motivation (and/or nearby entourage), e.g. to win the race, or the external goods they stand to gain thereby. Accordingly, it considers the broader context of institutions that create the rules in the service of a particular model of sport that goes unquestioned, most saliently a record seeking sport predicated on external values, viz., economic. Along these lines, Loland argues that record sports are unsustainable because they are predicated on continuous improvement within a closed and limited system (2001, 2006). Moreover, this is likely to result in doping and other performance enhancing methods where, 'Once one athlete has used these means and performed successfully, this seems to have a coercive effect on other athletes' (Loland 2006, 149). Loland forwards an alternative and broader palette of imaginative athletic contests where athletes can flourish (ibid.), and which would see Zhuangzi smile in complicit approval. As they stand, from a Daoist perspective, current policies are a nightmarish 'solution' for all involved.

Speaking of dreams, good or bad, and perspectives, Zhuangzi's most famous parable presents him as his own character,

> Once Chuang Chou [another transliteration for Zhuangzi] dreamt he was a butterfly, a butterfly flitting and fluttering around, happy with himself and doing as he pleased. He didn't know he was Chuang Chou. Suddenly he woke up and there he was, solid and unmistakable Chuang Chou. Between Chuang Chou and a butterfly there must be *some* distinction! This is called the Transformation of Things. (Chuang Tzu and Watson 1968, 49)

There is a multiplicity of ways this can be interpreted. We can see it in terms of a Cartesian dreaming versus waking conundrum, and consider how from *within* a dream we cannot tell whether we are dreamer or dream; we can consider what it says metaphysically about how things transform and change *in toto* or within the context of the Dao, and more. But to make this more pertinent to our purposes, this also illustrates how

HOLISM AND THE CULTIVATION OF EXCELLENCE IN SPORTS AND PERFORMANCE

the validity of our epistemic judgements depends on perspective, which in turn depends on the subject and her situation. In a similar vein to how Socrates thought that if he was wise it was because he did not think that he knew what he did not know, Zhuangzi believes that we should be modest with regard to our epistemic claims. In fact, for Zhuangzi, we cannot presume that what we 'know' *necessarily* corresponds to what is *objectively* the truth. In a way he was a sceptic. But slippery as he was, this does not mean that he simply said there is no truth, or objective reality, or that truth is *simply* relative. For the Daoist, language cuts the world in certain ways and therefore we cannot presume that our language-based truths correspond to objective truths. Thus, he was a sceptic with regard to *our ability* to know or be aware that we know those truths, not with regard to their existence. But Zhuangzi did not become a dogmatic sceptic or a relativistic and impotent observer. Being a sceptic for him already assumes a certain position, a negative view of knowledge and the world (namely that we do not know or cannot know either truth or that there is no such thing). Rather, Zhuangzi embraced a nimble perspectivism—much as Ortega but for different reasons—taking the position of the monkey keeper,

> But to wear out your brain trying to make things into one without realizing that they are that all the same—This is called 'Three in the Morning.' What do I mean by 'Three in the Morning'? When the monkey trainer was handing out acorns, he said, 'you get three in the morning and four at night.' This made all the monkeys furious. 'Well, then,' he said, 'you get four in the morning and three at night.' The monkeys were all delighted. There was no change in the reality behind the words, and yet the monkeys responded with joy and anger. Let them, if they want to. So the sage harmonizes with both right and wrong and rests in Heaven the Equalizer. This is called [the principle of] walking two roads [at once]. (Chuang Tzu and Watson 1968, 41)

The quickest way to the most expedient interpretation is to say that we should not be attached to what we think is true. When an athlete complains that she has to do three sets of 60-yard sprints in the morning and four in the afternoon she is making the same mistake as the angry monkeys. Of course, there are times when it *does* make a difference, as when doing the intense sprints first makes one tired for the longer sets (which can be done purposefully to train a different skill). But this is more to Zhuangzi's point, which is, that we should remain flexible without getting attached to any one particular 'truth' either as athlete or coach, martial artist or *sensei*, dancer or choreographer. *Phronesis* requires a good dose of this flexibility (besides the humility to realize we may not know what we think we do). Now, the story is also instructive regarding how to nurture a 'Daoist *phronesis*.' The keeper evinces what Zhuangzi refers to as 'fasting of the mind,' which entails calmness, serenity, equanimity and being absorbed, as Michael Crandell observes (1983, 112). If we adapt to situations, to the Dao, and follow it without strife, then we are at the centre, pivoting as we walk both ways: we are active and responsive but, crucially, without attachments. Hence, we change the plan for the day based on how *we* feel or see in those under our charge.

This combines *wuwei* with a liberating and most expeditious pragmatic perspectivism. Moreover, this perspectivism also entails different standards for different entities. Consider the story of Nie Que and Wang Ni for example, where the former wonders about whether all things are ontologically the same, and the latter proceeds to illustrate

Zhuangzi's perspectival stance by discussing how different conditions apply variously to diverse beings: a man sleeping in a damp place wakes up ill and sore on the back, whereas an eel thrives; the same goes for us living on tree branches, we become frightened compared to monkeys. Wang Ni asks 'Of these three [human, eel, monkey], which 'knows' what is the right place to live? (Zhuangzi and Ziporyn 2009, 17). These, as well as dietary tastes and needs, as the story goes on to explore, depend on the sort of creatures with which we deal. These distinctions for Zhuangzi do not result in ethical, aesthetic or ontological valuations, but rather they stay close to functional descriptions consistent with a Daoist holism. Upon Nie Que's insistence concerning the effectiveness of this insight for life, Wang Ni elaborates on how' 'The Consummate Person is miraculous, beyond understanding!' and goes on to detail how she is unfazed by flames, freezing weather, thunder … not even death and life change her (ibid.). To such a formidable person we now turn.

2. The Heart of the Matter: Xin 心 and Self-Cultivation

What did Zhuangzi understand by the consummate or perfected person? And how did this person come to be? The short answer is that such a person epitomizes thick holism. She is fully integrated: herself as a completely integrated being *and* with her environment. For Zhuangzi, the cultivation that leads to perfection begins with bodily action and, importantly and contra stereotypes, in the thick of things: his sages wander free and easy, pragmatically involved in every day life and affairs.

And to begin with the longer version, this person (all references from Chuang Tzu and Watson 1968): has no self (32); embraces things without discrimination (44); takes part in the ten thousand things and achieves simplicity in oneness (47); fasts the mind (57); lets the mind play in the harmony of virtue (69); sees fame and reputation as fetters (72), uses her mind like a mirror (97); dismisses benevolence and righteousness (151) and thus showing no partiality her virtue is complete (290); guards the pure breath (198); wanders free and easy, doing but not looking for any thanks (207); is imperturbable (231); acts like a child (253); is skilled in human and Heavenly affairs (259); and does not change herself for the sake of things (273). These, which are but a partial list of attributes, are engaged below as discussion unfolds. The *Zhuangzi* is thick with references to the perfect, consummate, sagely person of virtue. Centered on the person of excellence and how she flourishes, as Roger Ames states it is 'a philosophical text for the most part addressed to the project of personal realization' (1998, 1). However variegated the traits, spontaneity is the common thread needed for any and all of them to be actualized. It is the heart of the consummate person. But before looking into it, a few words on another heart that helps to better understand the foundation of Zhuangzian cultivation.

Ancient or traditional Chinese conceived of mind as *xin* 心, which stands for heart and mind in the fullest sense, the sum/interpenetration: emotions, reason and our vitality. The very character 心 represents a heart pumping blood. The richness of *xin* 心 and its disparity from the mainstream modern Western notion of the self, a Cartesian one, is patent. Charles Taylor has shown the fairly recent development of this rational and dualistic Cartesian self where the ghostly mind inhabits the body, to phrase it with a Rylean turn of phrase (1989). As Harold Oshima writes, mind and *xin* 'share little more than this common property of thinking. The area of congruence is small, the dissimilarities significant' (1983, 65). He adds that for Zhuangzi *xin* 心 literally refers to the heart—the organ—where thinking and feeling surge intimately intertwined, metaphorically to the perfected person's integration, and helpfully points out how the heart's function remained mysterious until the seventeenth century (ibid., 66ff.). For ancient Chinese people, a Western dualism of mind and body would be utterly foreign. Moreover, they did not have comparable concepts for 'unconscious', 'imagination' or 'ego'. Further, they placed more importance in lived and enacted practical knowledge as opposed to theoretical knowledge, which explains the importance of performing meditative and cultivating practices. Last, is the emphasis on every day, physically engaged activities as ways to nurture a cultivated spontaneity that leads to perfection under Zhuangzian methods, enlightenment for Chan Buddhism, or satori in Zen.

Henceforth in this section, I use the Chinese character 心, rather than its transliteration or the inadequate 'bodymind' or 'heart and mind' renditions to: (a) emphasize that the concept does not have an easy translation (short of very long and convoluted phrasings); (b) reduce the tendency to slip back into the overly simple, frequently used and very misleading 'mind'; and (c) foster thinking of it as the very complex phenomenon it designates (see more below) if only because of the initial awkwardness on encountering it without transcription. (An additional, ulterior reason is revealed in an endnote at the end of this section).

In addition to 心, the Chinese conception is more holistic than Western prevalent views because it includes other concepts that capture dynamics often lost to us. There is *shen* 身, which refers to 'spirit' understood as a living and lived body concerned with proprioceptive and kinesthetic dynamics that entails the idea of a self.[7] And there is *xing* 形, which denotes bodily shape as a process, e.g. a Lacrosse player who adapts her movements to the equipment and tactics specific to the game. Finally, successful integration means managing the internal *qi* 氣. This can be rendered as 'energy flow,' as Hay puts it (1993, 189). He explains, citing Porkert, that while similar to our Western concept of energy, it differs in that 'it always implies a *qualitative* determination of energy' (Ibid., 186, my italics). As mentioned with Ortega, we are all more or less attuned to the ebbs and flows of our energetic levels: we feel an electric-like excitement that runs from our toes to our head, we experience the calming spread of tender warmth, or a sapping emptiness that nails us to bed. Our breathing and heart, with their varied rates and qualities suffuse this. In the perfected person, all of these work harmoniously integrated with 心 as a holistic organism.

There are some parallels between *qi* and the Ancient Greek notion of *pneuma*, the human breath that animates the body or matter. But Jean François Billeter, a sinologist with deep and keen philosophical tendencies, explains that the key difference is that *pneuma* opposes matter and spirit, whereas *qi* 'animates the whole of reality [...] thus it excludes any opposition between matter and spirit' (2010b, 37, my translation). Chinese arts of meditation stress how this vital *qi* energy permeates the whole 心, from nervous system to metabolic processes to emotions and thoughts. In fact, for Zhuangzi, guarding the breath is one way of cultivating ourselves, and a hallmark of perfected persons: 'their breathing was deep. The Genuine Human Beings breathed from their heels, while the mass of men breathe from their throats' (Zhuangzi and Ziporyn 2009, 39). By adulthood, unless we are singers, or some martial artists and sportspersons who expressly work on this, such as freedivers, most of us breathe from the chest and not with the diaphragm—the full breathing to which Zhuangzi refers. Accordingly, we can understand 心 as a conglomerate of heart (emotions, sensations and desires), mind (thinking, imagining and volition) and vital energy that suffuses all bodily and mental processes, not forgetting the sociocultural environment that teaches us about this (Ortega's views are uncannily close to this). This holistic 心 is not a given, but must be developed. In fact, there is a tradition in ancient China of cultivating oneself (xiushen,修身) that spans Confucianism, Daoism and other schools whose goal is promotion of an integrated 心 to nurture our existence.

After discussing differences between Western and Chinese paradigms and explaining the most distinctive features of 心, it is time to consider what unites them. There are grounds for reconciliation. This is important if Zhuangzi's insights are going to prove revealing for us, who live in such a disparate world. Edward Slingerland writes in his comparative study of the *Zhuangzi*'s idea of self that, 'Despite the surface differences between, say, the Cartesian and Zhuangzian conceptions of the self, both of these philosophical conceptions grow out of and make use of a deeper metaphysical grammar that has its roots in a common human embodied experience' (2004, 323). In other words, our common, animate experience allows us to be able to understand 心 and Zhuangzi's use directly and not as an abstract concept like that of a 'triangle.' The one unifying element that issues from our animate holistic performances is spontaneity, for which perspectivism and harmony are pivotal. Dwelling on this sheds light on the workings of skillful performance and *phronesis*. Øyvind Standal and Liv Hemmestad close their discussion of *phronesis* in coaching by actually agreeing with criticisms that levy that the concept is inherently vague as to how it works, but deftly—with *wuwei* Daoist flair—make of this a strength by stressing its flexibility and openness (2011, 53–54). The following exposition of Zhuangzian ideas fills in the vagueness, but manages to maintain the limber qualities that bring flexibility to our concepts.

A first story to consider is that of Cook Ding, from an inner chapter tellingly titled 'The Secret of Caring for Life' (Chuang Tzu and Watson 1968, 50). Cook Ding is masterfully cutting up an ox for the ruler of Wenhui. More than butchering, his rhythmic movements make it seem as if he is dancing and making music. The ruler, fascinated, compliments him on his consummate skill, and the cook explains,

> What your servant loves is the approach of the *dao*, more advanced than any skill. When I first began to cut up an ox, I saw it in its entirety. After three years, I ceased to see it as a whole. Now I work with my spirit and not with my eyes. My senses no longer function and my spirit moves freely. Following the natural forms, the knife slides through large crevices and follows the big cavities as they are. [...] A good cook changes his knife once a year because he cuts. An ordinary cook changes his once a month because he hacks. Now my knife has been used for nineteen years [...] Nevertheless, whenever I come to a complicated part [...] I proceed with care and caution, keeping my eyes steady and moving my hands slowly. Then, with only a slight movement of the knife, the part is readily separated and falls as a clump of earth to the ground. Standing up, I look all around and with an air of satisfaction wipe the knife and put it away. (Höchsmann, Guorong, and Zhuangzi 2007, 99–100)

Cook Ding identifies three steps of his route to mastery. First, as a novice, he saw the whole ox. We can imagine him not only anxious but also handling the knife timidly, slowly and clumsily, much as a rookie basketball player, aikidōka or dancer who

HOLISM AND THE CULTIVATION OF EXCELLENCE IN SPORTS AND PERFORMANCE

ineffectively and ungainly tries to follow rules and brakes moves into steps. Secondly, after three years, he was able to focus on the parts at hand and not see the whole ox. The player, aikidōka or dancer has learned the sequence as a gestalt and needs no mental rehearsing for each step. And, finally, he works with his spirit, not the senses. Spirit here would be *shen*, the lived way of being dynamically attuned to proprioceptive and kinesthetic input (Ortega's vitality). This is expert skilled performance that is not burdened by any worries, able of complete concentration when needed

In terms of skill development, Billeter's analysis of this story is the most revealing in the literature. Before detailing his insightful examination, however, it is advisable to dispose of two misguided claims he makes. First, he writes that we are very familiar with this process of developing expertise, as when we learned how to adjust our grip when holding a glass being filled, or how to ride a bike. Secondly, he claims that Cook Ding's need to focus when something complicated comes up shows a lesser mastery (2010a). As to the first one, indeed we all are familiar with a *similar* process, and those experiences he mentions give us a window as to how this works. But a window makes for a way of spectating not doing. For most people, their level of expertise is nowhere near close to Cook Ding's or that of world-class performers even if they are devoted to their activities. This familiarity is misleading if it is meant to equate the two types of performance. The qualitative jump is too big to breach it with mere acquaintance, as *Riding the Wind* argues in more detail.

These stories are meant to help us do the jump ourselves not just intellectually but practically. In fact, only through our actual *attempts* will we understand. As to the second point, it seems that Zhuangzi's account captures better how consummate performers actually perform: they *are* fully attending to the situation at hand. They do not worry about their bodily movements, are emotionally centered, and their executive or volitional commands arise without deliberation or wavering, spontaneously. In fact, that kind of focus is the trademark of high performance. Surely, the focus is not piecemeal on the mechanics of movement. But neither is there absent-mindedness, as Billeter punctually intimates, or as Drefyus posits with his expert daydreaming driver who arrives at home without remembering how he got there—something that Breivik criticizes extensively (2013). Nevertheless, Billeter provides a perspicacious perspective on how these expert processes unfold.

He does this through the notion of what he describes as '"regimes or stages of activity", [régimes de l'activité] in the sense that one speaks of the gears of an engine, that is the different adjustments that one can make that result in different relations and have different effects in terms of engine power' (2010a, 43, my translation). Elsewhere he tries to clarify this notion by explaining that when listening to someone he can listen and understand the words attentively, but he can also think about other things or simply get sleepy, or he can suddenly come up with ideas in response to the interlocutor's that require him to ask for an interlude to allow these to form (Billeter 2010b, 18). All of these changes would amount to various 'regimes.' In essence, these are functional stages or levels of performance that change qualitatively and dynamically. Of import for us is that these take place through the body for him, which he understands 'not as the anatomical body or the body as object, but as the totality of our faculties, resources and capacities, known and unknown, that carry out our activity—so long as we conceive it thus, is our great teacher' (Billeter 2010a, 50). This is a thickly holistic view of performance and embodiment. There is a pivoting point to all these experiences, a before and an after when we realize we have learned the skill (ibid. 56). Thus, after many attempts to flip in the pool, 'nail' a 360 with the skateboard, or dance a cumbia without stepping on our partner, something clicks and it happens. This occurs when we finally forget ourselves in the movement. Other stories illustrate this and give a fuller view of the superior person.

Chapter 19, with another revealing title, 'Mastering Life' (Chuang Tzu and Watson 1968, 197), is awash with accounts of consummate people who, much like cook Ding, are supremely skillful. Among others, we read of a wheel carver, a bell-maker, a hunchback that catches cicadas, an old man swimming in such formidable rapids that even fish shun them, and a ferryman. It is worth highlighting again that these are stories of people immersed in life. They are all performers as well, in the active and holistic sense that matters here, not intellectuals ensconced in ivory towers. For Zhuangzi, the difference between the sage and the common man lies in how they use their 心. The former fasts the 心. Fasting is about listening with the 心 and *shen*, spirit (Chuang Tzu and Watson 1968, 57–58). One way to see what this entails is to think of it as forgetting, as in being focused in such a way that what captures people's attention actually falls from ours. Another way to look at it is in terms of Jamesian introspection and concentrated attention inclusive of the fringe of consciousness, and Ortega's emotive soul.

A number of stories show how this forgetting and fasting of 心 result in spontaneity—the mark of persons of excellence. To adapt Zhuangzi's account of the ferryman who handles the boat with supernatural skill and put him on a kayak (Chuang Tzu and Watson 1968, 200): novices get attentionally and literally caught up in the whirls and eddies of the rapids, but expert kayakers, free from any anxiety, glide through the water actually seeking turbulence. When asked about how he slides so imperturbably on the water, the Zhuangzian expert kayaker answers that 'a good swimmer will in no time get the knack of it. And if a man can swim under water [even with no prior experience] he'll know how to handle it!' (ibid.). Pressed for clarification, he says that the good swimmer has forgotten about the water, and the diver 'sees the water as so much dry land' and thinks nothing of capsizing, even if everything goes awry he will be serene (ibid). Just as the kayaker adapts himself to the fluid nature of water, riding it effortlessly yet fully attentive even when it ripples violently, the perfect person acts like a mirror flexibly adapting herself to the circumstances. Consummate coaches, *sensei* or mentors act much as the skillful person, mirroring the states of their charges, being responsive to each individual, and in the case of team sports or dance ensembles to both the individuals and the aggregated, more-than-the-sum-of-the-parts whole. Of course, there are times, particularly in competitive sports, when the envelope is pushed to the brink of breaking, and when it does, no amount of spontaneity will do. But generally, this occurs because the sportsperson overstepped the boundaries of her expertise.

Reaching this state takes training and habit, as the story of a hunchback that catches cicadas with a sticky pole demonstrates. When Confucius, as character in the story, asks how he had developed such uncanny ability, the hunchback details the different stages of training: several months before cicada season he begins to balance two balls at the end of the pole, increasing the number until he can balance five. Then he knows he can catch cicadas as if he were gathering them, and explains how his attention is fully given to the cicada wings and nothing else. Confucius then describes him as keeping 'his will and the spirit concentrated' (Chuang Tzu and Watson 1968, 200). That is, training and habit along with deliberate reflection throughout the process allow him to hone his attention and the spirit as a proprioceptively and kinesthetically attune-ment. Most are quick to allocate such skillful activity to subpersonal or unconscious pro-cesses, and Billeter discusses skill in terms of conscious and unconscious processes for the most part. But, on translating a particular character, rather shrewdly, he adds a fourth stage to the three we find with the cook. At this fourth stage, when we master a skill, we execute it with a reduced attention, leaving to the body the doing while we *watch removed*, with a certain ironic stance, as an spectator of the activity (2010a, 67–68). This watching need not be merely visual; we also 'watch' our kinesthetic and proprioceptive dynamics (which are more important in performance than visual ones). We can also observe these internal proprioceptive and kinesthetic processes in action or at rest (ibid. 95). By emptying ourselves (fasting or forgetting) in calm concentration we can be receptive to our *qi*, our vital energy and then our activity can perceive itself (ibid., 96–97). This process takes place not through intellectual analysis but by paying attention to our body and its dynamic processes. This ironic regard and the emptying of ourselves that Billeter speaks of, is fruitfully conceptualized with James' fringe of consciousness, and also plays a key role in trying to understand spontaneous action (in essay 6 it is conceptualized as a radically enactive and contentless cognition).

To speak of spontaneity then by considering a performative art of ancient China: calligraphy, one of the three 'arts of the brush' (painting, poetry and calligraphy). Corre-lated with the Western canon, calligraphy is closer to painting. In fact, paintings usually integrated calligraphy and poems as part of the very painting. Billeter has also written extensively on this art, peeling off many of its complex layers (2010c). Done with brush and ink, calligraphers mix the ink themselves to various levels of viscosity that range from watery to oily, and apply more or less pressure at various speeds to obtain star-tling effects on paper (or silk for some paintings, which is even more challenging). Because the paper used is very porous, the traces must be resolute and unwavering, as one cannot go back and try to erase or amend what is already on the page. This is a performing art where the traces on paper are but a record of the skilled movements of the entire 心. Unlike writing with a pen, doing so with a brush in Chinese and Japanese traditions means that stance and balance are important: the arm is not in contact with the desk; suspended mid air, it moves in flowing patters that start at the shoulder; in turn, this depends on the trunk and hip posture. Seventeenth-century Japanese Nō The-ater master Zeami Motoyiko wrote about *mushin* (no mind; see essay 7) and calligraphy stating that, 'One cannot fully reproduce the handwriting of a famous calligrapher effortlessly done in cursive style. This ease or freedom is achieved only after long years of training which began with writing in the square style' (McKinnon 1953, 223).

This in fact harks back to a much older Chinese tradition that, focusing on the past and its creations, seeks to pay homage to the master by *exactly* replicating his or her brushstroke and composition in a *spontaneous* way. As Arthur Danto points out, there was an important practice of imitating Ni Tsan in Chinese Painting (1994, 117). And this was not an isolated instance but the established and mainstream way of engaging with artistic creation. The differences we might ascertain between the master and his imitators would in fact be imperceptible to the Chinese eye of the times because they would be looking for very different things in the paintings (ibid.). The way the Chinese understood imitation makes it even more challenging than being original in the sense of painting something new or different– regarding talent and the type of effort involved. Danto explains this Chinese understanding of art:

HOLISM AND THE CULTIVATION OF EXCELLENCE IN SPORTS AND PERFORMANCE

'When every boulder or rock shows free and untrammelled inkstrokes, then the painting will have a scholar's air. If it is too laborious, the painting will resemble the work of a draftsman.' So wrote Ni Tsan. Here we can begin to see the extreme difficulty—one would almost say the impossibility—of imitation as the Chinese understood it, and so understand its challenge. One must paint as the Master painted and, *at the same time*, be free and untrammelled. The imitation cannot be outward indiscernibility: rather, the work must flow forth from the same internal resources, and painting in the style of Ni Tsan in consequence becomes a form of spiritual exercise. (1994, 119)

To spontaneously write calligraphy, paint, dance, perform a kata or play tennis *just* as someone else would borders the inconceivable. And yet, as the opening citation of Chad Harbach's *The Art of Fielding* (2011) suggests good players tend to be such good mimics that the lineage moving through certain players can be readily observed. If imitation is the highest form of flattery, or praise (depending on the intention), we are well equipped to do so. Aristotle first wrote about our natural and effective tendency to imitate, and current research shows that neonates are able to copy adult facial gestures shortly after birth (Gallagher 2005). Moreover, the much touted mirror neurons, which fire in our brains when we observe others' movement, also lend a copying hand or foot here. Elite performers are keen observers of other's successful movements, and while they eventually imprint theirs with a personal style, that kinetic signature, there are schools of athletes, dance, martial arts, that move with a recognizable style that learned eyes can recognize much as others identify painter's lineages and schools (unskilled or less skilful movement lacks style, as with the arts). If we consider not an 'adultist' view of sport, already fully formed and with expert players in place, but see how it develops, the importance of 'imitative spontaneity' is clear. Sports, martial and performing arts, and crafts are social practices. As such, they provide a framework for learning. In sport, we all begin by imitating those who succeed, whether it be gross motor action and observable techniques or (almost) imperceptible movements. Just as children learn how to walk, but with the advantage of already having experienced skill development and counting on counsel from others, we too start like Cook Ding. When, after many years a person is finally able to act and move *truly* spontaneously, without recourse to explicit rule-following or overt analysis, she has mastered the movements or techniques. Then she may develop her own style, albeit one that most likely will bear resemblances to a certain lineage.[8] To do so, she must forget herself and the specifics of the movement, what Zhuangzi would call 'emptying.' Forgetting herself and letting the move come through also means a certain 'necessity' or restriction.

There is a complex and interesting relation here between deliberate and conscious movement, and spontaneous movement. For Billeter and others, the former is the inferior, under control and often ineffective movement of humans; the latter is the more successful and superior movement of Heaven or *dao* (2010a; Slingerland 2003; Wu 1982; Wu and Zhuangzi 1990). Spontaneity seemingly wrestles control from us in that movements and action come unbidden, in a way similar to how the muses for Plato or inspiration for Romantic views of art impose themselves. Dynamic systems theory, takes away some of the charm and mysticism, but it mathematically captures how spontaneous synchronization takes place for systems at whichever length scale of description we choose, whether it be molecular, cellular, neural, anatomic (as when fingers synchronize spontaneously or people coordinate movements, e.g. two people will begin to swing their legs in unison

HOLISM AND THE CULTIVATION OF EXCELLENCE IN SPORTS AND PERFORMANCE

without intending it (Kelso 1995) (*Riding the* Wind discusses dynamic systems theory in the context of skill). In the end, these extemporaneous movements happen in spite of ourselves. That is, our reflective consciousness is not fully in command. The virtue in this lies in that 'Heavenly' advantage: spontaneous skilled movement allows for better performance in the case of experts. The case of novices differs, as psychological studies show the expedience of attentional focus for them but not experts (Beilock and Carr 2001). The vice or downside is presented by Benjamin Libet's experiments. These purportedly demonstrated that the brain initiates a voluntary act before conscious intention. This means that, 'unconscious brain events start the process of a voluntary act' (Blackmore 2010, 140). In other words, we are not in control, according to him. To put it differently and dramatically, free will is an illusion if our 'willed' movements begin before we consciously set them in motion. Is Ortega's cognitive volition, that phenomenological sense of I that wills and understands but an illusion? While this may be appealing to some wishing to discharge any and all responsibility, this is too simplistic an interpretation of the experiments. As Libet himself pointed out, we may not freely initiate actions, but we can veto them. That is, we are not free to do but are free not to do. To craft this in terms of Gallagher's analysis, we have a sense of ownership for our actions in spontaneous action, *we* experience the movement, but there is no sense of agency in that it is not us initiating it wilfully (2005). Nonetheless, even if there are methodological and conceptual issues with Libet's procedure and conclusions, they can still help shed some insight into the unbidden nature of spontaneity *as* we dispute them. Even if we take this overly restrictive reading of the experiment, there is a modicum of choice in and through spontaneous action. Put otherwise, spontaneity restricts but it also enables. The next three points open up a space within which to exercise our will.

First, we should look at spontaneous action within a much larger pragmatic framework. It is common to analyse the spontaneous *moment* itself in a piecemeal, discrete fashion. Libet's experiments zeroed in on the voluntary moment to flick a finger at one's will. Yet, when we act, unless directed by some eccentric psychologist in a lab, our actions and movements are part of much larger pragmatic contexts that: (a) endow our actions with meaning; and (b) open the door to conscious control. As for the former, it is more or less straightforward that a broader scope, seeing the golf ball hit as part of a tournament rather than a-moment-in-time-hit, enriches meaningfully the action. Regarding the latter, any given spontaneous action may take place subpersonally, but when placed in the larger context at which we normally operate, the fact is that we actually deliberate and choose on the course of action. An example that comes to mind is Barcelona's footballer Messi dribbling past four defenders and the goalie to score against Getafe in the Copa del Rey (1/16/2014). There may be 'reflex' movements as part of his repertoire of honed skills, but there is also a direction of purpose that a punctual model of spontaneity-as-automaticity cannot explain. As Gallagher writes, 'free will is about my purposive actions, which are best described in terms of intentions rather than neurons, muscles, reachings, etc.' (2005, 240) Surely, each dribble takes place and is concatenated at too fast a pace to plan and execute in a deliberate manner. Here James' fringe of consciousness becomes helpful to explain the spontaneous dribbling *functionally*—without recourse to either an unconsciousness that makes the fact that he scores but a lucky mystery (if it were truly out of his control the ball might as well go into his own net occasionally) or reifying the process as some neural network correlate that does not explain anything ultimately.

106

As he dribbles, Messi is effecting performative judgements that take place at the layer between unconscious processes where muscles fire and conscious ones where he responds to players coming at him. He is also able to attend to proprioceptive, vestibular, kinesthetic and kinetic cues regarding his own movements, the opposition and the ball's position and decide, in that fringe between awareness and automaticity, what to pay attention to. He empties himself as fully conscious actor to allow the game to fill him, but he does not relinquish control and awareness completely. Billeter's ironic perspective is another way to conceptualize this layer of awareness that is neither fully subpersonal nor reflective, and which allows for snap-of-the-fingers *judgements* (which can be *bodily* kinetic judgements not merely intellectual ones). Moreover, this does not happen completely out of his control, as he still has to maintain in mind the goal of scoring a goal, and the fact that this is part of a football match. During the totality of the football game, Messi is aware of what he is doing, there being moments where he deliberates on the tactics to use and other times where he is more spontaneous.[9] This opens up performative possibilities.

Second, as our movements become spontaneous—which, again, should be understood as part of a repertoire and not disconnected and punctual—the more spontaneous we can be, the better we perform in *other* aspects. By offloading cognitive, emotional, volitional and bodily resources, this frees attentional resources. As a result we are able to discriminate better across a wider range of phenomena, from proprioceptive and kinesthetic dynamics to environmental cues. Expert performers are not overburdened by incoming sensory data, which allow them to take on bigger challenges. What would end badly for even a competent downhill skier is but a relaxing glide for a consummate skier. Habit (and talent), as expounded earlier with Dewey, is the gateway to these performances where the performer can broaden the often narrow line between consciousness and unconsciousness, between constrain and possibility.

Zhuangzi's masters have honed their skills (Earth) through habit within a holistic system that includes their talents (Heaven, as spontaneous and cultivated action), and the broader environment. As an emotional boon, aligned with a holistic view we are afforded equanimity: a tranquillity to deal with the kind of quick decisions athletes, coaches, martial artists, sensei, performers and mentors often need to make at crunch time. This capacity for self-control across the full range of emotion, reason, will and bodily processes 'restricts our restrictions' and thereby increases our freedom. Another windfall is that this model addresses the paradox of willfully acting without effort, effortless action. As Slingerland puts it, the problem is that 'we need to *do* something first before we are ready to flow with the Way—that is we need to try not to try' (Slingerland 2003, 211). Other models, such as Wu's phenomenological reduction of *wuwei*, 'merely transfer the tension into a different set of philosophical terms' (ibid., 212). However, the fringe/irony model above allows to both be observer and actor through a functional account (see also radical enactivism in essay 6). To summarize, when a *cultivated* spontaneity takes over, our freedom increases.

Third and last, this unbidden spontaneity is also the gateway to a playful freedom that, when recast in terms of Suits' lusory attitude, opens creative possibilities that are both spontaneous and partially under our conscious control (1990). The lusory attitude demands that we willingly submit to game rules, which limit our options but at the same time encourage our creativity to meet the challenges specified by those rules. There is a structural parity between the process of cultivated spontaneity and a lusory attitude to game rules. In both cases, the restrictive is the gateway to creative expression. Playfulness, or a lusory attitude to life, is a key virtue of perfected persons for Zhuangzi. As Slingerland points out, 'wandering' or 'playing' is 'the most famous expression of Zhuangzian effortlessness and unself-consciousness. Its literal sense of physically easy wandering metaphorically represents an effortless manner of moving through the world' (2003, 196). Cook Ding's carving dance embodies this to perfection. 'The hands touch, the shoulders lean, the feet plant, the knees press; Swoosh! Swish! The bones leave the meat, the performing knife zings through the ox, hitting the tune of the Dance of the Mulberry Forest, the symphonic tune of the neck and the head,' thus translates Wu the opening lines of Cook Ding's story (1990, 316). He then concludes, 'All this is joy and expertise; and it is natural. To be an expert is to be experience, trailing, tracking nature, becoming natural' (Wu and Zhuangzi 1990, 317). In merry and serendipitous agreement, the dance and symphonic moves agree with neuroscientist's Aleksandr Luria's fertile idea of kinetic melody, which Sheets-Johnstone theorizes as,

> kinesthetically felt and [having] an affective character generated by the very movement that produces it at the same time that [said movement] is kinesthetically constituted as an ongoing qualitative affective-kinetic dynamic: it is heavy or light, moderately fast or solemnly slow, has swelling crescendos and fading diminuendos, and so on. (2011, 469; see also 2009, 254–258)

This fills in the internal dialogue between our bodily felt dynamics and the different layers of (un)awareness. Moreover, the playful (as lusory attitude), animates the dance. In this context, Crandell looks at the *Zhuangzi* from the perspective of Gadamer's analysis of play. He points out that even meditation, which is an advantageous way to develop the absorption requisite for equanimity and fasting or forgetting of the mind that results in stillness that can handle unruly monkeys (or ourselves), is not at odds with a lusory attitude (Crandell 1983, 112). We can concurrently meditate earnestly as we play earnestly, and in both cases, the underlying mirth and autotelic interest are fully present. Billeter's French translation highlights one aspect that others do not: when Cook Ding succeeds with the difficult part, he looks around *amused* (*amusé*), clearly in a playful and enjoyable state (2010a). Sages are playful and childlike in their simplicity. Laozi and Daoists thought of children and their ignorance as rather praiseworthy because in their simplicity and innocence they resembled the Uncarved Block.[10] Unlike the natural state of the child, however, the 'ignorance' of the sage is the result of conscious cultivation—and in that sense it has deeper roots. These sometimes go deep into suffering.

Lest readers think this is an overly florid or excessively joyful picture of performance and life at odds with a world where things often are messy and an ox can be unruly, we need but remember the turmoil that surrounded Zhuangzi. In fact, as Wu argues convincingly and originally, chapter three brings together a thriving life with affliction, 'there is the mutuality of nourishment and suffering. The title is concerned with nourishing our life, yet in five of its six parts the chapter tells us about cutting up an ox, amputation, harsh wild life, death, and fire—all external and destructive.' (1990, 305) But just as Ortega embraces the risk and suffering in life as a sportive affair, here 'in all this suffering we must live as if we were dancing [...] this is to nourish our lives. Nourishment occurs in and through dangers (Wu and Zhuangzi 1990, 301 & 305ff.). It is not about avoiding or enduring suffering but being able to enjoy things in the midst of

HOLISM AND THE CULTIVATION OF EXCELLENCE IN SPORTS AND PERFORMANCE

it, much as the athlete enjoys the pain of a good training session. In both cases, it is not a matter of enduring the suffering or pain, but rather these are integral to what it means and takes to embrace the experience. Thus, it becomes enjoyable and meaningful. This is reminiscent of Nietzsche's notion that what does not kill us makes us stronger, but with a merry disposition. Now, Daoism is about nurturing and preserving life, and for many this means, stereotypically, that one lives a quiet and careful life. Zhuangzi's zest for life is not restful, though it can be. As we see with the old man swimming in the perilous vortexes of the waterfall at Luliang, who incidentally explains his skill as involving spontaneous necessity because his actions are destined (Chuang-Tzu and Graham 2001, 136), there is a place and a time for dangerous endeavours should our skills be able to match the risks involved. Accordingly, a Zhuangzian ethos will also embrace risk sports as part of that mixture of suffering and nourishment that enriches our lives. In fact, such endeavours would be a superb ways to learn to control our fears and deepen our self-knowledge in a joyfully life-affirming way. But athletic or martial prowess is not sufficient. We need to also nurture a self-less attitude where concern for even our life becomes part of the endeavour. This is not the same as recklessness. Lie Yukou, Dean Potter and Shi Dejian exemplify this …

We meet Lie Yukou (another name for Liezi, the third figure of the Daoist philosophical canon) as a formidable archer who can shoot arrows and hit the bull's eye without spilling a drop of liquid from a cup resting on his elbow. Bohun Wuren says it is fine shooting, but not on a par with the kind of those who shoot without thinking about their shooting. He takes him to the top of a mountain, next to a precipice, and standing backwards, his heels over the chasm, asks Yukou to join him and shoot. Yukou, in a cold sweat, cowers to the ground. Wuren says, 'The Perfect man beholds the azure sky above, plunges into the yellow springs below […] without any change in his spirit or breath. But now your eyes betray your tremulous state. Your fear of danger is insurmountable in your mind!' (Höchsmann, Guorong, and Zhuangzi 2007, 216–217) That is, concern for the self gets in the way of the free and wandering ease exemplified by Zhuangzi's true master.

To avert attributions of 'mythical tales,' consider a contemporary real-life parallel that contrasts modern sport, climbing and *wushu* 武術, Chinese traditional martial arts. Dean Potter, a peerless climber, has 'soloed' (climbed without ropes or gear) the Eiger's North Face and then BASE-jumped from it. He has also slacklined—tightrope walked—on an inch-wide rope across a chasm over a thousand feet high in Yosemite, *without* a tether. And yet he confesses, 'that's always been the scariest part of climbing, falling … or right when you are gonna fall […] that would be it, it would be my death.'[11] Familiar as he is putting his life literally on the line, he still feels a whispering but firm tug from the self. Shaolin Kung Fu master Shi Dejian incarnates the Eastern ideal. Peter Gwin writes,

> Without warning he jumps up onto the low wall bordering the lip of the cliff, the wind filling his cape so that it flows out over the void […] standing on the ledge, he smiles at me. 'You are afraid?' he asks, seeing the look on my face. 'Kung Fu is not only training the body; it is also about controlling fear.' He hops lightly from one foot to the other, lunging, punching, spinning, each step inches from a horrifying fall. His eyes widen as he concentrates […] 'You cannot defeat death,' he says […] He kicks a foot out over the abyss, […] 'But you can defeat your fear of death.' (2011, 112)

Most of us would drop to our knees like Lie Yukou, but this is routine activity, however intense, for Dejian. The roots of his fearlessness, which he cultivates daily on the edge of precipices, are found in Laozi, 'if you aren't afraid of dying there is nothing you can't achieve' (1998, chapter 74). What may look like foolishness or recklessness to outsiders is otherwise for the consummate performer. The lack of fear in the case of Shi Dejian is not due to ignorance or an excess. To explain and exemplify with a very different scenario: *recortadores de toros* are people who have learned to dodge the bull by cutting out at the last moment when the bull charges and is about to gore them. This would be foolish for anyone else, but for them *this is precisely how their skill is tested*, by getting as close to the horns as possible as the bull punches with the horns (or by balancing on the rock for Shi Dejian—although in his case it is a bit more complex, since he seeks equanimity in the face of death). In Pamplona, during the running of the bulls, some foreigners confuse the bull with one of the wild cows let our in the ring for enjoyment, trying to emulate the *recortadores*. Their ignorance of the danger and lack of skills makes this reckless (and can be quite costly).

This ability to push the envelope is commensurate with one's talent and dedication, but *ceteris paribus*, dedication, knowing our limitations and taking on risks proportionate to our skills is a valuable way to improve and flourish as human beings. Taking on this kind of risk is also the way to freedom. As we read in the first essay with Sheets-Johnstone, freedom is predicated on personal involvement, and risk brings such involvement. Zen Master Deshimaru Taishen compactly summarizes this Daoist/Buddhist insight as he tersely commands, 'abandon egoism' (1982, 46). If we forsake our selfish, egocentric existence, we lose the 'damning' discriminations that set us apart from others, feed our desires and create anxiety. The idea is that a realization of our unity with the Universe or Dao ultimately leads to a loss of fear, even of our cherished life. Paradoxically, this results in true freedom to live. Whether we come to this realization by sudden or protracted process is unimportant. Buddhist views of self and attachment prove crucial to literally let go of any concerns for ourselves. Potter, while climbing, does so best when he forgets himself. In *Eiger, Unroped* (2011), a film of his solo Eiger climb, the moment he reaches an impasse, unable to reach the next handhold, the self appears with mortal virulence. These examples also show why spontaneity and perfected character, enlightenment, *prajna* or deep insight need to be lived and are a matter of praxis. Intellectually grasping the unreality of the self (akin to accurate arrow-shooting) is not sufficient when we are perched on a cliff fearing for life, literally if we are a climber, or anxious about the next arrow's chance for the gold medal. Only selfless climbing or shooting can help. Reaching this state requires actual practice. Which practices and methodologies are most fruitful is something we explore later alongside Japanese samurai (essay 9). For now, a few apposite and closing comments on selflessness and harmony.

Daoism seeks harmony between the *dao* and us. A harmonious life is peremptory to achieve the integration of our 心, with others and with the world. For Zhuangzi, we become too easily attached to external goods (power, fame, money and hedonistic pleasure), which saps our energies and increases our misery, bringing disharmony. Philosopher Victoria Harrison points out that 'a key part of such harmony is located within the individual' in terms of rational, emotional and vital conciliation, which interestingly 'fed into traditions of martial arts as well as into traditional Chinese medicine' (2013, 134). Thus, it is largely up to us to wilfully nurture harmony without being snared by

HOLISM AND THE CULTIVATION OF EXCELLENCE IN SPORTS AND PERFORMANCE

those external charms. Unsurprisingly, martial arts and Chinese medicine inculcate a certain asceticism that counters those tendencies.

There is also another aspect to harmony, to seek becoming one with the Dao, as Oshima writes (1983, 68). This asks to abandon the perspective of the self. Perspectivism is a way to achieve this decentring by allowing us to realize that our own perspective is but one among others. This has clear echoes in Ortega's views on love.[12] In fact, both Zhuangzi's perfected person and the Orteguian person of excellence nurture a kind of love where boundaries between self and others evanesce. Yet, another point of contact is that both acknowledge the role that circumstances beyond our control play in our lives.[13] Zhuangzi often points out that man plans and Heaven disposes, and that we should not fret about or sweat the small stuff of life (Chuang Tzu and Watson 225–226), while Ortega emphasizes how our life is like a shipwreck but that we should nevertheless press onward regardless in beautiful striving. Sport, under a Greek conception of *aretē*, sets rational conditions for competition, without external elements influencing the event, to obtain a measure of objectivity and minimize chance. Yet, the fact is that chance plays a big role in *any* competition, from untimely flat tires to muscles pulling or unexpected weather. In this case, a Zhuangzian attitude of not being attached to results and the Orteguian one of valuing the quality of the effort prove balsamic for the agonic disappointments of the aretaic model.

In short, Zhuangzi imaginatively and vividly explores a holistic model of skill development. Flourishing integrates form and function in ever refining levels that can range from virtuoso performances to the intellectual and emotional achievement of 'sages.' Living playfully, spontaneously, and in free and easy wandering (the title of chapter one in the *Zhuangzi*), richly nourishes our lives no matter what our initial talents, endowments and limitations are, as the next section shows.[14]

3. Dis~ability as the Fullness of Power

How would Chuang-Tzu help to empower the perception of and self-perception by persons with disabilities? His ideas further support those developed in the literature of sport philosophy (see Jespersen and McNamee 2008), and can contribute novel ways to conceptualize the issue (Jones and Howe 2005). Moreover, Zhuangzi's sensitive stance on the 'crippled,' to use his concrete yet non-pejorative word—*as* used by him —contrasts with, amends and supplements the perspicacious but impractical work of Michel Foucault. For the Frenchman, technologies of production, power, discourse and the self produce our bodies (1965, 1979, 1980). For example, his framework helps show how athletic bodies, under prevailing mores, are produced, inscribed and divested of power, but fail to provide a modicum of meaningful agency (Ilundáin-Agurruza 2008). Zhuangzi's writings supplement and amend this. Moreover, they are relevant to the cultivation of excellence and our skills generally, as they provide us with a broader and richer palette of pragmatic, existential and experiential possibilities. Finally, they also furbish alternative role models that expand current and confining ones that highlight the superficial at the expense of the essential (celebrities, spoiled athletes, etc.).

A few words on terminology before joining the Daoist: in the following 'dis~ability' intends to positively recast the term, and relies on the idea of complementary pairs that opens the essay. I borrow Kelso and Engstrøm's tilde '~', which they use 'not to concatenate words or as an iconic bridge between polarized aspects, but to

111

signify that we are discussing complementary pairs. Equally, if not more important, the tilde symbolizes the *dynamic nature* of complementary pairs' (2008, 7, their italics). Presently, it opens the conceptual space to discuss dis~ability as both *dynamically* limiting *and* empowering through its very conditions of functionality. The pair ability~disability would better fit the pattern, but besides being a cumbersomely long locution, the blending of dis~ability brings both sides closer conceptually. Taking it further, instead of merely pairing abled and disabled, it combines them such that they disappear in each other. Pragmatically, this means that all of us are dis~abled, being more or less able depending on the context. This is the dynamic aspect that takes place between modifier and adjective. Concrete examples will show how disabled people become dis~abled when performing and sometimes outperforming 'abled' people. When referring to work or ideas to be critiqued or outside the bounds of this ameliorative recasting, I use 'disability' in its customary sense but offset by quotation marks.

Discussion of dis~abled people takes place in the inner chapters in particular, chapters four and five mostly, and basically disappears afterward, so we can attribute to Zhuangzi himself the views discussed now. He presents a stance that does not essentialize 'disability,' but rather focuses on empowering functionality. Some of Zhuangzi's most unforgettable characters are dis~abled figures of undeniable charm and power who live in harmony with the *dao*, and whom he presents as examples to follow. This contrasts with the pervading coetaneous Chinese conception. Notoriously, those with physical imperfections were seen as unworthy and often rejected as social outcasts. This was so especially if their malformation was due to a penal sentence: the common punishment for criminals at the time was the amputation of toes, foot, nose or other body parts if recidivist. The fact that disfiguring and disabling a person was the punishment of choice shows the stigma associated with what today we think of as 'disability.' When speaking about hunchbacks, amputees, lepers, madmen or freaks, Zhuangzi's words neither solidify into hideous insult nor disintegrate into condescending euphemism. Rather they show his deep compassion. More crucially, they turn the limiting condition into an opportunity that embodies competence and charisma. With him, they are dis~abled but not 'disabled.' That is, they have endowments that arise out of their very (purported) limitations. Through this, Zhuangzi places at centre stage a segment of the population whose invisibility is directly proportional to the level of discomfort that they elicit in many. In the following story, he recasts how to look at a severely deformed person,

> Cripple Shu—his chin is buried down in his navel, his shoulders are higher than his crown, the knobbly bone at the base of his neck points at the sky, the five pipes to the spine are right up on top, his two thighbones make another pair of ribs. By plying the needle and doing laundry he makes enough to feed himself, and when he rattles the sticks telling fortunes for a handful of grain he is making enough to feed ten. If the authorities are press-ganging soldiers the cripple strolls in the middle of them flipping back his sleeves; if they are conscripting work parties he is excused as a chronic invalid; if they are doling out grain to the sick he gets three measures, and ten bundles of firewood besides. Even someone crippled in body manages to support himself and last out the years assigned him by heaven. If you make a cripple of the Power in you, you can do better still. (Chuang-Tzu and Graham 2001, 74)

HOLISM AND THE CULTIVATION OF EXCELLENCE IN SPORTS AND PERFORMANCE

Savvy Shu's operates within the pliable bounds of dis~ability, turning his condition into a boon. The last sentence pressures us into recognizing how far Shu goes not in spite of his limitations but because of them: he turns them into advantage (taking away many excuses we could forward for lacking in virtue). The closing line may insinuate a duplicitous appraisal that makes us better than cripple Shu. But Chinese is particularly difficult to translate, and other translations suggest other readings more in keeping with the overall gist of Zhuangzi's positive revaluation of dis~ability. Ziporyn renders it, 'And how much more can be accomplished with discombobulated Virtuosity!' (2009, 31)

The story also bespeaks of a holistic outlook where within the *dao*, even those seen as useless become functionally full and useful. Shu's story is part of chapter four which deals with affairs in the world of men. There, the Daoist highlights the usefulness of the useless. Several times in different scenarios, Zhuangzi writes of old imposing trees that are not cut down because they are perceived as useless, being too gnarly, the wood not of the desired quality, unfit for burning and so on. The trees speak to humans (in dreams) or other trees and point out that because of their very uselessness they are able to grow old and live unlike all the useful trees that are cut down and made into furniture, turned into firewood, etc. For Zhuangzi, the useless became tremendously useful precisely because it was *perceived* as useless. Sport, from a utilitarian and instrumental stance as we have seen with Ortega is also useless in this way, being a life-nourishing windfall that is seen as a ludicrous pastime by many. This turns upside down prevailing views. Crandell points out, adding another layer to our hermeneutics here, that this discussion of the useless is rather about promoting 'a *cheerful* indifference in the face of suffering, pain, and loss' (1983, 112).

Kretchmar discusses the power of holism precisely in the context of those who are considered handicapped, and brings an inspiring and contemporary 'Shu-narrative.' He writes of a gentleman he knew (Emil Dannenberg) who, on account of a gymnastics accident, had to have his neck vertebrae fused. As he explains,

> Remarkably enough, he chose the opposite [of a straight neck and upright head]—to have his head forever tilted downward, with his chin virtually affixed to his chest. He made the choice because he was a concert pianist, and he couldn't see the keys unless his head was slanted forward. Cynics would say he made the choice in order to preserve his livelihood.

> I would disagree. When sitting at the keyboard, Dannenberg was in his favorite playground. He made his unusual choice because he could not give that up. Dannenberg had a lovely play spirit and lived a long, productive, and happy life. He married, had children, and became president of Oberlin College. He found play in a lot of different places, not just the piano. Interestingly, *those with whom he regularly interacted never thought of him as handicapped in spite of his very odd appearance*. To be sure, his neck was disfigured, but the handicap wasn't in him. And neither was it to be found between him and the world because he was still able to access his favorite playgrounds. (Kretchmar 2013, 33, my italics)

There are two points I wish to highlight. First, there is a Zhuangzian playfulness to Dannenberg in so far as he nourishes his life in accord with his 'suffering' as we saw above. The second concerns the negative invisibility of 'disability' and positive

HOLISM AND THE CULTIVATION OF EXCELLENCE IN SPORTS AND PERFORMANCE

indiscernibility of dis~ability. 'Disabled' persons are often made invisible in various ways, from how we may turn away our gaze to how they are passed for jobs, or not even given the chance to be met for who they are. When visible, their 'disability' often constitutes their 'badge of shame.' In the context of sport, and to paraphrase the apt title by Purdue and Howe, we should see the sport and not the disability (2012, 189). Relying on Bordieu's habitus and capital, they explore the paradox of seeing the athletes' sporting performance *aside* from 'disability' within the context of Paralympics for abled audiences and also champion their 'disability' for a 'disabled' spectatorship (ibid., 194). While both stances are sensible within the current discourse, Zhuangzi would aim to reframe the issue altogether. We should make invisible the 'disability' *as* handicap, not the athlete or person as performer; we should highlight the ways in which they are dis~abled. This is connected to the specific practice where they functionally excel, and to this extent agrees with the argument by Purdue and Howe, but from a different yet non-antagonistic perspective. It permits to focus on the performance, the sport *and* the heretofore 'disability' now recast as a prowess, a power within *that* sport. To reiterate, we are to think of dis~ability in terms of how the *purported* handicap is actually a strength when wisely nurtured, one through which flourishing is possible.

In Zhuangzi's fifth chapter, which has been translated as 'The Sign of Virtue Complete' (Chuang Tzu and Watson 1968, 68); Höchsmann, Guorong, and Zhuangzi 2007, 110) or 'The Signs of Fullness of Power' (Chuang-Tzu and Graham 2001, 76), tellingly six out of seven stories feature dis~abled characters: three with feet cut-off, a hunchback, a person 'ugly enough to astound the world,' and another one with two persons suffering from severe ailments and disfigurements (Chuang Tzu and Watson 1968, 72). In one of them, someone whose toes have been amputated as a punishment is presented as teaching Confucius himself a lesson. The underlying tenor is that these dis~abled characters, overcoming their constraint, have mastered the art of life. The story of the cicada-catching hunchback is apposite here as well. But to read Zhuangzi again,

> Cripple Lipless with the crooked legs advised Duke Ling of Wey; the Duke was so pleased with him that when he looked at normal men their legs were too lanky. Pitcherneck with the big goitre advised Duke Huan of Ch'i; The Duke was so pleased that when he looked at normal men their necks were too scrawny. To the extent then that Power stands out [in the sense of *de* here, embodied virtue and capacity], we lose sight of the bodily shape. When men do not lose sight of what is out of sight but do lose sight of what is in plain sight, we may speak of 'the oversight which is seeing things as they are'. (Chuang-Tzu and Graham 2001, 80)

Such reversals become splinters that pierce the petrified trunk of prejudice or ignorance. Dannenberg's case himself validates this. Hence, we forget the body as substance and prize the functionality of the person (as a capacity, power or virtue, *de*). *Wuwei* is also an element that enables the process of dis~ability to unfold. Particularly relevant is the idea of turning weaknesses into strengths, and setbacks as opportunities (as Ortega would put it).[15] The opening saying, 'Embrace joyfully your limitations and weaknesses; Suffer gratefully your talents and strengths,' speaks to this.

On the subject of being functional, those seen as 'disabled' are praised for their fortitude and hard work ethic, often pointing out that they compensate by labouring harder, and thus being the equals of abled persons in terms of productivity.

HOLISM AND THE CULTIVATION OF EXCELLENCE IN SPORTS AND PERFORMANCE

This mistakes functionality as capacity with productivity in an economic or utilitarian sense. Such commendation, while rightly celebrating effort, makes this extra labour the price to be accepted as full members of society. In other words, this undercuts the praiseworthiness because it entails that unless they work harder they will not be seen as equal. If fails to realize the many barriers they have to overcome because of bias or thoughtlessness. Their specific dis~ability may be a limitation in a way, but it does not define them nor does it mean that if given the chance, they can live full, playful, meaningful, and yes, productive, lives. This happens in various ways. But the focus is on those that take place through performance.

Performers—athletes, martial artists, dancers, etc.—nurture and develop strategies that enable them to overcome their personal challenges in ways that turn 'disabilities' into empowering dis~abilities. The 'disabled' become paradigms of superior dis~ability when they compete on equal or even better terms with their abled peers, e.g. one-armed basketball player Zach Hodskins—now playing for the University of Florida's national top-tier team. They also develop alternate and novel techniques that allow them not only to cultivate existing internal goods of the practice. Analogously to how Jan Boklov forever changed the spot of ski jumping midair as he tried to avoid crashing and instituted the by now 'mandatory' V- wedge of the skier (Rieland 2014), dis~ably inspired movements also add creatively to the repertoire of kinetic possibilities. In addition, they can also take advantage of their very condition to present novel problems to competitors similar to how left-handed fencers or tennis players pose a different conundrum to their right-handed counterparts (left-handed people being another segment that has faced its own discriminatory practices). Dustin Carter is a young wrestler without arms or legs that manages to beat opponents in the 103-lb class at regular collegiate competitions. He has developed his neck muscles and alternative techniques to this end (Armstrong 2008).[16] Last, at times, the very 'disability' gives an edge in athletic endeavour, transcending their limitation to become 'over-able.' For example, Kevin Connolly is a skier without legs or hips whose lower centre of gravity allows him to sky where 'normal' skiers cannot (Solomon 2010).

To focus on movement and its quality now, when describing how dis~abled people move, they are often characterized as flawed and seen as ungainly. But here, the very dis~ability expands the available epistemological and aesthetic inventory. In the context of dance and bodily knowledge, Jaana Parviainen writes that, 'O'Donovan-Anderson reminds us that the motions of the disabled are no less epistemically valuable than are the more predictably smooth bodily motions of the 'fully-abled' (2002, 17), and raises the important question that we should ask what 'disabled' people know about moving bodies that fully-abled ones do not (ibid). A phenomenology that explores this would be very revealing about their and *our* movement dynamics. An Orteguian rather than Heideggerian attitude to technology is desired as well. Technological advancements, such as customized carbon fibre prosthesis, with suitable techniques to take advantage of these, open up possibilities not only for dis~ability, but for movement itself. Now legally troubled, Oscar Pistorius' Olympic performance illustrates this. Within the context of dance, we can think of how acclaimed dancer Alice Shepard redefines dancing from her wheelchair with rousing choreographies. These novel *I Cans* in the history of humankind—echoing Husserl's coinage—highlight a hybridization where technology and human bodies ask us to devise new conceptual paradigms and methods to comprehend who we are as animate bodies.

HOLISM AND THE CULTIVATION OF EXCELLENCE IN SPORTS AND PERFORMANCE

Having considered physical impairments we should also consider whether these perspectives apply to cognitive ones too. The Chinese sage would enthusiastically agree for the centrality of play and a lusory attitude when it comes to nourishing life, and would sympathetically but without condescension smile on the joy possible for those so challenged. Dewey pedagogically and Ortega existentially concur on the desirability of a ludic, joyful, even humorous for the latter, component to our learning. Kretchmar writes:

> Without downplaying the significance of mental disability, we still need to ask [...] Do they have access to any playgrounds? Can they laugh and find joy and meaning in life? If the answer is yes, or if skilled educators can lead them to their special playgrounds, then in an important sense, they (just like a disfigured pianist who can still play) are not so handicapped after all. (Kretchmar 2013, 33)

At this point, Zhuangzi's perspectivism also becomes useful by helping to call into question discriminations that in this case raise prejudices against cognitive and other impairments—as if holistically we could really split them—which is also more to the point of the Daoist's argument:

> What is acceptable we call acceptable what is unacceptable we call unacceptable. A road is made by people walking on it; things are so because they are called so. What makes them so? Making them so makes them so [...] For this reason, whether you point to a little stalk or a great pillar, a leper or the beautiful His-shih, things ribald and shady or things grotesque and strange, the Way makes them all into one. Their dividedness is their completeness; *their completeness is their impairment. No thing is either complete or impaired,* but all are made into one again. (Chuang Tzu and Watson 1968, 40–41, my italics).

We raise the spectrum of 'disability' as *necessarily* negative based on valuations that Zhuangzi finds problematic not only in terms of practical consequences, but also as a matter of principle. They arise from a partial (mis)understanding whereby people think they are dividing the world according to immutable essences rather than from particular perspectives. The sagely person is able to see through this, as Kretchmar does, and finds the same path and reasons to value playful and nourishing lives.

To summarize, Zhuangzi's discourse changes orthodox perceptions of so-called 'disabled' persons. His views encourage empowerment and value persons functionally, not in terms of anatomical looks or comparative biomechanics. Zhuangzi's cripples are dis~abled, skillfully moving about, resonating in consonance with the Dao, in harmony with life, unaffected and poised. They brim with self-confidence. Were they boats with a broken oar, they would speed ahead with their sails fully stretched out as symbols of might. Thus, they roam, freely and nonchalantly the way Zhuangzi did: in the fullness of power.[17] Exploring the felt dynamics of this fullness, for all of us are dis~abled, takes us to the third section, where we encounter contemporary analyses of skillful development, acquisition and refinement.

NOTES

1. For a more in-depth comparison among the different Chinese schools of thought within the context of Eastern Philosophy and the framework of sport philosophy see Ilundáin-Agurruza and Hata (Forthcoming).
2. Given the radically different translations available, I suggest comparing several. Presently, I choose the version that best fits the concepts to be explained from two deft translations: Red Pine's poetically attuned version and James Legge's more philosophical rendition (1981a, 1981b). I present the alternative in these endnotes. Legge translates these opening words thus: The Tao that can be trodden is not the enduring and unchanging Tao. The name that can be named is not the enduring and unchanging name (1981b).
3. For a similar argument applied to the concept of 'God', see Thomson (2003).
4. 'The best are like water/bringing help to all without competing/choosing what others avoid/hence approaching the Tao/dwelling with the earth/thinking with depth/helping with kindness/speaking with truth/governing with peace/working with skill/moving with time/and because they don't compete/they aren't maligned' (Red Pine 1996, 16).
5. 'Despacico y buena letra' in Spanish. The subsequent discussion on calligraphy makes this more pertinent.
6. When using names and spellings I rely on pinyin transliteration, except when quoting directly (which may use Wade-Giles or other alternative transliterations). Just as with Laozi's *Daodejing*, I rely on various translations that best fit the ideas under discussion. For various translations of the *Zhuangzi* see: Chuang-Tzuˇ and Graham 2001; Höchsmann, Guorong, and Zhuangzi (2007); Online see Legge's translation: http://ctext. org/zhuangzi/full-understanding-of-life; Chuang Tzu and Watson (1968); Zhuangzi and Ziporyn(2009).
7. Francisco Varela, in a video interview 'enviously' remarked how German conveniently distinguishes between 'leib' as a lived, vital and organic body, and 'Körper' as material body, allowing for finer discrimination (PERCRO 2013, http://percro.sssup.it/embod ied2013). Chinese affords more opportunities yet, and as we will see Japanese offers a real trove of conceptual riches.
8. Exceptions would be those who radically redefine the practice, e.g. Fosbury and his flop.
9. Gallagher (2005) uses the example of perceiving a slithering shape in our periphery, a snake. We jump out much as in Libet's experiments, unreflectively and instantaneously. But the wider pragmatic context and wider scope soon change matters, for should we be a herpetologist, upon realizing it is non-venomous, we can then willfully decide to study or even reach out for the snake.
10. In this context, it is telling that the character for *zi* 子, master, is also the character for child. Space limitations prevent discussing the idea of the Uncarved Block.
11. See *Eiger, Unroped* (2011), where Dean Potter soloes the Eiger. http://www.outsideon line.com/featured-videos/adventure-videos/climbing/123861004.html Accessed 7/18/ 2011. It literally ends on a cliffhanger.
12. Höchsmann, based on a German translation, interestingly interprets a story from chapter 14 on filial piety in terms of love rather than, as usually translated, benevolence and convincingly argues for the richer and more consistent interpretation of said passage as a sort of *'dao* of love' (2001, 54–57). This love is absolute, unconditional, without

HOLISM AND THE CULTIVATION OF EXCELLENCE IN SPORTS AND PERFORMANCE

attachment and self-less. Read this way, the rapprochement between Zhuangzi and Ortega is even closer.

13. Yet, another similarity concerns a problem that both face, what if one is good as a robber in terms of vocation? For Ortega, our vocation may be at odds with the moral values we hold—someone's talents may lie in theft, but he may be morally opposed to it. He digs the heels and insists that the best among us embrace our projects regardless of consequences. Zhuangzi's view is more flexible since his perspectivism permeates his ethics more than Ortega's. He considers that we can change our vocation depending on circumstances. Whereas Ortega finds consolation in the quality of the effort, Zhuangzi thinks, as Yearley explains, that we should embrace change and thus not value one thing or result over another, but rather be content with what it is (1983, 129).

14. As to the ulterior motive for using 心, it is but a didactic technique to exemplify the process of skill refinement: initially cumbersome to read at first for most readers, particularly if trying to keep in mind salient characteristics, the successive repetition and mindful attention result in a fluid but richer reading.

15. After three surgeries between ages 18 and 21, due to a degenerative disease in the right knee, the orthopedic surgeons opined that I would develop severe arthritis by my early thirties. Mild exercise seemed to be the course to take. This initial limitation and weakness set me on the road, literally, to a fulsome cycling career, with well over 225,000 miles and substantial elite racing over the last 20 years. There is not an inkling of said arthritis yet as my thirties are behind me. Lack of temperance and failure to further observe *wuwei* has resulted in other self-inflicted ailments, but this is something better left for another occasion.

16. In the rough and tumble world of Mixed Martial Arts, where no one can expect any favours, Nick Newell is a one-armed MMA fighter who, as of January 2014 had a perfect 11–0 record at the World Series (Gile 2014).

17. For this phrase, I borrow from A. C. Graham's translation of the title of chapter five as cited above.

REFERENCES

AMES, R.T. 1998. *Wandering at ease in the Zhuangzi*. Albany, NY: State University of New York Press.

ARMSTRONG, K. 2008. Ohio wrestler overcomes all odds. *Sports Illustrated*. Available at http://sportsillustrated.cnn.com/2008/writers/kevin_armstrong/04/30/carter.0430/ (accessed 13 March 2013).

BEILOCK, S.L. and T.H. CARR. 2001. On the fragility of skilled performance: What governs choking under pressure? *Journal of Experimental Psychology: General* 130 (4): 701–25.

BILLETER, J.F. 2004. *Etudes sur Tchouang-tseu* [Studies on Zhuangzi]. Paris: Éditions Allia.

———. 2010a. *Leçons sur Tchouang-tseu* [Lessons on Zhuangzi]. Paris: Éditions Allia.

———. 2010b. *Notes sur Tchouang-tseu et la philosophie* [Annotations on Zhuangzi and philosophy]. Paris: Éditions Allia.

———. 2010c. *Essai sur l'Art chinois de l'ècriture et ses fondements* [Essay on the Chinese art of writing and its basics]. Paris: Éditions Allia.

BLACKMORE, S.J. 2010. *Consciousness: An introduction*. Oxford: Oxford University Press.

HOLISM AND THE CULTIVATION OF EXCELLENCE IN SPORTS AND PERFORMANCE

BREIVIK, G. 2013. Zombie-like or superconscious? A phenomenological and conceptual analysis of consciousness in elite sport. *Journal of the Philosophy of Sport* 40 (1): 85–105.

CHUANG-TZŬ, A. and A.C. GRAHAM. 2001. *Chuang-Tzŭ: The seven inner chapters and other writings from the book Chuang-Tzŭ*. London: Allen & Unwin.

CHUANG TZU, A. and B. WATSON. 1968. *The complete works of Chuang Tzu*. New York, NY: Columbia University Press.

CRANDELL, M. 1983. On walking without touching the ground: 'Play' in the *Inner Chapters* of the *Chuang-tzu*. In *Experimental essays on Chuang-Tzu*, edited by V.H. MAIR. Honolulu: University of Hawai'i Press: 101–24.

DANTO, A. 1994. *Embodied meanings: Critical essays and aesthetic meditations*. New York, NY: Farrar, Strauss, Giroux.

DESHIMARU, T. 1982. *The Zen way to the martial arts*. Translated by N. Amphoux. New York, NY: Penguin Compass.

EIGER, UNROPED. 2011. *Online video*. Available at http://www.outsideonline.com/featured-videos/adventure-videos/climbing/123861004.html (accessed 18 July 2011).

FOUCAULT, M. 1965. *Madness and civilization; a history of insanity in the age of reason*. Translated by R. Howard. New York, NY: Pantheon Books.

———. 1979. *Discipline and punish: The birth of a prison*. New York, NY: Random House.

———. 1980. *The history of human sexuality*. Vol. I. New York, NY: Vintage Books.

GALLAGHER, S. 2005. *How the body shapes the mind*. Oxford: Oxford University Press.

GILE. 2014. Undefeated one-armed MMA fighter Nick-Newell promoted-to-BJJ black belt. *BJJ News*. Available at http://www.bjee.com/bjj-news/undefeated-one-armed-mma-fighter-nick-newell-promoted-to-bjj-black-belt/ (accessed 5 February 2014).

GWIN, P. 2011. Battle for the Soul of Kung Fu, *National Geographic Magazine* March issue, 94–113.

HARBACH, C. 2011. *The art of fielding: A novel*. New York, NY: Little, Brown.

HARRISON, V. 2013. *Eastern philosophy: The basics*. London: Routledge.

HAY, J. 1993. The human body as microcosmic source of macrocosmic values in calligraphy. In *Self as body in Asian theory and practice*, edited by T. Kasulis, E. Deutsch and W. Dissanayake. Albany, NY: State University of New York Press: 179–212.

HÖCHSMANN, H. 2001. *On Chuang Tzu*. Belmont, CA: Wadsworth/Thomson Learning.

HÖCHSMANN, H., Y. GUORONG, and ZHUANGZI. 2007. *Zhuangzi*. New York, NY: Pearson Longman.

ILUNDÁIN-AGURRUZA, J. 2008. Athletic bodies and the bodies of athletes: A critique of the sporting build. *Proteus: A Journal of Ideas* 25 (2): 15–22.

ILUNDÁIN-AGURRUZA, J. and T. HATA. Forthcoming. Eastern philosophy. In *Handbook for the philosophy of sport*, edited by M. MCNAMEE and W. MORGAN. London: Routledge.

JESPERSEN, E., and M. MCNAMEE. 2008. Philosophy, adapted physical activity and dis/ability. *Sport, Ethics and Philosophy* 2 (2): 87–96.

JONES, C., and DP. HOWE. 2005. The conceptual boundaries of sport for the disabled: classification and athletic performance. *Journal of the Philosophy of Sport* 32 (2): 133–46.

KELSO, J.S. 1995. *Dynamic patterns: The self-organization of brain and behavior*. Cambridge, MA: MIT Press.

KELSO SCOTT, J., and D. A. ENGSTRØM. 2008. *The complementary nature*. Cambridge, MA: MIT Press.

KRETCHMAR, S. 2013. Mind-body holism, paradigm shifts, and education. *Fair Play Revista de Filosofía, Ética y Derecho del Deporte* 1 (1): 28–43.

LAOZI. 1996. *Taoteching*. Translated by RED PINE (Bill Porter). San Francisco, CA: Mercury House.

———. 1998. *Tao Te Ching*. Translated by S. Mitchel. New York, NY: Harper Perennial.

LEGGE, J. 1891a. *Chuang-Tzu*. Available at http://ctext.org/zhuangzi/full-understanding-of-life (accessed 20 Febrauary 2013).

———. 1891b. *Tao Te Ching*. Available at http://classics.mit.edu/Lao/taote.1.1.html (accessed 4 February 2004).

LOLAND, S. 2001. Record sports: An ecological critique and a reconstruction. *Journal of the Philosophy of Sport*. 28 (2): 127–39.

———. 2006. Olympic sport and the ideal of sustainable development. *Journal of the Philosophy of Sport* 33 (2): 144–56.

MCKINNON, R.N. 1953. Zeami on the art of training. *Journal of Asiatic Studies* 16 (1/2): 200–25.

OSHIMA, H.H. 1983. A metaphorical analysis of the concept of mind in the Chuang-Tzu. In *Experimental essays on Chuang-Tzu*, edited by V.H. Mair. Honolulu: University of Hawai'i Press: 63–84.

PARVIAINEN, J. 2002. Bodily knowledge: Epistemological reflections on dance. *Research Journal* 34 (1): 11–26.

PERCRO. 2013. Available at http://percro.sssup.it/embodied2013 (accessed 15 May 2013).

PURDUE, D.E.J. and P.D. HOWE. 2012. See the sport, not the disability: Exploring the paralympic paradox. *Qualitative Research in Sport, Exercise and Health* 4 (2): 189–205.

RIELAND, R. 2014. *Five winter olympians who forever changed their sports*. Smithsonian.com Available at http://www.smithsonianmag.com/innovation/five-winter-olympians-who-for ever-changed-their-sports-180949589/?no-ist (accessed 15 August 2014).

SHEETS-JOHNSTONE, M. 2009. *The corporeal turn: An interdisciplinary reader*. Exeter: Imprint Academic.

———. 2011. *The primacy of movement*. 2nd ed. Amsterdam: John Benjamins.

SLINGERLAND, E.G. 2003. *Effortless action: Wu-wei as conceptual metaphor and spiritual ideal in early China*. Oxford: Oxford University Press.

———. 2004. Conceptions of the self in the *Zhuangzi*: Conceptual metaphor analysis and comparative thought. *Philosophy East & West* 54 (3): 322–42.

SOLOMON, C. 2010. Kevin Connolly will see you now. *Outside Magazine*. Available at http://www.outsideonline.com/outdoor-adventure/athletes/Kevin-Connolly-Will-See-You-Now.html?page=all (accessed 5 October 2012).

STANDAL, Ø. and L. HEMMESTAD. 2011. Becoming a good coach: Coaching and *phronesis*. In *The ethics of sports coaching*, edited by A. Hardman and C. Jones. London: Routledge: 45–55.

SUITS, B. 1990. *The grasshopper: Life, games and Utopia*. Boston, MA: David R. Godine.

TAYLOR, C. 1989. *Sources of the self*. Cambridge, MA: Harvard University Press.

THOMSON, G. 2003. *On philosophy*. London: Thomson-Wadsworth.

WU, K.-M. 1982. *Chuang Tzu: World philosopher at play*. New York, NY: Crossroad Pub. Co.

WU, K.-M. and ZHUANGZI. 1990. *The butterfly as companion: Meditations on the first three chapters of the Chuang Tzu*. Albany, NY: State University of New York Press.

YEARLEY, L. 1983. The perfected person in the radical Chuang-tzu. In *Experimental essays on Chuang-Tzu*, edited by V.H. Mair. Honolulu: University of Hawai'i Press: 125–39.

ZHUANGZI and B. ZIPORYN 2009. *Zhuangzi: Essential writings with selections from traditional commentaries*. Indianapolis, IN: Hackett.

SECTION III: HOLISTIC BRIDGES: THE MIND SCIENCES, PHENOMENOLOGY, AND OUR SKILLS

Jesús Ilundáin-Agurruza

This section rides on the back of the pragmatic dark horses we just encountered. Its conceptual and methodological boundaries, because of direct influence or philosophical affinity, are contiguous with the framework laid out by James, Dewey, Ortega, and Zhuangzi—whose foundational work is now referenced at specific points. They have helped build a holistic integration of skills where spontaneous action permits us to act creatively and successfully. The holistic bridges connect to this 'historical' work, span the present essays, and lead to the project's closing section. These three essays center on contemporary work across a diverse range of fields and methodologies: empirical studies by neuroscientists, cognitive psychologists and psychologists of sport, or work in the philosophy of mind and philosophical psychology. But phenomenology, however, leads the way. Breaking away from traditional accounts of skilled action that tend to automatize and make subpersonal (subconscious) the skillful aspect, an alternative model is developed based on a radically enactive cognition that eschews representations for capacities. This helps explain the unique phenomenology of expertise, which is recast as a skillful fluency that results in paragons developing kinetic signatures. Fractured action, concretized in the phenomenon of choking in sports, offers the underside of excellent performance. Nonetheless, failure may also be the source of valuable lessons.

6—WAKING UP FROM THE COGNITIVIST DREAM—THE COMPUTATIONAL VIEW OF THE MIND AND HIGH PERFORMANCE

Jesús Ilundáin-Agurruza

At that moment, when I had the TV sound off, I was in a 382 mood; I had just dialed it. So although I heard the emptiness intellectually, I didn't feel it. My first reaction consisted of being grateful that we could afford a Penfield mood organ. (Dick 1968, 5)

Maybe the only significant difference between a really smart simulation and a human being was the noise they made when you punched them. (Pratchett and Baxter 2012, 72)

When thinking hard, people will furrow their brow. Whether they countenance the conundrum of dialetheism (simultaneously true and false statements), ponder a bouldering problem, or visualize a complex pattern of choreographed dance steps or moves in a karate kata, furrowed brows wrinkle faces and ease tasks. It is neither accident nor wonder that we usually 'think' better when we move, from localized facial gestures to expansive whole-body dynamics. For example, hand and bodily movement lessen cognitive load and facilitate activities as abstract as mathematical problem solving (Brown and Reid 2006; Lakoff and Nuñez 2000). Of course, the claim is only interesting if somehow the movements are constitutive of, and integral to, the actual thinking and not a matter of mere contingency. A thick holistic and enactive conception of our cognition and abilities sees this as natural: a seamless continuity and overlap between body(mind) and (body)mind as we kinetically work our way through the world, perhaps with aspirations of an integrated bodymind. This essay begins to explore the intimate connection between movement, cognition, and excellence. Ultimately, their interactions result in phenomenologically rich lived experiences, and normative and ecological constraints and affordances of ethic and aesthetic dimensions, as the next essays will show. But before getting there, we need to show why other influential stances are no longer viable and find suitable a bridge.

The first section undertakes a critical overview of traditionally influential views on cognition given how deeply the mind sciences influence our understanding of skilled movement and its cultivation. The eye-catching National Geographic spreads of rainbow-hued brains and neurons firing like wondrous fireworks—as beautiful as *seemingly* innocuous—color perceptions and mislead with reifying duplicities and body–brain dualism. We wrongly adapt our expectations then, believing that our skills and excellence (or lack of) are simply a matter of different parts of the brain lighting up in different tones. The popular imagination and some neuroscientists do ascribe to neurons themselves capacities well beyond the evidence, such as the idea that discrete neurons can store psychological items (e.g. memories) (Sutton 2014). To temper this, three segments conduct a critique of the underlying cognitivist and computational, reductionist, and representational views of our bodymind, action, and movement. This leads to a transitional section on embodied cognition that discusses several of its salient conceptualizations. Last, radical enactivism is adopted as most advantageous to develop a thickly holistic account of expert skills where spontaneity and mindful but empty states are central and tested on the sharp edge of expert performance.

1. The Philosophical Woes and Foes of Cognitivism, Representationalism, and Reductionism

Presently, there are two main models that purport to explain our cognition and, by extension, our performances through movement, often conceptualized in terms of action: cognitivism, which has been at the forefront of the sciences of the mind (cognitive science, neuroscience, neurobiology, etc.) and embodied cognition, which is changing the terms of engagement, and may already be the new standard for some (Hutto and Myin 2013). Mainstream cognitivism advances a computational model of the mind. Our minds, conceived of as computers, process abstract symbols that encode representations of the world. In this sense, this is a representational view. In neuroscience, a representation refers to 'the complex neuronal firing patterns responsible for planning and carrying out bodily movement and action' (Gallagher 2012, 244). It also assumes a rule-based operating system where said rules are understood propositionally. Further, explicit awareness is the primary mode of cognitive function (Thagard 2012). Among our faculties, and aligned with a long-standing philosophical tradition, rational thought is favored. Simply put, according to cognitivism, we are rational beings who conceptualize experiences abstractly. A computational theory of the mind specifies this. Ontologically, this cognitive model is sometimes coupled to reductionism. This argues that our mental life reduces to neurons and the workings of the brain, where representations are encoded (Churchland 1988). Some, for example, Daniel Dennett (1991), take the more extreme but arguably more consistent step and embrace eliminativism. This dispenses with 'folk talk' as meaningful regarding minds. Functionalism, a related, though metaphysically independent view in philosophy of mind, holds that what matters to account for our minds, cognition, and consciousness is having the proper information and the operative rules not the specific physical support system (in principle, a silicon-based artificial intelligence is possible). Yet Paul Thagard observes, 'The claim that human minds work by representation and computation is an empirical conjecture and might be wrong' (2012, 15). Next, we examine three prevailing but problematic views: (1) computational approaches to cognition and action; (2) reductionism (presently, eliminativism serves under the reductive banner for practical purposes unless otherwise noted); and (3) representational theories of perception and cognition. All three face criticism. Sport philosophy is engaged to provide alternative reasons to further question these, at least in regard to their capacity to explain highly skilled performance.

HOLISM AND THE CULTIVATION OF EXCELLENCE IN SPORTS AND PERFORMANCE

1.1. Computational Conundrums

Computational cognitivists may dream of electric sheep when it comes to artificial intelligence, but realizing the dream of a full and solely computational account of the mind seems to be dissipating with the dawn of cognitively embodied approaches. The theoretical and scientific landscape has changed dramatically recently. Yet, Gualtiero Piccinini states, 'Computationalism is controversial but resilient to criticism' (2012, 222). Attesting to this, the pull of the mind sciences on the public sphere is phenomenal. They have taken by storm current discourse and research agendas on cognition. Despite its fruitfulness on a number of fronts, there are substantial reasons that cast a shadow of doubt over this scientific approach and its promise to *fully* explain how the brain works and gives rise to the mind, and above all to draw substantiated connections with our form of life *if* it remains committed to a reductionist model.

To the credit of computation, we are approaching the twentieth anniversary of IBM's Deep Blue victory over chess champion Garry Kasparov. Nowadays, even commercial computer games can beat the best human chess players regularly, and as journalist Finlo Rohrer puts it, 'Today, the world's best player, Magnus Carlsen, would be foolish to make a Levy-style bet': in 1968 David Levy's bet that by 1978 no computer would have beat him at chess (2013). He won the bet. But chess is a very special kind of game, highly formalized, where sheer computational power can crunch its way through vast numbers of calculations per second, as many as 33.86 petaflops (i.e. 33,860 trillion calculations) per second (O'Mahony 2013). Even more sobering, 'Experts even predict the arrival of "exa-scale" computers—which are 1000 times faster than 1-petaflops-level computers [...] by 2018' (Otake 2012). Computational accounts excel when it comes to accounting for and easily surpassing certain of our rational and mathematical endowments. The fanfare is somehow muffled when it comes to our linguistic abilities. Currently, no computer comes close to basic linguistic competency: double entendres, *le mot juste*, jokes, poetry, fiction, not to mention the suggestive charms of intonation are all a pipedream forever lost on computers, metaphorically speaking or not. Thus, even while staying within the 'intellectual' sphere, meaningful, pragmatic, and extensive computational success is elusive. Our biology, how we *actually* operate, and the phenomenology of our experience place further pressure on cognitivism and its computational promissory note.

When it comes to a full-blooded and fully bodied challenge, the computational account crashes. And if history and induction can serve as points of reference, the challenge is formidable: to date, emulating even simple movements any healthy human being performs routinely remains problematic. Neuroscientist Richard Firestein, in the context of extolling the epistemic importance of ignorance, writes, 'More than a century of robotics research has failed to produce a machine that can walk more than a few steps on two legs, let alone backward or up a slightly sloping plane, not to even mention steps' (2012, 128). Our everyday bodily movements, while mundane, are a marvelously finely tuned coordinative achievement that we simply do, and which we learn to carry out while our rational abilities are still lagging behind. Moreover, as Firestein clarifies, 'Walking around on two legs is in fact in many ways a more complex and demanding mental task than much of what goes on in the visual system' (2012). It is no coincidence that Firestein singles out the visual system, since that is the system that philosophers and scientists favor by default.[1] But as Firestein's assessment suggests, our motility is deserving of as much (if not more) attention and respect (leaving aside the issue of cross-modality). These are matters of biological 'fact,' of how we are put together.[2] To digress while making a related point: a bipedal and upright posture has done more to enable our cognition that any other evolutionary step we may have taken, the much-touted opposable thumb included. Before we could indulge in manual endeavors we had to first free hands and arms. This came courtesy of our feet and erect posture. How we have developed our motile talents brings on additional computational headaches. Performative endeavors pose particular challenges.

As mentioned above, computational models rely on explicit awareness of rules when it comes to primary cognitive function. This is problematic because many of our movements, from gross to refined, are beyond our *explicit* computational powers. In other words, accounting for common tasks computationally proves unfathomable for current models. Nonetheless, many of these complications are practical shortcomings of current technological capabilities that better engineering, computing power, and generous funding could potentially overcome. But, if walking is already a challenge, what are we to say in consideration of sports and activities where coordination, speed, and dexterity are crucial, even at the merely competent level, not to say the elite one? This is a good time to consider how expert performance in sport and other kinetic pursuits presents its own challenges for computational views of the mind. Some of these challenges seem technologically and conceptually insurmountable for computational accounts.

Birch's assesses the promises of neuroscience from the perspective of sport (2010). In particular, he questions neuroscientific/philosophical claims that (1) mental rehearsal is analogous to motor planning of natural movements, (2) that differences in performance lie in the neurons themselves, and (3) the shift from efficient to focused neural networks, offering a pointed critique that basically challenges their lack of discriminatory capacity (289 ff.). More broadly, while he also finds much to learn from the sciences of the mind, Birch argues that they are unable to cross the gap between phenomenal consciousness and reductive accounts (296). Birch's view is that the neurosciences (here referred to as mind sciences) are useful for understanding lower level workings of the brain that help address issues such as blocking pain to improve performance, but that when it comes to explaining phenomenal consciousness they do not make a difference (298). He does not develop his views beyond the critique and his careful assessment of Edelman's views on consciousness lie beyond the scope of this project. Yet, his affinity to phenomenology and some of his rejoinders, which point to the need to abandon brain-centered views for full-bodied ones, suggest that his views are amenable to or at least consistent with thick holism.

For his part, Vegard Moe (2005) develops a thorough critique of cognitivism in the context of sport relying on the phenomenological views of Dreyfus and Searle's analytic stance.[3] Both philosophical stalwarts are staunch critics of cognitivism. Their views are radically different methodologically and conceptually, yet both argue that a computational cognitivism problematically entails that we need to process a countless number of items of discrete information in a short amount of time. As already mentioned, high performance only accentuates this. Further, Moe explains how Dreyfus argues that cognitivism fails to account for a rich interpretive background and that, for his part, Searle contends that cognitivism does not consider how neurophysiological processes are ultimately biological facts.

Philosophical puzzles aside, cognitivism addresses the problems of speed and the need for explicit awareness and computation through a theory of automatization.

Schmidt and colleagues hypothesize a higher order executive level in charge of outputs at a lower level organized in a three-step process of stimulus identification, determination of the response, and motor organization adapted to the chosen action.[4] This seems like a sound move conceptually, because of the cognitivist and computational precept for explicit awareness and its emphasis on higher order thoughts; however, it actually complicates matters. Now there is a need to explain a gatekeeper that decides which rules to call upon and when to do so. That is, we encounter a homunculus problem that raises the issue of regression: we posit a gatekeeper that in turn needs another gatekeeper to act as 'decider' and so on. Elite sport and performances give the lie to computational automatization: performing at this level means that the speed to recall and then choose among these rules soon overloads the capacity for explicit processing. For example, a race car driver who must navigate unexpected debris on account of a competitor's crash requires instantaneous adaptations that prevent any sort of representational and rule-based operation of the sort that a two-level framework (automatic and explicit) can handle in real time. In other words, the sort of spontaneous Zhuang-zian execution is not feasible on this model. When performing, experts do not follow rules since doing so on the explicit, conscious neural pathways central to cognitivism soon overloads its limited bandwidth. Outsourcing the process to an unconscious and implicit system, however, fails because it does away with the need for computation in the strong sense the position needs.

A computational model cannot account for elite skillful action in sport, martial arts, and performing arts because it can neither representationally operate the skillful movements of high-level performers (in some ways it contradicts them) nor does it provide a satisfactory explanation of both subpersonal and spontaneous activity that makes such action possible (Krein and Ilundáin 2014). This does not mean that the role of conscious control and attentional awareness are out of the question in elite performances. In fact, as it will be argued throughout *Skillful Striving*, there is *need* for conscious awareness in expert performance, but in quite specialized ways that are best explained in terms of a blended holistic and enactive model. This also challenges the applicability of the hard and fast distinction between the implicit and explicit systems, *at least* for expert action. The fact is that our very bodies are essential to *how* we cognize and experience the world. It is because of our morphology and how we move that we experience the world *the* way we do, as the comments on bipedalism above suggest. Were we to slither around in serpentine fashion, our cognition and phenomenology would be adapted to perceive heat and vibrations over visual stimuli. This can be further conceptualized in terms of Gibson's (1979) notion of affordances, practical ways of engaging the environment and its objects in ways that allow us to use them. As phenomenologist Shaun Gallagher elaborates when considering the cases of a chair, a pencil, and a mountain, affordances 'are properties that depend on the agent who has a kind of body with bendable joints that will enable sitting, or who knows how to write, or who is in good physical shape for mountain climbing' (2012, 71). Because a computational cognitivism checks out at the door the extraneural or non-neocortical body, not to mention the environment, much that is phenomenologically crucial is left out.

This already points to a deeper problem that no amount of technological or biological modifications can tackle: the phenomenal aspect of performers' experiences. Cognitivism's strictly external and objectifying stance necessarily precludes any account of the *felt* realities of our experience. These are crucial to fully understand experience, cognition, movement, and action given their specificity to particular bodies and their environments. The idea is to capture also the qualitatively felt dynamics of movement such that our understanding of how we think and act are thereby validated experientially. To recast this in analytic terms, there is a phenomenal consciousness, which refers to the 'what it is like' to feel or think something; this is contrasted with access consciousness, which entails availability concerning use in reasoning and rational guidance of speech and action (Block 1995). While neuroscientific, anatomic, and biological accounts can describe and explain phenomena in objective ways and provide rich accounts of access consciousness and its processes, they fall short when it comes to phenomenal consciousness. It is doubtful that the only significant difference between a really smart computer simulation and a human being is the noise they make when you punch them ... especially if you are the one being punched. This makes all the difference. Phenomenological descriptions are versatile, capable of incorporating the former into their accounts as well, punches and all. They also provide a Janus faced look where we can observe the manifold and changing nature of our experiences while also finding an intersubjective validity that confirms the common structure of our experiences (essay 7 elaborates on this). It does not exclude findings from the sciences of the mind, but it reduces their aspirations.

1.2. Reductive Retreat

To recap the key idea from the preceding discussion and point it forward: reductionism is unable to bridge the subjective–objective gap or explain the phenomenal aspect of our experience. Even when cognitive scientists ostensibly embrace a holistic model, so long as it is embedded and reduced to the brain and neural systems, holism is but a misapplied label. Cognitive scientists Arne Dietrich and Oliver Stoll propose that consciousness is 'composed of various attributes, such as self-reflection, attention, memory [...] ordered in a functional hierarchy [...] this implies a *holistic view* in which *the entire brain* contributes to consciousness' (2010, 165, my emphasis). For them, holism is about the whole *brain*. Crucially, they leave out the rest of the body and the relations with its environment in *any* genuine sense. Yet, as Gallagher argues, filling the explanatory gap 'is not a matter of bridging it with intermediate elements, for example, with theoretical models, causal mechanisms, or representations. We need to work with *what there is* [...] to create a coherent and contextually rich background theory that supports and explicates the connections that actually exist among the elements of the embodied cognitive system' (2005, 6, Gallagher's emphasis). The culprit, however, is unabated reductionism and not the mind sciences per se. The latter provide bountiful insights into our cognition and abilities, but misfire when they pledge themselves to a philosophically suspect reductive model. Following John Dewey, we might say that if reductive approaches are 'the whole story, bodily action would be wholly assimilated to inorganic action, and the inclusion of the body in behavior that has a mental quality would be impossible' (1963, 307). Given the tenacious theoretical grip of reductionism, six further objections are advanced.

First, as Gallagher contends, the correlations that reductive methods draw between neural correlates and various phenomena 'do not constitute *explanations*, and indeed, such correlations are in part what need to be explained' (2005, 6, his emphasis).

Second, these reductive approaches never remain circumscribed to neural, cerebral, and physiological aspects. Eventually, the attempt is made to connect the purely physiological elements to meaningful processes, phenomena, and events in our lives. That is, correlations are drawn between the neural processes and, for example, specific emotions, experiences such as flow or choking, or overarching narratives that appeal to broader ideas in aesthetics, morality, and the like. Third, when neuroscientists and others fully embrace reductive tenets, this tends to result in misinterpreted data, mistaken assumptions, or partial understanding of the phenomena. For example, with a particularly known set of experiments on agency, Gallagher and Zahavi (2008) explain the experimenters asked good questions about pre-reflective agency, but were confused as to what it was they were actually testing. Chemero (2009), arguing against what he calls ruthless reductionism, discusses a similar problem where scientists were confounded, as he puts it. He reviewed 116 papers and found that 72% had methodological problems where the researchers 'gave little or no information concerning the specific objects that were given for exploration' [experiments concerned animal cognitive response to objects], which made 'the results difficult to interpret and virtually impossible to generalize across experiments' (Chemero 2009, 173). Fourth, there are also technological limitations that also affect methodology and results. As Scott Kelso (1995) points out, fMRI studies have a significant 2-s time lag between the vascularization in the brain and the neural activity measured; moreover most of these studies are linear ones whereas the brain is non-linear, parallel, and distributed. In sum, there is misrepresentation of the brain's structure and the images are not true to the dynamic neuronal processes. Moreover, extrapolations from studies are also seriously compromised. As Beall and Lowe (2014) show, even in the best cases there is a 30% chance of motion noise interference with cadavers, whose brains have no activity or motion at all (!). To put the nail in the coffin, sometimes the very empirical evidence disagrees and is open to contrasting hypotheses and interpretations. Jeannerod highlights how fMRI and metabolic brain-mapping are incongruent when it comes to capturing cortical activation of intentional actions (1997). A fifth, and deeper problem, considered at length next, entails the misattribution of the scope of psychological predicates, the resulting duplicitous 'brainbody dualism,' and its resultant phenomenological miscues.

No self-respecting neuroscientist would be caught brandishing the Cartesian dualist flag today. Rather neuroscience flies the banner of monistic naturalism, where brain bits account for the mental. And yet, when neuroscience is exclusively focused on the brain and embraces reductionism the result is 'brain dualism.' To explain, if cognitive neuroscience reduces the mind to neurons, neurotransmitters, and other elements of the central nervous system, the brain is not only necessary but suffices to explain the mental. Thus, to be in mood 382, or having one's memories implanted, as Blade Runner Deckard comes to learn in Philip K. Dick's novel, is but a matter of physically encoded neurons. Brain dualism results from splitting us into body and brain, where the brain accounts for the thinking element alone. Consistency then seems to lead to the conclusion that all we need is a brain in a vat (Putnam 1982), something Dennett ingeniously argued for (1981, 1991).[5] Even an anti-functionalist like Searle agrees with the scenario, as Gallagher (2005) writes, for when he champions neurobiology, Searle also appeals to the brain in the vat. This popular scenario in the literature does away with any nonneuronal input. In fact, if the brain is the wheel that makes things go around, there is no need for spokes, rim, or even roads on which to move about; there is no need for efferent or afferent neural pathways, a body, and much less a physical or social environment. A zany scientist and the brain to which he feeds a virtual world of experiences suffice (ignoring the fact that scientist and lab are already external to the vatted brain). Its *initial* plausibility and persuasiveness are clear. Based on the assumption that if experiences *really* take place in the brain, as the one necessary element without which thought is not possible, then proper stimulation will result in the world we would 'normally' experience. Such intuition pumps, much touted by Dennett, *seem* very persuasive. But analysis under a cooler head shows that they infuse a lot of hot air on an empty brain shell. A variety of reasons advise against brain dualism.

Bennett and Hacker (2003) argue that in so far as they adopt neurobiological reductionism Dennett, Searle, and neuroscientists such as Francis Crick and Antonio Damasio commit the mereological fallacy. This consists in attributing psychological states to the brain. As they put it, 'We know what it is for human beings to experience things, to see things, to know or believe things [...] But do we know what it is for *a brain* to see or hear, for *a brain* to have experiences, to know or believe something'? (Bennett and Hacker 2003, 70) Derisively, but clearly, they summarize: 'The brain does not hear, but it is not deaf, any more than trees are deaf' (2003, 72). They show that it is not merely a *façon de parler* or metaphorical speech, but rather a category mistake that fails to realize that ascribing psychological predicates to people or animals is *conceptually* bound with the meaning of the relevant predicate: 'Pain-behavior is a criterion —that is, *logically* good evidence for being in pain—and perceptual behavior [...] is a criterion for the animal's perceiving' (2003, 82). The reductionist mereological fallacy trades substance dualism for body dualism because it 'replaces the immaterial Cartesian mind by the material brain [which] retains the fundamental *logical structure* of dualist psychology' (2003, 111, their italics). Now we have an unthinking body and a thinking brain that is ascribed the psychological predicates that matter. Where Bennett and Hacker address the conceptual issue, phenomenologist Maxine Sheets-Johnstone considers the phenomenological facet.

Sheets-Johnstone has extensively argued against reductionism and Dennett's eliminativist and brain-centric views from a phenomenological perspective. For her, brains in vats are paradigmatic of what she calls the 'brain–body problem' (Sheets-Johnstone 2011, 374), the consequence of which is that 'in effect, a material brain ultimately eliminates a dispensable material body' (2011, 350). Her thorough and multi-pronged criticism exceeds the scope of the present essay, yet particular portions bear rehearsal for our purposes. First, the scenario sets up the scientists feeding the virtual experiences through neural stimulations. They have access to these simulations from a first person perspective, as if these were their own experiences. Otherwise, they would neither know what the brain is experiencing nor would they be able to feed suitable information. But doing this necessitates that someone *actually* have an animate body that experiences the world full force: proprioceptively, kinesthetically, and kinetically. Second, a vatted brain scenario cannot account for the experience of reflexive spontaneity because it is predicated on the fact that it is force-fed, and this is short of alchemical wizardry, as Sheets-Johnstone (2011) characterizes it. The sense of spontaneity here is one where the agent realizes it is her experience and actions (this is Gallagher's sense of ownership, see 2005). Third, how then are we to account for agency? How can we make the brain in the vat feel as if it is the agent of the actions fed into it? The point here is that much of our sense of agency is tried to the particular felt resonances of kinesthetic and proprioceptive qualities (Sheets-Johnstone 2011). We feel we are hitting a backhand because of the particular way wielding a tennis racquet feels when gripping it, feeling its tactile reverberation and resonances. Thus, when we wield the racket, in each instant of movement, the wieldiness of the racket is at play in my feeling of my moving body, as David Morris explains when he details the phenomenology of wielding objects (2002). Put another way, it is not a problem of replication per se. It is a matter of accounting for (a) how we *can* know that we reproduce the phenomenology of any given experience and (b) the spontaneity and agency, which in turn connect with the phenomenology of *how* we feel as moving agents. *Riding the Wind* investigates this.

Alternatively and additionally, almost a century ago, Dewey explained how a neuroscientific *bias* worsens the mind–body problem,

> It is one thing to employ, for example, the distinction between central and peripheral ori-gin of the existence of this and that idea as part of the technique of determining their respective cognitive validities, and quite another to assume that ideas and conscious con-tents are already intrinsically marked off in themselves [...] and that the problem is simply to find physiological equivalents for their distinction. As far as it is assumed that modes of consciousness are in themselves already differentiated into sensory, perceptual, concep-tual, imaginative, retentive, emotional, conative [...] physiological study will consist simply of search for the different bodily and neural processes that underlie these differences. The outcome is an exacerbation of the traditional mind-body problem. (1925, 341)

Dualism, whether Platonic,[6] Cartesian, or reductionist often leads to a mistrust or even a loathing of the body. The outcome favors the cerebral cortex, intellectualism, and a scientific and philosophical partiality toward our higher cognitive functions and thoughts. This supports a model of cognition that relegates all else to the 'dark dun-geons' of pre-human physiology and evolution. This is problematic because it is too partial to adequately explain the rich phenomena with which it deals. Further, the reductionist tendency to strictly favor a rational and theoretical model of knowledge for the higher operations of the brain's cortex then leaves out practical know-how as a les-ser kind of knowledge. Ironically, this view depends on said pragmatic knowledge to be able to carry out many cognitive tasks. In fact, it arises out of corporeal engagements with the world. For one, our 'purely' intellectual pursuits, predicated on this separation of theory and practice, are the result of habits and productions that soon overstep the narrow confines of intellectualized ivory towers and theoretical realms, 'intellectual habits like other habits demand an environment, but the environment is the study, library, laboratory and academy. Like other habits they produce external results, posses-sions' (Dewey 1988, 50). The case is that most of our comings and goings in life are *that*, practical affairs that engage our whole being. Even when the mathematician, in a frenzy, scribbles a proof's steps he is anything but *just* a mind thinking abstractions. His whole bodymind is engaged in the task, starting with the very excitement he feels, and the very fact that he *cares* about that proof, which manifests itself in perspiration, quick-ened breath, and yes, much necessary cortical activity. What to say of a fencer as she both performs cuts, lunges, ripostes, and parries while in the thick of the action.

When exclusively attended to and cut off from the practical and underlying habits, know-how, and skills, we end up with skewed philosophies less than true to the facts of life; we get intuition pumps; we effect artificial divisions. In athletics, we find the myths of dumb jocks and meatheads. These are propagated by how we organize institutions of higher learning (Reid 2012), or how the media and even managers speak of and to their athletes. The sport sciences, biomechanics, and physiology, when they adhere to strictly reductive and quantitative analyses, end up ignoring the deeper reasons that make those relevant in the first place. Aesthetics provides a concrete and instructive example of this bias. It is of interest for two reasons, because the arts nowadays have been legitimized as *intellectual* pursuits, and because the connection of many of them to bodily labor was an enduring stigma. Most of our 'fine arts' started as physically dependent, derided practices. Poetry, as the most intellectual and abstract of the arts, was held as the highest among them from Ancient Greece onward; those that involved physical and manual work, such as sculpture or painting, were demoted to the status of lowly craftsmanship. Michelangelo vigorously and testily fought to raise the status of sculpture once painting had been 'promoted.' Many would not be fully incorporated until the Illustration sharply distinguished fine arts from crafts in the eighteenth century (Beardsley 1966).

To remain with the arts, dualism rears its dual head and divides the very idea of self-cultivation. For Dewey, we are taught (with the support of science) that the art of the artist is merely repetition where skill without thought is the aim until 'suddenly, magically, this soulless mechanism is taken possession of by sentiment and imagination and it becomes a flexible instrument of mind' (1988, 51). Nine decades later, widespread views in the mind sciences and philosophy still support this view: effortless, superb performance is mindless we read (Bruya 2010; Dreyfus 1986). This is but another case of wizardry where the faux veneer of an answer is taken for the bright reflections that intimate deep understanding. Of course, there is repetition in the skill of the artist, performer, or athlete, but that on its own neither produces the greatness that master performers embody and enact nor does it explain 'mere' expert action. There is many a dedicated person who tirelessly works at it with respectable but no exemplary results. If there is room for empty minds, these are of a different nature than the 'mindless' as we shall see. Experts evince a higher degree of integration of their holistic bodymind. Coaching or mentoring, luck, and talent (these days often couched as genes), and disciplined hard work are ingredients in the recipe for success.[7] Mere appeal to either environment or genetic makeup, or a combination, does not constitute a full and satisfying answer. For now, there are further reasons not to jump on the reductionist train.

It is instructive to consider the morphogenesis of life, that is, how the origin of life results in particular life forms in the literal sense of specific bodies. Zoologist Theodore Torrey writes, 'Protoplasm exists solely in the form of organisms and any consideration apart from living things is a meaningless abstraction,' (Feduccia and McCrady 1991, 3). He explains, 'the word protoplasm does not describe a homogeneous something which, like water, possesses distinctive chemical properties [...] the term is a pervasive one that describes all the permutations of form and function in living systems' (Feduccia and McCrady 1991). If we exchange brain for protoplasm, we have a parallel for the arguments displayed above. That is, biology, which should be a discipline closer to the neurobiological constructs beloved by reductionists, gives us a model that advises against positing a mereological and dualist brain. Put differently, biology also endorses a functional perspectivism since the 'very stuff of life,' protoplasm, is not a *something* but a term that describes permutations of form and function, as Dewey would argue. This last point leads us to the sixth and last problem, reification.

HOLISM AND THE CULTIVATION OF EXCELLENCE IN SPORTS AND PERFORMANCE

Body–brain dualism also reifies the mind (and cognition, and movement) as a substance, thereby committing to an ontological quagmire. Positing a substance and reducing animate dynamics to stuff, to the brain and its neural and motor structure and processes, stultifies the very living and energetic qualities we wanted to study. It turns them into dead specimens much as taxidermy, in stuffing the animals, cannot but give an ersatz impression of the animated and beautiful creatures they once were. Alternatively, the problem is how to explain the life of the (body)mind, its subjectivity, when all there is supposed to be is neural tissue, a brain, and its physiological operations. This mirrors the mistake that modern philosophers such as Descartes, Locke, and Berkeley made when conceiving of ideas as 'things.' Not until a post-Kantian and phenomenological view that could understand ideas not as objects but as *ways of experiencing* could the impasse be broken. A philosophical shift is required: we should think and speak in terms of *how* we experience things—the conditions of experience—rather than *what* we experience; we should give precedence to functionality over mechanisms. This is readily applicable to a holistic phenomenology and is crucial to a proper description and understanding of the sorts of functions and processes that result in supreme skills. It is also of import to facilitate and conceptualize the cultivation of sporting expertise. Before getting there, we must examine and set aside representation.

1.3. Representational Redundancy

Plato, ostensibly a dualist was quite unlike a Cartesian dualist—which is the tradition that has channeled prevailing Western views. He may have seen the body as a shackle to the mind, yet he recognized its instrumental value in terms of education and character building. In particular, he appreciated the role of gymnastics and training, lauding this in many works, as Reid details (2007, 2010, 2012). On the other side, he was deeply mistrustful of mimesis. As a re-presentation and copying of (formal) reality, mimesis was never to be trusted nor trifled with for the broad shouldered former wrestler. When it comes to the (body)mind and its workings, this mistrust of representation is something we best be mindful of. Not to be misled by ambiguities that multiply as in a Borgesian game of mirrors, it is advisable to specify what representation stands for presently.

Gallagher (2012) explains that a representation in neuroscience refers to our movements and actions' complex neuronal firing patterns. These are given symbolic and formal 'meaning' that can stand for rules or patterns we use to move, think, and act. This can incorporate, but at a lower level of description, 'representation' understood as visual imagery, as Breivik (2013) does when discussing consciousness and athletic practice. He uses the notion of representation to speak of how elite performers often picture their own body images and movements when engaged in performance. Breivik is not concerned with computational models that engage representation as symbolic structures or motor images. Visual self-representation poses its own challenges, mostly in terms of epistemic misrepresentation of what one's movements actually are or look like, e.g. as Downes details regarding his own misperception of what he looks like when bouldering—rock climbing boulders without ropes of harnesses (2010). The focus now is on the empirical rather than the conceptual level (Fodor 1975, 1987; Pylyshyn 1984), which Hutto and Myin (2013) extensively critique. Because empirical work concerning

HOLISM AND THE CULTIVATION OF EXCELLENCE IN SPORTS AND PERFORMANCE

representations is rarely discussed in sport philosophy and performance studies, the ensuing may be somewhat technical (the most complex facets are left for the end-notes). But, it is it is important to engage it as a primary source to capture representations in detail and see both its possible contributions and limitations for performative activities and expert skillfulness. The findings themselves are not as problematic as much as the hypotheses when these stay too close to reductive and computational commitments. In fact, if informed and corroborated by phenomenology, these can mutually support each other, as Gallagher's work (2005, 2007) shows. Neuroscientist Marc Jeannerod's work is of particular interest.

In *The Cognitive Neuroscience of Action*, Jeannerod (1997) argues for a representational cognitive model of action at the neuronal level. He propitiously straddles the cognitivist and the embodied camps, so his work acts as a link. It further allows a clear and detailed view of how neuroscience theorizes representations based on experimental data. Jeannerod's main concern is with how the central nervous system generates actions, and specifically, how these actions are represented. Neuroscience tackles this problem by mapping mechanisms, which, at different levels, involves neuronal pathways and clusters, as well as neo-cortical, cortical, or subcortical regions. In short, it locates anatomically the numerous areas of the cerebrum that are activated when we act. Then, it theoretically conceptualizes these as representations and schemas.

Jeannerod develops a sophisticated framework of internal models that *somehow* represent external events in both a reactive and predictive way. Revealing this 'somehow' is the focus of his research. These internal models are representations. His notion of representation is broad and 'can apply to global aspects of an action (or even to an action in its entirety), as well as to more local aspects of that action' (Jeannerod 1997, 165). With the concept of a schema, he connects the different levels of description, viz. 'a given neuronal population can "represent" the complete action (e.g. press targets 1, 2, and 3 in a given order to get a reward), whereas other populations can "represent" more limited aspects (e.g. move the right arm to target 1, or move the eyes to target 2)' (Jeannerod 1997). Jeannerod hypothesizes that there are neurally pre-coded motor elements that constitute motor representations (1997, 51), and the existence of motor schemas (1997, 55), which he uses to argue for motor imagery. Unlike visual imagery motor images 'are experienced from within as the result of a "first person" process where the self feels like the actor' (Jeannerod 1997, 95). For him, during motor imagery we feel ourselves as executing the action, which can entail a body part, as in finger pointing, or the whole body, as in running.

At this point, Jeannerod switches from motor imagery as coded neuronal schemas to a sense of agency and sensations as *felt* that belongs to a very different level of description, a first personal one where *feeling* is supposed to validate the former. This is a substantial jump. On his way to a full scale neuronal reduction, he finds himself appealing to non-neuronal levels: 'Depending on the connections and inputs of each individual neuron, the sustained charge encodes, not only the spatial characteristics of the target, but also its *semantic value* and the *emotional context* of the task' (Jeannerod 1997, 148).[8] Semantic value and emotions are not neuronal-level processes, however, and this belies his goal of providing a strictly neural account of action. Neurons certainly play a role in our emotions and semantic engagements, as well as in expert performance. But, the 'nerves' of the target shooter are more than just the actual nerves and neuronal firings. They are nerves felt in the pit of the stomach, the dry mouth, and

133

jittery hands; they are emotionally laden nerves elicited because of the meanings he associates with the high-stakes competition and his worries about remaining calm and focused. These need a different explanation.

To this end, Jeannerod resorts to various kinds of schemas, from localized motor schemas we rely on for simple movements such as grabbing, to component ones we depend on to make coffee, to more global ones, source schemas, used in complex actions such as preparing breakfast (Jeannerod 1997, 160). The latter would be those pertinent to playing a game of volleyball, purportedly. These are coded differently representationally.[9] Motor representation includes only activated schemas, those selected for the intended action. Since motor representations, for Jeannerod at least, are dynamic structures, they must be reassembled anew for each action: external constraints differ and the context in which the action takes place changes, so that the same action is never repeated several times exactly the same way (174). This dynamic aspect is an important improvement over more static models.[10] Yet, some readers may already be thinking that this process (particularly as described in endnote 9) is too complex to explain actions and movement *if* conscious awareness of representations and suitably fast response times are needed, much more so in the real time situations that sports and performative endeavors involve. This is the computational problem of speed and bandwidth redux. Realizing this, Jeannerod asserts, somewhat understatedly, that the comparison mechanism has to be very fast (1997, 176). He addresses this issue in various ways. These range from ready-made schemas (e.g. throwing darts) to new ones (learning a new choreography), from goal-mapping mechanisms to subpersonal processes, and last, to decoupling mental imagery from execution.[11]

Breaching several cognitivist dogmas, these are sound moves on Jeannerod's part. His work is some of the most 'avant-garde' neuroscientific research and provides a tantalizing description of the neuroscience of action. It rightly presents a distributed (not linear), scaffolded, and dynamic neural model that moves him past classical cognitivism and problems concerning computation processing. But, it is still highly reductive, since representations for him entail neural motor codings. In response to Jeannerod's emphasis on brain processes, Gallagher levies the following that, as he avows, is favored by Sheets-Johnstone, Merleau-Ponty, and others,

> brain processes, whether they are motor, emotional, perceptual, or cognitive, cannot explain everything that we need to explain in regard to such aspects of experience. As emphasized above, body schemas are not purely brain schemas; they involve more general constraints placed on action by the whole body as it moves through an environment. In this regard a conception of a dynamical system that extends across these different dimensions, that is enactive, embodied and ecological, and consistent with a Husserlian conception of time-consciousness, avoids the implicit reductionism. (2005, 246)

This ties our previous arguments against reductionism to Jeannerod's representational schemas. These are challenged first, because of their inherent reductive commitments. But even if these are bypassed, a *fully* representational account faces further obstacles.

Let us recall that for Jeannerod a representation 'can apply to global aspects of an action (or even to an action in its entirety), as well as to more local aspects of that action' and that 'a given neuronal population can 'represent' the complete action [...], whereas other populations can "represent" more limited aspects …' (1997, 165) The fact that he brackets the notion of representation in quotation marks is telling. Indeed, it is not clear just how such neural codings actually represent—present anew—either internal or external signals and data. It is not some sort of virtual snapshot, as we are dealing with motoric phenomena and not visual ones. It could be a matter of neuronal patterns that somehow but consistently code pertinent phenomena, but then, the problem arises of how *we* recognize this (if at the conscious level), or how can neuronal patterns determine that what is *re*-presented matches the perceived object or event. The 'neurons' (staying within Jeannerod's reductive framework and forsaking any mereological issues) cannot determine that there is an accurate representation unless they have a third template to compare it to, and so on ad infinitum.[12] In a sense the neural codings for schemas act as memories, but as Birch (2010), puts it referencing Edelman, memory is no more a representation of the outside world than an antibody is a representation of a virus. Representations, whether as neural or symbolic codings, *may* be pertinent very punctually as when training a very specific skill, say the entry angle of the hands in the butterfly. Not so in real time and full-blown competitive or performative actions.

Hubert and Stuart Dreyfus, influenced by Merleau-Ponty, pioneered the critique of cognitivism. A key target was the notion of representation itself, because *as* representation it should be explicit and conscious yet, they argued, this excludes expert coping, which needs to be absorbed, that is subpersonal or not explicit. Jeannerod, we have seen, actually makes representation implicit to some extent in order to deal with the speed and bandwidth problem. But this solution is not without problems. The reason is that the more he shifts matters to a subpersonal level under the threshold of awareness, the less *meaningful* feedback is possible, since it must take place at the conscious level. Neural codings are not accessible; we do not have conscious access to neuronal clusters much less to single ones. But these must make sense to us at some point if we are to actually modify our movements and actions based on feedback that fits the situation. Jeannerod could rejoin that motor codings are pertinent and capture neural processes correctly, and that what we are privy to is feedback in particular cortical or other central and peripheral nervous systems regions. Yet, as he admits regarding how things are organized in serial generation mechanisms, 'It is difficult, if not impossible, to isolate processing steps (like intention, planning, etc.) from each other on the basis of anatomical localization: the system involved in the representation of action is a highly distributed one' (Jeannerod 1997, 172). The very distributed organization precludes shifting awareness to regions in the brain. We cannot perceive specific regions in the brain, or even the brain itself for that matter.

To make this work, Jeannerod shifts the descriptive level from neuronal to a higher level of descriptions and phenomena, writing about how we *feel* this or that, or how emotions are involved, as mentioned above. There is a broader ecological setting within which action needs to make sense: why is the slalom skier trying to maneuver in between the gates? Focusing solely on the hip and knee biomechanics and their purported neural codings leaves too much out. At this point, neural representations are not operative. It is a matter of empirical fact that we do have access to feedback, or else we would not readjust and recalibrate our movements or actions. This is what needs to be explained, and we can do so without recourse to neural motor representations. This does not mean that neuroscientific evidence and modeling are irrelevant, of course: the model he uses to explain the feedback mechanism via efference, efferent copy, afference, and reafferentation (see endnote 9) is sensible and coheres with our phenomenology of kinesthetic and proprioceptive dynamics. In other words, kinetic and proprioceptive dynamic patternings provide the intermediate yet immediate and meaningful link between whatever processes in the nervous and motor system take place, and how we *feel* ourselves as animate beings (essay 7).[13] Finally, the preeminent perspective and phenomenology under scrutiny are those of performers not observers. We are concerned foremost with the athlete, martial artist, dancer and actor, not the spectators or scientists. This needs a first-person phenomenology of movement as foundation for our skillful strivings (which can in turn support a neuroscience of action). Recent developments in the area of embodied cognition bring us closer.

2. The Many Faces of Embodied Cognition

The sport philosophy literature has largely and extensively engaged classical phenomenology, such as Heidegger (Breivik 2007, 2008, 2010; Martínková 2011), Husserl (Kretchmar 1974, 2014), Merleau-Ponty (Morris 2002, 2004; Standal and Moe 2011; Torres and McLaughlin 2011), Sartre (Culbertson 2011), besides analytic treatments of cognition (Moe 2005, 2007). But it has paid scant attention to the emerging Embodied Cognition (EC) paradigm. Given the genuine theoretical affinity between EC and thick holism, *Skillful Striving* addresses this—in a fashion. The very plurality of approaches within EC means that not all members are suitable companions for the way ahead. Hence, the subtle but important qualifications noted below. The general overview below also sets up conceptually pertinent arguments, ideas, and theorists so that they can be satisfactorily incorporated into subsequent essays.

The previous section has shown that we need to look elsewhere than the cognitivist camp if we are going to fruitfully assess skills, abilities, and excellence in performance. Fittingly, cognitive scientists Calvo and Gómila (2008), referencing the work of Kirsch and Haugeland, compare a game of chess with one of pool: the former is a formal game that can dispense with our bodily input, but in the latter we cannot get past the fact that we need to actually hit the white ball with the cue. Cognitivism and connectionism have made cognition a matter of chess, of explaining a formal system with neural networks, whereas as is obvious, much of our cognitive interactions with the world involve cues and sticks. This is the domain of EC. As with thick holism, one of the virtues of this alternative is that it corroborates how we *actually* experience ourselves in the world. Varela, Thompson, and Rosch's (1991) seminal study-manifesto *The Embodied Mind* laid out the groundwork. After a thorough critique of cognitive science and representational stances, they advanced a phenomenological alternative coupled to Buddhism that defended the codetermination of organism and environment. Nonetheless, as Thompson candidly avows in a later work, they started on the wrong foot when they criticized Husserl's phenomenology and opted for the Buddhist analysis due to insufficient familiarity with Husserl's work (2007, 413–416). Regardless, this work set the field of cognition, the sciences of the mind, and philosophy of mind on a new course.

Pared to the bone, an embodied view considers that our cognition is at least partly constituted by extra-neuronal elements that are not reducible to the brain and involves the rest of the body to varying degrees. This is readily appealing to sport philosophy and its concerns. The embodied camp encompasses a heterogeneous group of interrelated but distinct views. Some of EC's most salient versions—in an ever-growing field—comprise:

(1) *Embodied* views, as just mentioned and referenced, these posit extraneural bodily elements as constitutive of mental processes (see also Shapiro 2011).

(2) *Enactivist* versions, which, relying on phenomenology and conceptual analysis, argue that cognition and perception are partially informed by action (Noë 2004; Thompson 2007). A radically enactive version based on Hutto and Myin (2013) is built into *Skillful Striving's* thick holism.

(3) *Externalist* stances that consider how our cognition should relate appropriately to the environment (Clark 2011; Rowlands 2010). There are various accounts:

   (a) *Extended* ones argue that cognition is located in the external environment to varying degrees, are amenable to representations and functionalism, but down-play the role of the body (Clark and Chalmers 1998; Menary 2010).

   (b) *Embedded* accounts consider cognition to be coupled with the environment in mutual codetermination (Gallagher and Zahavi 2008).[14]

   (c) *Extensive*, the most extreme, in so far as cognition is not extended in degrees but full-fledged and integrated with the environment already (Hutto and Myin (2013).[15]

(4) *Situated* cognition, in addition to environmental aspects, also includes social and historical aspects among others (Gallagher 2008, 2009). *Everything Mysterious under the Moon* incorporates this stance.

Philosophers in the EC camp often uphold a combination of these, for example, Gallagher has enactivist, embedded, and situated credentials (among others) but takes exception to extended ones. All basically agree on the importance of the body for cognition (the lesser commitment to this by extended partisans noted). Thick holism is amenable to many if not all of their overall ends, as stated. In fact, some of the flagship theorists of the cognitively embodied model, such as Gallagher's phenomenologically situated and embedded approach (essays 7 and 10), Hutto and Myin's radical enactivism (essays 7, 9, and 10), or Varela's (1999) enactive ethical views (essay 10) are profitably incorporated into the present holistic model, with more or less explicit and drastic adaptations.

There are some controversies associated with an embodied cognitive model, how-ever. As Uriah Kriegel points out, the embodied cognition program is 'highly energetic but often conceptually confused' (2014, 5). One such confusion concerns the role the body plays in cognition, whether it is merely ancillary, plays a causal role of varying importance, or is fully constitutive. Sheets-Johnstone raises another serious challenge when she contends that the label 'embodied' is but a 'lexical bandaid' (2009, 215) and redundant when we speak of processes that cannot but be of qualitatively felt, moving *bodies*. That is, such cognition is 'by definition corporeal; it is thus not an abstract knowledge but a corporeally resonant knowledge that is tied to meaning [which is] embedded in experience' (2011, 231). In this regard, the issue is terminologically and conceptually contested terrain to the extent that specific articulations connote different descriptive levels more or less apt to capture the phenomena they purport to explain. The convention adopted now is to generally avoid the 'embodied' label because, among other reasons, it emphasizes the body(mind) to the exclusion of a truly dynamic and integrated bodymind (even if most of us are far from realizing such integration).

Skillful Striving defends a thick holistic model where a situated, embedded, and enactive bodymind is constitutive of our cognition—a cognition that includes front and center performative know-hows. This stance calls for friendly exclusions, exceptions, and amendments to EC partisans. Excluded are those methods, descriptions, and concepts that reify dynamic processes by turning them into mechanisms, as discussed already *in extenso*. The exceptions concern vocabulary preferences that come with problematic commitments for a genuinely holistic stance. Aside from lexical bandaids, for instance, it is the EC literature's penchant to largely adopt a neuroscientific vocabulary (sensorimotor processes or contingencies, neuronal clusters, efference copy, etc.). This is done for the cogent and justifiable purpose of connecting phenomenological and analytic work to the mind sciences. But, often this is adopted to the exclusion of a fuller phenomenological description that captures how we feel and think when moving. That is, it does not engage the issue at the pragmatic level at which we normally perform and think/feel. Moreover, it often has reifying and reductive tendencies. It would be best to include both, properly contextualizing and pruning the scientific terminology from reductive tendencies. In terms of friendly amendments, many could be made to the EC views detailed above. We begin with a concrete case to show how certain underlying theoretical allegiances come at a price. Sport psychologist and cognitive scientist Sian Beilock has conducted groundbreaking work on choking in sport (and other spheres) (see essay 8). She supports an alliance between EC and sport science, because EC opens,

> a new kind of window into sport psychology by predicting the interaction of the mind, body, and environment in ways that conventional information processing theories do not [and] sport science work is able to give back to the embodied movement by demonstrating what experience on the playing field buys one on the pitch and beyond. (Beilock 2008, 28)

Unfortunately, her endorsement of representation limits the traction she can get from an embodied approach. This affable censure is derived from the enactive commitments of thick holism, specifically when considering expert performance, which advises forsaking representations. In fact, as adumbrated above, enactivism is particularly suitable for this project. But, because some versions are more suitable than others the amendments and refinements continue in the next section.

3. Holism and Enactivism: Two Peas in a Pod?

Put simply, enactivism entails 'the performance or carrying out of an action' as Thompson specifies in his landmark *Mind and Life* (2007, 13), where he advances an autopoietic enactivism centered on self-organizing living organisms. Sheets-Johnstone clarifies that to 'enact' etymologically, '... means to "bring [something] into a certain condition or state," precisely as in the word's common usage: to make into a law' (2011, 454). For her, when we enact we put something into a specified form, for example, a kinetic form we use to go through the motions, as when we smile in pretense at someone detested (2011). This is the basis for her sympathetic, if thorough, critique of enactive approaches, Thompson's specifically, which she faults on two counts: bypassing the link to affect, and packaging movement into a deed of some kind that makes of kinesthetic/dynamics no more than a labeled act like 'walking' (Sheets-Johnstone 2011, 455). With the proviso, to avoid any reifying innuendoes, that rather than *something* being put into a form, we may best note that the phenomenon is a dynamic moving or acting, her point is well taken. After all, the concern lies with the qualitative dynamics inherent to how we experience movement when we perform, which her second criticism makes clear. Observing this, we can keep a sense of enactivity whereby we realize kinetic patternings (see essays 7 and 10), whether novel or 'learned,' where the dynamics are well alive. But, before continuing this line of inquiry it is best to discuss further aspects and variants of enactivism (Thompson's autopoietic account is revisited at the end of this section).

Sensorimotor enactivism, as developed in the work of O'Regan and Noë (2001) and, most fully, in the latter's *Action in Perception* (Noë 2004), defends the stance that action, perception, and our perceptual experiences are irremediably tied together. Perception is not concerned with inner representations but instead amounts to how organisms interact with their environments. Noë sums up this enactive approach thus, 'Perception is a way of acting. It's not something that happens to us, or in us. It's something we do' (2004, 1). Rightly, our perception is directly connected to action in this enactive account. But, this is not the kind of enactivism that best suits the aims of *Skillful Striving* for three reasons. First, as Gallagher recommends, Noë (and fellow-minded enactivists) should not 'reduce phenomenal experience to what [Noë] describes purely in terms of sensory-motor contingencies and embodied skills (there is clearly more to the body than just this' (2012, 98).[16] This is in line with the above exclusions and exceptions. The next reason, much as the three musketeers were actually four (positing an interesting ontological issue), is numerically singular but amalgamates a number of critical strands.

Second then, Hutto and Myin (2013), in distinguishing their own account extract some inherent tensions. The main tension is between Noë's partiality for practical and non-propositional knowledge that is about knowing how to do things and the endorsement of representationalism, to which he seems committed to avoid the charge of being a closet behaviorist (Hutto and Myin 2013, 25–28). This mediating knowledge grounds the organism's dispositions to act, but if so, it needs to be active and not passive, as Noë seems to suggest at times. Moreover, sensorimotor enactivism is attached 'to the idea that perceptual experience is inherently *contentful*' (Hutto and Myin 2013, 30, my emphasis), yet Noë also sees concepts as practical skills not representations. When we experience a cube it is the concept 'cube' that gives the content to the experience, yet the concept on his account is 'nothing but primitive sensorimotor skills' (Hutto and Myin 2013, 31). In which case then, the practical skill (the concept) needs to be understood in terms of how it is used, redundantly collapsing onto itself. Another reason that rules out this type of enactivism, particularly for a project centered on superb performance as is ours, is that in Noë's account:

> The bar for being a concept user is set very low if all that is required is having a skilled capacity for engaging with specific kinds of things in reliably expectant ways. For it is surely part of our attributional practice to count infants and animals as

perceiving something on just these grounds, even though we would not necessarily credit them with a mastery of the concept of what they are perceiving or experiencing. (Hutto and Myin 2013, 31–32)

There is a need for a model that can account for both, the developmental aspects of skills and their most refined expressions. The remainder of *Skillful Striving* develops this.

Third, in enactive accounts such as Noë and Thompson's (2002) and the aforementioned work by O'Regan and Noë, vision and visuomotor processes are primordial whereas the role of tactility and movement as resonant and primary qualities of our enactive endeavors is often downplayed or ignored. That is, vision, even when ascribed cross-modal tactile qualities, is overemphasized. This is something quite widespread with philosophers and scientists, as Chemero says (2009, 154). Having criticized this agenda elsewhere from an ecological perspective that calls for more realistic research and theory (Ilundáin-Agurruza 2013), it is advisable to tackle this from a different angle that suitably enlists neuroscientific evidence. Jeannerod leads the way again. Consider grasping, one of our most basic movements. Common sense and theoretical assumptions tend to weigh in favor of the visual when first considering how we calculate reach and grasp size. Neuroscientific evidence shows that there is a specific neural system that is devoted to object-oriented movements. As Jeannerod explains, the type of grip we use is the result of a motor sequence that begins well ahead of the actual grasping (1997, 35). This reflects higher visuomotor mechanisms that detect the shape of the object (Jeannerod 1997, 37). But, very interestingly, visual feedback is *not* very important for grip formation and coordination, as Jeannerod observes (1997, 38). Rather, active touch, which calibrates a number of attributes such as size, texture, weight, etc., and grip force seem more important for grip accuracy (Jeannerod 1997, 39). This evinces that sometimes tactile and kinetic dynamics prevail over visual ones. It also suggests that vision works cross-modally with other senses, in this case tactility. Collingwood's (1958) observations about Cezanne's painting having a primordially tactile quality are instructive in this regard, as is Sheets-Johnstone's (1990) analysis of Paleolithic cave art and the tactile and three-dimensional qualities of the line. There are more insights to be grasped yet.

Anticipating arguments to come in the remaining essays we can appeal to Gallagher, who makes the case for the 'body-*as-subject*—bodily experiences that have an effect on the way that I experience the world' (2012, 95). Our kinesthetic, proprioceptive, and nociceptive (pain) dynamics affect our perceptions markedly. If I am in pain, this affects how I perceive objects. When my leg hurts or even when my mood is gloomy, the hill looks steeper when I ride or run toward it (Bhalla and Proffitt 2000; Riener et al. 2011). Thus, it 'is not simply the fact that the size and shape of the thing, and the fact that I can reach it with this hand, constitute the "grabbiness" of the thing —if my pain prevents or slows my reach, then the thing is no so grabby' (Gallagher 2012, 97). Even our postural readiness to act can influence how we perceive color, as Gallagher (2012) states. The green disk for the racecar driver is not merely a color, but signals a whole set of complex actions and events. If he has lower back pain, this also modulates his readiness-to-action. This further shores up the point that, while analysis can be performed at small anatomic length-scales, it is the *whole bodymind* that consummates the action and is the preferred frame of reference with respect to which *make sense* of the evidence.

HOLISM AND THE CULTIVATION OF EXCELLENCE IN SPORTS AND PERFORMANCE

Sports, martial arts, the performing arts, and crafts stand out when it comes to tactile kinetic engagements. Skiers not only feel, and feel *with*, their skis, but also discriminate the different consistencies of the snow, besides sensing their bodies adapting to the rises and falls of the slope; martial artists feel the *bo* or staff while adapting and adopting it as a extension of their body much as Merleau-Ponty (1962) described the blind man and his cane; a violinist exquisitely blends finger, hand, and arm motions with the strings and resonances of her instrument; a master swordsmith feels with the hammer as he moves around the hot steel as if it were malleable clay. All of them are better guided by a deeper attunement to tactile, aural, and kinetic-kinesthetic dynamics rather than purely visual ones.

There is one enactive approach that suits very well the parameters of thick holism. This is, perhaps unsurprisingly, the most extreme version: radical enactivism, championed by philosophers Hutto and Myin (2013), which they term REC for short.[17] They take an even more drastic step against representation, doing away with it *completely* when it comes to basic minds. REC opens up enticing opportunities to rethink skills and abilities across a broad swath of contexts, from commonplace ones to the very specialized and highly refined contexts in which we are interested. They describe the sort of activities that basic minds effect:

> Catching a swirling leaf, finding one's way through unfamiliar terrain, attending and keeping track of another's gaze, watching the sun rising at the horizon—the vast sea of what humans do and experience is best understood by appealing to dynamically unfolding, situated embodied interactions and engagements with worldly offerings. (Hutto and Myin 2013, ix)

We could paraphrase and expand on their list thus: catching a ball in third base, finding the waypoints in an orienteering race, attending and keeping track of the opponents blade, watching the sun rising off starboard during a sailing regatta, matching our steps to the dance partner's, and on and on. In these activities, we find 'basic minds' which 'do not represent conditions that the world might be in' (Hutto and Myin, ix). That is, they do away with phenomenality and content. 'At its simplest, there is content wherever there are specified conditions of satisfaction. And there is true or accurate content wherever the conditions specified are, in fact, instantiated' (Hutto and Myin 2013, x). In short, they argue against contentful cognition. Hutto and Myin's goal is to argue against the view that cognition necessarily involves content, which they refer to as CIC. Assuming that 'many sophisticated embodied engagements constitute mentality and are best explained with reference to nothing more than habits of mind, without the need to invoke the existence of any content-involving or representationally informed cognition whatsoever' (Hutto and Myin 2013, 14–15). A Deweyan pragmatism gives the nod to this. Not so those supporters of CIC such as Andy Clark, Jerry Fodor and a long list of illustrious philosophers. The attack of CICers and defense of REC makes up the book's bulk. But we best center on our skillful strivings.

To elaborate on the basis of their stance, basic minds successfully interact with their worlds in rich ways that dispense with representations of any kind. 'To think otherwise, as many do, is to ascribe features and characteristics to basic minds that belong only to enculturated, scaffolded minds that are built atop them' (Hutto and Myin 2013, ix). Indeed, as Hutto and Myin insist, 'creatures are capable of dealing with aspects of their environments, sometimes in quite remarkable and sophisticated ways (ways that count as properly mental and cognitive), even if the capacity for content-involving deliberation or planning never develops' (2013, 14). This does not mean that cognition is never contentful, or to ignore that 'some very important forms of cognition essentially depend on the interactions between propositional attitudes' (2013). Rather, what we associate with propositional thought or cultural practices, the thinking we do when doing philosophy, comes much later, and builds on more basic abilities. Indeed, as they explain, the REC stance on basic minds best understands them 'in terms of capacities' (Hutto and Myin 2013, 151). This readily blends with the view of skills presented in *Nothing New Under the Sun*. More interestingly and auspiciously REC, when judiciously combined with thick holism, allows explaining masterful performance at different levels and across a number of contexts.

In this model, integrated bodyminds whose performance is superb act as basic minds whenever they are performing in 'full-on' mode. Pragmatically, their movements are 'empty' of representations, rules, or deliberate patternings but fully effective and adapted to the challenges of the moment. This adaptation, at the moment of the performance, is contentless, with no facts of the matter so to speak. Hutto and Myin state that,

> it is not knowledge (embodied know-how) that gives perceptual experiences their intentionality and phenomenal character; rather; it is the concrete ways in which organisms actively engage with their environments. But in so engaging with their environments there is not a set of facts that organisms know, or need to know, at any level. (2012, 30)

In the case of expert performers actions disappear in their bodymind, forgotten as the initial knowledge has been integrated. This is examined in more detail with Japanese samurai Yagyū Munenori[18] in *Reflections on a Katana* and the analysis of *mushin*, 無心, (no mind). We begin acting as basic minds developmentally, atop of which we build more refined skills in addition to complex ways of articulating and (mis)understanding them (see essay 7). Masters have a wide register of (en)action to create patternings, innovative or ingrained, as well as to operate at different attentional levels. This means that they are able to skillfully and ably phase between basic and scaffolded minds, between subpersonal and reflective consciousness, between mindful and spontaneous fluency, and mindless coping and automaticity. It is important to note that these are phenomenological continua and not mutually exclusive ontological opposites.

Theoretically advantageous, this account is more parsimonious than alternative cognitivist accounts where content, representations, computation, and complex mechanisms are used to account for action. If the latter ran afoul when it came to explain expert skill, particularly in certain risk sports where rapid response to challenges is requisite, a holistic and enactive account shines. There is no problem with regard to processing speed since there is *nothing* to process. The performer is not encumbered at any moment with rules, calculations, or any kind of content. To be clear, this does not mean that there is no room for deliberation and articulation. In fact, as posterior essays argue and explain, this is integral to a holistic and full account of excellent performance. But, the *transparent* rather than opaque magic happens in the empty spaces that basic minds open up. Our success is built on these.

HOLISM AND THE CULTIVATION OF EXCELLENCE IN SPORTS AND PERFORMANCE

To till the ground a stipulative terminological distinction follows. Hutto and Myin argue that perception for basic minds is not contentful. Nevertheless, to distinguish between basic and scaffolded minds, 'sensation' and 'perception' are differentiated henceforth. The former is reserved for the non-interpreted, non-representational, and contentless experiences of basic minds interacting with their environment. The latter is used to refer to interpreted, propositional, and contentful experience proper of acculturated and scaffolded bodyminds. The very specific kinesthetic and nociceptive dynamics of doing maximum sprints to the point that nausea ensues and the teeth hurt is quite a sensation unto its own. On the one hand, as a primal experience, the sprinter can only feel the pain as a raw sensation that overtakes his whole bodymind. There is no room for any kind of articulated thinking. He disappears with the rowing, as we saw with Kaag and James (essay 2; see also Nishida in essay 9). On the other painful hand, when he talks about it with his coach or fellow teammates or competitors *afterward*, then it is interpreted as extremely painful and unpleasant, and it becomes a perception. Humans, as complex organisms, switch between basic states and acculturated ones quite frequently and rapidly. The sensation and the basic mind are foundational to the latter genetically—in terms of when they develop. But this does not mean the scaffolded bodymind is irrelevant. Rather it allows us to discriminate and understand better and enjoy more the former. At least sometimes, in other occasions it simply and most inconveniently gets in the way of the performance, as essay 8 details. So far, holism and enactivism are two peas in a pod.

Yet, for all the, perhaps natural, affinity and like-mindedness between thick holism and REC, there are three points of dissension worth noting. First, thick holism even if enactive, might be a bit too expansive for Hutto and Myin, or be at least something they are not willing to fully embrace. For one, they 'remain neutral toward other, more extravagant claims associated with the original version of enactivism' such as 'the thought that organisms "enact" or "bring forth" their worlds— that enaction enables a world to "show up" for individuals' (Hutto and Myin 2013, 5). Given the situatedness and embeddedness I profess along with Ortega (essay 4), this all but warrants their neutrality *for now*. Second, thick holism is avowedly non-reductive, whereas REC's commitments flirt with it to at some points. Yet, Gallagher charges that 'enactivists should not attribute experience only to neural activity, citing Hutto and Myin' words as one such case' 'Radical enactivists hold that phenomenality is nothing other than specifiable sorts of activity—even if only neural activity' (2012, 207 fn. 3).[19] This, they state when discussing the phenomenality of qualia. It is not clear that they are committed to such reductive level, particularly given their view of the mind as extensive and scaffolded. Regardless of their stance, there is no reducing of experience to the neural level for thick holism. Third, John Sutton (2014) argues against Hutto and Myin's 'nothing-but-ism,' because they ground the significant aspects of an organism's cognition in terms of nothing but its history of previous interactions. In Sutton's view (2014), and because their book is directed at criticizing CIC, this limitation of the scope to organismic history is insufficient in the absence of a positive research program. Granted, they clarify that they 'restrict [their] ambitions to promoting REC' (Hutto and Myin 2013, 5), and surely one must clear the ground before one can build but it remains suggestive at best. For them, 'The ultimate task is to explain how basic minds make the development of contentful forms of cognition possible when the right supports, such as shared social practices, are in place' (Hutto and Myin 2013, 36). To this extent, *Skillful Striving* offers ways to envision the positive case for radical enactivism, offering if not a complete explanation at least meaningful glimpses of how basic minds subtend socially rich practices that result in excellent skills and performances.[20]

A thick holism that accommodates such an enactive account is extraordinarily broad ecologically. For lack of better terms, it is Catholic in its application and ecumenical in its interdisciplinary and methodological inclusiveness (the last essay will show how inclusive and expansive it actually is).[21] It examines phenomena horizontally across the performative, cognitive, normative, and socio-historical domains. It considers them vertically, ranging from the level of neurophysiology to the bodymind as integrative and performative, and on to the environment within which the organism lives. More germane to our interests, a holistic and enactive account proves most useful to elucidate the kind of action that superb performers carry out: spontaneous and mindful. This extends into the normative sphere, where we find a beautiful and morally praiseworthy spontaneous action (essays 7 and 9). This model challenges two widespread but questionable tenets of expert performance, namely those that see experts coping mindlessly and relying on automatized skill. These present us with a model of passive performance where the 'agent' is not in charge of the action, as it happens in spite of herself. On the other side, as noted above, a holistic and enactive model forwards an active performance where the agent is fully engaged, switching her attention spontaneously and ably in sync with the needs of the moment. It can also explain how the 'self' may disappear, tools are incorporated, and the knowledge is 'forgotten' in cases of expertise as the upcoming essays show. In between a fully conscious, deliberate, and attentive awareness and a subpersonal, pre-reflective and mindless operation there is a continuum where experts perform, making use of a Jamesian Background or fringe of consciousness (essay 2) and the sort of mentality that a holistic and enactive model explains.

One final amendment to *all* the aforementioned EC and enactive authors is that they invariably articulate bodymind dynamics in ways that keep them anchored to a not so veiled dualistic framework and vocabulary, i.e. they still speak of the body *and* the mind even as they insist on the inapplicability of this division *while* profusely using embodied and mental appellatives; they phrase matters in ways that emphasize the importance of the body for movement and the mind for thinking. Even when holism is mentioned (very rarely), it is adjectivized or becomes ancillary while the bodily and mental are substantively and substantially singled out, pace Bongrae Seok in the context of embodiment and Confucian philosophy,

> By including the body in the main process of cognition, the embodied approach often develops a holistic viewpoint that combines not only the body and the agent, but also the environment, the history of development, and particular conditions of the interaction between a cognitive agent and her (physical, social, and task) environments (2013, 9).

The issue is that we are still writing of the body/mind separately even *as* we argue to bring them together. To revisit Thompson's autopoietic enactivism in this context, he makes a formidable case for an enactive account rooted in biology and phenomenology. As Hutto and Myin observe, 'Thompson sees the enactive approach as a way to put aside the mind–body problem once and for all' (2012, 33). Yet, when discussing the convergence of enactivism and phenomenology he writes, 'The *mind* brings things into awareness; it discloses and presents the world [...] Things show up, as it were, having the features they do, because of how they are disclosed and brought to awareness by the intentional activities of our *minds*' (Thompson 2007, 15, my emphases). Subsequently, discussing phenomenology and embodiment, he states that, 'To say that the habitual *body* acts as guarantee for the *body* at this moment is to say that one's *lived body* is a developmental being [...] These sedimented patterns are not limited to the space enclosed by the *body's* membrane; they span and interweave the *lived body* and its environment' (Thompson 2007, 33, my emphases). His non-dualist credentials are impeccable, but these two examples show how he remains grounded in the very tradition his work seeks to overcome. This limitation may be largely due to inherent shortcomings of the English language (and many other languages when compared, for example, to Chinese and Japanese). But, referring to the body and the mind discretely, even when the context helps elucidate the sense, keeps the Cartesian split painfully open. It goes beyond the mere use of the 'old words' and categories for lack of better ones, if only because there is no explicit attempt at disowning them or devising alternatives. If we recall the first essay, we adopted a terminological convention to overcome this quandary.

Said convention enables to work flexibly with the notion of the bodymind and its different levels of integration. It calls for parenthetic bracketing of the one aspect to be de-emphasized, which concurrently emphasizes the other. This bracketing can be due to various reasons, such as lesser integration of bodymind functions (the bracketing denoting the 'weaker' facet), or merely the need to highlight one function over the other when making theoretical claims. Thus, body(mind) stresses the former component and (body(mind) does the reverse while underlining the mutual and inherent codependency and the ever-changing dynamics of their relationship. Lack of brackets then may refer to an integrated and harmonious bodymind such as during *mushin* states (essay 9) , or simply be a neutral way to refer to the bodymind generally under the rubric of thick holism (the context makes clear how to read it). In short, because the bodymind is contiguous and coterminous, the shifting parenthetic bracketing captures the fluidity of its qualitative dynamics. In this way, we can better describe and conceptualize the complex patternings of a thickly holistic system. In the context of performance, we can speak of the athlete's or martial artist's (body)mind when we discuss facets of awareness or attention usually discussed in terms of the mental, and of body(mind) when discussing what elsewhere refers to sensorimotor processes, muscles, nerves, bones, and other 'corporeal' aspects. This brings to the forefront the interactive nature of our functions and emphasizes the continuities that underlie them. Accordingly, in the conceptual spaces opened by this convention we find room for kinesthetic and proprioceptive dynamics that *constantly* take place, affectively and performatively permeating our every experience, whether reflectively or not. In *Everything Mysterious Under the Moon,* the Japanese nomenclature comes to the fore, interweaving its much subtler and richer conceptualization and articulation.

These closing comments amount but to a minor spat among friends; thick holism is complementary to EC approaches and contemporary scientific practice rather than antagonistic (so long as theoretically reductive imbroglios and reifying labelings are avoided). Within this fluid relation of the bodymind lie kinesthetic, proprioceptive, affective, and emotional dynamics that permeate and punctuate more or less explicitly and intensely said bodymind. As will be seen throughout, thick holism also incorporates developmental history, a codetermined relation between organism and environment, a distributed and scaffolded architecture, and broader cultural and historical elements. While it can be labeled enactive, embedded, situated, and so on, it sometimes parts ways in terms of the proper descriptive level suitable for the kind of phenomenon under consideration. Awakened for good from the cognitivist dream, we explore next the phenomenology of our skillful ways and how this relates and contributes to the kind of superb performances about which fabled tales are told.

DISCLOSURE STATEMENT

No potential conflict of interest was reported by the author.

NOTES

1. For a critique of this in the context of sport and movement see Ilundáin-Agurruza (2013).
2. I concur with Mike McNamee's suggestion that this is similar to Wittgenstein's notion of 'primitive reactions.'
3. Concerning Searle, Moe (2007) meticulously examines his complex account of intentionality and his notions of the 'Network,' 'Background,' and 'Connection Principle.' Moe reaches the conclusion that Searle provides a very useful 'internal' perspective of the mechanics of expert coping, but his neurophysiological account cannot underwrite his conceptual apparatus.
4. Moe (2005) discusses and critiques Schmidt in detail on pp. 159–160.
5. While Dennett is foremost an eliminativist materialist, his brain in the vat ideas apply as readily to reductionism. The arguments laid out below apply equally for the most part to his views.
6. NeoPlatonic thinking, rather than Plato, tied to certain theological interpretations, is much to blame for the Christian disregard for the body.
7. Our genetics is also a matter of luck for now. However, gene therapy and modification may soon alter this. For a cautionary assessment see McNamee's 'Whose Prometheus? Transhumanism, biotechnology and the moral topography of sports medicine' (2008) and Sandel's *The Case Against Perfection* (2007).
8. The actual process is rather more complex, since it 'requires a representation of the body as the generator of the acting forces, and not only of the effects of these forces on the external world' (Jeannerod 1997, 95). This is one of the very few references to the external world he makes. He considers that describing visual images is easy, but describing or coding the motor image is very difficult, e.g. it is easier to show movement coordination for swimming than to describe it. Motor representations are accessible through either mental movement time measurement or matching imaged movement with real movement. Experiments in which we either time an imagined task or compare timing imagined and performed tasks, say actually crossing a number of unevenly spaced doors and envisioning it, show this (Jeannerod 1997, 97). Because we rarely cross doors just to cross them, we need to account for the wider context in which actions are performed, with intermediate steps that must precede attainment of a goal.

HOLISM AND THE CULTIVATION OF EXCELLENCE IN SPORTS AND PERFORMANCE

Planning is crucial then. Jeannerod postulates that the ensemble of actions are represented in an 'action plan': a complex process whereby the function of action planning is 'to select, from the stock of available motor schemas those which will have to be performed, relate them to the proper internal and external cues, and organize them into an appropriate sequence. Selecting a given set of motor schemas implies inhibiting the non-desirable ones, specially those that may relate to intervening stimuli or distractors' (Jeannerod 1997, 127).

9. In the following description, 'efference' refers to outgoing neural signals from the central processor, the pertinent area of the brain, 'afference' concerns the feedback sent from muscles, skin, and such, 'efferent' copy is the duplicate used to calibrate both efferent and afferent signals. An internal Model Comparator (MC) channels the flow of inputs and outputs. He depicts the internal structure of motor representations by relying on comparator models where there is a command signal from the motor center to the effector of the movement, while the MC also sends an efference copy to another center. The effector produces a reafference that goes to the same center and the copies are compared. If they match closely nothing else happens, if they do not match, compensatory action ensues (Jeannerod 1997, 168). 'Corollary discharge and efference copy thus represent two nearly identical formulations of the fact that the nervous system can inform itself about its current state and use this information to monitor and regulate its own activity' (Jeannerod 1997). This provides a model for internal, reflective feedback on our movements.

10. Yet, what needs to be explained is precisely how these are coded such that they can capture the fluid dynamics of performing, for it is an ongoing event we are concerned with. It is far from clear that this encodings can play this role, since motoric mechanisms tend to reify processes. Jeannerod does develop a more rigorously dynamic view of schemas elsewhere (2006; Jeannerod and Gallagher 2002), but the descriptive level does no seem to do justice to the richness of the *felt* dynamics.

11. First, for him there are two qualitatively different ways to do a task, either applying well-learned routines or building new representations. For some actions, we have ready-made schemas (getting dressed, preparing breakfast) and for others actions, we need to implement more steps, plan, and calculate timing. For example, if we were to climb on a new area. Second, he also hypothesizes a mechanism that represents the goal of the action (final configuration) not the action itself (kinematics, joint rotation). Third, at one point he opens the door for subpersonal processes when he explains that findings suggest that, 'whereas frontal cortex is critically involved in establishing the motor routines, the basal ganglia [they handle non-conscious routines] have the function of handling these routines for carrying out the action' (Jeannerod 1997, 158). And fourth, he argues that in normal execution there is no awareness of the content of representation at *any* level; no image is experienced. To explain this, he argues that motor imagery and execution have different time constants: imagery implies subjective awareness (and would be delayed if it appeared at all), unlike execution, especially of fast movements (Jeannerod 1997, 179).

12. This is evocative of Aristotle's third man problem. For a full discussion and critique from a phenomenological stance see Gallagher and Zahavi (2008, 90–93).

13. Sheets-Johnstone (2009, 2011) gives an insightful account of congruency between emotions and kinesthesia.

HOLISM AND THE CULTIVATION OF EXCELLENCE IN SPORTS AND PERFORMANCE

14. As Gallagher and Zahavi write, 'The environment directly and indirectly regulates the body so that the body is in some sense the expression or reflection of the environment' (2008, 138). Dewey's, Ortega's, and Uexküll's ideas are clear forerunners.

15. Whether non-representationalism and the concept of the 'extensive mind' are orthogonal to the internalist–externalist dispute, with a framework of distributed cognitive ecologies sufficing, as Sutton (2014) argues, or being central to it, as Hutto, Kirchhoff, and Myin contend (2014) is indeed orthogonal to the aims of this project presently. Put differently, *Skillful Striving*'s holism cuts perpendicularly through this issue since its notion of the bodymind is as broadly distributed or extensive as these concepts can go.

16. As he also explains, Noë should not reduce 'experience to being enacted purely by sensory-motor contingencies understood in the logic of if-then bodily movements that constitute skilled sensorimotor behavior or know-how' (Gallagher 2012, 207 fn. 3).

17. Adapting Hutto and Myin's acronym, we could refer to the combination of thick holism and radical enactivism as WREC, from a holistic stance where the *whole* bodymind and environment act ensemble and perhaps, sometimes, even 'wreclessly.'

18. Family name comes first with Japanese names.

19. The original can be found in Hutto and Myin (2013, 8).

20. Hutto and Myin undertake the 'more modest claim […] [but arguably primary task of] understanding how mentality can be intentionally directed yet also wholly embodied and enactive' (2013, 36).

21. Considering the author's name and his irreligiosity the use of these two terms is not without irony. There is another paradoxical irony in the juxtaposition of holism's inflationary and encompassing tendencies and enactivist self-effacing leanings. But it is resolved easily since the totality of holism is permeated to the core by the nothingness of enactivism.

REFERENCES

BEALL, E.B. and M.J. LOWE. 2014. SimPACE: Generating simulated motion corrupted BOLD data with synthetic-navigated acquisition for the development and evaluation of SLOMOCO: A new, highly effective slicewise motion correction. *Neuroimage* 101 (1): 21–34.

BEARDSLEY, M.C. 1966. *Aesthetics from classical Greece to the present: A short history*. New York, NY: Macmillan.

BEILOCK, S.L. 2008. Beyond the playing field: Sport psychology meets embodied cognition. *International Review of Sport and Exercise Psychology* 1 (1): 19–30.

BENNETT, M.R. and P.M.S. HACKER. 2003. *Philosophical foundations of neuroscience*. Malden, MA: Blackwell.

BHALLA, M. and D.R. PROFFITT. 2000. Geographical slant perception: Dissociation and coordination between explicit awareness and visually guided actions. In *Dissociation but interaction between nonconscious and conscious processing*, edited by Y. Rossetti and A. Revonsuo. Amsterdam: John Benjamins.

BIRCH, J. 2010. The inner game of sport: Is everything in the brain? *Sport, Ethics and Philosophy* 4 (3): 284–305.

BLOCK, N. 1995. On a confusion about a function of consciousness. *Behavioral and Brain Sciences* 18: 227–87.

BREIVIK, G. 2007. Skillful coping in everyday life and in sport: A critical examination of the views of Heidegger and Dreyfus. *Journal of the Philosophy of Sport* 34 (2): 116–34.

———. 2008. Bodily movement—The fundamental dimensions. *Sport, Ethics and Philosophy* 2 (3): 337–52.

———. 2010. Being-in-the-void: A Heideggerian analysis of skydiving. *Journal of the Philosophy of Sport* 37 (1): 29–46.

———. 2013. Zombie-like or superconscious? A phenomenological and conceptual analysis of consciousness in elite sport. *Journal of the Philosophy of Sport* 40 (1): 85–105.

BROWN, L. and D.A. REID. 2006. Embodied cognition: Somatic markers, purposes and emotional orientations. *Educational Studies in Mathematics* 63: 179–92.

BRUYA, B. 2010. *Effortless attention*. Cambridge, MA: MIT Press.

CALVO, P. and A. GÓMILA. 2008. *Handbook of cognitive science: An embodied approach*. Amsterdam: Elsevier.

CHEMERO, A. 2009. *Radical embodied cognitive science*. Cambridge, MA: MIT Press.

CHURCHLAND, P.M. 1988. *Matter and conciousness*. Cambridge, MA: MIT Press.

CLARK, A. 2011. *Supersizing the mind: Embodiment, action, and cognitive extension*. Oxford: Oxford University Press.

CLARK, A. and D. CHALMERS. 1998. The extended mind. *Analysis* 58: 7–19.

COLLINGWOOD, R.G. 1958. *The principles of art*. New York, NY: Oxford University Press.

CULBERTSON, L. 2011. Sartre on human nature: Humanness, transhumanism and performance enhancement. *Sport, Ethics and Philosophy* 5 (3): 231–44.

DENNETT, D. 1981. *Where am I? The mind's I: Fantasies and reflections on mind and soul*. New York, NY: Basic Books: 217–29.

———. 1991. *Consciousness explained*. Boston, MA: Little, Brown & Company.

DEWEY, J. 1925. *Experience and nature*. Chicago, IL: Open Court.

———. 1963. *Philosophy and civilization*. New York, NY: Capricorn Books.

———. 1988. *Human nature and conduct; An introduction to social psychology*. New York, NY: Holt.

DICK, P.K. 1968. *Do androids dream of electric sheep?* New York, NY: Ballantine Books.

DIETRICH, A. and O. STOLL 2010. Effortless attention, hypofrontality, and perfectionism. In *Effortless attention*, edited by B. Bruya. Cambridge, MA: MIT University Press: 159–78.

DOWNES, S.M. 2010. Are you experienced? What you don't know about your climbing experience. In *Climbing—Philosophy for everyone. Because it's there*, edited by S. Schmid. Malden, MA: Blackwell: 195–205.

DREYFUS, H. and S. DREYFUS. 1986. *Mind over machine: The power of human intuition and expertise in the era of the computer*. New York, NY: The Free Press.

FEDUCCIA, A. and E. MCCRADY. 1991. *Torrey's morphogenesis of the vertebrates*. New York, NY: Wiley.

FIRESTEIN, S. 2012. *Ignorance: How it drives science*. Oxford: Oxford University Press.

FODOR, J. 1975. *The language of thought*. Cambridge, MA: Harvard University Press.

———. 1987. *Psychosemantics*. Cambridge, MA: MIT Press.

GALLAGHER, S. 2005. Dynamic models of body schematic processes. In *Body image and body schema*, edited by H. De Preester and V. Knockaert. Amsterdam: John Benjamins: 233–50.

———. 2007. *How the body shapes the mind*. Oxford: Oxford University Press.

———. 2008. Understanding others: Embodied social cognition. In *Handbook of cognitive science*, edited by P. Calvo and T. Gomila. Amsterdam: Elsevier: 439–52.

———. 2009. Philosophical antecedents to situated cognition. In *Cambridge handbook of situated cognition*, edited by P. Robbins and M. Aydede. Cambridge: Cambridge University Press: 35–50.

———. 2012. *Phenomenology*. Basingstoke: Palgrave Macmillan.

GALLAGER, S. and D. ZAHAVI. 2008. *The phenomenological mind*. London: Routledge.

GIBSON, J.J. 1979. *The ecological approach to visual perception*. Boston, MA: Houghton-Mifflin.

HUTTO, D., M. KIRCHHOFF, and E. MYIN. 2014. Extensive enactivism: Why keep it all in? *Frontiers in Human Neuroscience* 8 (706): 1–11.

HUTTO, D. and E. MYIN 2013. *Radical enactivism: Basic minds without content*. Cambridge, MA: MIT Press.

ILUNDÁIN-AGURRUZA, J. 2013. Moving wisdom: Explaining cognition through movement. *Fair Play: Journal of Philosophy, Ethics and Law* 1 (1): 58–87.

JEANNEROD, M. 1997. *The cognitive neuroscience of action*. Oxford: Blackwell.

———. 2006. *What actions tell the self*. Oxford: Oxford University Press.

JEANNEROD, M. and S. GALLAGHER. 2002. From action to interaction: An interview with Marc Jeannerod. *Journal of Consciousness Studies*, 9 (1): 3–26.

KREIN, K. and J. ILUNDÁIN-AGURRUZA. 2014. An east–west comparative analysis of mushin and flow. In *Philosophy and the martial arts*, edited by G. Priest and D. Young. New York, NY: Routledge: 139–64.

KRETCHMAR, S. 1974. Modes of philosophic inquiry and sport. *Journal of the Philosophy of Sport* 1 (1): 129–31.

———. 2014. A phenomenology of competition. *Journal of the Philosophy of Sport* 41 (1): 21–37.

KRIEGEL, U. 2014. *Current controversies in philosophy of mind*. New York, NY: Routledge.

LAKOFF, G. and R. NUÑEZ. 2000. *Where mathematics comes from: How the embodied mind brings mathematics into being*. New York, NY: Basic Books.

MARTÍNKOVÁ, I. 2011. Anthropos as Kinanthropos: Heidegger and PatoČka on human movement. *Sport, Ethics and Philosophy* 5 (3): 217–30.

MCNAMEE, M.J. 2008. *Sports, virtues and vices: Morality plays*. London: Routledge.

MENARY, R. 2010. *The extended mind*. Cambridge, MA: MIT Press.

MERLEAU-PONTY, M. 1962. *Phenomenology of perception*. London: Routledge.

MOE, VEGARD F. 2005. A critique of cognitivism in sport: From information processing to bodily background knowledge. *Journal of the Philosophy of Sport* 32 (2): 155–83.

———. 2007. Understanding the background conditions of skilled movement in sport: A study of Searle's 'background capacities'. *Sport, Ethics and Philosophy* 1: 299–324.

MORRIS, D. 2002. Touching intelligence. *Journal of the Philosophy of Sport* 29: 149–62.

———. 2004. *The sense of space*. Albany: State University of New York Press.

NOË, A. 2004. *Action in perception*. Cambridge, MA: MIT Press.

NOË, A. and E. THOMPSON. 2002. *Vision and mind*. Cambridge, MA: MIT Press.

O' MAHONY, J. 2013. Chinese supercomputer is World's fastest at 33,860 trillion calculations per second. The Telegraph. Available at http://www.telegraph.co.uk/technology/news/10129285/Chinese-supercomputer-is-worlds-fastest-at-33860-trillion-calculations-per-second.html (accessed 6 July 2014).

O'REGAN, J. and A. NOË. 2001. What it is like to see a sensorimotor theory of perceptual experience. *Synthese* 129: 79–103.

OTAKE, T. 2012. 10,000,000,000,000,000 Calculations per second: Paying a visit to the fastest computer on Earth. The Japan Times. Available at http://www.japantimes.co.jp/life/2012/02/12/general/10000000000000000-calculations-per-second/#.U7pJQRYspuY (accessed 6 July 2014).

PICCININI, G. 2012. Computationalism. In *Oxford handbook of philosophy and cognitive science*, edited by E. Margolis, R. Samuels, and S. Stich. Oxford: Oxford University Press: 222–49.

PRATCHETT, T. and S. BAXTER. 2012. *The long Earth*. London: Transworld.

PUTNAM, H. 1982. *Reason, truth and history*. Cambridge: Cambridge University Press.

PYLYSHYN, Z.W. 1984. *Computation and cognition*. Cambridge, MA: MIT Press.

REID, H.L. 2007. Sport and moral education in Plato's republic. *Journal of the Philosophy of Sport* 34: 160–75.

———. 2010. Athletics and philosophy in ancient Greece and Rome. Contests and virtue. *Sport, Ethics and Philosophy* 4 (2): 109–234.

———. 2012. *Introduction to the philosophy of sport*. Plymouth: Rowan & Littlefield.

RIENER, C.R., J.K. STEFANUCCI, D.R. PROFFITT, and G. CLORE. 2011. An effect of mood on the perception of geographical slant. *Cognition and Emotion* 25 (1): 174–82.

ROHRER, F. 2013. The unwinnable game. BBC News Magazine. Available at http://www.bbc.com/news/magazine-25032298 (accessed 6 July 2014).

ROWLANDS, M. 2010. *The new science of the mind*. Cambridge, MA: MIT Press.

SANDEL, M. J. 2007. *The case against perfection: Ethics in the age of genetic engineering*. Cambridge, MA: Harvard University Press.

SCOTT KELSO, J. A. 1995. *Dynamic patterns: The self-organization of brain and behavior*. Cambridge, MA: MIT Press.

SEOK, B. 2013. *Embodied moral psychology and confucian philosophy*. Plymouth: Lexington Books.

SHAPIRO, L. 2011. *Embodied cognition*. London: Routledge.

SHEETS-JOHNSTONE, M. 2009. *The corporeal turn: An interdisciplinary reader*. Exeter: Imprint Academic.

———. 2011. *The primacy of movement*. 2nd ed. Amsterdam: John Benjamins.

STANDAL, Ø.F. and V. MOE. 2011. Merleau-ponty meets Kretchmar: Sweet tensions of embodied learning. *Sport, Ethics and Philosophy* 5 (3): 256–69.

SUTTON, J. 2014. Remembering as public practice: Wittgenstein, memory, and distributed cognitive ecologies. In *Mind, language, and action: Proceedings of the 36th Wittgenstein symposium*, edited by D. Moyal-Sharrock, V.A. Munz, and A. Coliva. Berlin: Ontos-Verlag: 409–44.

THAGARD, P. 2012. Cognitive science. In *Stanford encyclopedia of philosophy*, edited by E.N. Zalta: 1–21. Available at http://plato.stanford.edu/archives/fall2011/entries/cognitive-science/(PDF).

THOMPSON, E. 2007. *Mind in life: Biology, phenomenology, and the sciences of mind*. Cambridge, MA: Harvard University Press.

TORRES, C. and D. MCLAUGHLIN. 2011. Sweet tension and its phenomenological description: Sport, intersubjectivity, and horizon. *Sports, Ethics and Philosophy* 5 (3): 270–84.

VARELA, F., E. THOMPSON, and E. ROSCH. 1991. *The embodied mind*. Cambridge, MA: MIT Press.

7—RIDING THE WIND—CONSUMMATE PERFORMANCE, PHENOMENOLOGY, AND SKILLFUL FLUENCY

Jesús Ilundáin-Agurruza

Lieh Tzu [Liezi] could ride the wind and go soaring around with cool and breezy skill, but after fifteen days he came back to earth. As far as the search for good fortune went, he didn't fret and worry. He escaped the trouble of walking, but he still had to depend on something to get around. If he had only mounted on the truth of Heaven and Earth, ridden the changes of the six breaths, and thus wandered through the boundless, then what would he have had to depend on? Therefore I say, the Perfect Man has no self; the Holy Man has no merit; the Sage has no fame. (Zhuangzi)[1]

The racing bicycle is the extension of the body and the ultimate skin of thought and awareness. The intense presence of the winds of the world, whistling through hairy arms and legs, gets sharpened: the gaze anticipates the activation of the brake; ominous gravel and holes are sensed faintly, even before they are within eyesight; the eyes in the back of one's neck become suspicious of an overtaking elite biker in the imaginary rear-view mirror, and they can 'see' a menacing car in a switchback behind me while I, in perfect balance and with no fear, descend Mont Ventoux—the windy, white mountain—at 80 km/h. (Steen Nepper Larsen)[2]

This essay continues the exploration that began with the critique of cognitivism. Its goal is to examine the continuities that thick holism offers as sensations become perceptions and movements become perfected, acquiring richer meanings. The performative activities under study best showcase this intimate continuity of normatively laden thinking-in-movement from the ground up and from the sky down, so to speak. In the most admirable cases, performers execute with seemingly unrivaled and exemplary skillful fluency. One fancies they are able, like Chinese sage Liezi, to ride the wind. What sort of process results in the ability to ride the wind—we imagine much as legendary Kelly Slater surfs the waves—with aplomb and immaculate cool?

We develop a phenomenology of skillful movement presently. After a brief primer on phenomenology to characterize its current application (given the plurality of approaches, some of which are quite dubious), we describe proprioceptive and kinesthetic dynamics central to active pursuits that act as experiential and enactive doors toward superb performance, developing a model and a phenomenology of expertise. Then, we consider exemplary execution under the rubric of skillful fluency, specifically discussing its normative aspects. After examining the many different ways of moving

HOLISM AND THE CULTIVATION OF EXCELLENCE IN SPORTS AND PERFORMANCE

meaningfully that we have devised, and changing the paradigm of expertise from skillful coping to skillful fluency, we close with an analysis of how such superb skills develop.

1. The Phenomenology of Skillful Performance

Consider the ways we can describe the final game of the 2014 World Cup between Argentina and Germany, a performance by the Alvin Ailey Dance Company, the final bout of the All Japan Kendo Federation Championship or Cate Blanchett's performance in *Blue Jasmine*. In which ways can we felicitously capture or describe what these performances are about? Would we think that there is *one* true way of capturing their 'truth' or describing the event? Most would remiss to think there is an underlying ultimate essence, Platonic or material, or a singular exclusive and authoritative description. Yet, when it comes to matters of the mind, body, and action (recalling that in our notion of the bodymind, these are seen as unitary; see essay 1), many favor a crude scientism that reduces mental life to materialist and scientific claims of neural regions, particles, and electrical activity. Much that we take essential to those phenomena is missing in such accounts, beginning with the drama that makes any of these events interesting in the first place. Of course, we are asking different kinds of questions; one poses an ontological issue about *what* X is, and the other an experiential about *how* we experience and describe X. Ontology or description, that is, the question.

Philosophers Garrett Thomson and Philip Tureztky (1996) argue that in looking at these kinds of issues, it is best to embrace the goal of description in lieu of ontological explanation, which makes claims about what exists and its nature. We have already critiqued ontologically predominant views on the bodymind as well as the sorts of reductive, reifying descriptions (representations) they adhere to. There is a place and moment for ontology (should it be non-reductive), but after four centuries of internecine disputations, we still are at an impasse. The alternative is to pay attention to our experience, particularly as it concerns performative bodymind dynamics. In fact, *Reflections on a Katana* will argue for a way to bypass the body/mind split *performatively*. Beforehand, we need preparatory work. To this end, we must begin by determining the proper level of description for the phenomenon we want to understand, as Scott Kelso (1995) advises.[3] There are two basic kinds of descriptions we can make, each possibly incorporating various descriptive levels. The following presents an argument against extensional and for intensional descriptions that validates the phenomenological analysis to come.

On the one side, extensional or physicalist descriptions describe the physical world: 'this book weighs 385 grams'; 'snowboarder and skater Shaun White's amygdala shows high electrical and vascular activity.' Such descriptions can capture the physical world at various levels, from the macroscopic to the nanoscale. On the other side, intensional or mentalistic descriptions are concerned with meaning and semantic ascription: 'I find this book appealing if a bit heady'; 'Shaun White is anxious upon facing the 80 degree slope.' Thomson and Turetzky explain, 'We can describe a game of baseball as movement of molecules, or as people hitting a piece of leather with bits of wood,' two extensional descriptions at two different levels, 'or as a game with rules, an etiquette, and winners or losers,' an intensional description (1996, 448). Consider an intensional description summing up the career of Dave

153

Bergman, who won a World Series with the Detroit Tigers in 1984: 'Fans and teammates loved him, probably a little more than you'd expect for a utility man who was a career .258 hitter [...] While Bergman wasn't a star, he did one thing really well — he was a master of the hidden-ball trick.' (Oz, 2015) It takes on added meaning when we find out that this was written the day after Bergman prematurely died of cancer on February 2, 2015. This cannot be captured in a purely extensional way as the following explains further.

We can describe any of the aforementioned events via Cartesian coordinates that ascribe different positions to the various particles in place at different time scales. Choosing the proper level and length scale is already a problem. Should the pertinent 'particles' be: players, dancers, and *karateka*; or different markers in their joints, face, and other body parts if biomechanic criteria are used; or cells and molecules when biological and chemical criteria prevail; or atoms or smaller particles if the ultimate reduction is performed by physicists? Would we use minutes for performance length, seconds for specific moves or pieces, or milliseconds for neural and muscular reaction times? The selection of a suitable extensional level of description is problematic. We can opt to capture an infinite number of physical properties and their relations. We can choose mass, or velocity vectors and trajectories, or acceleration, or elect to match some particular chromatic resonances over others, or for that matter, percussive properties. For example, we could say that particle 08 and particle 03 coincided at time 245, with particle 35 crossing vector DF5366-BW2353 at time T-16:00:001. But, there is the practical impossibility of carrying this out in detail, no matter which computational resources we pick. How would we describe a cricket game capturing all positions for *all* relevant data points if we were to pick subatomic particles?[4] Besides, the long strings of numbers would leave out precisely the very aspects that make us *care* about these sorts of events. Precise as to the trajectories and positions of bodies or particles, they would completely miss the significance, the very meaning of saying that the ball kicked by Mario Götze crossed the Argentine goalposts. The extensional rendering leaves German and Argentine fans unfazed; the intensional one dispenses ecstasy and agony, respectively. Extensional descriptions *alone* are literally meaningless (for us). Of course, which level we *do* choose depends on what we wish to describe. Yet, none is a better candidate on extensional grounds. That is, which aspects of reality we pick *already* comes with a built in normativity that appeals to the very intensional level and criteria that scientism and reduction seek to reduce or eliminate: there are reasons we must bring to prefer one level over another, and to the extent that these are meaningful, they are intensional.

Crude scientism and reductionism try to deny the applicability of intensional descriptions or to reduce them to extensional ones. This means that the real issue lies not in ontology, but in the relationship between these two modes of description. We can reformulate the issue as follows: 'How can there be true intensional sentences if the whole universe can be characterized entirely extensionally?' (Thomson and Tureztky 1996, 449) Much as we have done already, Thomson and Turetzky consider and reject reification, reductionism, and eliminativism, concluding that we need not accept the premise that extension suffices to describe reality, nor abide by any of their strategies to reify, reduce, or eliminate (ibid., 452). Consistent with thick holism, they conclude that we need to: (a) formulate creative cognitive connections, (b) formulate an understanding through posture and use of our bodies, and (c) care about phenomena, etc., as demonstrated 'through the projects a person undertakes and the commitment

HOLISM AND THE CULTIVATION OF EXCELLENCE IN SPORTS AND PERFORMANCE

manifested in her actions over a long period of time and in he context of social interactions and relations' (ibid., 456). They close with the 'intriguing suggestion [...] that we should give up the claim that extensional descriptions are a paradigm of understanding and clarity and somehow see intensional descriptions as somehow more basic' (ibid., 457). In an auspicious footnote, Thomson and Tureztky state that phenomenology undertakes this (ibid., 458 fn. 37). The remainder of this essay focuses on intensional and phenomenological qualitative descriptions (occasionally supplemented with extensional ones from the mind sciences when suitable). After the short overview of phenomenology (others have recently provided this in detail in the context of sports, Martínková and Parry, 2011, 2013), we delve into the rich details of performance as felt, explore some illustrative phenomenological descriptions of movement and skills, and begin the process of tying these to normative elements.

1.1. A Phenomenological Primer

Phenomenology deals richly with the intensional level, our meaningful and *lived* experience, but allows for intersubjective corroboration and objective congruence. Phenomenology, through *epoché* or bracketing, suspends the natural attitude that science and everyday life bring with them, as well as any concerns with existence, and allows us to develop an insightful understanding of our experience. This lays a solid stance for in-depth phenomenological perspectives and analyses of skills in sport and related performative endeavors that help vet scientific causal claims and enrich our lives with meaningful articulations and experiences. Even if this is concerned with our lived experience, it is not mere subjectivism. Rather, phenomenology seeks to uncover the invariant structure of experience or mode common to any given class of entities or phenomena. In addition to the *epoché*, it also implements a phenomenological or eidetic reduction to analyze the different correlations among specific structures of subjectivity *as* experienced: when we look at a dancer's body on stage, we perceive it in profile, yet cannot help to 'see' it as whole (we do not see it as lacking a back or right side); then, we proceed to determine the common aspects of perspectival human vision and its underlying processes, such as the 'filling in.' Without a laboratory, but after rigorous training, we can each conduct our own phenomenological inquiry. Yet it is not so much the *personal* but the universal that we seek to ascertain, not the 'what' of a specific experience but the 'how.' Martínková and Parry,[5] clearly state that phenomenology has 'to do with the universal-personal, not the particular-personal. It emphasizes experience (personal experience), but not subjective experience' (2011, 190).

It is important to emphasize this because some social scientists and philosophers of sport mistakenly think that phenomenology is but subjectivist opinion. Not any intensional description (or extensional) will do as well as any other one, particularly with phenomenologically rigorous ones. Husserl's eidetic variation and the invariant structures his method delivers do not mean lack of differences. This is where intersubjective validation comes: we contrast our findings with those of others. It is not any different from scientists, who also test one another's hypotheses and experiments. Besides, there are many ways to cut the cake, many delicious ways to examine and describe (sporting) experience. The beauty of this approach is that it prompts scholars to find universal structures to our experience that underwrite cross-cultural differences, as well as refined modes of description that better articulate the ever-elusive *je ne se quoi* of experience.

HOLISM AND THE CULTIVATION OF EXCELLENCE IN SPORTS AND PERFORMANCE

The principal phenomenological aim is disclosure—in Heidegger's (1962, 1971) sense of *aletheia*—of the universal structure, the dynamics as felt qualities, of our experience of movement, action, and skills in sports and other performative activities. Besides helping to better understand the phenomena in question, this will elucidate the deep connection between the normative—ethical, aesthetic, and existential standards of excellence—and the psychophysical processes of our bodymind. The work of Heidegger, Husserl, Merleau-Ponty, and Sartre underlies and deeply informs this examination. But, the focus is on contemporary phenomenologists more directly connected with the objectives of this study, notably Breivik, Gallagher, and Sheets-Johnstone among others. Some, such as sport philosopher Spencer Wertz, may not strictly be phenomenologists, but they still conduct keen phenomenological analyses.

1.2. Movement and Skill Dynamics in Performance

Engaging their skills, athletes and performers *feel* movement in rich and various ways—as the rest of us do within the limits of our own capabilities. But clarifying and describing aptly these feelings is challenging. When discussing the felt dynamics of movement and skills in performances, it is advisable to begin by considering feelings as sensations *and* perceptions before setting them, as gems on precious metal, on a proprioceptive and kinesthetic context. For Wertz, feelings are either perceptual, of objects (snow under your feet, or the change in one's pocket), or feelings as sensations (1991, 165–166). This differs from our distinction in the previous essay whereby perceptions are interpreted sensations. Perceptions for him concern external objects, while sensations are of inward phenomena. Because of reasons to be elucidated below, we make no inside/outside distinction of *meaningful* phenomena. Henceforth, we treat sensations of external objects and inward ones (kinesthetic, proprioceptive) in the same way and restrict 'perception' to any interpreted phenomena.

This aside, and in full agreement with Wertz now, what the feelings of perceptions and sensations (in his or our sense) share is that to be able to sense them requires the exercise of a skill and ability: people come to know them through use of limbs and cues (Wertz 1991, 166). In handling a tennis racket or throwing a javelin, we feel sensations specific to that implement and its handling which, coupled to how *we* wield them, in the best cases, come to be integrated into our bodymind through Deweyan habit (an active and deliberate cultivation). Wertz points out how G. E. M. Anscombe rightly distinguishes between sensations that can be described separately of X and those that cannot. Perceptively, he argues that the latter are characteristic of sport: 'the sort of sensations one has in the whole action of the service motion [in tennis] are ones simply not available unless a person has mastered the skills that make those sensations possible' (Wertz 1991, 172). As mentioned in essay 6 with regard to representations and Anders Ericsson's views (2003), the action and the kinesthetic dynamics are necessarily connected. Wertz dissents from Anscombe, however, because the inseparableness gives us clues in knowing those sensations. For him, 'there are elements in our experience that we do treat as cues in trying to master a given skill, and athletes in particular learn to recognize these early in their careers.' (Wertz 1991, 172) In this case, intimate experience and cue sensitivity serve to correct misguided conceptual analysis of performative phenomena from the couch. Perception is an intricate affair.

HOLISM AND THE CULTIVATION OF EXCELLENCE IN SPORTS AND PERFORMANCE

The complexities of perception are made clear by neuroscientist Michael O'Shea, who explains that it is feasible 'to perceive what is not sensed, not to perceive what is sensed, and to construct more than one perception from the same sensations,' as with the famous illusion of the painting by W. E. Hill, *My Wife and Mother-in-Law*, where we can either see a young woman or older one (2005, 64–65). Given the tremendous quantity of sensorial input, we can only become reflectively aware of a small slice of it. Thus, movements and sensations *sometimes* become perceptions, since these depend on being ascribed meaning. When speaking of cues, complex patterns of sensations, and other elements in the flow of movement as perceptions, it is better to speak of interpretation. As sensation becomes perception and linguistically articulated, it undergoes an interpretive process that is hermeneutically specific to the phenomenon in question: it is not the same thing to interpret a poem, painting, bullfight, handball game, dance, or sumo match. Even though the hermeneutic practice is analogous *qua* interpretive means to explore and co-create the phenomenon (along with the performer and the object or action), each may require *inter alia* different criteria, familiarity with the history of the practice, and its own standards of taste and excellence.[6] This underwrites the underlying perspectivism of *Skillful Striving* (essay 4). We may sense the 'same' putative object or phenomenon, but as we learn to identify and discriminate, we end up with different perceptions. Ortega (2006) gives the example of a hunter, a farmer, and a painter facing a landscape. Each will see three different landscapes as they lift from the river of sensations different elements. They can see the same group of trees, but the hunter sees there a hiding place for deer, the farmer a source of chestnuts, and the painter, a focal point for his painting. In other words, the interpretation we ascribe to experienced phenomena makes *all* the difference for us: we end up with different percepts and as such different felt 'realities.' Nonetheless, they are subject to the same interpretive process in terms of method and structure.

In the case of sport and active pursuits, phenomenological analyses of performance detail how sensations become interpreted and articulated perceptions that we can then weave into richer narratives about the performance, and ultimately its place in our life's overarching narrative. Therein lies the challenge, in learning to discriminate and articulate a largely subpersonal world about which Dewey says,

> we continually engage in an immense multitude of immediate organic selections, rejections, welcomings, expulsions, appropriations, withdrawals, shrinkings, expansions, elations and dejections, attacks, wardings off, of the most minute, vibratingly delicate nature. We are not aware of the qualities of many or most of these acts; we do not objectively distinguish and identify them. Yet they exist as feeling qualities, and have an enormous directive effect on our behavior. (1963, 299–300)

Kinesthetic and proprioceptive *perceptions* are those explicitly paid attention to, discriminated, and interpreted. The point to stress is that we should avoid reifying kinesthetic and proprioceptive perceptions or even sensations (when referring to them) into discrete object-like referents of our words. Wertz writes, 'This particular feeling is not localized by a specific object, but it is still 'localized' in some sense by a *whole* set of objects—there is a matrix of physical geometry that encompasses the court and the players' (Wertz 1991, 166 my emphasis). The emphasis here should fall on the 'whole' rather than the 'set of objects,' a *fluid* whole whose objects' interrelations dynamically vary. Alternatively, we can think of this holistically in terms of the kinesthetic and proprioceptive dynamics within the context, in tennis, of the court and players. Further, the very relations change qualitatively also, differing from game to game, and moment to moment. Yet, amid variability, Sheets-Johnstone finds the common thread. It is.

> kinesthetically felt and has an affective character generated by the very movement that produces it at the same time that [said movement] is kinesthetically constituted as an ongoing qualitative affective-kinetic dynamic: it is heavy or light, moderately fast or solemnly slow, has swelling crescendos and fading diminuendos, and so on. (Sheets-Johnstone 2011, 469; see also 2009, 254–258)

A serve is not just a movement, of course, but it comes with those qualitative kinesthetic, affective, and kinetic dynamics. It can begin moderately fast and increase its speed then come to an abrupt end to give a specific spin to the ball, and underlying affectivities invariably accompany it, for example, it may be modulated by certain desultoriness on account of fatigue or with buoyant verve and excitement because of the anticipated match game point.

With these elucidations in place, we can proceed to integrate them into the broader context of proprioception and kinesthesia. Many fail to distinguish the two, while others subsume kinesthesia under proprioception.[7] This is misguided. Proprioception has to do with limb and body position and here indicates what Gallagher (2005a) refers to as proprioceptive awareness, that is, being aware of our own body; it differs from proprioception as theorized by neuroscience, which sees it as subpersonal, that is, non-conscious. While both are fully integrated experientially (ibid.), for our purposes, it works best to keep the former sense of awareness forefront. Moreover, proprioception presently is also Gibsonian (Gibson 1979) in that it is part of an ecological holistic environment. Mindful of Sheets-Johnstone's (2011) apt criticism that Gibson's proprioception is static and positional, we should conceive of it as radically dynamic and correlated with and largely dependent on the kinesthetic. We are directly connected to the environment in resonant ways, and vice versa, the environment also responds to us. This much should be clear from the incursions into this topic by way of Dewey and Ortega (essays 3 and 4 respectively), who suitably stress the relevance of the organism–environment coupling as well as the role of our inward sensations (not inner): pace Ortega's views on body, soul, and vitality and Dewey's evocative writings on the role of these at all cognitive and emotional levels. Nepper Larsen illustrates this dynamic relation between us and the environment (inclusive of tools), articulating it in a way that incorporates both, the extensional and neuroscientific descriptive level and the phenomenological and intensional one. He writes,

> When the neuronal couplings that concern the bike are grounded and formed in the brain, the synapses are influenced by spatial interpretations, the sensual quality of rough rides, the linguistic exchanges in a group of tense riders heading towards the final sprint, the appraisal of new asphalt with no hole. This happens via the muscular conquests through which you become aware of the power you possess, the future performances, and the options to which the roads of the world might invite you. We are doomed to search for meaning. We can't help ascribing sense to things and events while we swiftly move sitting on slim gel-filled saddles, calm and stoic on steel, aluminium, or carbon frames. (Nepper Larsen 2010, 28)

HOLISM AND THE CULTIVATION OF EXCELLENCE IN SPORTS AND PERFORMANCE

Many of these dynamics, on which we build our meaningful narratives, are first wrought and experienced through those muscular conquests, that is, kinesthetically. Kinesthesia is 'a sense of movement through a sense of muscular effort' (Sheets-Johnstone 2009, 164 fn. 13). We are aware of our limbs and bodily position proprioceptively largely through kinesthetic dynamics: we feel our movement in virtue of the muscles' tensional qualities (or absence thereof). On the basis of these sensations, we form perceptions as *meaningful* pressures and forces—in sport often of the painful kind. (We also weave them into narratives that justify these exertions within the framework of practices.) Proprioceptively, we *can* tell the position of our limbs without movement sometimes. As Gallagher explains, 'static' proprioceptive awareness is sufficient to tell knee position, which entails a pre-reflective pragmatic and *non-objectifying* bodily awareness (Gallagher 2005a, 46). But, it is through kinesthetic feelings (both sensations and percepts) that we ascertain limb and body position *as* we move. We learn to recognize this mediated through movement, for as Wertz's explains, 'sensations and bodily position cannot be equated' because as sport makes clear, the spatial relations of our limbs are learned and mediated, not known directly (1991, 169). Even in the absence of movement, we determine limb or other positions—our ribs expanding or contracting, our spine straight or curved—often by contrasting kinesthetic feelings coupled to proprioceptive markers. Other relevant dynamics are vestibular ones, those inner-ear fluctuations that inform us of spatial orientation, or nociceptive ones, that is, perceptions of pain, which in active endeavors are commonplace. There is a danger, however, that these phenomenological dynamics be construed as purely inner or subjective in a private sense, as pain is often and mistakenly presumed to be.

It is important to stress that this phenomenological analysis does not presuppose an 'inner phenomenon' as a *private* sensation. Proprioceptive and kinesthetic dynamics are not any more inner, private, and accessible only through introspective ostensiveness than the food in the stomach and the digestive system's operations are. These days all it takes is a tube-fed camera for the doctor to see our dietary epicurean or stoic habits. In both cases, these are functions of the body(mind), 'bodily' processes, and as such not 'subjectively private sensations' *even* if I am the only one who can feel my sensations as mine. This is similar to how feeling and thinking my actions as intentionally mine and as I experience it through my senses of agency and ownership respectively does not presuppose a private world (more on these senses below). Inward sensations may be empirically validated and correlated in various ways (observation, behavior, self-reports, EEG, ECG, fMRI, etc.), and more importantly, they become meaningful *only* through a public, intersubjective context. In agreement with Wittgenstein's argument against any private language, we reject the meaningfulness of a private 'inner' world. We mark this difference by adopting the term 'inward', which directs our attention but does not locate, as opposed to 'inside,' 'inner,' and similar labels (the last essay delves into this further). Nonetheless, some in the Wittgensteinian camp have sensible reservations.

David Best, in an attempt to preserve the relevance of empirical methodology and conceptual analysis,[8] shows misapprehension concerning 'much phenomenological thought, which mistakenly assumes that it makes sense to suggest that it is possible to exclude contextual and therefore conceptual factors in order to concentrate on what it supposes to be the movement *itself*' (1979, 93, his emphasis). He is correct in his charge concerning those thinkers who make that claim. We do not perceive movement itself. Yet, none of the above exposition asserts or implies this. Rather, we feel in our

HOLISM AND THE CULTIVATION OF EXCELLENCE IN SPORTS AND PERFORMANCE

bodymind certain fluctuations that mark the *experience* of movement. Best (1979) criticizes Eleanor Metheny's stance on movement as dualist by underlining the difference between connotation and logical meaning after she divides the meaning of movement into overt and inner behavior. He states that,

> The range of possibilities of human movement provides a unique variety of experiences, but not because movement is a unique symbol of meaning, or a symbol of unique meaning, or a unique symbol of unique meaning. It is because the *feelings* which can be experienced while moving cannot be experienced in other ways. (Best 1979, 137, my emphasis)

Precisely as phenomenologically analyzed here, it is the feelings themselves that provide the unique structure of our bodies in movement, and not movement (as intentionally originating in the agent) or motion (as bodies moved in space, e.g. being pushed and falling).[9] Best could not make that claim unless he were first and personally aware phenomenologically of what movement feels like. Also, let us recall (essay 1) that we understand our own actions on the highest pragmatic level possible, that is pragmatically, intentionally, and ignoring lower level descriptions and mentalistic interpretations (Gallagher 2005a). The experience of movement and its phenomenological analysis do not lead to either diving into a private introspective world or a dualist division of our bodymind dynamics.

But, we can dive phenomenologically into these *felt* kinesthetic and kinetic qualities of the *experience* of movement with what Sheets-Johnstone calls the 'four cardinal structures of movement' (2009). Building on her career as a professional dancer, she developed a phenomenological description of the invariant qualities of the dance experience. She identifies four basic qualities common to *any* movement we may experience as a unified flow, separable only analytically (Sheets-Johnstone 2009, 204–207).[10] We can present these using platform diving as explanatory subject. There is (1) a *tensional* quality, which captures the felt effort when moving, here the initial percussive effort to launch from the platform; (2) the diving flight's *linear* quality concerning the path she takes, quite complex on account of the gyrations and twists along the diver's own axis while spinning along the vertical path travelled; (3) an *amplitudinal* quality, 'the felt expansiveness or contractiveness of our moving body and the spatial extensiveness or constrictedness of our movement' (ibid., 207), when in a pike, the diver is compressed, to unfold herself as she begins her twists and becomes fully stretched, arms and pointed toes, just before contact with the water 30 feet below; and (4) a *projectional* quality, how the energy is released, from the initial immobility of the starting position to the explosive takeoff, the quick release of the tuck as she begins her aerial maneuvers, and the final stiffening as she lines up the entry. Proprioception is crucial in this process, and again separable only conceptually. Important in this sport are also the vestibular dynamics, which tell the diver her position in the air, orienting her in space, visual ones that inform her when to stop rotating (called 'visual spotting'), tactile ones as she enters the water, and sometimes nociceptive ones, the wrists hurting, depending on the angle of impact on the water. Underscoring this there is an emotional tonality, which can range from calmness to anxiety. This emotional tonality is tightly connected with processes of self-cultivation and high performance, as *Reflections on a Katana* shows.

HOLISM AND THE CULTIVATION OF EXCELLENCE IN SPORTS AND PERFORMANCE

Our sensorimotor processes in charge of motor control, connected to perceptual processes, allow us to monitor and guide the intentional aspects of our actions, Gallagher (2012) explains. Yet, in terms of how this is felt and manifested to us, it is better described phenomenologically in terms of the kinesthetic dynamics we experience as we move. We do not feel sensorimotor processes even if we are steeped in neuroscientific research. Rather, we experience our body as we move, .for example, during a set of ten 200-m freestyle in the pool or sprints in the running or cycling track the muscles, lungs, and joints hurt in very specific ways that neither swimmer, cyclist, or runner would confuse for the other should they swap places—something any triathlete is very familiar with.

Observant of Gallagher's prescription for a pragmatic descriptive level, kinesthesia and proprioceptive dynamics emphasize the experience and perspective of performers, staying closer to their felt realities. Moreover, as Steel writes,

> knowing the muscular movements, that is, knowing how the action takes place on the level of anatomy, is not the same as knowing how to actually perform the action. Teaching someone how the muscles move does not teach him how to serve. In fact, thinking about the muscle movements when trying to serve would inhibit, even paralyze action. We are not learning a series of muscle movements, but a *whole flowing action*. We do not see the forest when we look only at the trees. We do not see the action when we look only at the muscle movements. (1977, 99, my emphasis)

This flowing action comes in degrees and kinds, depending on the agent's skill. We cannot equate the flowing actions and feelings of novices and experts. (*Fractured Action* discusses how choking gets in the way of such flowing action.) Interestingly, the specific feelings, not to say quality of flowing movement, correlate with the performer's skill level. Empirical evidence in cognitive science and sport psychology show how experts process information differently than novices and demonstrate more refined automatized processes that bypass rule implementation, e.g. keep the wrist aligned with the racquet's handle, rotate the hip,. when it comes to cognitive resources that pertain to memory (Beilock, Wierenga, and Carr 2003), attention (Beilock and Carr 2001) and sensorimotor skills (better articulated as skillful movement) (Beilock and Carr 2004). Our paragons of excellence are not simply quantitatively faster, stronger, or more flexible, but they are qualitatively better in *how* they operate (to include their ability to discriminate sensory input). They move differently to put it simply. Although Dewey speaks of an artist, much the same goes for performers,

> The fact, the scientific fact, is that even in his exercises, his practice *for* skill, an artist uses an art he already has. He acquires greater skill because practice *of* skill is more important to him than practice *for* skill. Otherwise the natural endowment would count for nothing, and sufficient mechanical exercise would make any one an expert in any field. A flexible, sensitive habit grows more varied, more adaptable by practice and use. (1988, 51–52, his emphasis)

Dewey concludes that while we do not understand the physiology of mechanical routine and artistic skill, both are habits. Even if we did understand it fully, these would be best cultivated as Deweyan habits. This practice *of* skill is what the better athletes and

HOLISM AND THE CULTIVATION OF EXCELLENCE IN SPORTS AND PERFORMANCE

performers do most of the time. Zhuangzian spontaneity (essay 5), where superb performers match skills to challenge, results from practice *of* skills that are pushed beyond current capabilities. Dan Hutto (2014) argues that spontaneous action necessitates practice not because practice makes perfect, but rather because it makes us *poised, practiced, and prepared*. The poise and preparation—a Deweyan process—prepare us to meet performative challenges with spontaneity rather than automaticity (alone). Those better and most practiced will perform better, all things being equal (see subsection 1.3).

We may wonder how we find the fit between our talents, skills, and suitable practices at which we may excel. Luck plays a big role, of course, not only in terms of the talents we are endowed with, but also in finding a matching practice that suits them. A Bedouin born and raised in the hot sands of Arabia built like Michael Phelps is unlikely to fulfill his latent talent and become a master swimmer. But, it is not only the vagaries of chance that determine this. Being adventurous is also important. Exploring widely, striking out and trying a good number of sports, dances, instruments, and so on increases our chances. When there is a match between talents, disposition, and hard work, we right away find that joyful agreement that fuels passionate dedication. Our skills find ways of performing that, as the saying goes, fit like a glove. There is much to be said for natural endowment; those who excel as paragons are amply endowed. But should we find the match (or the match find us), it still needs that practice *of* skill and cultivation. Regardless, and to retake Ortega again, this is no reason for anyone not to try to reach his or her personal perfection. And learning is something we all can attempt. That said, not all learn in the same way and, as we progress, our learning strategies change.

Novices learn piecemeal through rule implementation and attention to specific movement and body parts. Masters 'forget' rules and specifics.[11] Part of the process of mastery involves developing a sense for the holistic feel of a whole and flowing movement complete in itself. Able skiers do not simply (learn to) dip the hips into a skiing turn if they begin to lose stability, rather they integrate the position of knees, arms, head, torso into a kinetic unity that they tell is 'right' not so much from the result, stability and newfound control, but also the recognition of what *that* feels like. They learn to fall and be comfortable with it. As Erik Bendix explains,

> Alpine skiing is all about slipping and sliding and falling, but instead of aiming to make us laugh [as compared to a falling clown], it aims to transform the act of sliding downhill into a long slow-motion dance with gravity. [...] Skiers who have learned the dance well are able to settle those panicky movements down into something much smoother and more sustained. The skier still falls, but in a slow controlled motion that can stretch down an entire mountainside. Instead of fighting the pull of gravity, the more comfortable skier yields to it and finds ways to play with its force. Skiing then becomes a thing of beauty. (2014, n.p.)

This takes place on a slope, atop slippery snow, on skis, all of which are relevant to the body's adaptation and dynamics. Becoming proficient entails recognizing the right dynamics *as* one moves rather than abstractly breaking them down (of course, this is also important, but by itself or if prevalent, it will not do). Yielding requires trust and confidence. And this means feeling comfortable. To reiterate Steels' point, we learn a

HOLISM AND THE CULTIVATION OF EXCELLENCE IN SPORTS AND PERFORMANCE

whole flowing action and not a series of muscle movements. Insightfully, Wertz specifies that feelings become the 'right' feelings of a good serve or butterfly kick 'only *after* the acquisition of the physical skill in question. Commonly athletes do not know what it feels like until they have felt it, and they cannot judge how it is going to feel. If they try to, they may be surprised.' (1991, 167) Wertz's insight legitimates the perspective of the performer, something already foreshadowed in his correction of Anscombe. Adapting the phenomenology to excellent performance and performers' experiences leads to some modifications of current analyses.

1.3. Animating Description

Gallagher makes a very useful distinction between body schema and body image that we can modify to give a better account of performative dynamics. This draws a conceptual distinction to capture two operating systems that structure our experience. They form a seamless process unless pathological disruptions (e.g. schizophrenia, choking in sports) split them asunder. They are neither mechanisms nor anatomic or physiological constructs, but rather two ways in which we phenomenologically structure the experience of our bodymind. Gallagher defines body image as 'a system of (sometimes conscious) perceptions, attitudes, and beliefs pertaining to one's own body,' and body schema as 'a nonconscious system of processes that constantly regulate posture and movement—a system of motor-sensory capacities that function below the threshold of awareness, and without the necessity of perceptual monitoring' (2012, 234). He and Sheets-Johnstone have cordially and extensively contested the suitability of these concepts. Among other things, the core of the latter's charge is that these concepts are too static (2009, 328–340), which Gallagher has accommodated by highlighting the dynamic character of body schema, and the fact that the body image is not meant to capture such dynamics and is congruent with evidence from deafferented subjects (those who lose sensory input of a body part) (2012, 239–244). She proposes a different terminology, 'corporeal-kinetic patterning,' because it captures the kinetic dynamics (2009, 339). In order to avoid polemics but profit from their insightful exchange, the proposal is to deploy a modified nomenclature that combines their ideas. It reflects the inherent dynamics and avoids a reification and stultification both wish to avoid. Accordingly, these are reframed as 'bodily imaging' and 'bodily schematizing' patterns. The gerund precisely emphasizes the changing, dynamic qualities of our movement, while 'patterning' underscores that they are indeed procedural and not constructs.[12] While some might object that bodily imaging may not need to be characterized as dynamic, as Gallagher (2005b) suggests, he elsewhere intimates its flexible and dynamic nature, as it can be affected by posture, health, fatigue, nutrition, and so on. That is, it changes in synchrony with surrounding conditions affecting the system. The reframed concepts capture a crucial aspect of how our experience is structured: there are underlying patternings of movement that 'move' us such that we have a conceptual notion of what our body is/feels/looks like. This connects with William James' views.

As we saw in essay 2, Mark Johnson highlights the continuity in James' thinking between concepts and percepts, being but 'two aspects of a continuous flow of feeling-thinking' (2007, 87) and urges us to speak of the *act* of conceptualizing. This is precisely the sense in which to take the various uses of the gerund regarding bodymind functions: emphasizing the continuities and dynamic ebbs and flows. Thus, there is a flowing schematizing of the movement as the left wing, relying on moves that have become apparently 'instinctual,' dodges the oncoming defender and seamlessly heel-kicks the football to a striker running behind him; there is an imaging of the body as the dancer slowly rolls from the back of her partner and onto the floor as she visualizes her head driving the motion and her spine curving. Both, schematizing and imaging work in tandem—separated here for explanatory purposes only—and rely on kinetic, kinesthetic, and proprioceptive input.

Gallagher rightly claims that in everyday actions we mind the body only when conditions warrant. Bodily schematizing, in charge of subpersonal postural control, 'pushes the body into the recesses of awareness,' (Gallagher 2005a, 34). This frees us to be able to pay more attention to our surroundings than to our body. Accordingly, the schematizing handles many functions and movements offline, freeing up bandwidth to pay attention to the task itself (and bypassing the cognitivist problem concerning computational speed). Gallagher's (2005a) analysis of action in sport also correctly details how bodily imaging can contribute to movement control, for instance, when learning new techniques, steps, and refining one's game of tennis. This helps explain novice learning and characterizes some of the steps toward expertise.

For Gallagher (2005a) the subconscious proprioceptions tied to the bodily schematizing, which he calls 'proprioceptive information,' modulate most of our interactions in everyday life as we move about the world performing movements unconsciously, for example, holding a book or moving about a room. Gallagher correctly says that when 'learning dance or athletic movements, focusing attention on specific body parts can alter the established postural schema' (ibid., 141 fn. 6). Indeed, this remaking of bodily schematizing patternings requires attention to the relevant limb(s), but this remark is incomplete. To prefigure the discussion of expertise next, this happens when learning, but *also* when refining already expert movement. It is not a matter of simply focusing either. Such restructuring requires deliberate and continued attention, a *mindful* repetition of the movements in question until they become part of a flowing movement. Deweyan habit is the name of the game. Moreover, what guides experts is not the 'feel' of the specific body part but consummate wholes: in training, they may focus on hand entry position in their freestyle, but it has to feel right as a complete movement.

Discussing action and agency elsewhere Gallagher emphasizes how our sense of agency, phenomenologically, allows us to feel and claim *we* are the ones intentionally acting, without the need for introspection (2012, 168). Nor does it require explicit monitoring of our bodily movements, which we normally do not attend to (ibid., 169). For instance, when catching a ball in a game our attention is solely on the ball, predicting its speed and flight, and not our locomotion in relation to it (Gallagher 2005a, 26). He presents this example alongside one of walking across the room to meet someone. He writes that typically '[t]he body in action tends to efface itself in most purposive activities' (ibid., 26). By contrast Gallagher (2005a) observes how walking a narrow ledge over a precipice may involve a large amount of willed conscious control of the limbs. This concurs with James's principle of parsimony of consciousness, which is supposed to apply to most actions and movement in ordinary life. As James explains,

> We walk the beam the better the less we think of the position of our feet upon it. We pitch or catch, we shoot or chop better the less tactile and muscular [...] and the

HOLISM AND THE CULTIVATION OF EXCELLENCE IN SPORTS AND PERFORMANCE

more exclusively optical [...] our consciousness is. Keep your *eye* on the place aimed at, and your hand will fetch it; think of your hand, and you will very likely miss your aim. (Shusterman 2008, 165)

James, discussing attention with regard to our ideas of kinesthetic feelings and fluent action, determines that *'as a rule*, such feelings and ideas thereof have no substantive interest; our interest lies with the ends that our movements seek' (James 1890, 813, my emphasis). Indeed, when most people engage in a game of ball or practice a kata, or walk a ledge, they forget about their body and train the eyes on the ball focusing on the specific moves in the sequence, or willfully inch forward with eyes locked on the feet and the ground just ahead of our toes, sweating, swearing profusely, praying, or some combination thereof. This explains some features of everyday experience and sports. Expert performance is different. Not observing this leads to common misperceptions.

1.4. The Unique Phenomenology of Expert Performance

Through poise, practice, and preparedness, masters of their art acquire broader skillful repertoires and deeper performative registers. Since the dynamics and feel of sportive and performative flowing actions are tied to the skill level, this means that the qualitative experience of elite and superior performers differs from that of average performers. Hence, we cannot merely extrapolate if we wish to describe it accurately and understand it properly. Excellent performance in sport and performative endeavors means very specialized and refined skills with very narrow applications that draw heavily on psychophysical, social, and environmental resources. To study this duly and fully, we should complement empirical and theoretical studies with a suitably adapted phenomenology. After all, as a method, phenomenology relies on *personal* analysis even when ultimately it is subject to intersubjective scrutiny. This leads to correcting three common misunderstandings, delineating recommendations for phenomenological analyses, and underscoring performers' perspectives.

The first misunderstanding concerns misjudging the actual skills and dynamics of performance. The most visible example involves visual tracking. Consider vision in baseball, cricket and similar sports. Conventional wisdom in this case is mistaken regarding both average and expert performers. The speed of the ball batters face is too fast to keep normal eyes trained on it. Yet this is a popular belief to which even academics ascribe. In one of the few instances when Richard Shusterman engages sport at some length, surprising given that his thorough and insightful somaesthetic work seeks to legitimize 'the body as 'our tool of tools,' he writes that the batter needs to keep the eye on the ball (2012, 3; also 40). We know better nowadays.[13]

Knudson and Kukla (1997) note that at speeds that go beyond that of a person walking three mph (five kph) six feet (2 m) away from us, our eyesight needs saccades (the eyes jump and go blind for an instant).[14] Tracking fast moving objects is challenging even at 'slower' speeds and relies on saccades and recalibrations that estimate where to see the object next in between blind moments. But the spheres thrown in professional sports, such as baseball with its 95 mph (150 kph) fastballs or tennis with its 120 mph (190 kph) serves, exceed saccadic scanning. Our eyes cannot track the ball and estimate trajectory by jumping ahead in the projected path. To put it in perspective, our eyes would be 15 feet behind schedule, which means we would get hit by the balls (Anwan 2013). Knudson and Kukla state,

> 'In striking sports (baseball, tennis) teachers often use cues telling players watch the ball till it hits the bat/racket. Ball/bat collisions in baseball and softball only last 1 or 2 milliseconds (0.001 s). It is unlikely that any athlete can *consistently* see the ball hit the bat. Batters cannot use smooth pursuit to track the ball to the point of impact, even in slow pitch softball (Watts and Bahill 1990)!' (1997, my emphasis)

Thus the usual admonition to watch the ball hit the bat is actually counterproductive to the better one of watching its release (Knudson and Kukla 1997). This informs batters of the trajectory the ball will take and allows them to adjust appropriately should they have sufficient experience. While this inability to follow fastballs is true of all, novices, proficient players, and experts, *how* they handle visual and cognitive limitations differs. Novices and less abled athletes look at the ball; elite athletes do not focus on the ball but instead use bodily cues, reading their opponents' movements to guide them (Mann 2014). In fact, they only need a blurry image to accurately determine trajectory. They are able to accurately determine the path of much faster moving objects *because* they do not look at the object at all, nor do they try to do so. In other words, they embrace the 'invisibility' of the ball that most of us try to closely 'watch.' This means that we are mistaken when we claim to see the ball, all the more so if we attribute this to experts. They do not even try to observe the ball. Consequently, this should inform our phenomenology.

The insight that experts do not act in accordance with 'common sense' and popular views holds across other sports and active endeavors even when heedful of their specificity. Claims about walking on ledges or ropes as described by Gallagher, James, and others are based on a phenomenology of average performers that *is* correct for most of us, as stated above. But, expert slackliners who walk tightropes across gorges do not willfully look at the rope or their feet. They look straight ahead, intent on their task, reaching the end of the rope. And what and how they feel and move is unlike most of us. As such, the phenomenology differs, beginning with how attentional focus is managed. Work by Wulf and Lewthwaite (2010) in cognitive science validates this external/task orientation rather than internal/self-focus orientation. Performers move more efficiently and effectively when paying attention to external objects or goals rather than centering on body parts. Experts better performance and correlated biomarkers attest to this external focus. The internal focus, they argue may lead to self-consciousness and result in 'a series of 'microchoking' episodes with attempts to right thoughts and bring emotions under control.' (Wulf and Lewthwaite 2010, 94) For them, this gets in the way of automatized movement control that leads to economic and efficacious performance. This reliance on automatism to account for expert performance leads to a related second misstep that we revisit in more depth.

Automatization that bypasses explicit steps and subpersonal processes where body, rules, and detailed directions are forgotten has long been prescribed as the way to superior performance. As referenced the in previous essay, the Dreyfus brothers (1986) characterize expertise as mindless coping, positing that expert performances follow the automatized patterns of everyday activities and skill levels. The basic idea is that most skilled performance takes place offline. In other words, and to cast it in a

HOLISM AND THE CULTIVATION OF EXCELLENCE IN SPORTS AND PERFORMANCE

Zhuangzian way, we perform best when we forget the body. Gallagher characterizes this as *'performative forgetfulness of the* body' (2011, 305, his emphasis). There is much to endorse this in everyday life, sport, and performance at *all* levels. But, as usual, and as argued throughout *Skillful Striving*, it actually is more complicated than learning explicitly as novices and acting automatically as experts—even if this is how it *seems*.

Countering this tendency Shusterman (2008, 2012) emphasizes somatic consciousness and reflection as the way to improve performance. His views are largely agreeable to our holistic and enactive account. Shusterman sides with Dewey rather than James at this point, stating that Deweyan 'control of unreflective habit,' brings that habit 'into conscious critical attention in order to refine it so that one can actually do with one's body what one intends to do.' (2012, 63) With words that align him with a holistic and enactive view, as quoted by Shusterman, Dewey writes: 'True spontaneity is henceforth not a birth-right but the last term, the consummated conquest, of an art—the art of conscious control.' (Ibid.) Amenably also, Shusterman argues for a phasing process where an unconscious background and reflective foreground cooperate, the primary role of the former notwithstanding (2008, 2012). In arguing against Merleau-Ponty's advocacy of the 'hidden mystery of the body' to counteract abstract representations of body parts (Shusterman 2008, 59), Shusterman seeks the middle ground with a 'lived somaesthetic reflection, that is, concrete but representational and reflective body consciousness'[15] (Ibid., 62). Putting this representational aspect in the service of habit improvement to restore spontaneous perceptions, he contends that '[r]epresentational and reflective consciousness [...] can serve alongside somatic spontaneity as a useful supplement and corrective' (Ibid., 68). Finally and importantly, when considering that maybe most of us are insufficiently trained to simultaneously pay attention to do more than one thing, he conjectures, 'Perhaps those more experienced and skilled in attending to bodily behavior can combine such explicit or reflective attention with smooth effective performance that equally attends to the targets of action' (2012, 209). Indeed, that *is* the case—as will be extensively argued and explained in the remainder of the project. Superb performers are able to move fluidly between forgotten body and full attention (as explained in more detail below and in the remaining essays from different angles). In spite of the preponderant consonance, there are two points to contend and one adjustment to make.

First, one of his main goals is to legitimize the body and make it matter as broadly and deeply as feasible. He aestheticizes and intellectualizes it to great effect. Yet, his conceptualization and terminology remain deeply grounded in the conceptual dualism critiqued in the previous essays and that thick holism bypasses. Second, we may wonder with Gallagher why or how an enhanced somatic awareness leads to better sensory performance and doubt that 'constant monitoring of our golf swing will result in an improved game' (2011, 308). Gallagher's misgivings are justified, as it is not clear how or *if* this works in average performers. The way to show clearest the why and how is precisely by examining expert performance (which may show just how it is unique and where ours differs from theirs). To work effectively with the much greater challenges they undertake neither fully automatized, unconscious processes nor fully reflective ones work. There is the need for both, and then some as explained shortly. As Gallagher concludes, 'It would seem that knowing *when* and *how* to use body consciousness is important for the argument presented by Shusterman' (2011, 309, my emphases). Truly, this is a dynamic process where attentional focus on body(mind)

167

movements come forth punctually but deliberately (see below). This capacity is foreclosed to beginners, as this results in poorer performance, being engaged more proficiently as skills improve. Further, such expert capacity is dependent on the performer's state of form and the whims of chance. As for the adjustment, most of Shusterman's writing conceptualizes representations as visual images (e.g. of how we view our own body). But, when discussing his fourth metacognitive layer of consciousness, he takes a fully representational turn when he writes that, 'we monitor our awareness of the object of our awareness through its representation in our consciousness' (Shusterman 2008, 55). This metalevel then seems to involve symbolic representation. Problematically, he does not specify the role these representations play. That is, he would need to clarify the extent to which and the context in which we rely on them. If representations are part of that spontaneity they ameliorate through habit, this is problematic because, besides being theoretically dispensable, they arguably compromise spontaneity by slowing it down.

Expert performance requires a difficult to enact *responsive* balance between subpersonal, automatized, and pre-reflective processes below the level of awareness, and very focused, deliberate, reflective monitoring of our movements via kinesthetic, proprioceptive, and other dynamics that often needs to be creative and spontaneous. Elite performers are anything but mindless (see also Breivik 2007, 2013, and essays 8–10). Unlike novices and even competent performers, experts are able to concentrate on their objective *while* monitoring their bodymind and kinesthetic signals, switching flexibly and dynamically between conscious, fringe, and subpersonal levels. They specifically train this. To revisit the perilous tightrope, they monitor vestibular, kinetic-tactile, proprioceptive and kinesthetic dynamics that incorporate a sense of balance, wind, rope feel, line tension and angle, and their own minutely calibrated movements in ways the rest of us neither feel, interpret, and work with as effectively and efficiently. Attending to these dynamics allows them to look ahead and not at their feet. They remain focused on the end of the rope concurrently, putting more or less emphasis on the dynamics depending on what happens at *that* moment. Should they feel the rope sag or the ball of the foot slide, they adjust appropriately without looking. They can execute feats such as Dean Potter, a climber extraordinaire who slacklines for training and fun: he has regularly performed walks without a security tether over chasms above 1000 feet (300 m) high at Yosemite. This risky affair is part of his training, of his Deweyan practice *of* skill.

In addition to automatization and intense focus, to account for the fluidity, we need another layer *during* action—precisely the one that allows for the fluid shifting between the other two levels. If James assigns higher performance to a somatic background that remains unconscious,[16] it is not without some irony that this second-order thinking can be postulated to work, phenomenologically, at the level of James' fringe of consciousness (essay 2). This fringe helps regulate the flow of awareness and judgment. Sports with complex tactics make this most obvious. The fluid relation among all three levels enables the basketball shooting guard to run the sideline to attack from the corner, putting pressure on the defenders, monitor defense and offense, keeping the tactical plan of action in the Jamesian fringe, and pass for a layup to the awaiting center. Body(mind) dynamics are not fully in the background, or there would be no reaction to a mishandled ball. Both fluidity between and function of the different levels are a matter of underlying capability and skillful operation and hence subject to

HOLISM AND THE CULTIVATION OF EXCELLENCE IN SPORTS AND PERFORMANCE

cultivation and refinement. Masters assiduously do this to extents and in ways that most people do not fathom, as section 2 further explores.

A holistic and enactive account provides a simpler and better explanation of experts' flexible and spontaneous action than alternatives. Just as we engage conscious, fringe and subpersonal layers, at a higher level we find that a holistic and enactive bodymind coordinates with pre-performance deliberation and post-performance reflection (essays 8–10). This is also a thoroughly situated process where social and other environmental factors are vital (essay 10). Pragmatic and holistic accounts of skill cannot ignore the role of the environment: our bodymind and the proprioceptive awareness of it, even at the pre-reflective and non-conceptual level, forms part of an ecological structure (Gallagher 2005a, 106). It posits a dynamic environment within which movement happens and is meaningful. Israel Scheffler (1965) perceptively distinguishes between 'closed' and 'open-ended' skills. The former have a limit to their development, e.g. double-declutching, spelling, or walking. The latter require 'constant application of the powers of observation, attention, judgment, modification and correction,' such as 'those called for in conducting a philosophical argument, driving a car over a journey, or performing a downhill ski run' (Aspin 1976, 100). Open-ended skills are clearly situated. This situatedness also implicates bodymind imaging and schematizing patternings. As Gallagher explains, 'conceptual and emotional aspects of the body image no doubt inform perception and are affected by various cultural and interpersonal factors' (2005a, 26), which, during sporting practice also affect schematizing ones. As the next remaining three essays will show, this broader focus is an important part of the story when it comes to elite sportspeople and performers. For now, there is a third misunderstanding to consider regarding expert skill.

When considering skills, it is often assumed that expert skills are the same as those of others, only more developed.[17] That is, there is a difference of degree and not kind between the two. David Aspin, in discussing Scheffler's analysis of know-how, explicates that, 'Know-how is thus, in *some* sense, a continuum' (1976, 100, my emphasis). But how to interpret this 'sense' is not straightforward. As Aspin remarks on his way to the preceding citation, Scheffler makes another important distinction between mere competence (intelligent performance that learned patterns of behavior exemplify) and genius 'presumably of the sort that we see in a Fischer, a Fangio, a Tourischeva or a Killy' (1976, 100). This is because, he goes on to cite Scheffler, 'knowing how to do something is one thing, knowing how to do it well is, in general, another, and doing it brilliantly is still a third, which lies beyond the scope of know-how altogether, tied as the latter notion is to the concept of training' (Aspin, ibid.). This continuum may line up the totality of skills of a particular practice or endeavor, and even be applicable to distinct skills. Nonetheless, this belies an underlying complexity where we find qualitative differences of kind, not just degree.

An analogy may help. Take two native speakers who read a particularly rich book in terms of literary figures, allusions, imitation and subtexts—any by Umberto Eco, Italo Calvino, or Jorge Luis Borges will do. The sophisticated reader can appreciate the parody, sarcasm, puns, and allusions, all of which are utterly lost on the artless reader, even if both understand the sentences. Their reading skill can be suitably compared within a continuum, perhaps in terms of vocabulary. But the 'sense' and degree of their ability here means that the experience of the cultivated reader is much richer qualitatively. It is not the size of the vocabulary or the meanings associated with the words per se, as

169

these could be the same (and hypothetically the artless reader could 'know' more words). Rather, it is *how* the sophisticated reader is capable to engage the texts. The result is an incomparably richer literary world.[18] Similarly with performative skills, if a person cannot do a single pull up, he does not *know* (not can kinesthetically 'imagine') what it is like to work the gymnast's rings. Performative abilities intelligently and intelligibly open worlds of movement—with all their rich dynamics. In short, the performatively brilliant and skillful know-how is a third kind of thing. It is not a given either, as it must be trained, refined, and maintained.

But when expert performers are sharp and on top of their game, they have much richer registers to act on and to experience. Moreover, and to elicit Ortega's view on the reality of the landscape, experts see richer and different landscape possibilities. What to most people is but a stunning and forbidding 130-foot drop of impossible raging waters in Keyhole Falls in British Columbia, for Spanish kayaker Aniol Serrasoles, the first person to ever descend the cascade, it is but an alluring possibility to expand his repertoire of skills and experiences.[19] This requires observation, attention, judgment, modification, and correction, besides much practice; all premised on that Deweyan practice *of* skill that, to further improve, needs the challenge of the until-now-unachievable. Open-ended skills, in virtue of their situatedness, are amenable to continued improvement *in principle* (until age, boredom, injury, or other unpredictables put a stop). To suitably describe such formidable experiences, we cannot just remain as observers, no matter how sensitively observant.

To consider how to methodologically adapt our phenomenology, we can ponder on Wertz's (1991) point that we may be surprised by the quality of our movements when we actually experience them. Likewise, many a phenomenologist would be astonished were he or she to experience the movements of elite performers. Yet, reaching such levels of expertise is often at odds with the requirements to become a top phenomenologist and academic. Few of them have the inclination or luxury to indulge in such pursuits and acquire the requisite ability. Empirical studies can palliate this to some extent. They can provide quantitative data to draw objective comparisons between average and talented performers. For instance, we can consider physiological VO2 Max differences between elite endurance athletes and average people. VO2 Max measures the maximum volume of oxygen that athletes can use and is measured in milliliters per kilogram of body weight per minute (ml/kg/min). Average, untrained males have values in the range of 35–40 mL (kg-min), whereas elite athletes can score in the 70–80 range, with Tour de France 5-time winner Miguel Induráin having a value of 88 mL (kg-min) at his peak.[20] But such descriptions leave us cold. They fail to capture the what it is like of performance at such levels: The lung and muscle burn of the untrained person who 'blows up' after a few minutes of effort is not comparable, nociceptively or kinesthetically, to the sustained 'world of hurt' of the elite athlete who keeps going for one hour (or several). Various phenomenological methodologies can address this.

Neurophenomenology helps because it is premised on basic instruction and training of subjects who are then debriefed and interviewed (Gallagher 2012; Gallager and Zahavi 2008; Thompson 2007). But, this alone does not suffice. There are obvious limitations with performers' ability to adequately examine their own experience. There are also methodological issues with the narratives and answers thus obtained because they may rely on clichés, tropes, and cultural memes the more open ended they are, or

HOLISM AND THE CULTIVATION OF EXCELLENCE IN SPORTS AND PERFORMANCE

alternatively may be too influenced by researchers' prompts. To deal with cases when the subjects should not be privy to the goal of the task, as it would influence the results, Gallagher (2003) has developed frontloaded phenomenology that 'builds experimental design on or around phenomenological insights developed in phenomenological analyses to inform the way experiments are set up' (Gallagher and Zahavi 2008, 42). But this is applicable to experimental design. Its applicability is reduced or excluded outside of that context, as when examining real-world performance. In short, helpful as these alternatives are, we *still* need to complement the phenomenology of the observer with that of the participant. What we can call ethno-phenomenology, where the phenomenologists embed themselves in the practice, supplements them. That is, the phenomenologists are or become performers.[21] Two examples follow for illustrative purposes.

Breivik (2011) conducts an analysis of risk sports along five variables: body posture, skill, spatiality, temporality, and decision-making.[22] Using his own experiences (his abilities range from the expert level to proficiency), he analyzes skydiving, kayaking, and mountain climbing to show the particular lifeworlds of experience they afford. Complementing Heidegger, who leaves the body behind, with Merleau-Ponty and Todes, Breivik shows how in 'some sports we use fundamental characteristics of the environing world in a mode of playfulness' (2011, 314). Each sport shows specific experiential qualities that reveal exceptions to phenomenological 'givens,' for example. We learn that the body posture in skydiving is special, since we are not acting against gravity, not resisting it, but using it, working with it. Skydiving is thus 'an exception to Todes's idea of verticality being the primary dimension [... in skydiving] Horizontality is the primary reference dimension.' (Breivik 2011, 324) Taking Breivik's analysis we can see that verticality upends our normal experience and expectations, particularly when risk is involved. Because this throws into disarray our normal bearings, we need to retrain our orientating capacities and relationship to a basic axis that structures everyday life. Further, we can see how skydiving also provides the chance to confront death in unique ways: it requires overcoming our deep-seated fear of falling to our death. Skydivers must willingly give into it. The moment they jump off the plane, and until the parachute deploys, skydivers are effectively dead (as some very unlucky ones come to find out).[23]

Elsewhere I (2008) examine another risk activity: the running of the bulls (*encierro*). Having run for six consecutive years (in younger, more foolish times), I analyze the *encierro* as the interplay of death, fear, and joy and the corresponding emotional attunement. Heidegger's and Sartre's respective views on death enable us to examine the anticipation of death and our attitude toward it in the moments leading up to the event, from the early hours in the morning to the seconds before the herd is released. Anxiety prevails, with the possibility of our demise concretely taking on the shape of two horns. Interestingly, for experienced runners the angst vanishes the moment the bulls are in sight. Then, the possibility to enjoy the run becomes also concretized on the very same horns that moments earlier drained the blood from the face. The *encierro* then becomes transformative when our ordinary lives can experience, however briefly, the extraordinary, as Nietzsche (1968) argues. In the civilized world, it is rare to have the opportunity to confront risk with untamed and dangerous animals, much less as part of a ritualized event that permits the development and refinement of skills. Some runners have cultivated their ability to run in front of the bulls in spaces and for lengths foreclosed to most of the thousands of other people in the event. Being close to a 1300 lb (590 kg.) bull when one is leading it (not running from it, as people unfamiliar with the event believe or do) is a primal and atavistic experience of communion with a mythic animal that begs its own phenomenological analysis from the inside out. This event and similar ones, literally not just figuratively, attest to Ortega's idea that the very risking of life turns out to be the strongest affirmation of its importance and enjoyment.

Phenomenological analyses of sports and performative activities from the performer's perspective, particularly elite ones, reveal qualitative facets of the experience that would go unrecognized otherwise. These experiences are intense, rich, and highly modulated by unique dynamics. And, the execution and appreciation takes place through the very skills, as the enacted skill and the capacity to inhabit the movement are one and the same. There is a deep connection between the normative—ethical, aesthetic, and existential standards of excellence—and our skills and abilities. On the road toward excellence, the next section begins the explicit rapprochement between skills and norms.

2. Exemplary Skills and Skillful Fluency

What is the normative connection between our skills and the phenomenological analysis of our experience of skills? There seems to be too big a gap between our values and our creaturely movement. Phenomenology can describe the quality of our experience as we engage in sports, martial arts, or dance, but it is not a prescriptive endeavor. The challenge is an old one: how do we get from description to prescription, from facts to values, and from 'is' to 'ought'? This section and the following essays have the goal of meeting this challenge by way of thick holism and its integrative ways, starting with our skills, sporting, martial, and performing. Here begins the rapprochement between virtues and skill in a way that, without conflating them, reinforces a 'natural' affinity under the rubric of excellence.

In keeping with the tenor of thick holism, what we seek are continuities and processes rather than distinctions and discrete entities while keeping pertinent conceptual differences. Oil and water neither mix nor dilute in each other, but once surface boundaries and differences are pointed out the interesting and beautiful facets lie in how they interact, the surface tensions, and the interplay of watery and oily iridescences. After briefly reviewing salient differences and similarities between virtues and skills, we delve into the latter, trying to show how kinesthetic and kinetic surface tensions result in virtuous iridescences.

As we saw in *Nothing New Under the Sun*, both skills and virtues are excellences. Skills exhibit crucial similarities with virtues: we can cultivate excellences of skills as well as those of virtues; both contribute to the flourishing of our lives, particularly within the framework of communities and practices; both are imbued with normativity. They also evince marked differences: virtues are dispositions exhibited variously in actions and practices. Skills are also dispositions (we all have bad days when we fail to properly display them), but those of performative pursuits have narrower technical applications. Skills cultivate excellences proper to the skills themselves, thus badminton develops those abilities that allow us to hit the shuttlecock (bird) with a Danish wipe, a drop, a flick serve, and a push shot, and while general athletic skill may serve us in other

HOLISM AND THE CULTIVATION OF EXCELLENCE IN SPORTS AND PERFORMANCE

sporting or performing events needing speed, flexibility, and coordination, the very unique skills of handling the badminton racket and the peculiar shape of the shuttlecock are restricted to the badminton court. Virtues such as fairness or courage seemingly have much wider applications, for example, we can be fair and honest when it is against our best interest in doing so in a relationship or when facing whether to call a crucial shot against ourselves that the opponent has been unable to watch after tripping. The gap seems as phenomenal as that between phenomenal consciousness and materialist accounts of mental life. How do we get from the specific sensations, perceptions, and interpretations of our animate bodies as they perform, to some sort of open normative ground, one where technical skills are also more widely applicable?

Writes Sheets-Johnstone, 'Archetypal corporeal-kinetic forms and relations *embody* concepts, precisely in the sense in which we say that someone is the *embodiment* of courage, or that someone *embodies* the qualities we value. They are conceptual instantiations of such concepts as *insideness, thickness, thinness, animate being, power, verticality, force,* and so on [...] They are structured in and by *corporeal concepts.*' (2009, 221, her italics) We approach the relation between concepts and embodiment from the opposite direction to find how such fine semantically significant embodiments of corporeal concepts connect with ethical and aesthetic values. Thick holism frames this.

Thick holism, as it builds on the previous essays, does not simply fill in the metaphysical gap, rather it does not let it form in the first place. Likewise, as far as normativity goes, there is no is/ought gap; we find instead stronger or weaker connections within continuities. The crux of the argument is that just as biological facts are intrinsically normative, our morphology, our kinetics, and the accompanying proprioceptive and kinesthetic dynamics described above also help ground a rich normative element that is aesthetic, ethical, and existential. We have already noted the affinity between virtue ethics and thick holism, usually couched as embodiment in the literature. Virtue ethics permits us to walk the difficult plank between abstraction and concreteness, reason and emotion. John Russell rightly argued for the continuity thesis, for which 'the moral values that are most fundamental to sport—namely, those that are constitutive elements of sport—are expressions or reflections of more basic moral values found outside of sport.' (2007a, 52) Thick holism advances ontological, ethical, aesthetic, social, and environmental continuities.

In fact, this approach cuts at a right angle the entanglement between broad internalism (Russell 1999, 2004, 2007; Simon 1999) and conventionalism (D'Agostino 1981; Morgan 2004, 2012). It is not an alternative that settles the issue but an Aristotelian strategy to find the middle term and common ground.[24] As a naturalistic stance, thick holism offers an objective basis for values based on the phenomenological structure of our experience as well as biological and morphological factors. It is 'universal' in so far as it applies to our form of life, but the very practices and institutions that populate our life form circumscribe this universality. Additionally, thick holism also remains concrete and connected to our life in meaningful ways. Further, it allows for rationality but keeps our emotions close. The flourishing of human life sits at the center of its normative and existential concerns; it anchors these in the seamless integration of faculties and modes of being we enjoy as 'bodyminds' that amalgamate physical, psychic, emotional, social, and environmental facets. When discussing integrity, which Russell considers' the internal principle of sport,' as a means to promote such flourishing, he highlights a key aspect of sport for a holistically thick account, 'Sporting games

HOLISM AND THE CULTIVATION OF EXCELLENCE IN SPORTS AND PERFORMANCE

institutionalize the production and development of excellences that contribute to such human flourishing by promoting certain physical, emotional, and intellectual excellences.' (2007a, 61) These three excellences, which unfold in the social context of institutions and practices fit perfectly within a holistic framework. Indeed, sports have the potential to contribute to such excellences under a holistic roof.[25] They surely institutionalize this production and development, but beneath this causal role, at the very source of values also lay the phenomenological structuring of our experience and biological and morphological factors. To finally turn to the skills as just discussed in this context, we might title the following subsection by alluding to one of James' works.

2.1. The Varieties of Meaningful Movement

Our physical endowments are quite modest compared to those we find in the animal world. As the runts of the litter, we are nowhere the fastest runners or swimmers, neither the strongest, nor most agile. Yet, we excel in two ways that no animal species comes even close: the abundance of our kinetic ways, and the exquisitely refined quality of our movements.

Concerning the first way, our very limitations and restrictions become affordances and possibilities. As Ortega would look at it, setbacks are springs for opportunities. Through Zhuangzian spontaneity and Orteguian exuberance, we have developed an incredibly fertile and fine palette of kinetic ways. From the hundreds of sports, to the untold number of dances and the dozens of martial arts, our repertoire of movements is unmatched. Each of these cultivates very specific movements whose expert practitioners are most intimate with. Even as simple a task as the high jump, with only two formal requirements (clearing the bar and taking off from one foot), developed the Western roll and straddle, the Eastern method or scissors, and Dick Fosbury's innovative 1968 flop. The dynamics for each are radically different, as one is an upright jump, the other takes place rolling over, and the latter arching over on one's back. Incidentally, this shows how in competitive sport effectiveness prevails as a criterion over others, e.g. an aesthetics of simplicity and efficiency. The flop is more complex than the alternatives, but allows for higher jumps. It also illustrates the specific adaptation to a sporting context that provided a landing mat, as the scissors or the roll would be more useful in the 'real world' because jumpers see where they are falling. Free runners, practitioners of parkour whose mantra is fluid and efficient movement, illustrate this: they diligently cultivate their high jumping ability, but none do Fosbury flops. Often, our movements require complex interactions with others' bodies, collaboratively, as in dance, antagonistically, as in martial arts, or competitively as in sport, with all the kinesthetic, kinetic, and proprioceptive nuances these bring to play. Frequently, we engage tools. This can be as 'simple' as a stick with which we devise the most astounding *kata*, choreographed to lethal perfection, to something as complex as an single-handed offshore sailboat, with its complex rigging and great number of sails, not to mention the navigational and meteorological expertise needed. Some more details are worth discussing.

Within this variety, each movement (type) is expressed and felt qualitatively differently, along those four cardinal structures of movement, and with different meaningful possibilities as the earlier phenomenological descriptions show. As Sheets-Johnstone explains, 'The qualitative nature of movement, notably the movement of *animate forms*, makes possible systems of formal values that define in each instance a qualitative kinetics.' (2009, 233, her italics) These formal values come with subtle distinctions:

> Formal kinetic values are verbally condensed in terms like "sudden," "attenuated," "smooth," jagged," "large," "small," "weak", "strong," "angular," "rounded," and so on. Such terms pinpoint different formal qualities of movement: its tensional quality or degree of forcefulness; its linear quality — the linear design of the body and the congealed-to-expansive range of the body's movement; its manner of execution, that is, the way in which force is released — abruptly, ballistically, in a sustained manner, and so on. (Sheets-Johnstone 2009, 233)

These formal qualities are not discrete nor separately existing, they flow from one to the other. And this presents a challenge concerning how to properly articulate our experiences. It seems that we either leave out the dynamic facet or exclude its formal qualities. For example, when we describe extensionally something as smooth, we leave out any temporal aspects of our experience of smoothness. But, if we describe a phenomenon intensionally, as when using affective terms (cautious, excited, aggressive), then 'without calling attention to any particular formal quality, they impart the sense of an overall spatio-temporal-energic dynamic.' (Sheets-Johnstone 2009, 233) Jeannerod expresses the same point, as we saw, stating how it is much easier to show how a move is made than to describe it. We reconsider this under the guise of discrimination in the context of skillful fluency below, and return to the issue of articulation in the last essay.

Regarding the second way, an Orteguian drive to perfect 'our moves' through Deweyan habit has enabled us to invent myriad movements. It also has permitted us to improve them in ways that no other animal can approach, given similar challenges. Sports, martial and performing arts excel in this refinement. To be able to hone them, we need to have the ability to work skillfully, and fluidly with the conscious, fringe and subpersonal layers, making judgments as to what constitutes the right kinds of movements, the most effective or efficient or beautiful. All of these judgments entail normative criteria. In order to draw such judgments, we must be finely attuned to the way our limbs and muscles feel. Kinesthetic, kinetic, tactile, vestibular, proprioceptive qualities come to the forefront then. These enable us to describe and interpret our sensations into meaningful perceptions, and to connect them to prescriptive judgments.

For performers, the quality of their experiences is essential to their proficiency and enjoyment of the practices they cultivate. What may be minute or imperceptible differences to the uninitiated can make all the difference to those with requisite expertise. A fencer may prefer saber to foil or epée on account of the slight variations in grip and shape of the blade, whereas for most people, the three are just sword-like tools. Being attuned to the different dynamics enriches performers' experiences. Observers also can derive similar experiences and discriminations. The recent discovery of and subsequent research on mirror neurons (Rizzolatti and Sinigaglia 2008) shows that spectators can rightly and vicariously share similar (if much attenuated) movement dynamics to those of performers. When observing another's action, motor circuits in the observer's brain that activate on performing the same action also activate. That is, mirror neurons fire in the brain of the observer in a pattern that replicates that of the performer. But there are specific and interesting limiting adaptations that reveal degrees of difference. When one grips the handle of a blade different neurons are fired by comparison to the gripping of a baseball bat, or merely clenching one's fist in a grip-like shape. In other words, they are object-oriented neurons whether the action is performed or observed (Jeannerod 1997, 50).[26] Conceptualizing these difficulties is not a straightforward affair. It is not that neurons feel the other's movement, but that a whole person does so. Additionally, it is because observers *already* have the experience of what it is to feel those movements that they can recognize them (see also Sheets-Johnstone 2009, 231 fn. 10). In the end, the performer's experience and perspective cannot be equated or reduced to the observer's. There is a non-reducible element to what it is like to move and experience it ourselves.[27]

We use these sensations and perceptions for more than merely feeling our way. The primary role they play is that of enabling us to tell the postural and kinetic differences in our movements. But, this ability to discriminate has a deep repercussion in the context of active pursuits, and of sports in particular. It is through such kinesthetic and proprioceptive dynamics that we can regulate our movements, refine them, and integrate them into the structure of a game or sport. In fact, it is because we feel the different dynamics that we can actually be held accountable for breaking constitutive rules, those that define the structure and give personality to the game, for example, because we can control our hands and arms by feeling their location proprioceptively and their speed kinesthetically, in football we can justifiably penalize their purposive use to displace the ball or an opponent (holistically this should also integrate our intentionality and social factors; these are built into this framework in the ensuing essays). It is because of such dynamics that we can improve the rules of skill as well, and the skills themselves. That is, our skills, as specified and highlighted by different sports depend on our ability to discriminate and control the subtle dynamics that take place subpersonally, at the fringe, and reflectively.

Formalism (Suits 1990) underscores the essential role of constitutive rules. For him good gamewrights and suitable rules depend on these being properly adapted to our skills as afforded by our biological possibilities (morphological, physiological, biomechanical). Games have to be designed for what humans *can* do. This cuts both ways. Our abilities constrain game design but in turn these very rules and constraints help us develop our abilities. In turn, this may mean adapting the game, and so on. We could have a rule against dunking the basketball from behind the midfield line or against using our ears to fly over the pole vault bar; since we lack kinetic possibilities comparative to those of fleas and our auricular appendages cannot emulate Dumbo, these rules are unnecessary. On the other hand, we have seen how such rules adapt as our skills and techniques improve. In the javelin throw, the balance of the javelin was moved forward to shorten its flight and keep other competitors and spectators safe; in swimming competitions now it is not allowed to swim underwater further than 15 meters in response to swimmers' improved abilities and techniques that enable them to go over half the pool underwater at a faster speed than on the surface.[28]

Rules, then, are designed around specific humanly possible motilities, our athletic skills in the sporting context. Kinesthesia and proprioception finely tune these skills. But rather than merely playing a causal role of more or less importance, they are integral to the skills themselves. To explain how these dynamics thoroughly effect and affect the very motion of a backhand: a strong backhand that returns a difficult serve integrates racket, hand, arm, hip rotation, foot placement and many other such dynamics. Additionally, it is infused with an affective tonality or mood, for instance it can begin with the buildup of tension in anticipation of a match point, a tension that is held when the ball contacts the cords and released with the follow through upon seeing it clear the net. And it is connected to an overarching tactic. The tactic adapts to and is devised in accordance to how the player feels. When fatigued, shots are less accurate, daring, and imaginative. Further, these dynamics form the basis for normative judgments, in terms of performance quality, as per the internal rules of the games. We determine the quality of a stride and its efficiency, or the finesse of an arm moving in a dance or in ice-skating not only by the result or goal, but also the actual quality of the movements, as *felt* by performers and observed (and 'felt') by spectators. These are derived from performance ideals and parsed from past performances (whether personally carried out or observed, or both). Nonetheless, there are better and worse ways of moving and achieving the goals of a game that the constitutive rules establish (lusory goal, in Suits' parlance, 1990). These ways are as much performative (in terms of goal achievement) as aesthetic and ethical.

The very inefficiency built into sports makes them the best case to observe the contact point between underlying dynamics, skills, and norms. As we saw with Ortega and Suits (essay 4), sports and games are characterized by prescribing inefficient means to achieve the stipulated goals. Means that we willfully embrace because they make the activity possible in the first place. This entails that there are ways to achieve the goal according to, bending, and breaking the rules. Whereas during actual performance there is a holistic process where kinesthetic, technical, moral, aesthetic, social, and environmental elements make up the movements and their inherent qualities, we can phenomenologically and conceptually separate them, as we are gradually doing presently. To focus now on the normative elements sandwiched between the personal/individual facets and the more external ones (again separable but in concept only), there are two Ancient Greek concepts that help fasten the normative facet *in* the inward dynamics.

Both *kalon* (καλόν) and *kalokagathia* (καλοκαγαθία) fit beautifully a virtuous framework where *aretē*, which encapsulates excellence, skill, virtue, prowess, valor, nobility among others, is both target and arrow.[29] *Kalon*, etymologically and initially referred to the outwardly beautiful, but it has come to adopt other normative values that extend from the aesthetic to the ethical, thereby referring to the noble, honorable, and beautiful in a moral sense.[30] As it reflects an ideal of physical and moral beauty, we can render it as a beautiful and noble gesture. *Kalokagathia* is the character and conduct of a *kalos kagathos* (καλὸς καγαθός), a beautiful and moral person. If *kalon* is the act as noble gesture, we can say that *kalokagathia* is an educational ideal. Reid similarly writes of *Kalokagathia* (2010, 2012a, 2012b, Forthcoming). She connects athletic beauty to goodness as she explains how the balance and harmony of the statues was meant to represent the desired state of their souls (Reid 2012a). Moreover, the muscular beauty achieved through athletic training was supposed to 'evoke *aretē*, first and foremost as evidence of voluntary hard work.' (2012b, 286) Given that education for *aretē* is meant to bring harmony among the three parts of the Platonic soul, the discipline and hard work to sculpt the body is transferred to the soul as well. But as Reid argues 'kalokagathia is something more than virtue, something beyond social responsibility, something further than knowledge of and abidance by ethical codes' as it implicates 'personal, social, and aesthetic aspects' (Fortchoming).

Both are beautifully noble because they can supererogatorily offer the opponent generous help. Italian bobsledder Eugenio Monti and teammates, during the 1963

Innsbruck Winter Olympic sledding event, lent a simple but crucial screw to the British team, which would otherwise have to withdraw (Ecenbarger 2008). The Britons went on to win the gold, while Monti and the Italians had to settle for bronze. As Cléret and McNamee (2012) argue as they compare Coubertin's Olympic values and Nietzsche's will to power, such acts show that competition is less about domination than about generating human excellence. Even when this happens in much less glorious back-drops, it is just as impressive and beautiful. Spanish runner Iván Fernández Anaya acted in accordance to these ideals in a cross-country race in Burlada (Navarre) held December 2, 2014 (Arribas 2014). He was second by a significant distance when the saw Keniata Abel Mutai stop a ways before the actual finish, believing he had won. To the dismay of his coach, former marathon world champion Martín Fiz, when he caught up, rather than taking the victory, Fernández Anaya stayed behind Mutai and guided him with hand gestures to the finish (Mutai did not understand Spanish). Fernández Anaya, much like Monti, was not interested in winning in that way. Others could argue that knowing where the finish is should be part of running a cross race. They have a point. But it is empty and formal. Fernández Anaya knew who was the best runner on that day.[31] Both were *kalos kagathos*. As such, for Reid, they have *aretē* and 'something more, a certain kind of disposition, a particular *way* of exercising [their] goodness, a kind of moral beauty.' (Forthcoming, my emphasis) Extending Reid's analysis in a way that would seem to fit with her move to broaden the sphere of *kalokagathia*, we can argue that this particular way, in fact, happens through our very skills. They actually enable us to act *better* morally, aesthetically and athletically.

Kalon and *kalokagathia* can enhance play in virtue of the higher skill they make possible. It is often the case that sportspeople bend or break rules willfully (sometimes conventionally accepted as part of the game, as strategic intentional fouls in basket-ball).[32] Yet, those who observe the rules and manage to prevail demonstrate superior skills. This is morally praiseworthy and virtuous, and it is achieved as much through character as through their very skills and their interwoven dynamics. Ilundáin-Agurruza and Torres sum up using football as an example,

> We admire a verily difficult feint and half-turn pass to avoid a charging defender for the right reasons: not just because of the technical skill (it'd be easier to handle with a dirty play), but because this silky move has been developed and implemented pre-cisely to handle a difficult situation minding the rules. It is a beautiful move kinestheti-cally, aesthetically, and ethically. Nothing's lacking! (2010, 195)

In other words, better skills give performers the opportunity to act more nobly and without recourse to cheating. Yet, if *kalon* and *kalokagathia* are holistic in their blending of values, there are analyses of the aesthetic dimension that split matters.

Best (1979, esp. 99–122) divided sports into purposive sports and aesthetic sports. Purposive ones such as swimming, basketball, or tennis achieve their end scoring or winning, independently of the means of achieving said goal. Aesthetic sports, as ice-skating or rhythmic gymnastics, cannot achieve their purpose independently of the manner of achieving it.[33] A holistic approach cuts across this division, since purposive sports' achievement *of* their goal is not independent of *how* it is done. An ugly win detracts from it, as does one done by bending or breaking the rules, as both Best (1979) and Stephen Mumford argue (2011, 2012). Although concerned with buttressing the

HOLISM AND THE CULTIVATION OF EXCELLENCE IN SPORTS AND PERFORMANCE

connection between aesthetic and moral values, both positively and negatively, Mumford argues against such separation. Cheating or breaking the rules detracts from the beauty of the performance. Sports have a way of pushing persons to their limits and showing publicly our mettle (much as being onstage in front of the public for performers, or engaging in combat for martial arts). Under duress, we are also more tempted not to honor the implicit agreement to use less efficient means.

Indeed, competitive sports can bring out the best, and worst. How athletes have trained shows in competition clearest. All the defects that have not been polished during training will show in the intensity of competition. This applies to both purely technical skills as well as character traits. Endurance sports show this clearest since the very duress participants endure over time whittles them to the core. If one has not truly embodied the mechanics of a high elbow in swimming, as fatigue sets in, it will show. Likewise, some, pushed to the limit, will take the shortcut in the path ahead whereas others will still go around as stipulated by the rules of the game. Lally's (2012) account of his training race where only one of the competitors did not skip the final bend at the cost of losing places illustrates this beautifully (essay 4). We admire the competitor who honors the initial agreement and gallantly welcomes Lally into the community with a smile and not a single word about the top five finishers who cut the course. Excellent performances are beautiful *and* virtuous *and* skillful—consider an *excellent* boxing uppercut, for example.

Cesar Torres also argues against the idea that internalism in sport commits the 'separatist mistake' that splits the ethical from the aesthetic to show how 'interpretivism is a theory of sport in which moral and aesthetic concerns and evaluations are strongly interconnected' (2012, 313). Truly, his discussion fits the holistic framework in deep ways, not the least because he sees the aesthetic and ethical as bivalent, that is, without primacy of one over the other, and that 'this makes not only for a more coherent account of sport but also for a more fulfilling life' (Torres Ibid., 314). This occurs through the very sport specific skills that sportspeople develop, as Torres writes,

> The footballer whose deft of touch and dribbling deactivates what seems an impenetrable defensive scheme carves out and embodies such possibilities. In short, what is worthy of repaid attention and commendation are skilful play and the strategic arrangements that facilitate its manifestation. (Ibid., 311).

The one concession to make, to be more consistent with holism but also standing on its own (see Edgar 2013), is that beauty may be too narrow an aesthetic concept to capture the ways in which skills can embody aesthetic *and* ethical values. Indeed, we find original, admirable, radical, and other ways of investing our movements and actions with aesthetic, ethical, and existential meanings. This expansive ways are often carried out by the likes of footballer Alfredo Di Stéfano, Dancer Isadora Duncan, or *Aikidō* founder Ueshiba Morihēi. While all of us rely on the aforementioned dynamics to gauge our efforts and improve our skills, there are some who stand out far above the rest of us, acting as beacons of what is possible. Paragons of excellence, to whom we return after this long phenomenological and foundational hiatus, sport a different way that is qualitatively different from ours in significant ways. They exhibit skillful fluency.

2.2. Changing the Paradigm—Skillful Fluency

The convention in the literature on expertise is to write of 'skillful coping' when discussing these superb performances and those who enact them. Referring to the struggles most of us undergo as we strive to perform well, it makes sense to speak of coping. Yet this seems woefully inadequate to capture the level of excellence of truly exceptional masters. They are not just proficient, or even experts, rather they stand on a category of their own. A more fitting way to mark the difference between paragons and the rest is to conceive of this as *skillful fluency*. 'Fluency' according to the New Oxford American Dictionary means 'gracefulness and ease of movement or style,' being derived from the Latin *fluere*, to flow. In the East, the Chinese speak of *wushin* and the Japanese of *mushin*. The usual and literal translation of no-mind is misleading.[34] The idea is that the mind is supposed to be unstoppable, in the sense of being immovable, as Buddhist monk Takuan (1986) explains in essay 9. The outcome of this state of performing grace is that skillful individuals achieve a greater unity and integration of bodily and mindful processes. Fluent sportspeople do not cope but excel—elegant even in their suffering.

Qualitatively, they are on a different level in terms of performance, the inherent dynamics of their movements and their ability to discriminate. Their performances speak for themselves. Consider surfer Kelly Slater who, to date, has won the ASP World Tour Championship 11 times, five of them consecutively. Domination over such a long time is extraordinary, and puts him alongside legendary Milo of Croton, the Greek wrestler who won the wrestling title in six Olympic Games among many other crowns at the other games (Pythian, Isthmian, and Nemean), and Michael Phelps with his 22 Olympic medals in three games thus far. Slater is in a class of his own in the world of surfing. Alex Wade (2012) clarifies that while today's surfers can execute aerials and tricks that were unthinkable a few decades ago, these are done when the pressure is off, not during competition. When all other contestants cap a difficult wave with a 180-degree turn, Slater will do a 360-degree rotation. That ability to do what no one else dares, and predictably pull it off, requires extraordinary talent. Above all it asks for the backbreaking habit to not only surf but to steel oneself against the siren song of self-doubt. This is built on the kind of discipline that few are capable or willing to endure. Someone supposed to be a prodigy to whom things came easy stated, 'People make a mistake who think my art has come easily to me. Nobody has devoted so much time and thought to composition as I. There is not a famous master whose music I have not studied over and over' (Kilham 2008, np.). Wolfgang Amadeus Mozart reputedly said this.

Peerless swordsman Musashi Miyamoto writes of the need for one thousand days of training to develop and ten thousand days of discipline to polish oneself (Tokitsu 2004).[35] Such dedication is in itself formative and normative, it builds character. Built *through* Deweyan habit it is cause and effect, since it plants the seeds from which further expressions of it grow. Of course, it need not result in an admirable and wholesome moral character, as many a vile sportsperson makes patent. Skills and 'performative virtues' are specific. Dewey writes, 'The sailor is intellectually at home in the sea, the hunter in the forest, the painter in his studio, the man of science in his laboratory' (1988, 123). But as MacIntyre (1984) would argue, only those character traits that extend to the rest of our lives are worthy of being categorized as virtues. This is considered further in succeeding essays. The point, for now, is that such talent *and* dedication result in capacities that seem unfathomable for others.

HOLISM AND THE CULTIVATION OF EXCELLENCE IN SPORTS AND PERFORMANCE

The very prowess and skill of exceptional performers manifest also in their discriminatory abilities. In the thick of things, they are able to discern kinesthetic and proprioceptive dynamics that go unnoticed to most because they are able to offload skills and movements into learned patterns that 'feel' right at the level of the fringe while not taxing their ability to focus on the most relevant elements that maximize performance, e.g. they look at the body of the opponent not the ball. An analogy can help to understand the level of refinement that masters achieve. From different angles, both Churchland (1981) and Nelson Goodman (1968) speak of the extremely refined discriminatory powers of oenologists, wine tasters.[36]

Churchland, whose examples also cover music and astronomy, is concerned with a reductionist account of introspection. His position obviously is at odds with thick holism, but his overall point in this regard applies just the same. Goodman is concerned with how to differentiate between original and fake artworks, and he appeals to the example of the wine taster's ability to discriminate after the arduous learning process. Goodman (1968) concludes that we cannot be sure that we will not learn to see relevant differences between two identical pictures, a fake and an original, once we are aware of the situation. Many of us would be hard pressed to tell the difference between a merlot or a pinot noir, some will barely taste the grapes in the wine, but for the 'practiced and chemically sophisticated wine taster [...] the "red wine" classification used by most of us divides into a network of fifteen or twenty distinguishable elements ...whose relative concentrations he can estimate with accuracy' (Churchland 1981, 15). What is mastered for Churchland is 'a conceptual framework—whether musical, chemical, or astronomical—a framework that *embodies* far more wisdom about the relevant sensory domain than is immediately apparent to untutored discrimination.' (Ibid.) Learning brings about sweeping perceptual transformations. For both, the key idea is that cultivation of certain skills awakens discriminatory capacities that seem outlandish for the rest of us.

In the same way, remarkable athletes, artists, and martial artists who ride the wind master kinetic and discriminatory skills that, circumscribed to their areas of expertise, are integrated into a performative framework. Proprioceptive and kinesthetic dynamics, sensations, and perceptions tied to tools should they be used (as incorporated into the bodily schematizing and even imaging), environmental fluctuations that would be unfelt by most are a lush world open to them and closed to the rest. Dewey very perceptively wrote,

> I do not usually, for example, hear the sounds made by the striking of the keys; hence I therefore bang at them or strike them unevenly. *If I were better trained or more intelligent in the performance of this action*, I should hear the sounds, for they would have ceased to be just stimuli and become means of direction of my behavior in securing consequences. Not having learned by the 'touch-method,' my awareness of contact-qualities as I hit the keys is intermittent and defective. [...] there is no consciousness of contact 'sensations' or sensa. But if I used my sensory touch appreciation as means to the proper execution of the act of writing, I should be aware of these qualities. *The wider and freer the employment of means, the larger the field of sensory perceptions.* (1925, 335–336, my emphasis)

Great masters employ more freely and widely their consummate talents such that not only do they discriminate better, but are better able to process information, and adapt their skillful performances accordingly. This means they can handle with aplomb circumstances beyond the range of even other experts, let alone proficient performers or novices. Their discerning abilities bring about sweeping changes that allow surfers to feel minute pressure changes in the water and board balance and adjust themselves with extreme precision working in that Jamesian fringe where the gestalt is felt and kept just below the surface, much as the underside of their board. If the tail begins to slip sideways, this comes to the fore then. Surfing is interesting in this regard because of the very fluid nature of water, which dynamically and constantly changes in ways both subtle and dramatic, as Douglas Anderson (2007) shows in his insightful reading of water in the context of surfing and paddling 'alongside' Bergson and James.[37]

This is a kinetically *wise* process. That is, epistemologically it is not a narrow cognitive process where deliberation and rationality predominate. It validates Varela's (1999) argument for an ethical process where true expertise is spontaneous and not deliberative, concrete and not abstract (see essay 10). It is also mindful of our emotions and incumbent social ramifications. Carl Thomen, in an incisive article on surfing and Slater in terms of the sublime and the spectator's viewpoint, writes how good surfers produce aesthetically pleasing movements. They can do this through much practice, but also instinctively, because they know how to distribute the weight over the board, which part of the wave they needs to be on at any time, and what type of manoeuver is best. He explains,

> Although these responses require time to develop, their development has much more to do with feeling and intuition than the more 'rational' progression of skills we see in other sports; after all, no two waves are the same. It stands to reason then that those surfers who allow their bodies to be responsive to the changing dynamics of the wave the most will, over a period of time, come to understand better any given surfing situation pre-conceptually, and will therefore respond in a more appropriate manner. [...] When we talk about the body being spontaneous, what we are lacking 'is reflective control and analysis of the movement'. (Thomen 2010, 324)

Thomen correctly highlights how spontaneity is an essential part of this process, and the aquatic particularities of surfing (relatable to others such as whitewater kayaking). Nevertheless, this does not mean that other sports follow a more 'rational progression,' and in fact, any expert performative activity follows a non-deliberative process that aims at spontaneity to reach and refine expertise. As the next three essays show in more depth, this spontaneity, while not strictly reflective, does require pre-performance deliberation and post-performance reflection. In fact, true masters analyze their experience very keenly and deliberately. It does not mean either that there is no focused awareness (that a Jamesian fringe modulates). Experts excel in their ability to switch or phase through the different layers of awareness.

What needs to be further explained is how such an iterative process takes place. As discussed above, the Jamesian fringe, along with emotive control, works with the other layers and integrates with the other elements thick holism lays out, such as Zhuangzian spontaneity, and attunement to skills and their dynamics. Arguably, a way to reveal how this process works is to look at those times when those equally gifted and in possession of the requisite skills fail dramatically, as happen when sportspeople choke (essay 8). For his part, neuropsychologist Alekxandr Luria writes of chains of

HOLISM AND THE CULTIVATION OF EXCELLENCE IN SPORTS AND PERFORMANCE

isolated impulses that are reduced, that is simplified, and become complex movements that eventually form a single kinetic melody, just as when we learn to write we go from single letters to our writing style (1973, 32–36).[38] But his work, focused on the patho-logical, is directed toward breakdowns of these melodies (ibid., 37; 182). Fluidity and order live in perennial battle with chaos and entropy. Performers need to be able to balance this uneasy relationship, itself a skill (or rather a meta-skill).

Gunnar Breivik and Kenneth Aggerholm have pointed out the chaotic element in the performance of elite sportspersons in some sports, such as football (Aggerholm 2012) and downhill skiing (Breivik 2012, personal correspondence). Caused by either contraries' unpredictable reactions or because they push things to the limit on the slopes, this brings out to the fore again the specificity of sport, and the danger of mak-ing sweeping claims about *specifics*. Their examples show that some sports and activi-ties make it very hard to achieve skillful fluency, particularly if we visualize it as a sort of grace or beauty under pressure and 'silky' movements. And yet, there are ways these manifest themselves even amid chaos (which does not mean that there cannot be catastrophic failures as just mentioned). Our movements have a heterochronic quality: even skillful fluency is not a matter of synchronous kinetic melodies. Gallagher explained how movement is synchronic, a matter of flows, and diachronic:

> Dynamics is not just about the flowing sequence of change of movement or experi-ence, but about forces and structures implicit in that change. Sheets- Johnstone emphasizes the diachronic aspects of dynamics; but dynamics also involves syn-chronies that constrain and structure movement. Body schematic processes are not simply about change of position over time, the pure kinetic flow, but about the com-plex interactions of different parts of the body that are changing relationships throughout the movement, but that also impose limits on that movement. Synchrony is not something like a momentary snapshot—as if relations between e.g. hand and mouth were frozen in a simple linear way in any particular moment. (2005, 243)

Even fluid motions need to account for limitations and disruptions. Part of maintaining that fluidity is about learning how to absorb the bumps of diachronic elements in our experience. Few events are as chaotic as the *encierro*, with thousands of people vying to get close or away from the bulls. Televised images belie the intensity and brutality of the affair. And yet, there are some outstanding runners whose performances cannot be described except as fluid and graceful: they consistently manage to find the space in front of the bulls, surfing on what looks like a wave of horns and receding runners. As they say in conversation, they try to create aesthetic runs and mind an ethical code where helping others even at the risk of their own life or not bothering the bulls is pri-mary (Ilundáin-Agurruza 2007a, 2008). This does not mean that all or even most of their runs are beautifully fluid. Of course, *eventually* everyone who runs often and close to the horns falls or gets hurt. (But those fleeting moments stolen from anarchy are well worth it for those who know why they do so.) To work within chaos in this way requires a tight rein on the emotions.

To bring the theoretical framework closer to Aristotelian praxis, the question becomes, how do we refine or increase the integration within our bodymind? Imbalances may lead to body(mind) or (body)mind maladjustments. To sketch this as a parody: the muscular meathead or the incapable intellectual respectively at the

183

HOLISM AND THE CULTIVATION OF EXCELLENCE IN SPORTS AND PERFORMANCE

extremes. Our emotions play a pivotal role in the (dis)integration of our bodymind. If the spontaneity for acting and learning that characterizes our initial years in this world often becomes mired in reflective thinking as we grow, we can also fare no better when our emotions hijack us, take John McEnroe's tantrums on the court, or when our desires lead us by the nose in spite of knowing better. In either case we lose the natural integration we embody; we become shackled and our freedom is lost. This can result in fractured action (essay 8).

Key to a wise attunement of the emotions is the learning process.[39] Self-cultivation, learning, and philosophy as a way of life lie at the center of the philosophical dark horses' views, as we have seen. A full incorporation of emotion is a sine qua non. Before following an Eastern path toward this integration, however, a few reflections to plant seeds to be reaped later.

Spinoza is the clearest antecessor of this organic unity, and arguably first modern philosopher, to make of the emotions the keystone of his philosophical framework in the West. Whatever the merits or problems with his method, his ontological stance understood mind and body as two attributes of the same substance while it also emphasized the role of emotion in our thinking and acting. This makes him a legitimate predecessor to thick holism. Spinoza (1948) argues against dualism and for a unified view in Part Two of his *Ethics*. In Proposition XIII, he discusses how the body is the object of the mind, and after detailing his proof concludes that, 'we thus comprehend, not only that the human mind is united to the body, but also the nature of the union between the mind and body.' One way to explain this is to say that for him we are both mind and body through and through, and that the duality only arises from the manner in which we describe these attributes: from one perspective, an objective and external one, we speak of the body, whereas from a subjective stance we refer to the mind. This follows the descriptive rather than ontological route.

Spinoza knew the importance of emotive attunement and control if we were to become experts and wise in the ways of the world, such that we could find a modicum of freedom amid a deterministic universe. Because freedom is determined from within, not externally like the imagination, this enables us to understand our own reasons for action.[40] Spinoza makes of 'intuition,' his *amor intellectualis* a blend of reasoned emotion that liberates us from the grip of what he classified as negative emotions. Paradoxically, we find a modicum of freedom after we contextualize the emotions and realize the universal necessity at work in God/Nature.[41] If we understand our reasons for action *thus* we can grasp the truth of the matter internally. Thereby, negative and binding emotions evanesce since we are freed from external causes and incomplete understanding. Unsurprisingly, Ortega and Arne Naess, the father of deep ecology, are both intellectual admirers and heirs of Spinoza. Naess (1998) in particular balances the scale by emphasizing the positive side of the emotions as sources of motivation, giving us in particular the motivation for change. Moreover, for him, we 'can learn properly only what engages [our] feelings' (Naess 1998, 139).

One of the most interesting, radical, and attractive proposals to bring pedagogical, existential, and aesthetic dimensions together comes from the pen of Kretchmar (2013), undoubtedly the staunchest defender, in theory and praxis, of holism—as we saw in essay 4. He argues for a holistic educational model that presents the charisma and challenges of a holistic education in a way that engages our feelings and cultivates the motivation for change.

HOLISM AND THE CULTIVATION OF EXCELLENCE IN SPORTS AND PERFORMANCE

As apprentices (Kretchmar's word for students in a holistic pedagogy) begin to develop their skills and appreciate the practice. He elucidates:

> Slowly the charms of playground begin to reveal themselves. Slowly the player gets 'play-grounded' as skills and values required by it seemingly cross permeable membranes and seep into him or her. And reciprocally, the playground gets 'played' as the individual's own story, habits, and traits shape the playground in question. Interestingly, we do not even have a ready vocabulary that would allow us to talk about this. 'Play-grounded?' 'Played?' It would appear that pedagogical earthquakes caused by holism require not only new thinking and behavior but a new lexicon too. (Kretchmar 2013, 35)

Much as we need anew a richer lexicon to capture the rich dynamics of our animate life in ways that do not rely on reductionist and reifying 'neuro-talk,' we need better ways to describe the existential dimensions of our playful activities in ways that capture how the game and geo-social environment affect us, play-grounding us, and how *we* also shape game and environment, playering it.

The very idea that how we ride our bike up a mountain, swim in the pool, run the track, play football, practice a kenjutsu kata, or dance a tango defines the practice, rather, personifies the nature of thick holism in the best possible manner. When we give ourselves to the practice, this is kenotic through and through just in the sense adduced in the opening essay (from kenosis, self-emptying; see also essay 10). Understanding how this unfolds means revisiting our childhood.

2.3. *Childish yet Consummate and Risky Steps*

So far, we have developed an analysis of movement that might be termed adultist, that is, centered on the abilities of mature and fully developed persons. But we should not forget that this process starts in our learning years. The novice, we often read, learns by means of rules, unlike the expert. But, children, specifically those at the pre-linguistic age, learn to walk, to grasp, to attribute intentions to others (Gallagher 2005a), and to make assumptions about the persistence of objects through space and time obviously without rule-guidance. In a way, they learn spontaneously. The Chinese view of the sage as a child takes on a deeper meaning now (in fact, the character for sage and child is the same, 子). The difference is that sages control their emotions and willfully cultivate that forgetfulness of the 'learning steps.' There is much to learn from and with children. As Ortega states, maturity is not suppression but integration of infancy (Ortega 2004, 130) Thelen and Smith's (1994) nonlinear dynamic systems theory is instructive in this regard, as it shows that infants' walking is not due to some sort of inevitable developmental process, but results from a convergence of rich and multilayered opportunities that range from their anatomy, developmental history, the ground, or their parents.[42]

Let us consider kicking, since grasping and the hand have been predominant (after all bipedalism, as mentioned earlier, is something we should consider as more primordial than the hand). Thelen's research on spontaneous infant kicking, which happens for various reasons and postures, and can result from nonspecific arousal to instrumental behavior (Thelen and Smith 1994, 78), shows that is much more complex than appeal to a central pattern generator (CPG) affords, as the dominant views endorse. The muscles and nerves displayed considerable springlike qualities (that a CPG cannot explain), and which when given a burst of energy self-organized like a simple spring (ibid., 81). In other words, this follows the pattern into simpler self-organizations proper of dynamic systems. Two insights they derive from this research are that, 1) self-organization 'is an essential feature that gives behavior its ruled-based appearance without the need for specific rules.' (Ibid., 83) This is of import to views of skill development, particularly if we aim at exemplary movement and skill, because, (1) it validates the insight that skill without rules is not only the domain of expertise, and (2) it also shows this to be formative. Further, the resulting pattern organization is quite context specific. 'Kicking is not a goal-directed or goal-corrected activity, yet it is organized with respect both to the gravitational field and the internally generated energy pulses that initiate the movement.' (Ibid.) Both infant and environment determine the collective features of what we call a kick. This also coheres with the rich specificity found in sports at all levels, from the kinesthetic dynamics to the constitutive and prescriptive rules.

The rich bodily dynamics that learning to walk and the dynamics of kicking entail are characteristic of thick holism: a moving wisdom of the bodymind that heterochronically and spontaneously organizes itself in meaningful patterns at various levels of expression, from the cellular to the overtly intentional and semantic. Learning to walk and becoming proficient kickers are but the beginning of our skillful strivings. To paraphrase Laozi, it all begins with one step. Sometimes this step can be a risky one.

We develop our skills by pushing the boundaries of what we can do. Risk is integral to skill development then. To achieve skillful fluency, we need to seek risk. Slater risks more than any of his competitors, as we have seen. We also need to be comfortable with failure, as we will see in the next essay learning how to handle it is part of becoming successful and learning how to handle it. Sometimes, this means courting danger—early on. Russell (2007b) brings attention to the importance of allowing for risky activities in children's lives. Controversially but compellingly, he argues that we should permit for risks 'greater than necessary to promote the developmental goods' that these activities make possible (Russell 2007b, 177). He has in mind activities like gymnastics, diving, American football, cheerleading, horse riding, and similar sports that can result in serious injury or death. We find the opportunity to cultivate self-affirmation in these endeavors (see Russell 2005, and essay 9). This allows children to discover who and what they are (Russell 2007b, 182). More important, in terms of development and childhood, is the fact that some of our strivings and skills come with expiration dates. 'Indeed, by the time adulthood is reached, the capacity to acquire and practice certain physical skills is often diminished or even eliminated altogether' (Ibid., 187). And even once there, these are often short lived and hard to maintain (ibid.). This is particularly

HOLISM AND THE CULTIVATION OF EXCELLENCE IN SPORTS AND PERFORMANCE

the case with some sports and activities such as diving or gymnastics where starting early confers a big advantage or is needed to reach the requisite level to master the activity. These are biographical windows of opportunity that, if missed, we will not be able to develop them to the expert level. Something we may come to deeply regret. In short, exemplary skill development may require taking risks even before we are mature enough to realize the benefits of prudence. But it may still be a bet worth taking, particularly if guided by the right hands.[43]

An alternative account of learning that can set us on the road to holistic excellence would look at our skills in an ecological manner, not a computational one. The work of Araújo and Davids (2011) gives such perspective. In agreement with Thelen and Smith's insight, ecological dynamics in skill acquisition 'assumes an organism-environment mutuality and reciprocity in which both combine to form a whole ecosystem' (Araújo and Davids 2011, 13). This approach repudiates the thinly disguised dualism of the subjective–objective dichotomy of cognitive theories and embraces the ecological reciprocity just mentioned. The ecological view entails the physics of the environment, the physical and mental capacities of the individual, perceptual information, tasks demands, and more, which constrain the acquisition of skill (Ibid.,15). Obviating their ironically *own* dualistic articulation, this essentially adopts thick holism and enactivism. The process of skill acquisition in an ecological view involves an *education of intention, perceptual attunement,* and *calibration.*

In this way, (1) we pay more attention to more useful variables to achieve an end or learn which sources of information to attend; (2) thus, we can extrapolate from partly useful characteristics, how a ball bounces, to more useful information, recognizing early flight path to hit the ball (ibid., 17); (3) in turn, we can adapt our bodily dynamics, for instance to tools that alter our dimensions (rackets, golf clubs); and (4) this leads to a process that is dynamic and adapts to changes (training or aging) and requires recalibration (ibid., 17–18). The upshot is that this process better captures the dynamics of how we learn skillfully. We do not store some sort of representations, but rather become more skilled at navigating environments. Fittingly, they close suggesting a reconceptualization of skill acquisition into skill adaptation or attunement, as the latter emphasize the relationship between the individual and the environment in a specific performance context (ibid., 19). Once we acquire the skills, however, we need to refine them. This brings us back to that Deweyan practice *of* skill. This process can leave an imprint, a signature of sorts, in our bodymind.

As part of our species-typical development into adulthood, we acquire a *somatic style* to our movement in sports and other activities: we walk with a certain gait, we move our arms with a style all our own—just as we do when we swim or hit the ball. Yet, Sheets-Johnstone rightly notes, we recognize others' styles (their qualitative kinetic dynamics) far more readily than our own, because to 'recognize our own style requires us to turn to our own experience of movement and to witness the truths of our own experience' (2011, 499). Those who excel at witnessing their own experience learn to discriminate and perform better. And, those skillfully fluid and fluent develop a *kinetic signature*. A signature, through assiduous practice of patterned movements becomes uniquely ours; it is not simply our name in our handwriting.[44] So does a corporeal-kinetic signature imbue masters' movements with a recognizable quality all their own. While we are not be able, nor would we want, to learn how to *exactly* copy their signature, this can serve as an inspirational template for our self-cultivation.

We have explored the experiential riches that skillful fluency makes possible. But, just as Liezi, who could ride the wind, *had to* come down after fifteen days, eventually masters fail. Learning to cope with defeat may be one of their best assets, in fact. But for some failure, instead of a lesson and window of opportunity, can become pathological. Skillful fluency and its kinetic signature then turn into fractured action and a erratic scribble. Understanding this darker and antithetic facet to supreme skill can be very instructive for our skillful strivings. The next essay examines this.

DISCLOSURE STATEMENT

No potential conflict of interest was reported by the author.

NOTES

1. Zhuangzi and Watson (1968, 32).
2. Larsen (2010, 30).
3. Scott Kelso's groundbreaking work in dynamic systems theory advocates different levels of description, i.e. from neuronal activity to biomechanical angles and higher. He stresses the point that 'no single level of analysis has priority over any other' (ibid., 2). The underlying pragmatic criterion is that these adjust best to the phenomenon to be described, which is quite consistent with the thick holism here defended and the idea of different descriptive levels just argued for. Kelso develops a theory of coordinated human behavior—from neuronal level to mind—that is governed by generic processes of self-organization. This results in the spontaneous formation of dynamic patterns that are independent of the stuff that realizes them and the level at which they are observed (ibid., xi–xiii). With this, we can explain any phenomenon, from molecular behavior (ibid., 6–8) to coordination dynamics of limbs, say someone doing a biceps curl (ibid., 80), and from social coordination and coupling of limb synchronies (ibid., 93–99) to neural and mental processes (Ibid., 260ff). As he sees it, 'Instead of trying to *reduce* biology and psychology to chemistry and physics, the task now is to *extend* our physical understanding of the organization of living things.' (ibid., 287) Given the complexity of his views as well as space limitations, drawing a fuller connection between both programs is beyond the scope of this project. Related work on developmental research by Thelen and Smith is considered later.
4. Not taking into account that describing subatomic particles in motion is subject to Heisenberg's Uncertainty Principle: in particle physics, we cannot possibly locate and determine a particle's trajectory concurrently. An 'ultimate' extensional description at its most fundamental level is thereby impossible in principle.
5. This landmark collection of essays brings sport under the gaze of phenomenology and some of the best sport philosophers, with analyses that engage Heidegger, Husserl, Merleau-Ponty, Patočka, Sartre, and others as well as topics such as performance enhancement, risk sports, movement, the sweet tension in sport, and feints in football. Some of these are incorporated when directly pertinent, but the present analysis attempts to bring to the table an alternative *and* complementary perspective.
6. See Ilundáin-Agurruza (2000) for an elucidation of interpretation in the context of the arts but with ready and obvious application to other practices and phenomena. It

HOLISM AND THE CULTIVATION OF EXCELLENCE IN SPORTS AND PERFORMANCE

argues that ontology depends on the creative hermeneutic process and that artworks (or other created phenomena) are the result of a collaborative enterprise that integrates artwork, artist, audience, and historical context anchored by a caring disposition he calls attendance. The notion of attendance is incorporated in essay 10.

7. Breivik (2008) criticizes O'Saughnessy's view of proprioception, which takes proprioceptive dynamics for kinesthetic ones in ways that misconstrue how we actually feel said processes. Citing Todes, Breivik amends the account and aligns it with a holistic approach concerning how we move during sporting activity (348–349).

8. Best's Wittgensteinian leanings, with which I largely sympathize, point out how concepts cannot be true or false themselves since they are the standards of meaning, and as such cannot be criticized externally but only internally in terms of contextual consistency (1979, 135). The soundness of the point standing, it is instructive to complement his point by pointing how some of our concepts originate from movement, as Sheets-Johnstone notes in several instances appealing to the fact that for Husserl, the 'I move' precedes the 'I can do' (1990, 29, 2011, 116). Moreover, in *The Roots of Thinking* (1990), she shows how many of our central concepts originate in our bodymind. She sums this up elsewhere when she writes that, 'corporeal powers give rise to corporeal concepts, fundamental human concepts such as grinding, sharpness, hardness, and so on' (Sheets-Johnstone 2011, 116). Let us also remember Ortega's insight concerning how our bodily perceptions inform our concepts.

9. Space limitations prevent a discussion of agency and ownership regarding our actions, body schema, and body image. For a fuller account, see Gallagher (2005b).

10. For further exposition on these qualities, rhytmicities, and kinetic melodies, see Sheets-Johnstone (2009, 233, 273–274, and 317).

11. There is a rich sense of 'forgetting,' rooted in Zhuangzi's ideas, is more fully developed in essay 10 and its appendix. It necessitates further preparatory work, undertaken in essay 9, before it can be fruitfully discussed.

12. Gerunds are verbals that end in '-*ing*' but work as nouns. As such they express action or a state of being. But because gerunds function as nouns they take the position that nouns ordinarily take, e.g. as direct object or subject. Presently, the idea is that a gerund emphasizes the dynamic and fluid nature of bodymind schematizings and imaginings and deemphasizes or discourages thinking of them, however surreptitiously, as static entities or objects. In essay 10, Minamoto's idea of *kata* is discussed as a patterning as well, enriching the idea of animated and dynamic patternings.

13. Gallagher is aware of this research, much of which post-dates his analyses on the matter (personal conversation). His phenomenological analysis can be easily adapted to cover these cases.

14. In fact, even reading needs saccades. We do not need to see every letter to make sense of the text. And in fact we do not. A smiple epxirmnt sufgices: we nrsd olty the ferdt and ledt lertre to unftrstknd a tmxt. Knudson and Kukla explain, 'When there is slow relative movement between an observer and an object, the eyes can smoothly move together following the object until visual angular velocities reach 40 to 70 degrees per second,' that is the speed of a person walking at 3 mph six feet away (1997). These are the kinds of speeds at which we can smoothly follow objects. But in sport most movements require saccades such that we only observe actions partially. In volleyball, angular velocities exceed 500 degrees, and although we can handle 700 degrees, 'the eyes basically turn off so they saccade to the next fixation' (Knudson and Kukla 1997).

HOLISM AND THE CULTIVATION OF EXCELLENCE IN SPORTS AND PERFORMANCE

15. As Gallagher points out, Shusterman mistakes Merleau-Ponty's view, taking it 'as a negative description of 'representations of body parts and processes" when 'Merleau-Ponty simply wants to say that he can move without knowing anything about or being aware of the subpersonal processes of motor control' (2011, 310, fn. 1). Nonetheless, this does not affect the ulterior point that both, subpersonal an reflective, representational processes supplement each other.

16. Shusterman cites James, 'spontaneous action is always best' (2012, 62).

17. Polanyi writes, 'Skilful knowing and doing is performed by subordinating a set of particulars, as clues or tools, to the shaping of a skilful achievement, whether practical or theoretical. We may then be said to become subsidiarily aware of these particulars within our focal awareness of the coherent entity that we achieve' (Polanyi 2005 [1958], 2). But this tacit dimension, important as it is, remains too opaque. This project strives to bring some light.

18. Upon being asked by the deficient reader how he was able to uncover the secrets of the text, the latter may reply that 'reading while sunbathing has made him well red,' to the puzzlement of the former.

19. Serrasoles descended Keyhole Falls, after more than a year of preparation, in January of 2015 (Rogers 2015). First he had to rappel 300 feet of disintegrating volcanic rock. See the video at http://www.redbull.com/en/adventure/stories/1,331,696,054,636/the-scari est-waterfall-drop-you-ve-ever-seen

20. The author was tested at the age of 16, while he was a swimmer and produced a value of 75 mL (kg-min). Subsequently in his early 40s, he still had a value of 76–77 mL (kg-min) when trained. Given his solid but non-stellar competitive results, such factors are far from good predictors for athletic excellence in competition.

21. We may question whether the reflexivity requisite to become aware of the quality of one's movement affects said movement (in terms of skill) and its *felt* experience. Conversely, we can also wonder whether the level of skill influences the experience and gnostic possibilities of movement in kinetically intensive practices such as sports or performances. Is it changed, like some sort of motile Schrödinger's cat, when one looks into it? These are questions best left for another occasion, but worth noting.

22. The first part of this article (2007a) discounts various empirical, sociological, and anthropological misinterpretations of the *encierro* to then, conceptually and phenomenologically, describe its meaning.

23. Breivik conducts a Heideggerian analysis of skydiving (2010), Ilundáin-Agurruza (2007b) examines Skydiving and risk sports in terms of the Kantian sublime.

24. This is not the time to address this complex topic as fully as it deserves. For a rigorous and thoughtful assessment of Morgan's pivotal article (2013) and Russell's work that engages the ideas of Habermas and Gadamer see López Frías (2014a, 2014b). In the latter, he states the need for and his agreement with a more holistic account for ethics (2014b, 54–55).

25. Institutionalization is both problem and solution; we are too aware of current challenges that threaten to subvert sports' potential to flourish, to wit cheating, doping, or the inordinate influence of commercial interests. For a critical and balanced assessment of MacIntyre's uncompromisingly negative view of institutions see McNamee (2008); for a discussion of this issue and an in-depth application of virtue ethics to a concrete case, Turkish soccer, see Ilundáin-Agurruza and Kuleli (2013).

HOLISM AND THE CULTIVATION OF EXCELLENCE IN SPORTS AND PERFORMANCE

26. Jeannerod and colleagues show how hand-related parietal neurons play a specific role in visuomotor processes of grasping (1997, 46), and further that different neurons are encoded for either precision grip, finger prehension, or hand prehension, which in turn are used for grabbing different shaped-objects, that is, different neurons are used to grab a sphere, which requires all fingers, than a cylinder, which requires palm opposition (ibid., 48). Hence, grasping a tennis racket or the *tsuka* (handle) of a katana engage different neurons and for the agent *feel* dissimilar at the pragmatic level at which the object is engaged (Jeannerod 1997). Interestingly, the hands pre-reflectively shape differently as the object is approached, based less on vision than on previous experiences of grasping and their tactile qualities. Moreover, even when the *same* muscles contract, different neurons fire for different grips, for example, precision versus power grabbing (Jeannerod 1997, 41). Extrapolating from this, we can hypothesize how the same muscles contracting can result in different kinematics, dynamics, and feelings (sensations and perceptions) when used with different tools and with different rules of engagement that change the position of the grip, as in fencing (thereby allowing to explain both the physiological level and the pragmatic one of why the fencer prefers the sabre).

27. To reframe this with Gallagher, 'the body *actively organizes* its sense experience and its movement in relation to pragmatic concerns' such this is not reducible to neural and physiological operations even if these operations are necessary (2005a, 142).

28. Essays 9 and 10 explore the socio-historical aspect of our ways of moving in relation to Marcel Mauss.

29. For a discussion of *kalon* in the broader context of the Ancient Olympics see Ilundáin-Agurruza 2012.

30. See entries for κάλος, κάλως, and καλοκαγαθία in the *The Online Liddell-Scott-Jones Greek-English Lexicon* (2009).

31. Monti still showed superior *kalon*, for he actually forsook an Olympic medal. Fernández Anaya states that he believes he would have passed him to win a World or European championship (Arribas 2014).

32. Warren Fraleigh (1982) argues against such fouls in a widely cited piece. Addressing this issue as it merits lies beyond the feasible scope of this project, unfortunately.

33. Oda and Kondo (2014) discuss the unique case of Kendo, which seeks a purposive result, to eliminate the opponent, yet how this is to be achieved aesthetically (see essay 9).

34. For a critical analysis of skillful coping, flow, and *mushin* within an East-West comparative framework see Krein and Ilundáin-Agurruza (2014).

35. In *Reflections on a* Katana we will read more in depth about Musashi and expand on these ideas.

36. McNamee reminds me that Polanyi (2002 [1958]) also analyzed this under the notion of connoisseurship.

37. For an insightful reading of water in the context of surfing and paddling alongside Bergson and James, see (Anderson 2007).

38. Sheets-Johnstone (2009, 2011) and Thompson (2007) profitably incorporate Luria's framework.

39. For a holistic pedagogy of sport that discusses the ideas of Dewey, Ortega, Naess, Savater, and Spinoza among others, see Ilundáin-Agurruza (2014).

40. Nishida Kitarō (1990) founder of the Kyoto school comes to a similar conclusion independently; see essay 9.

HOLISM AND THE CULTIVATION OF EXCELLENCE IN SPORTS AND PERFORMANCE

41. The views summarized here reflect the content of Parts III and IV for the emotions, and Part V for freedom. For a lucid exposition of these ideas, see Garrett Thomson (2012).

42. Thelen and Smith 'approach the mystery of human development with the conviction that the acquisition of mental life is continuous with all biological growth of form and function' (1994, xiii). They rely on principles of nonlinear dynamic systems, whose premise is to understand the central question of 'how complex systems, including developing humans, produce *patterns that evolve over time*' (ibid., 51). Another key element is that dynamic principles are based on thermodynamic realities that describe the way the universe works, and which are independent of the level of observation or the particular material instantiation (ibid., 52ff. 71). This makes it very powerful, as it can account for any phenomenon without getting caught up in a reductionist trap. And being dynamical, it also avoids any reifying boxes. For instance, when considering the dynamic principles of development in the context of leaning to walk (something robotics is still struggling with) instead of ascribing locomotor development to a logically inevitable process, this is seen as the 'confluence of available states within particular contextual opportunities': normal human infants learn to walk upright because of anatomical and neural elements tied to the species' history, contingencies of humans' own developmental history, a strong urge to move efficiently, support surfaces, gravity, things to hold on to, parental guidance, etc. (Ibid., 72). The result is that, 'Walking self-organizes under these constraints because non-linear, complex dynamic systems occupy preferred behavioral states' (Ibid.). Further, their research shows that 'the central nervous system (CNS) is not a computer controlling an electronic output device [one of the dominant views, unsurprisingly congruent with cognitivism]. Rather, the CNS must translate intentions and plans into moving limbs and body segments. The body constitutes a complex linked system, with mass, elastic, energetic, and inertial properties, which has multiple sensory linkages within it and between the organism and the outside world.' (Ibid., 75) The pervasiveness of continuities and multiple but related levels bespeak of thick, dense holism.

43. See Ilundáin-Agurruza (2011, 2014, forthcoming) for a consideration of this issue from various angles.

44. Redolent of Luria's explanation of a kinetic melody (1973, 32), this was developed before I was aware of his work.

REFERENCES

AGGERHOLM, K. 2012. Elite-Bildung: An existential-phenomenological study of talents developing in football. PhD diss.

ANDERSON, D. 2007. Reading water: Risk, intuition, and insight. In *Philosophy, risk, and adventure sports*, edited by M. McNamee. Oxon: Routledge: 71–9.

ANWAN, Y. 2013. Hit a 95 mph baseball? Scientists pinpoint how we see it coming. *Berkeleyan Newsletter*. Available at http://newscenter.berkeley.edu/2013/05/08/motion-vision/ (accessed 14 January 2014).

ARAÚJO, D. and K. DAVIDS. 2011. What is exactly acquired during skill acquisition? *Journal of Consciousness Studies* 18 (3–4): 7–23.

ARRIBAS, C. 2014. El Valor de un Gesto. *EL País*, 14 December. Available at http://deportes.elpais.com/deportes/2012/12/14/actualidad/1355506756_770952.html (accessed 16 December).

HOLISM AND THE CULTIVATION OF EXCELLENCE IN SPORTS AND PERFORMANCE

ASPIN, D. 1976. 'Knowing how' and 'knowing that' and physical education. *Journal of the Philosophy of Sport* 3 (1): 97–117.

BEILOCK, S.L. and T.H. CARR. 2001. On the fragility of skilled performance: What governs choking under pressure? *Journal of Experimental Psychology: General* 130 (4): 701–25.

———. 2004. From novice to expert performance: Attention, memory, and the control of complex sensorimotor skills. In *Skill acquisition in sport: Research, theory, and practice*, edited by A.M. Williams, N.J. Hodges, and M.L.J. Court. Abingdon: Routledge: 309–28.

BEILOCK, S.L., S.A. WIERENGA, and T.H. CARR. 2003. Memory and expertise: What experiences do athletes remember? In *Expert performance in sports: advances in research on sport expertise*, edited by J.L. Starkes and K.A. Ericsson. Champaign, IL: Human Kinetics: 295–320.

BENDIX, E. 2014. Fear of falling. Unpublished Manuscript.

BEST, D. 1979. *Philosophy and human movement*. London: George Allen & Unwin.

BREIVIK, G. 2007. Skillful coping in everyday life and in sport: A critical examination of the views of Heidegger and Dreyfus. *Journal of the Philosophy of Sport* 34 (2): 116–34.

———. 2008. Bodily movement – The fundamental dimensions. *Sport, Ethics and Philosophy* 2 (3): 337–52.

———. 2010. Being-in-the-void: A Heideggerian analysis of skydiving. *Journal of the Philosophy of Sport* 37 (1): 29–46.

———. 2011. Dangerous play with the elements: Towards a phenomenology of risk sports. *Sport, Ethics and Philosophy* 5 (3): 314–30.

———.2012. Personal Correspondence. September 14.

———. 2013. Zombie-like or superconscious? A phenomenological and conceptual analysis of consciousness in elite sport. *Journal of the Philosophy of Sport* 40 (1): 85–105.

CHURCHLAND, P.M. 1981. Eliminative materialism and the propositional attitudes. *The Journal of Philosophy* 78: 67–90.

CLÉRET, L. and M. MCNAMEE. 2012. Olympism, the values of sport, and the will to power: De Coubertin and Nietzsche meet Eugenio Monti. *Sport, Ethics and Philosophy* 6 (2): 183–94.

D'AGOSTINO, F. 1981. The ethos of games. *Journal of the Philosophy of Sport* 8 (1): 7–18.

DEWEY, J. 1925. *Experience and nature*. Chicago, IL: Open Court Pub. Co.

———. 1963. *Philosophy and civilization*. New York, NY: Capricorn Books.

———. 1988. *Human nature and conduct: an introduction to social psychology*. New York, NY: Holt.

DREYFUS, H. and S. DREYFUS. 1986. *Mind over machine: The power of human intuition and expertise in the era of the computer*. New York, NY: The Free Press.

ECENBARGER, W. 2008. El Espíritu Olímpico [The Olympic spirit]. *Selecciones de Reader's Digest* 98–105.

EDGAR, A. 2013. Sport and art: An essay in the hermeneutics of sport. *Sport, Ethics and Philosophy* 7 (1): 1–171.

ERICSSON, K.A. 2003. Development of elite performance and deliberate practice: An update from the perspective of the expert performance approach. In *Expert performance in sports: Advances in research in sport expertise*, edited by J. Starke and A.K. Ericcson. Champaign: Human Kinetics: 49–83.

FRALEIGH, W. 1982. Why the good foul is not good. *Journal of Physical Education, Recreation, and Dance* 53: 41–2.

GALLAGHER, S. 2003. Phenomenology and experimental design. *Journal of Consciousness Studies.* 10 (9–10): 85–99.

———. 2005a. *How the body shapes the mind.* Oxford: Oxford University Press.

———. 2005b. Dynamic models of body schematic processes. In *Body image and body schema*, edited by H. De Preester and V. Knockaert. Amsterdam: John Benjamins: 233–50.

———. 2009. Philosophical antecedents of situated cognition. In *The Cambridge handbook of situated cognition*, edited by P. Robbins and M. Aydede. Cambridge: Cambridge University Press: 35–52.

———. 2011. Review article: Somaesthetics and the care of the body. *Metaphilosophy* 42 (3): 305–13. Available at http://onlinelibrary.wiley.com/enhanced/doi/10.1111/j.1467-9973.2011.01686.x/ (accessed 15 October 2013).

———. 2012. *Phenomenology.* New York, NY: Palgrave McMillan.

GALLAGHER, S. and D. ZAHAVI. 2008. *The phenomenological mind: An introduction to philosophy of mind and cognitive science.* New York, NY: Routledge.

GIBSON, J.J. 1979. *The ecological approach to visual perception.* Boston, MA: Houghton-Mifflin.

GOODMAN, N. 1968. *Languages of art: An approach to a theory of symbols.* Indianapolis, IN: Bobbs-Merrill.

HEIDEGGER, M. 1962. *Being and time.* New York, NY: Harper.

———. 1971. The origin of the work of art. *Language, Poetry, Thought.* New York, NY: Harper & Row.

HUTTO, D. 2014. *Personal Communication.* September 5, 2014.

ILUNDÁIN-AGURRUZA, J. 2000. ... In the realms of art: A conceptual inquiry of the genesis of the work of art. Ph.D. Thesis, University of Illinois at Urbana-Champaign.

———. 2007a. Between the horns: A dilemma in the interpretation of the running of the bulls—Part 1: The confrontation. *Sport, Ethics, and Philosophy* 1 (3): 325–45.

———. 2007b. Kant goes skydiving: Understanding the extreme by way of the sublime. In *Philosophy, risk and adventure sports*, edited by Mike McNamee. London: Routledge: 149–67.

———. 2011. *Weaving the magic: Philosophy, sports and literature.* In Philosophy of sport: International perspectives, edited by A. Hardman and C. Jones: 50–71.

———. 2008. Between the horns. A dilemma in the interpretation of the running of the bulls —Part 2: The evasion. *Sport, Ethics, and Philosophy* 2 (1): 18–38.

———. 2014. The quest for meaningful and lifelong learning. In *Philosophy, sport and education: International perspectives*, edited by M. Isidori, F.J. López Frías, and A. Müller. Viterbo: Sette Città: 43–69.

ILUNDÁIN-AGURRUZA, J. and C. KULELI. 2013. A new heart for turkish soccer: A MacIntyrean analysis of the beautiful game. *Soccer & Society* 13 (5 & 6): 667–86.

ILUNDÁIN-AGURRUZA, J. and C. TORRES 2010. Embellishing the ugly side of the beautiful game. In *Beautiful thoughts on the beautiful game*, edited by T. Richards. 185–96.

ILUNDÁIN-AGURRUZA, J. forthcoming. The eye of the hurricane: Philosophical reflections on risky sports, self-knowledge and flourishing. *Journal of the Philosophy of Sport.*

JAMES, W. 1890. *The principles of psychology.* New York, NY: Henry Bolt and Co.

JEANNEROD, M. 1997. *The cognitive neuroscience of action.* Oxford: Blackwell.

KELSO, J.S. 1995. *Dynamic Patterns: the Self-organization of Brain and Behavior.* Cambridge, MA: MIT Press.

KILHAM, L. 2008. *MegaMinds: How to create and invent in the age of google.* Self-Published.

HOLISM AND THE CULTIVATION OF EXCELLENCE IN SPORTS AND PERFORMANCE

KNUDSON, D. and D. KUKLA. 1997. The impact of vision and vision training on sport performance. *Journal of Physical Education, Recreation and Dance*. Available at http://sportsci.org/news/ferret/visionreview/visionreview.html (accessed 14 January 2014).

KREIN, K. and J. ILUNDÁIN-AGURRUZA. 2014. An east–west comparative analysis of *Mushin* and flow. In *Philosophy and the martial arts*, edited by G. Priest and D. Young. New York, NY: Roultedge: 139–64.

KRETCHMAR, R.S. 2013. Mind-body holism, paradigm shifts, and education. *Fair Play. Revista de Filosofía, Ética y Derecho del Deporte* 1 (1): 28–43.

LALLY, R. 2012. Deweyan pragmatism and self-cultivation. In *Pragmatism and the philosophy of sport*, edited by R. Lally, D. Anderson, and J. Kaag. London: Lexington Books: 175–98.

LARSEN, N.S. 2010. Becoming a cyclist: Phenomenological reflections on cycling. In *Cycling— Philosophy for everyone*, edited by J. Ilundáin-Agurruza and M. Austin. Malden, MA: Wiley-Blackwell: 27–38.

LÓPEZ FRÍAS, F.J. 2014a. William J. Morgan's 'conventionalist internalism' approach. Furthering internalism? A critical hermeneutic response. *Sport, Ethics and Philosophy* 8 (2): 157–71.

———. 2014b. Mejora Humana y Dopaje en la Actual Filosofía del Deporte. Valencia. Doctoral Thesis.

LURIA, A.R. 1973. *The working brain: An introduction to neuropsychology*. London: Penguin Books.

MACINTYRE, ALASDAIR. 1984. *After virtue: A study in moral virtue*. 2nd ed. Notre Dame, Indiana: University of Notre Dame.

MANN, D.L. 2014. Do as I do, not as I say: Elite athletes and their awareness of the visually-guided actions they perform. First International Conference in Sport Psychology and Embodied Cognition.

MARTÍNKOVÁ, I. and J. PARRY. 2011. An introduction to the phenomenological study of sport. *Special Issue. Sports, Ethics and Philosophy* 5 (3): 185–201.

MARTÍNKOVÁ, I. and J. PARRY. 2013. Eichberg's phenomenology of sport: A phenomenal confusion. *Sport, Ethics and Philosophy* 7 (3): 331–41.

MCNAMEE, M.J. 2008. *Sports, virtues and vices: Morality plays*. London: Routledge.

MORGAN, W.J. 2004. Moral antirealism, internalism, and sport. *Journal of the Philosophy of Sport* 31 (2): 161–83.

———. 2012. Broad internalism, deep conventions, moral entrepreneurs, and sport. *Journal of the Philosophy of Sport* 39 (1): 65–100.

MUMFORD, S. 2011. Aesthetic and ethical values in sport and their interconnection. International Association for the Philosophy of Sport, 39th International Conference – Rochester, NY.

———. 2012. *Watching sport: Aesthetics, ethics and emotions*. London and New York: Routledge.

NAESS, A. 1998. *Life's philosophy: Reason and feeling in a deeper world*. Athens & London: University of Georgia Press.

NIETZSCHE, F. 1968. *The will to power*. New York, NY: Vintage Books.

O'SHEA, M. 2005. *The brain: A very short introduction*. Oxford: Oxford University Press.

ODA, Y. and Y. KONDO. 2014. The concept of Yuko-Datotsu in Kendo: Interpreted from the aesthetics of Zanshin. *Sport, Ethics and Philosophy* 8 (1): 3–15. doi:10.1080/1751132 1.2013.873072.

ORTEGA Y GASSET, J. 2004. El Quijote en la Escuela. *Obras Completas* II: 401–30.

―――. 2006. Corazón y Cabeza, in *Teoría de Andalucía y Otros Ensayos. Obras Completas* [Heart and head. In theory of Andalusia and other essays. Complete works]. VI. Madrid: Taurus: 208–11.

OZ, M. 2015. Dave Bergman, master of the hidden-ball trick, dead at 61. *Big League Stew*. Available at http://sports.yahoo.com/blogs/mlb-big-league-stew/dave-bergman–master-of-the-hidden-ball-trick–dead-at-61-212803914.html (accessed 2 February).

POLANYI, M. 2002 [1958]. *Personal knowledge: Towards a post-critical philosophy*. London: Routledge.

REID, H. 2010. Athletics and philosophy in ancient Greece and Rome. Contests and virtue. *Sport, Ethics and Philosophy* 4 (2): 109–34.

―――. 2012a. *Introduction to the philosophy of sport*. New York, NY: Rowman & Littlefield.

―――. 2012b. Athletic beauty in classical Greece: A philosophical view. *Journal of the Philosophy of Sport* 39 (2): 281–97.

―――. Forthcoming. Kalokagathia: Understanding olympic ethics in terms of beautiful goodness. International Olympic Academy: Proceedings of the 2014 International Session for Directors of NOAs.

RIZZOLATTI, G. and C. SINIGAGLIA. 2008. *Mirrors in the brain: How our minds share actions and emotions*. Oxford: Oxford University Press.

ROGERS, S. 2015 The wildest waterfall drop You've ever seen. Available at http://www.red bull.com/en/adventure/stories/1331696054636/the-scariest-waterfall-drop-you-ve-ever-seen (accessed 14 February).

RUSSELL, J.S. 1999. Are rules all an umpire has to work with? *Journal of the Philosophy of Sport* 26: 27–49.

―――. 2004. Moral realism in sport. *Journal of the Philosophy of Sport* 31 (2): 142–60.

―――. 2005. The value of dangerous sport. *Journal of the Philosophy of Sport* 32 (1): 1–19.

―――. 2007a. Broad internalism and the moral foundations of sport. In *Ethics in Sport*, 2nd ed., edited by W.J. Morgan. Champaign, IL: Human Kinetics: 51–66.

―――. 2007b. Children and dangerous sport and recreation. *Journal of the Philosophy of Sport* 34: 176–93.

SCHEFFLER, I. 1965. *Conditions of knowledge: An introduction to epistemology and education*. Chicago, IL: Scott Foresman and Company.

SHEETS-JOHNSTONE, M. 1990. *The roots of thinking*. Philadelphia, PA: Temple Univerisity Press.

―――. 2009. *The corporeal turn: An interdisciplinary reader*. Exeter: Imprint Academic.

―――. 2011. *The primacy of movement*, 2nd ed. Amsterdam: John Benjamins Publishing Co.

SHUSTERMAN, R. 2008. *Body consciousness: A philosophy of mindfulness and somaesthetics*. Cambridge: Cambridge University Press.

―――. 2012. *Thinking through the body: Essays in somaesthetics*. Cambridge: Cambridge University Press.

SIMON, R. 1999. Internalism and the internal values in sport. *Journal of the Philosophy of Sport* 27 (1): 1–16.

SPINOZA, B. and A. BOYLE. 1948. *Ethics [of] Spinoza*. London: J.M. Dent and Sons.

STEEL, M. 1977. What we know when we know a game. *Journal of the Philosophy of Sport* 4 (1): 96–103.

SUITS, B. 1990. *The grasshopper: Games, life and utopia*. Ontario: Broadview Press.

TAKUAN, S. 1986. *The unfettered mind*. (Translated by) W.S. Wilson. Tokyo: Kodansha.

THE ONLINE LIDDELL-SCOTT-JONES GREEK-ENGLISH LEXICON. 2009. Available at http://www.tlg.uci.edu (accessed 27 December 2014).

THELEN, E. and L. SMITH. 1994. *A dynamic systems approach to the development of cognition and action*. Cambridge, MA: MIT Press.

THOMEN, C. 2010. Sublime kinetic melody: Kelly slater and the extreme spectator. *Sport, Ethics and Philosophy* 4 (3): 319–31.

THOMPSON, E. 2007. *Mind in life: Biology, phenomenology, and the sciences of the mind*. Cambridge, MA: Harvard University Press.

THOMSON, G. 2012. *From Bacon to Kant: An introduction to modern philosophy*. Long Grove, IL: Waveland Press.

THOMSON, G. and P. TURETZKY. 1996. A simple guide to contemporary philosophy of mind. In *The experience of philosophy*, edited by D. Kolak and R. Martin. Oxford: Oxford University Press: 444–58.

TOKITSU, K. 2004. *Miyamoto Musashi: His life and writings*. Boston, MA: Shambhala.

TORRES, C. 2012. Furthering interpretivism's integrity: Bringing together ethics and aesthetics. *Journal of the Philosophy of Sport* 39 (2): 299–319.

VARELA, F. 1999. *Ethical know-how: Action, wisdom, and cognition*. Stanford, CA: Stanford University Press.

WADE, A. 2012. *Amazing surfing stories*. West Sussex: Wiley Nautical.

WERTZ, S.K. 1991. *Talking a good game: Inquiries into the principles of sport*. Dallas, TX: Southern Methodist University Press.

WULF, G. and R. LEWTHWAITE. 2010. Effortless motor learning? An external focus of attention enhances movement effectiveness and efficiency. In *Effortless attention: A new perspective in the cognitive science of attention and action*, edited by B. Bruya. Cambridge, MA: MIT University Press: 75–102.

ZHUANGZI and B. WATSON. 1968. *The complete works of Chuang Tzu*. New York, NY: Columbia University Press.

8—FRACTURED ACTION—CHOKING IN SPORT AND ITS LESSONS FOR EXCELLENCE

Jesús Ilundáin-Agurruza

A minute ago he'd felt fine, or thought he felt fine, but now the possibility of failure had entered his mind, and the difference between possible failure and inevitable failure felt razor slight.Chad Harbach, The Art of Fielding[1]

Everyone knows that masterpieces, ironically enough, sometimes arise from the midst of such defeat, from the death of the spirit. Mishima Yukio, Sun & Steel[2]

Accounting for the abilities of skillful performers presents a formidable challenge. Yet those who *already* possess the requisite skills but *fail* to perform pose an even bigger conundrum. John McEnroe had a stellar 1984 season, entering the French Open undefeated. Playing Ivan Lendl, he dominated the first two sets. Then, tied 1–1 McEnroe became furious at a cameraman and went on to lose in five sets (Morrison 2012). At the 2011 US Masters Rory McIlroy, leading with ease, hit a triple bogey and had a staggering 43-shot back nine, only good enough to finish tied for 15th Place (Viner 2011). Underwhelming performances or, rather, overwhelming underperformances, are ubiquitous in many practices, such as the arts, public speaking, academics (test taking), and even sexual activity, but their nature is uncertain. 'Choking' in sport is, however, the paradigm. Insight into this quandary will result in a better understanding of skilled action generally and in sport and other performing activities specifically. In a deep way, expertise and choking are two sides of the skillful performance coin. After all, it is not whether experts, even paragons of excellence, will fail or not; sooner or later all will. We are human all too human. What matters is how experts handle pressure and failure. Here, we explore the quick sands of failed expertise to gain understanding of such an enigmatic phenomenon. This sets up the argument that failure can be a key element to success and even beneficial for self-cultivation.

This essay begins with brief overviews of the concept of choking and empirical work on it. It then conducts an extensive examination from a holistic and ecological standpoint. An abridged phenomenological model of the experience of choking developed elsewhere (Ilundaín-Agurruza 2015) leads to adiscussion of two rarely discussed aspects of choking: 'slumps' or prolonged patterns of failure, and team chokes. Finally, it draws some lessons and sketches a remedy for fractured action that leads to the next essay on the Japanese practices of self-cultivation. Vignettes from Chad Harbach's maiden novel *The Art of Fielding: A Novel* are interspersed throughout,

HOLISM AND THE CULTIVATION OF EXCELLENCE IN SPORTS AND PERFORMANCE

as they deftly capture the troubling and blundering dynamics of choking.[3] The first one gets the ball rolling.

1. Choking in Sports: The Basics

In *The Art of Fielding*, we meet college-bound Henry Skrimshander, a peerless baseball shortstop. The shortstop is the most dynamic position in the field because, standing between first and second base, he is in the path of many, and some of the trickiest, hits. Skrim or Skrimmer, as nicknamed by his teammates, on account of inspiring and inspired playing and exemplary coaching by an older classmate turns around his college's (Westish Harpooners) longstanding dismal record. As part of his development, Henry has read and mastered a book, eponymous with the novel, written by (fictional) legendary shortstop Aparicio Rodriguez. Aparicio's *Art of Fielding* is an eclectic manual whose numbered Zen-like epigrammatic reflections mix pragmatic advice and cryptic pronouncements. To wit, we read 'The true fielder lets the path of the ball become his own path, thereby comprehending the ball and dissipating the self …' (2011, 16). Echoing a famous Chan poem[4] by Qing-yuan Wei-shin, it asserts: 'Rule # 3. There are three stages: Thoughtless being. Thought. Return to Thoughtless being. Do not confuse the first and third stages. Thoughtless being is attained by everyone, the return to thoughtless being by a very few' (Ibid.).[5] These are balanced by hands-on explications, '147. Throw with the legs' (Ibid.). Henry embodies the book's title and essence, epitomizing expert skill:

> Henry turned his back to the infield and took off, unable to see the ball but guessing its landing point based on how it had come off the bat. Nobody else was going to get there […] He stretched out his glove as he bellyflopped on the grass, lifted his eyes just in time to see the ball drop in. Even the opposing fans cheered. Putting Henry at shortstop—it was like taking a painting that had been shoved in a closet and hanging it in the ideal spot. You instantly forgot what the room had looked like before. (2011, 46)

This is the kind of athlete and elite performer who simply does not fail: always quintessentially poised, as Harbach depicts him. Not a flicker of doubt. Just as Henry's hand and his well-worn glove are perfectly molded to each other, there is a harmonious match between Henry and the challenges he faces on the diamond: without undue strain or distracting thoughts he just acts, meeting the needs of the moment in ways unrivaled by others. Explaining how someone as gifted and confident can come apart begins now.

At its simplest, a choke in sports happens when the athlete severely underperforms in relation to the requisite skills she has *already* mastered. Choking is best described and understood within the holistic model as developed to this point by previous essays. Accordingly, it is not *just* a matter of particular neural circuits or motor skills gone awry. Rather, it is a complex phenomenon with broad ecological ramifications that extend beyond the 'brains' of troubled performers. Choking dynamics vary depending on the type of activity, the performers' skill level, their level of fatigue, and other personal and environmental variables. Choking occurs across a wide range of expertise levels, from beginners with basic training to confident and competent performers.

Beginners who have mastered a few rudimentary skills may fail to enact these when trying to display them in public, for example. Choking is most clearly revealed at the expert level because of the wide differential between successful and failed performances. The disparity between high skill level set and subpar performance is much bigger in their case. Theoretically, it is also hardest to explain because *mastery* of applicable skills should result in effective performance *ordinarily*. In other words, experts have the skills and should be less likely to fail so catastrophically given that part of their skill set should be the ability to cope with difficult situations. The importance of context and the environment shows that there is more to successful or failed performance than skill and definitely more than neural misfirings.

Wertz (1986) conducted the first in-depth analysis of choking in the philosophical literature. Engaging Davidson's causal theory of intention, he considered whether choking is an intentional action or a bodily movement, and if so, whether it would be controllable. Wertz diagnoses choking as both bodily movement and intentional action on account of its complexity, concluding that it is best to ask '*when* is choking an action?' (Wertz 1986, 104). He discusses two commonly attributed conditions for action that are often associated with choking. One, being conscious, which for him is certainly met as a criterion since, if anything, when choking 'there is too much consciousness on the part of the victim' (Ibid., 98). But, 'from an Asian or Zen perspective, it may be too restrictive' depending on 'what is meant by "conscious"' (Ibid., 99). And two, having moderate control of the action at the time (Ibid., 98). Wertz finds this more problematic because in determining what is meant by 'moderate control' sometimes there is no such control but 'there are some choking cases that are controlled' (Ibid., 99). He refines both in the context of martial arts and its view of *mushin* (no mind) action and consciousness. Through this fruitful line of inquiry, he concludes that, 'choking occurs when these two components [conscious and unconscious] are out of synch' (Ibid. 99).

Ultimately, for Wertz choking is an interpretational construct: it is a representation of an action whereby we fail to carry out the intended action, and instead, we perform a (poor) representation of it (1986, 103). This is congenial to the interpretive stance endorsed for our perceptions and their meaning (in themselves, and as they connect to biographically more extended narratives). Considering the concerns raised regarding representation in essay 6 and the alternative enactive model, however, this requires some careful analysis. He appeals to a semantic analysis with an identity rule where 'the action *choking* is semantics-impregnated in that the accompanying movements or events involved a judgment or an interpretation to make the identifiable as such' (Ibid.). And he characterizes the interpretational constructs of rules, traditions, practices, etc. as the context for choking actions. Further, he details several possible descriptions (all extensional) of a golf putt and determines that, 'Choking would be one act description of a given episode' (Ibid., 102). Simply put, representations and the actions they represent are semantically encoded for him. If this is applicable to any sporting action, this is problematic for all the reasons adduced in essay 6. This notwithstanding, we could actually modify his analysis to account for choking while exonerating it from otherwise troublesome representational commitments.

We could argue that, whereas skillful fluency is radically enactive and without representations, the fractured action of choking is representational. As Wertz rightly describes movement, based on Margaret Steel's ideas (1977), sporting actions are flowing wholes. But, choking disrupts this flow. One possible reason being that we attempt to 'represent' the action, thereby fragmenting it into body parts and movements. The latter are in place in a training context where the point is to do that, but not in the context of full-blown performance, as in competition. Then, this can lead to self-monitoring, or distraction, emotional disruption and more, all identified as causal factors by various theories (see below). We still could maintain his representational account as part of a scaffolded framework, however. At the level of interpreted perceptions, how athletes and others articulate the experience of choking, we have representations and interpretational constructs as rules, traditions, values, frames o reference, etc. But these semantic articulations arise from the frontlines of performance, where the sweat and pain are literally produced through muscular work. That is, contentful interpretations are built on contentless, enactive movements. This matter aside, Wertz's fine analytic disquisition opens the door for a pluralist and ecological conception of choking as the one developed presently and elsewhere (Ilundáin-Agurruza forthcoming-a). Such an ecological account should discuss empirical evidence and hypotheses that the mind sciences (cognitive science, sports psychology) bring to the table.

2. Empirical Theories of Choking

Two kinds of empirical views in cognitive science and sport psychology are paramount nowadays to clarify the underlying mechanisms in choking: the most prominent are self-focus or self-monitoring theories (SFTs), and the alternative are distraction ones (DTs). SFTs and DTs basically posit that choking ensues from paying too much attention (SFTs) or not enough (DTs) to the task at hand, oneself, or both. They can be contrasted (Beilock and Gray 2007) and even integrated (Beilock and Carr 2001). SFTs argue that performance pressures negatively affect self-consciousness, which then affects performance, either directly (Baumeister 1984; Baumeister and Showers 1986), associated with but independent of task-monitoring (Carr 2014), or even tied to explicit skill knowledge (Masters 1992). The common element among these positions is that automated and subpersonal (non-conscious or pre-reflective) processes and mechanisms enhance performance, with the reverse pattern being detrimental to performance (this essay challenges this). SFTs have the virtue of showing empirically how novice and expert skillful strategies and failure dynamics differ (Beilock and Carr 2001; Beilock and Gray 2012). For their part, DTs show how various pressure conditions that affect working memory disrupt fluid movement routines (Eysenck and Calvo 1992). Their virtue lies in being ecologically broader than SFTs because they incorporate non-neural aspects as pressure conditions, for example, anxiety. After all, emotional temperance plays a key role in both skillful and choked performance. For all their explanatory power, there are some shortcomings with both models.

Basically, these two theories, whether singly or jointly, are unable to address broader environmental or ecological issues that any successful theory of skill and choking needs to address: real-world conditions across diverse contexts as opposed to artificial experimental ones, or the role of pragmatic interests that motivate performers, e.g. emotional investment such as the different effect a local or international competition will have on athletes. Most empirical tests conducted have inherent limitations, and hence, the hypotheses formed upon them are suspect. These tests are very helpful to isolate specific elements that affect performance (distraction, motivation, and so on) and to ascertain differences between experts and novices in *very specific* yet somewhat *contrived* situations. In some cases, they attempt to overload cognitive resources with dual tasks, for example, as they try to mimic high-pressure situations that call upon polished skill resources that may lead to choking (or a clutch performance): players of varying abilities putt in a laboratory setting while playing for small amounts of money (10–15 USD) or while doing arithmetic calculations so that a distraction is added in order to compromise working memory or attention. As already cited above, empirical research has amply showed that novices and experts handle attention, memory, and other elements differently. But that is just the beginning of the story.

We should think twice before betting it all on the experimental evidence and hypotheses. The issue is not that data is misinterpreted or that the hypotheses are misconstrued; rather the problem lies in the design of the experiments. Protocols to conduct scientifically sound studies and laboratory limitations limit their applicability. If they were ecologically valid, that is, done in realistic settings, researchers might be surprised. It should be pointed out that neither choking nor mental training studies compared pragmatically relevant targets that might really motivate the actor. The tendency, justified by experimental control conditions, is to simplify the scenario. But this falls short of real-life conditions. These make a world of difference. Just as we grasp diverse handles differently, we are also motivated variously. The intensity, feeling, and movements of grabbing the sword or the bat would differ when merely playing around with them compared to grasping them for a duel to the death or batting for the World Series title in the last inning with all bases loaded and down by three runs. A small sum hardly compares to what really moves athletes; adding numbers as a dual task is a far cry, sometimes literally, from the distracting pressures of hazardous environments that, for example, a sailor faces in a storm when the boat's systems go down and, making things more interesting, a leak springs up or the main mast breaks. Moreover, choking studies are too narrow in another sense, as they rarely consider cases of team choking, when a group catastrophically fails collectively. Another problematic issue, for SFTs in particular, is the prominent role they give to both automaticity of cognitive processes and subpersonal or mindless coping to the exclusion of reflective and conscious control (as Wertz does as well).[6]

To draw a lesson from a related issue, consider the much-touted effect of mental training, which has sprouted a whole cottage industry. Its ameliorative effect on performance has been widely and long reported. And yet, the interpretation of the effects remains very ambiguous. For some, such as Paivio (1986), this is a matter of motivation, while for others like Finke (1979), such imagery actually benefits neural mechanisms (Jeannerod 1997, 120). It would have to be seen whether the imagery is useful as a training tool that may interfere with performance if the athlete attempts to visualize him or herself during the performance. It seems that this is the case: (a) it is in line with the analysis just suggested in response to Wertz's representations; (b) aligned with SFTs, it is also problematic because we are self-conscious when we visualize ourselves while performing that very action; and (c) it additionally concurs with the assessment of DTs because this doubling up of performing the movement and visualizing it can be distracting (this during veritable performance or competition, not training).

In essence, choking is too complex a phenomenon for current models.[7] Partially, the issues result from the mind sciences' penchant to subscribe to a cognitivist model that stresses symbolic representation and operationalization, neural correlates, and

HOLISM AND THE CULTIVATION OF EXCELLENCE IN SPORTS AND PERFORMANCE

sensorimotor processes—amply critiqued already. The next section contrasts and situates expert performance and choking in a wider holistic framework that enactively and ecologically takes into account a broader range of factors that affect performance and that should be considered to better understand failure and, ultimately, skillful performance.

3. An Ecological View of Choking and Expertise

A thickly holistic account of choking and skill cannot ignore or downplay environmental factors, which include geophysical aspects and also social, emotional, and practice-specific facets. In this regard, it is amenable to situated views of cognition and skills (see also essay 10). Situated cognition brings the environment to bear on our cognitive processes, typically engaging a close relationship between agents, actions, and perception such that learning skills reflects how they are used in real life (Collins 1988). Congruent with the philosophical dark horses' views (essays 2–5), a situated view of consciousness takes into account how a community and its practices help constitute our cognitive strategies, besides other environmental elements, that are often ignored by most cognitive accounts. Here, this means looking at how sports and performing practices experts *actually* operate in such a broad context. These various variables in turn entail a broad ecological critique that, for expository reasons is apportioned; they form part of a gestalt of performance. Sequentially, it considers five variables: consciousness-related aspects, training versus competitive contexts, sports specificity, varied environmental conditions, and performers' fitness and exertion.

3.1 Consciousness, Mindless Coping, and Expertise

Until recently a strong current in philosophy, cognitive science, or psychology viewed expert performance in concordance with Hubert Dreyfus' (Dreyfus and Dreyfus 1986) phenomenological analysis as non-thematic, unconscious, pre-reflective, and taking place in the dark recesses of the body regarding its fine-grained kinematic elements. Because this subsection argues against the prevalent notion that success is predicated on the subpersonal and that choking results from reflective processes, it goes in depth into this. Dreyfus, who should be applauded for spearheading a phenomenological alternative discourse to prevailing computational accounts in the 1960s an onward, in addition to also rejecting representation, remains a point of reference. He also brought attention to the pragmatics of everyday life through Dewey and, predominantly, Heidegger. His views capture much that is correct regarding expertise. Detailing five levels, performers progressively rise through the ranks of novice, advanced beginner, competent, proficient, and expert (Ibid., 16–51). (The actual number is less important than the progression.)

Among these, novices attempt to follow rules, a method gradually phased out in lieu of automatization and mindless coping. When first pursuing a practice within a community, initially performers learn skills by explicitly relying on rules and piece-meal focused attention on specific movement and body parts.[8] If they become experts, as Dreyfus outlines it, they operate pre-reflectively when successfully coping with difficult circumstances. For him, experts drive their cars or pedal their bikes to a destination with minimal input from awareness and with little recourse to attentional resources. Because Dreyfus wants to argue against the prevalent computationalism and establish

HOLISM AND THE CULTIVATION OF EXCELLENCE IN SPORTS AND PERFORMANCE

unconscious absorbed coping for human beings in everyday life, he needs to 'democra-tize' expertise and make it a hoi polloi phenomenon.[9] In his model, *average* individuals become 'experts' as a matter of course: given enough time and sufficient but ordinary talent, they are bestowed the title. Notwithstanding the suitability of the analysis for highly skilled action, we should discuss several problems when comparing Dreyfus' mindless experts and their skill level with the skillful fluency of performative paragons.

First, while Dreyfus' analysis marks a certain level of expert competence, the standard he sets should not be categorized as truly exceptional. Both cohorts, Dreyfusian experts and exceptional performers, such as elite sportspersons, have much in common. They overlap in terms of skills cultivated and chronological and sequential learning path, but there are critical differences. Not the least is the amount of time and effort required, coupled to other factors, e.g. talent. This results in *extraordinary* skills. If Dreyfusian expertise takes a few years to develop, elite-level performance often takes a minimum of three or four hours a day for ten years for many performers (Anders Ericsson 2003).[10] (*Performative* virtuous excellence is spread over a lifetime—the conceptual contours and commitments of this virtuosity are specified in essay 9.) The Dreyfusian model fails to properly, (a) denote the level of excellence commensurate with the exceptional level it purportedly designates, because (b) it does not describe the phenomenology and functional operation of expertise. In short, it misrepresents or misconceives how superb performance operates and feels like to performers. That is, it does not properly discriminate the qualitative uniqueness of outstanding expert action. Objectively, Dreyfusian expertise embodies a low standard of performance that can be mediocre in comparison with elite performers' capabilities. It is related to subjects' internal states but is not connected to the outcome or quality of the performance (Breivik 2013, 90). Nor is it only a matter of results either. This segues into the second problem.

Even if we limit ourselves to the so called 'internal' states, the very fact that Dreyfusian 'experts' carry out the task on automatic pilot belies this. True, in everyday life such expertise does marvelously well: being off-line permits us to use more effi-ciently our limited attentional resources. Nevertheless, there is no continuous and com-pletely subpersonal or unconscious coping. If this were so then our reaction to unexpected stimuli, such as a deer or child running across our path as we drive 'mind-lessly,' would not be possible. Dreyfus can accommodate this: mindless coping need not be all pervasive; if the braking occurs it is because the driver is not paying attention to the foot shifting and stepping on the right pedal, in the first place. We need to dis-tinguish between automatization and mindless coping which, though related, are inde-pendent mechanisms. What Dreyfus needs to emphasize then is not the mindlessness, which is the daydreaming or black box idea of coping, but rather the automatization. We automatize certain tasks involved in the mechanics of the activity, shifting, steering, and so on, under normal conditions, those that we learned the through rules if you will (and also imitation, trial and error, imagination, and more). This automatization is what makes the mindlessness possible in the first place. Many, from the advanced beginner to the expert level at times often simply shoot some hoops, swim some laps, run a cou-ple of miles, go for a spin, or lift some weights; they are disconnected, relaxed, having fun. *If* we so choose we can use our automatization-freed resources thus. But this automatization is not sufficient to explain the full spectrum of expertise and mastery.

Third, Cappuccio (forthcoming) pointedly asks whether the cognitive processing of expert motor skills is entirely pre-reflective in nature, or rather compatible with

HOLISM AND THE CULTIVATION OF EXCELLENCE IN SPORTS AND PERFORMANCE

reflective self-awareness and attentive monitoring of one's own actions. Along with Breivik (2007, 2013), here, we develop the view that elite sportspersons and performers are not embodied black boxes that *must* rely on such unconscious processes to cope skillfully.[11] Indeed, they are able to keep much in focus; only not what most people would in similar circumstances because they lack the requisite performative skills. These include enhanced discrimination and integrated emotional abilities. Exceptional performers act spontaneously, actively and creatively in contrast to passive and mechanically automatized behavior. Of course, we all move and act spontaneously sometimes, but while this is unplanned for most, masters can act spontaneously 'purposefully' and reliably (see the analysis of *mushin* in essay 9).

The emphasis must be not so much on the fact that there are automatized processes, but rather that many of these *can* be accessed when needed; not all are completely subpersonal all the time. The orthodox view is that we become aware of these only when something goes wrong, following Heidegger and his famous example of the broken hammer. Again, this is applicable to common practice in sports and performative pursuits. It is true that the more common case is that we pay attention when malfunction occurs. Yet, both competent and superb performers do, in fact, access different subpersonal dynamics routinely as part of practice (see subsection 3.2 below) and during full-fledged performance or during competition. They *willfully* scan and 'lift' different kinesthetic and proprioceptive dynamics as well as other stimuli from the stream of sensations (that *may* become interpreted perceptions): they may pay attention to the burning sensation in their thighs or arms, or the flow of terrain or medium they are immersed in, exploring it richly, like the bouquet of a good wine. Where extraordinary performers excel in comparison with Dreyfusian experts and competent performers is in their ability to switch among attentional foci.

World-class exceptional performers or those who train for competition to be the best among their applicable bracket (this would include national caliber teenagers or even seniors) are quite different from even Dreyfus' experts. Breivik observes how much is left to automatic processes, with the athlete toggling back and forth between focus and automation (Breivik 2007, 130). Comparative work on flow and *mushin* (Krein and Ilundáin-Agurruza 2014) corroborates this: expert martial artists in a state of *mushin* as well as athletes or performers in flow remain highly focused *but* attentionally flexible; they are able to switch or move their attention fluidly as the situation requires. Masters rely on both unconscious processes that reduce the cognitive loads *and* focused high-level attentive monitoring of the situation at a *reflective* level. What needs to be explained is how such a switch takes place. As we have seen in essays 2 and 7, the layering of the Jamesian fringe (itself another attentional mode) acts as the hinge through which the shifting takes place. Along with emotive control, this enables fluid and efficient process phasing when integrated with the other elements thick holism engages (Zhuangzian and enactive spontaneity, attunement to skills and their dynamics, deliberation, and reflection within a broad ecological context). Because top performers need not explicitly pay attention to the immediate and most salient interface, for instance, the skis' edge placement, they can scan a wider range of conditions than less skilled performers, such as the snow conditions and terrain well ahead during a 60 mph (100 km/h) downhill descent.

As mentioned the kinesthetic and proprioceptive abilities of masters (both in terms of discernment and performance) allow them to handle much more difficult situations. Situations that require extraordinary focus, not mindlessness. World Rally Champion Carlos Sainz might drive to the store thinking about which kind of beer to buy, but when racing through off-road mountain passes, he was definitely focused and paying attention to road conditions, speed, shifting, and his co-pilots' instructions, quickly shifting among these stimuli. Breivik makes this clear with ultramarathoner Bernd Heinrich, whom he quotes as saying,

> Even the tiniest inefficiencies of movement can make a huge difference over a long distance. I often noticed that muscle tenseness could be relaxed by conscious effort. I then focused attention on my calves, thighs, arms, trying to relax them even during training runs, so that the most essential running muscles would be exercised. For a mile or so I would monitor and hence try to control the kick of my arm swings, to make sure no energy was wasted in side-to-side motion. (2007, 129)

Third, the sort of competitive environments and situations in which elite athletes[12] and high performers engage are not of the ordinary kind. They are *limit* situations. Then, they must engage their whole accumulated expertise—bodymind dynamics, performative, discriminatory, and tactical skills. This is conceptually distinct but forms a unified gestalt experience. Limit situations can be specific moments, such as a golfer's or an archer's crucial last shot with victory of loss on the line, or the more protracted intensities of offshore sailing, such as the Vendée Globe race that has solo sailors race to be first to circumnavigate the earth without any stops and unaided. Since their races can last three months or more, there is an overarching intent of purpose, but clearly no racer stays focused throughout it all. Rather, there are moments and conditions that require much focus, and others where none in particular is needed. When a skillful cyclist like Italian Paolo Savoldelli, nicknamed *Il Falco* (the hawk) on account of his breakneck descents, hurtles down a mountain pass at 65 mph (110 km/h), he is anything like a Dreyfusian expert. He monitors continually and intensely the road conditions, the way his bike frame, handlebars, pedals, saddle, and tires transmit the 'road feel,' and his own body(mind) dynamics. A more extreme case is that of wingsuit flying, when sportspersons fly through canyons, over valleys, and next to mountain faces as they direct their fall at speeds over 100 mph (160 km/h).[13] Dreyfusian experts have not steeled themselves to the limit situations that those pushing the envelope of performance have.

Jørgen Eriksen conducts the best defense of Dreyfus in the sport literature by correctly emphasizing the merit of his non-representational stance (2010). Dreyfus (2002) convincingly argues, relying on Merleau-Ponty's phenomenology of skillful coping, for actions without representing goals. This coheres with the non-representationalism of *Skillful Striving*. But, his model cannot account for a particular kind of expertise: risk sports. As Eriksen contends, the Dreyfusian analysis takes a monolithic view that is not applicable to all sports (Ibid., 74–75). Eriksen (2010) highlights the role of deliberation in the Dreyfusian model to accommodate some of Breivik's (2007) criticisms. For indeed, there is room for deliberation and planning, something that Breivik does incorporate in his later work (2013) (*Skillful Striving* highlights this below and in the next two essays). Nonetheless, as Eriksen (2010) details risk sports pose a special problem for Dreyfus because these prevent deliberation yet require attention and not mindlessness, which is in line with Breivik's (2013) view that elite sportspeople do not cope mindlessly even in fast paced events.

HOLISM AND THE CULTIVATION OF EXCELLENCE IN SPORTS AND PERFORMANCE

The relevance of this for choking and unflappable expertise is that contrary to what is commonly assumed in the empirical and philosophical literature, focus, attention, reflective consciousness, etc. are not only not necessarily connected with poor results or even choking but rather play a vital role in superb performance. Put differently, choking is not a matter of being distracted or bringing reflective consciousness into the performance and thereby paying too much or too little attention to self, task, or explicit skill knowledge. On the contrary, the *right* kind of attention enhances performance. It is a matter of how this attentional focus is managed. If the tripartite layering is fluid and acts with non-representational spontaneity, it is positive for performance. What fractures performance and leads to choking is combination of factors to be briefly discussed in section 4. There are further angles to consider that affect our abilities and require specific adaptations.

3.2 Training and Competitive Contexts

The next variable to consider pertains to training and competitive contexts. Each offers related but unique insights into how sportspeople and performers actually operate, and how choking and skillful performance relate to them. Most laboratory tests do not replicate or take these factors into account. Because of this, their ecological validity is compromised. But taking a broader perspective is instructive. Training and competition not only improve or test our skills, but they also act as bulwarks against choking.

Training is paid scant attention, but it is what athletes and performers do most of the time. Training for elite sportspeople means carrying out drills and doing repetitive actions that require explicit, reflective awareness, discrete engagement of kinetic body-mind dynamics (subtended by the gestalt flowing feeling), and kinesthetic and proprioceptive feedback, besides tactical and strategic elements, and evaluative self-assessments. Depending on the sport, this may also include extensive time strategizing, observing the actual venue when pertinent and possible, and visualizing and reflecting on matters that escape most of us. Surfers, mountaineers, kayakers, stage racers, and countless other sportspeople spread among hundreds of sports, and other performers, spend inordinate time and energy planning the minutest details. This is often ignored given the focus by media and spectators on the feat and the moment of competition. It leads to a misunderstanding of performative endeavors and their phenomenology. This also affects how we explain expert performance and failure. For instance, received 'wisdom,' abetted by an unimaginative media that perpetuates empty clichés, sees risk sport practitioners as simply adrenaline junkies.

Marsh (2012) interviewed Gerard Butler after he had filmed *Chasing Mavericks*. The film is about surfing icon Jay Moriarty, who died while doing underwater static breath holding as part of his training to surf Jaws, and his mentor Frosty Hesson. The interview is dense with empty talk about adrenaline rushes that, far from shedding light on the qualitative experience of a surfer's ride, hides the intensity, beauty, and terror of the experiences Butler enjoyed and suffered. Many in the literature (Ilundáin-Agurruza 2007, forthcoming-b; Krein 2007; Russell 2005) have argued elsewhere that what athletes actually seek are veritable challenges to match or help advance their skills; the flow, the rush, and the like are but very enjoyable by-products. As professional surfer Mark Visser says, 'I really want to push myself on a whole range of different levels' (Wade 2012, 14). Preparing to ride Jaws *at night*, a famed Hawai'i surf break with 60+ feet waves, Visser

HOLISM AND THE CULTIVATION OF EXCELLENCE IN SPORTS AND PERFORMANCE

spent *three years* working with submarine lighting engineers to design the most adequate illumination, not to speak of time spent on other details to set up jetskis, helicopters, and months of intense preparation that included safety teams, special forces members, fitness coaches, and even paddling in shark infested waters for up to six hours to prepare for the unpredictable and learn to stay in control (Ibid., 14–16). With no hyperbole, we can say that he had spent his whole surfing career preparing for this. This challenge was summation of previous skills and potential consummation of his flourishing abilities. There are much easier ways to enjoy such rushes that do not take years of preparation and such devoted efforts. This preparation not only instills confidence but, if done properly, can mimic situations that can bring about choking by pushing the athlete to the very limit while other variables are kept under control, thereby doubling as training against choking.

Competition or formidable tests such as ascending K2 or surfing Jaws push performers to new levels. They also show flaws in training and preparations, if these have been inadequate, or if one is not up to the task. They are contests of truth, as Reid would conceptualize it (Reid 2010). Whether public or not, the test or contest shows us our mettle, athletically (are we up to the task?) and morally and aesthetically (can we meet it as per the rules? Is it the kind of accomplishment we can proudly lay claim to in the sense of *kalon*?). To answer positively requires discipline and the courage to take the risk of finding out we may not be who we thought we were. Moreover, competition and such tests are best understood not as ends, but as ways to further refine our skills (see essay 10). Then we really perform the ultimate practice *of* skill, as Visser does. This in turn is but one way to develop the capacity to face possibly choke-inducing situations head on with the requisite confidence. Being able to cope with situations at the limit of our skills requires inordinate dedication to *quality* training.

The Art of Fielding's aptly captures the punishing nature of Henry's workout regime during summer recess at his college,

> They met at five thirty every morning. When Henry could run up and down all the stairs in the football stadium without stopping, Schwartz bought him a weighted vest. When he could run five seven-minute miles, Schwartz made him do it on the sand [... then] with the lake water lapping at his knees. Medicine balls, blocking sleds, yoga, bicycles, ropes, tree branches, steel trash cans, plyometrics [...] After his shift [...] Schwartz set up the pitching machine and the video camera. Henry hit ball after able until he could hardly lift his arms. Then they went to the VAC to lift weights. In the evenings they played on a summer team in Appleton. (Harbach 2011, 46)

But even such Spartan regimes may not be enough to ensure peace of mind. For some, training so hard to then fail is unthinkable, and avoiding contests is one way to evade potential failure. If they do decide to go ahead, there is no room for hiding. Visser prepared for the unexpected in that harrowing night surf, when he would hear the roar of the shape-shifting mountain of water behind him but not see it. Yet, every day the week before the set date, he woke up in cold sweat at 5 a.m. (Wade 2012, 15). Deweyan habit, inscribed through conscientious practice into the core of our way-of-being, is one manner of overcoming the persistent murmurs of fear and self-doubt. Excellence is not built on one hard memorable workout. Predictable and repetitive patterns are *sine qua nons*. For Henry, 'Every day that summer had the same framework, the alarm at the

HOLISM AND THE CULTIVATION OF EXCELLENCE IN SPORTS AND PERFORMANCE

same time, meals and workouts and shifts and SuperBoost at the same times, over and over, and it was that sameness, that repetition, that gave life meaning' (Harbach 2011, 47). Deweyan habit incorporates meaning into our lives; devoted sportspeople and performers understand this bone to bone (essay 10 considers the issue of meaningfulness in the context of means and ends). This can take the shape of seemingly mind-numbing repetitive drills. But in actually they require exceptional attention. As Anders Ericsson, Krampe and Tesch-Römer state,

> A necessary precondition for practice, according to Auer (1921), is that the individual be fully attentive to his playing so that he or she will notice areas of potential improvement and avoid errors. Auer (1921) believes that practice without such concentration is even detrimental to improvement of performance. On the basis of an extended study of Olympic swimmers, Chambliss (1988, 1989) argued that the secret of attaining excellence is to always maintain close attention to every detail of performance 'each one done correctly, time and again, until excellence in every detail be-comes a firmly ingrained habit' (1989, p. 85). (1993, 371)

Swimming is a sport that, when limited to doing lap after lap, makes it a top contender for the title of 'most Sisyphean' sport. It is very easy to get into a state of Dreyfusian mindless coping and do what Phelps referred to in an interview as 'G.Y' after a particularly bad session, shorthand for 'garbage yardage' (Forde 2014). But competitive swimmers tend to be anything but mindless most of the time. Legendary swimmer Jim Montgomery says with regard to what he thinks,

> As soon as I jump in the water, I begin to *concentrate* on my stroke deficiencies. Am I carrying my head too high, dropping my right elbow midway through the pull, or not finishing through with my left arm? All these things can occur in my freestyle stroke when fatigue sets in. (Montgomery and Chambers 2009, 35, my italics)

What specifically is attended to depends on the goals and needs of the moment. Breivik highlights that elite athletes conduct substantial conscious thinking and analysis of their performance with coaches and technical staff (2013, 92). This is important because we are often poor judges of our own movements, as mentioned in essay 6. Through them, superb performers learn how to pick what will impact performance most. And, they also conduct extensive post-performance review and reflection for both competition and training (Breivik 2013, 93).[14] This process reveals weaknesses. When left unattended, they develop the wrong kind of patternings; this can lead to failure and choking. Again, the right kind of attention builds fluency. Even in the thick of competition athletes are attentive. One competes the way one trains. Martina Moravcova, a world-class butterfly specialist, speaking of the many aspects of her stroke she focuses on *while* she races the 100-meter fly says about the last 15 meters, 'I focus on entering my arms shoulder-width apart in order to catch the water effectively, even if my shoulders and back are tightening up. In addition, I increase my tempo, thus maintaining my stroke rate into a strong finish' (Montgomery and Chambers 2009, 59). Any of the elements she mentions require reflective attention at various times that happen heterochronically, as indicated in essay 7. Performance, even skillfully fluid and fluent, partakes of synchronies and diachronics as athletes and performers must adapt to unpredictables. Contests and risky activities shine at throwing unexpected wrenches into the spokes of performance. Experts excel at dealing with such surprises. And paradoxically, learning to deal with the unexpected is largely built on the repetitive and predictable—when attentively accomplished.

Not being attentive during training and competition in this way develops the conditions that lead to detrimental habits and paying the *wrong* kind of attention. Then, a number of concatenated factors that begin quite disparately eventually coalesce into inadequate performance. They can become so dense that the performer then chokes. Improper, inattentive training and competition produces misadjusted kinematics; kinesthetic sensations fail to match expectations and are interpreted as unpleasant perceptions; instead of fluidly scanning through the different sensorial dynamics the performers become mired in particular facets, the painful 'side stich' between lungs and abdomen, the competitor pulling ahead; self-defeating thoughts take over. Small, unattended details have a way of growing hidden. Until, merciless, they burst. Much as the Little Prince says that one must destroy the bad seeds of Baobab trees 'the very instant that one recognizes it' lest they grow and choke one's planet, quality is built on the small, painstaking details readily being taken care of (Saint-Exupéry 1971, 21). The ethos to forestall choking before it begins is built on Orteguian *pundonor*—that deep commitment to doing things thoroughly and to the utmost of one's ability (essay 4). And, this needs not only a healthy dose of honesty to admit shortcomings but a heaping serving of resolve to look for them.

A world-class swimmer who set many records, Montgomery candidly admits he has deficiencies. This kind of focus does not allow for boredom or thoughts of absurdity; rather it requires full commitment to the activity in the moment and to excellence in and over one's life. Very hard sets of sprints or putting oneself in perilous situations are, respectively, so painful or terrifying that ennui is all but impossible. Montgomery's expertise is unquestionable, but his attitude is broadly ameliorative: he pays exquisite attention; to do so, he is able to shift through automatized skills as needed so that when he does drills he can focus *mindfully* on specific needs (in a way he is able to act as both expert and novice, whereas novices are stuck with one format); he considers a wide range of possible deficiencies, he does not assume he has but a few and very small flaws to polish (actually, the smaller the flaw the harder to fix); this attitude also keeps him fresh to learn, and another perk, it keeps tedium away. There are no short-cuts, however. As the Little Prince states regarding the Baobabs, 'It is a question of discipline' (1971, 23). Of course, this is no guarantee against failure, but part of this discipline means handling it properly and squarely so that it does not grow into a choking Baobab too big to uproot.

While expert skills are functionally highly refined, procedurally embedded, and very efficient in comparison with those of novices, the kind of attentional resources and drills used to improve are conducted at the explicit and reflective level. This entails the close monitoring of specific movements, body parts, and tactics at the reflective level, while taking advantage of other aspects of the flowing movement being automatized, and others at-the-ready at the fringe level. Put simply, elite-level sportspeople and performers engage in training that often is painful, requires inordinate but *attentive* repetition, discipline, and reflection. There are further angles to consider, however, which affect our abilities and require specific adaptations. And these come in a plethora of flavors.

HOLISM AND THE CULTIVATION OF EXCELLENCE IN SPORTS AND PERFORMANCE

3.3 Sports Specificity

This brings us to the next theme, the particularity of sport skills. Each sport requires unique skills as required by the constitutive rules that specify how to obtain the goals of the activity (Suits 1990). There are clusters of closely associated skills: rugby, American football, and Australian football are quite similar, but the rules result in subtle deviations for each sport. For example, the sorts of tackles proper to each of these games are quite different. That sports develop exclusive skills does not mean we cannot draw some general conclusions. Much as Scheffler (1965), Breivik (2013) makes an insightful distinction between closed and open skills in the sporting context. Some sports control performance through fixed sets of movements—gymnastics and archery—which improve through attentive and deliberate practice. Significantly, '[b]y the gradual automatization of a repertoire of sport-specific basic movements, one can concentrate on higher level features such as rhythm, timing, strategy and so forth' (Breivik 2013, 92). Open skill sports—football and surfing—require adjusting to competitors or environmental changes, but still allow for apportioned training of specific skills, such that 'Conscious attending is therefore gradually replaced for these sections by a more automatic execution of skills' (Ibid.). Thus, even if sports' skills differ in this respect, functionally they end up with automatization of processes by different means. (We should be mindful that spontaneity, however, is the crucial element in masterful performance.)

Because sports involve training specific physical skills that result in automatization, and spontaneity in the best cases, the question now becomes, whether specificity makes a difference in terms of choking when we consider physiological, environmental, and social factors.[15] To focus here on the role of attention primarily from a physiological stance, consider the following five sports: sharpshooting, biathlon, apnea, boxing, and football. Arguably, sustained attention—that is, 'attention that is voluntarily concentrated on a single factor of stimuli' (Bruya 2010, 17)—is essential to all five. Yet, it is differently realized. For both sharpshooting and biathlon, visuomotor processes are central. Putative solutions to choking issues would arguably and correspondingly center on quiet eye gaze (Vickers and Williams 2007). Sharpshooting hinges on *maintaining* a calm state where breathing, heart rate, and other physiological responses are kept in check to best train the rifle or pistol on the target. But for biathlon, one of the most aerobically demanding sports, the goal is to *induce* such calmness to shoot at targets while cross-country skiing a challenging course. Constant weight apnea with or without fins requires a curious combination of both strenuous effort and calmness: in the initial dive phase until divers reach 60 feet (20 meters) in depth they work hard to descend, then negative buoyancy takes over and they drop at a sustained rate of three feet (one meter) per second when they must remain as passive and calm as possible to save oxygen, upon turning around the hardest effort in the whole dive is required to return to the surface. Throughout, the emphasis is on staying focused monitoring body position to maximize being streamlined and obtaining maximum glide per stroke with the least energetic expenditure. Monitoring proprioceptive kinesthetic and vestibular dynamics correlated to diaphragmatic nociceptive sensations, to gage oxygen depletion and CO_2 accumulation, is crucial: the *kind* of pain felt is the key. Choking during the event means passing out from lack of oxygen and possibly drowning (choking underwater by any other name!). In boxing, besides speed of reflexes, power, and stamina, the ability to withstand pain and maintain that focus is peremptory when fighters' cognitive abilities are being compromised by painful hits to the head and other body parts. Moreover, many fighters shun relaxed states for excitatory ones to incorporate intimidation, confidence, and a hormonal rush to forestall pain. In football, a variety of stimuli fight for players' attentional resources: position of teammates and opponents (in relation to themselves) keeping in mind pitch boundaries, ball position, level of exertion, specific role in the team, and intricate tactics. Visuomotor processes are relevant, but in so far as they play a role in the larger context of tactical and geometric elements where they contend with opponents and locations for players, ball, and field lines. The relations with other players make it a very different kind of competition from that of biathlon, where players contest in parallel but do not engage one another directly, or apnea, which is a solo event, or the mutual antagonism of boxing. This brings complex interpersonal dynamics where the element of surprise, missing from some other sports mentioned, adds another dimension. A corollary of this is that each sport affords unique phenomenological experiences, as we saw in essay 7, even if there are common invariant underlying dynamics. That is, the variety of sports and their unique qualitative dynamics means that failure (or its flipside) can manifest very differently. Accordingly, our theory should extend to cover, meteorological, topological, and other environmental conditions.

3.4 Varied Environmental Conditions

Prima facie, such differences suggest that, given that the conditions to excel and the skills drawn upon are so different, choking will differ as to its genesis, manifestation, and phenomenological structure. Environmental elements also bolster this line of argumentation. These include external factors such as meteorology, topography, sport venue, or social aspects as sources of adaptive requirements and pressure. In many outdoor sports such as mountaineering, sailing, and stage-race cycling, athletes must deal with changing and complicated meteorological and topographic factors whether competing or training. In some water sports, the fluid nature of water adds yet another complicating dimension, e.g. kayaking a 30-foot waterfall that comes after a complicated chute, or big wave surfing a 45-foot (15 meter) wave that shifts shape depending on wind, rock formations, and currents. Other sports take place in controlled situations and facilities but with audiences up and close, as in combat sports, gymnastics or platform diving. Being on-stage in front of big crowds can either motivate or affect perniciously the athletes' performance. This is especially the case when performers compete at events or locales of personal significance or amenable to exert inordinate strain, for example, mythical and intimidating venues such as Maracaná or Wimbledon, or events like the Olympics. Nevertheless, the key lies in the event or locale being ascribed importance by the agent in question. Sometimes, a training session with *very* difficult goals might result in a choking incident where the athlete performs woefully below par. Even theatricality, as an expressive quality through which contestants create the game or compete can play a crucial role that goes beyond the mere functional value of behavior (Aggerholm 2013). Others' behaviors can positively or negatively affect our performance (including one's own teammates, as we see in section 3 with team choking). Hence, social elements are also pertinent. Relationships with what here are called primary social factors, those with whom the athlete directly interacts (teammates, competitors, and

HOLISM AND THE CULTIVATION OF EXCELLENCE IN SPORTS AND PERFORMANCE

coaches) and contrasted with secondary social factors (public and media), offer yet more affordances and constraints for success or failure.[16] Much as with performers in the arts, these conditions can increase possibilities for choking. As can other conditions tied to one's readiness.

3.5 Performer's Fitness and Exertion

Montgomery also mentions another often-ignored variable in studies that is a given in competition and training: fatigue. Weariness brings out our weaknesses. These can be moral as well as technical: we are more likely to cheat and become sloppy. Refined and exceptional skill in sport not only necessitates arduous and repetitive practice within the context of a recognizable athletic community, but is also highly contingent on the sportsperson's fitness level and exertion or effort. While the old adage that we never forget how to ride a bicycle largely holds regarding the mechanics of some learned skills, their *quality* fluctuates with the highs and lows of athletic form; form is crucial to the finesse and fluidity requisite to excel—even for the most formidable of performers. There is a big difference between an athlete being in shape and out of it— the epithet suitably indicates the way practice sculpts athletes' bodies.[17] In many sports, skill, fitness, and workload are cumulative, and years of practice also result in adaptations, for example, physiological ones that allow more efficient use of energy sources (one can ride or run longer using lipid sources rather than glycogen) or coordinative processes that lead to more refined handling skills (and are affected by metabolic processes in turn). In other sports like archery or fencing, being in shape takes a different form altogether, but invariably, the dexterity and expertise to place the arrows in a tight group around the bull's eye or parry and riposte an attack is also subject to analogous ebbs and flows. To better understand the *entente* between skill and choking, we need to look at effort.

Effort has two variables: objective, marked by physiological and metabolic processes, and subjective, singled out by the feeling of exertion (Bruya 2010, 5). In cases of peak performance, often but not always, a sense of effortlessness accompanies them, usually conceptualized as flow.[18] In flow states, objective effort is not aligned with subjective effort, and experienced effortlessness may even lead to improved objective performance (the next essay discusses this further). Alas, fitness is capricious. The contingency and evasiveness of being in top form play a key role in success and failure and thus are intimately connected with choking. Fatigue affects the ability to excel. Unsurprisingly, strenuousness has been shown to be relevant for choking processes (Hill 2013). And with attention compromised, given the high metabolic and *computational* drain that even as 'simple' a movement as walking places on neural processes and cognition, judgment is also compromised (Dietrich and Stoll 2010). The athlete will dive into a tailspin that leads to self-monitoring, distraction, overload, or other personally tailored process of becoming undone. Ullén et al. (2010) detail the clear physiological correlates of flow: decreased heart period, increased cardiac output, and respiratory rate and depth. In choking, these processes are reversed. We can expect increased heart rate and compromised respiratory processes such as hyperventilation that affect performance negatively. Endurance sports afford the clearest case of the fitness-skill-choking dynamics because athletic fitness directly affects skill implementation and also correlates with the perceived level of effort.

HOLISM AND THE CULTIVATION OF EXCELLENCE IN SPORTS AND PERFORMANCE

In the case of choking, there are many causal factors that intertwine to diverse degrees for different athletes. These include psychosomatic, pragmatic, and even existential elements (the latter tied to vital evaluative processes, e.g. questioning one's commitment to the activity on a larger sale). Often there is a vicious circle. For instance, we can diagnose several of these in the case of speed ice skater Dan Jansen at the 1992 Olympics in Albertville. As world record holder, he was set to win medals in the 500 and 1000 meters, yet in the wake of his sister's death, he finished fourth and 26th(!) respectively (Morrison 2012).[19] We find cause for emotional turmoil and a progressive and markedly worsening performance. That drop is significant, for it shows that it was not simply a matter of not having been able to train and focus (although this was surely impacted), and thus being out of shape. His initial fourth place in the shorter event shows that he was good enough to compete with the best, though not to dominate. Moreover, if it were truly a matter of his being unfit, this would not qualify as a case of choking.

Firstly, fitness is a matter of a continuum, it is improper to speak of an exceedingly out of shape underperforming athlete as choking. Being out of shape means the athlete's skills just are not there. Unfit athletes will not experience a flow state nor will fluidity and fluency mark their performance. It follows, therefore, that they cannot thereby experience choking because of their failure, which is attributable to, and fully explained by, their being out of shape. Secondly, this is too loose an extension of the term. It derives its sense from the appropriate case where mastery of skills and fitness are, in fact, matched. In his case, we find that Jensen was distraught to the point of distraction, and though initially able to forestall any negative thinking and processes in the first event, he came apart for the second. Choking entails the interplay between the performance's objective elements (speed, goals scored) and the subjective feelings (effort, pain), as well as self-expectations (which can be induced by others). This is tied to the athletes' actual fitness level *and* their self-perception of the same. Many athletes are perfectionists or insecure. In either case, this leads to a self-defeating overtraining or second-guessing that is instrumental for failure and the choke. In turn, processes that are better automatized are recalled, 'am I pulling through with the club?' 'Do I dip my hip enough into the turns and lean on the skis' edge?' The flowing motion is lost.

It is time to hear from Skrimmer again. On the verge of breaking Aparicio's all time record for 51 consecutive wins, Henry was about to throw the ball as he had done thousands of times …

> His arm was moving forward, there wasn't time to think, but he was thinking anyway, trying to decide whether to speed up his arm or slow it down. He *could feel himself* calibrating and recalibrating, adjusting and readjusting his arm […] As soon as the ball left his hand he knew he'd messed up. (Harbach 2011, 201, my italics)

Henry's choke begins with one bad throw whose origin Harbach wisely leaves uncounted for. He does relate it chronologically to emotionally upsetting events that eventually develop into vomit-inducing nerves. How performance deteriorates from one bad throw to a subpar performance to a choking episode and on to a slump is a complex phenomenon affected as these five variables show.

The very plurality an ecological model affords can give the impression that the choking experience will be equally variable. The next subsection presents the common elements that any and all choking experiences share.

HOLISM AND THE CULTIVATION OF EXCELLENCE IN SPORTS AND PERFORMANCE

4. Rudiments of a Phenomenological Model for Choking[20]

There are four factors that phenomenologically disclose the common structure of the choking experience: (A) disruptive proprioceptive and kinesthetic dynamics, (B) a faulty Jamesian fringe of consciousness, (C) disrupted time dynamics, and (D) emotional interferences. When an athlete or performer chokes, these factors will organize her experience. These are not strictly causal mechanisms. But, when concretely manifested some of them can play an assisting role, as when a strong emotional reaction becomes overwhelming. These factors are derived from miscellaneous but interrelated sources that include analysis of theoretical and empirical research, ethnomethodology, and personal experience.

As to the first factor, the model primarily focuses on those salient phenomeno-logical features on our experience that result from *unfolding* performative skills and their attendant dynamics. *Riding the Wind* discussed these extensively. The actual *feeling* that athletes experience depends on three elements: proprioceptive and kinesthetic dynamics pertaining to the patternings of bodily schematizing and imaging, the four cardinal structures of movement, and the notion of hyperreflection. This kinesthetic and proprioceptive dimension is intimately connected with environmental stimuli. As already discussed, expert performers efficiently and effectively switch among pertinent stimuli, and their attentional resources are superior to those of normal or pathological subjects (specific sports parcel these out differently). This permits them to adapt to rapidly changing conditions on the edge. Yet, in the case of experts, their higher sensitivity is a double-edged sword. It helps them enjoy a richer experience, and opens the possibility of better performance. But, should performers begin to lose their grip, they can become overwhelmed precisely because they are dealing with a much more complex situation. Talented jugglers drop more balls when they fail; skilled performers in limit situations have more calamitous breakdowns.

Functionally, the *right* feel of skillful movement is a whole flowing action. Choking gets in the way of such smooth process: there is fragmentation and not flow. This is reflected differently in our bodily schematizing and imaging. Remember that these are not actual mechanisms but rather help structure our experience, with the former non-consciously organizing processes that regulate posture and movement, and the latter being the sometimes conscious perceptions, beliefs, and attitudes we have about our body(mind). The two smoothly interweave under normal conditions. Choking disturbs or severs this connection. When athletes or performers choke, spontaneous action and automatized skills are arrested in development. The schematizing and imaging are dis-jointed. An informational influx overloads the schematizing so that neither its scope nor processing speed can handle. And, the imaging pushes forward segmented skills and body parts. When discussing Wertz, we adumbrated how representations could play a role in choking. Experts normally integrate skills enactively. This allows for spontaneous and successful response. Should they begin to 'represent' the movement, after some mishap or other, they will begin to fragment the process. The imaging will take over the schematizing. Then, contentful representational processes replace contentless ones on which the spontaneity of movement is predicated. In short, this reverts to a novice-like process with representations of basic skills. A choking breakdown also parallels schizophrenic hyperreflection, Gallagher's (2005) term for obsessive and pathological reflection upon oneself. This excessive reflection monitors both task execution and self.

HOLISM AND THE CULTIVATION OF EXCELLENCE IN SPORTS AND PERFORMANCE

Imagine a hammer thrower whose performance deteriorates progressively. The hammer is a very demanding discipline that requires exquisite coordination and body mechanics to spin the weighed end around one's own axis and manage to throw it at a suitable angle and in the direction desired. Its technique is also more complex than that of the shot put or discus throw, since the windup that has the thrower spinning requires a complex coordination between the heel and the toe, rocking back and forth, that needs to be synchronized with the weighted ball at the end of the steel cable. If the thrower, for whatever reason, focuses overly on the toe-heel mechanics, actively representing the different biomechanical elements, she can throw off the timing with the hammer itself; alternatively, paying attention to the spinning, or the release, can disrupt the other elements such that the hammer throw fails. With this imbalance, her flowing gestalt movement increasingly deteriorates into compartmentalization. As she becomes hyperreflective and emotionally agitated, the other aspects just discussed bring about failed performance. Sheets-Johnstone's (2009) four cardinal structures of movement (essay 7) help describe the overall quality of choking. These capture the *qualitative* dynamics of our choking movement *as* experienced: tensionally, the initial windup can be compromised by setting off on the wrong foot, literally; linearly. her gyrations will be off kilter to the weight; the amplitudinal quality also reflects a constricted and forced early or late release, and the projectional quality is released spasmodically and misaligned, ejecting the hammer diagonally into the surrounding safety net.

William James' fringe of consciousness gives insight into how the how and why of choking as felt. As explained in essay 2, James' (1918) background or fringe of consciousness provides phenomenological evidence for an intermediary layer between conscious awareness and reflective processes, and subpersonal mechanisms and pre-reflective awareness that relates to automatized skilled movements. Any of us can validate this experientially. This very essay has a certain 'form' that stays with the readers as they move forward; it is not based on exact remembrance of every sentence, but threads its way through keeping a sense of what it is about. The fringe acts as a flexible hinge and layering itself between the two layerings of consciousness and unreflectiveness. The tip-of-the-tongue phenomenon, when we strive to remember a name, shows this clearest. Choking is analogous but involving our movements, which are arrested as we struggle to bring them forth. We have a sense, kinesthetic and proprioceptive, for the right movement but cannot effect it, just as we cannot recall a name; we know we have the requisite skills the way we know that we 'know' the name or word and can judge whether any of the forthcoming ones is correct we calibrate and recalibrate the arm just as we stutter or trip over syllables. The hammer thrower can tell right away whether she is on to a good throw or not. As a functional process, the fringe is more parsimonious and allows for a *transparent* connection between the conscious and subpersonal levels that works with what there *is*. It does not need to posit an intermediary *mechanism* or structure, ideational, physiological, or computational. When choking, the sportsperson becomes unhinged. We find the hammer thrower unraveling as she feels the wrong kind of 'sensations'—as sportspeople often speak of their introspective self-assessments. Untimely disruptions further complicate this.

Edmund Husserl's analysis of time can refine our understanding of choking (and fine performance as well). Temporal disruption dynamics in schizophrenia are particularly revealing. Choking involves a desynchronization that leads to a process of hyperreflection that is connected to emotional strain. We experience time in very elastic

HOLISM AND THE CULTIVATION OF EXCELLENCE IN SPORTS AND PERFORMANCE

ways. We feel 'time' speeding and slowing down depending on variables of an affective nature, say interest, boredom, enjoyment, or pain. For Gallagher, 'perhaps anxiety or some such emotion can cause a desynchronization in the system' (2005, 189). In other words, emotion acts as an explosive's fuse. Lack of synchrony results from a decoupling between the sense of agency we have when acting, thereby feeling and judging we intentionally moved and carried out the act, and the sense of ownership of said actions, the sense that these are our own. Much as bodily schematizing and imaging, these operate united and seamlessly. But, in pathological cases, the schizophrenic retains the sense of ownership while feeling as if the actions come unbidden and are not his own. Gallagher relies on Husserl's analysis to explain how this happens. Hijacked by emotion, choking mirrors this.

We can present Husserl's views most efficiently if we adapt Gallagher and Zahavi (2008). Protentions and retentions structure our sense of time. The former are expectations with forward looking intentional content; the latter look backward and retain previous intentional content, they are memories in short. Protentions and retentions meet in a primal *impression* that acts like a nodal point. This we call the present or now. In the following example, these are hewn quite roughly for simplicity. Primal impression 1 is the hammer thrower spinning the weight once around her body. It becomes retention 1. She then has the anticipatory sense of another spin following as she now begins to turn herself, which her impression 2, while she carries the sense of retention 1. As the hammer goes once more around this brings the anticipation of another turn, protention 2, and so on. The retentional aspect stitches together our experience. Doing so, it unifies the sense of consciousness that makes our experiences *ours*. These retentions and protentions are richly imbued with kinesthetic and proprioceptive dynamics (Sheets-Johnstone 2009, 2011).

Protentions furnish the intentional sense that more will happen. But for schizophrenics, the protentional phase goes awry: the surprise is not tied to the agent any more. As Gallagher (2005) explains, without the sense of agency, and dependent on the protentional aspect, the experience of unbidden thoughts for example cannot be tied to our passive cognitive system; they appear as if from nowhere. But because the retentional aspect works, schizophrenics retain their sense of ownership. Feeling out of control, with thoughts and actions happening to them, anxiety, fear and negative emotions begin to derail the train so that accumulating this disruption leads to that

> hyperreflection that brings to the forefront prenoetic [hidden] processes that normally remain in the background' which can also 'generate a body image that exaggerates proprioceptive and kinesthetic sensations, and interferes with the normal functioning of the *normally* tacit body schema. (Gallagher 2005, 205, my emphasis)

This framework can describe both schizophrenia and the process of choking. When people choke, their expectations are thwarted such that they are unable to fluidly move through the protention–retention phases. This compromises the protentional facet. They become mired in the retentional phase, which disrupts schematizing patternings and processes. Automatized processes and skill-fragmenting representations come forth from the fringe into awareness, interfering with attentional bandwidth and negatively affecting performance. Neither hammer thrower nor Henry feel in control; they cannot release the ball or hammer as they recalibrate and second-guess themselves. Choking athletes feel helpless and unable to take over. The hyperreflective process that stays with the retentions relinquishes agency. Differently put, ownership displaces agency. With this in place, we can examine the remaining element, emotion.

Emotion completes the puzzle of the choking experience. We choke because we *care*. Arguably too much. In this case, this is the pragmatic level at which we make sense of things. Emotions are situated, sociocultural phenomena as much as psychophysiological, since we learn to understand our emotions through others.[21] Fear, one of the six basic emotions, anchors the affective tonality of choking at its simplest, most pragmatically expedient level. Under its rubric, we fit anxiety, worry, unbridled nerves, and even anger (as a reaction to the flight or fight response, and thus explaining McEnroe's tantrum-induced choke). Thomas Merton renders a famous passage in the *Zhuangzi* as a poem:

> When an archer is shooting for nothing/He has all his skill./If he shoots for a brass buckle/He is already nervous./If he shoots for a prize of gold/He goes blind/Or sees two targets—/He is out of his mind!/His skill has not changed. But the prize/Divides him. He cares/He thinks more of winning/Than of shooting—/And the need to win/Drains him of power. (1992, 158)

What we were able to do easily becomes virtually impossible when anxiety about our performance creeps in. Instead of focusing on shooting well, the archer fears missing the target and not winning the prize. The solution for Zhuangzi is to forget the self. A self-forgetting that historically became progressively more prominent in later developments at the intersection between philosophical/religious views and praxes in East Asia, especially Japan (see essays 9 and 10). Remaining with Western athletes for now, should we take choking athletes to the *palestra* and strip them, we will find fear: the fear that they will be found wanting. Other worries such as their contract being on the line still depend on their performance as a first level concern that ties more directly to fear (and related emotional states just mentioned). When anxiety affects the protentional phase, this separates normal operation and removes the very agency that begins this process. If we expand our scope ecologically, all DSTs and DTs theories will find fear's tracks ranging all over the performative landscape of choking. When athletes choke, the emotional tonality of fear is manifested not only as worrisome or anxious thoughts but, concurrently, as kinesthetic and proprioceptive dynamics: they worry and feel themselves tightening up as their muscles stiffen, limbs congeal, and their breathing quickens. This is bad. But it can get worse, as when it becomes a pattern or it 'infects' others.

5. Varieties of Choking: Slumps and Teams

In addition to the paradigmatic case of an athlete choking during a particular performance, there are also cases where an athlete may *consistently* choke, a *slump*, as well as those where a whole team of players buckles under the pressure. The following explores these two types of choking phenomena.

5.1 Slumps

As Jackson and Beilock point out, there is a distinction to be made between short, acute instances of poor performance, a typical choke, and *slumps* that are

HOLISM AND THE CULTIVATION OF EXCELLENCE IN SPORTS AND PERFORMANCE

prolonged and chronic (2008, 105). Wertz's (1991) analysis of a slump is instructive and, presciently *avant la lettre,* cognitively embodied. The feeling of confidence that tennis player Stan Smith lost in his 1974 slump,

> was tied to those instinctive shots and movements that were replaced with calculative thinking about the moves, production of the shots, and the results. In other words, the feeling of confidence is not just *an emotional feeling* [...] but a *bodily feeling* [...] involving sensations and perceptions of a specific temporal order that belong to an individual's personal, subjective history. (Wertz 1991, 163–164, his emphasis)

Ably, this encapsulates much of the general tenor of the phenomenology of (un)skillful movement from this and the previous essay. The emotional and body(minded) feelings of moving in a foreign way from what we are used to, our kinetic history, become more and more entrenched, inscribed in our kinetic repertoire. Harbach's novel superbly depicts Skrimshander's initial blunder, how it becomes a slump, and how that wicked repertoire becomes etched in us. This is how he describes Henry falling prey to the second-guessing typical of slumps,

> At the last moment he sensed the throw would be too hard for Ajay to handle so he tried to decelerate slightly, but no that was wrong too, but it was too late. The ball left his hand and began sliding rightward, out into the path of the charging runner. (Harbach 2011, 321)

Eventually, this becomes a pattern for Henry. In a slump, discrete instances of choking add up to a chronic state resulting from the dislocations between schematizing and imaging, hyperreflection, and subjectively 'feeling the wrong sensations' proprioceptively and kinesthetically. A slump is but a harmful Deweyan habit. It is actually *cultivated* every time we give into the triggers that set off the choking event. As such it becomes an ingrained patterning that is engraved literally in the body(mind): the brain's neuroplasticity readapts the neural pathways into self-defeating patternings (this does not mean that the choking can be reduced to these, of course). Henry's initial prowess becomes a weakness the moment he cannot fathom how to face failure. If this can happen to as gifted and confident a player as Henry, it can happen to any of us. Or a whole group altogether.

5.2 Team Choking

A 'team choke' presents its own explanatory challenge. A team is made of discrete units but, when successful, it operates as a collectivity that is more than the sum of its parts—unless its synchronization is compromised. But just how does an individual choking process spread to the group?

Ackerman and Bargh elucidate that, 'the basic neural architecture in social coordination may be innate, but the expression of particular forms of coordination may often be moderated by goal-relevant features of the social interaction' (2010, 344). In this case, cohesiveness is a goal to the further purpose of victory. Ackerman and Bargh further explain that our social interactions are pervasively organized, and often tend to result in automatic social coordination, which should help develop cohesion and *esprit*

HOLISM AND THE CULTIVATION OF EXCELLENCE IN SPORTS AND PERFORMANCE

de corps. Dynamic systems theory is one of three primary routes to social coordination where spontaneous harmonization between similar elements of a system results in synchrony where people show alike patterns of entrainment, as when people match the rate of swinging legs (Ibid., 339). Teams practice many long hours to achieve said synchrony deliberately. For Wertz, choking in team sports counts as the same action if we treat the team distributively rather than collectively: 'The team use is an extended sense of the individual use' (102). Nonetheless, because a team is meant to operate as a seamless entity this works for choking in so far as it is a disruption of such putative unity. Accordingly, the key is to show how this discrete and distributed element becomes syncretic and collective in a way that applies conceptually and causally. We need to explain how the phenomenon can spread to the team even when it begins with one particular player's mistake and subsequent undoing.

Henry's undoing also affects the team negatively. His self-doubt, coupled to Schwartz's, his mentor and friend, and the coach's 'loyalty to a fault' mentality means that their unparalleled season, on its way to win their championship (they had been losing for decades before Henry's arrival), is also compromised. As it becomes clear that Skrim is as likely to throw the perfect ball as much as to botch the throw, what was a tight team begins to break at the seams, with players arguing in the locker room, becoming frustrated on the field, and simply not playing well. Skrim's lack of confidence becomes the team's insecurity. It is not until Skrim quits the team and that his protégé competently assumes his role that things turn around for the Harpooners.

To further refine this, we can consider the role of automatic social coordination and felt effort in this context. Ackerman and Bargh explain that deliberate coordination around goals that entail psychological synchronization is difficult 'when it concerns complex, high skill tasks' of which 'team sports are another example: learning the fundamentals of a sport like basketball or soccer takes a considerable amount of time and effort, and individual mastery is no guarantee that one will be able to effectively function within the team environment' (2010, 342–43). For them, the answer to the effort and intensive training required for such seamless and coordinated performance may be found in automaticity, which subtends a process of flow and is evident in 'the ability to coordinate under conditions of high objective effort without the corresponding increase in subjective effort [...] characteristic of high-performing sports teams' (Ibid. 357). Rather than automaticity, we would propose spontaneity. The former is mechanical and predicable, unlike the latter. Success in team sports is not about carrying out automatized and planned plays only. It is actually about being spontaneous *while* relying on automaticity. The best and toughest contraries present unexpected problems that do not fit drills and tactics. The need then is to be prepared to creatively respond. Automaticity cements the coordination to initiate the process of becoming a *team*, but spontaneity brings out the success on which the team thrives as a collective.

When an individual chokes during crucial moments of the game or worse, falls prey to a slump, we can argue that this propagates to the team on two levels: (1) a case of choking means that he will be unable play at his expected skill level. This reduces overall coordination by disrupting established synchronizing patterns such as tactics and player role; other players cannot count on him fulfilling his role. It is not that he fails once or has a bad play, but that his performance is so dismal that others cannot make up for it eventually. (2) This in turn leads to a lack of automaticity and spontaneity in terms of social coordination. While not necessitating that all players or instances

HOLISM AND THE CULTIVATION OF EXCELLENCE IN SPORTS AND PERFORMANCE

of poor playing constitute an act of choking, this replicates the phenomenon *collectively* as a ripple effect: unskillful action propagates, first to those teammates most directly connected to the choking athlete.[22] If the baseballs going in his direction are lost, there is no finding them for other teammates.

Empirical evidence, dynamic systems theory, and phenomenology can help account for the 'contagion.' Behavioral cues are shared intersubjectively. Mostly unreflectively, we pick up on others' behavior and imitate them or adopt their behavioral patterns (this does not mean we cannot become aware and inhibit the imitative process sometimes). Someone's frown or smile affects us readily, and we tend to mimic it. This applies to complex behaviors, and begins very early—in infancy. Gallagher cites Rakoczy et al., whose research suggests that 'around 1 year of age the actions that children learn "are not just individual, idiosyncratic behaviors, but cultural conventional forms of action." And many of these forms of action are rule governed and normatively structured …' (2012, 198). This transfers readily and quickly to other domains in sophisticated ways: 'by the time they are 2 or 3 years of age they adopt strict norms about how to play a particular game, following rules arbitrarily set by the experiments,' with the children protesting vehemently when a puppet played the game the 'wrong' way (Ibid.).

Our other-oriented outlook then permeates games and performative enterprises from the very moment these begin to form part of our performative and existential landscape. Additionally, dynamic systems theory explains how this socialization leads to the transmission of behavior. Entrainment, the matching of physiological and behavioral movements and events, has been amply documented in infancy, showing a qualitative spike at 8–10 months (Thelen and Smith 1994). That is, from early on we adapt others' rhythms as our own. There is evidence to strongly suggest that social coordination follows the same patterns as intra-organismic coordination, as Scott Kelso's (2006) work has shown across different scales, from organisms, to limbs, to people. For example, this operates when two people start by tapping or swinging their legs asynchronously and end up in synchrony without intending to do so. The upshot is that in nature there is a push for coordination from cells all the way to social interactions. Last, phenomenologically, Gallagher and Meltzoff (1996) argue that understanding other persons is primarily a form of embodied practice. Gallagher writes that,

> in cases of interaction ones intentions are not just formed in one's individual body as the result of an isolated subjective process, but depend in a dynamic way on the other's elicitations and responses. *Intercorporeity* involves a mutual influence of body schemas, a reciprocal, *dynamic* and *enactive* response to the other's action, taking that action as an affordance for further action and interaction. (2012, 200, my emphases)

This can result in affordances and the adoption of improved behavioral patterns and movements. But, in can also mean the adoption of constrains and negative patterns. An athlete who chokes is going to bring a very different and more acute patterning that will eventually interfere and disrupt the reigning synchrony. Those closest to her will be influenced first, but, ultimately, this can affect enough team members to lead to a systemic team-wide choke. Whether personal or collective, choking is a most unfortunate and unpleasant experience. Yet, exploring choking and failure further can lead to some positive lessons and point toward a possible remedy for choking.

221

6. Lessons from Failure and Choking

To hear from McEnroe as cited by Wertz, 'Choking is a part of every sport, and part of being a champion is being able to cope with it better than everyone else. But there isn't any set way of doing it; everyone finds what's best for him' (1986, 101). McEnroe is spot on when he asserts that champions cope with choking better than others. There may be personal nuances when dealing with choking, but there are also useful techniques and theoretical frameworks to that end. This is about dealing with failure. Now that the difference between possible failure and *inevitable* failure feels razor slight, how can we address and redress this?

An erstwhile major league player tells Henry, 'The name of the game is failure, and if you can't handle failure you won't last long. Nobody's perfect' (2011, 172). *Everyone* fails at some point. No one likes it. But a difference between those experts we might call *virtuous* masters and most others is that, in consonance with the maxim 'keep your enemies closer than your friends,' they do not fear failure but *learn* to deal with it. When they do fail, they embrace it. This does not mean that because they appreciate the value of failure, they think along the lines of 'because I learned so much from my mistakes, I am going to make more!' What it does mean is that failure and choking can impart some valuable lessons concerning performance and life. As Ueshiba Morihei wrote, 'Failure is the key to success: each mistake teaches us something' (1992, 87).

The fact is that failure or imperfect performance is the norm in sport and performative endeavors. In the case of virtuous experts, choking and failure are learning tools toward personal perfection and creative performative possibilities. In this way, they can avoid the fragmentation by fear of failing, taking in stride failure and unmet expectations. Failure can be motivational. It is a matter of shifting our perspective. On a practical level, it can motivate us to practice harder to minimize its occurrence. But considering that success and perfection are moving targets, it is better to take this to a philosophical level. There we learn to learn from and through it. Choking and failure then are hidden opportunities for self-growth, for self-cultivation understood as a life-long skillful striving (see next essay). In this view, it is the struggle itself that gives value to victory *and* defeat, as we see below in a fuller context. The rich ground for this begins with a reconceptualization of failure.

Fractured action can be the source of creative responses that add to our repertoire. That is, failures *themselves* can be resources for creative and spontaneous additions to our kinetic repertoires. And, the analysis of Zhuangzi's (essay 5) views showed how the limitations of dis~abillty are actually empowering and full of playful and creative possibilities. For his part, and relying on Michael Polanyi, Peter Hopsicker tantalizingly argues for a reconceptualization of the value of the inexact or even failed motor behavior to transcend the usual negative connotations associated with these. As the ensuing shows, this is in line with a venerable tradition of thinkers engaged throughout *Skillful Striving* for whom it is the striving, the struggle that moves us to move. One advantage, as Hopsicker puts it, is that through this attitude we have the opportunity to bring 'uncharted domains under our control' (2013, 79). Mistakes, failures, and errors are sources of new ideas. Beyond ideas, we could argue that they are the source of performances which, bound to fall short of their ideal, are but part of the never-ending process to refine ourselves as we come to know ourselves. Hopsicker argues,

> In contrast to seeing the athletic world as a finalized series of detailed and accurate motor performance techniques, or as a quest to perfection, perhaps we should instead equate human sport exploration to a 'fumbling progress' or a 'plunging reorientation' toward a greater understanding of ourselves. (2013, 80)

This reorientation is indeed Socratic in its quest for self-knowledge. Such explorations and reorientations seem destined to fumble and plunge their way through the thicket of small and big failures and occasional successes. Nonetheless, Hopsicker here seems to have in mind an Aristotelian or Hurkian view of perfection (essays 1 and 4), that is, absolute. His sensible point, however, is compatible with the kind of personal perfection we have developed with Ortega: one where we pursue our own perfection fumbling and plunging in our own personal way. Moreover, in *this* context, this is in line with the Deweyan view of deliberation as one that attempts to unify competing tendencies rather than the Aristotelian linear account (essay 1).

Learning from failure in this way needs patience. It is a lifelong process surely. But also, in the narrower context of our more immediate goals and challenges, it asks for perseverance. We need to deal with the rawness of our emotional disappointment and then take steps to instill better Deweyan habits. In the context of athletic competition, the athlete may have to wait months or years, as with the Olympic Games. Decathlete Dan O'Brien was the current world champion before the US Team trials, but he choked, missing *all* his pole vault attempts. He never made it to the Barcelona '92 Olympics. He did redeem himself after four years of hard work and uncertainty when he stood on top of the podium at the Atlanta Games (Morrison 2012). But, sometimes, there is no redemption. Chinese hurdler Liu Xiang, who won the gold medal at the 2004 Olympics, failed in both his 2008 and 2012 bids due to injury during heats. Eight years of single-minded effort ended with the sad story of an angry country, having hailed him as a hero at first, upon finding out that Xiang and officials had conspired to keep quiet the fact that he had been injured (Moore 2012). Samurai Tsunetomo Yamamoto, author of the celebrated *Hagakure* (葉隠), writes,

> It is said that one should not hesitate to correct himself when he has made a mistake. If he corrects himself without the least bit of delay, his mistakes will quickly disappear. But when he tries to cover up the mistake, it will become all the more unbecoming and painful. (1979, 42)

Had Xiang faced the fact that he was injured before lining up at the start, his fall from grace would have been graceful, even inspiring for the grit and devotion he had shown; had he followed the Delphic command to know himself better, he might have realized what his weaknesses and strengths were. But, it is not only a matter of identifying these. It is also about realizing that our talents and strengths are ours to be gracefully suffered as much as our limitations and weaknesses are to be joyfully embraced. Xiang's autochthonous Daoism and Zhuangzi (essay 5) would have been wise guides. *Wuwei*, 無為, effortless action, takes into account both talent and limitations and teaches us how to make of our weaknesses strengths and vice versa. But, sometimes, no amount of self-knowledge can avert simply back luck or worse.

When failure is calamitous and protracted, a slump or much worse, it is an opportunity to develop what, for Russell (2014), is the quintessential sportive virtue:

HOLISM AND THE CULTIVATION OF EXCELLENCE IN SPORTS AND PERFORMANCE

resilience. Zen Monk Deiryu (1985–1954) encapsulated tenacity and resilience in the face of failure when he wrote alongside a scroll painting of a Daruma doll (the Japanese version of a roly-poly toy), the following saying, 'Seven Times Down, Eight Times Up!' (Stevens 2002, 34–35).[23] The idea being that the natural state is standing upright, and that setbacks are temporary and, if we recall Ortega, also opportunities. Masters embody and enact this (in the sense now of laying down a path to follow). In *Reflections on a Katana,* this will be recast in terms of *shugyō* as resilient and lifelong skillful striving. In sports, French cyclist Raymond Poulidor clearly shows resilience in the face of defeat. In 14 starts to the Tour de France, he was second three times and five times third. He finished a remarkable 12 Tours, racing his last one when he was 40 years old. Poulidor became known as 'the eternal second.' Unluckily for him, his career overlapped with two greats of cycling, each of whom won five tours, Jacques Anquetil and legendary Eddie Merckx. Yet, as a racer he never lost heart. His efforts are admirable *precisely* because he did not win. Full of panache, he persisted. Outside of sport, this might be obduracy. Within, it may be the ultimate example of resilience as he perseveres without previous wins to motivate him. We can even reconsider the idea of 'victory' with him. On record he is a 'loser.' But, the very effort is what becomes admirable, giving him a 'virtuous victory' *because* he never wins.[24] Even if failure fails to open the key to success, there is a deep meaningful beauty to unrequited performance.

Ortega viewed life as a shipwreck ultimately. What matters most, we learned, is the struggle itself. The suffering and discipline opened up opportunities for growth, creativity and even joy. Revisiting Japanese novelist Mishima Yukio proves worthwhile. Inspirational enough he wrote, 'Everyone knows that masterpieces, ironically enough, sometimes arise from the midst of such defeat, from the death of the spirit' (1982, 48). The words that take this thought to its consummation, however, deflate this inspiration to some extent. But better for our purposes, they replace it with lucidity. The kind of lucid awareness that makes of the nebulous ideas we inhabit a solid realization. Mishima continued,

> Though I might retreat a pace and admit such masterpieces as victories, I knew that they were victories without a struggle, battleless victories [...]. What I sought was the struggle as such, whichever way it might go. I had no taste for defeat—much less victory—without a fight. (1982, 48–49)

There are victories not worth having, and failures on which it is worth staking one's life. Paradoxically, this lucidity where we fully give ourselves can open the door to overcome choking. Babe Ruth said, 'Never let the fear of striking out get in your way' (Stewart 2007, 675). If the fear of loss or a poor performance stiffens limb and will, the ultimate 'failure,' death, stiffens us all at once. In Henry's copy of Aparicio's book we read, 'Death is the sanction of all the athlete does' (Harbach 2011, 17). This initially puzzling statement acquires sense in the context of what Tsunetomo says, 'The way of the Samurai is found in death [...] by setting one's heart right every morning and evening, one is able to live as though his body were already dead, he gains his freedom in the Way' (Yamamoto 1983, 17–18). For samurai death by the sword was a real possibility and *the* one fear to overcome—an ethos that risk sports adopt nowadays (Ilundáin-Agurruza forthcoming-b). The 'simple' idea is to serenely confront what we most fear at any given moment.

The rub lies in how to achieve this. How do we return to an enactive and empty state of spontaneous and contentless thinking when we are dead worried? Precisely by performing enactively… by not thinking *when* thinking becomes contentful; by avoiding representations that either as rules or body(mind) imagings fracture performance. Zen Monk Takuan mentions an old saying, 'To think, "I will not think"—/This, too, is something in one's thoughts./Simply do not think/About not thinking at all' (1986, 34).[25] And now, it is Aparacio who sheds light when he writes, 'The shortstop has worked so hard for so long that he no longer thinks. Nor does he act. By this I mean that he does not generate action. He only reacts, the way a mirror reacts when you wave a hand before it' (Harbach 2011, 305). This is what in Japan they call *mushin,* 無心, no mind. The remainder of this project addresses this more fully in the context of actual practices. There we find a holistic and enactive performance where masters perform like active mirrors: without contentful and representational thinking, they can be empty to spontaneously create and successfully respond to the situation at hand. For now, the parting thought is that there is opportunity in failure and misfortune, should one *make* ready for it.

We leave Henry with a bad case of Steve Blass' disease, as it is commonly called in baseball because Blass was the first prominent player in major league baseball to suffer a career-ending slump. How to continue on the way to peerless mastery may entail risking a life-ending cut by a razor sharp edge. This directs us easterly, to those islands of the rising sun that Izanami and Izanagi created with the water droplets falling from their spear, Japan. There the faint echoes of these lessons are consummated as deeper insights where performance and normativity become fully integrated into lifelong practice.

NOTES

1. Harbach (2011, 320).
2. Mishima (1982, 48).
3. I am grateful to Andrew Edgar for bringing this novel to my attention.
4. Chan Buddhism is the Chinese precursor to Japanese Zen.
5. Qing-yuan Wei-shin's poem reads: 'Before I had studied Zen for thirty years, I saw mountains as mountains, and waters as waters. When I arrived at a more intimate knowledge, I came to the point where I saw that mountains are not mountains, and waters are not waters. But now that I have got its very substance I am at rest. For it's just that I see mountains once again as mountains, and waters once again as waters' (Watts 1957, 126). This is the terse Chinese version: 老僧三十年前未參禪時、見山是山、見水是水、及至後夾親見知識、有箇入處、見山不是山、見水不是水、而今得箇體歇處、依然見山祇是、見水祇是水.
6. Wertz states, 'Our bodies perform the actions without our minds being aware of the movements on more than a surface level' (1986, 99). For him we know how to execute a kick but do not know how we do it. As stated in earlier analyses, there is indeed much that happens offline and subpersonally, but both reflective consciousness and the Jamesian fringe play a larger role than he assumes, giving us more awareness than he attributes to our sporting and performative movements. As discussed earlier, it is possible to pay attention, become aware, and discriminate much that can show us

HOLISM AND THE CULTIVATION OF EXCELLENCE IN SPORTS AND PERFORMANCE

plenty about how we kick—particularly if the expert makes this an important aspect of her practice.

7. Christensen, Sutton, and McIlwain (forthcoming) propose a broader and more flexible model, which they call 'Mesh.' The holistically and ecologically broader basis allow for an optimistic outlook.

8. Contrarily, infants and pre-linguistic children do not learn thus originally, with imitation, trial and error, and coordinative dynamics prevailing (essay 7). Of course, once language (itself a skill) is in place, the efficiency of rule-based learning and teaching takes over (this is particularly expedient for the adults), even if arguably many skills are best learned by doing and being shown rather than through verbal instruction.

9. This 'democratization' or devaluing and watered down normalization of expert skill is adopted across a wide disciplinary spectrum. It influences even philosophical analyses, interpretations, and translations of Chinese classical texts such as the *Zhuangzi*. Chris Fraser's conception and analysis of 'forgetting' in performance in said text follows suit (see also appendix). He speaks of us as 'virtuoso walkers' that 'need not attend to our shoes' since when they fit we forget them (Fraser 2014, 207). But as Scheffler's (1965) analysis of 'closed' and 'open-ended' skills shows, walking is a closed skill that bears no improving after a certain level, so speaking of 'virtuoso' walkers is hyperbolic and detracts from true virtuosity in other activities where we find that (tight rope walking for instance). For his part Billeter, to explain the performance of the consummate per-former, states 'we all have experienced it [consummate performance]' as he refers to the common experience of learning to ride a bicycle (2010, 57, my translation). Surely, this works well to illustratively give a sense for what it is like to operate at a superior level. But this also elides true expertise with our more common and less refined actions and movements. Nonetheless, there *is* a sense in which we can improve even 'closed' skills to some extent. Chozansi explains through the mouthpiece of 'the Demon: 'Again, look at someone who is walking. Because most people are usually more conscious of the upper parts of their bodies, they walk counterpoise to their heads, while others walk moving their arms or entire bodies. A person who walks well does not move his body from his waist up, but rather walks with his legs. Thus, his body is serene, his internal organs are not stressed, and he is not worn out' (Chozan 2006, 160).

10. Of course, this ten year/10,000 rule is not hard and fast. Some take a considerably shorter time to become experts while others never reach expertise.

11. In addition, Breivik raises a number of issues against Dreyfus' phenomenological account elsewhere. For example, he shows how Dreyfus' expansion of the Heideggerian view on tool use overreaches Heidegger's own account and then develops an alterna-tive theory of absorbed coping (2007).

12. Athlete presently refers to sportspeople who are competitive and train assiduously, not to recreational sportspeople.

13. For a beautiful and transfixing short video of some of the best wingsuit women and men see professional skydiver and BASE jumper Sommer's (2013) compilation at https://www.youtube.com/watch?v=WRqnTODwvEA

14. Crucial to this is the social context of communities within which athletic, martial, and performing arts practitioners become wise in the ways proper to them, and through which the practices flourish (essay 10).

15. For purposes of analysis and clarity, not because these are separate from a holistic perspective.

HOLISM AND THE CULTIVATION OF EXCELLENCE IN SPORTS AND PERFORMANCE

16. In Gibson's sense of agent and environment interaction that creates behavioral possibilities for the former (1988).
17. This does not mean that the body will resemble a Greek statue, for athletic practice molds athletes into shapes congruent with the demands of the sport. For a critique of the athletic build see Ilundáin-Agurruza (2006).
18. Flow states differ from peak performances. Superb performance, whether in states of flow or not, presents challenges to computational, Dreyfusian and Searlian accounts, see Krein and Ilundáin-Agurruza 2014.
19. He redeemed himself with a gold medal in the 1994 Lillehammer Olympics.
20. See Ilundáin-Agurruza (forthcoming-a) for the fully developed version of this model. This subsection summarizes the main features. In a way, the ecological analysis as presented here, and the full model combine to constitute the full holistic account of the phenomenon of choking. The present summary however, does include some additional elements, e.g., the discussion on representations.
21. This does not imply that emotions are solely cultural and thus inherently and always relative. Diversely exhibited across cultures and varying by person, there is also a pan-cultural and common structure to how we experience them. See Sheets-Johnstone (2009, especially 207–210.
22. Interestingly Ackerman and Bargh go on to state that, 'Additionally, redirecting the cognitive resources typically involved with self-monitoring to other-monitoring (where the self becomes an observer) may help prevent "choking" under pressure' (2010, 357). Although we need not endorse SFTs as the singular way to account for choking, this centrifugal notion where we efface the self finds echoes in traditional Japanese martial arts treatises, as the next essay shows.
23. Russell also makes reference to this saying. This reference was antecedently and independently incorporated into the text before learning of his use.
24. In the last essay, the notion of kenosis, the complete giving of ourselves with no expectation of anything in return will add another layer to this.
25. Cleary translates it, 'Intending not to think is still thinking of something; do you intend not to think you won't think?' (2005, 125).

REFERENCES

ACKERMAN, J.M. and J.A. BARGH. 2010. Two to tango: Automatic social control and the role of felt effort. In *Effortless attention: A new perspective in the cognitive science of attention and action*, edited by B. Bruya. Cambridge, MA: MIT University Press: 335–72.

AGGERHOLM, K. 2013. *Elite-Bildung: An existential-phenomenological study of talents developing in football*. Ph.D. diss., Department of Sport Science, Aarhus University.

BAUMEISTER, R.F. 1984. Choking under pressure: Self-consciousness and paradoxical effects of incentives on skillful performance. *Journal of Personality and Social Psychology* 46: 610–20.

BAUMEISTER, R.F. and C.J. SHOWERS. 1986. A review of paradoxical performance effects: Choking under pressure in sports and mental tests. *European Journal of Social Psychology* 16 (4): 361–83.

BEILOCK, S.L. and T.H. CARR. 2001. On the fragility of skilled performance: What governs choking under pressure? *Journal of Experimental Psychology: General* 130 (4): 701–25.

HOLISM AND THE CULTIVATION OF EXCELLENCE IN SPORTS AND PERFORMANCE

BEILOCK, S.L. and R. GRAY. 2007. Why do athletes choke under pressure? In *Handbook of sport psychology*, edited by G. Tenenbaum and R.C. Eklund. Hoboken, NJ: John Wiley & Sons: 425–44.

———. 2012. From attentional control to attentional spillover: A skill-level investigation of attention, movement, and performance outcomes. *Human Movement Science* 31: 1473–99.

BILLETER, J.F. 2010. *Leçons sur Tchouang-tseu* [Lessons on Zhuangzi]. Paris: Éditions Allia.

BREIVIK, G. 2007. Skillful coping in everyday life and in sport: A critical examination of the views of Heidegger and Dreyfus. *Journal of the Philosophy of Sport* 34 (2): 116–34.

———. 2013. Zombie-like or superconscious? A phenomenological and conceptual analysis of consciousness in elite sport. *Journal of the Philosophy of Sport* 40 (1): 85–105.

BRUYA, B. 2010. *Effortless attention: A new perspective in the cognitive science of attention and action*. Cambridge, MA: MIT Press.

CAPPUCCIO, M. Forthcoming. Unreflective action and the choking effect. *Phenomenology and the Cognitive Sciences*. Special issue.

CARR, T. 2014. practicing, playing, and playing well under pressure: What do cognitive and sport psychology have to say to coaches and athletes? 1st International Conference on Sport Psychology and Embodied Cognition. United Arab Emirates University- Al Ain, 24–27 February.

CHOZAN, N. 2006. *The Demon Sermon of the martial arts*. Translated by W.S. Wilson. Tokyo: Kodansa International.

CHRISTENSEN W, J. SUTTON, and D.J.F. MCILWAIN. Forthcoming. Putting pressure on theories of choking: Towards an expanded perspective on breakdown in skilled performance. *Phenomenology and the Cognitive Sciences*.

COLLINS, A. 1988. *Cognitive apprenticeship and instructional technology*. Technical Report No. 6899. Cambridge, MA: BBN Labs Inc.

DIETRICH, A. and O. STOLL. 2010. Effortless attention, hypofrontality, and perfectionism. In *Effortless attention: A new perspective in the cognitive science of attention and action*, edited by B. Bruya. Cambridge, MA: MIT University Press: 159–78.

DREYFUS, H.L. 2002. Intelligence without representation: Merleau-Ponty's critique of mental representation. *Phenomenology and the Cognitive Sciences*. 1: 367–83.

DREYFUS, H. and S. DREYFUS. 1986. *Mind over machine: The power of human intuition and expertise in the era of the computer*. New York, NY: The Free Press.

ERICSSON, K.A. 2003. Development of elite performance and deliberate practice: An update from the perspective of the expert performance approach. In *Expert performance in sports: Advances in research in sport expertise*, edited by J. Starke and A.K. Ericcson. Champaign, IL: Human Kinetics: 49–83.

ERICSSON, K.A., R.T. KRAMPE, and C. TESCH-RÖMER. 1993. The role of deliberate practice in the acquisition of expert performance. *Psychological Review* 100: 363–406.

ERIKSEN, J. 2010. Mindless coping in competitive sport: Some implications and consequences. *Sport, Ethics and Philosophy* 4: 66–86.

EYSENCK, M.W. and M.G. CALVO. 1992. Anxiety and performance: The processing efficiency theory. *Cognition & Emotion* 6 (6): 409–34.

FINKE, A.F. 1979. The functional equivalence of mental images and errors of movement. *Cognitive Psychology* 11: 235–64.

FORDE, P. 2014. Camp Bowman: Michael Phelps and world's elite swimmers sign up for unique blend of grueling training and pain with eyes on Rio. *Yahoo Sports*. Available at https://www.yahoo.com/?err=404&err_url=http%3a%2f%2fsports.yahoo.com%2fnews%2fcamp-bowman-michael-phelps-and-worl%25E2%2580%25A6nd-of-grueling-training-and-pain-with-eyes-on-rio-191017440.html (accessed 21 June 2014).

FRASER, C. 2014. Heart-fasting, forgetting, and using the heart like a mirror. In *Nothingness in Asian philosophy*, edited by J. Liu, D. Berger. London: Routledge: 197–212.

GALLAGHER, S. 2005. Dynamic models of body schematic processes. In *Body Image and Body Schema*, edited by H. De Preester and V. Knockaert. Amsterdam: John Benjamins: 233–50.

———. 2012. *Phenomenology*. Basingstoke: Palgrave Macmillan.

GALLAGHER, S. and A.N. MELTZOFF. 1996. The earliest sense of self and others: Merleau-Ponty and recent developmental studies. *Philosophical Psychology* 9: 211–33.

GALLAGHER, S. and D. ZAHAVI. 2008. *The Phenomenological Mind*. London: Routledge.

GIBSON, J.J. 1988. Exploratory behavior in the development of perceiving, Acting, and the acquiring of knowledge. *Annual Review of Psychology* 39: 1–41.

HARBACH, C. 2011. *The art of fielding: A novel*. New York, NY: Little, Brown.

HILL, D. 2013. Choking in sport. Available at http://insight-dev.glos.ac.uk/academicschools/dse/research/pages/chokingSport.aspx (accessed 23 April 2013).

HOPSICKER, P.M. 2013. 'The value of the inexact': An apology for inaccurate motor performance. *Journal of the Philosophy of Sport*. 40 (1): 65–83.

ILUNDÁIN-AGURRUZA, J. 2006. Athletic bodies and the bodies of athletes: A critique of the sporting build. *Proteus: A Journal of Ideas* 25 (2): 15–22.

———. 2007. Kant goes skydiving: Understanding the extreme by way of the sublime. In *Philosophy, risk and adventure sports*, edited by M. McNamee. London: Routledge: 149–67.

———. Forthcoming-a. From failure to fluency: A phenomenological analysis of and eastern solution to sport's choking effect. *Phenomenology and the Cognitive Sciences*.

———. Forthcoming-b. The Eye of the hurricane: Philosophical reflections on risky sports, self-knowledge and flourishing. *Journal of the Philosophy of Sport*.

JACKSON, R. and S.L. BEILOCK. 2008. Attention and performance. In *Developing elite sports performers: Lessons from theory and practice*, edited by D. Farrow, J. Baker, and C. MacMahon. London: Routledge: 104–18.

JAMES, W. 1918. *Principles of psychology*. New York, NY: Dover.

JEANNEROD, M. 1997. *The cognitive neuroscience of action*. Oxford: Blackwell.

KELSO SCOTT, J.A. 1995. *Dynamic patterns: The self-organization of brain and behavior*. Cambridge, MA: MIT Press.

KREIN, K. 2007. Risk and adventure sports. In *Philosophy, risk, and adventure sports*, edited by M. McNamee. London: Routledge: 80–93.

KREIN, K. and J. ILUNDÁIN-AGURRUZA. 2014. An east–west comparative analysis of Mushin and flow. In *Philosophy and the martial arts*, edited by G. Priest and D. Young. New York: Routledge: 139–64.

MARSH, S. 2012. Modern Maverick. *Delta Sky Magazine* 63–65 (80): 82.

MASTERS, R.S.W. 1992. Knowledge, nerves and know-how: The role of explicit versus implicit knowledge in the breakdown of a complex motor skill under pressure. *British Journal of Psychology* 83 (3): 343–58.

MERTON, T. 1992. *The way of Chuang Tzu*. Boston, MA: Shambhala.

MISHIMA, Y. 1982. *Sun and steel*. Tokyo: Kodansha International.

MONTGOMERY, J. and M. CHAMBERS. 2009. *Mastering swimming*. Champaign, IL: Human Kinetics.

HOLISM AND THE CULTIVATION OF EXCELLENCE IN SPORTS AND PERFORMANCE

MOORE, M. 2012. Anger at Chinese hurdler Liu Xiang's 'staged' Olympic race. *The Telegraph*. Available at http://www.telegraph.co.uk/sport/olympics/news/9497212/Anger-at-Chinese-hurdler-Liu-Xiangs-staged-Olympic-race.html (accessed 21 February 2015).

MORRISON J. 2012. The top 10 biggest sports fails of all time. *Smithsonian Magazine*. Available at http://www.smithsonianmag.com/history-archaeology/The-Top-10-Biggest-Sports-Fails-of-All-Time-160728725.html#ixzz2jNyOL476. (accessed 12 September 2013).

PAIVIO, A. 1986. *Mental representations: A Dual Coding Approach*. Oxford: Oxford University Press.

REID, H.L. 2010. Special issue: Athletics and philosophy in ancient Greece and Rome: Contests and virtue. *Sport, Ethics and Philosophy* 4 (2): 109–234.

RUSSELL, J.S. 2005. The value of dangerous sport. *Journal of the Philosophy of Sport* 32 (1): 1–19.

———. 2014. Resilience. Warren P. Fraleigh Distinguished Scholar Lecture delivered at the International Association for the Philosophy of Sport annual meeting, 6 September, Natal (Brazil).

SAINT-EXUPÉRY, A. 1971. *The Little Prince*. San Diego, CA: Harcout Brace.

SCHEFFLER, I. 1965. *Conditions of knowledge: An introduction to epistemology and education*. Chicago, IL: Scott Foresman.

SHEETS-JOHNSTONE, M. 2009. *The corporeal turn: An interdisciplinary reader*. Exeter: Imprint Academic.

———. 2011. *The primacy of movement*. 2nd ed. Amsterdam: John Benjamins.

SOMMER, J. 2013. Winfsuit best moments. Available at https://www.youtube.com/watch?v=WRqnTODwvEA (accessed 19 February 2015).

STEEL, M. 1977. What we know when we know a game. *Journal of the Philosophy of Sport*. 4 (1): 96–103.

STEVENS, J. 2002. *Budo secrets: Teachings of the martial arts masters*. Boston, MA: Shambhala.

STEWART, W. 1990. *The gigantic book of baseball quotations*. New York, NY: Skyhorse.

SUITS, B. 2005. *The grasshopper: Game, life, and Utopia*. Boston, MA: David. Godine Publisher.

TAKUAN, S. 1986. *The unfettered mind: Writings of the Zen Master to the sword master*. Tokyo: Kodansha.

———. 2005. The inscrutable subtlety of immovable wisdom. In *Soul of the samurai*, translated by by T. Cleary. North Clarendon, VT: Tuttle: 100–41.

THELEN, E. and L. SMITH 1994. *A dynamic systems approach to the development of cognition and action*. Cambridge, MA: MIT Press.

UESHIBA, M. 1992. *The art of peace*. Boston, MA: Shambhala.

ULLÉN, F., Ö. DE MANZANO, T. THORELL, and L. HARMAT. 2010. The physiology of effortless attention: Correlates of state flow and flow proneness. In *Effortless attention: A new perspective in the cognitive science of attention and action*, edited by B. Bruya. Cambridge, MA: MIT University Press: 205–17.

VICKERS, J. and M. WILLIAMS. 2007. Performing under pressure: The effects of physiological arousal, cognitive anxiety, and gaze control in Biathlon. *Journal of Motor Behavior*. 39 (5): 381–94.

VINER, B. 2011. Famous sporting chokes: What becomes of the sporting imploder? *Belfast Telegraph*. Available at http://www.belfasttelegraph.co.uk/sport/famous-sporting-chokes-what-becomes-of-the-sporting-imploder-28608205.html (accessed 23 November 2013).

WADE, A. 2012. *Amazing surfing stories*. West Sussex: Wiley Nautical.

WATTS, A. 1957. *The way of Zen*. New York, NY: Vintage Books.

WERTZ, S.K. 1986. Is 'choking' and action? *Journal of the Philosophy of Sport* 13 (1): 95–107.

———. 1991. *Talking a good game: Inquiries into the principles of sport*. Dallas, TX: Southern Methodist University Press.

YAMAMOTO, T. 1979. *Hagakure*. Tokyo: Kodansha International.

SECTION IV. EAST AND WEST TEAMWORK: A COMPARATIVE ANALYSIS OF SKILLFUL PERFORMANCE

Jesús Ilundáin-Agurruza

The two essays in this last section consolidate the preceding into a comprehensive model. They explore the connections among individuals' skillful performances, social context, and the ethos of excellence. *Skillful Striving* has argued for an ecological understanding whereby spontaneous, skillful, and successful performance is premised on a number of factors that help constitute it: holistic and enactive skills, deliberation preceding performance, and post-performance reflection. A 'reflective intuition' is added now to complete the model. The enactive domains of performance, normativity, cognition, and the socio-environmental context help contextualize and explain the deep and broad registers of consummate performers. Looking eastward, to Japan, the essays interweave a number of strands that run throughout *Skillful Striving*. They recast skills and virtues as continuous wholes when performed by performative paragons. Theory and practice are amalgamated in Japanese *dō*, practices of self-cultivation, where our integrative bodymind is an achievement. Delving into the ideal of *shugyō*, self-cultivation is reformulated as a lifelong skillful striving to excel. Here, Nishida Kitarō, whose seminal and complex thought looms large, joins the ranks of the dark horses. The comparative tenor of this section also extends to a comparison between martial arts and sports. Ethical choice as spontaneous action and disposition and the means/ends relation are reframed in order to incorporate a holistic and enactive model of performance. Pedagogy and communities lie behind excellent performances, with kenotic and attendant attitudes modulating this process. This engages a situated intersubjectivity where historical conditions and a shared language enable us to better understand and articulate our skillful strivings.

9—REFLECTIONS ON A KATANA – THE JAPANESE PURSUIT OF PERFORMATIVE MASTERY

Jesús Ilundáin-Agurruza

One moon shows in every pool; in every pool, the one moon. (Zen Saying)[1]

Thirty spokes converge on a hub/but it's the emptiness/that makes the wheel work/pots are fashioned from clay/but it's the hollow that makes a pot work/windows and doors are carved for a house/but it's the spaces/that make a house work/existence makes something useful/but nonexistence makes it work. (Laozi)[2]

Not think:
Before and after,
In front, behind;
Only freedom
At the middle point. (Poem about Kendō)[3]

Japanese culture has a distinctive talent that suits admirably well the underlying personal perfectionism of *Skillful Striving*. This gift turns a putative weakness into a strength. Cultivating its own 'personal' perfection, Japan has turned apparent limitations into patent opportunities. The land is not particularly endowed with natural riches, and its people have not been disposed to change the world through radically original contributions.[4] Customarily, they have looked to other cultures for inspiration. To explain in the context of martial arts, these were largely incorporated from Chinese *wushu* (武術), traditional martial arts. They also imported metallurgical knowledge for weaponry: their Chinese imitation swords broke or bent when confronting the Mongol invading troops arrived in Japan in the thirteenth century. The much-touted relation between Zen and the samurai, which resulted in the warrior code of *bushidō* (武士道), and lucid acceptance of death, was largely due to the introduction of Buddhism in the sixth century. Native *Shintō* (神道), literally way of the spirit, was quite averse to any serious consideration of death. Likewise, the *bunbu ryodō* (文武両道), the two ways of the pen and the sword, was also, if not imported, then at least preceded by the Hwarang warriors from the Silla Kingdom in what today is Korea. In short, none of these developments originate from or are unique to the Japanese. What the Japanese *did* do was to adopt and refine them to unparalleled levels.

Martial arts acquired levels of sophistication as *educational* practices nowhere else matched; their famed katana swords improved on the Korean and Chinese blades, far surpassing these and perfectly adapted to their martial needs. By the time of the second invasion, the katana could take on any Mongol warrior. They also improved on European-imported technologies: during the brief period of time during which they used firearms for warfare they greatly improved the European's original models.[5] This pattern is replicated across Japanese culture, whether it be technology or cultural practices. Much the same applies to the cultivation of excellence through various praxes, many of them performative. Accordingly, in Japan we find an advantageous way to continue this inquiry, specifically, in its *dō*. As arts of self-cultivation, *dō* are outstanding contemplative *and* active paths toward excellence: they combine theory and praxis, and moreover seek to integrate and refine a genuinely holistic and enactive bodymind (See Hutto and Myin 2013 and essay 6). In fact, the argument is that philosophical analysis from this Eastern perspective of sport and other performative pursuits, particularly in their most refined expression, can bypass the mind–body problem and traditional western ontology. Rather than dueling with it on ontological grounds, a deft sidestepping à la *Aikidō* can redirect the momentum toward functionality and a personalized view of any individual's holistic integration.

This essay takes up again one argument laid out in the opening essay, *Nothing New Under the Sun*. Therein, it was discussed how Reid (2012), along with MacIntyre (1984), argued that virtues and skills differ because the former can be expressed in various ways, whereas the latter have very narrow applications. Generally true for most people in many situations, the stated intention was to reclaim a thick and vigorous normativity for skills. In *refined* expressions, skills are virtuous because they make the virtues realizable, while the virtues display the skills in their fullest form. Given our holistic commitments, virtue and skill *can* be continuous wholes distinguishable only conceptually. Those are instances of skillful and fluent striving. The following shows that, even more than an ideal to inspire us, this vision is actually *already* embedded in concrete practices (which does not mean that particular manifestations may not fall short of these practices' own ideals). As such it is even more inspiring because we find the ideal incarnate in outstanding individuals. While we were 'riding the wind' in the seventh essay, this skillful fluency was connected with a radically enactive spontaneity that is cognitively contentless. Presently, we fill this void with nothing(ness).

We begin with Japanese ideas as they relate to a holistic bodymind, contemplating the many ways these allow to engage the bodymind. Following this, we explore the ways Japanese *dō* cultivate our skills and character. Nishida's thought acts as a bridge between *dō* and our skillful strivings as we endeavor for perfected execution. Then, we expound on spontaneity, and show how these arts, in particular the way of the sword, are theoretically wise concerning expert skill, cohere with contentless cognition, and are practically shrewd as a remedy for fractured performance. This closes with a comparison between martial arts and sports primarily.

1. The Japanese Integrative Bodymind

The Japanese conception of bodymind follows closely the Chinese one as described in *Zhuangzi—Playful Wanderer*. Japanese people call the bodymind *shin* and use the same pictogram, 心 (called a *kanji* in Japanese). Nonetheless, Japanese culture affords a level of discrimination regarding the holistic bodymind that, in consonance with the opening paragraph, is nothing short of astounding. Varela bemoaned the fact that English, compared to German, lacks the convenient distinction between the body as lived and vital, *leib,* and the material, purely physical body, *körper* (2013). This is but the most basic distinction the Japanese draw. The objective of this section is to review the Japanese view on the bodymind and explore the remarkable affinity with thick holism and the 'existential pedagogy' that animates both. It furnishes us with outstanding descriptive and classificatory possibilities.

The Japanese have developed a sophisticated taxonomy that emphasizes functional aspects of the bodymind over ontological classification. That is, various factors—kinesthetic, organic, performative, cultural, social, and political—specify the role that the bodymind plays.[6] The following presents the most crucial categorizations pertinent for this section, although more aspects could be discussed. Redolent of a target with its concentric circles, this begins with the 'individual' spaces and gradually expands its scope to social ones. Unlike the target, there are no clear or specific demarcating lines, and rather than being a two-dimensional affair this is a multi-dimensional phenomenon with psychophysical, spatial, social, and temporal/historical expressions.

In consonance with the Germanic distinction, the Japanese use *karada* (体) to capture the idea of the Greek *soma* or anatomical body, and *shintai* (身体) to refer to the acting and lived human body (this is analogous to the Chinese notion of shen (身). *Shintai* is obviously suitable to discuss performative skills. Presently, rather than lived body, and to keep consistently with the emphasis on the gerund, it is preferable to render *shintai* as *living* body. Were we discussing the performance of a table tennis player, say his quick reflexes and hand–eye coordination, *shintai* would be the term to use; describing the muscles and tendons involved in the gripping of the racket, *karada* is applicable. Yet, and expanding on the Germanic notion, even *karada* is amenable to being coupled with living processes in some contexts without eliding into *shintai*. Fukumoto (2013) discussed how *karada-hogushi,* a pedagogical technique introduced in Japanese physical education classes, seeks to heighten awareness of the bodymind processes, improved bodily regulation, and enhancement of communication skills.[7] In other words, *karada*—as the soma—can also be part of a dynamic pedagogy as anatomical and biomechanical structures are contextualized within techniques that rely on *shintai*. This is similar to the Chinese *xing* (形) as bodily shape engaged in movement. When they wish to specify the psyche, the Japanese use *shin,* (神) and 'is indicative' of the 'core' of the mind, as exemplified by '*sei-shin* (精神 = energy + mind = psychological)' (Sakai and Bennett 2010, 147). *Seishin* is sometimes translated as 'spirit,' but as Yuasa specifies, unlike the disembodiment it suggests in the West, it actually 'means both material and spiritual energy' (1993, 197, n. 5).[8] Ortega's (essay 4) phenomenological analysis of 'spirit' as involving both cognition and volition, 'soul' implicating feelings, and 'vitality' as concerned with sensations is well aligned with this framework where what matter are functional continuities and not ontological entities. In this case, *seishin* is concerned with the nervousness of a cliff diver as she is about dive from 20 meters. High cliff diving gives pause to even the most seasoned professional. Orlando Duque, with nine world championships and two Guinness world records avows how before each jump he is seriously worried—until he jumps (Murphy and Yasukawa 2013). It is not simply the very idea of the jump, or the apprehension or anxiety, but how the trepidation is actually felt: it resonates kinesthetically radiating outwardly from the abdomen. Put otherwise, anxiety (or elation) is not at one extreme of the body(mind) (the 'mental' in a non-holistic framework) but rather is experienced as part of a fulsome animate being.

HOLISM AND THE CULTIVATION OF EXCELLENCE IN SPORTS AND PERFORMANCE

The closer counterpart to the minimal notion of a holistic bodymind presently operative is the Japanese *shinshin* (心身). It stands for an *integrative* bodymind where the three former notions are functionally incorporated and regulated in virtue of how they are executed performatively. In this case, and indicative of the continuity that underlies bodymind functions, the kanji are homophonous: respectively, they refer to 'mind' (心) and 'body' (身). But, they work in unison and context also imbues them with a flexibility that, as with *karada*, means that they are not statically grounded as either soma or psyche.[9] In fact, and very expediently, *shinshin* can also emphasize the requisite bodymind function as needed. Reversing the order of the kanji stresses one or the other aspect. Thus, 心身 has a tendency to emphasize the 'mindful' function, whereas 身心 accentuates the bodily facet. Again, these are never split as autonomous and separate entities; they are functionally continuous and in a dynamic process of integration or disintegration. The convention of parenthetic bracketing regarding the bodymind and thick holism amenably coheres with this analysis. Body(mind) then is functionally equivalent to 身心, and (Body)mind is so for 心身. When emphasizing a gymnast's anxiety and loss of concentration on the balance beam, (body)mind—心身 characterizes this, as the psychic supersedes the bodily; when the increasing pain in a runner's hamstring sets off thoughts of self-doubt, Body(mind)—身心 indicates where the imbalance is accentuated. Of course, given the dynamic nature of our coming and goings, these can, and often do, change quickly. For example, pain in the hamstring can set off worries that may in turn cause more tension in the leg, and so on, with the corresponding switches of emphasis in the bodymind dynamics.

These Japanese terms bring a level of refinement, precision, and terseness not possible in Indo-European languages.[10] To give this more bite, oftentimes translation of Japanese texts lose these nuances. For instance, Yuasa's book title, which would refer to *shintai*, is translated simply as *The Body* (1987). The richness and subtlety of his analysis and taxonomy are a translator's nightmare; they are also the readers' loss every time they encounter the word 'body' and the usual associations with the objectified *karada* or *körper* are elicited. When reading translations from Japanese texts, it is therefore advisable to keep forefront that terms like 'body', 'mind', or 'spirit' rarely have Western connotations. The easiest way to handle this is to simply realize that *any* of them are holistic. In one way or another, they concern the bodymind but simply emphasize different functional aspects.

Most notably, this integration is not a factum but something we are to achieve. It is integrative rather than integrated because the latter suggests an accomplished achievement, whereas the former specifies this as an ongoing process: it is integrative in the sense that the unification of the bodymind comes in various degrees and is subject to a continuous process of either improvement or deterioration, much as an athlete's form. In the context of skills, actual performance is required. It is through the very execution that our skills 'become', not only giving evidence of integration to others and us, but above all because they can only happen through performance. On the tennis court, we cannot simply think our way to a *perfected* smash. At its highest level, there is a specific characterization, *shinshin ichinyo* (心身一如), which can be translated as 'oneness of bodymind.' It seeks Zhuangzian spontaneity through discipline, and for Yuasa, it leads to superior execution (1987, 200). At this level, the performer, putatively in a state of *mushin* (無心, *wushin* in Chinese) unfolds as a non-deliberative acting intuition as per Nishida Kitarō (Section 2) where action and judgment, will, thought, and emotion fluidly coalesce. A master *kendōka* (剣道家) parrying an attack and instantaneously responding with a simultaneous riposte and countercut operates as harmonized bodymind. Its opposite counterpart is not the mere lack of skills, as it may be supposed, but the choke and its failure of already mastered skill. Dewey is right at home here. Shusterman exposes how Dewey's bodymind, rather than ontological is a 'progressive goal of dynamic, harmonious functioning that we should continually strive to attain' where 'integration is an achievement rather than a datum' (2008, 165).

Additionally, *kokoro* captures our bodymind's ever-present emotional tonality. It is another functional term with very strong affective connotations. It proves difficult to translate; Saito translates it as essence or spirit (1985). While this is adequate to suggest a general sense for her purposes, it needs refinement. Its conceptual range makes it coterminous with *shinshin*, but it emphasizes the emotional component and relates it to our willfulness. As such, it is closer to the original pictogram of the heart pumping blood, and fittingly uses the same kanji 心 to denote it. We can speak of someone having a big or small *kokoro* as someone having more or less courage, for instance. Describing the serenity of the target shooter to remain calm as the clock time runs would rely on *kokoro*. It is a particularly important concept in Japanese aesthetics and its arts, where its function is to enable us to sympathize with natural objects and situations (Saito 1985). This means that it is ecologically broader, and that its sphere of applicability extends from our self and into the environment, social and natural.

The wider social context, as noted at various points, is crucial for the refinement of skills and the very existence of those manifested through specific sports, martial arts, and performative endeavors. There are also unique Japanese terms to describe our bodymind from the social perspective; these are situated notions cognitively speaking. Two are relevant now: *mi* (身) and *mi bun* (身分). Simply—if a bit loosely—*mi* denotes the personal facet, and *bun* the social one. *Mi* refers to *our* bodymind as socialized.[11] In other words, it is our deportment, the appearance and bearing with which we conduct ourselves, including our very way of moving. It is imbued with ethical connotations and also assesses character in relation to behavioral cues and actions. In the West we say that the eyes are the 'window to the soul' or that someone's character is 'etched on their face.' Poetic as these are, they are less apt to capture the complex relation between character, body, and socialization. The former's appeal to the immaterial soul places a veil of mystery while the latter simply alludes to the process that has etched character the way rain shapes the passive rock. Our character is shaped actively, however, by our habits and our interactions with the broader sociohistorical environment. When a rider becomes the *patrón* or boss of the Tour de France after years of domination, as Eddy Merckx, Bernard Hinault, or Miguel Induráin did, it is not only the distinctive yellow jersey that marks them. The way they carry themselves in the *pelotón*, projecting confidence, means that other riders move aside as the *patrón* moves around the pack. *Mi* affords normative judgments in terms of ethical comportment as virtuous or vicious, or other personal qualities, as when we assess someone as thoughtful or kind. In short, *mi* perceptually and performatively manifests *our* qualities to others.

Looking at this now *from* the others' perspective readily leads to the intersubjective term of *mi bun*. It adds more explicit and richer social and political connotations that require familiarity with institutions and cultural mores. This time, *mi bun* captures our social standing and includes not just our bearing and behavior as in *mi*, but also our clothing, hairstyle, and other marks of social station such as kind and quality of

HOLISM AND THE CULTIVATION OF EXCELLENCE IN SPORTS AND PERFORMANCE

professional implements. This would permit to differentiate between samurai (侍), literally those who serve, and *ashigaru* (足軽), regular levied troops, for example. The former would not only behave and walk differently, demanding deference by those of lower status; they would be dressed more smartly and carry two swords rather than one or none. *Mi bun* then brings into play sociopolitical assessments. Originally, in Japan's feudal caste system, it was tied to social class, and it denoted higher or lower status. In contemporary Japan (and elsewhere where there are no castes), we can connect this more deeply to social respect as warranted by our achievements also. For instance, in the context of sports, consider a softball or baseball coach and her or his players. They stand in this relation of respect in virtue of station, demeanor, attitude, and in recognition of expertise and accomplishments. One last point is that to discriminate suitable attributes *bun* requires to be privy to apposite social and historical connotations, that is, we can ascribe to the softball or baseball players a samurai spirit, or aretē to a track athlete, *only if* we know enough about samurai and bushidō, or understand the role the Ancient Greek ideal played for the Greeks.

We can analyze these psychosocial aspects of the bodymind further, and see how the personal *mi* facet happens in and through the social one from the very beginning (the historical component is explored further in *Everything Mysterious Under the Moon* in connection with generative phenomenology). Our unique morphological characteristics are affordances and constraints that no doubt restrict as much as enable the ways we can move: a longer or shorter Achilles tendon gives more or less bounce and elasticity to how we run or jump. But, the incisive work of French anthropologist Mauss (1950) shows how our upbringing within a specific society gives us our basic movement patternings, bringing affordances and constraints of its own.[12] Clearly, we learn through and from others how to walk, swim, or use eating utensils, and this within a set of synchronized patternings, as Thelen and Smith's (1995) work on dynamic systems shows. There are, moreover, culturally prevalent ways of walking or swimming that we adopt and to which we sync up as we develop our habits through instruction, overt or implicit. For instance, American women walked very differently than French women in the 1930s, and Japanese people swam with different stroke styles than European ones (Mauss 1950). This takes place not only during our childhood, but also anytime we become habituated to a new practice, for example, the varied ways armies march in different countries.

The martial, performing, and sports worlds clearly demonstrate these social patternings. In the martial arts, Kono Yoshinori, the most renown Japanese sensei of *koryū* (古流), literally 'old style,' or traditional martial arts that hark back before the Meiji Restoration (1868), illustrates the intricacies of Mauss' ideas. He describes how martial arts instruction brought deep changes to the pupils' movements (Tamaki 2010). In a recent video, Kono shows how the 'ancient' martial artists avoided twisting, bracing, and energy build-up, staples of today's martial arts (Kono and Geikiryudojo 2012). Samurai had a peculiar way of walking, legs spread apart and with a low center of gravity focused on the *hara* (腹) or lower abdomen, always on the ready. They also held the sword differently than nowadays is taught, with the hands close together and near the *tsuba* (鍔), guard, rather than apart and further from the guard. Purportedly, these were the normal and established patternings that samurai adopted that Kono tries to inculcate. Educated eyes can pick out different and distinctive ways of running, swimming, dancing, fighting, or playing a game. For instance, consider the distinctive Brazilian

HOLISM AND THE CULTIVATION OF EXCELLENCE IN SPORTS AND PERFORMANCE

creative *jogo bonito* style of playing football, with its genial and jovial spontaneity (excepting the recent tenure of national coach Luis Felipe Scolari); in the world of dance, choreographers' 'progeny' is remarkably patent as we see with Merce Cunningham's, Pina Bausch's, or Alvin Ailey's dancers. In today's ever more globalized world, fashions spread and bring more or less uniformity precisely in this way; acculturation provides for and shapes our habits (of course, this does not determine how we may personally modulate them). This offers further insight into how a 'kinetic lineage' may be inherited (see *Zhuangzi—Playful Wanderer*), with players inheriting kinetic patternings from *sensei*, mentors, or schools. The opening citation in that essay described how Izzy, a teammate of Skrimshander, mirrored the former's batting stance just as Skrimmer evoked Aparicio's stance. *Mi* (and) *bun* capture and probe the complex personal but culturally modulated qualities of our bodymind and our performances.

This level of discrimination and ability to describe our bodymind provides a better way to conceptualize its dynamics, if not by adopting the terminology, then at least by showing us the conceptual spaces and explicitly making us aware of them. The terminological exactitude also affords further analytic precision. Shusterman (2008) points out that Dewey measured a culture as more civilized the less it differentiated between the mental and the physical. Japanese culture would be the zenith for the pragmatist, then. This nomenclature also offers interpretive possibilities that cannot be fully pursued presently. But to sketchily discuss one to suggest the tantalizing prospects, we can profitably relate *kokoro* to scholar Motoori Norinaga's (1730–1801) influential theory of *mono no aware* (物の哀れ). Saito translates *mono no aware* as 'sensitivity or pathos of things', which 'refers to the essential experience of sympathetic identification with natural objects or situations' (1985, 243). It basically permits an empathic identification where our emotional state matches or is attuned to the situation. This ability to harmonize with the state of a natural object or a situation can be adapted to the sporting and martial scenario in terms of attunement between whitewater kayaker and water, climber and mountain, cyclist and mountain pass or trail, or martial artist and sword. Further, this also offers interesting possibilities to reconceptualize the normative ethical and aesthetic unity, being conceived performatively and in terms of achievement.

The elucidations in *Riding the Wind* on *kalon* and *kalokagathia* are pertinent in this contest also. Similar interpretations and connections are possible for the above terms. The main idea to highlight, pursued next in more depth, is that the bodymind unity is conceived as a performative achievement. Unsurprisingly this accords with Dewey, for whom, let us recall, 'Integration is an achievement rather than a datum' (1988, 30). Moreover, as Asian scholar Ames writes, 'the body is a variable statement of meaning and value achieved in effort to refine and enhance human life within the changing parameters of context' (1993, 166). While he asserts this in the context of Chinese philosophy, the trickle effect to this exposition is clear. The framework of the arts of self-cultivation will detail how discipline and dedication affect the meanings of the bodymind.

Some preliminary distinctions between West and East frame this examination. Mainstream views in the West tend to consider matters ontologically. The relation between and the metaphysical status of the mind and the body abut on the hard problem of consciousness (Chalmers 1995). In Japan, however, Kasulis and Nagatomo expound in their introduction to Yuasa's work, theories focus on performances and achievements, and study baseball and batting over simpler actions such as

HOLISM AND THE CULTIVATION OF EXCELLENCE IN SPORTS AND PERFORMANCE

spontaneously raising an arm to demonstrate non-determined movement (Yuasa 1987). The questions they raise are threefold, 'What are the relationships among the intellectual *theory* of the swing, the somatic *practice* of the swing, and the integrated *achievement* of the skill?' (Yuasa 1987, 4, their emphasis). This helps highlight three ideas.

First, the view that this integration is about achievement: different people are at different stages of bodymind integrative harmony and more or less advanced levels of proficient action. In the West, the average performer establishes the norm and is the object of study. We see this in the numerous studies in biomechanics and physiology that draw general conclusions from target populations. Moreover, Kasulis and Nagatomo explain how the focus falls on the universal rather than the exceptional and, interestingly, also the diseased or pathological is what captures the attention of most researchers (Yuasa 1987). There are good reasons for this, as Gallagher and Zahavi argue, 'Pathological cases can function heuristically to make manifest what is normally or simply taken for granted' to gain distance from the familiar (2008:140). And yet, there is something to be said for considering the exceptional. As Yuasa explains, Japan favors exemplary individuals who excel and embrace *shugyō* (lifelong practice, see below*)*:

> the traditional Eastern pattern of thinking takes as its standard people who after a long period of training have acquired a higher capacity than the average person, rather than the average condition of most people. It proceeds to investigate the mind-body relationship in light of exceptional cases such as, for example, a genius or the masters of various disciplines. (1993, 61)

These exceptional cases establish the norm. Here, 'norm,' then does not take on the sense of 'average,' but rather is to be taken as the norm to be followed. It is normative, and as such it can be inspiring. 'It is both the ideal state and the potential state which promise a *possibility* to all people' (Yuasa 1993, 62–63 his emphasis).

Second, the underlying assumption is that, 'we are capable of increasing levels of integration' (Kasulis 1993, 298). The level of bodymind integration that a beginner sailor has developed is incomparably far less developed than, for example, Ellen MaCarthur. In 2005, she broke the record for the fastest solo sailing circumnavigation of the globe. We can echo Kasulis words, adapted to our purposes, and wonder about how strange it is that Occidental philosophy assumes that the bodymind is equally integrated in both sailors. And third, this framework also means that we can test this integration through actions. We actually see how we perform, and this readily informs us as to our level of integration just as athletic competition bears witness to our ability in that context.[13] This is relevant because oftentimes one hears claims about mysterious, private, and occult 'mental' powers. Before forging ahead, it bears saying that there are many and rich points of contact between East and West, as this project itself shows. Nonetheless, it is in the differences that we find insights for now.

There is a deep Buddhist framework on which Japanese thought builds. Two Buddhist monks stand out because of their philosophical and phenomenologically sophisticated writings: Shingon school founder Kūkai (774–835 C.E.) and Soto Zen patriarch Dōgen (1200–1253 C.E.). Both, idiosyncratically, emphasized the key role of the *living* bodymind, *shintai*, as it develops toward the integration of *shinshin ichinyo*, the oneness of bodymind that seeks spontaneity through discipline and results in superior execution. For Kūkai, we become Buddha through our very *shintai*; Dōgen stresses the

HOLISM AND THE CULTIVATION OF EXCELLENCE IN SPORTS AND PERFORMANCE

role of seated meditation, *shikan taza* (只管打坐), thereby emphasizing the role of practice, bringing in the notion of achievement as part of the process, and a Zhuangzian self-forgetting.[14] As a practitioner progresses from the initial insight of *kenshō* (見性) toward *satori* (悟り)—*samādhi* in Sanskrit), and ultimate enlightenment, the idea is to remove (sa) distinctions (tori) to attain an absolute stillness where the dichotomy of body and mind falls off and subject and object unite.[15] Person and movement, agent and action, become one. This is decidedly and radically enactive as it is best accounted for in terms of capacities and contentless cognition. Herrigel writes in his famed *Zen in the Art of Archery*, 'bow, arrow, goal and ego, all melt into one another, so that I can no longer separate them. And even then the need to separate them has gone [...] Now at last, the Master broke in. "The bowstring has cut right through you".' (1999, 61) Suzuki, in his preface to Herrigel's book says that,

> In the case of archery, the hitter and the hit are no longer two opposing objects, but are one reality. The archer ceases to be conscious of himself as the one who is engaged in hitting the bull's-eye which confronts him. This state of unconsciousness is realized only when, completely empty and rid of the self, he becomes one with the perfecting of his technical skill. (Herrigel 1999, viii)

Herrigel then explains that state of mind sought is 'charged with spiritual awareness and is therefore also called "right presence of mind." This means that the mind or spirit is present everywhere, because it is nowhere attached to any particular place' (1999, 37).

The esoteric flavor of such statements needs to be unpacked if we are to engage them with a philosophical rigor that leads to a better understanding.[16] What does it mean to become one with any object, movement, or action? How does the mind not reside anywhere? As Hyland (1990) elucidates, there is a certain aura of inaccessibility due to Zen's rhetoric. Moreover, Yamada and 山田奬治 (2001) also cast doubt on the accuracy of Herrigel's account, arguing that the Zen aspect of his *kyudō* (弓道), way of the bow, training is overwrought since his sensei Kenzo Awa was just beginning to develop his ideas. There are two sides to East Asian esotericism from a Western perspective. One results from the expected difficulties of translation between such divergent languages and lack of familiarity with the traditions that inform these statements. Language and concepts that would be readily clear to many in East Asia sound arcane. But this is no different from how much of the West's philosophical or Judeo-Christian tradition would have sounded to the Japanese in the early twentieth century. This is largely a cultural matter that suitable contextualization can redress to a large extent. The other side pertains to dubious claims of mysterious functions, powers, or abilities that defy belief. Tales of lore are indeed embellished, and what was perhaps a warrior's victory over half a dozen adversaries becomes an army. *Ki* or *qi* 氣, life force or vital energy (Japanese and Chinese transliterations respectively), already discussed with Zhuangzi, elicits much skepticism also. Some claims, particularly when connected with geomancy (earth divination) and divining powers, are indeed dubious. Yet much of it is similar to how we explain bodily processes in terms of energy and electrical and chemical signals (which many Westerners understand nothing about beyond their familiarity with the electric current that powers their gadgets and homes). Next, Yuasa helps refine and elucidate *dō* and set up the subsequent discussion in Section 3 of Nishida's complex views, which explain how this seemingly mysterious unity and presence of mind comes to be.

241

2. The Arts of Self-cultivation—Japanese *Dō* and the Path of Skillful Striving

Japanese *dō* are paths toward excellence. Contemplative and *active*, they also integrate theory and praxis. Prominent examples, some already enumerated in *Nothing New Under the Sun*, are *sodō* (書道), art of calligraphy, *Nō* (能) acting, *yakimono* (陶磁), art of pottery, *chanoyu* (茶の湯), *sadō, or chadō* (茶道) which refer to the way of tea, *ike-bana* (生け花) or *kadō* (華道), art of flower arrangement, and of course, martial arts such as *Kyudō*, sumo (相撲) wrestling, and *kendō* (剣道) as the way of the sword. Each *dō* has methodological particularities that amount to different routes to the same ultimate goal. In a deep sense, *dō* realize an old saying known as *mumonkan* (無門關), The Gate-less Gate: 'The Great Way is gateless/Approached in a thousand ways/Once past this checkpoint/You stride through the Universe' (Sekida 2005, 26). They are all methods, ways, to get to enlightenment should they be engaged properly.

These paths are remarkable practical and normative ways that impart ethical, aesthetic, and existential principles and values. Steeped in the millennial Eastern traditions of *Shintō*, Confucianism, and Buddhism, particularly the latter's quintessential Japanese manifestation of Zen, they are soteriological practices in so far as they seek enlightenment through personal perfection. Yamamoto Tsunetomo (1659–1719) stated, 'Throughout your life advance daily, becoming more skillful than yesterday, more skillful than today. This is *never* ending' (1979, 27, my emphasis). In advance of the later focus on swordsmanship,[17] we can conceive of the process of engaging in a *dō* as self-cultivation much like the making of a sword blade, which can be a path. Ueshiba Morihei, founder of *Aikidō* (合気道), the way of harmonious spirit, affirms that, 'iron is full of impurities that weaken it, through forging, it becomes steel and is transformed into a razor-sharp sword. Human Beings develop in the same fashion' (1992, 56). Ueshiba is thinking of how swordsmiths refine the steel by pounding and folding it to the count of several million layers, a process called *tanren* (鍛錬), which translates as disciplining or forging. This perfection is an ideal to be sought endlessly, as Tsunetomo says. Staying with theme of the blade, renown swordsmith Kunihira Kawachi inscribed in the tang of a Katana 'discipline your mind with this sword' (Kawachi and Manabe 2006, 27); and Michael Bell, who continues Yoshihara Yoshindo's lineage of sword making writes that, 'when I polish a sword several hours a day for three months, I am polishing my soul' (2012).[18] Ueshiba summarizes this ethos nicely, 'Those who are enlightened never stop polishing themselves' (1992, 52). As performative praxes, that is, activities that need to be performed, these are not simply paths to enlightenment, but enlightenment in them-selves; something Kasulis corroborates from a different angle (1993). The very procedures, techniques, and movements *constitute* the path (hence also the specificity).

How one must understand praxis in this context is as a mode of expression and not a technique to achieve a goal (Kasulis 1993). It is telling that religious practice halls, and those of other *dō* such as martial arts ones, are called *dōjō* (道場). Its Sanskrit roots mean 'place of enlightenment' (Suzuki 1993, 128). To sum up, following the path of a *dō* means engaging an enlightening practice reflectively and with full dedication. And this, for a *long* time—ideally for a lifetime. This lifelong dedication, framed by specific standards of excellence takes us to the realm of *shugyō* (修行).

Usually rendered as lifelong self-cultivation, *shugyō* is a complex concept. It derives originally from the Buddhist practice of *sennichi shugyō* (千日修行), one

HOLISM AND THE CULTIVATION OF EXCELLENCE IN SPORTS AND PERFORMANCE

thousand days of practice. Embedded in traditional *dō*, *shugyō* objectively and performatively grounds excellence. In essence, it is an endeavor to excel in a lifelong commitment (this does not mean one has to stay with one particular practice; it is about the habit). It begins by training the living body, *shintai*. And generally, it happens in and through movement, however, deft or delicate this may be, as the just-so turning of a wrist in *sodō, the* art of calligraphy. It involves our bodymind and demands relentless dedication to generate that elusive integration that seeks to avoid either body(mind) or (body)mind imbalances. As Carter specifies, 'It is never a casual undertaking but an ultimately serious journey as some form of spiritual awakening, or realization' (2008, 4). Sakai and Bennett cite *kendo* master Mochida,

> It took me fifty years to learn the fundamentals of kendo with my body. It was not until turning fifty that I started true kendo training. It was then that I could do kendo with all my heart (*kokoro*). When I became sixty, my legs and back weakened. It was my spirit that enabled me to compensate for this weakness [...] When I became seventy years of age, my entire body weakened. The next step was to train by not moving the spirit [...] When I turned eighty, I achieved a state of immovable spirit, but sometimes random thoughts entered my mind. I continue striving to eradicate such superfluous thoughts. (2010, 325)

This clearly exemplifies the kind of endeavor that *shugyō* demands. Even when one's faculties diminish because of age or illness, one adapts and presses on. As it is clarified below, in the end, it is not about prowess or technique but mastery over oneself. This requires a habit, dedication, and discipline that few are willing or able to endure. Sport philosopher Abe Shinobu says regarding his own *kendō* practice, 'I see practice as a never-ending struggle with myself to correct my faults' (1986, 47). Musashi Miyamoto (1584–1645), Japan's most renowned swordsman, won sixty duels to the death (some against multiple combatants) between the ages of 14 and 29. Luckily for his would-be challengers, Musashi had an epiphany and never killed any one else after coming to his realization. Instead, he simply outmaneuvered opponents with a *bokken,* 木剣 (wooden sword). In his *Go Rin No Sho* (五輪書), *Book of Five Rings*, he tells that it was not until he turned 30 that he realized he was lacking in true understanding; training from morning until night he was 50 when he finally saw the deepest secrets (Sakai and Bennett 2010; Tokitsu 2004; Wilson 2004). At the end of the Scroll of Water Musashi writes, 'A thousand days of training to develop, ten thousand days of training to polish' (Tokitsu 2004, 167). The former number correlates with empirical research, which postulates either 10 years or 10,000 hours of deliberate practice (Ericsson, Krampe, and Tesch-Römer 1993). But, the second one is equivalent to about thirty years of eight-hour days. Musashi did train relentlessly everyday until his death. He also appreciated all too well that such prowess is subject to the ebbs and flows of 'being in form.' During his later years, he pursued, quite successfully, other arts such as painting or sculpture.

Perhaps a popular saying attributed to various people can help think of this in a brighter manner: 'We do not stop playing because we grow old, we grow old because we stop playing.'[19] *Shugyō* then is this eternal spirit to remain playfully dedicated. Such dedication is in itself formative and normative, it builds character. Carter's assessment is that, 'There is nothing like these understanding in the West, which does not employ its arts and crafts, or its sports to achieve spiritual self-transformation' (2008, 4). Now,

HOLISM AND THE CULTIVATION OF EXCELLENCE IN SPORTS AND PERFORMANCE

because of its centrality in Japanese *dō* and for this project, as well as its inherent complexity and difficult translation, it is important to provide detailed analysis and contextualization.

The kanji for *shugyō* derive from the Chinese characters 'to master' and 'practice,' so literally it means to master a practice (Yuasa 1993, 196, n. 1). As Yuasa's translators Nagatomo and Hull clarify, the term 'self' is not part of this and is adopted in deference to the West's individualistic orientation (Ibid.). This works for the initial stages of the process but because the 'ultimate goal is to achieve the state of "no-mind" or "no-self" it does not do justice to the full meaning of the original phrase' (Ibid.). Yuasa further considers the adequacy of 'cultivation,' its connection with tilling the land and raising crops, and related notions like refinement and education. He then concludes, 'It appears difficult for European languages to express the connotations by the Japanese word [...] which carries the sense of strengthening the mind (spirit) and enhancing the personality, as a human being, by training the body' (Yuasa 1993, 10). (Here, *seishin* and *shintai* are the pertinent words for 'spirit' and 'body'; (body)mind and living body(mind), respectively.) He considers 'austerity' and 'asceticism' but rules against them on account of their dualistic roots in monastic values that chastised the body. Self-cultivation is the default, if somewhat misleading, translation adopted in the literature.

In order to sidestep these complexities, *shugyō* is reformulated in a way that situates it with the aims of this project as a resilient and enduring *skillful striving*. The applicable notion of resilience is derived from Russell's (2014) insightful analysis of this virtue. His working definition sees resilience 'as the ability to come back from or to respond effectively to some sort of setback, failure, or adversity,' and further considers that it is 'arguably the central virtue in sport' (Ibid.). Indeed, resilience is a virtue that sports, martial arts, and life need in spades—but competitive sport particularly so. The notion of endurance is related to resilience, but emphasizes the fact that this is for the *long* run. The Japanese saying cited in the previous essay, 'Seven times down, eight times up!' becomes fully meaningful in the context of *shugyō*. It is not about 'toughing it out' for the duration of a long and hard event, not even a three-week bicycle race or a Himalayan summit attempt that might take weeks in deplorable conditions; tenacity is more appropriate in these cases as Russell argues (ibid.). It is about enduring significant adversity over a considerable span of our life and fostering this virtue over its whole course. This is an ethos that is Orteguian to the core (as seen in essays 4 and 8) for we are to persevere even when we (know that we) are destined to suffer shipwreck. Finally, *shugyō* is also about developing and refining skills with which to tackle challenges.

Life requires performative skills, and *dō* are precisely such endeavors. In the context of these endeavors, and in terms of how the bodymind is engaged, we can conceptually distinguish two main emphases: (a) a body(mind), for example, morphologically, the strong and lean legs of runners, the muscular torsos of gymnasts; or kinetically, in the way we move, say energetically, lethargically, elastically and (b) as (body)mind that expresses our *ki*, inner energy (our vitality *and* soul for Ortega). These two modes give us our kinetic signature—the uniquely personal mien with which we impart our movements. When harmonized we get a holistically fluid bodymind. Ueshiba writes, 'A good stance and posture reflect a proper state of mind' (1992, 68). In this case, *mi*, how we carry ourselves reflects our *seishin* (not forgetting its connection to *shintai*, the living body). This bearing is the result of our habits, as Dewey would emphasize. Last, it is something we strive to achieve. *Shugyō* is modulated according to our talents and limitations. This also elicits an Orteguian attitude where we do our best given our abilities when what counts is the quality of the effort. In agreement, Ueshiba states: 'Everyone has a spirit that can be refined, a body that can be trained in some manner, a suitable path to follow' (1992, 13). These further show the genuine and rich conceptual overlaps between *shugyō* and this project, further supporting its rendition as 'skillful striving.'

With *shugyō* and self-cultivation recast as skillful striving, we can further explore its implications and its connection with *dō*. Given its epiphanic qualities, existentially rich gnostic truths are readily available within its framework. These truths are tightly bound with how we feel, with the proprioceptive and kinesthetic dynamics that speak the language of our moving bodies. We pursue certain performative paths because our tastes or preferences are premised on narrative (sometimes theoretical) affinities, affective undertones, and kinetic dimensions that fit our ways-of-feeling-and-moving-in-the-world. They are also performative truths that necessitate being acted out (sometimes to find out whether we are found wanting, sometimes for the sheer joy of it). Hence, *shugyō* grounds excellence performatively while circumventing reductionist temptations and tendencies and emphasizes the Jamesian continuities in our experiences. In short, the goal is the holistic development of the person and her abilities, where holism means bodymind integration within an ecologically and socially rich context.

Shugyō has a strong normative dimension, both ethical and aesthetic. In its skillful striving after personal perfection, it follows specific standards of excellence. Thus, beyond, or rather, behind lies a community that provides said standards and values. Given the scope of *shugyō*, its congruence with MacIntyre's (1984) argument that virtue should be expressed across one's life in a uniform way is noteworthy. In the case of *dō*, it involves, particularly if not uniquely, those virtues inscribed in *bushidō* inherited from a larger socio-historical context. Emphasizing process and reflection, *shugyō* becomes truly educational in its aspiration to bring out the best in us. With this difference in mind, we can consider just how skills (and not just virtues) become normatively rich and extend over our life in the context of *dō*. In the setting of the Confucian virtue of *li* (礼), Ames highlights how rites and rituals can provide order and allow to formalize natural processes as rules of conduct in a way that 'integration represented by physical efficacy is a characteristic of the consummating person' (1993, 167). Analogously, performative *dō* become formalized kinetically and through bodymind functions.

Carter stresses the normativity of *dō*. He premises *The Japanese Arts of Self-Cultivation* on the hypothesis that 'ethics is primarily taught through the various arts, and not learned as an abstract theory' (2008, 2). He explains further that in Japan ethics falls within the scope of virtue ethics, centered on character, rather than dealing with metaethical disquisition on criteria for right or wrong actions (Ibid.). And, expanding on the idea mentioned above that these paths are themselves enlightenment, through *shugyō* 'each of the arts is a pathway, a road [...], and also signifies a way of life [...] leading to a transformation of who a person is. In short, each of these arts, *if seriously engaged in, is itself enlightenment in some form*' (Ibid. 3, my emphasis). They are transformative in and of themselves. The very way of engaging *dō* means their constitutive skills can be virtuous in two ways. First, the mode, manner, and attitude when performing the various skills can be virtuous themselves. Under the aegis of *bushidō*, tasks are accomplished with an explicit and pervasive sense of honor and service, in this case to the task and the way. It is very much like the Orteguian *pundonor* (essay 4), a high

HOLISM AND THE CULTIVATION OF EXCELLENCE IN SPORTS AND PERFORMANCE

sense of honor in doing things in the best possible way. The second way—more controversial but interesting—is that the very skills enact virtuous dispositions, or rather, that in enacting themselves they become virtues. This is a matter of performing mindfully in the present, with dedication to perfected execution and technique, *and* engaging the practice reflectively afterward such that insights coalesce.

For Aristotle, this reduces *aretē* to *technē*, which he would object to. If anything, this underscores the difference the underlying sociocultural milieu and the competing philosophical paradigms make. In an Ancient Greek context, and under an Aristotelian framework, such reduction would impoverish *arête*. Yet, in the Japanese context, they enrich each other mutually as the very performative skills are the path or enlightenment itself. Further, the Deweyan sense of deliberation supports the Japanese case in the context of a holistic and enactive account. As we saw with Wallace (essay 1), Dewey's deliberation is exploratory and integrative as it strives to harmonize opposing dispositions (which parallels the pursuit of an integrative bodymind). This does not mean discarding an Aristotelian account of virtue (as pointed out in the first essay, his views of deliberation are applicable in contexts with clearly set goals). In fact, and as the next point shows, there are legitimate points in common.

Putatively, a virtuous character that exercises phronesis is reflective. Issai Chozansi (nom de plume of Chozan Niwa, 1659–1741), a samurai who embodies the *bunbu ryodō* (two ways of sword and pen) to a superlative degree, wrote *Tengu Geijutsuron* (天狗芸術論), the *Demon Sermon of the Martial Arts*. This is a difficult yet discerning work that turns swordsmanship into a diaphanous reflexive practice. He writes, speaking through the mouth of the *Tengu* (Demon),[20] 'Generally speaking, the person who has gained proficiency in an art is constantly employing his mind' (Chozan 2006, 120). Readers will surely think of the many athletes that unfortunately reaffirm the stereotype of being 'unthinking blokes.' Proficiency then is not to be equated with thoughtfulness generally but exceptionally. Perhaps. But, *now*, we need to realize that (a) this 'mind,' as *seishin* or even *kokoro*, *still* is incarnate; (b) this applies to *dō*, not sports; (c) it involves *shugyō* not *keikō* (稽古), training (see below); and (d) here, the purported mind is not a Cartesian one but rather a bodymind in a specific stage of integration and development through apposite skills. Thus, as progress (or regress) is made, this reflexivity happens through the body(mind) not just the (body)mind.

Accordingly, technique, implemented through the various *waza* (技), specific and specified techniques, is the means, the very conduit for skillful *and* virtuous practice. The virtue is embodied in the skill in this context. As the *kendōka* (剣道家) performs the various sequences of moves in a *kata* (型), form as choreographed patterns of movements, each movement is mindfully performed with *pundonor*, and embodies *kalon*. The very movements and the accompanying kinesthetic, kinetic, and proprioceptive dynamics become meaningful patternings where the very performative standards are embedded and felt: these move the *shinai* (竹刀), bamboo sword, in precise sequences where minute deviations are felt, which the *kendōka* endeavors to correct and perfect. Coupled to reflection, technique and principle merge, as Chozan constantly states and explains in many different ways. At one point, the *Tengu* explains, 'As you become skillful in technique, ch'i harmonizes and the principle of the place that contains that ch'i is manifested on its own. When this has completely penetrated the mind and no more doubts remain, technique and principle become one' (Chozan 2006, 96–97). This integration happens through practice.

HOLISM AND THE CULTIVATION OF EXCELLENCE IN SPORTS AND PERFORMANCE

Three examples illustrate how the skills as performed movements become virtuous. 'The practitioner of the *Jigen-ryū school* of swordsmanship conducts *"Asa ni sanzen, yu ni hassen,"* (3,000 in the morning and 8,000 in the evening) blows with his wooden sword' (Turnbull 2010, 53). These are meant to be 'mindful' blows where the person concentrates her *ki* on each blow. The art of drawing the sword, *iaidō* (居合道) provides another extreme example. In the temple of Hayahizaki, there are records of *iai* masters who drew their swords thirty or forty thousand times over several days, with three of them having drawn over ninety thousand times in a week (Tokitsu 2004). Yamaoka Tesshū (1836–1888) was a veritable *kensei* (剣聖), sword saint. This refers to a truly peerless master and implies not only exceptional skill but also a high degree of moral perfection. As Stevens (2001) details, his top students were tested in a ruthless way: a seven day, 1400 set of combat matches (200 a day) with *bokken* (木剣), wooden swords, where the candidate dueled bout after bout against fresh opponents.

Such almost abusive training regimens aim at: (a) surpassing one's limits while (b) cultivating skillful fluency through bodily integration by (c) quieting thought through mindful and strenuous yet precise work to (d) teach what cannot be taught verbally because it entails gnostic truths (again another point of contact with the enactive view presently endorsed). Within the context of Buddhist soteriology, each stroke, draw, cut, parry, or countercut whittles away at the self or ego. This renders the performer selfless and enables a state of mindful presence, *mushin* (this egolessness, central to this Japanese paradigm, is clarified with Nishida, and especially in Section 4; it also engages enactive bodyminds). Such practice further tested the performer's tenacity. Being a matter of *shugyō* means that resilience will be needed, as life spares no one of turmoil. In the case of Tesshū's students, this meant bravery to face the fresh opponents knowing that after a few dozen matches the blows would come unstoppable. The overt lessons and reflection that accompany such practice are drilled into the bodymind, literally, through strenuous practice. The moral lesson needs to be performed and felt in the flesh: egolessness is only achieved in the doing and paring away; bravery becomes courage of character as it is pounded in blow by blow.[21] There are no shortcuts.

Merely reading or being told about this, no matter the stature of the *sensei* (先生), master, does not suffice. Chozan recounts the story of an old and slow but matchless cat when it comes to prevailing over a rat that has bested all the cats in the neighborhood and even a sword-wielding samurai (2006). The story concludes with the cat declaring, 'A teacher can only transmit a technique or enlighten you to principle, but receiving the truth of the matter is something within yourself' (Chozan 2006, 190). Nonetheless, we should not think that any given *dō* in itself suffices: our concerns must be broader. The necessary and central role of practice is a banality that sport psychology and cognitive science validate. But as Janelle and Hillman write, the question must 'move forward to understanding the *what* and the *how* of practice' (2003, 28). Unless we know how and what to train, the effort could be misspent. We need to take this further.

A truly ecological and holistic model would also add, *why?* A story in the *Liezi* (列子) presents the eponymous Daoist sage as a character where he describes how when he learned archery and became a good shot he asked the opinion of Guanyinzi (関尹子). The latter asked him if he knew *why* he hit the target. As expected, a dumbfounded Lieze replied negatively. Guanyinzi sentenced, 'Then you are not good enough yet' (Lao-Tzu, Tzu, and Tzu 2013, 201). After three years of assiduous practice, he returns to

247

HOLISM AND THE CULTIVATION OF EXCELLENCE IN SPORTS AND PERFORMANCE

the same question 'Do you know *why* you hit the target?' Upon Liezi's affirmative answer, Guanyinzi's retort was 'In that case all is well. Hold that knowledge fast, and do not let it slip' (Ibid.). Blind commitment to a practice will not suffice.

Realizing these deeper reasons is what makes the practices themselves meaningful in the first place; they are the source of a deeper motivation where it is not merely about shooting the target to bits or getting a medal. In fact, truly facing this 'why' with a gnostic attitude also has consequences for the quality of our performance. Barry Allen (2013) argues that martial arts are unique, compared to sport and dance, in that the intention of the movement is essential for it to count as a genuine successful and beautiful martial arts action (as we argued in essay 7 this is also the case for sports and other performative endeavors). Indeed, there is a certain commitment required to effect some of these movements. In swordsmanship, (in both the East and the West) there are certain techniques that require total commitment. Kim Taylor explains they 'require the swordsman to stay directly on the line of attack,' we present a target to draw the opponent and wait until he is 'committed to his swing' (2010, 133). He continues 'once this happens, there is little time to react and defeat him [...] everything is bet on a single swing and response. There is no room for error or adjustment. They either work or they do not' (Ibid.). We must have very good reasons to do this. Lacking good enough reasons our commitment wavers and we become stale—or are cut down. Anders Ericsson, whose psychological work centers on expertise, writes, 'At some point in their career, however, some experts eventually give up their commitment to seek excellence. They stop engaging in deliberate practice and focus only on maintaining their performance, which results in automatism (and "arrested development")' (2003, 65). This marks the point of inflexion where the reasons behind the 'why' do not match the sacrifice. Moreover, this automatization means that we become disengaged from the process, and that our very skills begin to deteriorate. Automatization is useful to drive efficiently to the grocery store while thinking about a project, but it is a death knoll to our creative, flourishing and inspiring skillful strivings. Better answers to the 'why,' in this context, give us better reasons to become better versions of ourselves.

This way of conceiving a practice then expands the frontiers of the MacInterian view on skills, and addresses the old Aristotelian problem whereby excellence in any given practice does not necessarily lead to overall or moral excellence. Superb artists, outstanding scientists, or wondrous athletes sometimes incarnate moral turpitude. The tight connection between the actual techniques, *waza*, and moral development in Japanese *dō* brings a continuity that leaves no gaps. If a person is to truly exemplify the spirit of the practice, moral excellence is *also* her goal. And technique, as mentioned earlier does not suffice. Carter cites Saotome, 'Physical technique is not the true object, but a tool for personal refinement and spiritual growth' (2008, 46). This growth and refinement are intimately tied to and becomes virtuous as just argued. Therefore, we find moral exemplars and not merely role models. Put differently, exemplarity is already structured as part of the praxes themselves, just as the soteriology toward self-awareness and enlightenment. When the distinction needs to be drawn for the sake of precision and rigor, and with this in place, exemplarity and excellence are henceforth reserved for moral exemplars whose virtues extend beyond the practice, and 'expert' and 'expertise', and similar epithets are applied to role models within a specific practice (otherwise neutral terms such as 'superb' and the like are used to cover both cases). To return to the argument, Carter explains that it seems better to think of the goal in terms of self-awareness rather than self-realization, because the former entails an awakening to our selflessness and spontaneous forgetting of the self (1997, 114). This is not only better aligned with the Buddhist ethos but also the objective of *mushin* as means toward that self-awareness.

If so, self-awareness is both process and terminus and underscores that (a) we become more skillful by practicing the skill itself not merely theorizing about it and (b) it is a process with no end in sight except the continuous improvement. Moreover, such enlightenment can take place through martial arts practice. Becker discusses the sense in which enlightenment as world-transforming is grounded in Martial Arts (1982). He speaks of three levels: (1) a basic one where animal movements are turned into martial moves; (2) as ritual that changes the practitioner's mores; and (3) 'a more elevated level [… where] we gain knowledge of the ebb and flow of the universe itself by forming the forms and dancing the dances of the martial arts' (Becker 1982, 25). This is thickly holistic, as 'it is founded upon a different, more wholistic, and more *living* view of the universe' (Ibid.). In advance of the last section that contrasts East and West, we can ask: Might this not be part of Western athletics?

Discussing how the endurance athlete (some insights are sport specific) embodies the cultivating process, and in particular, the dedication it takes, Lally writes, 'What is necessary is the profound feeling that such efforts improve the person, connecting the athlete to a world larger than himself, one that is rich in meaning. This realized improvement within training does not come to the athlete in the form of an epiphany, exploding in one's consciousness as a single moment of clarity' (2012, 180–181). Lally then characterizes this athletic cultivation as an 'unfolding' of our diffused everyday existence into something that transcends it (Ibid., 181). Given Dewey's holistic credentials, this is close to *shugyō* methodologically, and to *dō* ontologically. But it is not the same either in terms of the richness of the qualitative experience itself or the extent of its integration into a practice with an *explicit* normative telos. And, this is so not merely because of the truism (perhaps) that there are cultural differences (there is a way to deepen this that transcends the intellectual poverty of cultural relativity; see the last essay). Nor is this less eligible because it is about some sort of instantaneous epiphany. There are Zen schools that favor both instantaneous enlightenment (Rinzai) and gradual awakening (Soto). The difference lies in the very method, process, and goals.

As to the method, the issue is that the quest for normatively rich gnostic insights is not built into the framework of endurance or other sports the way it is into *dō* (see Section 5). Concerning the process, there is another relevant concept that pairs up with *shugyō*, namely *keikō* (稽古), training, and which captures better the sort of activity most athletes engage in day in and day out. *Keikō* stresses physical effort, training, tactics, and results. Thus, *keikō* or training better capture what most endurance athletes do. This is the emphasis in the West and in modern 'sportified' martial arts (Asian or Western). Even if, as stated above, the normative insights happen through and are built into the techniques, it is not reduced to this in the case of *shugyō*. Techniques are necessary for all, whether gifted and average, but not sufficient, as mentioned above. The literature emphasizes unanimously this, from early medieval manuals on Zen or martial arts all the way to contemporary writers (Chozan 2006; Suzuki 1993; Yagyū 2003; Yuasa 1987, 1993). In short, *keikō* training is not about gnostic insights but achieving athletic goals, while the reverse is true of *shugyō*. And, as far as the aim, because of the influence of Zen, *shugyō* seeks to actually dwell into the 'ordinary' experience; it

HOLISM AND THE CULTIVATION OF EXCELLENCE IN SPORTS AND PERFORMANCE

does not seek the transcendence Lally mentions. To clarify, it seeks to make of the extraordinary but ordinary while preserving the character of both. Explaining this conundrum, which has broad implications for skillful and expert action, takes us to Nishida.

3. Nishida—Finding Unity in Difference

Nishida Kitarō (1870–1945) was Japan's Twentieth Century preeminent philosopher. He spearheaded the Kyoto school of philosophy. Nishida is another philosopher who *lived out* his philosophy. As Yuasa points out, Nishida's living experience *taiken* (体験) and his *zazen* (坐禅), seated meditation, deeply informed his views (1987).[22] The kanji for tai, 体, should alert readers that it is the living bodymind in active practice. Dewey's notion of *an experience* fits well this Japanese framework, which also includes *keiken* (経験) to refer to self-conscious experience and reflection upon the living experience. That is, *taiken* is concerned with experience itself, the kinesthetic and proprioceptive dynamics for example, and is imbued with ineffability; *keiken* has to do with the articulation of that primal experience. The import of this is that *taiken* is where we *live*-in-the-doing, and that *keiken's* articulation complements it. Living experience and reflection go hand in hand. In a simplified way, bringing these into full integration was Nishida's aim. Overall, he sought to bypass the traditional dichotomies that beset philosophy: subject/object, one/many, mind/body, and particularly is/ought since it directly connects with how we live our life. Because the complexity and breadth of his thought precludes full discussion, the focus is on those ideas that help understand the integrative and enactive bodymind: pure experience, acting intuition, logic of place, absolute nothingness, and unity of contradictories.[23]

William James' views on pure experience were seminal for Nishida's own development as he sought to overcome the is/ought gap while maintaining a meaningful connection to Japanese culture generally and Zen specifically.[24] Nishida's 1911 maiden work, *An Inquiry into the Good* (1990) first explained this integration in terms of pure experience, one without any deliberative discrimination at all. For Nishida, pure experience lies beneath ordinary experience. It is not to be transcended but accessed. In fact, for Nishida, pure experience is normatively the richest of experiences, as Dilworth says, when understood in terms of Zen emptiness or nothingness (Carter 1997). And this is normative since we cultivate our capacity to experience it through meditative practices. The emphasis in Asian traditions is on the method, the means or path to our insights, and not necessarily the answer itself. They focus on the 'how' rather than the 'why'; but a deep 'how' that ironically functions as a why as it reveals experience without relying on language (Ibid.). Nishida initially conceptualized this process whereby we access pure experience as an intellectual intuition. His early writings suggest that this unity is achieved through the (body)mind, where the intellectual facet prevails over the bodily one. Interestingly, and foreshadowing a later stance congruent with an integrative bodymind, he exemplifies this with an inspired painter where he and brush move spontaneously. This sets up his later notion of *acting intuition*.

Whereas intuition traditionally has been cast as passive, in Nishida's mature thinking it becomes creative and active. As he writes in one of his later works when discussing the act of consciousness as a dynamic interpenetration of subjectivity and objectivity,

250

HOLISM AND THE CULTIVATION OF EXCELLENCE IN SPORTS AND PERFORMANCE

> My concept of active intuition as a transformational vector is a formulation of this. It is the creative world that transcends the self in the depth of the self. The more the self becomes aware, the more it realizes it [...] Intuition always has this significance of dynamic, historical expression. (1987a, 84)

Yuasa (1987) explains that there are two levels in Nishida's acting intuition, a surface one, the intuition, which is conscious and passive, and a deeper and unconscious one, the acting component. This reflects the state of ordinary experience and the level of the empirical self. But when we advance toward the absolute nothingness, this is reversed, and intuition becomes active and the acting component passive (Yuasa 1987, 68). Then intuition becomes creative. As far as the mind–body relationship within this schema (as per the translators' words; bodymind dynamics would be more apt), Yuasa elucidates that in the everyday self, while body (objectivity) and mind (subjectivity) 'are inseparably conjoined, they are still distinguishable into subjectivity [mind] and objectivity [body],' which 'means that the respective functions of the mind and body are not completely one' (1987, 69). The deeper acting intuition brings about the transformation; we become integrated. Of note are two aspects now. One, Nishida stresses that this intuition 'is a transformative structure' (Ibid., 102). As such, acting intuition is a normative affair: the pure intuition bypasses any subject and object divide into a unity of contradictories that comes in degrees and can be improved upon through disciplined striving (cultivation). And two, and specifically relevant for performative endeavors, this highlights the bodymind in action on its path toward *shinshin ichinyo*, that oneness of the integrative and harmonious bodymind. As integration improves, the aim is a balanced bodymind. How this engages active pursuits is illustrated after presenting the concepts of nothingness and contradictories.

Nishida's stance is decidedly holistic. His acting intuition integrates intellect, emotion, and volition already in his early stages of thinking (Nishida 1990) and is only accentuated in later ones (Nishida 2011a), where intersubjectivity also becomes prominent. The union of the subjective and objective, and in turn, the union of 'I' and 'thou', is to be found in the state of pure experience. Eventually this expands to include the environment as co-created in mutual influence with us. Detailing Nishida's views on the environment and our relation to it lie beyond the scope of this project. Briefly, his conception sees a mutual influence between the environment and us. This is in line with Dewey, Ortega, and situated enactivists, but he does give it a more sophisticated twist. Carter explains, 'Either way, the interaction is *mutual*. And therefore, the contradiction is also mutual: the individual is (partially) negated (changed) as an individual through its encounter with the environment; the environment is (partially) altered (negated) by the individual acting on it' (1997, 68). His personal imprimatur is that the coupling and adaptation is not seamless; he keeps alive the tension that his unity of contradictories affords (explained momentarily). In his last period Nishida (2011b) pushed by Tanabe Hajime's criticisms and work (Tanabe 2011), included a historical dimension that firms up even more his holistic commitments (the historical dimension is addressed in the last essay). In these late writings, Nishida also makes it clear that this acting intuition is a continuous process, 'At the depths of our self-awareness, there is something that transcends our self. The deeper our self-awareness grows, the more this holds true' (2011b, 665). Usefully recapitulating several key ideas, Nishida scholar John Maraldo states that what acting intuition emphasizes 'is a bodily achievement, the performance of an

HOLISM AND THE CULTIVATION OF EXCELLENCE IN SPORTS AND PERFORMANCE

embodied individual who in turn is formed by the world; again, both body and world must be conceived as historical' (2012, 18).

Nishida developed a complex framework around the logic of *basho* (場所), place or topos (after Plato), to further his analysis. This transcends both the empirical and the transcendental self (which he calls 'being' and 'relative nothingness', respectively) and embraces absolute nothingness, *mu* (無). As Abe (1987) states, *mu* becomes Nishida's primary concept. This is the place where the subject and object distinction is overcome, becoming an action—Nishida's acting intuition. In other words, in absolute nothingness the dissolution of our self brings about the integration of pure experience with reality. In the context of knowledge and spirituality Nishida writes,

> The workings of cognition come about in this contradictory self-identity of the knower and the known … This is precisely what I mean by 'acting intuition'. […] The true self functions "immanently *'qua'* transcendently, transcendently qua immanently," that is, in a contradictorily self-identical manner […] acting intuition is the dialectical process mediated by this kind of negation. (2011b, 665)

Maraldo clarifies that Nishida used 'the language of transcendence to explain absolute nothingness, saying it transcended the opposition between being and non-being for example; but language did not indicate any thing, power, or consciousness beyond the world' (2012, 13).

Absolute nothingness establishes the unity of contradictories, or a contradictory unity of opposites, where the perennial dissonances of philosophy, the dichotomies abovementioned, can be harmonized as a higher but still tensed chord. 'Nothingness *is* the world as contradictory identity' (Carter 1997, 69, his emphasis). The unity of contraries keeps the tension between one/many, unity/difference, and mind/body, without solving it for either one. As Carter explains, 'the one is self-contradictorily composed of the many, while each of the many are self-contradictorily one with all of the others, forming a unity' (1997, 70). Unlike a Hegelian synthetic solution to the thesis–antithesis entente, Nishida keeps the conflict inherent in both opposites; they remain separate yet conjoined. Thus, there is no 'synthesis, but a unity-in-contradiction, an identity-of-opposites,' yet, and coevally, 'absolute nothingness as the ultimate and final universal […] is itself beyond all characterization, and therefore beyond all contradictoriness' (Carter 1997, 70). In other words, instead of an Aristotelian logic of contradiction and a Hegelian synthesis, Nishida advances a logic of both/and (Zhuangzi also posited such logic, if less robustly). Simply put, Nishida underlines how opposites are connected while keeping the inherent tension. Nishida illustrated this highly abstract notion with art, as adduced above: 'when inspiration arises in a painter and the brush moves spontaneously, a unifying reality is operating behind this complex activity' (1990, 32). Maraldo elaborates,

> Both artist and work are formed mutually and are reflected in one another. While this mutual formation can be described in terms of a causative process taking time, with the person first intuiting or internalizing and then acting or externalizing, Nishida described it in terms of the place or topos wherein intuiting entails acting and acting intuiting, and wherein the difference between internal and external collapses. (2012, 18)

HOLISM AND THE CULTIVATION OF EXCELLENCE IN SPORTS AND PERFORMANCE

This situation is applicable not only in the arts, but extends to all disciplined behavior (Nishida 1990). Martial arts, dance, musical performance, combat and team sports incarnate this process in a more interesting, or at least complex, way than the arts arguably: even if for Nishida canvas and painter change and affect each other mutually, performative endeavors involve much more dynamic relations where mutual intersubjective and environmental adaptation in-the-moment is paramount. As the ice hockey players glide in myriad combinations, slamming into one another, passing the puck, making formations and plays, there are constant *and* variable encounters of opposites. Both contraries *and* teammates are opposites precisely because they *inter*act with each other, whether it be a passing play or one where the puck is blocked or stolen. Two players are inherently distinct yet they become one for the duration of the mutual action they create during a play. The play is enacted, constituted, and made possible because of this meeting of opposites. Ultimately this resolves not in a duality or even mutuality, but a complete unit. In such action, there is 'the state of oneness of subject and object, a fusion of knowing and willing. In the mutual forgetting of the self and the object, the object does not move the self and the self does not move the object […] we find 'simply one world, one scene,' writes Nishida (1990, 32). In sport, if we follow Nishida, we pursue the action itself, the very process of exercise (Abe, 47). Abe helps clarify, 'Applying Nishida's theory to sport, in sport the self is lost but finally the true Self is found. The moment an athlete putts the shot, the instant a kendo master's sword strikes his or her opponent—every moment the athlete springs into action—body and mind are integrated as an action of the self. At that brief moment, mind is transformed to body and body to mind' (Abe 1987, 46). The details of this process are yet to be laid out as fully as needed. Fukasawa begins this task when he explains,

> the Judoka sometimes experiences a moment when he/she can flip down his/her opponent without all the might in his/her body. At that moment, he/she becomes unconscious and doesn't have the awareness of flipping the opponent, nor the opponent has the awareness of having been flipped. What it seems that happens is that both bodies automatically move together. As they become nothing their experience are [*sic*] something they cannot express with words at that moment. But after having flipped the opponent they may try to articulate or remember it. (2004, 50)

This aptly describes the unity found through an identity of opposites. The claim that the archer, the bow, and the shooting and target become one is not so mysterious anymore. The last two sentences evoke the notions of *taiken*, the experience itself, and *keiken*, its conceptualization. For now, there is one amendment to Fukasawa's apt narrative. It concerns the moment of fusion where the opponents are unaware of being flipped. His narrative is sensibly aligned with prevailing views in the literature on this point: experts operate at a subpersonal and automatic level where the implicit system takes care of skill and the 'physical' side of things (looked at from the conventional perspective). Nevertheless, that moment of unity is a more complex phenomenon than seems; even in the fusion of perspectival horizons and the spontaneous movements, there is room for creative spontaneity as well as judgment and awareness. To show this, it is requisite to open the scope of the examination in various ways to capture the intricate layering and dynamics involved, during, *and* before and after (see next subsection and essay 10). Next follows another amendment, to Nishida now.

HOLISM AND THE CULTIVATION OF EXCELLENCE IN SPORTS AND PERFORMANCE

For Nishida, the process just described 'is an extremely ordinary phenomenon' (1990, 32). Yuasa criticizes Nishida on this point because he does not 'demarcate ordinary experience from the experience of *basho*' (1987, 72). What Yuasa means is that the experience of unity, of fluid performance (e.g. in a state of *mushin*) is not as common as Nishida would have us believe, even if it underlies all experience. It needs to be revealed. We do 'so through *practice*. [...] Thus, the disintegration of the distinction between consciousness as subjectivity and the body as objectivity is overcome; the functions of mind and body become one' (Ibid., 70, his emphasis). Put differently, it is an experience to be *earned* through assiduous practice, not a given. That is, it is a normative achievement and not an ontological entitlement. There are various stages, as befits increasing expertise and skill development. In ordinary experience, there is a lack of harmony in the bodymind, with either body(mind) or (body)mind imbalances. An uncoordinated dancer who tries to think through her steps clearly shows the latter, whereas an inexperienced runner who begins at too fast a pace a long race evinces the former. But, there is hope, for as he says, 'Nonetheless, by training the body-mind continuously, it is possible for even an ordinary person to have a *glimpse* of this dimension' (Yuasa 1987, 200, my emphasis). He illustrates this superior dimension across a broad range of performative endeavors when he eludicates that the

> smallest gap between the movements of the body and mind on such occasions as a gymnast's [*sic*] performing his or her best techniques in a state of no-mind, or a master pianist's [*sic*] performing in total absorption, or an experienced actor's [*sic*] acting out his role on a stage, becoming the role itself. These people are [...] in a state of 'the oneness of body-mind' (*shinshin ichinyo*). (Yuasa 1987, 200)

In methodological terms, we can say that Nishida's thinking is a philosophical *dō* engaged in the spirit of *shugyō*. He rethinks intuition as active, and provides a flexible and expedient conceptual framework that keeps opposites in a constant dynamic dialogical tension. This brings a more sophisticated intuition into the realm of performance. It enables us to understand movement and action in a subtler way. His key contributions to this project are that he accounts for how experience is structured phenomenologically *and* logically *and* constitutively without resorting to a transcendental step. An additional benefit—that evokes Zhuangzi's usefulness of the useless—is the expediency nothingness (or emptiness if considered functionally) has in terms of cognition and performance. This enactive stance is further developed in the next section (and in the appendix).

4. Mushin—Freedom and Creativity in Mindful Awareness

In the context of skillful fluency and expertise, much like Cerberus, the three-headed dog from Hades, we can speak of the tyranny of automatization, mindless coping, and attentional focus. They are connected through a common theoretical body, for automatization allows mindless coping to a large extent, and this also makes selective focus possible. *All* three clamp on our ability to act spontaneously, creatively, and effectively to changing circumstances. Having dealt with the middle head of mindless coping in essay 7, it is time to finally muzzle the first one, automatization, and tie the second one, attentional focus. This opens the way to enjoy the freedom of mindful awareness—*mushin*.

HOLISM AND THE CULTIVATION OF EXCELLENCE IN SPORTS AND PERFORMANCE

If there is one claim collectively held as true by laypeople and academics alike, it is that we perform skillfully better when we leave matters to automatized and subpersonal processes. There is indeed a justified appreciation for the role that automatized functions play in evolutionary terms, but those who have wrestled with the issue also realize there is a tension that means one of the heads seems to always free itself to bite. The next three academics exemplify this from different angles. A preliminary clarification is necessary though. First, length constraints advise against separate and detailed exposition on attention, focus, awareness, and mindfulness, which are instead briefly explained *in situ* as and where pertinent.

Bruya (2010) centers on what he calls 'effortless attention.' It can be briefly summarized as the ability to focus attentionally such that it improves our performance at no extra or even at a lessened cost (metabolically or subjectively). Action and attention correlate positively with effort; the higher the demands of the task the more effort that we need to be attentive and efficacious. In short, attention and focus come at a price. But, 'there are times, however, when attention and action seem to flow effortlessly, allowing a person to meet an increase in demand with a sustained level of efficacy but *without an increase in felt effort*—even, *at the best of times with a decrease*' (Bruya 2010, 1, my emphasis). Researchers differentiate between objective effort, which incurs in metabolic expenditure, and subjective one, effort as *felt*. Of course, and besides difficulties in measuring quantitatively subjective felt effort, this seems to contravene the law of conservation of energy (and its associated maxim that there is no free lunch in the universe!). But, the longstanding skepticism is receding. In fact, there is recent empirical evidence for this kind of effortlessness on both counts, objective and quantitative, and subjective (Ibid.), as many of the essays in Bruya's (2010) anthology show.

Bruya discusses automaticity in the context of attention, which researchers disagree on whether it comes early or late in attention. He cites Jeannerod, who 'suggests that the automated steps of an action come in for conscious access when there is discord between intention and actuality—when the perceptual representation does not match the action representation' (Bruya 2010, 15). (See essay 6 for Jeannerod's views on representation.) Bruya also mentions how findings suggest that 'much more behavior than previously thought is outside of voluntary consciousness' and acquiesces that this 'would help explain why effortless action often seems outside of conscious awareness' (Ibid., 16). Yet, Bruya makes the tension palpable when he notices the risk of leaving it all to a subpersonal level beyond the reaches of reflective consciousness. He asserts, 'it would also seem to leave a high-level effortless action as purely automated, thereby seeming to preclude credit to a subject for creativity, insight, emotional expression, and so forth' (Ibid.). The issue is how to account for the effortlessness without giving up all control. Next, a Japanese analysis arrives to the same place through a different route.

Suzuki (1993), from the perspective of Zen Buddhism as it relates to samurai and swordsmanship, *frequently* alludes to the role of the 'unconscious' to explain states of performance in a *mushin* state.[25] He considers that *mushin* 'may be regarded in a way as corresponding to the concept of the unconscious' (Ibid., 94). (*Mushin* is more accurately discussed later.) He elaborates, already building some tension as he attempts to bridge this back to consciousness,

Psychologically speaking, this state of mind gives itself up unreservedly to an unknown "power" that comes to one from nowhere and yet seems strong enough to possess the whole field of consciousness and make it work for the unknown. Hereby he becomes a kind of automaton, so to speak, as far as his own consciousness is concerned. (Suzuki 1993, 94)

Suzuki wants to leave some room for the role of consciousness, but yet he is still strongly swayed by the powers of the unconscious, turning the performer in the state of *mushin* into a robot. Dreyfusian mindless coping fits with this view also (Dreyfus and Dreyfus 1986). Yet, in the very next sentence he states, 'But as Takuan explains, it ought not to be confused with the helpless passivity of an inorganic thing, such as a piece of rock or a block of wood.' (Suzuki 1993, 94) Obviously, Zen monk Takuan Soho (1573–1645) has a sharper view than Suzuki, who settles for the person in *mushin* being 'unconsciously conscious' or 'consciously unconscious' (Suzuki 1993, 94–95). A number of issues arise here.

First, this makes it quite patent that the swordsperson is not really an automaton, else she would hack at the opponent or any old tree trunk nearby. Takuan's keen analysis (discussed momentarily) is perceptive and fits better the facts. For him, it is not an automaton but rather a performer able to work and switch between such states fluidly. Ironically and interestingly, Suzuki keeps explaining the experts' performance by validating the role of the unconscious while denigrating that of conscious action, 'The man must turn himself into a puppet in the hands of the unconscious' (Ibid., 117; see also 110, 119, 127, 165, fn. 19, 191, 209 among others). Yet, he at times echoes *again* Takuan's analysis in the context of Buddhism's nirvana (Suzuki 1993, 140) or swordsmanship as a free and creative performance (Ibid., 142, fn. 3). In addition to the strain between the two levels and how they relate to each other, it is hard to see how something truly unconscious and not under our control can be said to be a matter of choice and freedom (it can be a matter of degree, but he does not consider this).

Second, Suzuki mentions how Takuan sees that *mushin* 'means the "everyday mind" (*heijo shin*), and when this is attained, everything goes well' (1993, 147). Suzuki explains that once technique is mastered, any kind of conscious dwelling will interfere. Ironically again, since he was close to Nishida in a scholarly and personal way (Yusa 2002), his analysis does not afford the possibility of a flexible bridge between or alternative to the two levels of awareness and action. Nishida's views on the relation between ordinary experience and acting intuition allow to explain more subtly and accurately the relation between the two levels and between everyday mind and superb performance while keeping that tension between the two alive. Nonetheless, Suzuki's translations and analyses of treatises on swordsmanship in relation to Japanese culture and Zen are still quite revealing in other respects. If anything, this stresses the difficulty of capturing just how *mushin* unfolds in exemplary and expert performance and what the relation between subpersonal and reflective processes is. This is made more patent when as careful and insightful a commentator of Nishida as Carter also mischaracterizes unfolding expertise in the moment.

Carter brings Nishida to bear on this when he discusses the Japanese philosopher's acting intuition. He writes about the master swordsman who anticipates the opponent's movements 'without calculation or analysis, and without a decision taken which is at all separate from the initial intuition. The surface consciousness is not engaged, nor are its tools of deliberation and calculation involved' (Carter 1997, 106).

HOLISM AND THE CULTIVATION OF EXCELLENCE IN SPORTS AND PERFORMANCE

Rightly, and echoing the critique advanced earlier against computational views of the mind and performance (essay 6), he adduces that, 'There simply would not be time, for what is required is instant recognition of the circumstances, and an intuitively instantaneous response (which, nonetheless, has been honed by years or even decades of preparatory practice' (Ibid.). Correctly also, he speaks of the long period of training and spontaneity. But, just in what sense said spontaneity is intuitive needs to be spelled out. Carter cites Nishida, for whom judgment and meaning are necessarily states of disunity, whereas in 'the state of pure experience, self and other, subject and object, true and false, meaning and the meaningless, "are mutually submerged, and the universe [as unity] is the only reality ..."' (1997, 5). In this case, we could argue that judgment and propositional meaning parenthetically bracket the bodymind as either (body)mind or body(mind). Yet, the pure state, as a contradictory unity, makes it possible to operate at both levels in a contentless state, as posited by radical enactivism. Nonetheless, Carter's analysis still emphasizes offline processes.

In a different work, Carter cites Masino in the context of the *dō* of Japanese garden design (日本庭園), 'In other words, when the mind, hands, body, time, and materials merge into one, then an unconscious mind, which goes beyond the bounds od consciousness, is responsible for creating things' (2008, 64). Carter then goes on to explain that a

> martial artist responds to any and all situations without thinking, a Nō actor becomes the character and the gestures depicted, the *sumi-e* [ink-wash painting] artist becomes one with the branch of the cherry tree which she is about to paint in a series of almost instantaneous strokes on rice paper which allows no hesitation or reconsideration; the tea master folds the ceremonial napkin *without thinking*, yet is *fully aware* [...] Virtuosity always appears effortless and graceful. (Ibid., 65, my emphases)

As with Bruya and Suzuki, Carter's account captures much of what goes on in superb performance. He also rightly clarifies that even if mastery appears spontaneous and effortless, 'it is achieved through great effort, constant practice, and the unrelenting courage to continue' (Carter 2008, 65). Nonetheless, the tension between the 'without thinking' and the 'fully aware' goes unnoticed. It is precisely in that tension that Nishida's ideas prove powerful and helpful shortly (as does an enactive account).

Effortless automatization, unconscious operation, the implicit system, offline processes, all work wonderfully well for many tasks and for *competent* performance. But, it is inherently contrary to a skillful striving that deliberately seeks continuous thriving and improvement in the most challenging circumstances. First, they do not account for outstanding performance, or rather they fall short of explaining how it works. Hence the difficulty all three have in working with the tension, whether aware of it as Bruya is, or not fully 'conscious' of it, pace Suzuki and Carter. Moreover, from a merely pragmatic stance, automatization is also counterproductive for superior performance. Anders Ericsson explains,

> Based on an earlier account [...] my proposal is that the development of typical novice performance is prematurely arrested in an effortless automated form; experts however, engage in an extended and continued refinement of mechanisms that mediate improvements in their performance [...] most amateurs do not improve their performance only because they have reached (in their minds) and acceptable level! (2003, 63)

HOLISM AND THE CULTIVATION OF EXCELLENCE IN SPORTS AND PERFORMANCE

Anders Ericsson mentions how this applies to some experts. This rightly emphasizes deliberate practice, which as presented in essay 8, is indeed a major component many researchers often ignore. On the other side, we must limit the scope of this deliberateness functionally, conceptually, and chronologically. Functionally, it need not be necessarily a representational affair (even if Anders Ericsson makes it so). We can deliberate kinetically, kinesthetically, and proprioceptively as we try to figure out whether sweeping with the sword overhead and downward has the right feel and meets the opponent's blade at the suitable angle. Conceptually, it helps to distinguish between being deliberate in our practice as being willful or mindful, and deliberating in the sense of calculating. The latter implicates a more theoretical and intellectualized approach that, again, may but need not be the case (see the closing comments on Dewey's alternative view of deliberation below). Lastly, deliberation and reflection take place during training for the most part, not during 'moments' of truth' and competition (in fast paced sports, or 'on' moments in more protracted sports). These previous deliberate reflections and training set up the spontaneity, often misconstrued as automatization.

Handling the tension between deliberation and automatization, and between representation and non-contentful cognition may be like playing with a two-edged sword and courting a bad cut on the unforgiving edge of contradiction between mutually exclusive phenomena. In Japanese, *ai uchi* (相打) refers to a mutual kill between two swordsmen. This is better than getting killed and having the opponent gloat over one's dead body, but hardly. The desirable outcome is an *ai nuke* (抜き), a mutual escape, where shared admiration over polished swordsmanship leads to a toast. An understanding of *mushin*, Nishida, and radical enactivism averts the deadly and contradictory outcome and splits matters right down the middle. A few historical remarks help contextualize the role that swordsmanship plays here.

Among *dō*, swordsmanship and Japanese medieval training manuals are particularly suited to show what *mushin* is and how it is related to cognition and skillful striving. Primarily because,

> it involves the problem of death in the most immediately threatening manner. If the man makes one false movement he is doomed forever, and he has no time for conceptualization or calculated acts. Everything he does must come right out of his inner mechanism, which is not under the control of consciousness. He must act instinctually and not intellectually. (Suzuki 1993, 182)

It is the lethality of the practice that makes it particularly relevant. With so much as stake, it is imperative to learn what to automatize, but also when to have ready and explicit access to specific and even basic skills if need be. And how to remain mindfully aware. Suzuki and most commentators commit the fallacy of the excluded middle, as it were. Not everything should be relegated to either instinctiveness or explicitness.

Nowadays, *kendo* has formalized and sublimated the mortal element, but the times when many of the authors and sensei to be enlisted next lived were fraught with deadly 'opportunities'. There was a common practice in medieval Japan called *musha-shugyō* (武者修行), a sort of wandering pilgrimage similar to feudal knight errantry that some samurai undertook as part of their education. In its most severe manifestation, it involved looking for the strongest swordsmen and challenging them to a duel that sometimes was deadly. This explains Musashi's 60 fights to the death. The point is that the insights discussed below were attained as part of a practice where death was indeed a likely possibility. Today we often speak of 'do or die' situations when feeling substantial pressure, as in closing a major business deal or putting a difficult golf shot on which the championship hinges (Beilock 2010), however, excepting risk sports, few activities carry a veritable deadly threat.[26]

What began as *kenjutsu* (剣術), deadly warrior techniques with the sword, during the Tokugawa era (1600–1868) gradually became the less lethal *kendō* (all other *jutsus*, each specific to a weapon, became *dō* as well). This period marks the unification of Japan after centuries of an internecine warfare that gave the samurai much opportunity to sharpen their skill in the kill. During the first few decades of this era, and with many samurai becoming *ronin* (浪人), masterless warriors (wave men, literally), there were occasions aplenty for duels either to test skills or impress potential employers, among other reasons. The frequency and bloodshed led to an eventual ban on duels by the *bakufu* (幕府) or shogunate government, but the initial decades impressed the need to develop techniques to survive. Here, Zen Buddhism with its emphasis on detachment from desires and life proved a boon. This began a slow process where concern with killing the opponent and outward focus turned into self-development and an inward awareness. That is, the deadly sword, through *shugyō*, became a way of the sword and life, a *dō*. This also changed the code of *bushidō* (of which there are many different versions) as a warrior's code into *budō*, a set of principles and attitudes within a framework of service and self-growth.

In the way of the sword, one of these principles is *ki ken tai no ichi* (気剣体の一), which can be translated as 'spirit, sword, and body as one.' *Ichi* in this context refers to 'one' in the sense of unity.[27] In concert with thick holism, the idea is that all these elements are in agreement and work seamlessly as one: the person's *ki* or vital energy, the living body, and the sword as a tool integrated into her schematizing and body-mind in what fencing masters refer to as '*le sentiment du fer*,' the feeling of steel where the fencer and sword become one much like Merleau-Ponty's (1962) blind man and his cane. Achieving this requires much practice and refined techniques. But even if necessary, they do not suffice. In accord with Suzuki, Abe points out that technique was not sufficient, that the swordsman 'had to overcome fear of death and delusion' (1986, 47). Once a sufficiently high level of expertise is achieved, emotional control in those 'do or die' situations is paramount. *Mushin* is the way to this unflappability.

After some prefatory comments, the discussion turns to spontaneity before returning to the aforementioned tension with Nishida.[28] There are two common misperceptions, held by lay people and academics alike, that it behooves us to correct. First, *mushin* is often equated with flow in sports. They share much functionally and experientially, but ultimately there are two important differences on account of the cultural framework: the experience is structured differently in some key aspects, and, unlike flow in sports, such state is explicitly cultivated whether it be in the context of Zen and *satori* or martial arts and *mushin* (Ilundáin-Agurruza and Hata 2015). Krein and Ilundáin-Agurruza write, 'Even if it were assumed that the two phenomena begin with the "same" raw sensations, when they are filtered through Japanese culture, and martial arts conducted under the aegis of a *dō,* the two will differ phenomenologically' (2014, 159). Further, given the different cultural context, the two will 'in the long run, acquire different qualitative properties' (Ibid., 160–161). This stated, because of the rich overlap and

HOLISM AND THE CULTIVATION OF EXCELLENCE IN SPORTS AND PERFORMANCE

to simplify matters, unless the context clearly applies to *mushin* alone both are discussed together. To avert any translation-prone misleading connotations, the Japanese term is used when it is specifically tied to Japanese writings or contexts. Otherwise, 'empty mindfulness' is the more neutral term employed to capture states of performative excellence by a holistic and enactive bodymind. The second confusion concerns its literal translation as 'no-mind'. Since it relies on spontaneity and results in superior performance generally, it is usually related to mindless coping states and automaticity, as just seen. The aims now are to dispel this and build a positive case that clarifies the tension without doing away with it. This is important, functionally, for successful *mushin* states, and theoretically for a better understanding of the phenomenon.

It helps to consider first what *mushin* (or flow) is not. It is anything but no-mindedness, automaticity, or mindless coping. The sort of performance that it produces requires a finely tuned and fluid responsiveness to a changing situation where much is on the line. For this reason, and as just seen above, those erroneous epithets are often mixed with attributions of being concentrated, paying attention, or staying focused. Leaving the unresolved tension aside, 'concentration' is not a good descriptive choice because this emphasizes effortful focus. *Mushin*'s operative awareness takes effort, obviously, but as seen with Bruya, whether as flow or *mushin*, it is felt as effortless. Second, *mushin* states are more economical and efficient on account of this lessened cognitive load. Third, and partially from the previous two points, it is more effective than concentration allows *ceteris paribus*, unless extraneous elements interfere, e.g. a mishap with equipment or similar unpredictable event (and even then, a performer in *mushin* will likely handle these better). As legendary samurai Yagyū Munenori (1571–1646), author of the *Heihō Kadensho* (兵法家伝書) says, 'Whatever you do, if you keep the idea of doing it before you do it with singleminded concentration you will be uncoordinated' (Yagyū 2005, 121). This reflection comes from the pen and sword of a man who singlehandedly killed six enemy samurai bent on killing his lord. 'Paying attention' is less contentious but not adequate. It overly narrows the attentional scope to a specific stimulus and is too static to account for the fluidity at play. 'Staying' or 'being focused' is the default go-to phrasing. Yet, 'focus' lacks clarity and relatedly is guilty by association, given its close conceptual bond with the former two notions, as their common interchangeableness in usage shows.

In their stead, 'mindful awareness' is the descriptor that best corresponds to the phenomenon. 'Mindful' brings with it the requisite sense of attentiveness without the literal hang-ups of the aforementioned terms. It also fits readily the notion of emptiness in a paradoxically suitable way, as the ongoing discussion shows. Further, it retains 'mind' in the phrasing. 'Awareness,' since it comes in degrees, from subpersonal to partial to acute, takes on naturally the requisite connotation of fluidity, and above all works as a capacity for performative perception. It also can be directed outward or inwardly. This results in the specialized spontaneity characteristic of *mushin*. Said spontaneity is characterized by a dynamic and active *engagement*. It is deliberate yet displays skillful fluency. It is a Zhuangzian spontaneity that results from a forgetting and fasting of the bodymind characterized by calmness, serenity, equanimity, and being absorbed, but mindfully so, even in the midst of turmoil, like the ferryman in the rapids (see essay 5). That essay also lays the first cornerstone of the conceptual explanation: the notion of emptiness. Verily, emptiness is full of possibility. It is in virtue of its very nothingness that a plenitude of performance is possible (which also relates to Nishida). It endows

HOLISM AND THE CULTIVATION OF EXCELLENCE IN SPORTS AND PERFORMANCE

mushin states with creativity as well: we can generate novel responses to best suit environmental constraints and to turn these into affordances and opportunities. This coheres with the holistic and enactive account here developed (see also essay 10 and the appendix). A slightly built *aikidoka* (合気道家) not only uses her agility but her opponents brawn and reliance on size and power to maneuver him effortlessly by redirecting the inertia of his movements; she empties herself of intent and works with the spaces around her to redirect him.

Performers in *mushin* are fully and smoothly engaged in the action and disengaged from themselves. They are skillfully fluid and fluent. Their bodymind is unstoppable, in the sense that it is immovable. This 'means unmoving,' Takuan Soho explains in his *Fudōchi Shinmyōroku* (不動智神妙録), a long and dense letter he penned for Munenori (Takuan 1986, 20). Cleary clarifies that here 'immovable' means 'imperturbable' (2005, 103).[29] Janelle and Hillman inform how studies report that, 'Elite athletes appear to be both capable of regulating reactions to anxiety-producing stimuli as well as perceiving potentially threatening situations as either positive or challenging' (2003, 37). The control of any distracting thoughts as well as emotions is paramount for elite performers, particularly those in contemporary risk sports or any who had to face a sword-wielding opponent. Munenori elucidates what it means practically for our bodymind to flow unperturbed, '…there will be actions in your arms, legs, and body but none in your mind […] and neither demons not heresies will be able to find it. Training is done for the purpose of reaching this state. With successful training, training falls away' (Yagyū 2003, 75). 'Training' here can also take the broader meaning of 'learning' in the context of *dō* and Zen if we take Cleary's translation (Cleary 2005, 24). Takuan (1986) also speaks of this fluidity as the no abiding mind, which is meant to 'abide where there is no abiding' as Suzuki puts it, reflecting a Zen paradox (Suzuki 1993, 172, fn. 25). Importantly, 'Fluidity and emptiness are convertible terms' as Suzuki states (1993, 158). Both swordsman or risk sportsperson are to cultivate a state of emptiness that avoids obstructing action. Now, how can we account for this emptiness conceptually in a satisfactory way?

Laozi's opening citation shows the Daoist roots that inform emptiness in East Asia, and which go deep into Buddhist and Hindu notions of Śūnyatā (Ilundáin-Agurruza and Hata (2015); the next essay and the appendix examine this further). Effectively then, *mushin* is a capacity. The underlying idea is that we are capable of emptying ourselves of the self, thoughts, desires, ambitions, fears, distractions, and, of course, in a suitably enactive fashion, any sort of 'mental chatter' that articulates thoughts propositionally. To bring this back to the concrete world of performance with Takuan,

> If we put this in terms of your martial art, the mind is not detained by the hand that brandishes the sword. Completely oblivious to the hand that wields the sword, one strikes and cut his opponent down. He does not put his mind in his adversary. The opponent is Emptiness. I am Emptiness. The hand that holds the sword, the sword itself, is Emptiness. Understand this, but *do not le your mind be taken by emptiness*. (1986, 37, my emphasis)

Analogously, in one of his later works Nishida writes, 'It is by truly emptying itself that the field of consciousness is able to reflect objects just as they are' (1987a, 656). We

HOLISM AND THE CULTIVATION OF EXCELLENCE IN SPORTS AND PERFORMANCE

can illuminate these remarks in connection with Nishida's mature views and radical enactivism.[30] Let us recall that contentless cognition does away with representations, posits basic minds, and thinks of these as capacities. This lack of content is conceptually congruent with an Asian notion of emptiness. Contrary to what the labeling of basic minds might suggest, this can be observed not just in simple actions, but also is characteristic of complex actions and particularly of the highest expression of skillful performance. Beyond representations, explicit rules, words, categorizations, and specified conditions of satisfaction, the subpersonal and the reflective, the explicit and implicit systems become one in action. We do not operate at a subpersonal level or with deliberate control and focus. Rather there is a seamless transition between the two in action that, without becoming a synthesis, keeps the dialectic fluid as the circumstances need. Therein lies the geniality of Nishida's and the Asian path. A synthesis that blended the two would result in a metaphysically distinct third element with neither empirical nor phenomenological basis. The dialectical tension means that both are separate yet united in the action; it does away with the distinction functionally while remaining ontologically parsimonious; expert performers move seamlessly between the two levels as they adapt to the situation and its outward and inward stimuli (James' fringe plays the role of this emptiness, a hinge that phenomenologically structures our experience and not a mechanism).

In less complex terms, because *mushin* and flow lack representational cognitive content—being capacities-in-the-happening—both sides of the equation are empty. In acting intuition, successful performers just act: the swordswoman becomes one with her sword, archer, bow, and shooting become integrated. They act spontaneously, engaged, fluid, and empty. It is the realization of capacities attuned to the moment, tools (if needed), and environment, and of the latter becoming integrated with the former. Skydivers, BASE jumpers with wing suits, hang gliders all work with the air, their suits or gliders, and the wind currents, and these also adapt, respectively, with surfaces and shapes offered to wind and performer to them. We find that the fluidity of boundaries and the switching between the implicit and explicit systems cancel each other out in the very acknowledgment of each other. If the Jamesian fringe of consciousness explains this process phenomenologically, and Billeter's view of Zhuangzian spontaneity as an ironic and removed regard does so perspectively, Nishida provides the conceptual underpinning.

It is worth citing the *Tengu's* words in Chozansi's work at length while commenting on them,

> Following the perceptions of the mind, the speed of practical application is like opening a door and the moonlight immediately shining in [...] Victory and defeat are the traces of practical application. But if you don't have *conceptualization*, form will not have aspect. Aspect is the shadow of concept, and is what manifests form. If there is no aspect to form, the opponent you are supposed to face will not exist. (2006, 118, my emphasis)

This lack of conceptualization and immediacy of reaction is readily incorporated into a radically enactive framework. It does away with concepts that manifest form and discriminations. The *Tengu* continues,

HOLISM AND THE CULTIVATION OF EXCELLENCE IN SPORTS AND PERFORMANCE

> This is what is meant when we say that neither my opponent nor I exist. If I exist, my opponent exists. Because I do not exist, even the insignificant thought of good or evil, perversion or properness, by the man coming at me will be reflected as in a mirror. And *this is not reflected from me*. It is simply that he arrives and moves on [...] If I tried to divert it from myself, *it would become a thought* [...]. (Chozan 2006, 118–119, my emphasis)

This illustrates the unity of contradictories just discussed, whether it be the opponent or the antagonism between implicit and explicit cognitive systems, or the subpersonal and reflective levels of awareness. The *Tengu* observes,

> The person who comes and goes like a god neither thinking not enacting the unfettered mysterious function—this is the swordsman who can be said to have attained enlightenment. (2006, 19)

Once the self (empirical and transcendental) is overcome as absolute nothingness, there is noself, only action and the unity of opposites. This selflessness, *muga* (無我), is crucial in Buddhist soteriology to overcome attachments to desire and life, and surmount the fear of death; it is crucial to performative activities in 'do or die' situations to conquer anxiety; it is crucial for cognition to be truly contentless. *Dō* are designed to instill the capacity to reliably operate so.

Zen monk Deshimaru Taishen, who also popularized Zen in the West, vacillates as he describes action in Japanese martial arts, but more pertinently,[31] engages contentless thinking,

> There is no choosing. It happens unconsciously, automatically, naturally. There can be no thought, because if there is a thought, there is a time of thought [when an instantaneous flash is needed] and that means a flaw. For the right moment to occur there must be a permanent, totally alert awareness of the entire situation. (1991, 32)

The context Deshimaru uses is that there must be a complete unity of mind, technique, and body—*shin*, *waza* (技), *tai*—clearly a holistic understanding. Indeed, spontaneous action predicated on deliberation, habit, and reflection underwrites this ability to work in the radically enactive space of contentless minds. Wertz, insightfully calls attention to Deshimaru's idea of *hishiryo* (非思量), non-thinking 'a state of thought beyond thought' (1991, 10), and which he relates to Heidegger's *Gelassenheit* as he explains that this refers to 'a state of meditative thought beyond calculative thought' (138; also 238 endnote 38). In Western terms, the better way to think about this thinking beyond thinking and calculation is in a holistically and radically enactive way.

Chozansi makes reference to a mirror and the moonlight shining above. Both tropes, the moon reflecting on water and the mirror have a long tradition in Asia, and Buddhism especially. They are popular images to capture what and how *mushin* is supposed to be like when confronting an antagonist (whether human, animal, or other, as when climbing mountain). Munenori (Yagyū 1986, 1993, 2003, 2005, 2008) expounds at length as he weaves Buddhist exegesis with technical advice to keep the bodymind fluid and avoid tarrying. The *Tengu* elucidates that the moon on water 'is a metaphor for when you can move and respond with spontaneity and No Mind' (Chozan 2006,

133). Both Munenori and Chozansi make it clear that it is a matter or instantaneous action that happens faster than a blink, something only a contentless cognitive system can produce. This instantaneity is built on patient work, however, as essay 10 explains.

Similarly, a mirror *itself* is contentless and reflects instantaneously—but in East Asia, it has a richer meaning. Oshima details the strength of the metaphor discussing what mirrors were like in Zhuangzi's time (fourth century BCE): they were made of bronze, and crucially, imbued with magical properties given that they could not only reflect, but also generate fire from the sun at certain times of the year, be like calm water (and thus like sages at rest), and also produce water through condensation on moon nights (1983, 74–79). Thus, the underlying sense is that mirrors are creative and productive, not merely passive reflectors; much like Nishida's acting intuition and contentless bodyminds in action. In a suitably Daoist fashion, the limitations of mirrors (contra Plato's misgivings) are turned into advantages.

Scottish trials cyclist Danny MacAskill embodies wonderfully expertise as a non-Asian mastery that fits the above performatively (phenomenologically, flow is a different matter as mentioned). In his latest 7-minute online film, *The Ridge,* he goes to the 'Isle of Skye in Scotland to take on a death-defying ride along the Cuillin Ridgeline' (Thomson and MacAskill 2014). As he rides up and down the ridge, at times on a sliver of ground barely a foot wide and sheer drops on either side, the ease and nonchalance is obvious, as is his patent mindful awareness. He creates movements and possibilities through his skills where no one else would find spaces. Emptiness, nothingness, and no-self are full of creative opportunity and displayed in all their glory in the film. For Suzuki, emptiness harbors 'infinite possibilities' (1993, 149). How to actually and effectively choose the right or better course of action can be a problem onto itself. Much as the rules in games and sports create possibilities, the constraint of practice is the door to freedom in performance.

The spontaneity of *mushin* is not a matter of unplanned movements and reactions either. It is the result of much practice and training, and deliberation. For Nishida acting intuition at its creative best is a deliberate and arduous process (even if the performance itself may seem effortless, this is built atop relentless discipline). He writes, making a point that easily extends to performative endeavors, 'Artistic intuition, for instance, though it appear simple and unreflective, is never without an element of reflection, and its obedience to [...] reflective self-development can involve a strenuous and painful effort' (1987b, 34). *Mushin* and flow are the result of Deweyan habit. Dewey's unorthodox views on deliberation shed further light (see essay 3). For him deliberation 'responds in action to the stimuli of the environment' (Dewey 1988, 139), and is a 'dramatic rehearsal (in imagination) of various competing possible lines of action' (Ibid., 132) that arises from an excess of preferences (Ibid., 134). Deliberation checks overt action and rehearses imaginatively the possibilities, until the right confluence, which he calls the 'object of thought' leads to the energetic release (Ibid.) Contrary to common assumptions, it is wonderfully efficient: 'Nothing is more extraordinary than the delicacy, promptness and ingenuity with which deliberation is capable of making eliminations and recombinations in projecting the course of a possible activity' (Ibid., 135). *This* kind of deliberation is a mark of consummate experts. They train for calamity; they carry out these imaginative deliberations continually, running scenarios of possible mishaps, possibilities, and 'unpredictables.'

HOLISM AND THE CULTIVATION OF EXCELLENCE IN SPORTS AND PERFORMANCE

Ski guide and author Allen O'Bannon once fell 300 feet while ice-climbing. Florence Williams describes this experience thus: 'Time slowed. An image came to his mind from a conversation he'd had with another ice climber who'd survived a fall […] O'Bannon pulled in his arms and legs until his rope finally arrested him […] Now 50 and a risk manager […] he tells his clients, mostly scientists, about the power of preparation' (2014, 84–85). O'Bannon explains that in a crisis while some panic and some stay cool, most people fall into what he terms 'the bewildered state' and pretty much do nothing. As for O'Bannon, Williams quotes,

> 'I push training in as many simulations as you can,' […] 'At what distance will you pull your bear spray' How will you react when you fall into a river? The idea is to know what failure is like. If you can't train, visualize. Then your response becomes automatic. (Ibid., 85)

Visualization is a technique that Tsunetomo already in the seventeenth century recommended, telling in gruesome detail to imagine all kinds of deaths to get used to the possibility of death (Yamamoto 1979). Much like O'Bannon, many mistakenly conceptualize their responses as automatic, intuitive, even unconscious processes. Yet they do remember in detail what they do, and their in-the-moment 'reactions' owe their effectiveness to Deweyan processes of habit and deliberation. These scenarios are not run as mere hypotheticals, but rather hinge on the present, for our 'judgment of future joys and sorrows is but a projection of what *now* satisfies and annoys' us (Dewey 1988, 142, my emphasis). As Dewey explains,

> The moral is to develop conscientiousness, ability to judge the significance of what we are doing and to use that judgment in directing what we do not by means of direct cultivation of something called conscience or reason, or a faculty of moral knowledge, but by fostering those impulses and habits which experience has shown to make us sensitive, generous, imaginative, impartial in perceiving the tendency of our inchoate dawning activities. Therefore the important thing is the fostering of those habits and impulses which lead to a broad, just, sympathetic survey of situations. (1988, 144)

The opening poem to this essay about *kendō* speaks to this: 'Not think:/Before and after,/In front, behind;/Only freedom/At the middle point.' Freedom lies at the middle point between past and future, in the here and now. Our present interests then modulate our choices. This lays down habits, which furnish the necessity of forward action in one case as instinct does in the other. Carter explains how practice and spontaneity come together in *dō*, as these are ways 'towards spontaneity via disciplined cultivation' (2008, 107). These are the source of Deweyan habits. Again, freedom is found within constraints, like Kant's dove needs the air's resistance to fly.

The end result of *mushin* is utterly philosophical (and congruent with the lessons that failure affords us, as seen in the earlier essay). The *Tengu* concludes at the end, 'In both learning and swordsmanship, just consider it to be your main business to know yourselves' (Chozan 2006, 170). At heart, *mushin* involves a process of self-knowledge that seeks to transcend itself immanently (contrary to sport experts and flow, it explicitly seeks this). Sword master Hori Kintayu says to his pupil Kimura Kyuho, as per the latter's account, that whether one succeeds technically is not important, 'the main business is to seek it [deeper understanding] not in things external but within oneself' (Suzuki 1993, 135). Two final ideas: first, it needs to be stressed that this is not a matter of purely intellectual insight, propositional knowledge, or rational process, but that it is a gnostic truth that is lived and cultivated through the bodymind in action; second, and foreshadowing a theme the last essay delves into, *mushin* is an existential pedagogy. *Mushin* is not only about superb performance primarily or about self-enlightenment, but about transmission to others.

To close now on a redemptive note for Henry Skrimshander's comeback to baseball (readers interested in reading the novel should skip the rest of this paragraph). Emptiness is much at the core of his return from that catastrophic slump that ends his baseball career and wrecks his life. One morning we find him returning to the diamond—just to throw some balls. Then, we read how he 'spun his hips and whipped his arm, feeling nothing, less than nothing, no sense of foreboding and anticipation, no liveliness, no weight, no itch or sentience in his fingertips, no fear, no hope. The ball bore through the morning mist on what seemed like a true path' (Harbach 2011, 512). When Henry allows this nothingness to fill him, he is back where he started. Only all the wiser, much as mountains are mountains, the ball is the ball (see essay 8, fn. 4). Once again.

5. East & West—Martial Arts and Sports Face-off

Aparicio's fictional book 'The Art of Fielding' within Harbach's eponymous novel deftly combines Western mores with Eastern lore. But, off the pages of fiction, how do both 'worlds' relate, specifically, within the scope of sport and performative practices? There are a few studies of such comparative nature in the philosophy of sport. Some evaluate philosophically martial arts on their own (Abe 1986; Bäck and Kim 1979; Becker 1982; Oda and Kondo 2014), others compare them in relation to sport (Wertz 1977), art and dance (Allen 2013), virtue (Reid 2010), Nietzschean self-overcoming (Monahan 2007), enlightenment (Bäck and Kim 1979),[32] or provide an eclectic collection of essays (Priest and Young 2014). Rather than a detailed commentary and re-exposition of what others have covered, punctual comments engage pertinent ideas in line with *skillful striving* (taken now as both process of self-cultivation and this project itself). That is, skills and abilities are the prism to look at these sources.

Having said that, it is worth beginning with commentary on a seminal piece. Spencer Wertz was one of the first sport philosophers to conduct comparative analyses of sport and Asian practices (1977, 1984).[33] Contrary to Becker's (1982) dismissal of these as strewn with cute Zen-like phrases, they are perceptive examinations. Wertz (1991) provides two main lines of inquiry. One considers the way Western sport shares in *mushin*-like states, what today we refer to as flow. He explores this in the world of tennis through the work of Tim Gallwey. The other considers Zen monk Deshimaru's (1991) book on Zen and martial arts, where Deshimaru draws a sharp contrast between both practices. He uses the former to establish some putative cases of excellent performance in *mushin*-like states that may match those of Eastern masters. This is not contested nowadays, but was doubted then (we should also keep in mind the differences). He looks at such cases in order to dispute some of Deshimaru's claims and find genuine

HOLISM AND THE CULTIVATION OF EXCELLENCE IN SPORTS AND PERFORMANCE

affinities between Western sports and Eastern martial arts, Zen, and Yoga. Of note is that Deshimaru's stance on sport 'reflects the concept of *recreation*' (Wertz 1991, 131, his emphasis).

This last point should encourage us to keep in mind the diversity of sports and martial arts vertically and horizontally, that is, their historical and geographical extensive manifestations. Both have evolved in very complex ways, sometimes interrelated over time in numerous places. Insights applicable to some sports and martial arts may not be appropriate to others. Just as we find competitive, recreational, and risk sports for instance, each with specific manifestations, in East Asia *alone,* there are a number of classifications. We have already mentioned *koryū,* traditional martial arts as *jutsus* or warfare techniques; and while they directly precede *dō,* they are quite different.[34] We find also *kakutogi* (格闘技), sportified martial arts, for example, karate (空手), *tae-kwon-do* (태권도), or *kungfu* (功夫, *gongfu* in pinyin). And today there are the popular *sogo kakutogi* (総合格闘技), mixed martial arts. In the ensuing, and for reasons of practicality, the rubric of traditional martial arts covers both *Koryū* and *budō.*

Wertz also points out how many of Deshimaru's claims regarding sporting short-comings vis à vis martial arts are true of 'the experience of sport for *average* athletes' (1991, 140, his emphasis). This is consistent with the study of the normal as average in the West generally, as mentioned above with Yuasa. But when we consider the exceptional, there are significant differences. Sometimes these are positive, as much of the foregoing evinces. Sometimes these are negative. Next, we consider some differences. How they could benefit from each other, and other salient themes—for instance, the means and end (process and results) entente, or competition—have their philosophical denouement in the last essay.[35]

A number of studies have remarked on some unique differences between the martial and sportive worlds. As we saw Allen writes of the different kind of aesthetic value and beauty that martial arts manifest, as it happens only when the movements are effective and intentional in actual engagement (2013). Oda and Kondo's (2014) study of *kendō* highlights the role that *zanshin* (残心), a relaxed awareness that maintains intent and alert posture after a successful strike, plays. It is a unique aesthetic judgment on two counts that sets it apart from other aesthetic sports as per Best's (1979) distinction between purposive and aesthetic ones: the judgment takes into account the intention of the performer, and how this needs to determine 'a subjective, internal state by appealing to intersubjective criteria: the observation of the kendo-ka's actions' (Oda and Kondo 2014, 13). A more contested difference considers the moral tendencies of both practices.

For Bäck (2009), martial arts are sources of good moral character while sports stand out for their vice-inducing tendencies. He argues that we are better off taking up martial arts rather than sports, and giving up competition (the last essay forwards an alternative model of competition immune to his critique). Nonetheless, he takes a rather monolithic view of sport, lumping all of them and their different categorizations together. McNamee (2008) has challenged the reliability of his sources (see also Reid 2012). Nonetheless, some of Bäck's points are applicable to the subset of competitive and elite sports. Morgan's (2006) extensive and deep analysis of American sports shows the complex ways in which institutionalized and corporate interests, and free market values can 'encourage' misbehavior.[36] Let us suppose for argument's sake that virtues in sport do exist, but they do not transfer as readily to other areas in comparison to

267

HOLISM AND THE CULTIVATION OF EXCELLENCE IN SPORTS AND PERFORMANCE

martial arts. How do we account for this? This issues from crucial methodological differences. Succinctly, the martial sphere explicitly sets out to cultivate character, unlike the sportive one.

There is no overarching philosophical and spiritual framework that enfolds the training in sports. As Carter states, 'There is nothing like this understanding in the West, which does not employ its arts and crafts, or its sports, to teach the deepest religious and ethical thoughts of its culture' (2008, 3). Sports may inculcate sportsmanship, he continues, but only in Japan is this overtly about self-transformation (Ibid., 4). Takuan specifically unites the two: 'Technique and principle are like the two wheels of a cart' (1986, 4), where principle is the underlying philosophic and religious framework that frees one from attachments and effortful focus. If Takuan writes about it, Munenori embodies this. He was a consummate swordsman yet reflective and cultured, and his treatise magisterially combines Buddhist phenomenological insight and practical know-how in contrast to Takuan's strictly philosophical writings and Musashi's more prosaic, tactical, and practical *Book of Five Rings*.

In the West, we find psychological procedures meant to help athletes either improve attitude and focus or mitigate specific stressors or neuroses with the narrow goal of performance; it is not about self-realization. Japanese (and Asian) ways opt for indirect ways to induce and cultivate existential realizations (still connected to the practice at hand). As Takuan writes with regard to the acquisition of existential insights 'there is no transmitting it by words or speech, no learning it by any doctrine' (1986, 89). Thus, the role of hard work is to teach the lessons to facilitate a gnostic realization. Moreover, *outstanding* martial (or sporting) performances and actions cannot be 'taught' propositionally, as mentioned earlier. They are not reducible to rules. Says Takuan, 'There is no established rule for manifesting this ability' (1986, 91).[37] Through all this, these masters remain reflectively aware that any given *dō* is nothing more than that, and that a full skillful striving is much broader and deeper. This applies well beyond martial arts or Zen. As Herrigel puts it, 'What is true of archery and swordsmanship is true of all the other arts' (1999, 77). Lest we get carried away, Chozansi has a sobering rejoinder, 'Though one art may seem trivial, one should not take it lightly. But again, do not make the mistake of considering that art to be the Way' (Chozan 2006, 93).

Finally, Yuasa specifies, 'the standpoint of praxis has been regarded as more important than that of theoria (1993, 35), explaining how sports begin from the mind while the martial arts start with the body (Ibid., 30). It is telling that Sekida states, 'only after we have dealt with the practical aspects of Zen training [...] do we go on to consider its theoretical and philosophical aspects' (1985, 37). In other words, martial arts integrate mindfully technical and philosophical facets with the actual pragmatics of the practice at hand. This is exemplified most dramatically in how this process extends to the very tools they rely upon. Chozansi asserts, 'The highest principles are contained within the techniques and follow the self-nature of the utensil' (2006, 96). Athletes, of course, achieve an equivalent mastery and identification with their tools, yet, there is a difference akin to that between *mushin* and flow. The saying goes, 'the sword is the soul of the samurai.' In Japan, the tool becomes integrated as part of the holistic bodymind as a performative element but is also imbued with deep spiritual meaning.

If martial arts may look as polished as the blade of a katana, closer inspection shows some imperfections. Some are easily buffed away. As already mentioned, their esotericism makes them overly cryptic quite often. But suitable translation and

HOLISM AND THE CULTIVATION OF EXCELLENCE IN SPORTS AND PERFORMANCE

contextualization can handle this. Martial arts are also often associated with the supernatural, with common attribution of superpowers to some practitioners. This is but a *peccadillo*, as already addressed. Moreover, Dohrenwend clarifies, these exaggerated legends that attribute extraordinary and often supernatural skills to legendary masters are stories 'traditionally used for entertainment purposes in China, and Chinese acrobats are trained specifically for their representation' (2012, 10). Those familiar with the tradition will take them as such. This is an issue only when dealing with the gullible or gross mischaracterization by frauds. Bäck and Kim (1979), among others, satisfactorily address objections regarding the incongruence between the violent origins and techniques of martial arts and the view that they develop character and promote non-violence. But some blemishes may indicate a corrosion that needs a more thorough polishing.

Bäck's extols how martial arts face real danger, and thus virtues learned through them are extensible to our complete lives (2009). He writes,

> Again, a martial art is not play, despite its training conventions. Nor is it merely dance, despite its emphasis on formal patterns. Its danger and its preoccupation with handling violence and aggression give it a realism lacking in play or art. If you are wounded in a war dance, you are not really hurt; excelling in a war dance does not make you a warrior. Here a martial art has some common ground with dangerous sports: fostering virtues of perseverance and courage, but perhaps without the drawbacks. (Bäck 2009, 230)

Their virtues can extend across a whole life and permeate character—they go beyond the *dōjō*'s walls—but for reasons that have little to do with *real* danger (or at least not *necessarily* so, unlike risk sports). Martial arts nowadays are not dangerous in the ways that saw Suzuki write about swordsmanship and the problem of death. To validate his point, Bäck speaks of soldiers' use of martial arts in combat. But, that is an *application* of martial arts in combat by *soldiers* (who may train in martial arts as they train in CPR). It is not different from how running is also useful for soldiers, or swimming for Navy Seals. We would not think running itself as dangerous because soldiers in combat run. Today few, if any, martial artists emulate kung-fu master Shi Dejian's exercises on cliff tops (essay 5). Thankfully, *budō* prevailed, and today casualties are the rarest occurrence in the *dōjō* when considering fully fledged martial arts practices. To compare, between 1998 and 2007 there have been 2 deaths in mixed martial arts and 70 in boxing (Impact MMA 2011). In fact, in boxing there have been 339 deaths from head injuries between 1950 and 2007 (Baird et al. 2010). In mountaineering, arguably the most dangerous sport in terms of fatalities, deaths are counted by the hundreds (or thousands over the years): just in Mount Everest alone over 200 people have died since 1922 (Adventure Stats 2015). Granted these compare different timescales and variables, but they do give a fair estimate of the respective relative danger.[38]

Why martial arts virtues extend to our complete lives has to do more with their underlying framework of explicit character development as *shugyō* than with danger, be it real or not. The true heirs to the martial spirit are actually the very dangerous sports he associates with the ills of sports in general. Molinuevo explained, in the fourth essay, how for Ortega the 'sportsman is the heir of the warrior who has disappeared' (1995: 26, my trans.). Risk sports and activities may not be the historical heirs to martial sobriety in the face of death, but are closer as existential and performative inheritors.

HOLISM AND THE CULTIVATION OF EXCELLENCE IN SPORTS AND PERFORMANCE

They must perform in situations analogous to those that gave rise to the keen insights that swordsmanship afforded *mushin*. Accomplished martial artists and adventurous sportspeople evince comparable bodymind integration in the face of danger. That said, what kind of insights they draw are likely to differ, not because sports are 'vicious' and martial arts are virtuous, as Bäck suggests, but because sports do not inculcate explicitly reflection on their experience—nor do they preclude it either.

Bäck rightly states that, 'there are other options, other ways to acquire those same virtues [e.g., self-affirmation]' namely, 'training in the martial arts' (224). Interestingly, he then ties martial arts to danger. Given the tenuous connection to veritable danger, this undercuts the connection between martial arts and virtue. Bäck also wonders about what values dangerous sport may provide (2009, 234, fn.6). In addition to Russell's (2005) value of self-affirmation, here are a number of possibilities: (1) they can encourage an ethos of authenticity when encountering nature (Anderson 2001); (2) truly facing the possibility of death can lead to an appreciation of the sublime itself as part of a performative process where the very structure of the sublime is paralleled by our bodymind dynamics (Ilundáin-Agurruza 2007); (3) they make possible a particular kind of self-knowledge of one's self in nature and remote places (Howe 2008); 4) they provide meaning-conferring encounters with death or meaning-depriving meetings with our finitude, and can be transformative in a Nietzschean way while embracing an Orteguian aesthetic sense of life (Ilundáin-Agurruza 2008); (5) in addition to self-affirming values, there are self-negating ones (Sailors 2010); and (6) they can also be the source of gnostic truths and alternative values such as self-abnegation or uniquely sporting ones like the cultivation of 'style' (Ilundáin-Agurruza forthcoming-b).

Bäck builds on Russell's (2005) admission that his views are more prescriptive than descriptive in so far as self-affirmation is embodied by the best exemplars, and points out that for Russell, 'winning the competition, the contest, seems to have dropped out. He seeks to return to the Victorian conception of sport—or perhaps to transform a dangerous sport into something like a martial art' (2009, 224). Bäck advice is to do away with competition, as mentioned. Recent developments in the martial word, however, cast doubt on their ability to advance moral character and seem to bring martial arts closer to the prescriptive sphere. Malizszewski explains on developing trends he has observed over the last twenty years since he began writing on martial arts: 'there has been a decline in the depth that has characterized the more traditional systems' (2010, 18). He continues, 'The spiritual or meditative focus is more "generic" in the sense that any loose association with the ethereal is deemed spiritual or metaphysical' (Ibid.). The core of what sets them apart has eroded.

In a related manner, whenever there is a lack of *veritable* competition (versus staged) in the *dōjō*, this impoverishes the martial arts. Or, at least, it limits their ability to cultivate values that can be found best or only through these modes. They lose their backbone for self-knowledge as an epistemic virtue, on which other virtues may build, e.g. this happens whenever that deference for the *sensei,* due to rank and respect (or intimidation), reflects less than the performers' actual abilities (whether deliberate or unintended). Many a 'contest' between *sensei* and students has the former reign supreme. Surely, the context is often one of training or demonstrations; but the fact is that students often hold themselves back (even if inadvertently). Outside of athletic-like competition as one where our capacities are tested to the maximum (which Bäck rules

HOLISM AND THE CULTIVATION OF EXCELLENCE IN SPORTS AND PERFORMANCE

out), we cannot determine the *actual* abilities of the performer under pressure. Numerous online videos show matches where the *sensei*, usually older, even venerable, throws around much stronger, faster, and younger opponents (of advanced rank), who patiently wait their cue to attack; we see how the *sensei*'s *bokken* finds the mark every time while the challenger's always slices well outside of the line of cut. Actually, there is a sense of competition, as taking the risk to find out our actual ability, that Bäck does not consider. This would redeem martial arts to some extent. *Kyudō*, a very safe martial art (short of standing on the wrong end of the *dōjō* when shooting is taking place), is a truer martial art in this respect. Onuma Hideharu sensei says, 'The bow never lies. It is honest and unbiased, an excellent teacher of truth' (1993, 4).

It is true that we are more likely to find moral exemplars in *traditional* martial arts, *koryū*, than in sports and 'sportified' martial arts, *kakutogi*. But, if sports could do with more explicit (self)reflection and educational aims, *traditional* martial arts could bring more contest-like intensity.

Finally, sports and martial arts are both found wanting in one aspect. To put it bluntly, some striking martial abilities and astonishing athletic skills, and their accompanying theoretical and philosophical inclinations, are not the fruit of intellectually admirable qualities. Suzuki explains how Zen's directness, simplicity, practicality, disregard for strict and explicit moral training, and applicability to handle death (foremost for warriors) was 'a natural fit for the comparatively *unsophisticated mind* of the samurai' (1993, 61–63; 72, my emphasis).

Competitive athletes and zealous sportspeople share much in common with samurai in this regard. Many of them (misguidedly as seen above) think they react automatically, instinctively, and underplay the role of deliberation and spontaneity (shortchanging themselves in the process). The very internal goods and ways of achieving them necessitate this lack of reflectivity sometimes: the practical problems that samurai faced, namely the problem of death (Suzuki 1993, 124), and that sportspeople engage require immediate, unreflective action. Then the need for quick and unreflective action may become impulsive. This is not *necessarily* negative. Turning a weakness into a strength, we can say that there is a virtue in this. As Suzuki puts it, scoring one against those academics who like to pontificate from their chairs,

> One great advantage the sword has over the mere book-reading is that once you make a false move, you are sure to give the opponent a chance to beat you. You have to be on the alert all the time [which] keeps you true to yourself: that is to say, you are not allowed to indulge in idle thinking. (1993, 132–133)

And what goes for the swordsman goes for the superb sportsperson or performer. There are times when rational, calculating, representational thinking gets in the way, as the discussion on *mushin* shows. Instead, those moments on the edge call for spontaneous and radically enactive action. This does not mean that there is no room for deliberation before or after—and this is where those walking a *dō* differ from many athletes and risk sportspersons. The mutually lifesaving *ai nuke* takes place in the next essay. There East and West collaborate within the context of social practices where holistic and enactive ways are taught and flourish.

HOLISM AND THE CULTIVATION OF EXCELLENCE IN SPORTS AND PERFORMANCE

DISCLOSURE STATEMENT

No potential conflict of interest was reported by the author.

NOTES

1. Shigematsu (1981, 23).
2. Laozi (1996, chapter 11, 32).
3. Deshimaru (1991, 78).
4. Of course, as happens with generalizations, this is easily falsified, we need only think of Shikibu Murasaki's *Tale of Genji* (源氏物語 *Genji monogatari*), touted as the world's first novel. There are, however, recognizable patterns that sustain these generalizations.
5. See Perrin's (1979) *Giving Up the Gun* for an account of the Japanese reversal from the gun to the sword. Japan is the only culture that has deliberately given up technologically advantageous warfare technology, and this due to a number of normative factors that included aesthetic, martial, and ethical considerations. See the next essay for further elaboration in the context of situatedness.
6. I am very grateful to Fukasawa Koyo for his explanations regarding this complex terminology and his patient consideration of all my questions.
7. Following Japanese custom, family name is given first; with some historical figures first name is used afterward.
8. Yuasa has developed the most sophisticated analysis of *shintai*, in recent Japanese thought. Nagatomo Shigenori's *Attunement Through the Body* (1992) gives a clear and thorough account of Yuasa's views. Nagatomo's own views are expressed in this book as well. Space limitations preclude integrating his otherwise original and insightful ideas.
9. Context helps determine the sense in which to read different kanji with the same pronunciation, as here with *shinshin*; alternatively we can have the same kanji but different words and concepts, as with *shin* 身 and *mi* 身.
10. I happily learned about this coincidence with the much more elegant Japanese changeable emphasis once I had adopted the bracketing convention for bodymind. I am thankful to Aramaki Ai for pointing this out, as well as for her help with ensuring the correctness of the kanji concerning the bodymind terms.
11. Interestingly, in consideration of the role that swordsmanship plays below, *Mi*, in addition to the body as one's self and station or condition of life, also takes the meaning of the edge of a sword blade (Hepburn 1873, 164). *Mi bun* refers to social position in the sense of rank or condition (Ibid.).
12. He directly influenced Foucault's ideas on the care of the self (1988) and power (1979, 1980) and Bordieu's on the *habitus* (1984). See Ilundáin-Agurruza 2008 for an analysis of the Athletic body and the bodies of athletes in terms of aesthetics and power relations.
13. To further contrast, West and East consider the issue of the mind/body relationship as it relates to free will. The Occidental view of this relationship places it on the empirical level, neuroscience probes the brain for clues to our mental life, and free will is seen as either being present or not: your choice to read these words right now is conceptualized in terms of whether free will is operative depending on whether causality is binding at *all* levels. The Japanese stance finds a correlative interaction between mind and body that implies there are degrees of freedom, whether you are more or less compelled to read this hangs on a number of factors, foremost among these being whether

you have good or better reasons to justify it (this essay being *really* interesting being a very good and self-serving one for both of us). See Nishida (1990) for a contemporary elucidation of this.

14. Yuasa (1987) expounds on their views in chapters six and seven. See also the last essay and the appendix for further analysis of fasting of the self.

15. These concepts are deeply intertwined with Chinese practices, and these in turn derive from Indian Hindu and Buddhist ones. This is too complex to discuss presently. See Ilundáin-Agurruza and Hata (2015) for a discussion of related issues in the context of Eastern and sport philosophies.

16. Some claims of 'superhuman' strength or ability, such as the 'unraisable body,' where three people cannot lift the *sensei*, can be explained through physics. What may seem mysterious is simply good technique aligned with the forces of physics. See Daniel (2004).

17. 'Swordmanship' covers both genders presently. Unlike other adaptations such as 'sportspersonship,' the epithet 'swordspersonship' proves too cumbersome even for the most open ears.

18. In Japan, each different part of the sword is crafted by a different person, with a sword-smith forging the blade, the polisher sharpening and giving it the mirror finish, another person making the *saya* (鞘) scabbard out of wood, etc. Yoshihara was a maverick that mastered all the arts and could make a complete sword. Michael Bell is another con-summate artist who also makes the whole katana, from blade to accouterments such as the *koshirae* 拵え. I have been fortunate to forge two blades with him and learn much about the making of katana and its rich tradition. For samples of his splendid work, see http://dragonflyforge.com/photo-galleries/katana-photo-gallery/.

19. This has been attributed to a number of people, such as Benjamin Franklin, George Bernard Shaw, and others. Apparently, the original source is Karl Groos. http://en.wik iquote.org/wiki/Growing_old (accessed October 12, 2014).

20. *Tengu* were mythical creatures, half-human half-bird that inhabited the forests and came in different degrees of mischievousness, from the prankster to the dangerous. They were famous and feared for their martial skills.

21. Courage is here seen as a central virtue that permeates our whole character, with brav-ery in the physically active portion being instrumental to it (I follow McNamee [2008] in this).

22. This distinction is relevant for the discussion of the articulation of experience in essay 10.

23. From early on, Nishida emphasizes religion, among many reasons, because it is a phe-nomenon familiar to all (1987a). But his views apply deeply across the board. His coinages are difficult to translate, and there are various versions for many of them. Pre-sently, I choose those that best fit the underlying argumentative tenor of this project or that are clearest for the concept at hand. When citing, the translator's choice is used.

24. See Ilundáin-Agurruza, Fukasawa, and Takemura (2014) for a discussion of Nishida and sport philosophy.

25. Becker has a fairly critical view of Suzuki on account of historical inaccuracies and for muddling terminology (1982, 24 & 28 fn. 6). This is true to some extent. But Becker's (at times caustic) demeanor is prone to throw the baby with the bathwater. Outright dis-missal is not advisable either; there are insights to be gleaned from a cross-sectional analysis of his words with those of other writers as well as conceptual analysis, as done presently.

HOLISM AND THE CULTIVATION OF EXCELLENCE IN SPORTS AND PERFORMANCE

26. See Ilundáin-Agurruza (forthcoming-a) for an analysis of risk activities in terms of self-knowledge in an East–West comparative framework.

27. Shrewdly, Mike McNamee remarks how, after all the subtle conceptual distinctions, this is the same word as when counting the numerical; rather than a different or specific 'one' attuned to organic complexity.

28. For more in-depth discussions of *mushin* in relation to flow, see Krein and Ilundáin-Agurruza (2014); in connection with Eastern philosophy generally, see Ilundáin-Agurruza and Hata (2015); and in relation to choking in sports, see Ilundáin-Agurruza (forthcoming-a).

29. This is a short but complex text of notoriously difficult translation. See Takuan (1985, 1986, 2005). Sato's translation (Takuan 1985) has a commentated translation; Cleary's (2005) translation is also annotated. Much the same applies to Yagyū Munenori's treatise, of which the following are recommended (1986, 1993, 2003, 2005, 2008). Suzuki (1993) translates most of Takuan's work and paraphrases many of Munenori's key ideas. Similarly, for Musashi's book recommended translations are 1993 and 2004, and Tokitsu's 2011 translation.

30. Asian thought and praxes have broad theoretical affinities with a radically enactive view of cognition as contentless that stays close to our experiential dynamics. It has traditionally been suspicious of language as an adequate method toward the truths of experience. This does not mean that we should do away with attempts to articulate experience, as essay 10 discusses. Also, we need to distinguish between an account of these experiences and of highly refined skills themselves in terms of nonrepresentational capacities, and the very articulation of this, which, of course, is propositional.

31. The underlying assumption is that non-thinking or lack of content needs to be subpersonal, unconscious, and automatic. This is that false dichotomy again. Unsurprisingly, and like Suzuki, he says in the very next page that, 'Only consciousness can seize upon the opportunity for action, the empty space in which one must act' (Ibid., 33). Deshimaru also makes the erroneous claim that martial arts happen in a flash while in sports there is a moment of doubt (Ibid.). Wertz corrects this (1991, 132).

32. They consider how engaging in martial arts promotes moral character, no-violence, and leads to enlightenment. They associate the latter to *Samādhi* and *satori*, which they relate, problematically, to the analytic clarity of the Cartesian methodology (1979 27–28), since the overly rational process they describe leaves the bodymind behind.

33. In his 1991 book, he incorporates expanded versions of both.

34. See Tamaki's (2010) interview of Kono Yoshinori for his interesting and iconoclastic reflections on this.

35. For an alternative comparative consideration of sport and martial arts, see Ilundáin-Agurruza and Hata (2015). To summarize briefly some of the more pertinent differences *not* mentioned presently: the West emphasizes physiological quantitative approaches and psychological techniques inclusive of neuroimaging, and there is a preponderance of explicit instruction. It also stresses training (*keikō*), and flow states are ancillary and secondary to results in competition (or health is chief for many non-competitive sportspeople). Emotional control and temperance are secondary to performance as outbursts by amateurs and professionals alike show; sometimes these are means toward victory, i.e. consider trash talking and verbal intimidation. On the other side, Asian *traditional* ways center on *shugyō*, see results as less important than the process, and bodymind integration prevails. Additionally, spiritual meaning and emotional control are crucial for the martial arts, see Yuasa (1993).

HOLISM AND THE CULTIVATION OF EXCELLENCE IN SPORTS AND PERFORMANCE

36. The recent 2011 scandal in sumo wrestling is an exception that also validates Morgan's analysis in the Japanese scene, since finances were central. Interestingly, yet unsurprisingly, given the Confucian communitarian values in Japan, it also differed radically from the more individualistic Western model in that many of the fixed matches were arranged to help opponents either move up or not lose their standing or job. In a way, this also then stands in contrast to Western prevalent mores and may signal how Western sporting, individualizing, and free market values may be a pernicious influence as Morgan contends.

37. Incidentally, this can be fruitfully contrasted with Kant's ideas on genius.

38. We could compare martial arts to other sports in terms of number of injuries and their seriousness. Martial arts are on the whole safer and less injury prone than other sports. In mixed martial arts, 'The injury rate in MMA competitions is compatible with other combat sports involving striking. The lower knockout rates in MMA compared to boxing may help prevent brain injury in MMA events' (Bledsoe et al. 2006). This can easily be extrapolated to other combat forms in martial arts. There are always risks associated with injuries from sprains or misdirected hits, but this is not the kind of danger Bäck is considering, as his target are dangerous sports.

REFERENCES

ABE, S. 1986. Zen and sport. *Journal of the Philosophy of Sport* 13 (1): 45–8.

———. 1987. Modern sports and the eastern tradition of physical culture: Emphasizing Nishida's theory of the body. *Journal of the Philosophy of Sport* 14 (1): 44–7.

ADVENTURESTATS. 2015. Available at http://www.adventurestats.com/tables/everestfatilities.shtml (accessed 22 February 2015).

ALLEN, B. 2013. Games of sport, works of art, and the striking beauty of Asian martial arts. *Journal of the Philosophy of Sport* 40 (2): 241–54.

AMES, R. 1993. The meaning of the body in classical Chinese philosophy. In *Self as body in Asian theory and practice*, edited by T. Kasulis, E. Deutsch, and W. Dissanayake. Albany, NY: State University of New York Press: 153–74.

ANDERSON, D. 2001. Recovering humanity: Movement, sport, and nature. *Journal of the Philosophy of Sport* 28: 140–50.

BÄCK, A. 2009. The way to virtue in sport. *Journal of the Philosophy of Sport* 36 (2): 217–37.

BÄCK, A. and D. KIM. 1979. Towards a western philosophy of the eastern martial arts. *Journal of the Philosophy of Sport* 6 (1): 19–28.

BAIRD, L.C., C.B. NEWMAN, H. VOLK, J.R. SVINTH, J. CONKLIN, and M.L. LEVY. 2010. Mortality resulting from head injury in professional boxing. *Neurosurgery* 67 (5): 1444–50.

BECKER, C.B. 1982. Philosophical perspective on the martial arts in America. *Journal of the Philosophy of Sport* 9 (1): 19–29.

BEILOCK, S.L. 2010. *Choke: What the secrets of the brain reveal about getting it right when you have to.* Edinburgh: Constable & Robinson.

BELL, M. 2012. Personal conversations on sword making, Bushidō, and Zen, April 2011, May 2012.

BEST, D. 1979. *Philosophy and human movement.* London: George Allen & Unwin.

BLEDSOE, G.H., E.B. HSU, J.B. GRABOWSKI, J.D. BRILL, and G. LI. 2006. Incidence of injury in professional mixed martial arts competitions. *Journal of Sports Science Medicine* 5: 136–42.

HOLISM AND THE CULTIVATION OF EXCELLENCE IN SPORTS AND PERFORMANCE

BORDIEU, P. 1984. *Distinction: A social critique of the judgment of taste*. London: Routledge.

BRUYA, B. 2010. *Effortless attention*. Cambridge, MA: MIT University Press.

CARTER, R.C. 1997. *The nothingness beyond god: An introduction to the philosophy of Nishida*. St. Paul, MN: Paragon House.

———. 2008. *The Japanese arts and self-cultivation*. Albany, NY: State University of New York Press.

CHALMERS, D.J. 1995. Facing up to the problem of consciousness. *Journal of Consciousness Studies* 2: 200–19.

CHOZAN, N. 2006. *The Demon Sermon of the martial arts*. Translated by W.S. Wilson. Tokyo: Kodansa International.

CLEARY, T. 2005. *Soul of the samurai: Modern translations of three classic works of Zen & Bushido*. North Clarendon, VT: Tuttle.

DANIEL, J.A. 2004. Unraisable body: The physics of martial arts. Available at http://www.aikidore public.com/aikiphysics/unraisable-body (accessed 1 October 2014).

DESHIMARU, T. 1991. *The Zen way to the martial arts*. New York, NY: Compass.

DEWEY, J. 1988. *Human nature and conduct; An introduction to social psychology*. New York, NY: Holt.

DOHRENWEND, R.E. 2012. Martial arts history from one era to the next. In *Asian martial arts: Constructive thoughts and practical applications*, edited by M. De Marco. Santa Fe: Via Media Publishing Company: 10–3.

DREYFUS, H. and S. DREYFUS. 1986. *Mind over machine: The power of human intuition and expertise in the era of the computer*. New York, NY: The Free Press.

ERICSSON, K.A. 2003. Development of elite performance and deliberate practice: An update from the perspective of the expert performance approach. In *Expert performance in sports: Advances in research in sport expertise*, edited by J. Starke and A.K. Ericcson. Champaign, IL: Human Kinetics: 49–83.

ERICSSON, K.A., R.T. KRAMPE, and C. TESCH-RÖMER. 1993. The role of deliberate practice in the acquisition of expert performance. *Psychological Review* 100: 363–406.

FOUCAULT, M. 1979. *Discipline and punish: The birth of a prison*. New York, NY: Random House.

———. 1980. *The history of human sexuality*. Vol. I. An Introduction. New York, NY: Vintage Books.

———. 1988. *The care of the self*. New York, NY: Vintage Books.

FUKASAWA, K. 2014. The potentiality of empathy with others in competitive sport: A suggestion from Nishida's 'pure experience', and 'I' and 'Thou'. *International Journal of Sport and Health Science* 12: 47–52.

FUKUMOTO, M. 2013. The principle of somatic learning by Thomas Hanna: The common viewpoints for decoding various bodywork systems. Presented at International Association for the Philosophy of Sport, Fullerton, CA, 5 September.

GALLAGHER, S. and D. ZAHAVI. 2008. *The phenomenological mind: An introduction to philosophy of mind and cognitive science*. New York, NY: Routledge.

HARBACH, C. 2011. *The art of fielding: A novel*. New York, NY: Little, Brown.

HEPBURN, J.C. 1873. *Japanese-English and English-Japanese dictionary*. New York, NY: A.D.F. Randolph.

HERRIGEL, E. 1999. *Zen and the art of archery*. Translated by R.F.C. Hull. New York, NY: Vintage.

HOWE, L. 2008. Remote sport: Risk and self-knowledge in wilder spaces. *Journal of the Philosophy of Sport* 35 (1): 1–16.

HUTTO, D. and E. MYIN 2013. *Radical enactivism: Basic minds without content*. Cambridge, MA: MIT Press.

HYLAND, D. 1990. *Philosophy of sport*. New York, NY: Paragon House Publishing.

ILUNDÁIN-AGURRUZA, J. 2007. Kant goes skydiving: Understanding the extreme by way of the sublime. In *Philosophy, Risk and Adventure Sports*, edited by M. McNamee. London: Routledge: 149–67.

———. 2008. Between the horns. Part II: An existentialist solution to the dilemma on the running of the bulls. *Sport, Ethics, and Philosophy* 2 (1): 18–38.

———. Forthcoming-a. From failure to fluency: A phenomenological analysis of and eastern solution to sport's choking effect. *Phenomenology and the Cognitive Sciences*.

———. Forthcoming-b. The eye of the hurricane: Philosophical reflections on risky sports, self-knowledge and flourishing. *Journal of the Philosophy of Sport*.

ILUNDÁIN-AGURRUZA J., K. FUKUSAWA, and M. TAKEMURA. 2014. The philosophy of sport in relation to Japanese philosophy and pragmatism. In *A companion for the philosophy of sport*, edited by C. Torres. London: Bloomsbury: 66–82.

ILUNDÁIN-AGURRUZA, J. and T. HATA 2015. Eastern philosophy. In *Handbook for the philosophy of sport*, edited by M. McNamee and W. Morgan. London: Routledge: 98–114.

IMPACT MMA. 2011. Available at https://impactmma.wordpress.com/2011/04/18/mixed-martial-arts-how-safe-is-mma/ (accessed 22 February 2015).

JANELLE, C. and C. HILLMAN. 2003. Expert performance in sport: Current perspectives and critical issues. In *Expert performance in sports: Advances in research in sport expertise*, edited by J. Starke and A.K. Ericcson. Champaign, IL: Human Kinetics: 19–47.

KASULIS, T. 1993. The body—Japanese style. In *Self as body in Asian theory and practice*, edited by E. Deutsch and W. Dissanayake. Albany, NY: State University of New York Press: 295–316.

KAWACHI, K. and M. MANABE. 2006. *The art of the Japanese sword*. Tokyo: Floating World Editions.

KONO, Y. and GEIKIRYUDOJO. 2012. Yoshinori Kono. The way samurai moved. Available at https://www.youtube.com/watch?v=cSIJ2Te-Jsc (accessed 21 January 2015).

KREIN, K. and J. ILUNDÁIN-AGURRUZA. 2014. An east–west comparative analysis of Mushin and flow. In *Philosophy and the martial arts*, edited by G. Priest and D. Young. New York, NY: Routledge: 139–64.

LALLY, R., D. ANDERSON, and J. KAAG. 2012. *Pragmatism and the philosophy of sport*. London: Lexington Books.

LAO-TZU, L., C. TZU, and L. TZU. 2013. *Tao: The way—The sayings of Lao Tzu, Chuang Tzu and Lieh Tzu*. Translated by L. Giles and H.A. Giles. Special ed. El Paso, TX: EL Paso Norte Press.

LAOZI. 1996. *Taoteching*. Translated by Red Pine (Bill Porter). San Francisco, CA: Mercury House.

MALIZSZEWSKI, M. 2010. An optimal elixir: Blending spiritual, healing, and combative components. In *Asian martial arts: Constructive thoughts and practical applications*, edited by M. De Marco. Santa Fe: Via Media Publishing Company: 18–23.

MACINTYRE, A. 1984. *After virtue: A study in moral virtue*. 2nd ed. Notre Dame, IN: University of Notre Dame.

MARALDO, J.C. 2012. *Nishida Kitarō, The Stanford encyclopedia of philosophy*. Edited by E. Zalta. Available at http://plato.stanford.edu/archives/sum2012/entries/nishida-kitaro/ (accessed 24 January 2013).

MAUSS, M. 1950. *Les Techniques du Corps* [The techniques of the body]. In Sociologie et Anthropologie [Sociology and anthropology]. Paris: Presses Universitaires de France: 364–86.

MCNMAEE, M. 2008. *Sports, virtues and vices: Morality plays*. London: Routledge.

MERLEAU-PONTY, M. 1962. *Phenomenology of perception*. London: Routledge.

MONAHAN, M. 2007. The practice of self-overcoming: Nietzschean reflections on the martial arts. *Journal of the Philosophy of Sport* 34 (1): 39–51.

MORGAN, W.J. 2006. *Why sports morally matter*. Abingdon: Routledge.

MURPHY, C. and O. YASUKAWA. 2013. 'The Duke' of cliff diving: Orlando Duque. *CNN International Edition News*. Available at http://edition.cnn.com/2013/10/23/sport/orlando-duque-cliff-diving-colombia/ (accessed 21 February 2015).

MUSASHI, M. 1993. *The book of five rings*. Translated by T. Cleary. Boston, MA: Shambhala: 3–92.

———. 2004. Writings on the five elements. In *Miyamoto Musashi: His life and writings*, edited by K. Tokitsu. Boston, MA: Shambhala: 137–96.

NAGATOMO, S. 1992. *Attunement through the body*. Albany, NY: State University of New York Press.

NISHIDA, K. 1987a. *Last writings: Nothingness and the religious worldview*. Honolulu: University the Hawai'i Press.

———. 1987b. *Intuition and reflection in self-consciousness*. Albany, NY: State University of New York Press.

———. 1990. *An inquiry into the good*. New Haven, CT: Yale University Press.

———. 2011a. The logic of place. In *Japanese philosophy: A sourcebook*, edited by J. Heisig, T. Kasulis, and J. Maraldo. Honolulu: University of Hawai'i Press: 649–59.

———. 2011b. A religious view of the world. In *Japanese philosophy: A sourcebook*, edited by J. Heisig, T. Kasulis, and J. Maraldo. Honolulu: University of Hawai'i Press: 662–8.

ODA, Y. and Y. KONDO. 2014. The concept of Yuko-Datotsu in Kendo: Interpreted from the Aesthetics of Zanshin. *Sport, Ethics and Philosophy* 8 (1): 3–15.

ONUMA, H. 1993. *Kyudo: The essence and practice of Japanese archery*. Tokyo: Kodansha.

ORTEGA Y GASSET, J. 1995. *El Sentimiento Estético de la Vida (Antología)*. Edited by J.L. Molinuevo. Madrid: Editorial Tecnos S.A.

OSHIMA, H.H. 1983. A metaphorical analysis of the concept of mind in the Chuang-Tzu. In *Experimental essays on Chuang-Tzu*, edited by V.H. Mair. Honolulu: University of Hawai'i Press: 63–84.

PERRIN, N. 1979. *Giving up the gun: Japan's reversion to the sword, 1543–1879*. Jaffrey, NH: David R. Godine.

PRIEST, G. and D. YOUNG. 2014. *Philosophy and the martial arts: Engagement*. Abingdon: Routledge.

REID, H.L. 2010. Athletic virtue: Between east and west. *Sport, Ethics and Philosophy* 4 (1): 16–26.

———. 2012. *Introduction to the philosophy of sport*. Plymouth: Rowan & Littlefield.

RUSSELL, J.S. 2005. The value of dangerous sport. *Journal of the Philosophy of Sport* 32 (1): 1–19.

———. 2014. *Resilience*. Warren P. Fraleigh Distinguished Scholar Lecture delivered at the International Association for the Philosophy of Sport annual meeting, 4 September, Natal (Brazil).

HOLISM AND THE CULTIVATION OF EXCELLENCE IN SPORTS AND PERFORMANCE

SAILORS, P. 2010. More than meets the I: Values of dangerous sport. In *Climbing—Philosophy for everyone. Because It's There*, edited by E. Schmid Stephen. Malden, MA: Blackwell: 81–92.

SAITO, Y. 1985. The Japanese appreciation of nature. *The British Journal of Aesthetics* 25 (3): 239–51.

SAKAI T. and A. BENNETT. 2010. *A bilingual guide to the history of Kendo* [Nihon kendo no rekishi : eiyaku tsuki]. Tokyo: Sukijanaru.

SEKIDA, K. 1985. *Zen training: Methods and philosophy*. Boston, MA: Shambhala.

———. 2005. *Two Zen classics: The gateless gate and the blue cliff records*. Boston, MA: Shambhala.

SHIGEMATSU, S. 1981. *A Zen forest: Sayings of the masters*. New York, NY: Weatherhill.

SHUSTERMAN, R. 2008. *Body consciousness*. Cambridge: Cambridge University Press.

STEVENS, J. 2001. *The sword of no-sword: Life of the master Warrior Tesshu*. Boston, MA: Shambhala.

SUZUKI, D. 1993. *Zen and Japanese culture*. New York, NY: Princeton University Press.

TAKUAN, S. 1985. Divine record of immovable wisdom. In *The sword & the mind*, translated by H. Sato. Woodstock, NY: Overlook Press: 111–20.

———. 1986. *The unfettered mind: Writings of the Zen master to the sword master*. Tokyo: Kodansha.

———. 2005. The inscrutable subtlety of immovable wisdom, in *Soul of the samurai*, translated by T. Cleary. North Clarendon, VT: Tuttle: 100–41.

TAMAKI, L. 2010. Yoshinori Kono: Le Virtuouse du Bujutsu [Yoshinori Kono: The virtuous one of Bujutsu]. *Samourai* 4: 12–8.

TANABE, H. 2011. The logic of the specific. In *Japanese philosophy: A sourcebook*, edited by J. Heisig, T. Kasulis, and J. Maraldo. Honolulu: University of Hawai'i Press: 671–83.

TAYLOR, K. 2010. Niten-Ichi-ryu and Shinto-ryu. In *Asian martial arts: Constructive thoughts and practical applications*, edited by M. De Marco. Sana Fe: Vai Media Publishing: 132–5.

THELEN, E. and L. SMITH 1995. *A dynamic systems approach to the development of cognition and action*. Cambridge, MA: MIT Press.

THOMSON, S. and D. MACASKILL. 2014. The ridge. Available at http://www.youtube.com/watch?v= xQ_IQS3VKjA (accessed 3 October 2014).

TOKITSU, K. 2004. *Miyamoto Musashi: His life and writings*. Boston, MA: Shambhala.

———. 2011. *The complete book of five rings*. Boston, MA: Shambhala.

TURNBULL, S.R. 2010. *Katana: The samurai sword*. Oxford: Osprey.

UESHIBA, M. 1992. *The art of peace*. Boston, MA: Shambhala.

VARELA, F. 2013. Video interview. Available at http://percro.sssup.it/embodied2013 (accessed 16 June 2013).

WERTZ, S.K. 1977. Zen, yoga, and sports: Eastern philosophy for western athletes. *Journal of the Philosophy of Sport* 4 (1): 68–82.

———. 1984. The Zen way to the martial arts (Zen et arts martiaux). *Journal of the Philosophy of Sport* 11 (1): 94–103.

———. 1991. *Talking a good game: Inquiries into the principles of sport*. Dallas, TX: Southern Methodist University Press.

WILLIAMS, F. 2014. Yellow streak. *Outside Magazine*, November Issue: 80–88.

WILSON, W.S. 2004. *The lone samurai: The life of Miyamoto Musashi*. Tokyo: Kodansha International.

HOLISM AND THE CULTIVATION OF EXCELLENCE IN SPORTS AND PERFORMANCE

YAGYŪ, M. 1986. Family transmitted book on swordsmanship. In *The sword & the mind*, translated by H. Sato. Woodstock, NY: Overlook Press: 20–109.

———. 1993. The book of family traditions on the art of war. In *The book of five rings*, translated by T. Clearly. Boston, MA: Shambhala: 93–164.

———. 2003. *The life giving sword*. Translated by W.S. Wilson. Tokyo: Kodansha International.

———. 2005. Martial arts: The book of family traditions. In *Soul of the samurai*, translated by T. Cleary. North Clarendon, VT: Tuttle: 8–99.

———. 2008. The book of the house of Yagyū transmission of the art of war. In *The sword & the mind*, translated by W. Ridgeway. Birmingham, AL: Cliff Road Books: 11–85.

YAMADA, S. and 山田奨治. 2001. The myth of Zen in the art of Archery. *Japanese Journal of Religious Studies* 28 (2): 1–30.

YAMAMOTO, T. 1979. *Hagakure*. Tokyo: Kodansha International.

YUASA, Y. 1987. *The body: Toward an eastern mind-body theory*. Albany, NY: State University of New York Press.

———. 1993. *The body, self-cultivation, and ki-energy*. Albany, NY: State University of New York Press.

YUSA, M. 2002. *Zen & philosophy: An intellectual biography of Nishida Kitaro*. Honolulu: Univeristy of Hawai'i Press.

10—EVERYTHING MYSTERIOUS UNDER THE MOON—SOCIAL PRACTICES AND SITUATED HOLISM

Jesús Ilundáin-Agurruza

The most beautiful thing we can experience is the mysterious. (Albert Einstein[1])

Though there is a reflection,
    The moon reflects itself
Without thought.
    Without thought, too, the water:
    Hirozawa Pond (Emperor Sutoku[2])

Nothing under the sun is greater than education. By educating one person and sending him into the society of his generation, we make a contribution extending a hundred generations to come. (Jigoro Kano[3])

Yūgen -幽玄. This Japanese concept stands for a unique sense of mystery. According to Yuasa (1993), it means profound or suggestive mystery. Literally, it signifies 'dim', 'deep', esthetic or 'mysterious' (Woolley 2012). It is fittingly imbued with an aesthetic sensibility. The mysterious is also is related to mysticism, riddles, and a philosophical disposition. In fact, Huizinga (1955) finds the birth of philosophy in the riddles of the ancient Indian Vedic texts. Appreciating *yūgen* requires an active role on the part of both performer and observer (should there be one), as the observations on 'attendance' below explain. The moon is also rich in connotations. It plays a key role in Buddhist writings and *kenjutsu* manuals, as seen in the previous essay. The mystery under a midnight moon is the *yin* (陰) to the *yang's* (陽) intellectual clarity of the high noon sun. Yet, appreciating the mystery means dwelling deeply in it, not leaving it untouched. Only then do we develop the kind of gnostic insight that allows us to *feel* our way to a perspective where nothingness and everything, spontaneity and deliberation, emotion and reason, means and ends, is and ought, and the subpersonal and the reflective are unified in contradictorily Nishidan tension. The catalyst is an imaginative education. Through it, the mysteries of *mushin* as a skillful striving are both unraveled and reconnected through a joyful pedagogical lens where a holistic enactivism is built into the rich framework of practices and communities. In the end, the remaining challenge is how to articulate the dark and deep mystery of the *living* experience such that we may gain insight without erroneously believing that we have disclosed its deepest secrets.

HOLISM AND THE CULTIVATION OF EXCELLENCE IN SPORTS AND PERFORMANCE

This final essay explores enaction and holism in the context of spontaneous action and ethical choice. This leads to an analysis of East Asian views on enactive ethical action. A reflective intuition (another fecund tension) that shines in performative scenarios precedes reconceptualization of the means/ends relation. Performance is then prescriptively regulated by a caring attitude of 'attendance' and what is here called the kenotic paradox. Subsequently, situatedness and intersubjectivity help explore the role of geo-historical circumstances from a phenomenological perspective. Last, the discussion turns to the challenge to articulate our felt experience in the context of Wittgenstein's argument against a completely private language. The emphasis is on a comparative approach, where East Asian and Western philosophical perspectives are more extensively present and explicitly combined.

1. A Holistic and Enactive Ethics of Spontaneous and Superior Performance

Australian swimmer Cecil Healy's actions at the 1912 Olympic Games were exemplary. They exuded sportspersonship. Unmistakably. Healy was one of the best swimmers of his time, having equaled world records and won many Australian and international championships (Walsh 1983). During the qualification series at the Games, Hawaiian Duke Kahanamoku was the only other swimmer to best him. The US team, because of an error by its management, was late to the semi-finals classification event. This in effect meant that Healy was poised to win the gold medal. But, in opposition to many other delegations, Healy decidedly intervened and helped with the appeal to allow the Americans swim an ad hoc classificatory race (Eccenbarger 2008). This in spite of, or *because*, it was clear the Hawaiian was the fastest. Once classified, Kahanamoku handily won the final. Healy settled for silver. He obviously wanted what was best for the competition, even if that meant not winning himself.[4] This is a wonderful example of *kalon*, as discussed in *Riding the Wind*.

A *traditional* Western ethical explanation would account for Healy's actions either in terms of deontology, that is, appealing to rules, duty, and intentions, or in terms of consequentialism and calculations, pleasure, and outcomes. In both instances, a rational model is applied. Healy either deliberates and acts dutifully or calculates and seeks to maximize the best outcome for all involved (supposing that we could settle on a ranking of duties or decide whose best interest to favor). Dewey remarks rightly how both theories, as most opposite extremes in philosophy, suffer from the same mistake. They 'ignore the projective force of habit and the implications of habits in one another. Hence, they separate a unified deed into two disjointed parts, an inner called motive and an outer called act' (Dewey 1988, 33). Moreover, because both suppose an immutable background from which to assess our deeds, whether transcendental or empirical, both also 'deny the relevancy of time, of change to morals. While time is of the essence for the moral struggle' (Ibid., 38).

Virtue ethics avoids both of these errors, since it is predicated on habit-developed character and its emphasis on good judgment according to the situation is time sensitive. But, in most accounts, such as Aristotle's (2011) or MacIntyre (1984), it is also

HOLISM AND THE CULTIVATION OF EXCELLENCE IN SPORTS AND PERFORMANCE

a matter of rational analysis and a *telos*-oriented deliberation. The intent now is to redirect the moral compass as well as modify its virtuous scope so as to rethink these in terms of capacities in accord with the holistic model of skillful action and striving. The rapprochement between Asian and Western stances continues hereafter and provides a clearer view of how a holistic enactivism assimilates the domains of performance (enacted capacities or skills), normativity (ethics and aesthetics), cognition (gnoseologic continuum), and the socio-environmental. These are referred to as the 'enactive domains' for short. In the most refined cases, these are but different descriptions and perspectives on the same unified phenomenon that is expressed in expert performance. That is, what we can call consummate performers are not only superior technically, but their performances exhibit beauty and moral goodness. Thus, they serve as role models. They are great athletes, martial artists, performers, but just as much, they shine because of their polished character.

Paragons of excellence respond to difficult situations like Sutoku's mirror: without hesitation, their response matches the demands. This does not mean that there is no prior foundational rational process involved that can set up intuitive action heuristically. As presented in sections three and four of this project, excellent and virtuous performance relies on the four factors of deliberation, reflection, intuition, and empty cognition. In virtue of our skillful capacities, these can structure our moral acts. Dewey (1988) puts at the center of our moral compass habit, which, again, for him is acquired, systematizing, dynamic, and projective. This engages the good will, which disposition guides, consequences measure up, and is to be acted out. Dewey explains how the dispositions that guide the good will are 'a potential energy needing only the opportunity to become *kinetic* and overt' (Ibid., 34, my emphasis), while the ever relevant consequences 'include effects upon character' (Ibid, 35). This sets the stage for the discussion on Zhuangzian fasting of the mind (see appendix also). It also agrees with our emphasis on actual kinetic manifestation in performance *and* keeps together intention and result. Unlike MacIntyre's approach to virtue ethics, this is not tied to an Aristotelian goal-oriented deliberation (essay 1) nor is it narrowly rational. A holistic ethics is ecological and enactive: it encompasses aesthetic and performative constituents and conjures from nothing spaces to circumvent the strictures of rational moral approaches. This turns constraints into affordances. Such ethics also explains better many, if not most, of our routine ethical undertakings as well as other complex scenarios where focused performative expertise is needed. It relies on spontaneous and successful action, or put differently, instantaneous and effective response.

In many everyday situations and specialized contexts, suitable courses of action require *immediate* and non-calculative responses. They ask for intuitive and spontaneous acts that adapt to the needs of the moment and are not decided rationally (whether deontologically or consequentially is beside the point). This model explains Healy's actions as prompted by an impulse to redress what he saw as an unfair situation, athletically and ethically. What *actually* dictated his actions is largely irrelevant for the purposes at hand; the ensuing develops a 'just so' theoretical explanation. Below, other more 'hands-on' examples will help illustrate different elements of enactive ethics. But, the choice for Healy's non-performative account of moral *choice* (if ultimately related to one) underscores how its scope can accommodate more complex and traditional scenarios. Healy's intervention was predicated on a deep appreciation for the internal goods of excellent swimming. He also recognized the sacrifices and training needed to manifest Kahanamoku's talent, was deeply aware that competition to determine the worthiest and ablest competitor necessitates a selfless commitment, and genuinely embraced a compassionate regard for others. But, what prompted Healy to act was neither determined in accord with maxims nor by weighing consequences. Rather, there was an initial spring to action not unlike how he dived from the blocks into the pool after the starting gun fired. Good starts are prepared beforehand and are observed for ethically sporting reasons and sportingly ethical reasons: they reward athletically well-honed fast reaction times that have been earned through disciplined training, but the sense of the skill is derived from an appreciation for a fair contest. Similarly, Healy sprang to act on Kahanamoku's behalf because of his sense of fairness *within* the context of a swimming competition (which ideally is derived from a comprehensive notion of fairness). Such sense is established by previous experiences and related deliberations and reflections on past moral engagements that help build an intuition that acts without the need for explicit, rational, and contentful cognition (and of course, the community from which he derives such ideas; a facet to be expanded upon in Sections 5–7). This does not mean that he is reacting unthinkingly like a spring pushes back when the pressure is released or that the rational processes are forsaken.

These processes play preceding foundational and subsequent reflective roles that help develop heuristic normative shortcuts to swift actions. They are also pertinent when the situation extends in time, needs explicit argument, careful analysis, or outcome assessment. But, once we have figured out a modus operandi for certain types of ethical cases, we need not run moral algorithms to determine the course of action. We simply, but effectively, act. The underlying sense of rightness issues from a non-rational, intuitive fit between the needs of the situation and our abilities and response. Being dispositional, the sense of rightness is open to change, obviously, when conditions alter, counterarguments are persuasive, or the person's open mindedness allows. In Healy's case, and given that the issue involved an appeal process, argumentation was requisite, of course. In other instances, such as when someone has a mishap and we rush to help without giving it a moment's thought, rational thinking is distinctly at play. A thickly holistic enactivism best explains cases with blended performance, norms, and know-how. Put differently, skillful striving as an ethos of personal growth holistically combines performative, epistemological, and normative elements: we *know* how to act suitably and adapt to the situation with the engagement of our bodymind. Truly exceptional individuals achieve such a level of integration that they act like active and malleable mirrors. Biologist turned philosopher Varela's (1999) *Ethical Know-how: Action, Wisdom, and Cognition* proves a valuable source to further examine spontaneous actions that are not only successful but also *kalon*: morally praiseworthy in an ecological, situated, and enactive way.

Varela's commitments are aligned with enactivist and cognitively embodied stances. He expresses the core idea behind this reflective intuition thus, 'a wise (or virtuous) person is *one who knows what is good and spontaneously does it*' (Varela 1999, 4, his emphasis). For him, as just discussed, many of the things we do in everyday life, which may also involve unexpected occurrences such as accidents and our responses to them, involve ethical actions that 'do not spring from judgment or reasoning but from an *immediate coping* with what is confronting us' (Ibid., 5, his emphasis). From the urge to help someone who slips and falls in front of us, to the words of consolation, we may offer someone distressed, these come forth unbidden. As just presented, ethical judgment also happens through careful and rational evaluation and consideration. But this is not the paradigm. In skillful performance cognitive, normative, and performative factors do not operate only or best (in many cases) in this way. In opposition to a tradition of thinking based on rationality and abstraction, Varela develops a model where the 'proper units of knowledge are primarily *concrete*, embodied, incorporated, lived; [where] knowledge is about situatedness' that also takes into account its historicity and context (Ibid., 7). There is an obvious affinity between his views and those espoused here.

Varela correctly argues for the relevance of 'the immediacy of a given situation' (1999, 9). We often live in the hustle and bustle of everyday life, but sports and other performances stand out when it comes to presenting us with 'urgencies' that require immediate responses. Take for example, a paraglider who is surprised by an in-flight wing deflation, when the canopy collapses and he begins to fall in flight. He needs to instantly pull from the proper line (cord) and counterbalance the fall if he is going to remain airborne. Echoing Heidegger, Varela observes that 'Our lived world is so ready-at-hand that we have no deliberateness about what it is and how we inhabit it' (Ibid.). To recast his sedate 'seating at lunch' example into something more vigorous, when we assiduously play tennis or golf, hitting some balls or playing a few holes demands us to handle the tools, move about, converse and more, all of it 'without deliberation' such that 'we could say that our [playing]-self is transparent' (Ibid.). This makes for a 'readiness-for-action' he calls 'microidentity' that is 'proper to every specific lived situation', which he terms 'microworld' (Ibid.). These are historically constituted (Section 6). Analogously to how fractured action is ripe with opportunity for creative and spontaneous expansion of our skillful repertoire, for Varela, breakdowns are the hinges that articulate microworlds that act as 'the source of the autonomous and creative side of living cognition' (1999,11). Paragliding mishaps have resulted in a rich repertory of new skills that permit novel and more sophisticated maneuvers.

Living cognition is enactive knowledge for Varela: (1) perception is perceptually guided action and (2) cognitive structures arise from sensorimotor patterns that guide action perceptually (1999, 12). Varela's view is suitably dynamic, decentralized, and distributed, with complex processes being the result 'of coordinated activity of simple elements, (Ibid., 53). For him, the speed and transiency of our behavioral processes is achieved at all levels. Specifically those of,

> sensory interpretation and motor action' [and ...] the entire gamut of cognitive expectations and emotional tonality central to the shaping of a microworld'—by the binding of neuronal ensembles that result in sensorimotor couplings, and ultimately action and the *behavioral mode for the next cognitive moment, a microworld*. (Varela, et al. 1991, 51, his emphasis)

But, as argued in essay 6, theoretical conceptualization of processes in terms of sensorimotor couplings and capacities, when these bear the whole weight of the explanation and eschew a more kinetically and kinesthetically fluid perspective, is problematic. This is largely why a holistic and radical enactivism is endorsed in lieu. Nonetheless, there is much to gain from Varela's ideas yet.

Varela frames the issue correctly for the most part: 'most of our mental and active life is of the immediate coping variety, which is transparent, stable, and grounded in our personal histories' (1999, 19). And, he perceptively examines and rightly emphasizes what we can call the 'micromoment'—to adopt a nomenclature parallel to his—where the slice of action singled out takes place, e.g. the actual moment of 'coping' when the paraglider first notices the wing collapse and succeeds in arresting the fall. He also acknowledges the relevance of deliberation and analysis, 'It is at the moments of breakdown, that is, when we are *not* experts of our microworld anymore, that we deliberate and analyze, that we become like beginners seeking to feel at ease with the task at hand' (Varela 1999, 18). Yet, there is need to release a tension that builds in his view here (shared by those accounts he bases his on, such as Dreyfus' model of coping). Varela makes deliberation and analysis a matter of novices, but earlier he finds these breakdowns to be the source for that autonomous and creative cognition he so keenly analyzes. Novices do not succeed in dealing with breakdowns in creative and autonomous ways. Rather, that is what experts do. Moreover, the latter also rely on rational and deliberative processes, and not merely when dealing with breakdowns. For one, they are engaged as preparation and planning for possible tribulations and mishaps. Deliberation and reflection are a matter of expertise also and play a key antecedent and subsequent role, respectively, *particularly* for those who *truly* excel. Nonetheless, the creativity and swiftness characteristic of excellent action issue forth from intuition and contentless cognition. We now turn to explore this. The point of origin lies in the East.[5]

2. An Eastern Account of Performance, Normativity, and Cognition

Varela's discusses in detail what he calls the teaching traditions of the East: Daoism, Confucianism and Buddhism (1999). He develops primarily the latter two. He relies on Megnzi, 孟子 (Mencius), second in stature within the Confucian tradition to Kongzi 仲尼 (Confucius). He espoused a view of human nature as being originally good: we are borne with compassionate feelings. Seok develops a cognitively embodied analysis of Confucian virtues, stressing that Confucian moral philosophy has a 'strong orientation towards the embodied moral mind' (2013, 50). He also singles out Mengzi and focuses repeatedly on his example where we see a child about to fall in a well. We *instantaneously* and bodily feel the compassionate pull to save the child. There is no need to run benefit-cost analyses or deliberate on which rules we should adhere to. Seok's analysis is largely congruent with much of the above, except that some of his stances are open to the criticisms raised earlier (essay 6) to an embodied program of cognition that is narrowly brain-centered. For his part, and a bit too cavalierly, Varela equates such 'natural' impulses to Laozi, 老子, *wuwei*, 無爲, and the Mahayanistic cultivation of *prajñā*, (Buddhist wisdom) and its Buddhist ideal of the *bodhisattva*, बोधिसित्तव, the enlightened and compassionate person helping others reach *Nirvāṇa*, नर्िवाण. His emphasis, however, is on Mengzi and Buddhism, particularly its goal of an empty self or selflessness (see *Śūnyatā* in the appendix). Yet, a holistic and radical enactivism and a thicker account of Daoism, specifically Zhuangzi's, 莊子, rather than Laozi's, explain more transparently than either Varela or Seok this kind of effective and efficient spontaneous performance, ethical and otherwise.

We begin with that impish Daoist sage, Zhuangzi, and the fourth chapter in his eponymous book, 'In the World of Men'. It regales us with a story where, in order to explain virtuoso action, he casts Kongzi as a character advising his favorite disciple, Yánhuí, 顏回.[6] The disciple is bent on going to dispense advice to a young and reckless ruler who is causing great harm to his people. As Fraser explains, the disciple intends

HOLISM AND THE CULTIVATION OF EXCELLENCE IN SPORTS AND PERFORMANCE

to handle the tyrant 'according to fixed formulae determined in his heart' (see *xin*, 心 below) (2014, 202). After quizzing Yánhuí, about his strategies, all of which have faults that will land Yánhuí in trouble, Kongzi advises him to fast the 'mind'. He explains to Yánhuí, puzzled by what this fasting is about, that he must,

> Make your will one! Don't listen with your ears, listen with your *mind*. No, don't listen with your mind, but listen with your *spirit*. Listening stops with the ears, the mind stops with recognition, but *spirit* is empty and waits on all things. The Way gathers in *emptiness* alone. Emptiness is the fasting of the mind. (Chuang Tzu and Watson 1968, 58, my emphasis)

This state of being and acting will enable Yánhuí, to act in consonance with the circumstances, spontaneously and successfully. It permits to attend to situations that require immediate and spontaneously effective response. Because there are many rich layers of philosophical import for a holistic and enactive account of norms, these are discussed in the appendix. It examines the translation and interpretation of three vital words: (1) *mind*, 心 (*xin*), which is best understood as 'heart-mind,' stressing the bodymind and its vital continuities when it comes to thinking, action, and feeling (essay 5). (2) *Spirit*, 氣 (*qi*), better rendered as 'vital energy.' Pervading organic and inorganic matter, it is the very energy that animates our lives and *moves* us to move. (3) *Emptiness*, the most complex of the three, and which is analyzed in terms of 無 (*wu*) nothing, which expands on the Nishidan analysis from the previous essay; 空 (*kōng*) emptiness, in its two main pertinent senses, Daoist and Buddhist; *and* 虛 (*xū*), void or empty, the actual character in the text, and which most directly connects to the characteristic of basic contentless bodyminds in spontaneous, effective action. It is important to stress that these are not merely abstract concepts. Their import lies precisely in the fact that they are incarnated in the consummate person, the 真人 (*zhēnrén*). Her heart-mind harmoniously blended with the psychosocial environment, this person enacts, in the original sense, as she lays down a path of conduct predicated on her spontaneous, successful responses to environmental challenges as she 'fasts' and forgets her bodymind: her attention fully invested in the moment.

The upshot of this passage (and the views discussed in the appendix) is that emptiness need not be a subpersonal process, completely out of reach; neither are intense concentration or focus to avoid distractions tantamount to relinquishing skills to the subpersonal. Rather, the specificity of our practical engagements requires a dynamic implementation of skills that are scaffolded and called upon during the performance at different levels of awareness. Moreover, acute discernment is also a capacity itself. In this case, it integrates a cross-modal array of perceptions, tactile, visual, aural, even olfactory, with a plurality of skills applicable to kinetic and kinesthetic engagements with our bodymind, tools, and world chosen from our skillful repertoire. Awareness is requisite to retain any phenomenological sense of agency and ownership, as well as to play an active role in our goings and undergoings. Furthermore, *awareness* of what Fraser calls unconscious processes is a problematic idea, since by definition we cannot be aware of what is truly subpersonal. To avoid this, Billeter hedges his bets. He points out that consciousness either 'disappears, or partially disappears, or changes in terms of function, or is transformed', and develops a positive and fruitful account in terms of an ironic regard through which we reflectively observe our own actions (see

HOLISM AND THE CULTIVATION OF EXCELLENCE IN SPORTS AND PERFORMANCE

essay 5) (Billeter 2010, 66, my translation). In other words, he realizes that some level of attentional awareness and pre-reflective consciousness are needed to be able to describe, as Cook Ding does, 'how things work at all' (Ibid., 60, my translation). Such rich phenomenological descriptions are a first step to a better understanding.

Thick holism and the enactive model precisely allow for integrated and learned skills that operate at different levels—subpersonal, Jamesian fringe, conscious—as part of a performative and cognitive continuum that persons develop to different degrees. It is a dynamic model wherein skills transform in response to ecologically broad environmental elements that range from the surroundings to our past performative history (previous undertakings with a particular practice; for some, this may be the origin of self-doubt that can lead to fractured action). Compared to superlative experts, competence, mindless coping, and automatization are lesser ways of performing—sophisticated as it may be to be able to daydream while driving a car. It is never a purely automatic matter in cases of superb performance, much less in extremes cases where the performer may be literally on the edge … of a ledge, as stunt cyclist Danny MacAskill illustrates once more.

As the short video *The Ledge: Danny MacAskill Making 'The Ridge'* shows, MacAskill carefully allowed for the forgetting and learning to happen (Thomson and MacAskill 2014a).[7] He confidently and speedily rode down on shale and broken rock on a narrow cornice, barely one foot-wide (.3 meter) at some points, with a sheer 500 feet (165 meter) drop on either side at times. There is a very dangerous point a foot-wide with a big rock jutting out, where he had to come to a full stop, bunny-hop the front end to the top of the rock and then turn 90 degrees before continuing the harrowing ride. MacAskill was not attending to the handlebars the way Billeter describes his and most casual riders' experience: trying to 'maintain the equilibrium by modifying the position of the handlebars' (2010, 57). Expert cyclists turn and maintain the equilibrium not with the front end of the bike (stem, fork, and handlebars); rather, they use subtle hip movements. Just as Cook Ding upon reaching a knotty point pauses (essay 5), MacAskill also paused. All three levels in the consciousness continuum interacting fluidly: when there was need to deliberately and attentively *think* how, where, and when he is going to bunny-hop the stone outcropping, he did so; what he could relegate to the fringe, for example, how his hips counterbalance his bike's front end, he did so; what had to be automatized, the pedaling, was duly done—until he had to reassess how to sync his pedal stroke to clear the rock without bumping himself off the ledge with the inside pedal. MacAskill was *very* attentive to the path ahead of him, and aware of what *he* was doing, mindfully so. Empty of self-monitoring and worries about his skills or what might happen to him, he moved resolutely. This rather plain and dull account belies the hair rising descent (many commenters on the online thread mention how *they* were sweating just watching).

Analyses often ignore the habit-inducing *practicing* that underwrites this process. In fact, Fraser is wary of habit-dependent protocols. His motivation justifiably seeks to maintain flexible and responsive skills and to keep a creative openness that does not succumb to 'habits and preconceptions' that breed 'cognitive sclerosis or blindness to anything that does not fit neatly into the existing framework of our skill' (2014, 210). Yet, we should note that such worry only applies to the traditional passive conception of habit, not Dewey's active and creative one. Such habit liberates us, opening those empty spaces within stricture, just as the restrictions imposed by the rules of games

HOLISM AND THE CULTIVATION OF EXCELLENCE IN SPORTS AND PERFORMANCE

open creative possibilities. MacAskill's integration is partly, but crucially, built on his already amazing prowess, technique, and nerve. But, the development of his talents is achieved through habit-forming practice, or rather through doing habit-forming movements, which better captures the way the actual process happens. (The role other practitioners play is considered in Sections 5–7) As *The Ledge* and the other accompanying *Making of The Ridge* short videos show, even as talented a rider as MacAskill, practices over and over to extend his abilities by pushing himself beyond what he has done before. As we learned with Dewey (essay 3), this going beyond what we can achieve is the only way toward skillful growth. This squarely addresses the concerns Fraser raises. Yet, he brings up a different and more troublesome issue.

Perceptively, Fraser asks, 'If spontaneous responses issuing from the empty, *xū*, state are actually grounded in habit, prior training, and our existing self-understanding, how can we distinguish insensitive, heedless responses from sensitive, adaptive ones? How can an agent confirm she is not being guided by baseless or suboptimal prejudices?' (2014, 211). There are two related issues here, successful performance and the moral quality of the response. He appeals to practical efficacy as a possible criterion. Just as Cook Ding and MacAskill do, when facing a knotty moment, they pause, concentrate, and allow their skill to spontaneously meet the challenge, 'thus advancing beyond [their] original level of skill' (Ibid.). This addresses the former but does not assure the rightness of the action.[8] *we* can still have amazing skills with an unchecked depravity to match. As to this knotty issue, *we* need to pause.

A solution, congenial to Fraser, is to contend that superb performance *is* normative through and through, as *Skillful Striving* maintains. The truly exceptional performer is not only technically efficacious, but also ethically and aesthetically outstanding. Eugenio Monti's actions (essay 7), much as Healy's, show a superior handling of the situation all around. Not only were Monti's technical and athletic skills excellent, but his sportspersonship and appreciation for the internal goods of the tradition were on par. Of course, we can find many exceptions, defective cases that lack integration and resort to cheating, for example. These give us sordid victories, not admirable ones. Fraser's stance lines up with the holistic and enactive view here developed whereby there is a fit between all the enactive domains in fluid synchrony. He states, 'This ethical work is an ongoing process of developing greater sensitivity to our circumstances, cultivating a calm, centered constitution that allows [...] to respond to opportunities [...] allowing room for novel, effective responses that shatter existing biases' (2014, 211). The point to emphasize is that this ethical work, in the best cases, happens also in and through performative skills.

Nonpareil surfer Kelly Slater once more helps illustrate how unparalleled performance happens through the empty openings of *xū* while engaging character cultivation and its connection to skills. Less striking a case than Monti's or Healy's, it offers a broader existential slice that shows how gnostic truths take root while crucially intertwining with normative and cognitive elements. On 17 October 2014, in Portugal, Slater pulled a move on his board that rippled through the surfing world with the power of a rogue wave. Albeit, the wave he actually rode was quite unremarkable. On it, he has been the first surfer to ever successfully complete a 540°, which stands for the rotation degree. Landing backwards into the wave, he then gracefully turned and exited the wave.[9] This is remarkable on its own. What astounds most is that Slater is pulling off these moves aged 42—twice the age of many of his competitors. Having surfed over

HOLISM AND THE CULTIVATION OF EXCELLENCE IN SPORTS AND PERFORMANCE

37 years, with 22 as a professional, and 11 ASP World Tour Championships, he is still at it. Such longevity at the highest competitive level is unrivaled in modern sport.[10] And this baffles most people. His age-cohort of surfing competitors has long moved to other endeavors or surfing challenges. Approaching this biographically and existentially within the current framework sheds light.

When he first took on the world of surfing, he was brash, abrasive, and fellow surfers resented him. As Roberts puts it, 'Slater dominated with his technical precision, innovation, and ruthless competitive drive' (2015, 62). He excelled athletically, checking the performative and cognitive boxes. But, 'As he's confessed many times, he was a miserable winner' (Roberts 2015, 62). He once won a US Open taking advantage of a technicality to a chorus of boos. Slater states, 'I had such a feeling of emptiness and loneliness back then [...] I wanted to win so badly that it got in the way of other things' (Roberts 2015, 63). Sometimes emptiness is a bad thing too. He first retired in 1998. But, 'since the end of his first retirement, in 2002, Slater has worked at cultivating a more balanced approach to life and surfing' going 'deep into a process of self-reflection and emotional recovery' (Ibid.) Roberts, who has interviewed Slater several times since 2005, depicts a candid Slater whose tears flow speaking of the kindness of people and has found a middle ground between the battle mentality for competing and a more relaxed existence. This re-forging of character is admirable and remarkable because it has happened while still being in the midst of his professional career, with all the associated pressures and distractions, and temptations. And he has kept on winning; and winning admirers for the right reasons. There is a harmonious consonance between his skills, how he competes, and his personality. The way Slater looks at competition is telling, 'It's really like a Zen practice' because 'for most elite athletes, a personal challenge feeds their desire to be good at something. So to get to a point where you're happy and you're still able to push yourself competitively, you have to find different reasons' (Ibid.). This has paid off.

His different reasons amount to one thing: motivation. He has found the way to enjoy what he does and remain enthused. This avoids the burn out that plagues others, and which for many is the limiting factor rather than physical deterioration. When he pulls off something special, he says, 'It just feels natural' explaining, 'I get the affirmation that I'm doing what I was meant to do in life. When I landed that maneuver in Portugal, I felt like I was eight-years old again and my dad was on the beach watching me do my first off the lip' (Roberts 2015, 92). The emptiness that plagued his younger winning days has given way to an emptiness that allows him to embrace the demands of competition at the highest level with the enthusiasm of an eight-year old, the accumulated knowledge of someone who has surfed for 37 years, and the insight of a reflective and thoughtful individual who has learned to appreciate his talents.

The foregoing has explained how the enactive bodymind operates within an Eastern–Western comparative framework. It is a 'theoretical manifesto' for a holistic and radical enactivism where the contentless cognition of basic minds—emptiness as theorized above—operates fluidly to create fulsome spaces for skillful responses. Regarding *xū*, Fraser explains that '*emptiness* enables and open, "reflective" response that allows our capacities to function at their fullest'. As we saw with Hutto and Myin, the cognitively non-representational and enactive minds are 'best understood in terms of capacities' of just the sort examined presently (2013, 151). Excellent performance does not happen in spite of but precisely through this 'empty cognition'. Much as a fasting

HOLISM AND THE CULTIVATION OF EXCELLENCE IN SPORTS AND PERFORMANCE

operates though dietary parsimony and restriction, and in a Zhuaungzian ethical account results in superior performance, an enactive fasting endorses cognitive, normative, and performative simplicity that effects holistic expertise. The last two subsections discuss the scaffolded nature of this cognitive and normative holistic stance, where the situated and social environment comes to bear. Now, some may denigrate this as an account where performance is of a 'shoot-from-the-hip' kind. It is indeed so. The actions are spontaneous, cognitively empty, and the normative assessments of the better way to respond (say adjusting our limbs in a particular way) are also non-propositional and non-representational. But, shooting from the hip requires even more training and developed talent if we are to hit the target at all! Wild West's Annie Oakley sharpshooter's celebrated marksmanship is proof of this.

> Her typical program which demanded both concentration and speed, included shooting coins tossed in the air, firing in rapid succession at small bull's eyes, splitting a playing card held edgewise [at 90 feet with a .22 bullet], sighting in a table knife to shoot objects behind her, hitting five targets thrown up at one time, clipping off with a repeating rifle piece after piece from a potato held on a stick, snuffing out cigars held in an assistant's fingers, and smashing marbles so small that only puffs of white dust gave evidence of their destruction. (Riley 1994, 84)

In other occasions, she also bounded 'over a table and then [shot] two glass balls already in the air when she began to jump' (Riley 1994, 52), or even 'aimed at .22 cartridges tossed in the air, driving each out of sight' (Ibid., 181). As if these were not enough, her 'skill with horses also assumed legendary proportions' (Ibid., 52). Oakley's reliable prowess was built not on sheer luck, no husband however trusting would repeatedly volunteer to have bits of cigar blown off his mouth by a bullet (no matter what sins he had to atone for); it was not built on natural talent *alone*. Her own motto explains it best: 'Aim at a high mark and you will hit it. No, not the first time, nor the second and maybe not the third. But keep on aiming and keep on shooting for only practice will make you perfect. Finally you will hit the bull's eye of success' (Ibid., xiv). This advice almost hits the bull's eye, since practice does not make us perfect but poised to act. Eschewing metaphysical flights into abstractions, we keep our sights trained on the *zhēnrén*.

Billeter explains that the exceptional person is 'empty like the Heavens' (1994, 324, my translation), and we find in her 'nothing intentional, calculative, artificial, restrictive or constrained' (Ibid., 325, my translation). Contrary to average people in the way in which she is and acts, the sagely person seems empty like the heavens because we do not discern any ambition. Billeter clarifies this through the notion of '*agir selon*' (to act or behave in accordance with) that he uses to freely render the text's original *yuán*, 缘, 'which means "to follow"—to follow a way, for example' (Ibid.).[11] That is, she behaves in accordance with the needs of the moment, which is predicated on a 'spontaneous reaction' (Ibid.). For instance, imagine two dancers improvising. One, with legs straight, is bent forwards on her waist at a 90° angle, when at one moment, her partner jumps while leaning on her shoulders, to then, unexpectedly for both, she pushes off backwards to roll on the first dancer's back, at which point she assumes the former dancer's position. These kinds of novel and improvised off-the-cuff moves happen through 'voiding' or 'emptying'. Therein, spontaneity unfolds unencumbered by planning and calculation. As argued throughout, such movements are not either solely or mostly the result of 'black box' automatized and unconscious processes. Rather, they build on habituated past movements that become our *kinetic inventory* to be deployed and recombined. The result is enhanced action. In short, the voiding or emptying reveals windows of opportunity. Windows are built beforehand by means of Deweyan habits and deliberations.

We may rightly wonder about the range of expertise of the swordsman, athlete, sharpshooter, or performer in comparison with that of the consummate sage. It seems that the capabilities of the former are much more limited and 'parochial'. There are two related but distinct facets to expertise here. One concerns the range and the other the focus of said range. The focus helps determine the range: the breadth of the expertise, whether it permeates our whole character or spans all enactive domains or not, depends on the performer's focal point or aim. This takes up again, but from a different angle, the schism between virtues and skills. The person of excellence has a broad scope that goes beyond punctual performance, no matter how accurate or formidable. Varela states that the comparison between the expert athlete and the *bodhisattva* is useful to illustratively legitimize the claims Eastern teaching traditions make, but we should not confuse them, particularly in terms of 'the range of expertise' (1999, 35). The assumption is that the latter is superior, as his later comments suggest. Simply put, the sagely path seeks the loftier goal of spiritual insight whereas the athletic one pursues victory. Moreover, it is also often assumed that these two domains are mutually exclusive. To wit, Varela argues explicitly that we must not 'identify skillful means [which he ties to wisdom and Buddhism] with ordinary skills like learning to drive a car or play the violin' because 'mastery of the skillful means of ethical expertise results in the elimination of *all* habits so that the practitioner can realize that wisdom and compassion can arise directly and spontaneously out of wisdom' (Varela 1999, 72, his emphasis). For him, it is not a matter of learning and adding skills, but of removing obstacles to the expression of our inherent skills. His assessment that these practices, when used for self-improvement, reinforce the very egotism they are meant to dispel is well founded—within a Buddhist context that aims at *śūnyatā*, that is. There is prima facie merit to these claims.

They also run contrary to two central claims in *Skillful Striving*: (1) the propounded continuity among performative (skills), moral (virtues), aesthetic, and socio-environmental domains within a multidimensional normative continuum, and (2) the prescription that performers aim at a holistic excellence that reflects the former continuum as an expression of their overall character. Our skillful strivings are holistic undertakings. As such, putative differences are not of kind, as it seems, but a matter of emphasis. There are four points that help refine the above analysis.

First, we generally devote ourselves to such practices for a number of *ranked* or *weighted* reasons, not a single and uniform one. These reasons can change, as can their relative value to one another. While different practices cannot be pursued simultaneously, some objectives may be achieved concomitantly and through various endeavors. That is, there is no necessary exclusion between practices (nor between means and ends, see next section). A monk may seek enlightenment *through* his martial arts practice, or hiking for that matter; an athlete may seek victory and the athletic capacity to obtain it *and* cultivate her character while imbuing her practice with aesthetic value. And any old way of achieving victory will not do, as Healy's case makes clear: he wanted an honorable and beautiful victory *or* loss.

HOLISM AND THE CULTIVATION OF EXCELLENCE IN SPORTS AND PERFORMANCE

Second, the partiality and preeminence of the intellectual and spiritual over the physical (to phrase matters in accordance to this stance) result from an implicit dualism that separates the bodymind, split skills from virtues (and the aesthetic), and prompt Varela to discard 'ordinary' skillful means, such as sportive or performative ones, as ways toward the spiritual. The ongoing argument is that there is no such primacy or distinction in an ontological sense but rather it is a functional matter of better or worse performative and functional integration within a broad ecological framework when it comes to fulfilling a thickly holistic excellence. When achieved, this excellence, though always capable of refinement, is the result of a harmonious bodymind that is itself an achievement. Moreover, this is at odds with Varela's enactive commitments and the overall aim and scope of his project. As he writes, 'Through appropriate extension and attention and by training over time we have transformed these actions [intentionless, self-less ones] into embodied behavior' (Varela 1999, 35). Our actions and behavior cannot but be embodied.[12] Living bodyminds (*shintai*) perform them; integrated ones (*shin-shin*) perfect them. Varela goes on to explain that the kind of enactive wisdom he defends 'must be developed and embodied through *disciplines* that facilitate the letting-go of ego-centered habits and enable compassion to become spontaneous and self-sustaining' (Ibid., 73, his emphasis). These disciplines are (en)active pursuits for which ordinary skills of just the sort he dismisses are integral to the spiritual awakening he prizes. Additionally, for many Asian teaching traditions (such as yoga, any *dō*, and some Western ones), which are at the root of both soteriological endeavors and Varela's views, meditation is central. This involves the bodymind thoroughly, e.g. seating properly in *zazen* for hours on end requires considerable effort and focus. Likewise, intense activity characteristic of sports and other active pursuits can be decisively meditative as Yuasa (1993) remarks in the previous essay (whether this excludes athletic pursuits squarely or instrumentalizes the activity are different matters to be discussed below). In the context of *qi* (see appendix), some very vigorous practices are meditative and also seek spiritual goals that happen through, or rather, are coterminous with the bodymind's movements and exertions. It is a matter of emphasis, as they seek and obtain different outcomes. Sportive and athletic individuals are to cultivate intellectual and aesthetic facets in their lives, but intellectuals and artists better follow performatively active paths as well.

Third, skills, virtues, and aesthetic values are not normatively distinct when performed. In fact, the very ethical transformation Varela extols can be achieved through 'non-ethical' skillful means (reflecting his terminology, which already accentuates and brings on divisions). When *properly* engaged, in the more refined cases, they are one and the same: the drawing of the sword and the realization that there is neither sword nor self happen together. This results in *kalon*, the beautiful deed because noble and skillful. A better way to understand things is to characterize them as various *ways* to inculcate values across the whole normative span. In other words, the issue is *how* performers engage the practice rather than the practice itself being meditative or athletic, or the former being inherently superior (besides, it is not as if no monk meditates poorly or that no sportsperson gains rich existential insights). There is a qualitative range, surely: outstanding performers achieve the harmonious integration, competent performers overemphasize one element over the other or fail to suitably synchronize them with the needs of the moment, and incompetent ones, novices, and those under the vise of fractured performance exaggerate blunders.

293

Fourth, we can bypass Varela's concerns with egoism. These skillful strivings, even those pursued within purely sporting disciplines, are best done for the sake of the activity not the self. The goals are to perform better running, shooting, or dancing, and to develop the requisite skills proper to the activity. The very process and effacement of the self or ego is enhanced when performers are mindful of the activity and view their talents as gifts not their own (precisely because they are gifted, and which behoove to be developed). The consummate person extends the pride she takes in doing things well on the court, the stage, or the *dōjō* to the rest of her life. *Shugyō's* lifelong pursuit is the proper existential framework (which can be coordinated to emphasize certain domains more at certain points in life). Right and better action is a capacity with joint moral, aesthetic, and skillful expression. And this is not simply a matter of a punctual (ad)venture or even an isolated practice. In the cases under consideration, it pervades the performer's character. By all accounts, Annie Oakley was a straight shooter in competition, performance, and life. She was a role model to women and young girls because her skills matched her upright and honest character. She never succumbed to trickery in her performances (unlike many contemporary performers) (Riley 1994). The lengths she went on to clear her name from a case of libel give a weightier indication, as she spent substantial amounts to set the record straight when an unscrupulous news editor falsely and deliberately besmirched her reputation to sell copy.

To summarize, this model explains Healy's actions, and MacAskill's, Oakley's and Slater's expertise, better than the narrowly rational alternatives. The master lives a fully fledged life that is active as it integrates all enactive domains. Zhuangzian masters 'simply' act in harmony with the situation. Fasting the heart-mind, 心, they neither ruminate nor second guess. They move energetically and fluidly. They act spontaneously yet decisively. They perform superbly and joyfully. One of the factors they rely on is conceptualized here as 'reflective intuition'.

3. Reflective Intuition

As it stands, the first impression is that a *reflective* intuition is infelicitous at best or oxymoronic at worst. Intuition is supposed to operate unreflectively, if anything. It is meant to bypass rational processes and bring immediate understanding. It would appear that unreflective intuition with no contribution from higher-order rational processes is the way to go for a holistic and enactive approach to performance. Put differently, it seems indeed contradictory to bring deliberation into the picture. Yet, much as Whitman (1903) could accommodate contradiction because he was large and could contain multitudes,[13] enlarging the intuitive scope dissolves any *seeming* inconsistency. It is possible to craft a flexible model that proves more expedient philosophically and pragmatically. The generous contours of thick holism bring together the two modes, spontaneity built on empty bodyminds and cognitive processes that may or may not involve representation. The next examination develops a hybrid and dynamic model of intuition in the context of performance that is connected to two aspects of reflection that interlace both strands, enactive and representational. This type of intuition, itself a capacity to be developed, is pivotal to excel in performative endeavors.

Suzuki writes, 'It is the intellect that raises the question, but it is not the intellect that answers it' (1993, 156). At times, our need for answers misleads us. To adapt this to performance and our purposes, while the intellect articulates the question,

HOLISM AND THE CULTIVATION OF EXCELLENCE IN SPORTS AND PERFORMANCE

understanding and spontaneous performance arise otherwise. There are performative conundrums that necessitate understanding—standing under and beholding the question—rather than specific answers. Sometimes, the puzzlements begin as wordless and gentle proddings; at other times, they may come as painful jabs. For example, a dancer explores flowing continuations to a set of improvised moves, pausing to reenact and attempt one line of movement at one speed, only to recalibrate and try again differently as she feels her way toward understanding the possibilities of the movements. This unspecificity does not mean either opaque or qualitatively poorer understanding. Rather, it is flexible, enactive, and efficacious in its own way: it can bring a deeper appreciation for the 'question', a more joyful expression of movement in consonance with the circumstances, or a 'successful' performance by criteria other than victory, such as richer insights or more flowing movement. Of course, this process can be engaged, in addition, discursively. In fact, in the best cases, it *is* at *some* point. It is only that propositional articulations, however, are not the *summum bonum* in performance, cognition, or our lives. They are but another piece to the puzzle. We can picture the two modes as the *yin* and *yang* of expert performance—in harmony at their best, forever united yet different. That said, it is time to explain how these pieces fit the puzzle. It begins with an examination of time dynamics.

Superior performance draws from both sources, but diversely and at different times. Timing and synchrony are central to this. They are a further facet of our integrative bodymind. In parallel with the functional fluidity we find among conscious, fringe, and subpersonal phenomena of consciousness, there is a continuous functional flux between our cognitively empty (body) mind states and representational ones. Although there is no counterpart to the fringe of consciousness, the relation between the two is similarly very dynamic: just as the athlete or performer scans through the different levels of awareness, she also engages either enactive or deliberative and rational processes. Which is relied upon when depends on the nature of the challenge, the environmental conditions, her skills, and a host of other psychophysical elements (motivation, fitness). This can go terribly wrong as we have seen with Henry Skrimshander in essay 8, or terrifically well, as Zhuangzi's consummate masters show. Masters whose bodymind is harmoniously integrative, with a flowing *qi* if you will, freely move between the two, matching their responses to the situations. Someone competent but with a (body) mind or body(mind) imbalance may be asynchronous and perform poorly. The emphasis so far has fallen largely on the performer, or *the* moment of the performance as defined by, for example, the 41 steps in 9.63 seconds that Usain Bolt took to win gold in the 100 meters at the 2012 London Olympic Games (Saxena 2012). This is when spontaneity and the enactive command the stage. But, how about the steps before and after the race? What do these contribute? As will be argued next, the leading steps before the performance *and* the following ones are crucial. Concordantly, we must assimilate the 'before and after' period enveloping performance into our account for a better understanding of excellent performance.

To explore the chronological facet of superior performance, the Japanese philosopher Minamoto Ryōen's views are advantageous because they make a compelling case and analyze insightfully the before-performance-after segment.[14] The idea of *kata* (型 or 形), which translates as 'form,' acts as the hub in his thinking. Basically, it refers to an organizing schema or pattern, just as a martial arts *kata* is a patterned and formalized sequence of movements. To stress its dynamic nature, and in keeping with the

HOLISM AND THE CULTIVATION OF EXCELLENCE IN SPORTS AND PERFORMANCE

convention adopted in essay 7, the gerund, 'patterning', is used instead when not using the transliteration from Japanese. Minamoto (2011) contrasts two kinds, the *kata* of form and the *kata* of style. The latter 'is a much wider and more fluent concept' than the former (Minamoto 2011, 931). In fact, the patternings of style include those of form temporally, conceptually, and functionally: 'Attending to the performance as a whole, the kata of style includes the kata of form—whether multiple or singular—to give form to beauty in the flow of time' (Ibid., 935). The scope of style is much broader. The patternings of form in the tea ceremony 'can be grasped visually in the act of receiving guests with the preparation of tea' (Ibid., 931). Bolt's 41 steps correspond to this. But the patternings of style of the tea ceremony, since they cover the whole 'stream of decorum from the time before the guests arrive until the time they are seen off, [affect] a much longer course of time' (Ibid.). Bolt's pre-run routine, warm up, and the cool down, celebratory run, and medal ceremony frame the 100-meter run and should be included as part of the performance's meaning-conferring context. The same year, London had a stage version of *Chariots of Fire* that brought 'the kinetic thrill of the athletics track to the theatre' (Hemming 2012). As play director Edward Hall remarked, the theater could 'tease out the emotion of the moment or suggest the way nerves seem to bend time for the participant' (Ibid.). For such an intense and short event as the 100 meters, the moments *before* leaving the blocks are qualitatively more important for Bolt. Again Minamoto explains, 'The kata of style appears in the act of controlling breathing as a preparation for the kata of form as well as in the reverberations that echo through the act of closure after a performance' (Ibid., 935). Likewise, to understand Bolt's performance, we can explain enactively his explosiveness, his reaction times, his immediate responses to the opponents should he feel any getting closer. We can also consider the role of rational and practical deliberations and articulations: how he actually thinks and speaks about his run before and after, as well as the myriad interactions with coaches, the press, and more, and which form part of the performative history of Olympic competition. E.g. some athletes deal poorly with media pressure; Bolt seems to thrive in it. Within this totality, there are lively alternations between the two modes.

As Minamoto elucidates, this applies to all sorts of performing and martial arts (obviously, we can add sports) (2011, 935). To wit, 'the manners of *sumō* wrestling that run through the short breaks in the bout, or the courtesies shown before and after drawing the bow in the Way of Archery, would then be further examples of the kata of style in traditional Japanese performing arts' (Ibid.). But, these manners of style are a lot less noticeable. Because the patternings of form are more visible to spectators, form is the one on which novices fix their attention exclusively. Verily, novices, pundits, and academics alike all too often focus on Bolt's 41 steps only to forget about the byzantine, complex elements that make that feat possible. Minamoto writes, 'Each performance contains a kata of form which tends to monopolize our attention, but if we include the long span of time before and after as part of the process, the kata of form is not possible without practice and performance' (Ibid.). In fact, without the patterning of style 'that includes what comes before and after, there would be no kata of form' (Ibid., 931). Those who really appreciate a practice are intimately familiar not only with what happens on stage during the performance, but also with the rehearsals, the backstage and front-of-house workings of the theater, the lighting, and subtleties that structure the performance and its preparation. This is foreclosed to dilettantes, as is the deeper beauty of sprinting to most casual fans.

HOLISM AND THE CULTIVATION OF EXCELLENCE IN SPORTS AND PERFORMANCE

A pity, for the patterning of style is richer and broader than that of form: embracing it 'within the stream of time', it has a flow that the one of form does not, 'allowing for the unexpected, the startling, the resourceful' (Ibid.). Style offers more yet, because it encompasses 'both things that are not included in the temporal element, such as literary style, as well as things that revolve about temporality as their core, such as manners' (Ibid.). Style then offers multivalent analyses of complex phenomena like sport, martial, and artistic performances; temporal, aesthetic, moral, cognitive, and social elements become pertinent and amenable to analysis. We can follow the reverberations of the patterings or *kata* of style well beyond Bolt's pre- and post-performance routines to include, beyond the two-week period of the Olympics and the walls of the Olympic Stadium, Jamaica and its sprinting culture. Or, we can analyze and contrast the phenomena of *mushin* and flow, or mindful awareness, as they are experienced by specific individuals within larger timescales than customary ones, and also examine them within their respective cultural frameworks according to Buddhist or sportive canons.

Last, whereas the patterings of form are 'general and universal to the extent that the name of the one who created [them] is forgotten, style has an individual face, as it does in the "taste" and "literary style" used in tea ceremony implements' (Minamoto 2011, 931). A *karateka* performing a *seisan kata*, which means 13, one of the oldest, follows the general and universal patterns as set by her particular school of karate. All students learn the same pattern and strive to perfect it. In terms of style, she will have her own kinetic style of moving, as manifested and modulated by her morphological qualities and even her energy level at the time. Were she to follow it as *karatedō*, as a way of life, and eventually become an expert, she will then develop a kinetic signature, a personal way of moving distinctively all her own that parallels kinetically a painter's style (essay 7). But, because the patterings of style are personal, as Minamoto explains, 'if we take continuity in its social dimension, the kata of style, in contrast to the kata of form, is unstable and fated to disappear' (931). *Our* style of doing things lives and dies with us.

The emptiness of spontaneous and enactive action can become part of the individual patterings of style as well. In a team of synchronized swimmers, they can all learn the same routine and movements for a performance, the formal patterings being the same. But, how each move is learned and internalized until it is owned and becomes spontaneous happens through the patterings that style affords. This framework then is ample enough to cordially accommodate the vibrant tension latent within reflective intuition.

The sense of reflective intuition under consideration is one where understanding and judgment are instantaneous, surely, but informed by previous deliberation and training and subsequent reflection on the performance.[15] 'Comprehensive reflection', is used henceforth to refer to both post-performance assessment and pre-performance deliberation as part of an ongoing process of valuations and revaluations. The intuition under consideration is a rigorous one that is also reflective in sophisticated ways. The words of Zen monk Takuan are doubly helpful. They reveal the role intuitive reflection plays in performative challenges and successful performances and contextualize this discussion while setting things up for a reconceptualization of the means/ends relation. Takuan writes:

297

> Consider the core of the mind to be a wagon, with willpower to be carried about in it. Push it to a place where there can be failure, and there will be failure. Push it to a side where there can be success, and there will be success. But whether there is success or failure, if one entrusts himself to the straightness of this wagon of the core of the mind, he will attain right-mindedness [flawless integrity] in either case. (1986, 56)

This right-mindedness operates much in the fashion of a spontaneously reflective intuition. As Takuan's translator Scott Wilson explains, 'The emphasis lies in the individual's [*sic*.] first setting himself right, through *self-reflection*, training, and discipline' (Takuan 1986, 96 fn.1, my emphasis). The rich reverberations of Ortega's *pundonor* (essay 4), striving after flawless integrity, Dewey's deliberative habit, as well as James' tough discipline should be clearly heard. The result is spontaneous, superior action. Rather than being fully subpersonal, this reflective intuition unfolds in varying degrees of awareness. It does so through subpersonally integrated kinetic patternings that respond to a tennis table ball's trajectory; it operates at the fringe level of consciousness, lifting certain kinesthetic features off our perceptual and cognitive river, as when a kayaker monitors the resistance of an eddy of water to her paddling movements; it in involved when self-reflectively aware, for example, a jumper's mounting anxiety as she waits seated on the rail of the world's largest ski jumping hill at Vikersundbakken in Norway.

In normal conditions, as we scan through these we are pre-reflectively aware of being the agent or experiencing something. Much as Deweyan habit is active and dynamic, this intuition drinks deeply from Nishida's acting intuition. This intuition is philosophically complex, skillfully resourceful, and practically full of possibilities as it carves out realizations for fulsome engagements with our environment. As such, it is its own terminus on an ongoing series of in-the-moment interactions. Ortega theorizes this in terms of Spinoza's *amor intellectualis*, which is an intellectual state superior to reason.[16] In Nishidan fashion, it allows for freedom within a deterministic system. Its inferences differ from those of reason in that they are immediate and require neither general rules nor intermediate reasoning steps. For our purposes, the idea is that a narrow rationality is not the highest level of skillful cognition. Rather, it needs to be amalgamated with other faculties (understanding, imagination), as well as emotional and social elements. To further elucidate reflective intuition and see how it works, it is useful to distinguish it from rational intuition, common sense, and intuitive snap judgments, and show how it bypasses their inherent problems.

Rational intuition is concerned with necessary propositions and inferences guided by reason's beaming light. It is involved when we 'feel' that modus ponens is a logically valid inference, for example. The immediate sense of correctness we get in this case is purportedly different from our intuitions concerning empirical facts, often labeled as common sense, say that the heavier object will fall faster than the lighter one or that the sun revolves around our stable earth. As Hales so aptly puts it, 'these plausible inferences have been laid waste by science' (2000, 135). These commonsensical intuitions are passed on along as proverbs, maxims and the like. Characteristic of them is that they are often endorsed uncritically. Further, for many of the adages, there is always a contrary one that seems just as intuitive. Experience has also other ways of proving our common sense intuitions and instinctive reactions wrong.[17] When faced with a charging bull people tend to run away in a straight line, or if handed a cape, they try to protect themselves by hiding behind it (incidentally, and to lay to waste

HOLISM AND THE CULTIVATION OF EXCELLENCE IN SPORTS AND PERFORMANCE

another cliché, the bull charges incited by movement, the red color doing nothing for it). This only lines up the bull perfectly for a goring. Counter to our intuition, the thing to do is to push the cape away from oneself or hold the charge of the bull to feint and cut to the other side at the last moment. No wonder many prefer to face the horns of logical dilemmas instead.

Rational intuition is impervious to this sort of empirical and performative epistemic reversals of fate. Even if many look at it with suspicion or derision, many other prominent philosophers such as Bonjour, Chalmers, Dennett, or Kripke, avow that it grounds their arguments (Hales 2000). But, for all its importance and prevalence in the thinking of many, either openly or closeted, it presents particular problems of its own. The bright light of reason harbors a dark secret. Hales, serendipitously with this essay's title, writes, 'There is a mystery in the dark heart of reason, a skeleton in all of our closets that we would jus as soon keep hidden from the light of day. This is the justificatory status of rational intuition' (2000, 135). Pithily put, rational intuition leads to an infinite regress. Hales advances a modest foundationalism as the preferable horn of a dilemma whose other horn advocates for accepting that 'philosophy grounded in the use of rational intuition is bunk' (145). Of course, this blending brings in a distasteful, for purists, taste to the pure bouquet of the necessary. Our present concern is not with this kind of intuition, whose headache comes from trying to establish an a priori nonfoundational account that is not viciously circular. Reflective intuition has a solid foundational basis, but it is unaffected by such purist concerns.

Beyond philosophical rational intuition, there are the kinds of intuitive judgments that fall under the rubrics of snap judgments or gut feelings. This slim intuition is best exemplified by the 'thin-slicing' thinking that Gladwell's book *Blink* popularized (2005). It is largely subpersonal, which he references as the 'adaptive unconscious', and is modeled after a computational model of the mind that supposedly informs our thinking and helps us make snap judgments within the first two seconds (Gladwell 2005, 11). There is merit to many of Gladwell's examples, particularly those where judgment is based on years of training, study, and experience (in which case these can be recategorized as reflective), while many others are more questionable. Nonetheless, as Brooks' (2005) incisive review points out, in addition to statistical analysis' superior predictive record over that of gut feelings, philosophers have written about thin-slicing, which they call wisdom, for eons. As seen with Varela, there is more to this initial two-second snap judgment that initially meets the eye. Where this analysis has merit, it is on purely non-intuitive grounds, that is, reflective ones.

Between the ever so fast and thinly sliced hunch and the comparatively slumbering and thickly rational thinking there is a flexible, spontaneous, and capable intuition that is rigorous and reflective in its own way. Reflective intuitions are not to be taken as self-evident and necessary. Likewise, they are not to be accepted unquestionably as common sense truisms in a self-justificatory series. Very flexible processually, reflective intuition *is* empirical but does not exclude reason across the board. Another way to put this is that *where* it is rational, this is foundationally based on experience. This is in keeping with pragmatism's affinity for naturalism. Reflective intuition is also genetically recursive. This is not concerned with some sort of epistemic DNA analysis, but rather appeals to the origin and history of the intuition. Initially, they all rely on a 'sense of (self)-evident truthfulness'. Reflective intuition has the broader scope of the three. Rational intuition is 'ahistorical' in virtue of its a priori nature, and the thin intuition of

HOLISM AND THE CULTIVATION OF EXCELLENCE IN SPORTS AND PERFORMANCE

gut feelings is short-lived. Reflective intuition, however, has a *history* of deliberation and analysis. Each particular intuitive instance is part of a broad web of cognitive and performative processes whose scope encompasses the aforementioned history of the immediate instantiation (not unlike the patternings of style). This means that its scope goes beyond the *immediate* judgment, understanding, or action of punctual intuitions. Moreover, it is not doomed to the dungeons of the subpersonal. It makes available higher discriminative powers that result in more refined skills that benefit from a history of careful deliberation and subsequent analysis. These comprehensive reflections in turn lead to learned patternings that dynamically change with the situation. This history typically begins with algorithmic-like iterations that over time are gradually optimized into heuristic shortcuts. The integration of low-level skills and refinement into clusters of higher-order abilities seen in performative endeavors exemplifies this very clearly.

Consider an example. Wind and flight aerodynamics are pivotal factors in ski jumping. A study of the aerodynamics comparing the top ten and top worst jumpers at the 1996 World Cup in Innsbruck found that the major differences 'can be attributed to the aerodynamics of the flight technique of jumpers, which is characteristically conditioned by the geometric distinctions of the body shape of ski jumpers during flight' (Jost et al. 1998, 248). This is why jumpers must remain fluid if they are to ride the wind like Liezi. Chozansi's *Tengu* (demon) would say they should allow their *qi* to pervade and move freely through the changing spaces of their acting bodymind. They begin with basic step-by-step instruction and acquisition of basic and discrete motor skills that are algorithmically and repetitively carried out as solutions to simple motor task challenges until they learn to appreciate the kinesthetic feel that results in the heuristically integrated skill of flowing movement. After our anxious ski jumper at Vikersundbakken has centered herself through breathing and imagery, she slides down and takes off, pushes off the lip and, *counterintuitively*, leans forward into the fall with the skis in a V-shape, and then prepares her landing. But, mid-flight a very strong gust pushes her body. She needs to quickly recalibrate to maintain lift, remain airborne longer, and land safely. Sometimes moving her arms slightly suffices. Here, the lineage of previous motor efficiencies, judgments, jumps, discussions with coaches and teammates, analyses of others' jumps, and reflection on her abilities inform her intuition that this time arm shifting will not work. Her response and its effectiveness reflect the *quality* of her intuitive spontaneous response's genetic history. This is what modulates and shapes her inherent talents and those unique bodymind psychophysiological parameters that geometrically distinguish her in flight. Again, given the specificity of skill to practice, in other sports or activities there may be more time for deliberation or preparation and less time for correction e.g. as when driving a golf ball or responding to an opponents' wicked sidespin playing tennis table. But no matter the activity, successfully spontaneous performances rely on this broader reflective intuitive process. It is methodologically rich, modally cross-referential, and intersubjectively validated.

As a process, reflective intuition tests and re-tests its assumptions, and relies on a broad methodological palette that can include phenomenological description, conceptual analysis, hypothesis testing, performance re-enactment, and cross-modal checks among different senses. E.g. a tennis player doing a mock slice serve engages several of these depending on the context: he may verbally rehearse a specific step, 'hit the ball at the 2 o'clock point and pronate', he also analyzes the various steps of the serve from various perspectives, kinematic (speed of the racket), biomechanical (elbow position), physiological (exertion level), which he gauges kinesthetically and proprioceptively, visualizes the move, and conducts mock serves without the ball. If he is also a philosopher or so inclined, he may analyze it phenomenologically for both theoretical and practical reasons: the theoretical analysis can enrich his descriptions and understanding of the what-it-is-like to serve, and this can help him refine the serve or enjoy it more (or less on both counts should he attempt this *while* serving!). In addition to his own experience as to the practical efficacy of his various intuitions and strategies, he also intersubjectively validates his conclusions with others' experiences and analyses. Pragmatic considerations aside, how justified are we *philosophically* in relying on this reflective intuition?

For those still worried about ultimate justification, the initial 'phenomenological feeling', suspect in a priori rational accounts, as Hales explains (2000, 138), is not problematic for reflective intuition because there is no 'qualitative' jump from the empirical to the a priori; there is a continuous thread. It does not rely on the 'long discredited faculty of psychology' that relies on belief-forming mechanisms among which we still need to justify why we would turn to intuition (Hales 2000, 144). We must concern ourselves with how properly to describe experience, processes, functions, movements, or actions at the proper level to facilitate our understanding. Rather than the light of day, the mystery is revealed like the magic runes in Tolkien's Middle Earth, under the light of the moon. This is the purview of phenomenology.

Phenomenology, as a method, helps articulate and describe our foundational perceptions, the building blocks of our meaningful experiences. It does so rigorously, and at various levels, from a static and transcendental one concerned with consciousness to a generative and historical level (see Section 6). It allows us to reflect on our experience because it pays close attention to the felt sensations of the moment; because it analyzes conscious and pre-reflective experiential phenomena; and because it can be part of a broader theoretical framework (as it is in *Skillful Striving*). For instance, and as shown in detail in *Riding the Wind*, we can consider the flowing feeling of efficient movements in kick boxing: kinesthetically, we can pay attention to how our knee feels when doing a round-house kick. Better or worse 'flowing feelings' are cashed out in terms of practical effectiveness. But, as noted, there is a higher conceptual and normative level where the various pertinent enactive domains unite into a whole where said movement is imbued with broader, deeper, and richer meanings: the movements become honorably beautiful actions or ignobly ugly ones, and these actions become part of our performative biographies, which in turn will inform our future intuitions and performances. On a larger scale yet, and as we have seen with Kretchmar (2013), these in turn re-constitute the very practice we engage; how we perform appropriates the very activity. It owns us as much as we own it. Best leaving these wider social aspects for later, we should begin to direct our steps toward reflection. Chozanzi's words are illuminating again.

The metaphysical centerpiece of his medieval swordsmanship treatise is the essence of mind, consciousness. But, its operation remains a 'Mysterious Function' whose 'principles cannot be known' (2006, 144). Yet, we can train it to act spontaneously and successfully by controlling our emotions, being focused during action, avoiding egotism, and being spontaneous. This depends on our intuition, which is, 'a knowledge that illuminates truth and falseness, perversity and propriety, with the spiritual clarity of the essence of the mind' (Chozan 2006, 145). This intuition is gnostic and

Socratic in the sense that its clarity is gained from self-knowledge and a lucid realization as to our place in the world. This requires reflexive and reflective thinking, for a mirror-like reflection from various angles, directed inward and outwardly.

Thus, two aspects of reflection are pertinent now. As to the first, it simply involves pondering on something carefully, with rigor, and depth. As mentioned, our reflective intuitions have a genetic history. Before and after the intuitive judgments and understanding, ahead of the spontaneous execution of movements and actions, masters think deeply about how to improve and rely on deliberative and analytic processes. In simple words, they reflect on their experiences. They can analyze their performance for weaknesses and strong points. Experts need to test their skills and push their boundaries to further refine them. In the case of risk sportspersons, whose activity is often questioned and superficially viewed as *merely* thrill-seeking behavior, it just so happens that their endeavors are dangerous and very thrilling. Performers can also examine *why* they do this at all, that is, inquire as to the role their activity of choice plays in their lives, as Slater exemplified earlier. In the case of risky activities, these can and should be the source for existential self-assessment and the possible gnostic truths to be gained (Ilundáin-Agurruza forthcoming-b). The role of comprehensive reflection is not simply reduced to pondering on possibilities, but also involves experiencing and reflecting on failure (essay 8). Indeed, excellence and its meaningfulness go hand in hand with embracing failures. MacAskill's many failed attempts to do a front flip with his bike over a tall fence, as shown in *The Frontflip* 'making of' video depicts this perfectly (Thomson and MacAskill 2014b). Moreover, paragons integrate all enactive domains. They adopt strategies to incorporate these processes enactively into their patternings of movements and dispositions to act. These constitute their personal kinetic signature.

Regarding the second, it has an altogether different notion of 'reflection' conceptually. It involves the idea of reflection as mirroring. Zhuangzi helps present how this mirroring works, 'The Consummate Person uses his mind like a mirror, rejecting nothing, welcoming nothing, responding but not storing. Therefore he can handle all things without harm' (Zhuangzi and Ziporyn 2009, 54).[18] This metaphor of the mirror is more apt than it seems. Mirrors reflect instantaneously, and our spontaneous action is best when it springs in the same manner. Surely, mirrors are passive, merely reflecting what is presented to them whereas we are active and creative. If we remember the kind of mirrors involved, harking back to Ancient China, these were 'productive': able to generate fire or water (through condensation), they were attributed magical properties, were made of different materials (e.g. bronze) and had varied shapes (convex, flat, etc.), which means that they did not simply reflect (see essays 5 and 9). More yet, just as mirrors require upkeep and dusting away to reflect at their best, reflective and enactive mirroring needs much disciplined training of our skills. This makes them a better fit to our creative, holistic, and enactive ways.

The beautiful opening poem by Emperor Sutoku is helpful now: 'Though there is a reflection/The moon reflects itself/Without thought/Without thought, too, the water: Hirozawa Pond' (Chozan 2006, 133). Chozansi, through the character of the *Tengu* explains it thus, 'At the heart of this poem is an enlightened state of mind concerning action and response with No-Mind and spontaneity' (Ibid.). This reflection that acts spontaneously arises from that state of mindful emptiness that is dynamically 'filled' with the moment. In other words, when a performer suitably acts to meet the challenge, her spontaneity and effectiveness does not rely on representational cognitive

HOLISM AND THE CULTIVATION OF EXCELLENCE IN SPORTS AND PERFORMANCE

processes *at* the instant of action. There is a mirroring between her empty state and the trial she faces. There is 'no self' that gives rise to worry, just the ability expressing itself in synchrony with the environment. But, as Chozansi writes, this 'is not what you would call empty-headedness. It is the foundation of the mind and has no form' (Chozan 2006, 188). As seen with Takuan in the previous essay, it is about not being distracted or stopping. Chozansi's advice is that 'You should never be taken by phenomena' because once 'you are the least bit taken by something, your ch'i will be drawn to it. And once your ch'i is even slightly drawn to something, it will be incapable of adaptability or openness' (Ibid.). Being taken by phenomena is when we pause, engage rational thinking, and become filled with representational content. To avoid damning distraction and attain superb realization, 'there is nothing more than following phenomena as they come, responding to them, and leaving no traces' (Ibid.). As usual, the hard part lies in actually being able to do this.[19]

Now, it may be adduced that mirrors represent, but our enactive ways are supposed to lack representations of *any* kind. Of course, these are two different senses of 'representation,' but to pursue this briefly: mirrors do not 'store' representations at any point; our cognitively and performatively empty ways merely reflect without storing or stopping either. To the extent that representations are involved—they are important for successful action—these are pre- or post-performance style patternings with extended histories. Conceptually, we need to distinguish between empty (body) minds and representational ones, surely. Practically, they work best ensemble, the way a well-honed relay team runs: sequentially and with impeccably precise transitions. Polishing our skills requires careful comprehensive reflection—some of our instantaneous responses can have very long fuses. Consequently, the former sense of reflection, that deep and meticulous thinking, is integrated into the genetic histories of intuitive reflection and spontaneous action. In short, when both kinds of reflection harmoniously coalesce, we find spontaneously enactive action and reflection.

On a recent sparring bout with student Gabriel Wells, working with blunt steel swords, we set out to solve the problem of how to stop a 'vertical' cut (the fastest and most powerful) without relying on any kind of high-guard counter, the obvious response. We decided on the middle guard, which holds the sword at waist height. Having worked on swordsmanship on and off over the years, and with *no* claim to *any* sort of mastery, my repertoire did not include any parries from this guard to a high cut. Purposefully, I avoided imagining or trying to figure out beforehand what line the sword could take. After the signal, he slashed at close to full speed. The resulting simultaneous parry and countercut was not one I had yet seen in manuals or learned before: stepping *into* the line of his cut, and catching the oncoming blade between his own crossguard and blade, I used the other blade's kinetic energy to instantly pivot on its own short edge (the one closer to the leading forearm and opposite to the second set of knuckles holding the grip) and cut the opponent's face (mistiming would have meant my head would be hit instead). Even though it was enactive through and through *when* performed, it was not a mere reaction. It was under tight control: the blunt but hard edge of the blade stopped after barely touching the protective metallic mesh on his fencing mask (there was no need to take his head off!). More importantly, previous deliberations, training, and sparring sessions informed this spontaneous movement and the control. It also needed repetition, and post-performance analysis, to see why it worked and to refine it in order to incorporate it to our repertoire. The important point is that the mirroring that *mushin*[20] and states of empty mindfulness make possible is inherently tied to comprehensively reflective processes.

The state of mindful emptiness can be shared intersubjectively, as when teammates operate in harmonious synchrony or opponents become one action, as Fukasawa illustrates with the *judōkas* in the previous essay. It can even be transmitted to and shared with animals. Consider the case of horses, animals that are very perceptive to behavioral cues we and other animals give—visual, tactile, or olfactory. Clever Hans was a horse believed to be able to do arithmetic operations. It was discovered that the horse responded to minimal behavioral cues that the trainer or others, completely unawares, transmitted through their body language. When a superb jockey and his horse connect to the point of identifying with each other, then, 'the horse forgets the man, the man forgets the horse, and their spirits are one and do not go in different ways' (Chozan 2006, 131). The horse and the rider mirror each other. And this can extend from the merely performative domain into the normative one. Japanese Olympic equestrian Shunzo Kido beautifully showed this during the 1932 Los Angeles Olympic Games (Eccenbarger 2008). He had a very strong bond with his horse. Performing exceptionally, they were leading and set to win the gold medal. Then, the horse staggered. Kido could *feel* instantly that it was not a mere misstep. Most riders would have pushed for the gold. Kido *unhesitatingly*, instantly, concerned for his horse, quit the race. Again, in the most splendid cases, the integration of the enactive domains results in such admirable cases worthy of *kalon* status.[21]

Accomplished experts respond to the situation like these mirrors. They match their response to the needs of the moment, whether these be purely athletic, martial, and artistic, and whether these involve other people or animals. Virtuous, beautiful, effective action is spontaneous but not capricious or intuitive in the sort of way Gladwell and the popular press, cherry picking from him, have popularized. Reflective intuition is a capacity. As such it forms part of our stock of skillful strivings—it can, and needs to, be cultivated. Such spontaneous action necessitates practice not because practice makes perfect, but rather because it makes us poised, practiced, and prepared as Hutto stated (essay 7). Lest this give the impression that these consummate experts are flawless and, indeed, perfect, they are all too aware that in life the unexpected is always around the corner. That is why those who have achieved the highest states are so comfortable with failure, and why the accept change in stride. This very acceptance, fruit of reflection in both senses, is also what allows them to practice, absorb, and be poised and prepared.

Even if we are sold on this kind of reflective intuition, if only because it *works* (better than the alternatives), we should question the role that reflection plays in performance and excellence. Leaving aside practical issues of whether reflection may hamper performance, the philosophical challenge is concerned with reflective thinking, philosophical justification, and the meaning of our endeavors.[22] Erin Flynn raises the following issue: 'No doubt post-performance reflection is (often) a crucial *means* to developing excellence, but it should not be confused with excellence or made a part of excellence' (2013, my emphasis). First, his point applies not just to post-performance reflection but also to comprehensive reflection. The line of argumentation in *Skillful Striving* commits us to defending the view that such reflection *is* an intrinsic constituent of excellent performance. Reflection is necessary for excellence. This applies also in specific contexts as

HOLISM AND THE CULTIVATION OF EXCELLENCE IN SPORTS AND PERFORMANCE

well. To lay out the case against reflection fully, Flynn continues, 'Many expert athletes seem to be very poor analyzers of their own performance, of what made it successful', similarly to some artists who fail to reflect upon their work with the brilliance of the critic (Ibid.). This is readily extensible to artistic, martial and other performances *qua* artistic, martial, etc. For the sake of brevity, comments and examples are restricted to sport. Flynn raises two main points that pertain to the role that reflection plays in excellence, and the idea of whether it enhances the *kind* of excellence in display, whether it be athletic, artistic, or martial. Sketches to two answers follow.

The first one simply admits that, given the *telos* ascribed to them, this is correct within current categorizations of performative endeavors. Strictly speaking, such performance assessment as part of excellence is not *athletic* itself. Moreover, said analysis does not necessarily mean better *athletic* performance. In fact, it may get in the way in so far as it can lead to over-analysis during performance if given too much importance (essay 8).[23] This answer, for all its intuitively commonsensical appeal, cannot be assimilated into the framework of *Skillful Striving*. The second answer makes of comprehensive assessment a prominent feature of excellence *as* athletic, martial, or artistic. It posits an expansive stand that expands the conceptual and practical scope of these practices and makes the boundaries more permeable. The strategy is similar to that in arguments about extensive (Hutto and Myin 2013) or extended minds (Clark 2008; Clark and Chalmers 1998; Menary 2010). Obviating important but ancillary differences for now,[24] the basic idea is that the 'mind' does not stop with the brain or nervous system but rather incorporates tools and even the environment. Analogously, we can extend the operative notions of excellence, performance, and athletics to include a much broader swath of phenomena, as argued with the patterning of style. In fact, this is more radical than the extended mind hypothesis. The underlying thick holism not only does away with 'mind' and 'body' splits and bodily boundaries, or does it include the environment, but, following Ortega, considers personal and collective histories to be integral—even phenomenologically.

Athletics and competition are not only about the result (by which we judge the two performances as the same) but above all the process. A full account of this process goes far beyond the podium. Accordingly, we can propose that the coach is an integral part of the athletic pursuit *as* athletic: the athlete is simply offloading a process to be able to perform better *athletically*. In the case of the superior analyst athlete, she enriches her performances athletically precisely in virtue of her more insightful analyses. Thus, the '*same*' performance in terms of result *is* not the same qualitatively, particularly in terms of what matters most: what it *means* to the athlete. This is similar to how an artist's painting may look the same as another's (suppose it is a contemporary painting in the style of Malevich's *Black Square*). The interpretation is what makes it not only richer but ontologically distinct (Ilundáin-Agurruza 2000). Moreover, her reflections may enhance *our* appreciation of the performance. Rare as it may be in the world of bland sports interviews and canned answers, some athletes give us golden gnostic nuggets, *pace* Clark Sheehan and Rich Lally (essay 3). This extends the scope of athletic performance to include other putatively non-athletic elements, such as reflective intuition, among others.

But, as we saw with Liezi and his archery in the previous essay, the ultimate question to be answered is, *why*? Reid aptly summarizing McFee's critique of MacIntyre writes, 'Sport should do more than train us to do an action. It should foster an under-

HOLISM AND THE CULTIVATION OF EXCELLENCE IN SPORTS AND PERFORMANCE

standing of why we do that action, (2012, 67).[25] Ultimately, athletic excellence should be a manifestation of a larger excellence—even it retains its 'identity'. *Skillful Striving* enlarges what counts as excellence in sport (or other endeavors) so that it is not only pure athletic virtue that wins all, so to speak. It is not just about the net result (win or loss) but *the way* it is achieved (some wins are more admirable than others). Delving into this means redefining the process-result relation. Put otherwise, we need to re-conceptualize means and ends.

4. Rethinking Means-Ends and its Repercussions for Performance

Spaniard Kilian Jornet Burgada is hard to categorize as a sportsperson. This may be because, much as legendary Dean Potter has invented sports combining BASE jumping with climbing and with slacklining, Jornet's combination of ultrarunning and alpinism (and skiing when need be) does not even have a name yet. He has 'run-climbed' the Matterhorn in 1 h 56 m, 'roundtripped' it in less than three hours, and done Denali, which usually takes two weeks to climb, in 9 h 43 m. His next project is to run up Everest. Only 27, he has set already an impressive number of records in mountains all over. But, philosophically, just as impressive as his feats is his attitude. Christopher McDougall writes, 'You can retire with a trophy case like that, but Jornet insists he's still apprenticing' (2014, 73). Jornet honors Shunryu Suzuki's preface opening words, 'In the Beginner's Mind there are many possibilities, but in the expert's there are few' (2010, 2, 147). Despite all his achievements, Jornet remains unassuming and willing to learn from anyone. He simply disappears into the mountains for seven or eight hours, daily, 'usually alone, yet stopping often to quiz random hikers and climbers about approaches and conditions. "It's important to keep your ears open" [Jornet says] You need to be humble' (McDougall, 73). Jornet is coming along for part of this gambol around means and ends. The goal is to redraw the conceptual map concerning means/ends relations that influences how we think of sports and performative endeavors. It results in a 'kenotic windfall' that redefines in turn how we look at education (coaching) and competition in sport and martial arts. John Dewey and Garrett Thomson help us rethink this in a profound way.

We need to distinguish between the means we use and the ends we seek when we consider processes.[26] *Usually* means find their worth extrinsically and are instruments to other goals or goods, while ends are associated with intrinsic worth and non-instrumental value. The conventional analysis tends to see specific activities, such as sports, instrumentally as means to obtain health, achieve recognition, or attain wealth. Health is attributed a dual role as valuable in itself but also a means to other activities. And, happiness is understood to be valuable in itself, an end. Garrett Thomson argues that this analysis is mistaken because this assumes that only ends have non-instrumental value and means are always instruments (2003a, 50). The implication is that the only facet that has non-instrumental value in any activity is the goal. If this is the case, then we are denying the action itself any value. Thomson considers we should never treat our 'actions merely instrumentally' (2003a, 51). For him, if something is instrumentally 'valuable,' then it has not value itself: supposing that a person's life consists of the activities she performs, if these are *purely* instrumental to the goal sought, then so would be her life: *She* would be but a means (Ibid.).[27] The best reason to engage in an

HOLISM AND THE CULTIVATION OF EXCELLENCE IN SPORTS AND PERFORMANCE

activity is because we enjoy the process. Moreover, it is because or when we engage people and activities non-instrumentally that they become meaningful to us. This in no way means that either ends or instrumentality are morally or even philosophically suspect.

In fact, as McNamee points out, 'sports are after all highly instrumental endeavours [...] Sports exalt instrumental action. Indeed we invent sports and games for their "gratuitous difficulties", as Lasch (1979:181) put it, in order to devise arenas for instrumentality or purposive action as Best (1978) put it, albeit of a non-utilitarian kind' (2008, 60).[28] Indeed, we can instrumentalize sport, and that provides one type of non-utilitarian value. It is just that instrumentality does not provide the kind of value often associated with it and that non-instrumentality goes much deeper. Non-instrumentality helps us connect with the internal goods directly and deeply; meaning itself is internal to the action. But, as McNamee (2008) reasons we are complex beings with multiple motivations. He advances a judicious 'balancing of internal and external goods gained from our engagement in shared practices such as sport' (McNamee 2008, 67). Consequently, we can do something or relate to someone in ways that combine the instrumental and non-instrumental; we can appreciate both internal and external goods. This means that which reasons for action we have and the balance between internal and external goods are even more important. Sports are highly instrumental, but that does not mean that is the only way to engage them; nor the best one. But to be clear, it is not a matter of emphasizing process over results, as often argued. 'It is a matter of how we should conceive the good: the good should not be defined as an aim' (Thomson 2003a, 52).

Instrumental rationality endorses an ethos of 'the ends justify the means.' Sportspeople are only too keenly aware of how this instrumentalizes their sport and condones cheating. Astutely, Thomson turns this on its head and rethinks the relation means–ends. To better express the non-instrumental value of the process, he phrases it strikingly and paradoxically: 'The ends are means to the means' or 'goals are means to non-instrumentally valuable activities, which are also means' (Thomson 2003a, 52). Dewey also puts it inimitably, 'Means and ends are two names for the same reality' (1988, 27). In other words, the idea is that we set goals and embrace them because they give us a reason to do what we enjoy. We climb the mountain to become a better climber. It is about improving our skills and mastery of the sport, and the goal of the mountaintop or finish line are very good motivations. For Dewey, 'Means are means; they are intermediates, middle terms. To grasp this fact is to have done with the ordinary dualism of means and ends. The "end" is merely a series of acts viewed at a remote stage; and a means is merely the series viewed at an earlier one' (1988, 26). Again, the patternings of style help put this in context, as the broader scope provides the contest where running is about more running in a series. As Dewey writes, 'The distinction of means and end arises in surveying the course of a proposed line of action, a connected series in time. The "end" is the last act thought of; the means are the acts to be performed prior to it in time' (Ibid.)

In the context of conducting a revaluation of martial arts Monahan states, very much in agreement with our view:

> What is special about the martial arts, however, especially from the Nietzschean perspective, is that it must always be a practice and never a product. Like one of Nietzsche's own favorite metaphors, dance (8: pp. 107–110 and p. 195; 7: pp. 245–248),

> the 'art' of the martial arts is only ever *rendered through movement* and is never a static 'artifact.' One's own body becomes the medium for a kind of artistic expression that is always transient and ephemeral. It is *kinetic* rather than static, a *process of becoming* rather than a manifestation of being. (2007, 42, my emphases)

This applies not only to martial arts or dance, but also sports, and performative endeavors, of course. It strikingly and compellingly highlights the active, processual, and dynamic facet of performance. Wise despite his youth, Jornet looks at his sport in just this way, 'This sport is about improving, not winning', he explains. 'You never learn from victory' (McDougall 2014, 73). It is about seeing the running as part of that series of means to more running. While it may seem that this 'learning outside of victory' instrumentalizes the activity into a learning activity, this is incorrect. It is learning about the activity itself; this is a non-instrumental interest in the activity. Of course, there may be gnostic truths that he can learn, but those are ancillary, an added boon. Jornet wants to get better at run-climbing. His enjoyment and love of the activity comes first. He finds value in the climbing not the finish per se. The finish is important, surely, but instrumentally. Finishing a climb means we can climb anew. Particularly if we have free soloed it like Alex Honnold or Dean Potter are wont to do, without any ropes or protective equipment! In the process, we will have refined our skills to boot. The activity, the climbing is valuable non-instrumentally while the ends become instrumental. In short, 'The end-state is instrumentally valuable because it leads to further activity' (Thomson 2003a, 52).

In *Nothing New Under the Sun*, we read about five-time Tour de France winner Miguel Induráin's lament that he had nothing to show for his efforts compared to anyone who made or produced something. This framework provides a deep and meaningful answer. It is not that the pedaling is meaningless compared to other activities that result in a ship being built, for example. It is that objectives and end-states, such as the finished ship, 'are not intrinsically valuable even if they direct and explain action' (Thomson 2003a, 53). Rather, much like Jornet's steps are but steps to more steps in the process of his running and climbing, these are like steps in a larger process. In the case of the goal of building, the ship is but part of a larger process that makes for more 'shipping business,' as it allows for more navigation. The ship is valuable as a means—it is instrumentally valuable—*even if* it was the goal. Thomson drives the point home and sails the ship to port: 'We uncritically assumed that the process of construction is a means to having a finished [ship] and, with a little reflection, we discover that [...] it is the goals of our activities that are instrumentally valuable; they are valuable to achieve because they lead to further worthwhile activities' (Ibid.). Induráin's cycling led to more beautiful opportunities to ride; the riding was *the* valuable element, not the finishes. Sports and performative endeavors, because they do not produce any*thing*, in this model, best exemplify non-instrumental value: they give us the opportunity to embrace them in themselves. Of course, they can be instrumentalized, but this is a travesty of their true nature. Deweyan habit makes these steps possible—turning things around, for him 'in fact a man who can stand properly does so, and only a man who can, does' (Dewey 1988, 24). The *kata* of style's framework shows that for any *activity*, ship-building or running, it is but part of a larger practice. Finally, and as a boon, the effort expended for nothing, as we argued with Ortega, is the best and most beautiful existential justification. We dance, pedal, and build so that we can do it again because for us they are worthwhile endeavors and strivings.

HOLISM AND THE CULTIVATION OF EXCELLENCE IN SPORTS AND PERFORMANCE

This may not fully answer *why* we engage in a specific activity, but it does bring a measure of insight as to where to look for it. 'We do not *know* what we are really after until *a course* of action is mentally worked out' (Dewey 1988, 28–29, his emphasis). We still need to find out why something is valuable for us, and figure out how to go about it. Surprisingly for the 'old way' of thinking about means and ends, habit helps find the course: 'Now the thing which is closest to us, the means within our power, is a habit. Some habit impeded by circumstances *is the source of the projection of the end*. It is also the primary means in its realization' (Dewey 1988, 28, my emphasis). Refreshingly at odds with the hyper-technological and over-managed world of elite sports, Jornet uses iconoclastic means of training with no coach or specific training plans. As we saw, he just goes for *very* long runs. His habit sets the path for the running and climbing.

Some may grumble that even if we agree to this reinterpretation, there are values and *values*. Sportive values rank at the bottom of the normative totem pole, being apparently less important than other kinds, e.g. artistic or moral (forsaking for argument's sake the holistic unity of values defended so far). We can respond with Schacht's that,

> These values [originating in sport] are not to be despised merely because they lack the aura of dignity and the purport of necessity and universality that 'real values' are supposed to have. Indeed, if Nietzsche is right, *they exemplify the only kind of 'real values' there are*; for while they are not written into the very nature of things, no other values are either. And the values engendered in and through the advent of sport have as much claim as any others to be heightened expressions of the basic thrust of life. (Forthcoming, my emphasis)[29]

Sport creates values, and these are uniquely positioned to show us how to enjoy and value our activities—the only way to *live* life is in the doing—in non-instrumental ways. There are very dignified values, virtues such as sportsmanship, of course. But, sometimes levity is the more profound statement, and the path to follow; there is also such a thing as taking oneself too seriously. Jornet comes with a real life riposte to the 'guardians of gravity.' He races almost on a weekly basis (25 on skis; 15 running) 'to stay sharp and in the moment' (McDougall 2014, 73), but he never takes himself too seriously, rather, 'the more he races, the more joyful he gets: in his first Western States, Jornet was going head-to-head with the two favorites when he leaped off a rock and clicked his heels like Fred Astaire. "Was that on purpose?" I ask. He laughs. "Yes, you have to make some fun. What we do isn't serious"' (Ibid.). And this is not born from thoughtlessness or glib naiveté but, we could argue, from being truly aware of how serious the stakes are when he runs on loose shale atop steep cornices: 'In 2012, he was inches away from his idol—Stéphane Brosse, the legendary French ski mountaineer—when Brosse fell to his death as the pair attempted a speed crossing of the Mont Blanc massif' (McDougall 2014, 68). This did not tamp down his spirit, however, as the next year he set a record on the same course. Life is best lived as a game—or so argue some thinkers worth listening to.

Plato writes in *Laws,* 'We should pass our life in the playing of games—*certain* games, that is sacrifice, song, and dance' (1961a, 1961b, 1398, 803c), which Ortega cites with approval as he defends a jovial attitude to life and philosophy (1960, 2001). Jornet unequivocally displays this playful and celebratory attitude. Dakota Jones, one of the few to beat Jornet, admits

That's something [his playfulness] I've got to learn from him [...] 'The week before Hardrock [the race he beat Jornet at], he ran like five hours on the course every day. Crazy! But he'd never been there before and wanted to check out the scenery.' Jornet confirms his no-taper approach: 'Such beautiful mountains! I went out, met people, ran the summits, the rivers. It's a shame if you just go there to race.' (McDougall 2014, 73)

Suits' grasshopper (1990), wiser and more fun than Aesop's ant-chastised one (1871), would applaud Jornet on this count. As Ortega, he understands the nature of games and sports to lie in the overcoming of unnecessary obstacles. He places this at the forefront of his utopian view of life: we are to spend it playing games, that is, overcoming superfluous challenges, and not tied to the strictures of the merely useful. To paraphrase Ortega, the most necessary is the superfluous. Here, we find the vein with the purest non-instrumental value: effort for its sake. In this, it differs from other performative endeavors in general (it is conceivable to do martial arts this way in training, but in combat superfluity will get you hurt—or killed in olden times). In this kind of generous effort that gives all for nothing we can find the most enjoyment, *value*, and, paradoxically, return on our energetic 'investment, ... but only *if* we do not look for it. This is what I term 'the kenotic paradox.'

5. The Importance of Being Earnest: Kenosis and Attendance

The concept of *kenosis* is theoretically most generous and germane. This is best explained with poet David Mutchslecner's words: 'The Kenotic act—the outpouring of oneself for others or for creation at large—contains a holy paradox. The degree to which one is poured out is the degree to which one receives back him or herself' (2013a). Etymologically, kenosis is derived from the Ancient Greek, κενός, 'empty.'[30] Providentially so, we could say by now given the preceding elucidations concerning emptiness in performance (see also the appendix). Its sense is derived from the idea of Christ emptying himself, making himself nothing, but it came to refer to one's self-emptying so as to receive God's will (Mutschlecner 2013b). The paradox is that we must give ourselves selflessly, genuinely not expecting to get anything, and only then does the miracle happen and we are rewarded beyond comparison. Sport can be kenotic, as just argued above. It does not exclude other benefits, such as psychophysical health or even making money if one is a professional, of course. This concerns now the metaphysical nature of sport and the phenomenological facet of the experience. Mutchslecner writes that 'the quality of its pouring out [is] equal to the inner integrity of its structure' (2013a, n.p.).

The superfluity that underlies sport underwrites its *kenotic* nature. The experience of sport can also be kenotic, at certain times. Paradigmatically this takes place when everything is on the line. The amply discussed states of mindful emptiness and *mushin* manifest this clearly. But, it also happens in extreme exhaustion. John Kaag (2012) conceptualized this for us in *Nothing New Under the Sun* with the pain of rowing when the rower disappears in that willingness to be as nothing. Additionally, and less often examined, we can consider the patternings of style. Then, we can see now how the athletes, martial artists, or dancers can prepare themselves for a genuine *kenotic* outpouring or even empty themselves in advance, through meditation for instance, or afterward, in

HOLISM AND THE CULTIVATION OF EXCELLENCE IN SPORTS AND PERFORMANCE

the taking in of what the consummation of their acts amounts to. This complete out-pouring for the sake of something or someone else displaces the performer to the periphery of the action (and our attention) now.

This inquiry has centered on performers and their experience largely; however, the next steps on this *kenotic* trek keep the present focus on the practices themselves, as constituted by the performer's attitude, to explore how it affects the performance's nature. This is theorized as 'attendance,' as derived from an 'attendant aesthetic' (Ilundáin-Agurruza 2000).[31] Once again, etymology is useful, if not to define, at least to clarify conceptual boundaries and give direction. *The Shorter Oxford English Dictionary on Historical Principles* (1964) specifies that:

> *Attend*: it derives from the Latin *ad+tendere*, to stretch. 1. To direct the mind and ener-gies to, to watch over, to wait for, expect. 2. To turn one's ear to, to listen, to turn the mind to, to consider, as well as to turn one's energies to something or someone. 3. To direct one's care to, to apply oneself to the care or service of. Middle English – sense 'apply one's mind, one's energies to'. In Old French *atendre*, give one's attention to.

Picture the way parents watch over their sick child. If you are one, surely you have endured some long nights where the feverish child commanded your attention. Fully. Watching the chest as it rises and falls belaboring every breath; the beads of sweat forming on the small forehead; the normally sparkling eyes now closed. Anxiously, you wait for a sign of reprieve. Wishing you could take the child's place. This intense attend-ing, tending to, is the only thing you can do. Yet, there you are. Alternatively, imagine a 'sunnier' process: a creative context where you nurture the child and her talents with the same intense dedication. Say, her first kicks of a football, pedal strokes on a small bike, or tentative moments afloat—all rites of passage for many children. There is guid-ance, love, mirth and the same unwavering attention. This is the kind of directed atten-tion and dedication that attendance asks of us.

Attendance parallels the holistic mien of *Skillful Striving*. A simple way to cast it is as intentionality plus a caring attitude. It is an attitude or disposition toward phenomena (people, living beings, performances, things, ideas). It is also a criterion to help determine the quality of the disposition. In this way, it parallels how *phronesis* can be both means toward virtuous action and end itself. Fully developed, it entails a philosophical way of living and of conducting philosophical thinking as it seeks to understand problems. After all, a 'problem' is originally what is put forth in front of us. Thus, an attendant attitude directs our attention and energies to what is in front of us. Importantly, it is not merely intellectual, as Husserl's intentionality, but performative and embodied. It demands that we attend in a deeply caring way, as the examples above show.[32] It could not be other-wise from a holistically thick standpoint. Further, this attendant ethos is kenotic through and through in the original sense of emptying oneself, that is, of complete surrender. In sports and performance, the running itself is above our personal goals, or rather our goals should be subservient to the running. Jornet's pursuit of records should be not for the glory of name, but to see if 'it' can be done: can someone run up and down Mount Everest? Can running–climbing match the mountains? He is but the medium. There is no need to actively avoid or reject external goods that may come along, but that is not *why* it is done. This asks for an effacement of the self, making the activity the center of our being, for literally we are expending our energy and attention for its sake. We strive

HOLISM AND THE CULTIVATION OF EXCELLENCE IN SPORTS AND PERFORMANCE

through and for the practice: it is not about being a better footballer or dancer but about allowing better football or dancing to be created through us. Yet, this improves our playing or dancing—and us, kenotically. It enhances the lived experience in the moment, since, having gotten our distractions out of the way, we are filled by it. How this translates practically is contingent on the particular kenotic object, but the functional role it plays remains structurally the same.

This is prescriptive. An ethos of attendance asks us to fulfill our talents. It is devotional. In the case of a practice, sportive, martial, artistic, it is expressed as a 'full dedication with a willingness to serve' the endeavor itself (Ilundáin-Agurruza, 2000, 468).[33] Ortega's take on love and education fasten the open latches in this argumentative line. For him, when we love someone or something, it is not about *our* feelings, needs, or wants. Rather, this is about that which we love: 'This is love—the love for the perfection of the beloved' (Ortega 1963, 32; 2004b, 747).[34] This should be at the center of our love: a devoted and devotional attitude to the activity or person loved. He argued that 'there is inside of each thing an indication of a possible plenitude' (Ortega 1963, 32; 2004b, 747). There are two implications for the lover. One, that we should make it our life's goal to perfect the loved one. And two, that we push loved ones to make them strive and face risks so they may reach their plenitude (or get as close as possible). In the case of practices, it is about seeking to take them further, being willing to drive ourselves, at the expense of risk, to see where they can be taken; much as Jornet does in the mountains. This is also thoroughly educational and has implications for mentoring, teaching, and coaching.

To educate, in the sense of *educere*, means 'to bring out'. The underlying idea is to bring out the best from our charges. Often, those who teach, or more likely, those who set curricula and study programs, begin with a set of 'items', whether intellectual or physical (as per current dualist programs), that all students need to master. Similar to the means–ends relation, this is wrongheaded. For Dewey (1906), the child's life is integral and a whole, yet the tendency is to divide the world into subject areas with which the child cannot connect in an organic and existentially workable way. And, for Ortega (2004a), we try to adapt the child to the adult he or she is supposed to become. And this will not do. Whereas our capacities grow from taking on bigger challenges than before, learning and challenges must be commensurate to the student's capabilities. Ortega, with his 'principle of scarcity' in education, argues that we 'should not teach but what can truly be learned' (2004a, 51, my translation). That is, the lesson must fit the student, not the other way around. Then, we will be pushing them rightly: making them the heart of the matter, and not the other way around, placing us and our knowledge at the center of what is to be learned. Whether coach, teacher, sensei, trainer, or mentor, the above attitude should characterize how they look at their pupils: with an attitude of attendance, fully committed to them and their talents. This requires a *personalized* education. Teachers, masters, or *sensei* can lead by example as inspiration for the students, inviting them to explore how they may develop their talents.[35]

Education is at the heart of performative endeavors and sports. As Teruyama Taro (2014) says, *mushin* is deeply connected with teaching. *Mushin* and states of mindful emptiness are thoroughly educational in two ways. One, they are educative to others and us. Through the spontaneity they afford, we develop best our talents and skills, thereby enhancing our life. Nevertheless, they are not ends but means, in the chain of ends-as-means, toward that fuller life that empty states make possible. Fully invested,

HOLISM AND THE CULTIVATION OF EXCELLENCE IN SPORTS AND PERFORMANCE

we can better experience and discriminate the qualitative possibilities open to us, then reflect comprehensively to enrich their significance. The key lies in the mechanism through which we learn said qualitative possibilities, as Teruyama mentions (Ibid.). This is gnostic terrain, one where truths cannot be taught directly or told, but must be lived. Because of that, an *exclusively* theoretical approach does not work. Chinese former NBA basketball player Yao Ming says in an interview describing his foundation, 'Teamwork, chemistry and leadership are not things you can learn from paperwork. If you read a paper on leadership 100 times you still don't get it. You have to experience it' (Walsh 2014, 76). Some truths need to be experienced or learned through our performance.

This process involves others, the second way. Loving the practice leads to sharing it with others. First, in keeping with Ortega's view on love, true love for the practice means seeking its flourishing. This necessitates others. Isaac Newton's words are fitting, 'If I have seen further than others, it is by standing upon the shoulders of giants'. It is in the company of others that our enterprises and practices thrive. Morally, gratitude underlies this. Dewey writes, 'There is sound sense in the old pagan notion that gratitude is the root of all virtue [...] the best we can accomplish for posterity is to transmit unimpaired and with some increment in meaning the environment that makes it possible to maintain the habits of decent and refined life' (1988, 19). Unsurprisingly, past martial arts virtuosos became *sensei*, teachers, who sought to share their art, pace Musashi, Munenori, Chozansi, Ueshiba, or Tesshū. What they were trying to pass on was *mushin* not for its sake but to instill appreciation for their *dō*, and more deeply, life. Most wrote treatises, they all emphasized the *direct* nature of the teaching and the need to reflect deeply on it. Words may help at some crucial junctures the way a Zen *koan* (公案, kōan) awakens the disciple.[36] But beforehand much reflection and practice, when performance is involved, are needed (whether it be *zazen* (坐禅) seated meditation, or running). Now, the West may be too explicit and direct in its teachings and expectations, but the East can be too implicit and frustrating. Their different goals result in a tension (that can only be explored but in the briefest manner here). Western coaches, for instance, seek technical development for prowess and results, while *sensei* seek to instill self-realization and focus on the quality of the performance itself. If Western coaches can be authoritarian and often, some Eastern *sensei* are notorious for hinting and not telling things directly, as Herrigel (1989) recounts of his experiences learning *kyudō*. Virtuously fitting, between the two extremes lies the idea of giving the right instruction at the right time for the right purpose; something that the better coaches and *sensei* do with a view to lifelong practice and learning.

We may rightly wonder, does this not instrumentalize sport or whichever practice, making it but a means to whatever path, lofty or low? If the end is primarily to seek truth, insight, fitness, or relaxation, the practice is an instrument. As adduced above, this is not inherently problematic. Only that there is more and better. With *kenosis,* we give it all and receive all because we do not look for it. We seek learning, but about the practice itself: the focus is on doing it as well as we can do it. This is non-instrumental because it is centered on the activity itself and its internal goods and ways of achieving these means properly. Moreover, in the best cases this takes place through *mushin* and mindful emptiness: learning to perform better happens in the empty space that allows us to fully inhabit the movements proper to the active endeavor. *This* very process teaches us about ourselves. This is the mechanism that Teruyama inquired after.[37]

313

HOLISM AND THE CULTIVATION OF EXCELLENCE IN SPORTS AND PERFORMANCE

This has consequences for competition. An attendant and *kenotic* method, where the self becomes a means to the performance redefines contests in sports, martial arts, and other activities. The contest as goal becomes the ends-as-means to more and (hopefully) better performances, the performers also another 'means'. This does not mean performers are instrumentalized. The *kenotic* paradox is that the more they give themselves the more they get and the less they become mere instruments. Their exertions become more meaningful through this because they transcend the self; the activity is enriched and provides a deeper and larger framework. Following our opening analysis of means-ends, the competition is why the athlete trains; this is a first-order 'why.' A second-order and more profound one reinvests the goal, the win, as part of the process.

Crucially, exertions and contest are shared. In this way, competition then becomes a *shared* skillful striving. It differs from the mutual quest for excellence (Simon 1991) and from the contest of truth (Reid 2009), in that it places front and center the activity, not the performer, *even if* it is realized through the performers and their efforts. Nonetheless, and as with Simon's account, the consequence is that the contestants share the win: they partake of the victory. Winners are not the sole victors. Their triumphs are an admirable expression of a common effort: on top of the podium of the Champs-Elysées only one rider stands, but he would not be there had not the other 197 made his feat possible. His victory is admirable to the extent that the others turned it into a contest where great cycling wrote epic tales of sweat and pain on the French roads.

This framework also helps explain why a performance that embodies *kalon* is something to be admired and cultivated into something that goes beyond the competitive framework. This shared skillful striving can lead to deep, beautiful relationships. German Lutz Long and American Jesse Owens competed against each other in the long jump event at the 1936 Olympic Games in Berlin, which Hitler kidnapped in the service of Aryan superiority. Long's actions beautifully upended the Nazi leader's plans. His advice helped Owens avoid fouling and disqualification, assuring him a place in the finals (Mandell 1971). This led to a thrilling competition until Owens prevailed in the last jump with a magnificent 'flight' beyond the 8-meter mark. Long congratulated Owens effusively in a show of friendship that profoundly touched Owens—after all Hitler was watching. Much as a Roman emperor had to oblige to the plebs' thumbs up or down vote, the stadium's reaction left Hitler little choice but to clap, all none too pleased (as captured in Leni's Riefestahl's controversial and splendid film *Olympia* (1938)). Long and Owens went on to forge a great friendship that only ended with Long's death on the frontlines during the Second World War. Similarly, Zhuangzi had a dear friend, Huizi, 惠子, a logician from the School of Names (the equivalent of contemporary analytic philosophy), and also a character in many stories in the *Zhuangzi*. The Daoist sage often sparred with Huizi on many topics, enjoying the spirited banter. In one story, as Zhuangzi follows a funeral, they pass by Huizi's grave. He then tells his followers about Carpenter Shi, who was able to lift a speck of plaster off his friend's nose with his ax without even grazing him (it is telling that again he uses an example where superb performance is key). The ruler of Song summoned Carpenter Shi and asked him to demonstrate. Shi replied that he could not do it because his partner had been long dead and he could pull that off only with him. Zhuangzi then ruefully says, 'Since Huizi died, I have no suitable man to work on. I have had no one with whom I could talk' (Höchsmann, Guorong, and Zhuangzi 2007, 242).[38] The lesson that illustrator Cài

314

HOLISM AND THE CULTIVATION OF EXCELLENCE IN SPORTS AND PERFORMANCE

Zhìzhōng (Tsai Chih Chung) draws is that: 'An adversary means opposition and competition. But not having an adversary means grief and loneliness' (Chih Chung 1992, 92). We had better appreciate our great adversaries before we end up missing them. They are a gift we should nurture in full attendance, *kenotically*. Sharing with others in this way can be deeply meaningful. Larger communities and their rich histories are the best ground for inspired teaching and learning.

6. A Holistic Tapestry: Situatedness and History

Situated approaches to cognition long predate the contemporary moniker, with Dewey and Ortega being two thinkers whose ideas clearly develop such a program (essays 3 and 4, respectively). A situated approach not only highlights the role of the bodymind, but also the social and environmental milieu. They co-creatively in*form* each other. Nowadays, the field of situated approaches includes, with some internecine theoretical disputations, embedded, embodied, enactive, and extended approaches. Thick holism cuts perpendicularly across these, as we have seen in essays 6 and 7. This section completes the holistic account of performative skills and excellence. If *Skillful Striving* has accentuated personal realization and the performers' perspective, the focus is now widened to situate the performer in the practices and communities within which they operate. An opening and brief consideration of Dewey leads to an expansion of the phenomenological approach. This considers historical, geo-cultural, and intersubjective phenomena. Then, the social facet is further examined in terms of practices and communities.

Dewey was at pains to stress the continuities between our psychophysical nature, our talents, and the environment. His ideas are thoroughly holistic and, by extension, inclusive of a situated approach. As Gallagher explains, Dewey's views go beyond stock enactive stances (Noë 2004; O'Regan and Noë 2001) where perception and motor action are assimilated because these fail to include social and intersubjective elements (2009, 38), and when included (Varela, Thompson, and Rosch 1991) Dewey is not mentioned (Ibid. 48–49, fn. 7). The social domain directly and pervasively shapes our performative skills: it gives us patternings of learning, behavior, criteria, and standards of excellence, as well as the words to express and deeply understand our experiences. The rich Deweyan corpus furthers these ideas. The pragmatist argues that communitarian backgrounds give us the material, cultural, and cognitive tools with which to develop said talents. He prizes individuals' cultivation foremost and, in agreement with Plato, argues that we are happiest when engaged in activities for which we are naturally talented (Dewey 1916, 105). But, he diverges from the Greek's (and Ortega's) preference for aristocracy, and instead sees that the goal of self-cultivation (skillful striving within our framework) as personal flourishing is maximized within the context of a *democratic* society. Nonetheless, as much as our society helps us develop, the extent to which we belong to a group that shares all our interests, interrelation to other groups restricts its freedom, in turn limiting the value of the activity for us (Dewey 1916). Compromises must be brokered. History, which also structures our experience phenomenologically, shows the complex interplay of interactions, affordances, and restrictions best. Hence, situatedness is now championed under its banner.

If a linguistic turn marked Anglo-American philosophy in the twentieth century, what we can analogously term the 'historic turn' also characterized phenomenology.

This significantly developed the method to include a wider set of phenomena. Wilhelm Dilthey's ideas on history and hermeneutics influenced a number of phenomenologists, most notably Ortega, Heidegger, Gadamer, and Ricoeur (Makkreel 2012). In fact, Ortega frequently critiqued Husserl's static phenomenology because it was ahistorical and lacked an appreciation for the intersubjective complexities of our lives. Paralleling how phenomenology shows the intricacies of our movement as felt, the geohistorical perspective opens our eyes to broader intersubjective phenomena that surround us, in mutual co-creation. We consider Ortega, Husserl, and, in the context of narratives, Watsuji Tetsurō, Japan's foremost twentieth century ethicist.[39]

Throughout his work, already in 1914 with his 'pedagogy of the landscape', Ortega phenomenologizes the relevance of the landscape as a fundamental generative element for how we become who we are. In other words, it has existential import for us. The landscape that surrounds us—the land we inhabit, its weather, the rocks, trees, water, and other inhabitants—shapes us vitally, but is constituted only by 'that group of objects or portions of this world that exist in a vital way for the animal' (2004a, 425, my translation).[40] For Ortega, this constitutes an *umwelt*, in Uexküll's sense where organism and environment mutually shape each other. Communities, which set the standards of excellence and methods of achievement, thereby guiding the development of sportive and performative skills, constitute *umwelts*. There are certain epistemic conditions to understand suitably these phenomena. As he writes, 'Each object—thing, happening or person—imposes on us, if it is to be observed well, its "peculiar distance." [...] The truth is precisely the contrary [of the Nineteenth Century's penchant for a subjectivist worldview]: we live surrounded by the exigencies that things present to us' (Ortega 2007, 751–754) We must adapt the scope of our philosophical vision. E.g. we cannot bring neuroscience into the sociohistorical, just as looking at a façade's bricks and their porosities is not suitable to behold the cathedral. Partially, the proper perspective here is historical.

Ortega's is a thoroughbred enactive and situated program where history plays as important an ontological a role as the landscape. As he famously said, exaggerating to balance unfettered biologism, 'Man, in a word, has no nature; what he has is—history. Expressed differently: what nature is to things, history, *res gestae*,[things done] is to man' (Ortega 1961, 217; 2006a). Our history and our historical conditions, what Ortega called our circumstances, referring all things that surround us constitute our radical reality and life. To capture the way we, and our fate, integrate with the environment, he wrote: 'I am I and my circumstance, and if I do not save it, I do not save it myself' (1963, 45; 2004b: 757, my translation). For Ortega, then, how our skillful strivings find expression is inherently tied to our immediate environment and our historical conditions. We are living projects that take shape historically, and given that we must tell stories to make sense, our actions provide the argument for historical narratives (Ilundáin-Agurruza 2013). To sum up, for Ortega, life is a historically reasoned narrative enterprise where we strive to perfect ourselves through authentic, sportive, and rigorous cultivation. Husserl helps to clarify further the role of history and geo-historical elements in our experience.

Husserl's ideas on generative phenomenology show how history and our circumstances shape our experiences. His thought underwent a marked evolution from a static phenomenology centered on a transcendental analysis of the ego, to a genetic one that is dynamic and intersubjective, to finally a generative one that describes our process of

HOLISM AND THE CULTIVATION OF EXCELLENCE IN SPORTS AND PERFORMANCE

becoming and the influence of generations in our lives, as Steinbock's groundbreaking work, which fleshes out such implicit theoretical evolution, shows (1995a, 1995b). Specifically, it considers geohistorical aspects where history, geography, even climate were of import, in addition to other cultural and normative aspects. Given the complexity of this work, it is best to center our discussion on Husserl's elucidation of homeworld, which is normatively significant in relation to an alienworld. These expand on the primordial role of the 'lifeworld' (*lebenswelt*), which refers to 'The "world of immediate experience", the world "already there", "pregiven", the world as experienced in our everyday and natural attitude' (Gallagher 2012, 159). The homeworld structures everyday, normal, comings and goings, establishing social norms of behavior and a world of rites, rituals, mores, and manners; the alienworld sets practical, existential, and conceptual 'borders' to the first.

To explain this by way of a concrete example: in Medieval Japan we find the homeworld of the Imperial Palace in Kyoto. As the capital of Japan at the time, Kyoto had a very sophisticated courtly life, much influenced by Chinese culture, where poetry and many of the Japanese arts were highly refined. The alienworld rose from the northern edges of the city: Mt. Kurama, thickly forested, was the legendary lair of *Tengu*, the mythical human-like winged creatures and fearsome fencers that impart knowledge in Chozansi's *Demon Sermon of the Martial Arts* (Chozan 2006). How we experience a walk in one or the other context is structured differently: in the homeworld there is familiarity and a sense of comfort, whereas the alienworld brings out a sense of danger and the otherworldly. The homeworld puts us at ease; the alienworld makes our hair stand on end. In setting the norm, the homeworld does not specify what is average but *typical* and best in terms of aesthetic and existential concerns. Put shortly, it gives us *our* world and sets its normative constraints and possibilities. To show how history and geography affect a form of life, and these in turn influence our kinetic and performative skills, we can consider Japanese history between the Muromachi Period (1338–1573) and the Azuchi Momoyama Period (1573–1867) and contrast this with suitable European counterparts.

This timeframe incorporates deep changes in the martial Japanese structure and way of life. It transformed from *bujutsu*, 武術, warfare techniques in the Muromachi era, to *budō*, 武道, martial ways, in the latter. Between these two periods, the code of *bushidō*, 武士道, became codified and refined into a way of self-cultivation (skillful striving) through habit and mindfulness seeking achievement of bodymind integration. Quite unique to Japan, these martial changes included an aesthetics and ethics of warfare that saw Japan deliberately give up firearms when it had amply surpassed Europe's firearm quality and combined stocks. This is the first time a country has willfully rejected an advantageous military technology. Nöel Perrin states there are at least five reasons to explain this, the two most relevant for our purposes are as follows: (1) the ratio of the population that belonged to the warrior class was much larger in Japan; and (2) the Japanese appreciation for a specific gracefulness of movement exemplified by the fluid movements of a swordsman and falsified by the 'ugly' stance of the arquebusier (1979, 32–45).[41] This is pertinent because they coalesced into specific kinetic and skillful ways that integrated performative capacities and character. Perrin explains, 'In Japanese aesthetic theory, there are some fairly precise rules about how a person of breeding should move his body, how he should stand or sit or kneel' (1979, 42). Samurai swordplay fulfilled many of these rules where aesthetics and pragmatics combined. These corporeal

317

HOLISM AND THE CULTIVATION OF EXCELLENCE IN SPORTS AND PERFORMANCE

techniques gave norms, *normal* patterns, that societies, and within these societies groups of people, embraced as ways of moving about in the world.

Perrin points out how at comparable times in Europe nowhere did the warrior class population exceed one percent (in England we find about sixty lords, five hundred knights, and 5800 squires and gentlemen), a mere 'six-tenths of one percent of the population' (1979, 35). Japan in 1597 had an astounding two million people who belonged to this class, about 8 percent of the total Japanese population (Ibid., 33). (Samurai women also trained as fighters with their *naginata* 薙刀, halberds.) Though the sheer size of the class is astounding in itself, the import lies in societal influence: it had disproportionate political and social clout given that the power rested in the hands of the *Daimyō*, feudal lords, and their armies rather than with the Imperial Family. The homeworld as normative locus then shifts from Kyoto to a decentralized model that makes of Kyoto the alienworld then: the refined manners do not belong in the coarser but performatively more complex and skillful world of warfare. Eventually, the *Pax Tokugawa* of 1603 unified Japan and effected the transformation from *jutsus* to *dō* where warrior practices became more stylized in various ways, some admirable, some useful, and others, self-defeating. Japanese geography, whose mountains and valleys led to many fiefdoms, its warring past, and the alliance between Zen and the samurai, imbued life with a martial quality that pervaded all human affairs. Ritualized and adopted as mores of a warrior culture, this could be seen in the way people walked, their hairstyles (even commoners often shaved their heads in that odd manner designed to wear a *kabuto*, 兜, or battle helmet), an other subtler ways, such as their high sense of honor and service, and which resulted in tensions between duty to one's superiors (*giri*, 義理) and an individual's conscience (*ninjo*, 人情). Mauss, (1950) work helps us connect this discussion to our kinetic ways again.

Our movements have both personal and unique as well as social and shared aspects. The former depend on our morphology and previous history of disciplined movements, the latter on the patternings that society instills on us. For Mauss (1950) in a sort of rapprochement to holistic and Eastern ways of the bodymind, the complete person ('l'homme total') is psychosocial and physiological. He highlights and details how we imbibe our corporeal manners from the surrounding society, from the way we walk, dance, and use eating utensils, to the way we swim move our hands in various contexts, or how armies march (see essay 9; Kono Yoshinori's ideas discussed alongside Mauss' are also relevant). While we imprint this with our personality, they also reflect strongly whence we come. In fact, the variations are not as much personal as social (Mauss 1950, 368–369). Congruently, Sheets-Johnstone writes that, 'corporeal and kinetic intentionalities and patternings develop on the basis of kinetic motivations into a kinetic repertoire that is at once both personal and social' (2009, 344).

Contemporary psychosocial research supports this transmission of skills, showing how associations between bodymind performance and abstract concepts are situated and informed by cultural imperatives, values, and habits (Leung et al. 2011). Further, these skills and patterns are learned intersubjectively, whether this be done reflectively and aware, as when we purposefully try to learn a new skill, or subpersonally and unawares the way we may adapt our gait to those of others around us (as dynamic system theory shows—essay 7). Social ways of moving become imprinted from the very start of our lives. Sheets-Johnstone, relying on empirical research findings, shows how movement is pivotal for an infant's world as early as the first day, with infants synchronizing movements to adults' speech (2000, 345). Further, she cites Lois Bloom, who observes how 'Children learn about relationships between objects by observing the effects of movement and actions done by themselves and other persons' (Ibid., 346).[42] In conclusion, intersubjectivity, intermodal learning, and adoption of social motile patterns are with us from the very beginning.

Returning to Japan, the immediate social outcome was a Japanese population where both warrior class and kinsfolk were well trained in martial ways, and which developed a keen sense of kinesthetic discriminations and kinetic patternings proper of martial movements. In contrast, Italy between the *duecento and quattrocento* was similarly split into a number of city states and also had a large number of armed conflicts among the different city states and with foreign powers. But, it relied largely on Condottieri (warlords for hire) and their companies of mercenaries. Machiavelli attributed this to the loss of native martial spirit and practices. Even if, as historian Caferro (2014) points out, this has been revised recently and misses some of the complex relations between the mercenaries and the local population, the fact remains that this outsourcing of martial ways made it unnecessary for natives to cultivate martial skills. Here, we have two forms of life and two very different sets of skills and self-realization. The Japanese took pride in martial ways that also included philosophical and religious tenets as part of their learning. In Italy this was missing, and Western coetaneous manuals lacked the underlying philosophical elements. Interestingly, we find a common socio-political methodology that channels ritualized martial ways. Similar to Mauss, and in advance of Foucault's ideas Dewey preternaturally diagnoses,

> Those who wish a monopoly of social power find desirable the separation of habit and thought, action and soul, so characteristic of history. For the dualism allows them to do the thinking and planning, while others remain docile, even if awkward, instruments of execution. Until this scheme is changed, democracy is bound to be perverted in realization. (1988, 52)

But if a community suffers deleterious effects when dominated by institutionalization, as MacIntyre (1984) argues, it is the also the social context wherein our practices flourish.

7. Communities and Norms as Paths to Flourishing

Crucially, this takes place best within the fertile ground that practice-specific communities provide.[43] These communities can be considered democratic when cooperative and characterized by an open, dialogic ethos. Said communities provide the standards of excellence, the means to develop our skills, and social and material support. MacIntyre's ideas (1984) on virtue, practices, and community are not explicitly discussed at length; they have already been considered and critiqued extensively in sport philosophy, e.g. McNamee (2008), McFee (2004) and others (Ilundáin-Agurruza and Kuleli 2012; Reid 2012), besides having been examined at various times in this project already, primarily in *Nothing New Under the Sun*. We continue with the praxis of considering alternative 'dark horse' sources amenable to thick holism. We begin with Schacht's Nietzschean salvo,

> As a part of human culture, the sport world—like the art world, the world of science, academic life, political life and other complex domains of our emergent human reality

HOLISM AND THE CULTIVATION OF EXCELLENCE IN SPORTS AND PERFORMANCE

> —requires participation at many levels if it is to survive, flourish and develop. And this is not only because it requires a 'feeder system' to produce stars at the top of the pyramid. It is even more because such large-scale participation is necessary in order to sustain the *environment of values* on which the whole thing depends. But the desirability of keeping such domains of culture going, as the only real way of rendering humanity more than just another species having its day in the sun on our little planet, is not the only Nietzschean justification of involvement in them. For another part of it has to do with making our lives worth living. (1998, 130, his emphasis)

This environment of norms, like that of values, similarly to the turtle that sustains the elephant on which the world rests in Hindu cosmogony, stands at the bottom of our practices. Deeper than values yet lies the fact that these norms structure our lives meaningfully. They guide our strivings to thrive. The norms themselves are means to another higher order ends-as-means that makes these meaningful in a wider, perhaps deeper or higher, context. The activities that fill our lives with the possibility of meaning grow from a cooperative spirit and shared bodies of knowledge and values: when both individual and community contribute and give themselves for each other's sake, they create the conditions for excellence. Nonetheless, conflict is bound to happen. James Wallace writes, 'The result, if the practice flourishes, is a moving, changing consensus often accompanied by considerable noise and some confusion' (2009, 15). This means that we must develop strategies to harmonize agreement and disagreement on essential points. We should not be too hopeful for permanent solutions.

Paralleling our personal lives' lifelong skillful strivings as *shugyō*, because of 'continually changing circumstances, any harmonization, any successful adjustment of practices to one another, is temporary; the need for readjustment is *never-ending*' (Wallace 2009, 17, my emphasis). When facing such 'perpetual' tasks—particularly from the span of a single life—a historical frame is all the more important to keep a measure of perspective to ground us and avert existential vertigo. More broadly and foundationally, the historical perspective is essential to the development of practices. For MacIntryre, '[a] living tradition then is an historically extended, socially embodied argument, and an argument precisely in part about the goods which constitute that tradition. Within a tradition the pursuit of goods extends through generations, sometimes through many generations' (1984, 222). This is made intelligible in terms of the larger history of the tradition as conveyed to us, which flourishes when relevant virtues are exercised. If phenomenology helps us understand how we personally integrate this meaningfully, to situate this within the broader social spectrum we take up the historical and particularist account of norms and practices that Wallace (2009) develops—a suitable bookend to his ideas on skills and virtues in the first essay.

The following citation interlaces a number of themes—situatedness, attendant care, performance, the continuities in the enactive domain, and the relevance of history—while setting the stage for the subsequent analysis,

> The developed activities become in themselves objects of *intense interest* and *appreciation*. A *good life* is not merely a life of subsistence; it involves absorption in useful complex activities that require practical knowledge for their *performance*. The acquired, refined *capacities and dispositions* that individuals need in order to participate successfully in these activities are excellences of thought and character—*skills, know-how, and*

HOLISM AND THE CULTIVATION OF EXCELLENCE IN SPORTS AND PERFORMANCE

> *virtues of character*. Not only is *community* necessary, but *sociality* also provides a necessary condition for developed practical knowledge cultivated know-how, and technical and ethical norms. (Wallace 2009, 124, my emphases)

For Wallace practices, which exist 'within larger communities' (2009, 13), consist on the acquisition of complex bodies of norms and practical knowledge learned from others largely. They 'are activities guided by a shared body of practical knowledge—knowledge of how to pursue the activity' (Wallace 2009, 11). Such knowledge is normative, being about how to do something properly, i.e. better rather than worse. Importantly, this knowledge and its transmission are frequently demonstrative *and* performative: 'often, the best way to exemplify a norm, say the right way to make a surgical incision, is by demonstrating the action' (Ibid.). Controversially but illuminatingly, he argues that ethical norms 'are found among the norms that constitute the practices that make much of our lives, and these norms, too, are items of (presumptive) practical knowledge' (Wallace 2009, 2). The controversy lies in how this makes such norms contingent and subject to the vagaries of historical practice. They change—improving or worsening. Because of their empirical status, this opposes any sort of norms derived from either the authority of reason or divinity. In keeping with thick holism and the enactive account of norms and action, these 'practices are *psychosocial* phenomena, ways of living that people in a community share', the component norms of which, ethical norms inclusive, 'are *also* psychosocial in nature' (Wallace 2009, 3, my emphases).

David Quammen, writing about the Native American relation to horses and tradition of horse riding, wonderfully encapsulates the spirit of such practices and their rich histories,

> You embrace your skills and a passion that have come down from your ancestors; you learn the skills from your elders and make the passion your own; you become proficient, then expert, then generous with your expertise; you care for your animals smartly and lovingly; you pass the favor along to younger kin. You make your family proud and whole. That's the ultimate Indian relay. (2014, 126)

An Indian relay is a competition where riders swap horses without stopping, jumping from galloping horse to galloping horse with the help of others standing at the ready at the transition point. This is a beautiful example and metaphor for the full generational circle of flourishing under practices. Attendance, kenosis, and educational devotion are in full display here. Notably, it also involves another species, as sometimes creatures other than humans are part of the process. Keeping such traditions alive and kicking, like a good and healthy horse, depends on well-honed skills, a caring, devoted attitude to the practice, and passing on the knowledge.

Kanō Jigorō 's opening words to this essay ripple through this as the waves of handed down learning undulate for generations. Wallace elucidates how this works: 'Activities and the norms that guide people in their practice exist only insofar as individuals master the requisite shared practical knowledge and practice it. The locus of these norms is to be found in the skills, know-how, dispositions, and concerns of individuals' (2009, 126). Further, and in allusion to Dewey's ideas, he specifies that these 'capacities and dispositions' must 'operate harmoniously and express themselves in "a unified course of action"' (Ibid.). Trouble in paradise arises not only from potential conflicts among practices, but rather is inherent to practices and norms. There are two facets to the latter, the change that our Heraclitean world imposes on our mortal creations, and the very structure of norms. Because the former is rather self-explanatory and is largely driven by the latter, we focus on norms.

Structurally, norms are like rules. As readers of Wittgenstein (1963) and those familiar with McNamee's (1998a) and McFee's (2004) applications of his ideas to sports know, rules do not determine their own application. Following a rule alone cannot specify what is correct (or incorrect) in all cases; its interpretation and application are not self-determined. This does not mean that norms or rules are arbitrary or merely subjective. But neither are they universal, necessary, or fully transparent. Rather, rules are conventionally agreed upon by a community that shares certain practices. As Gallagher elucidates, 'Following a rule in a language game does not involve a metacognitive interpretation of a rule that we somehow hold in our head. It is rather an ability that consists in nothing more or less than a practice, the mastery of which has been fine-tuned in particular settings (Wittgenstein 1963, § 201)' (2009, 46). When it comes to norms, some clarifications are in order.

Wallace uses Frederick Will's views to effectively show the distinction between manifest and latent aspects of norms. The former are those explicitly laid out as sets of instructions or rules, as 'templates for action' (Wallace 2009, 33). These are simple applications which precedent use guides, e.g. you must conduct periodic checks of a boat's rigging, or one must return the ball before it bounces twice when playing *pelota a mano* (Basque handball). The latent aspect of norms resists complete formulation and arises when faced with novel situations. Skilled offshore sailors worth their salt know-how to improvise beyond 'textbook' applications of good sailing practices, as they often encounter broken or malfunctioning parts of the rigging, from jammed cleats to ripped sails, and capable handball players know to score by ways other than having opponents miss the bounce. As these latent norms are connected to a web of other norms, it behooves us to understand this as fully as feasible if we are to succeed in facing challenges for which manifest norms are insufficient. Yet, '[t]he assumption in much philosophical thinking in all areas of philosophy that norms of thought and action guide us only by means of the specific direction provided by their manifest contents has the result that they offer no help in sufficiently novel situations' (2009, 54). Indeed, we cannot escape this predicament. Wallace cites Frederick Will: 'norms are *always* in some degree open, rather than closed with respect to their manifest aspects' (Wallace 2009, 35), my emphasis). Rational and intuitive attempts to meet this are inadequate.

Narrow rational approaches—deontology or utilitarianism—are bound to encounter conflicts not solvable within their own normative framework, hence the perennial clash among norms, tenets, or rules. Additionally, as Wallace diagnoses, 'There is not *a method* for applying rules in hard cases, but this is because the actual practical problems that qualify as hard cases are so various and because solutions to such problems often require improvisation' (2009, 110, his emphasis). If rational ways cannot accommodate novel cases, intuitionism cannot give a general account of how norms can be guides in hard cases or why specific choices are good (or bad) (Ibid., 111). In their stead, Wallace makes the case for what he dubs 'extreme particularism', which 'attempts to dispense with general practical knowledge altogether and attributes normative guidance to particular perceptions' (2009, 6). If socially, communities hand down a repository of successful procedures, ultimately, we must devise, individually or cooperatively, solutions to novel challenges. Quoting Dewey, Wallace explains that reasonable choice involves 'unifying, harmonizing, different competing tendencies' not in their original form but sublimated, 'reducing it to a component along with others in an action of transformed quality' (2009, 110). A reflective intuition, which incorporates Deweyan deliberation and post-performance reflection in addition to the holistic and enactive normative performance, which is creative and spontaneous, fits well along with his particularist account. In practice, particularism relies on holistic and enactive capacities and character.

Wallace writes, 'Practical reasoning *at its best* is improvisational and creative' (2009, 19). To effect this creativity and improvisation outside manifest rules and the strictures of rationality or the vagueness of intuition, we need to rely on a holistic and enactive normativity. If successful, we can aspire to an ever-tenuous harmony, not unlike the slackliner walking the rope, that rests on a particularism where spontaneous, creative, and enactive norms thrive. The skill to operate in this way is derived *in absentia* of specific rules (and representations) that have been internalized. In the long run, what is acquired is, by any other name, Deweyan habit: 'When an individual masters a particular practice and participates in it effectively, what the individual will have acquired is a complex Deweyan habit of acting in accordance with a body of norms' (Wallace 2009, 17). A holistic and radically enactive cognition operates analogously. Hutto and Myin explain when they argue for a scaffolded model of *shared* practices within the context of cognition:

> [w]hen an individual learns how to perform mental arithmetic, he or she does not do so by acquiring a capacity to manipulate bona fide internal symbols. Rather what is gained is an ability to perform operations that previously required the manipulation of external symbols but have now become possible in the absence of external symbols. (2013, 152)

Crucially, this scaffolded peformative account 'is not internal in any sense offensive' to radically enactive cognition, but becomes 'independent of context' (Ibid.). This 'focuses on the *communal and collective* resources that stably augment and expand upon the resources provided by our basic cognitive capacities' (Hutto and Myin 2013, 153, my emphasis). At the basis of, and scaffolding more complex elements that can be representational, e.g. a coach's verbal instructions, we find the underlying contentless and performative bodymind, our advanced skills being played out. This is a thoroughly psychophysical and social process. As bodyminds, we individually execute this, but a shared social background underwrites this. This relation between individual and community is not without its conundrums, however.

MacIntryre bemoans modern individualism and advances his communitarian view, yet he ironically relies on a strong narrative sense of the self. He clearly connects it to the community, 'For the story of my life is always embedded in the story of those communities from which I derive *my identity*' (MacIntryre 1984, 221 my emphasis). But, the very strength of his argument against Humean and Lockean empirical atomism or Sartrean ghostly role-playing needs a robust sense of the self. This brings back, under a different guise, the very individualism he wishes to expel from his community. Endorsing a different path to a similar end, the Asian and Japanese basis for exemplary moral and spiritual virtue relies not on the self but on selflessness. Between the two extremes we

HOLISM AND THE CULTIVATION OF EXCELLENCE IN SPORTS AND PERFORMANCE

find a shared model of self and community. McNamee's (1998b) examination of the conflict between methodological individualism and communitarianism provides a sensible model in the context of trusting relations in sport.

McNamee considers the limitations of practical rationality, particularly as concretized in game theory and similar strategies, concluding with the suggestion 'that any or all human relations and associations in sport should be conceptualised in ways other than contractual' (1998b, 165). He analyzes three versions of communitarianism (identity, virtue, and social), and by his own cognizance avoids falling 'into the trap of advocating one particular characterisation of human relations as paradigmatic' (Ibid. 167). McNamee does advance trust as a moral baseline that regulates the suitable sense of shared identity: trust 'on Baier's analysis is characterised as letting persons take care of something that is cared for or valued, where such caring involves the use of discretionary powers' (Ibid., 174, see also McNamee 1998a). This coheres with the attendant attitude presently advanced. To show the limitations of contractual stances and provide his alternative, McNamee carefully lays out an example of a swimming coach who sexually abuses a swimmer under his tutelage. As he indicates, regardless of consensuality or feelings of infatuation and 'love', 'it still remains the case that he has utilised his station to exploit a level of intimate trust over a valued and vulnerable person that make us revile him' (Ibid., 178).[44] Ultimately, he articulates a 'more perspicuous characterisation of close personal relations that are often characteristic of teacher and pupil, coach and young athlete; one that foregrounds notions of shared identities, the appreciation of vulnerability, and the appropriate virtues that accompany them' (Ibid., 177). As to the virtues, more follows momentarily, but before we explore further this shared identity with Watsuji, taking one last theoretical trip to Japan.

Watsuji Tesurō built his ethics on a Confucian and Buddhist legacy that also assimilated Western thought—he studied in Germany under Heidegger's auspices.[45] Originally, and diverging from Heidegger's (1962) phenomenological analysis of *Being and Time*, Watsuji (1996) advocated that spatiality was more primary than temporality on intersubjective grounds (of course, temporality is also important). Carter explains that, 'Space is inextricably linked with time, and the individual and social aspects of ourselves are inextricably linked as well, and our history and culture are linked to our climate' (2011, 12). But in the end, place precedes time in our relations and our own constitution as selves. The keystone to his system is the idea of *ningen*, 人間. It is derived from the Buddhist's concept *jinkan*, which shares the same kanji. This signified 'the human world as contrasted with the worlds of beasts and heavenly beings' (Yuasa 1987, 37) and refers to the common ground we share in human relations. The usual translation of *ningen* is 'in betweeness of human beings'. Watsuji, redolent of Nishida's unity of contradictories, finds that there is a dialectical unity between the individual and others. We can think of Fukasawa's judokas again (essay 9), but in this social context competitors, coaches, public, institutions stand in relation to the *judōka*. Further, to exist in betweeness is to exist with the life-space '[which] means nothing other than to exist as a human being in virtue of one's body [i.e., *shintai*, the living body]' (Ibid.). Through this living body we adopt the social and personal mores, the ways of walking or moving, that Mauss examines. In fact, Watsuji 'argues that we are foremost *both* social *and* individual and that the ethics is established [...] as a unity of these two, which leads to [...] a nonduality that expresses itself as benevolence' (1996, 331, Carter's emphasis). Ultimately, the betweenness prevails over the 'I', because our

intentional I is prescribed by the other and *vice versa* (1996, 51). The radical consequence is seen in that for a truly isolated person, a Robinson Crusoe, it is not even
possible to be either public or a private being, for the two states are dynamic and
interdependent (ibid., 146). But, even if this in betweeness structures formally all human
relations, it is culturally modulated.

Contrary to the West, which begins with the individual, as Carter explains, Watsuji
begins with 'the vast network of interconnections that serves to makes us who we are'
(1996, 329). This, he brilliantly theorized through his analysis of climate. Watsuji (1961)
was the first to conduct a fully developed phenomenological analysis of climate and its
relation to culture, in his case relating the monsoon weather patterns, and how this
had shaped the unique Japanese character. Watsuji reveals how the experience of feeling the cold weather already entails others: 'But as we have been able to use the
expression "we feel the cold" without any difficulty, it is "we" who experience the cold,
not "I" alone' (2011, 858). Climate binds us together as a people because, as Yuasa
explains Watuji, 'to exist in a climate, to exist in the concrete aspect of space, is to exist
in "living nature"' (1987, 39). Geography and weather are not mere addenda to our circumstances, but as Ortega argued inherent to the human experience as such. This
binds us together, and in the best cases it is expressed as benevolence.

To look at benevolence and the aforementioned 'appropriate' virtues then.
McNamee explains how,

> most philosophers of sport have taken MacIntyre literally on the exultation of justice,
> courage and honesty as the primary virtues required by and developed in sport. To be
> sure these are three of the four cardinal virtues (temperance notwithstanding) and it
> may be the case that justice, courage and honesty are our best travelling companions
> in that quest for narrative unity in our lives. (2008, 60)

But, these virtues of justice often conflict with those of benevolence. We may be inclined
to allow a young and dedicated runner to compete even if he does not meet the minimal required time, but this is at odds with the underlying idea of fairness that means the
time is the same for all, which ensures parity of competition.[46] Further, it is not at all
clear that these should be the guides in our normative and narrative travels. As Wallace
states with a well-aimed riposte, 'Virtues of benevolence [such as kindness] are the perfection of the concern for one another that gives virtues of justice their point' (2009,
129). My shared identity begins not with the idea of being just toward you but with my
caring to be so. This phenomenologically other-directed decentering of the self begins
with that attendant caring for the other's welfare. Fitting the auspices of thick holism,
this is a lifelong striving where our skills and virtues must be continually tended. 'A person's continual struggle to harmonize these competing tendencies is Dewey's version of
the Socratic mission of tending the soul' (Wallace 2009, 129). Tending the soul and being
able to harmonize competing tendencies begins by finding a common vocabulary. There
are two steps, articulating and finding agreement for our descriptions.

8. Primeval Words: Kinesthesia and Articulating Experience

So far, much of the discussion has discoursed on perceptions, kinesthetic and proprioceptive dynamics, and other inward phenomena that seem to take place deeply

HOLISM AND THE CULTIVATION OF EXCELLENCE IN SPORTS AND PERFORMANCE

and darkly within. To what extent can we meaningfully describe and understand these? How can we share these, if they are 'inner' sensations and phenomena? In other words, and to paraphrase Sheets-Johnstone's (2009) title, the remaining challenge is the languaging of experience. As she puts it, without mincing words, 'Everyday language is clumsy and inadequate when it comes to dynamics. It basically names things and tags a verb to the name: the waves are rolling [...] its concern is with objects and with what objects do, not with dynamics' (Sheets-Johnstone 2009, 363). This results in propositional statements about objects, not descriptive renderings of the dynamic phenomena themselves (Ibid.). Articulating the *felt* realities of experience, finding the suitable primeval words, in performative endeavors remains a challenge.

None, thinking, language, concepts, or meaning are necessarily or completely propositional. A dog making a v-line for food across the room rather than following the contours of the wall is thinking, but not propositionally. Successful action in many instances, as shown in this essay, takes place without propositions and with no representations. There are rich non-propositional languages in the arts and performance. We can also speak of kinetic concepts, i.e. the right feel and angling of a dancer's hand. Likewise, meaning is not the sole purview of propositional language. We think in and we mean through movement as well, e.g. the meaningful movements as the patternings of a *kata*. Sheets-Johnstone's 'Thinking in movement' (2009; 1981) considers the nature of improvised dance and its inherent spontaneity.[47] She prognosticates that in considering this issue, 'we will find that what is essential is a nonseparation of thinking and doing, and that the very ground of this nonseparation is the capacity, indeed, the very experience of the dancer, to be thinking in movement' (2009, 30–31). In the 1981 version of the essay Sheets-Johnstone states that, 'In such thinking, movement is not a medium by which thoughts emerge but rather, the thoughts themselves, significations in the flesh, so to speak' (400) that are 'being created by a mindful body; a kinetic intelligence [that] is forging its way in the world, shaping and being shaped by the developing patterns surrounding it' (404–405). This essay has already addressed the nature of spontaneity extensively. Concepts and meanings outside of propositions notwithstanding, we can look at this from the other direction: we can question whether or the extent to which language can articulate performative phenomena and corresponding dynamics.

Ueshiba states, 'Those who are enlightened never stop polishing themselves. The realizations of such masters cannot be expressed well in words or by theories. The most perfect actions echo the patterns found in nature' (1992, 52). Many martial arts masters who wrote manuals parallel Musashi. He constantly ends his lessons with admonitions such as, 'You must examine these well,' 'This should be examined with care', 'you should train these well', 'You must understand these well' (Musashi 1993, 2004). The idea behind these is threefold: first, to underscore that words do not suffice to impart the skill or knowledge; second, that thorough examination and intense training are the way to insight; and three, that the teaching must be direct, from sensei to disciple, the book being merely an ancillary aid and not a substitute. In relation to this, Musashi translator Tokitsu Kenji explains, based on his own martial arts experience (which he would record as notes), that often his own descriptions are shorthand annotations to act as reminders of movements and kinesthetic and nociceptive dynamics among others (Tokitsu 2004, 338–339). Part of the problem resides in asking words to do something not in their nature. We may be as gifted a food critic as the narrator in

HOLISM AND THE CULTIVATION OF EXCELLENCE IN SPORTS AND PERFORMANCE

Muriel Barbery's *Gourmet Rhapsody* (2010), but he cannot *give* the taste of that delectable crème bruleé to someone who has never eaten a similar food, much less the 'perfect' morsel he is after to existentially and gastronomically vindicate his life. Words, the *keiken* of our articulated experience, fail to capture the *taiken* of the experience itself (see essay 9). If language stands out for its capacity to abstract, it is limited when trying to capture the very concrete aspects of our living experience.

Yet, it seems that language *does* allow us to *communicate* and *understand* those sensations-that-become-perceptions. Kinesthetic, proprioceptive, tactile, kinetic, nociceptive, visual, olfactory, and the rest of sensations are *given* meaning with and in the company of other people. Others teach us how to interpret various sensations, turning them into interpreted perceptions. This is part of the scaffolded process of acculturation. Through such hermeneutic exercise, we learn how to discriminate (discrimination is a capacity) among sadness, nostalgia, and melancholy, or between pain from injury and from exertion, for example. These also result in different cultural expressions of our affectivities. They are often rooted in the truths of our body(mind), that is, corporeally. As Sheets-Johnstone argues (2009), fundamental linguistic concepts such as up or down are grounded in elemental corporeal concepts during infancy. We should remember Ortega's argument, foreshadowing Lakoff and Johnson, to the same purpose (essay 4). Additionally, it enables us to 'remember' past perceptions—that is, interpreted sensations—and share these. In fact, Tokitsu's shorthand notes being meaningful at all depend on 'public' meanings, as we see below with Wittgenstein.

When it comes to turning to experience itself, Sheets-Johnstone discusses, in addition to the three-spatial dimensions, a much ignored fourth coordinate other than temporality: that of inside and outside.[48] This 'inside/outside' coordinate pertains to 'the felt dynamics of one's movement' and 'the body itself', for example: 'heart flutterings, a gripping overall tension, stomach rumblings [...] attest to experience of "insides" and to their quintessential import' (2009, 365–366). In a holistically thick overture, she writes,

> In the experience of self-movement the mind/body 'problem' disappears; we are all of a piece in the experience, whether we are feeling the qualitative dynamics of the movement as it unfolds, focusing attention on its directional changes, for example, or its speed, or its degree of extension, thus attending objectively to some particular aspect of the movement. (2009, 366)

Once the wind carries the last mirthful echoes, we may *still* wonder about the inside dimension of these phenomenal and inward sensations—qualia. However commonplace in the philosophy of consciousness, qualia are a contested philosophical concept. Phenomenally, qualia are subjective, qualitative, and give us the 'what it is *like*' to experience something. From a kick to the shin playing soccer to a feather's tickling sensation on our skin. But, since these are supposedly inside, inner, private phenomena, how can we meaningfully describe, let alone share these? Appealing to pre-reflective embodied processes, Gallagher promisingly reframes the notion of qualia. He suggests that we give up on the vocabulary of qualia without abandoning the experience itself. As he phrases it, 'there is still *something it is like*. Not what *it* is like, but what *I* am like as I experience X—where "I" means the embodied agent rather than pure consciousness' (Gallagher 2012, 99). The bodymind anchors the sensations then. He concludes that this 'calls for further phenomenological investigation' (Ibid.). Ludwig Wittgenstein is

HOLISM AND THE CULTIVATION OF EXCELLENCE IN SPORTS AND PERFORMANCE

another philosopher whose credentials place him on the situated camp because of his 'externalist' views on language, as Gallagher explains (2009). He will be our guide to further investigate this.

9. The Last Word: the Private Language Argument

It is important to show how our inward dynamics are not hidden and private affairs. That is, making of them 'inner' qualia *we* alone experience is problematic. Philosophically, this precludes meaningful talk about them. Practically, it makes it impossible to communicate and hence to learn. In the context of performance, beyond vital demonstration, the right words by coach or sensei sometimes are the one element that crystalizes the insight of all previous practice. This is built on a common vocabulary that learner and teacher can share. Moreover, it is to the extent that we can articulate this inward dynamics that we can conduct theoretical and philosophical examinations.

Contentiously brilliant, and the subject of seminal studies (Jones 1971; Rhees 1963; Saunders and Henze 1976), Wittgenstein developed an argument against the possibility of a *completely* private language in *all* of its features (henceforth abbreviated as CPL). It is a 'logical apology' against private meanings and sensations to ensure objective and public meanings that are communicable. He first poses the argument in § 243:[49]

> [...] Could we also imagine a language in which a person could write down or give vocal expression to his inner experiences—his feelings, moods, and the rest—for his private use? [...] The individual words of this language are to refer to what can only be known to the person speaking; to his immediate private sensations. (Wittgenstein 1963)

This excludes secret codes or thoughts privately kept to ourselves, a common misperception whereby some (e.g. Gallagher 2009) posit such examples as cases of the kind with which Wittgenstein's argument is concerned. These 'private' languages are in fact meaningful because they *necessarily* use shared elements of a common linguistic practice. As Wittgenstein writes, 'When one says, "He gave a name to his sensation" one forgets that a great deal of stage-setting in the language is presupposed if the mere act of naming is to make sense' (1963, § 257). If sound, the argument cuts the Gordian knot that entangles much of our philosophic thinking. To set the stage duly, we briefly discuss how it affects epistemology and the philosophy of mind, before centering on the argument itself, and then considering the uniqueness of the kinetic and kinesthetic facets of performative endeavors. This categorically drives away any ghosts that might try to ensconce themselves within.

As far as epistemology and metaphysics go, the argument against a CPL is a game-changer.[50] Modern philosophers like Descartes, Locke, Berkeley, and Hume held that ideas are the direct objects of perception: we only perceive our own ideas. Since this validates our subjective experiences, it seems to make sense. The consequence of this view is that we are never in direct contact with the external world. This traps Descartes and colleagues in a mentally private world. However, Descartes never questions the meaning of his words when exercising his radical doubt. If his words are to be meaningful—obviously they are—then this very meaningfulness *already* places Descartes in the external world. Most coaches and sport psychologists have inherited this

328

HOLISM AND THE CULTIVATION OF EXCELLENCE IN SPORTS AND PERFORMANCE

framework. Wittgenstein's point, that our ideas are essentially public, redefines our thinking on language, knowledge, and reality. This also has repercussions for the holistically misnamed philosophy of mind.

Descartes' fully subjective, introspective model of the mind implies that we know its contents simply by *how they feel* (ideas are the immediate objects of perception). This cannot explain cases when mental states are not transparent, as when we mistake jealousy for anger, or instances of 'blindsight' (purportedly blind people who can see unaware). It also raises the problem of other minds. Privy only to our own mental lives, how do we know others have minds? Can we know whether they are in pain? Cartesians cannot answer this: they must assume a private language that obtains meaning from private inner sensations. Wittgenstein's argument challenges this and the direct identification of sensations, supporting how we actually answer such questions: first, conceptually, then with a connection to external causes. The latter could be behavior—a painful grimace from pulling a hamstring while sprinting—or events, such as drinking alcohol then feeling dizzy. This does not get rid of subjectivity or intersubjectivity, but demands a reconceptualization of both.

In a CPL, *all* of its features are private and refer to a person's inner mental life. From the nebulous contours and convoluted structure of the argument, strewn over 30 paragraphs in the *Philosophical Investigations*, we can extract two lines of argumentation. The first one denies the possibility of error; the second posits the need for an existing objective and shared linguistic practice. These are formalized for clarity's sake. As to the first, the idea is that a CPL lacks an independent criterion of correctness, which the ensuing makes patent:

> … I want to keep a diary about the recurrence of a certain sensation. To this end I associate it with the sign 'S' and write this sign in a calendar for every day on which I have the sensation […] a definition of the sign cannot be formulated [But] surely serves to establish the meaning of a sign. Well, that is done precisely by the concentrating of my attention; for in this way I impress on myself the connection between the sign and the sensation. But 'I impress it on myself' can only mean: this process brings it about that I remember the connection right in the future. But in the present case *I have no criterion of correctness*. One would like to say: whatever is going to seem right to me is right. And that only means that here we can't talk about 'right'. (Wittgenstein 1963, § 258, my emphasis)

We can call this 'the Criterion of Correctness Argument' and render it as a *modus tollens*: if a language is to be meaningful, then it must allow for the possibility of words being mistakenly used. A CPL does not allow for the possibility to distinguish mistaken uses of a word (because its only possible criterion for correct word use is that it *seems* correct to me, which can also result in an infinite regress). Thus, a meaningful CPL is impossible.

The second version we can name 'the Community of Speakers Argument.' We receive the very notion of having sensations and what these *are* from others. 'What reason have we for calling "S" the sign for a sensation? For "sensation" is a word of our common language, not of one intelligible to me alone' (Wittgenstein, 1963, § 261). As mentioned above, there is a lot of stage setting in place already. Moreover, we rely on others to establish the criterion. As Wittgenstein poposes in § 265,

Let us imagine a table (something like a dictionary) that exists only in our imagination. A dictionary can be used to justify the translation of a word X by a word Y. But are we also to call it a justification if such a table is to be looked up only in the imagination? 'Well, yes; then it is a subjective justification.'—*But justification consists in appealing to something independent.* (1963, my emphasis)

Whereas the former is subject to public criteria and scrutiny, the latter is not. Appealing to our memory to validate such instances is inadequate. To paraphrase him, it is like buying several copies of the same newspaper to ensure that what it says is true. There are two steps to the formalization, first a hypothetical syllogism, then a *modus tollens* (using the conclusion of the first as premise for the second): all meaningful word use requires the possibility of words being used mistakenly. The possibility of words being used mistakenly depends on the shared linguistic practices of a community of speakers (the stage setting and common language). Therefore, all meaningful word use relies on the shared linguistic practices of a community of speakers. But because, by definition a CPL does not depend on the shared linguistic practices of any community, then it follows that there cannot be a meaningful CPL.

To avert the 'privacy' of 'insides' and 'inner spaces' to which we are the only witnesses, the terms 'inward' and 'outward' have been endorsed throughout. These do not posit an ontology that differentiates between inside/outside or inner/outer phenomena. Rather, and congruent with the functional and perspectival commitments of holism, inward and outward are a matter of perspective on the *same* phenomenon. We direct our attention inwardly or outwardly: we feel embarrassment and the warmth of our blushing cheeks; there are no hidden inner *phenomena*.[51] Moreover, so long as the blushing or embarrassment is meaningful, it is because it is tied to a public language. Dewey's words carve out in bas-relief how to functionally connect this to a situated context if 'qualia' are to be meaningful:

> [...] organic preparation for varied situations having many factors and wide-reaching consequences is not so easily attained. Effective participation here depends upon the use of *extra-organic conditions*, which supplement structural agencies; namely, tools and other persons, by means of *language spoken and recorded*. Thus the ultimate buttress of the soundness of all but the simplest ideas consists in the *cumulative objective* appliances and arts of the community, not in anything found in 'consciousness' itself or within the organism. (1929, 347, my emphasis)

So far this has built a logical argument against private mental phenomena. Next, we can develop a causal argument based on kinetic and kinesthetic dynamics. These differ from the paradigmatic cases of sensation that Wittgenstein uses, such as pain, in important ways, as Peter Arnold persuasively argues. In the case of pain, he writes that,

> there is a logical connection between the expression of pain and the *concept* of pain, even though pain can sometimes be experienced without being expressed. In the case of kinaesthetic feelings [...] it is necessary to perform a specific action such as a tennis serve if kinaesthetic feelings appropriate to the action are to be experienced and identified as the ones they are. (Arnold 1986, 32, my emphasis)

HOLISM AND THE CULTIVATION OF EXCELLENCE IN SPORTS AND PERFORMANCE

That is, we need to serve a tennis ball to have the appropriate perceptions and dynamics proper to a tennis serve. As Arnold clarifies, a person serving

> without having access to an appropriate and identifiable kinaesthetic flow pattern would render the act hollow. It would be devoid of that particular kind of experience that necessarily, and naturally, goes with it. It would be comparable to saying 'I am in pain' without having the experience of pain. (1986, 31)

When we are distracted, we can serve while thinking about a dalliance, but unlike the necessary kinesthetic dynamics, those other amorous feelings are contingent to the action. This does not mean that we need to be conscious of the kinesthetic dynamics all the time, as argued at various points in *Skillful Striving*. Arnold explains this diaphanously. The point is not whether a person is conscious of said 'necessary' dynamics all the time, 'but whether such feelings are inextricably present and *available* to consciousness when a particular action is performed and attended to or when a particular statement is made' (1986, 31, his emphasis). What if we were to be virtually stimulated through a simulator such that the dynamics of movement were elicited when we were not moving? Would this not invalidate Arnold's point? In fact, it is dependent on it, for we need to have experienced that movement as such to recognize it virtual counterpart. In the case of kinesthesia and performance there is a logical connection and also a causal one, as Arnold argues. All this said, movements in performative endeavors make sense within suitable frames of reference. Outside of it, the movements of a tennis serve or a *jodan* stance in *kendō* would lack a 'conceptual connection between the doing [...] and what is publicly understood' by them (Ibid., 32) The movements themselves, as seen with Sheets-Johnstone above, can be meaningful *hors* parole, but the wider context of the practice of dance is what makes them meaningful as *dance* movements, improvised or not. More interestingly for our purposes, regarding the privileged perspective of paragons, Arnold writes, 'Without a reasonably mastered performative action by the agent, there would be no adequately structured kinesthetic perception of it' (Ibid.). In other words, mastery of the movement is needed to properly recognize reliably the kinesthetic flow patterning, only then 'would it be reasonable for the agent to claim that he or she *knows* the feeling of serving correctly' (Arnold 1986, 33, his emphasis).

Further, in terms of intersubjectivity, we can also say that other people experience the same kinesthetic feelings as ours if they perform a similar pattern of movement to the one we performed and refer 'in a way that they answer to the same description' (Arnold 1986, 31). This intersubjectivity happens in and through our *inter*acting body-minds and their intercorporeal resonances. Sheets-Johnstone states, 'Intersubjectivity is first and foremost an intercorporeality; it has to do with meanings engendered and/or articulated by living bodies' (1994, 54). We read and feel these meanings on each other's skin, sometimes literally. Gallagher explains in detail how this works,

> On the embodied view of social cognition, the mind of the other person is not something that is hidden away and inaccessible. In perceiving the actions and expressive movements of the other person in the interactive contexts of the surrounding world, one already grasps their meaning; no inference to a hidden set of mental states (beliefs, desires, etc.) is necessary. When I see the other's action or gesture, I see (I immediately perceive) the meaning in the action or gesture; and when I am in a process of interacting

HOLISM AND THE CULTIVATION OF EXCELLENCE IN SPORTS AND PERFORMANCE

> with the other, my own actions and reactions help to constitute that meaning. I not only see, but I resonate with (or against), and react to the joy or the anger, or the intention that is in the face or in the posture or in the gesture or action of the other. (2008, 449)

We resonate in consonance with others, even other species, as Zhuangzi's story of the happy fish shows. Walking by the river Hao with his philosophical sparring partner Huizi, Zhuangzi made a passing comment about how happy the fish darting in the water were. The dazzling dialog is worth citing in full,

> Hui Tzu said, 'You're not a fish-how do you know what fish enjoy?' Chuang Tzu said, 'You're not I, so how do you know I don't know what fish enjoy?' Hui Tzu said, 'I'm not you, so I certainly don't know what you know. On the other hand, you're certainly not a fish-so that still proves you don't know what fish enjoy!' Chuang Tzu said, 'Let's go back to your original question, please. You asked me *how* I know what fish enjoy-so you already knew I knew it when you asked the question. I know it by standing here beside the Hao. (Chuang Tzu and Watson 1968, 189, their emphasis)

Zhuangzi playfully turns Huizi's logic against himself to make the point that we can feel *directly* the states of other beings. We can be mistaken and fooled, of course, but this still is dependent on the fact that most of the time we do know. Else, *how* can you ask that question? If language, to be meaningful, entails that there are no 'private spaces' within our bodyminds, our bodyminds reverberate with and bond us with others. Even when we differ morphologically, cognitively, and otherwise from the zipping minnows we know what it is like to joyfully glide in water or move about in *our* environment. A situated approach underwrites this.

Nonetheless, even if we have public meanings, intersubjective communication and bonding, and performative resonance, the challenge still remains: how do we articulate this? Wittgenstein famously closes his *Tractatus* with, '7. What we cannot speak about we must pass over in silence' (1921, 74). And Zhuangzi says: 'Words exist because of meaning; once you've gotten the meaning, you can forget the words. Where can I find a man who has forgotten words so I can have a word with him?' (Chuang Tzu and Watson 1968, 302).[52] Are we to remain in the world of silent movement, however?

On the one side, and to understand phenomena philosophically, articulation is peremptory. On the other, there are ways to understand matters experientially that circumvent linguistic expression (whether transcendentally or immanently being best left for another time). But these are not mutually exclusive as much as complementary. We can develop a holistic hermeneutics where we combine both, linguistic articulation as well as performative interpretation. A plurality of interpretations is possible, depending on the many pertinent factors, from the agent's intention to those of others observing or interacting, and the overall context of reference (the same motion of throwing a ball within a court or outside can be a harmless passing of the sphere or warrant arrest). Accordingly, we can explore ever so briefly how language can become part of this process. To do this, we must follow the path of poetry.

Poetry, understood in the sense of *poiein*, creation, and meant to include literary production such as fiction and even criticism, is ideally suited to this task. Poets, in *this* wide sense, are the original minters of words and concepts, working with concrete metaphors (*all* language is rooted in metaphor, much of it corporeal as already

HOLISM AND THE CULTIVATION OF EXCELLENCE IN SPORTS AND PERFORMANCE

discussed) that reveal to us the sharp or dull, hard or soft, fuzzy or smooth, vibrant or soft textures of our unarticulated experiences. Sheets-Johnstone (2009) recourses to Shakespeare (Hamlet and Macbeth) to distill the inward workings of emotion and the experience of 'insides', showing how the bard's linguistic talents can contribute to philosophic and scientific research. One of Heidegger's essays, *The Origin of the Work of Art* presents truth not simply as propositional, but rather as *aletheia*, 'the unconcealed-ness of beings' (1971, 35). That is, truth as disclosure. For him, 'Language itself is poetry in the essential sense,' and further 'it is the essential sense in which beings first disclose themselves' (Heidegger 1971, 72). But such disclosure and truth are not propositional for him. Instead, they are grounded in the very experience of dwelling in the word. We can widen the notion of disclosure to include non-linguistic concepts (kinesthetic perceptions and movements purposefully undertaken) that result in corporeal and kinetic understanding. There is a corporeal, non-linguistic understanding of sequences of moves we may perform that we may not able to articulate *yet* (either mechanics, sequential steps, or what it feels like).[53] For example, a series of dance steps, a martial arts kata, or how to compensate ear-pressure underwater by controlling separately glottis and soft palate. But these are enriched through public discourse. Being able to develop a descriptive vocabulary that is qualitatively true is the remaining challenge. Poetry and narrative—metaphorical coinage and its analysis—can help articulate matters in ways agreeable to open minded phenomenologists and scientists. In short, we need performative poets or poets of performance that may guide our dynamic renderings, capturing the evocative truths of our experience.

Philosophy begins in wonder, Plato tells us in Theaetetus, 'I see, my dear Theaetetus, that Theodorus had a true insight into your nature when he said that you were a philosopher, for wonder is the feeling of a philosopher, and philosophy begins in wonder' (2013, 155 d). It also ends in wonder … a deeper kind of wonder where the mystery is not varnished with the veneer of false understanding. It begins and ends with *yūgen*; with mountains as mountains and movement as movement (see essay 8, fn.5). If the mysterious is the most beautiful thing we can experience, perhaps wonder is the most meaningful thing we can experience. Nothing is new under the sun, and yet, everything remains mysterious. But perhaps not necessarily meaningless. Between 'philosophia' as the reasoned articulation and the sensations themselves we find 'kinesophia' as moving wisdom and sophokinesia as meaningful movement.

Heeding the paean to poetic thought, this could be a way to summarize this project:[54]

Nothing new under the sun …

Yet—Pragmatic pioneers and experiential mavericks astride
   exuberant steeds
     p l a y f u ll y
    wander

waking from dreams of electric sheep
  they ride the wind
  overcoming frac tu red ac tion
Suddenly—reflections on a Katana mirror
  skillful strivings under the mysterious moonlight

333

DISCLOSURE STATEMENT

No potential conflict of interest was reported by the author.

NOTES

1. Einstein (1954, 10). Also available online at http://sciphilos.info/docs_pages/docs_Einstein_fulltext_css.html
2. Chozan (2006, 133).
3. Kano (2014). My gratitude to Fukasawa Koyo for providing me with this citation.
4. The legacy of his short life, he came to an untimely end at the Battle of the Somme in 1918, goes beyond his medal and this inspiring account. He perfected the 'Australian crawl', and 'played a pivotal role in the development of body surfing and popular surfing culture in Australia' (Rodwell and Ramsland 2000, 3).
5. For an overview of Asian philosophy in its three main traditions of India, China, and Japan in the context of sport philosophy, see Ilundáin-Agurruza and Hata (2015).
6. Given that the sage and the book are eponymous, the text is referenced in italics as the *Zhuangzi*.
7. Available at https://www.youtube.com/watch?v=wZjcTG141rs&spfreload=1
8. Fraser challenges the moral worth of the Cook's action: if he were not a butcher he would not have to bother with knotty junctures in the carcass of what would otherwise be a living, harmless animal.
9. See http://www.aspworldtour.com/posts/75272/slaters-mind-bending-540-rotation for a video of the feat (accessed 30 December 2014). The closing tongue-in-cheek comment refers to John John Florence, for whom Slater is a mentor figure. John John beat slater to win the Surfer Poll Award, which Slater had won consecutively since 2004. See http://www.grindtv.com/action-sports/surf/post/surfer-poll/ (accessed 12 August 2014).
10. Greek Wrestler Milo of Kroton (sixth century BCE) would be a worthy match in antiquity: He won the wrestling event in six Olympic games and seven Pythian Games. That is, his career spanned 28 years at the highest level. Jamaican sprinter Merlene Ottey bests this longevity, with seven Olympic appearances. At 52, she was still competing for the Slovenian national squad, having qualified for the 2012 European Championships.
11. Literally, it means 'along', 'predestined affinity', 'reason', or 'edge' (Chinese Dictionary, online).
12. The label helps stress the sense that this is done 'physically', but it does so redundantly and underscores the very dualism it seeks to overcome, as argued in section 3 (essays 6 and 7).
13. Whitman's famous stanza reads in *Leaves of Grass* states, 'Do I contradict myself?/Very well then I contradict myself, /(I am large, I contain multitudes.)' (1903, 108).
14. Minamoto's works, unfortunately not translated into English, fit remarkably well with the thick holism of *Skillful Striving*. As Heisig explains, Minamoto centers on and differentiates mind from no-mind and their unique relationship to the living body. In his view, artistic refinement, especially in the performing arts 'mediates between tacit awareness and explicit awareness' (Heisig 2011, 930). This achievement is fulfilled 'in no-mind where things cease to be external objects and the subject-object distinction breaks down' (Ibid.). In the following, I cite from the few pages that Heisig has translated.

HOLISM AND THE CULTIVATION OF EXCELLENCE IN SPORTS AND PERFORMANCE

15. Essay 8 and Breivik (2013) discuss the importance of these in the context of consciousness and sports.

16. Ortega emphasizes the emotional side, the amorous facet, seeing a plenitude in each thing or person. For Ortega, 'This is love—the love for the perfection of the beloved' (Ortega 2004a, 747; 1963, 32). As Marías explains in an endnote, the difference with Spinoza is that Ortega centers on the beloved whereas Spinoza focuses on the lover (Ortega 1963, 166–167). Ortega also argues, contra Spinoza, that love is neither about joy nor the intellectual (2006a, 856–857). As we saw with his analysis of vitality, spirit, and soul, thinking and willing are instantaneous, but love and the emotions, unfold in time (see also Ortega 2006b). This idea is pertinent for coaching and a pedagogy that seeks to cultivate the talents of the student rather than preconceived notions about what should be trained or taught.

17. Intuition is quite different from instinct, of course.

18. For alternative translations see Chuang Tzu and Watson (1968, 97), Höchsmann et al. (2007, 127), and Chuang-Tzŭ and Graham (1981, 98).

19. Not to preclude the possibility that a reader may find an insight that unlocks unparalleled performance, here is the rest of his explanation of spontaneity and no-mind: 'This is, moreover, like the single full moon shining in the sky while all of the ten thousand rivers and streams contain their own one moon. This is not a matter of the light being divided and then striking the water. If there were no water, there would be no reflection. Again, this is not a matter of the moon being reflected as soon as it is received by the water. Whether it is reflected into ten thousand streams or does not go beyond a single puddle, the moon is neither added to nor subtracted from. And again, it does not select either a large or small body of water. From this you should be awakened to the mysterious function of the essence of the mind' (Chozan 2006, 133). May it work for others better than for me.

20. As a reminder to readers, the reason for the scare quotes here is that *mushin* is properly attributed to states of bodymind in Eastern *dō*. It takes a very high level of integration and operates within a Buddhist framework (Krein and Ilundáin 2014). The author's personal example with the sparring bout simply illustrates a similar (but much lower) quality of empty mindfulness and performance that may be more relatable to readers.

21. Another reading of Kido's actions, conceptually complementary, would consider this in the context of instrumental and non-instrumental values (Ilundáin-Agurruza 2014).

22. These are easily sidestepped given that reflection is supposed to precede or follow performance or can be integrated as part of a training program. A different and unrelated worry is whether self-reflection in the sense of self-monitoring or self-consciousness affects performance. Essay 8 and Ilundáin-Agurruza (forthcoming-a) deal with the latter.

23. The case can be made that, as a *means*, it can be used to improve performance and thus lead to excellence, particularly through the guidance of a coach. But, this is external to the athleticism of the performance; it remains a satellite in the orbit of excellence, not an integral feature within its atmosphere.

24. As Hutto and Myin explain it, 'The difference between these claims is that the Extended Mind Hypothesis (EMH) doesn't rule out the assumption that biologically basic cognition is, by default, brain-bound. Thus, prominent versions of EMH assume that only in exceptional cases—for example, when non-bodily add-ons are required in order to make the achievement of certain cognitive tasks possible—do minds extend. By contrast, those

HOLISM AND THE CULTIVATION OF EXCELLENCE IN SPORTS AND PERFORMANCE

who endorse REC and thus the strongest version of the Embodiment Thesis assume that minds are already, in their basic nature, extensive and wide-ranging' (2013, 7).

25. McFee argues that because 'there are standards of excellence from the beginning' MacIntyre's ideas 'cannot explain the normativity inherent in a practice but, instead, depend on it' (McFee 2004, 80). Even if McFee seeks to find a non-circular *philosophical* foundation for the standards, perhaps a historical approach can help to bring meaning into the picture, as developed in this essay.

26. This examination of means and ends closely follows closely the discussion in Ilundáin-Agurruza (2014, 60–61).

27. More provocatively, he applies the 'principle of universality' to apply this to the micro-level of actions so as to claim that our actions are never instrumentally valuable. The points raised to above do not depend on this one.

28. Today McNamee would put it thus: 'we strive for maximum efficiency in a purposefully inefficient system' (Personal Communication, 23 February 2025).

29. The version cited is from his forthcoming *Sport? A Nietzschean Appreciation* (forthcoming). It is modified version from his *Nietzsche and Sport* (1998), where the citation above, with slight changes, can be found on pages 128–129.

30. See *The Online Liddell-Scott-Jones Greek-English Lexicon* (2009).

31. In Ilundáin-Agurruza (2000), it is developed in the context of aesthetics and the ontology of artworks as constituted by interpretation; an 'Attendant Aesthetics' focuses on the work of art, not the artist or audience. This is paralleled in the argument above.

32. There are parallels with Husserl's intentionality (1998). For one, both are about directing our attention to what is in front of us, and they structure our experience. But, Husserl's intentionality is purely intellectual. In fact, this presupposes an attitude of attendance: interacting with the world of ideas, once we bracket the existence of phenomena means that *already* we *care* about the phenomenon under consideration, *and* also about the very phenomenological method itself. It underlies any and all of our engagements, which we undertake because we care in the first place. In this way, this agrees with Heidegger's critique of his old mentor, and overlaps with his concept of care (*sorge*) (1962). Heidegger is concerned with the ontological level, not the ontic, and his analysis centers primarily on anxiety and the everyday. Nonetheless, attendance is not an abstract ontological *category*, but rather, performative and incorporated into and modulated by our bodymind in felt resonance not just with the other but the full environment that is alive for *us*.

33. 'Service' as complete observance of duty can be problematic. This imbalance plays out most dramatically in Bushidō during the Tokugawa era. The close bonds within the brotherhoods of warriors built around their leaders, that the Confucian ideal of filial piety underwrote, meant absolute duty to one's master or father. The imperative, all-binding duty to one's superiors, *giri* (義理), is opposed by *ninjo* (人情), which is an individual's conscience and feelings. Since *samurai* (侍) comes form *saburau* (侍う), to serve by one's side, their duty to follow orders sometimes meant carrying out obviously immoral acts that might clash with the warrior's personal beliefs. Yamada Yōji's *The Hidden Blade* brilliantly plays out this theme (2004). Attendance is about serving, but not blindly.

HOLISM AND THE CULTIVATION OF EXCELLENCE IN SPORTS AND PERFORMANCE

34. As we saw with his analysis of vitality, spirit, and soul (essay 4), thinking and willing are instantaneous, but love and the emotions, unfold in time (Ortega 2006b). Minamoto's ideas on *kata* are again applicable here.

35. Sometimes, it can be evoked to the exclusion of verbalization. George Steiner remarks that when he visited sculptor Henry Moore in his studio, 'if he talked politics, it was not too pleasant, because most of the time he said nonsense. But it was enough to cover one's ears and contemplate his hands to realize what a total and absolute intelligence is: Henry Moore's hands' (Steiner and Ladjali 2005, 95, my translation).

36. *Koan* rather than 'puzzles to be solved or intuited' as popularly believe, 'are expressions of awakening' (Fisher 2015). They are studied and pondered, but each of these marks the moment of enlightenment of a Zen student. Even if they are verbal articulations, they are nonsensical, so the very role of language is actually questioned.

37. Incidentally, this framework works for what I label 'paradoxes of self-defeat': those in which we are supposed to desire desirelessness, expressly abandon all thought, willfully relax, and similar. Suppressing the self (and its wants and needs) opens the space for the activity itself.

38. See also the following alternative translations, Chuang-Tzǔ and Graham 1981, 124; Chuang Tzu and Watson 1968, 269; Zhuangzi and Ziporyn 2009, 104.

39. Family name is given first, as customary in Japanese culture.

40. For Ortega, this landscape is species specific and entails a mutual adaptation of human or animal to landscape/environment and *vice versa*. Here, he follows the ideas of von Uexküll regarding the *umwelt*, see 2004a, and also, 2005. For a parallel use of von Uexküll's ideas see Sheets-Johnstone, 2009, esp. 139, 172, and 286. Ortega's delineation of the lifeworld/landscape can be found in 1963 and 2004b.

41. The other three are: (1) geopolitically, the fighting prowess of the Japanese and the inherent difficulty in invading islands fostered an isolation to pursue their own way, (2) the symbolic value of the sword, the samurai's soul, which also amalgamated pragmatism and usefulness, and (3) a general reaction against external ideas. To these we should add a sixth one, the underlying Buddhist, Confucian, Daoist, and Shintō worldviews, which directly impacted their warrior ways and honor code.

42. Others validate these findings. Dan Zahavi, arguing against the theory-theory of mind, discusses how infants after 24 hours can discriminate between external tactile sensations and proprioceptive double-touch sensations (2004). He also cites research that supports the idea that between two and six months of age we might be said to be in the most social period in our life, with the social smile in place and a preference for moving objects versus static ones (Ibid.; see also Gallagher 2007, 2009).

43. An alternative critique of communitarianism from within is possible when considering East Asian traditions, specifically those influenced by Confucian values, which bring to the table non-democratic and non-liberal stances. For an analysis of this in the context of a critical examination of Olympism see Hsu and Ilundáin (forthcoming).

44. This example is sadly and starkly all too relevant, as the recent scandal at USA Swimming makes patently clear; Sturtz's (2014) exposé could serve as a case study on how individual and institutional corruption has led to a pandemic and broken coaching system with many abused swimmers.

45. See also Ilundáin-Agurruza, Fukasawa, and Takemura (2013) for a discussion of pragmatism and Japanese philosophy and Watsuji's ideas.

46. The kindness may also harm the runner if he loses by a wide margin. Under the usual framework, it is disappointment either way: either he does not compete and is disheartened or he is humiliated and thus disillusioned. But, being young *and* dedicated means we can let our kindness guide us without flouting fairness: we can be explicit that we will work with them in earnest so they can improve enough to compete next time around. Wallace's example, from which this one is adapted, centers on academics (2009, 114–115, 127).
47. The 2009 essay is an expanded version of the original 1981 piece.
48. She examines a variety of perspectives on 'insides', from those we inhabit as caves, to our ontogenetical experience of them (e.g. a mouth) (2009), our breath, and shadows (367–378). Our use of the 'inward perspective' is aligned with hers, which nowhere suggests a privacy of mental life or meanings.
49. Following scholarly practice regarding this work, section number instead of page number is used.
50. The explanation and formalization of the argument are co-authored with Garrett Thomson (see also Thomson 2003b). The application to sport and kinesthesia is my own.
51. Of course, there is much that goes on inwardly that we are unaware of, valves opening and closing in our veins and arteries, chemicals rushing, electrical impulses, etc. Even if they are processes, these are not inward sensations, for we do not feel them. As such they are beyond any putative status as inner in the sense we would speak of inward sensations. Curiously, these are phenomena we can learn about and describe, but we do so only externally, through medical and scientific observation and procedures.
52. See also Höchsmann, Guorong, and Zhuangzi (2007, 264).
53. See Ilundáin-Agurruza (2011) for a recursive integration of play and literature as part of the philosophical process to understand the phenomenon of sports, play, and the imagination in the context of childhood and play.
54. Adapting a literary device in Calvino's (1981) brilliant novel *If on a winter's night a traveler*.

REFERENCES

AESOP. 1871. *Aesop's Fables*. London: George Routledge.

ARISTOTLE. 2011. *Aristotle's Nicomachean ethics*. Translated by R.C. Bartlett Chicago, IL: University of Chicago Press.

ARNOLD, P. 1986. Kinaesthetic feelings, physical skills, and the anti-private language argument. *Journal of the Philosophy of Sport* 13: 29–34.

BARBERY, M. 2010. *Gourmet rhapsody*. New York: Europa Editions.

BILLETER, J.F. 1994. Étude sur Sept Dialogues du Zhuangzi. *Études Chinoises* XIII (1–2): 295–343.

———. 2010. *Leçons sur Tchouang-tseu*. Paris: Éditions Allia.

BREIVIK, G. 2013. Zombie-Like or Superconscious? A phenomenological and conceptual analysis of consciousness in elite sport. *Journal of the Philosophy of Sport* 40 (1): 85–106.

BROOKS, D. 2005. Blink: Power hunch. *New York Times Book Review*. Available at http://www.nytimes.com/2005/01/16/books/review/16COVERBR.html?_r=1&pagewanted=print&position=& (accessed 15 November 2014).

CAFERRO, W. 2014. Mercenarios y Guerra en Italia, ss XiV-XV [Mercenaries and warfare in Italy, fourteenth and fifteenth centuries]. *Desperta Ferro Antigua y Medieval* 16: 6–13.

CALVINO, I. 1981. *If on a winter's night a traveler*. San Diego, CA: Harcourt Brace and Company.

CARTER, R. 2011. Watsuji Tetsurō. In *Stanford encyclopedia of philosophy*, edited by E.D. Zalta. Available at: http://plato.stanford.edu/archives/spr2011/entries/watsuji-tetsuro/. PDF version. 1–16.

CHIH CHUNG, T.1992. *Zhuangzi speaks: The music of nature*. Translated by B. Bruya. Princeton, NJ: Princeton University Press.

CHINESE DICTIONARY. Available at http://www.chinese-dictionary.org (accessed 28 December 2014).

CHOZAN, N. 2006. *The Demon Sermon of the martial arts*. Translated by W.S. Wilson. Tokyo: Kodansa International.

CHUANG-TZŬ and A.C. GRAHAM. 1981. *Chuang-tzŭ: The seven inner chapters and other writings from the book Chuang-tzŭ*. London: Allen & Unwin.

CHUANG TZU and B. WATSON. 1968. *The complete works of Chuang Tzu*. New York, NY: Columbia University Press.

CLARK, A. 2008. *Supersizing the mind*. New York, NY: Oxford University Press.

CLARK, A. and D.J. CHALMERS. 1998. The extended mind. *Analysis* 58: 7–19.

DEWEY, J. 1906. *The child and the curriculum*. Chicago, IL: The University of Chicago Press.

———. 1916. *Democracy and education: An introduction to the philosophy of education*. New York, NY: Macmillan.

———. 1929. *Experience and nature*. Chicago, IL: Open Court.

———. 1988. *Human nature and conduct; an introduction to social psychology*. New York, NY: Holt.

ECCENBARGER, W. 2008. El Espiritú Olímpico [The olimpic spirit]. *Selecciones de Reader's Digest*, July. 98–105.

EINSTEIN, A. 1954. *Ideas and opinions, based on Mein Weltbild*. New York, NY: Bonzana Books.

———. LIVING PHILOSOPHIES. Available at http://sciphilos.info/docs_pages/docs_Einstein_full text_css.html (accessed 8 January 2015).

FISHER, N. 2015. Nothing holy: A Zen primer. Available at http://www.dharmanet.org/lczen.htm (accessed 15 January 2015).

FLYNN, E. 2013. Personal communication. September 19, 2013.

FRASER, C. 2014. Heart-fasting, forgetting, and using the heart like a mirror. In *Nothingness in Asian philosophy*, edited by J. Liu and D. Berger. London: Routledge: 197–212.

GALLAGHER, S. 2007. *How the body shapes the mind*. Oxford: Oxford University Press.

———. 2008. Understanding others: embodied social cognition. In *Handbook of cognitive science*, edited by P. Calvo and T. Gómila. Amsterdam: Elsevier: 439–52.

———. 2009. Philosophical antecedents to situated cognition. In *Cambridge handbook of situated cognition*, edited by P. Robbins and M. Aydede. Cambridge: Cambridge University Press: 35–50.

———. 2012. *Phenomenology*. Basingstoke: Palgrave Macmillan.

GLADWELL, M. 2005. *Blink: The power of thinking without thinking*. New York, NY: Little Brown.

HALES, S.D. 2000. The problem of intuition. *American Philosophical Quarterly*. 37 (2): 135–47.

HEIDEGGER, M. 1962. *Being and time*. Translated by J. Macquarrie and E. Robinson. New York, NY: Harper.

HEIDEGGER, M. 1971. *The origin of the work of art. Language, poetry, thought*. New York, NY: Harper & Row.

HEISIG, J.W. 2011. Minamoto Ryōen. *Japanese philosophy: A sourcebook*. Edited by J Heisig, T. Kasulis, and J. Maraldo. Honolulu: University of Hawai'i Press: 930.

HEMMING, S. 2012. 'Chariots of Fire' comes to the stage. *Financial Times*. Available at http://www.ft.com/cms/s/2/2708eb7a-92ea-11e1-aa60-00144feab49a.html (accessed 14 January 2015).

HERRIGEL, E. 1989. *Zen in the art of archery*. New York, NY: Vintage.

HÖCHSMANN, H., Y. GUORONG, and ZHUANGZI. 2007. *Zhuangzi*. New York, NY: Pearson Longman.

HSU, L. and J. ILUNDÁIN-AGURRUZA. Forthcoming. An inquiry on compatibility between East Asian confucianisms and modern olympism—A humanistic and global perspective. *Journal of Chinese Philosophy*.

HUIZINGA, J. 1955. *Homo Ludens: A study of the element of play in culture*. Boston, MA: Beacon Press.

HUSSERL, E. 1998. *Idea pertaining to a pure phenomenology and to a phenomenological philosophy. First book*. Dordrecht: Kluwer Academic.

HUTTO, D. and E. MYIN. 2013. *Radicalizing enactivism: Basic minds without content*. Cambridge, MA: MIT Press.

ILUNDÁIN-AGURRUZA, J. 2000. … In the realms of art: A conceptual inquiry of the genesis of the work of art. Ph.D. Thesis, University of Illinois at Urbana-Champaign.

———. 2011. Weaving the magic: Philosophy, sports and literature. In *Philosophy of sport: International perspectives*, edited by A. Hardman and C. Jones. Newcastle upon Tyne: Cambridge Scholars Publishing: 50–71.

———. 2013a. Ortega y Gasset, José. In *International encyclopedia of ethics*. Edited by H. Lafollette. Wiley & Blackwell.

———. 2014. The quest for meaningful and lifelong learning. In *Philosophy, sport and education: International perspectives*, edited by M. Isidori, F.J. López Frías, and A. Müller. Roma: Sette Citá: 43–70.

———. Forthcoming-a. From unskilled failure to skillful fluency: A phenomenological analysis of an eastern solution to sport's choking effect. *Phenomenology and the Cognitive Sciences*.

———. Forthcoming-b. The eye of the hurricane: Philosophical reflections on risky sports, self-knowledge and flourishing. *Journal of the Philosophy of Sport*.

ILUNDÁIN-AGURRUZA, J., K. FUKASAWA, and M. TAKEMURA. 2013. The philosophy of sport in relation to Japanese philosophy and pragmatism. In *A companion for the philosophy of sport*, edited by C. Torres. London: Bloomsbury Editions: 66–82.

ILUNDÁIN-AGURRUZA, J. and T. HATA. 2015. Eastern philosophy. In *Handbook for the philosophy of sport*, edited by M. McNamee and W. Morgan. London: Routledge.

ILUNDÁIN-AGURRUZA, J. and C. KULELI. 2012. A new heart for Turkish soccer: A MacIntyrean analysis of the beautiful game. *Soccer & Society* 13 (5–6): 667–87.

JONES, O.R., ed. 1971. *The private language argument*. London: Macmillan.

JOST, B., F. VAVERKA, O. KUGOVNIK, and M. COH. 1998. Differences in selected kinematic flight parameters of the most and least successful ski jumpers of the 1996 world cup competition in Innsbruck. *Biology of Sport*. 15 (4): 245–51.

KAAG, J. 2012. Paddling in the stream of consciousness: Describing the movement of Jamesian inquiry. In *Pragmatism and the philosophy of sport*, R. Lally, D. Anderson, and J. Kaag. London: Lexington Books: 47–61.

KANO, J. 2014. Nothing new under the sun …. Available at http://100yearlegacy.org/english/Kano_Jigoro/pdf/kj_panph_English.pdf (accessed 24 August 2014).

HOLISM AND THE CULTIVATION OF EXCELLENCE IN SPORTS AND PERFORMANCE

KREIN, K. and J. ILUNDÁIN-AGURRUZA. 2014. An east–west comparative analysis of Mushin and flow. In *Philosophy and the Martial Arts*, edited by G. Priest and D. Young. Abingdon: Routledge: 139–64.

KRETCHMAR, S. 2013. Mind-body holism, paradigm shifts, and education. fair play. *Revista de Filosofía, Ética y Derecho del Deporte* 1 (1): 28–43.

LEUNG, A.K., L. QIU, L. ONG, and K.P. TAM. 2011. Embodied cultural cognition: Situating the study of embodied cognition in socio-cultural contexts. *Social and Personality Psychology Compass* 5 (9): 591–608.

LITTLE, W., H.W. Fowler, and J. Coulson, eds. 1964. *The shorter Oxford English Dictionary on historical principles*. Revised by C.T. Onions. Oxford: Oxford Clarendon Press.

MACINTYRE, A. 1984. *After virtue: A study in moral virtue*. 2nd ed. Notre Dame, IN: University of Notre Dame.

MAKKREEL, R. 2012. Wilhelm Dilthey. In *Stanford encyclopedia of philosophy*, edited by E.D. Zalta. Available at http://plato.stanford.edu/archives/fall2011/entries/cognitive-science/ PDF version. 1–39.

MANDELL, R.D. 1971. *The Nazi Olympics*. Champaign: University of Illinois Press.

MAUSS, M. 1950. Les Techniques du Corps [The techniques of the body]. In *Sociologie et Anthropologie* [Sociology and anthropology]. Paris: Presses Universitaires de France: 364–86.

MCDOUGALL, C. 2014. FKT up? Kilian Jornet's insane new sport. *Outside Magazine*, December, 68–73.

MCFEE, G. 2004. *Sport, rules and values*. London: Routledge.

MCNAMEE, M. 1998a. Celebrating trust; virtues and rules in the ethical conduct of sports coaches. In *Ethics and sport*, edited by M.J. McNamee and S.J. Parry. London: Routledge: 148–68.

———. 1998b. Contractualism and methodological individualism and communitarianism; situating understandings of moral trust in the context of sport and social theory. *Sport, Education and Society* 3 (2): 161–79.

———. 2008. *Sports, virtues and vices: Morality plays*. London: Routledge.

MENARY, R. 2010. *The extended mind*. Cambridge, MA: MIT Press.

MINAMOTO, R. 2011. Kata as style. In *Japanese philosophy: A sourcebook*, edited by J. Heisig, T. Kasulis, and J. Maraldo. Honolulu: University of Hawai'i Press: 931–5.

MONAHAN, M. 2007. The practice of self-overcoming: Nietzschean reflections on the martial arts. *Journal of the Philosophy of Sport* 34 (1): 39–51.

MUSASHI, M. 1993. *The book of five rings*. Translated by T. Cleary. Boston, MA: Shambhala: 3–92.

———. 2004. Writings on the five elements. In *Miyamoto Musashi: His life and writings*, edited by K. Tokitsu. Boston, MA: Shambhala: 137–96.

MUTCHSLECNER, D. 2013a. Kenosis in the Dante Etudes. Unpublished manuscript.

———. 2013b. Personal Communication. Several meetings. June–Agusut, 2013.

NOË, A. 2004. *Action in perception*. Cambridge, MA: MIT Press.

O'REGAN, J. and A. NOË. 2001. What it is like to see a sensorimotor theory of perceptual experience. Synthese 129: 79–103.

ORTEGA Y GASSET, J. 1960. *What is philosophy?* New York, NY: W.W. Norton.

———. 1961. *History as a system and other essays toward a philosophy of history*. New York, NY: Norton.

———. 1963. *Meditations on Quixote*. New York, NY: W.W. Norton.

———. 2001. *Qué es filosofía? [What is philosophy?]* Madrid: Alianza Editorial.

HOLISM AND THE CULTIVATION OF EXCELLENCE IN SPORTS AND PERFORMANCE

———. 2004a. El Quijote en la escuela. *El Quijote en la escuela. Misión de la universidad y otros ensayos sobre educación y pedagogía* [The Quixote at school. Mission of the University and other essays on education and pedagogy]. Madrid: Alianza Editorial.

———. 2004b. *Meditaciones del Quijote* [Meditation on Quixote]. Obras Completas. Vol. I. Madrid: Taurus: 747–828.

———. 2005. *Misión de la Universidad* [Mission of the university]. Obras completas. Vol. IV. Madrid: Taurus: 529–68.

———. 2006a. *Notas a la Edición* [Notes to the edited work]. Obras completas. Vol. V. Madrid: Taurus: 852–8.

———. 2006b. *Facciones del Amor* [Facets of love]. Obras Completas. Vol. V. Madrid: Taurus: 457–62.

———. 2007. *Particularismo y Acción Directa - Notas de Fenomenología Social* [Particularism and direct action—Notes on social phenomenology]. Obras Completas. Vol VII. Madrid: Taurus: 751–3.

PERRIN, N. 1979. *Giving up the gun: Japan's reversion to the Sword, 1543–1879.* Jaffrey, NH: David R. Godine.

PLATO. (1961a). Phaedrus. In *The collected dialogues of Plato*, edited by E. Hamilton and C. Huntington. Princeton, NJ: Princeton University Press: 475–525.

———. 1961b. Laws. In *The collected dialogues of Plato*, edited by E. Hamilton and C. Huntington. Princeton, NJ: Princeton University Press: 1225–513.

———. 2013. *Theaetetus*. Translated by B. Jowett. Project Gutenberg Ebook. Available at http://www.gutenberg.org/files/1726/1726-h/1726-h.htm (accessed 21 June 2013).

QUAMMEN, D. 2014. People of the horse. *National Geographic*, March, 104–26.

REID, H.L. 2009. Sport, philosophy, and the quest for knowledge. *Journal of the Philosophy of Sport* 36 (1): 40–9.

———. 2012. *Introduction to the philosophy of sport*. Plymouth: Rowan & Littlefield.

RHEES, R. 1963. Can there be a private language? In *Philosophy and ordinary language*, edited by C. Caton. Urbana, IL: Illini Books: 90–107.

RIEFESTAHL, L. 1938. *Olympia* [DVD]. Berlin: Olympia-Film.

RILEY, G. 1994. *The life and legacy of Annie Oakley*. Norman, OK: University of Oklahoma Press.

ROBERTS, M. 2015. The never-ending ride of the world's greatest surfer. *Outside Magazine*, January Issue, 60–63, 92.

RODWELL, G. and J. RAMSLAND. 2000. Cecil Healy: A soldier of the surf. *Sporting Traditions* 16 (2): 3–16.

SAUNDERS & HENZE. 1976. *The private language problem: A philosophical dialogue*. New York, NY: Random House.

SAXENA, S. 2012. Bolt and beautiful in just 41 steps. *The Times of India*, 21 August. Available at http://timesofindia.indiatimes.com/Bolt-beautiful-in-just-41-steps/articleshow/15383597.cms (accessed 12 January 2015).

SCHACHT, R. 1998. Nietzsche and sport. *International Studies in Philosophy* 30 (3): 123–30.

———. Forthcoming. Sport? A Nietzschean appreciation.

SEOK, B. 2013. *Embodied moral psychology and confucian philosophy*. Plymouth: Lexington Books.

SHEETS-JOHNSTONE, M. 1981. Thinking in movement. *The Journal of Aesthetics and Art Criticism.* 39 (4): 399–407.

———. 1994. *The roots of power: Animate form and gendered bodies*. Chicago, IL: Open Court.

HOLISM AND THE CULTIVATION OF EXCELLENCE IN SPORTS AND PERFORMANCE

———. 2000. Kinetic Tactile-Kinesthetic bodies: Ontogenetical foundations of apprenticeship learning. *Human Studies* 23 (4): 343–70.

———. 2009. *The corporeal turn: An interdisciplinary reader*. Exeter: Imprint Academic.

SIMON, R. 1991. *Fair play: Sports, values, and society*. Boulder, CO: Westview Press.

STEINBOCK, A.J. 1995a. *Home and beyond: Generative phenomenology after Husserl*. Evanston, IL: Northwestern University Press.

STEINBOCK, A. 1995b. Generativity and generative phenomenology. *Husserl Studies* 12: 55–79.

STEINER, G. and C. LADJALI 2005. *Elogio de la Transmission* [In praise of transmission]. Madrid: Siruela.

STURTZ, R. 2014. Unprotected. *Outside Magazine*. Available at http://www.outsideonline.com/outdoor-adventure/water-activities/swimming/The-Sex-Abuse-Scandal-Plaguing-USA-Swimming.html (accessed 1 October 2015).

SUITS, B. 1990. *The grasshopper: Game, life, and Utopia*. Boston, MA: David R. Godine.

SUZUKI, D. 1993. *Zen and Japanese culture*. New York, NY: Princeton University Press.

SUZUKI, S. 2010. *Beginner's mind*. Boston, MA: Shambhala.

TAKUAN, S. 1986. *The unfettered mind: Writings of the Zen Master to the Sword Master*. Tokyo: Kodansha.

TERUYAMA, T. 2014. Personal Communication. August 31, 2014.

THOMSON, G. 2003a. *On the meaning of life*. Belmont, CA: Wadsworth/Thomson Learning.

———. 2003b. *On philosophy*. Belmont, CA: Wadsworth/Thomson Learning.

THOMSON, S. and D. MACASKILL 2014a. The ledge: Danny MacAskill making 'The Ridge'. Available at https://www.youtube.com/watch?v=wZjcTG141rs&spfreload=1 (accessed 4 January 2015).

———. 2014b. The frontflip: Danny MacAskill making 'The Ridge'. Available at https://www.youtube.com/watch?v=FJ67I8sJ7Qo (accessed 4 January 2015).

TOKITSU, K. 2004. *Miyamoto Musashi: His life and writings*. Boston, MA: Shambhala.

UESHIBA, M. 1992. *The art of peace*. Boston, MA: Shambhala.

VARELA, F. 1999. *Ethical know-how: Action, wisdom, and cognition*. Stanford: Stanford University Press.

VARELA, F., E. THOMPSON, and E. ROSCH. 1991. *The embodied mind*. Cambridge, MA: MIT Press.

WALLACE, J. 2009. *Norms and practices*. Ithaca, NY: Cornell University Press.

WALSH, G.P. 1983. Healy, Cecil Patrick (1881–1918), *Australian Dictionary of Biography*. National Centre of Biography, Australian National University. Available online at http://adb.anu.edu.au/biography/healy-cecil-patrick-6621/text11401 (accessed 19 December 2014).

WALSH, B. 2014. 10 Questions. *Time*, 15 December.

WATSUJI, T. 1961. *A climate: A philosophical study*. Translated by G. Bownas. Tokyo: Printing Bureau, Japanese Government.

———. 1996. *Watsuji Tetsuro's Rinrigaku: Ethics in Japan*. Translated by Y. Seisaku and R. Carter. Albany: State University of New York.

———. 2011. A phenomenology of the cold. In *Japanese philosophy: A sourcebook*, edited by J. Heisig, T. Kasulis, and J. Maraldo. Honolulu: University of Hawai'i Press: 856–9.

WHITMAN, W. 1903. *Leaves of grass*. New York, NY: Doubleday Page.

WITTGENSTEIN, L. 1921. *Tractatus Logico-Philosophicus*. London: Routledge & Kegan Paul.

———. 1963. *Philosophical investigations*. London: Basil & Blackwell.

WOOLLEY, D.R. 2012. Word of the day: *yūgen* 幽玄. Available at http://just.thinkofit.com/word-of-the-day-yugen-幽玄/ (accessed 7 October 2014).

YAMADA, Y. 2004. *The hidden blade* [DVD]. Tokyo: Shochiku.

HOLISM AND THE CULTIVATION OF EXCELLENCE IN SPORTS AND PERFORMANCE

YUASA, Y. 1987. *The body: Toward an eastern mind-body theory*. Albany: State University of New York Press.

———. 1993. *The body, self-cultivation, and ki-energy*. Albany: State University of New York Press.

ZAHAVI, D. 2004. The embodied self-awareness of the infant: A challenge to the theory-theory of mind? In *The structure and development of self-consciousness: Interdisciplinary perspectives*, edited by D. Zahavi, T. Grünbaum, and J. Parnas. Amsterdam: John Benjamins: 35–63.

ZHUANGZI and B. ZIPORYN. 2009. *Zhuangzi: Essential writings with selections from traditional commentaries*. Indianapolis, IN: Hackett.

EPILOGUE

Jesús Ilundáin-Agurruza

As soon as you have finished a job, you start appreciating its difficulties

Chinese Proverb[1]

Socrates asked Phaedrus the seemingly innocuous question, 'Where do you hail from, Phaedrus, and where are you bound?' (Plato 1956, 3). Wiley hunter of gnostic truths, Socrates's question opened a path of inquiry that took into its scope not only the strapping youth's peripatetic destination, but particularly his whole life. More modestly, there are two issues to consider presently that help us see where we hail from and where we might be bound. The first one concerns eclecticism and heterogeneity, while the second deals with the extraordinary.

As to the first, a polite reader might put it this way, 'Why such a heterogeneous and eclectic mix of perspectives?' This is largely a methodological issue regarding the very diverse interdisciplinary path in *Skillful Striving*, with Asian philosophies, ethics, phenomenology, philosophy of mind, and pragmatism, primarily. The weakest, if partially correct, answer is that they complement one another. We could even argue that they do so quite well, highlighting that they have shed light on the phenomena under discussion: excellence, skills, and performative endeavors from a holistic perspective. Even if this is the case, this is unsatisfactory. The polite reader will rightly rejoin, 'But, why *these* and not others?'

The stronger answer is that this combination is the *minimally sufficient* one needed to account for excellence and the skillful strivings of performative paragons. Surely, we could add more disciplines, as the last essay discusses, with historiography, poetry, and others. Alternatively we could promote some from a supporting to a primary role, e.g. dynamic systems theory. This would amount to additional explorations that belong with the first answer. Performative excellence, the sort that is conquered through our strivings asks for nothing less than skillful virtuosity. To able to suitably describe, explain, and understand this skillful virtuosity—given the complexity of the issue, which intertwines performative, cognitive, normative, and social domains—brings us to the door of holism. As both review and justification, we proceed by looking at the path walked and by highlighting the methods, disciplines or thinkers we have encountered.

A thickly holistic account needs to unveil both overt and underlying continuities of matters of fact, even if in doing so, it paradoxically imposes divisions. Pragmatism, with James and Dewey, ideally highlighted these continuities. They are the two philosophers who have emphasized continuity most in their work. But, once we began this process of elucidation, a number of paradoxical, apparently contradictory, or disparate dualities arose, e.g. body/mind, action/reaction, automatization/deliberation, is/ought, aesthetic/ethic, etc. Dealing properly with these led to three strategies. (1) At times, it necessitated inventing or finding a third factor, as we did with James' fringe in order to account for our experience of expert action in a way that did not rely solely on a split between automatized and conscious processes where the former prevailed. His phenomenologically validated solution proves more parsimonious and affords better explanations than contemporary cognitive accounts that rely on mechanisms, whether anatomic or computational. (2) It also led to a Nishidan 'epistemic ethos' where an acting contradiction avoids the 'either/or' analysis to embrace a 'both/and' understanding of the phenomenon, e.g. the union of subject and object in action when two teams create 'playing' on the field. Nishida's views also helped to connect Western enactive accounts with traditional Asian praxes, Japanese *dō*, whose insights were sometimes vetted in the most extreme conditions, as we saw with swordsmanship; and/or, (3) it was a matter of reconceptualizing the issue, as with the mind/body problem. *Skillful Striving* self consciously sidestepped it. For, as we learned with Japanese philosophy, in the world of performative endeavors we are acting and living 'bodyminds' in various stages of integration when it comes to acting. This it is not an ontological issue but a performative one of achievement. To successfully develop these three strategies, the methodology and thinkers chosen were those that were necessary yet sufficed to explain the context of performative activities and excellence. There are further ways in which selected accounts, approaches, and thinkers are the best fit for the aims of this inquiry.

Excellence in performance begins, functionally and enactively, with the ecological development of our skills and dispositions. When the context allows for skillful strivings toward personal perfections, those that rich practices and communities modulate, skills can become virtuous. Some practices and ways of approaching them are deeper and richer than others, but as we learned, it is not so much what we do but how and why we do it. There are many paths to arrive at the Gateless Gate, true, but only so many ways to enter. It is about the quality of the effort, as we learned with Ortega, whose vitalist and existential phenomenology best draws out the implications of the superfluous effort that characterizes a sportive attitude to life. Daoist Zhuangzi's stories of masters who excel in the most varied scenarios brought us closer to an understanding of superb action: we perform best when we act spontaneously and unfettered. A *Zhuangzian* analysis of spontaneity is pivotal for any holistic account of expert action. And refining this led to examining alternatives to contemporary prevailing paradigms of expertise and cognitivist and phenomenological models.

A holistic and radically enactive approach—based on Hutto and Myin—that advances contentless capacities in lieu of representations transparently accounts for the kind of action on the edge that characterizes high-performance. In this way the philosophy of mind and philosophical psychology find their way into the project. But, understanding *just* how our bodyminds actually move and act in a skillfully fluent way meant a deep incursion into the phenomenology of movement, particularly with the ideas of Gallagher and Sheets-Johnstone. The descriptions of kinesthetic, proprioceptive, and other pertinent variables allowed us to (re)describe and understand the unique phenomenology of expert performance. Nonetheless, a full account of expertise cannot ignore the other side of the coin: failure. Fractured action or choking permitted us to incorporate an ecological model of performance as well as Wertz's and Breivik's work, and further directed us to a remedy found in Japanese culture. It uniquely offers the clearest fit between actual practice, with its *dō*, paths of self-cultivation, and theoretical understanding of the drive toward achieving personal perfection. *Shugyō* was recast as a lifelong skillful striving where we endeavor to integrate our bodymind through performance. Explaining this phenomenon required a full-blown situated account of enaction and holism in the context of spontaneous action and ethical choice. Fully integrating Asian and Western views, this reconceived the means/ends relation on its way to explore the crucial role of geo-historical circumstances and the challenge to articulate movement and *felt* experience meaningfully.

Throughout, certain arguments and ideas (skill and virtues, personal perfection, spontaneity) were reconsidered and refined as they accrued meaning when placed in different but interlaced contexts. Finally, it was the intent, as stated in the introduction, to engage thinkers and accounts *not* in the mainstream. The reason for this was not so much to march to the beat of a different drum for its sake, however worthwhile that may be on occasion. Rather, and crucially, it was because precisely these authors and approaches just discussed are the ones who could best illuminate the skillful strivings of experts in the context of excellence. *Mainstream* methodologies, accounts, and thinkers, as we have seen on various occasions, are inadequate or mistaken at key points. Rather than merely build a critical case, the alternative sources enabled us develop the positive side. This has resulted in an enactive wisdom that interlaces *kinesophia* and *sophokinesis*. It is sophokinetic in so far as wise movement results from suitable reflections, deliberations, and a reflective consciousness. It is also kinesophic because movement is wise as well, issuing forth from that enactive cognition where emptiness of content means fullness of action. The top-down and bottom-up approaches meet at the center, giving rise to the excellent performance of paragons, whom we discuss one last time.

Our courteous reader has one more question, 'Why do we need to examine extraordinary performance to explain ordinary skill?' In other words, 'Why focus on experts, rather than normal people?'

Truly, there are very good reasons to study the normal and the average. After all, they constitute the majority, so it behooves us to understand this. Likewise, there are important reasons to study the pathological, cases of deafferented or schizophrenics or choking in sports, for example. As we saw with Gallagher and Zahavi they can 'make manifest what is normally or simply taken for granted' (2008, 140). And there are many studies of both already (which does not mean these are enough). But, there is the simple matter that these are not mutually exclusive. We can and should study all three. Given that limited time, energy, and resources are always a concern, we need better reasons other than because we can do it. As a preamble, our concern here was *excellence*, this being the case, it is incumbent on us to look at the extraordinary. The average is not a suitable locus to study it. There are at least four other reasons to study the exceptional as embodied in performative paragons who enact it.

First, extraordinary performance is a unique, all too rare phenomenon interesting in its own right. We are rightly and naturally attracted by the remarkable and outstanding. The performances of superior athletes, artists, martial artists, and performers fascinate us. We could take Kant's (1951) lead and adduce that genius has no rule, effectively putting this beyond comprehension. But this is tantamount to avoiding the issue when we neither need to nor should. Our interest should go beyond merely 'enjoying' their accomplishments. We would endeavor to understand them better precisely because they are so remarkable, scarce, and poorly understood—which segues into the next reason.

Secondly, high-performance is often assumed to be like normal performance, only 'more'. But it is mistaken to think that it is a quantitative matter alone. Sometimes, given a sufficient quantitative critical mass, there are qualitative changes. Usain Bolt does not merely run faster than most of us. His running and that of a few elite runners is all a quality of its own; just as much out of reach as climbing Yosemite's the Nose without ropes and climbing gear, or diving 300 feet (100 meters) on one breath. These feats come with unique dynamics and abilities, as we have discussed at length. And they are tantalizing. If they have the power to elicit, 'How can that be?' we should have the resolve to try to understand them.

The reader may wonder now, 'If such performances are in a class of their own, and the performers are *so* different from us, does this not run the risk of confounding us?' We should worry first about not misconceiving these performances and performers. For instance, we saw how standard and prevailing computational and some phenomenological accounts were inadequate to explain expertise in, particularly but not limited to, risky activities. Moreover, it is only in studying them that we can compare with the ordinary and realize what the differences are in their practical and theoretical import. Only then can we draw meaningful similarities and differences and actually avoid mistaking one for the other. Finally, if the pathological can show the limits of theoretical claims, and the normal provides insight into how most people are, the superlative comes with other promises. This leads to the next reason, more controversial and interesting.

Thirdly, we should establish the norm according to these exceptional cases and not the average cases. One sense in which to take 'norm' is to mean the 'normal' as average or ordinary. It is a descriptive use. This is often how it is interpreted. Yet it need not be so. In the case of *excellence* it should not, because it is concerned with superior action. This other sense is a *normative* matter because it enacts a path to follow. Thus, this is 'both the ideal state and the potential state which promise a *possibility* to all people' (Yuasa 1993, 62–63 his emphasis). As we saw with Japan, this is the standard they adopt when they engage both the study and practice of the arts of self-cultivation (which we reframed as skillful strivings). In cycling, there is an oft-repeated truism that is applicable: 'if you want to ride faster, you need to ride with faster people than you.' Just as we would learn from those wiser, we should set up as the standard to follow those who excel when it comes to excellence performance. This means we need to study the exceptional. One outcome of studying the extraordinary is that it shows what is achievable, and expands the repertoire of possibilities for the rest of us. We may not be able to reach their level, but we can be inspired to strive and improve.

Fourthly, then, paragons and their performances are inspirational. They may be exemplary, but they are neither perfect (who is?) nor easy. They are the first to admit to striving and working hard. And they are the first to embrace failure as a spring to opportunities. Moreover, in keeping with the tenor of *Skillful Striving*, it is the striving that matters, the quality of that effort as we exert ourselves seeking our personal perfection (we can still make objective comparisons among people or apply external standards, of course). We should not let our own insecurities and fears get in the way

HOLISM AND THE CULTIVATION OF EXCELLENCE IN SPORTS AND PERFORMANCE

of attempting what we thought impossible for *us*. It is not about merely admiration but inspiration; it is not about imitation but emulation in our own way.

We are perennial works in progress towards flourishing. This is a target that should become a means to the process itself, because *there* we live our life, in the going, in the laying down of our path. Striving after an unattainable perfection may seem Sisyphean, but in the right perspective, our very bane can be our joy, our very limitation and weakness can be our strength. For one, if we enjoy the process, the means, the path itself, the activity we are engaged in, this just gives us more reason to keep doing it.

The result is a model that encourages lifelong enriching activities that non-instrumentally cultivate our abilities by accentuating the process while not excluding results. Many of us wrestle with adverse circumstances, undeveloped skills, emotional immaturity, intellectual blind spots, and social shortcomings. *Skillful Striving* examines the process to transform these limitations into opportunities to flourish. Devoted training, rigorous reflection, and emotive maturity nurture excellence into a *skill-full* and well-lived life. In these challenging times, it is well worth studying a process of personal growth within a social context where our models of excellence echo the ethos that Longfellow's poem intimated in the introduction:

> In the elder days of Art
> Builders wrought with the greatest care
> Each minute and unseen part;
> For the gods see everywhere. (1992, 108)

They themselves and their performances are the works of art they craft with the greatest care. Ultimately, *Skillful Striving* rethinks how we may blossom as members of communities that encourage exploration and cultivation of our abilities as shared skillful strivings for excellence.

The opening citation to this epilogue is sobering, but can also be inspiring as just discussed. With the blessed curse of hindsight comes the appreciation for the problems. Anew. Much as stepping across Heraclitus' river, however, neither the problems nor the crosser are the same now. And yet, to even realize what has changed or that *we* have changed we must do so against a core that remains the same in some way. Then we may realize they are once again the same waters and crosser. Weaving narratives, storied or theoretical, helps us do this, even if the words are written on water.

NOTE

1. DeMarco (2012, 155).

REFERENCES

DEMARCO, M. 2012. *Asian martial arts: Constructive thoughts and practical application*. Santa Fe, NM: Via Media Publishing.

GALLAGHER, S. and D. ZAHAVI. 2008. *The phenomenological mind*. London: Routledge.

KANT, I. 1951. *Critique of judgment*. New York, NY: Hafner Press.

LONGFELLOW, H.W. 1992. *Complete poetical works*. Boston, MA: Houghton.

PLATO. 1956. *Phaedrus*. New York, NY: Macmillan.

YUASA, Y. 1993. *The body, self-cultivation, and ki-energy*. Albany, NY: State University of New York Press.

APPENDIX—MUCH ADO ABOUT NOTHING

Jesús Ilundáin-Agurruza

Make your will one! Don't listen with your ears, listen with your mind. No, don't listen with your mind, but listen with your spirit. Listening stops with the ears, the mind stops with recognition, but spirit is empty and waits on all things. The Way gathers in emptiness alone. Emptiness is the fasting of the mind. (Zhuangzi)[1]

This short passage is thick with innuendo and rich in philosophical promise; it begs to be combed with a fine exegetical brush. Presently, we probe, once again, unparalleled performance and its normative ramifications and commitments by way of making three clarifications regarding Chinese concepts and characters in the original text and their translation.[2] Far from being an erudite sinological discussion, this proves revealing and fundamental for our understanding of spontaneous action in relation to our broad and holistic normativity and the corresponding guidelines for the well-lived life of the superior person. This explains in depth how emptiness operates in skillfully normative contexts.

The first elucidation concerns the character 心, *xin*, which most translators (Höchsmann, Guorong, and Zhuangzi 2007; Legge 1891; Chuang-Tzu and Watson 1968; Zhuangzi and Ziporyn 2009) render as 'mind,' excepting Graham, who translates it as 'heart' (Chuang Tzu and Graham 1981, 68).[3] According to the dictionary, it means 'heart,' 'mind,' 'feeling,' or 'intention'.[4] (See additional linguistic elucidations in essays 5 and 9.) Zhuangzi's Kongzi is not speaking of the mind in the Western sense, with the attendant associations of rationality and propositional thought, the proverbial 'know that.' He is concerned with a holistic faculty that amalgamates intellect, emotion, will, whichever abilities may be pertinent for the situation at hand (orienteering or singing skills, for instance), and fluid socio-environmental attunement. Chris Fraser, who also uses 'heart', explains that it was 'the organ that in Classical Chinese thought was typically assumed to guide action,' and in addition to emotion, it is also associated with cognition and self-consciousness (2014, 199). It is a know-how as discussed in the first essay: a broad *techné* where narrow rationality is supplanted by engagement born from Deweyan active habit. In outstanding cases, the integrated bodymind performs requisite tasks with remarkable ease and efficacy. In this passage, Zhuangzi is thinking of the perfected or consummate person in action that embodies this.

This person is referred to in Daoism as the 真人, *zhēnrén* (from 真 *zhēn*, 'real', 'true' or 'genuine', and 人 *rén*, 'person').[5] It plays a pivotal role in the book since it denotes the sage as role model. Chuang-Tzu and Watson translates it as 'true man' (1968, 77), as does Legge (1891), while Billeter opts for 'the true person' (1994, 317).

Others (Fraser 2014) opt for 'perfected,' but because this suggests that the agent has reached perfection, given the commitment to an ongoing never to be achieved perfection (essays 1, 4, and 9), and unless citing or echoing an author's words, either the pinyin transliteration of *zhēnrén*, or adjectives such as consummate, superior, excellent and synonyms are used henceforth.

The consummate person acts in a state of 自然, *zìrán* (*shizen* in Japanese), which literally means 'self-so' or 'of-itself-so.' It is derived from 自, *zì*, nose, which refers to the self with the connotation of one's perspective, and 然, *rán*, meaning 'thus'. As translator Scott Wilson points out, in ancient times it meant 'to burn': 'Thus 自然 indicated the self-igniting or self-thus' (Chozan 2006, 26). Liu notes the difficulty of translating this term in the *Zhuangzi* and suggests 'naturalness' (2014, 162).[6] At the heart of it is the very notion of spontaneity as presented in essays 9 and 10: the performer seeks that state of mindful emptiness, *mushin*, that allows her to act naturally, unaffectedly, and spontaneously in accord to the needs of the moment. Accordingly, the heart-mind does not get in the way through either hyper-rationality or exacerbated emotion. Rather, her heart-mind 心 is centered and in harmony with the situation. The *zhēnrén* then is the individual who incarnates an equanimous and balanced blending of all enactive domains in superb performance. This is accomplished through a fluid *qi*.

The second clarification concerns the character 氣, *qi*, which the same translators render as 'spirit.' The English term is imbued with associations to the notion of a soul, a disembodied psyche, and the like. These are misleading. In Chinese, it literally means 'air', 'gas', 'breath', 'smell', and derivatively 'spirit'. It combines the idea of steam, 气 emanating from rice, 米. Zyporin comes closest with his rendition of 'vital energy' (Zhuangzi and Ziporyn 2009, 26–7). As discussed in essay 5, it is richly and complexly imbued with dynamic and energetic properties that aim at evoking the life force of living beings as well as the energy in inorganic matter. This is the factor that accounts for fluidity in performance, as it is malleable and is in its nature to flow, becoming problematic when it stagnates. *Qi* permeates us inside out, connecting us to our environment. Hence, it is liable to being nurtured as a healthy *qi*—or squandered. Martial arts and traditional Chinese medicine rely heavily on it—with 太极, *tàijíquán* (taichi) uniting both in one practice. In the context of *tàijíquán*, Tien-Deng Yu explains how with a fluid *qi* performers can '"use the mind to circulate the *chi*" (以心行氣) and to "use the *chi* to move the body" (以氣運身) and attain the final unification of the mind and the body.' (2014, n.p.) Spontaneous action draws deeply from this source, as the *zhēnrén* must effectively and instantaneously adapt to the situation without missing a heartbeat.

We become skillful in any *dō*, from poetry to marksmanship, through training in technique. Chozansi clarifies, however, that functionally *qi* is 'what makes each one singular' (Chozan 2006, 115). In fact, *qi* lies at the center of Chozansi's whimsical but deep treatise. It discusses its philosophical underpinnings and relations to Daoist and Buddhist tenets, particularly those involving change and transformation, and the order of things in terms of *yin* 陰 and *yang* 陽; it explains the complex relations *qi* has with the heart-mind, the bodymind, consciousness, and form and principle; it even dispenses practical advice on how to center one's *qi*, starting with our breathing. If the untrammeled *qi* leads to spontaneity, the free-flowing *qi* is achieved through training. Put differently, a Deweyan habit that channels our skillful strivings or efforts at self-cultivation is requisite to balance and help integrate our bodymind. But, this must be done in the

HOLISM AND THE CULTIVATION OF EXCELLENCE IN SPORTS AND PERFORMANCE

right state of heart-mind: the idea is to enter that state of *mushin*. This is the way to be mindfully present, completely focused yet relaxed and spontaneous. Otherwise, we may end up with a distorted and clogged *qi* that results in fractured action.

In essay 8, we met fictional gifted baseball shortstop Henry Skrimshander. He exemplifies how performance is affected negatively when the *qi* is not flowing. For Henry, the arm releasing the baseball at one point just did not feel right, as we read, which congeals his thinking and stiffens the elbow simultaneously. His slump, analyzed from the present stance, is the result of deep psychosomatic and interpersonal imbalances; these accumulate the tension until he becomes unraveled by that one first bad throw. Chozansi writes, 'You should never be taken by phenomena. Once you are the least bit taken by something, your ch'i will be drawn to it. And once your ch'i is even slightly drawn to something, it will be incapable of adaptability or openness' (Chozan 2006, 188). Moreover, and in agreement with our holistic commitments, Chozansi determines that poor performance, which results from indolence and mindlessness, is also aesthetically lacking: 'when ch'i is distorted and has no life, neither the movement nor stillness of form, nor the continuity of hands and feet will be beautiful' (Chozan 2006, 159). The ongoing examination and essay 9 detail the way to a fluid *qi*. For now, and to sum up, rather than thinking of *qi* as some sort of spiritual 'entity', we should conceptualize it in terms of habits and cultivation, and its kinetic manifestation and kinesthetic resonances in dialogue between inner and outer energies. The gymnast, on vaulting off the parallel bars releases the kinetic energy accumulated through the swinging while the bar absorbs and releases the stored energy. The problem is that this takes effort, and effort expends our energies.

Life and sport are meaningfully predicated on the management of energy (Ilundáin-Agurruza 2012). Daoism seeks to balance the *qi* and seeks a harmonious flow of energies. A quietist attitude to life and desirelessness are central to mainstream Daoism, which emphasizes tranquility. The wise management of our energies is a must if we are to prudently live a long life (particularly so in the more overtly religious manifestations of Daoism). Zhuangzi admonishes against foolish squandering of our energies discussing with his dear friend Hui Shi, 惠施, a logician and philosopher in the analytic vein famous as a fearsome debater. Hui Shi 'found no peace in it [Dao; life] even for himself, scattering himself unceasingly into all things [... his] talents were fruitlessly dissipated running after things and never returning to himself. He was like a man trying to silence an echo or to outrun his own shadow. How Sad!' (Zhuangzi and Ziporyn 2009, 120).[7] This seems to run counter to Ortega and the celebration of exuberance and sport as meaningfully squandered energy (essay 4). The steed's out of proportion reaction to the spur's stimulus is an inspiring image of life for the Spaniard. Strikingly, Ortega states that the most necessary is the superfluous, sport being the best example (1961, 2004b). But this gratuitous expenditure of our limited energies seems ill-advised for prudent lives. We can always bite the bullet and even the gun's barrel, and ban prudence but for the timorous; we can reject the life of quietude. Yet, a more nuanced view of Ortega's views and Daoism finds rapprochement rather than discord.

A point of agreement is that they do not look at life with a utilitarian outlook, seeking to maximize our investments, energetic or of any kind. Neither sees material means (money) or social goods (fame, power) as worthy North Stars for our values. Both celebrate superb skill and the cultivation of our talents. Moreover, a broader look at the *Zhuangzi* shows that the aim of the sage's diatribes is an *ultimately* 'aimless busyness'

HOLISM AND THE CULTIVATION OF EXCELLENCE IN SPORTS AND PERFORMANCE

when pursuit of extrinsic goods prevails. Consummate Zhuangzian paragons we have considered (essay 5), the butcher, the cicada catcher, the swimmer in the rapids, the ferryman, all cultivate their talents through effort and discipline (besides reflection and deliberation). Zhuangzi would concur with the idea that the consummate person, the *zhēnrén*, minds Ortega's dictum that the criterion for a worthy life is that it be played as well as it may be possible (2004a, 469). The idea is to nurture life, an inspiring life, given our talents and circumstances. This fits readily with the *tempered* exuberance we have crafted with Ortega's ideas and which begins with sports as rule-limited inexpedient endeavors that require us to hone our skills. Unlike the horse, we can choose how to expend our energy. This is then modulated existentially into an ethos of life where energy is not to be hoarded but magnanimously and meaningfully spent. Liezi, 列子, who asks whether we know *why* we shoot the arrow at the target, would concur. A would Dewey. He also conceives of human nature as irremediably energetic, with infants being bundles of expressive energy to be harnessed through socially taught habits.

It may be countered that life is not a game or a sport but serious business. Yet, precisely that *is* the point that Ortega and Suits (1990) argue for independently. The no nonsense approach to life looks at it in terms of results and goals, outsourcing meaning. A more meaningful life is found *within* the exertions themselves, not outside. Sports and performative endeavors *create* meaning from inside out. And this begins with the muscles themselves. Many have seen the muscles as devoid of meaning themselves.[8] Hoberman says quoting Yukio Mishima, the Japanese writer who adored his own body, "'it is a special property of muscles' [...] that they [feed] the imagination of others while remaining totally devoid of imagination themselves." (1986, 26)

John Kaag provides an alternative and more stimulating account. He builds on the Jamesian comment that 'the ideas are in the muscle,' which we can describe as a muscular epistemological pragmatism through rowing: 'Learning to row is simply learning: a mode of inquiry. Indeed, the rower's experience of muscular fitness, with its initial ache and subsequent growth, exemplifies a moment of James epistemological approach.' (Kaag 2012, 59). The very kinesthesia of muscularity performs kinetic symphonies where flesh and idea are fully integrated in joyful and significant suffering in the case of sports. Essay 10 addresses the issue of meaning explicitly, with particular emphasis on kenosis. Some skillful strivings, practices of self-cultivation, are built on exertion to the point where, reaching one's limit, a profound sense of emptiness is all that is left. In essay 9, we saw how *shugyō* can require just such intense and *full* dedication. In some cases, the selflessness that Varela propounds is but the emptiness achieved through complete exhaustion, as the *iaidō* practitioners and Yamaoka Tesshū's students show. But there are ways and ways of engaging emptiness, as the following discourses.

The third elucidation looks at emptiness, then. What most translators render as 'emptiness' is a rather complex philosophical and exegetical matter, particularly in Eastern philosophy.[9] It is important to analyze this because of the varied implications this has for superb and skilled action. There are three concepts and characters, each with multiple connotations that are related to emptiness in various ways: 無, *wu*, 空, *kōng*, and 虛, *xū*. The underlying philosophical tenor of *wu* and *xū* is Daoist while *kōng's* is Buddhist. In fact, the *Zhuangzi* features *xū* prominently and is key to the *zhēnrén* and

HOLISM AND THE CULTIVATION OF EXCELLENCE IN SPORTS AND PERFORMANCE

her performance. There are marked similarities among these, but we should be wary of conflating them or bringing them as close as Varela does (essay 10).

The dictionary translates *wu* as 'nothing,' 'nil,' and 'without.' Philosophically, it is best understood as 'non-being,' 'non-existence,' 'emptiness,' and 'void, (Pregadio 2011 1042).' 'Nothingness' is perhaps the clearest and simplest way to put it. From this perspective, emptiness then resounds with Daoist reverberations of nothingness: Laozi, 老子, writes in chapter 77 of his *Daodejing* (道德經) that, 'The sage acts but relies on nothing' (Lao Tzu 2012, 159). Metaphysically, *wu* alludes to that formless and nameless origin of the *Dao*, 道 (see essay 5). It is contrasted with 有, *yǒu*, 'Being' or 'existence.' As Liu Xiaogan points out, *wu*, is not used philosophically in modern Chinese, but it is critical in Daoist texts not only metaphysically, 'but also as an idea that can guide social and political life, and individual self-cultivation' (2014, 151).

Accordingly, and functionally and existentially, *wu* carries over into the ideas of *wuwei* (effortless action) and 無心 *wuxin* (*mushin* in Japanese)—discussed correspondingly in essays 5 and 9. The following elucidations should be seen as complementary to Nishida's views on nothingness. Other echoes that now ring amplified are James' notion of pure experience and again Kaag's implementation as the athlete who becomes as nothing (essay 2). There is a marked contrast with Daoism, however, if we consider James temperament and his partiality toward the strenuous: the Chinese way tries to avoid precisely the strain that James sought. The Daoist sage, when acting from the vantage of *wu's* emptiness does so in accordance with the *Dao*: patience, quietude, ease, and desirelessness are her hallmarks. But also steadfastness. In other words, *wu* is concerned with a person's functional and psychological disposition. This should not be confused with a person who embodies emptiness in the Buddhist sense (even if they are not incompatible, and in many cases both find abode in the same individual). Laozi writes in chapter 11 of the *Daodejing*:

> Thirty spokes converge on a hub/but it's the emptiness/that makes the wheel work/ pots are fashioned from clay/but it's the hollow that makes a pot work/windows and doors are carved for a house/but it's the spaces/that make a house work/existence makes something useful/but nonexistence makes it work. (1996, 32)[10]

Here *wu* is translated as 'emptiness', 'hollowness', and related notions. Accordingly, void, emptiness, and nothingness are full of possibilities. Sometimes they open doors to opportunity, literally, or figuratively; sometimes they lead to spiritual fulfillment. Moreover, when profitably engaging the faculty of the imagination, *wu* is a boon for performative endeavors.

Imagination permits us to behold what is not present (whether real or not). Being related conceptually to the Greek ˅(*fantasia*; fantasy),[11] or appearance, it may be deemed un-philosophical because it deals precisely with what is not rather than with truth. But, for those who conceive of philosophy as perspectival (Nietzsche, Ortega, this author), it is inherently philosophical because it is *the* way toward compassion in ethics, alternative epistemological viewpoints, and varied interpretations in aesthetics. Imagination is fundamental for a philosopher's methodological toolkit. It is also a capacity liable to be refined, enabling us to harness and redirect passive and easygoing musings and daydreaming into active and creative explorations. Further, it is key for emotional attunement and empathetic resonance (Ilundáin-Agurruza 2011). Much like the hub's

355

emptiness and the space between the spokes make the wheel spin faster and more efficiently, a lively yet channeled imagination allows the world of sports and performance to flourish in ever creative ways. Imagination works within and without the spaces that nothingness as emptiness opens up. The affordances and constraints unique to sports' rule-defined inefficiencies or the expressive and kinetic repertoires of performances structure our imaginative flights much as the way the resistance of the air enables Kant's dove to fly (essay 3). Great performers find openings where others fail to see them; as if by wizardry, they imagine 'implausible possibilities' and enact them. Spanish novelist Javier Marías writing about the 2002 football European Cup remarks how as the first half came to a colorless end there was a moment when the ball simply hang mid-air. The ball's path had become but an uninteresting impossibility to all, players, fans, and commentators. Until Zinedine Zidane saw it come down. 'Only then did Zidane understand the chance, the improvised, unexpected nature of the ball: supernatural, a gift fallen from the sky. He did the rest. At times he also seems to have fallen from the sky. That's how he recognized it, and the gift became flesh, and then verb' (Marías 2008, 72–3). The realm of emptiness holds more good plays yet.

Kōng, influenced by Buddhism, specifically, conceives of emptiness as *śūnyatā*, शून्यता. Basically, obviating doctrinal and arcane differences among various Buddhist schools, this refers to the emptiness that underlies all worldly phenomena, and which causes the dependent origination that Buddhist practice seeks to overcome. Meditation is partly a soteriological process toward liberation. This is the second sense of emptiness: the cultivation of an empty stage of bodymind that seeks the realization that all is illusion, and aims at *nirvāṇa*. Victor Mair, in the extensive notes to his translation of the *Zhuangzi*, relates 'emptiness' in the Zhuangzian text to the Buddhist conception, stating that it 'is reminiscent of the Indian concept of *śūnyatā*, which is the void or nothingness conceived as a symbol of brahman [*sic.*] (the divine reality of the universe). In Buddhist Hybrid Chinese, the same word used by Chuang Tzu here for "emptiness" is used to translate' *Śūnyatā* (1994, 6). Nishida drinks deeply from both of these sources, and being quite familiar with both the *Laozi* and the *Zhuangzi* (Krummel 2014), he also includes Daoist innuendoes into his views on nothingness. Of course, these are posterior associations and developments that are not directly related to the perfected *zhēnrén* or Zhuangzi's ideas. Regardless, the *zhēnrén*, as superb performer, practically operates with (in) both senses of emptiness, Daoist and Buddhist: he spontaneously roams the world compassionately and selflessly, and with no attachment to worldly affairs.

Varela relates the emptiness achieved through Buddhist practice to expert performance, 'Every expert knows this sensation of emptiness well: in the West, for example, athletes, artists, and craftsmen have always insisted that self-consciousness interferes with optimal performance' (1999, 35). What he means by self-consciousness here can be contentious. If he intends that the performer is acting unawares, in Dreyfusian automatism, as his earlier comments on coping and allusions to Dreyfus seem to suggest, then this is not correct of expert performance, as has been argued throughout this work. There is always at least a pre-reflective sense of being the agent who is acting and experiencing, in addition to the dynamic shifting among the conscious, subpersonal, and fringe levels of awareness. Interestingly, his very phrasing shows that there is not a complete lack of awareness. For, if experts *know* the sensation, then they must be aware in *some* sense. They can claim to be the enactors and the actors, maintaining phenomenologically a sense of agency and one of ownership (essay 7). In short, there

HOLISM AND THE CULTIVATION OF EXCELLENCE IN SPORTS AND PERFORMANCE

is always a pre-reflective awareness, a phenomenological sense that the experience is ours. Superb performers are particularly deft at working mindfully within the empty spaces that are invisible to others. *Xū* characterizes this.

Xū figures prominently in the *Zhuangzi*. It marks the flawless *zhēnrén* and her embodiment of superlative performance. In the passage cited above, 'The Way gathers in emptiness alone. Emptiness is the fasting of the mind,' the original text uses the sinograph for *xū*: '唯 道集 虛 。虛者, 心齋也' (*Zhuangzi Yinde*, 9/4/28; ICS *Zhuangzi* 4/10/2-3, my emphasis*)*. But, this does not settle matters as to how to translate or interpret it. Most translators opt for 'emptiness,' but as just posed, 'emptiness' can take varied Daoist and Buddhist meanings (the latter of which would be anachronistic ascriptions to much of the *Zhuangzi*, definitely to the inner chapters with which we are working primarily). Besides, there are more possibilities for *xū*: the dictionary lists 'empty', 'void', 'unoccupied', 'false', or 'weak,' and the Chinese Text Project adds 'worthless' and 'hollow' to the list.[12] Zhuangzi's revaluation of the useless and *wuwei* offsets the negative connotations of 'worthless,' 'weak,' and even 'false' (essay 5). For now, the most fruitful senses to consider, in addition to 'emptiness,' are 'void,' and 'empty.' But, in keeping with the use of the gerund to emphasize the dynamics of holism (essay 7), it is best to reformulate them as 'voiding' and 'emptying': these reflect the active in-the-moment-by-moment responsiveness of agents to a situation. They spontaneously, instantly, and successfully meet its needs (which practically differ for different individuals). Taking advantage of habit-honed skills, and unimpeded by explicit and exhaustive rational processes yet at least pre-reflectively aware, they operate within the spaces that a naturalness and freedom from concerns provide.

Fraser explains that *xū* 'supposedly allows us to employ nature-given capacities without conscious ambition or distraction, clearing the heart so that we can respond promptly and directly to changing circumstances' (2014, 204). In the state of *xū*, the *zhēnrén* attains a 'blank, clear, or open psychological state' for Fraser (2014, 198).[13] 'Wandering' (遊, *yóu*) is the way that *xū* manifests itself. Through it, the superior person fluidly, spontaneously, and in a joyful and carefree manner approaches performance and engages the world. In the cases of virtuosos, the unification of all enactive domains is achieved with *apparent* ease (apparent because it is built on relentless dedication and habit). This wandering results in and is performed in a multiplicity of ways: 'The implication is that different agents, with different capacities, may flourish in a variety of ways' wandering and forgetting in a state of *xū* that is 'central to psychophysical health, personal flourishing, and judicious, efficacious action' (Fraser 2014, 201).

This flexible platform is crucial for a holistic ethics that purports to adapt to the talents of the performers, as argued with Ortega while placing the onus of striving or flourishing on them. Fasting of the heart-mind is also tied to the idea of 'forgetting', 忘 (*wàng*). This forgetting is a method to achieve the state of *xū*, that is, of embodying an active and creative emptying. In one way, it is about emptying the heart of outward worries and distractions to maintain an inward equilibrium (Fraser 2014). The fundamental agreement between Fraser's discerning interpretation of *xū* in the *Zhuangzi* and ours acknowledged, there is a critical point of departure concerning the level of awareness in expert performance and how this actually works as 'forgetting'. Before fully endorsing the fulsomeness of emptiness, Zhuangzian and enactive, we need to address this predicament.

The very term, 'forgetting', as used in the *Zhuangzi*, or at least Western translations and scholarly interpretations, strongly suggests a forsaking of conscious processes and elements. Most interpreters follow this. Billeter explains expertise in the *Zhuangzi* stressing an automatized unconsciousness that allows us to learn how to ride a bicycle, writing of 'the day when I learned to ride a bicycle. I had to learn how to stomp alternating between the two pedals, to maintain the equilibrium by modifying the position of the handlebars, and to ride in as straight a line as feasible' (2010, 57, my translation).[14] This becomes internalized and forgotten in the limbs, so to speak. Fraser's conception and analysis of forgetting in performance agrees with this, speaking of us as 'virtuoso walkers' that 'need not attend to our shoes' since when they fit we forget them (Fraser 2014, 207) (see also essay 8, note 9).

Billeter explains Zhuangzian expertise, which he calls 'superior knowledge' (*connaissance supérieure*), in terms of forgetting as a 'way of knowing *because* one has forgotten' (2010, 59, my translation and emphasis). Fraser speaks of the 'blank, receptive state of "forgetting" from which her actions ensue' (ibid. 207). This can be exemplified by basic skills being integrated in the acting bodymind. Now, the very term, 'forgetting', as used in the *Zhuangzi*, or at least Western translations and scholarly interpretations, strongly suggests a forsaking of conscious processes and support of automatism while dispensing with or minimizing the role of said processes in skilled action. Overemphasizing subpersonal and automatic processes to the detriment of a more holistic and ecologically situated model leads to a tension between duly integrated skills and creative control and awareness of highly skilled performance. This is relevant because it lies at the juncture between average performance by most people, and experts' superior performance, especially those who stand out across the whole spectrum of domains. The latter operates with a wider and deeper register. Considering this now also permits to directly connect previous key claims to the Asian outlook.

Fraser equates the kind of superior performance that engages holistic and enactive processes with transcending self-awareness, self-consciousness, or self-conscious cognition (Fraser 2014, 205ff.). Nonetheless, self-awareness is never quite transcended phenomenologically, as he realizes. Barring fractured action or pathological cases, there is no complete transcendence of self-consciousness, but rather a sense of both agency and ownership, as well as a pre-reflective sense of self that accounts for us 'knowing' it is *us* who are undergoing the experience. Fraser also describes forgetting as the automatic and 'instantaneous way a skilled virtuoso responds to her context' (ibid. 207). Efficacious performance by someone very skilled happens 'because his skills transform along with the things he encounters, requiring *no conscious monitoring* form the heart' (ibid. 206, my emphasis). (For him, the heart grounds cognitive processes.) What's more, stressing the negative role of consciousness, he specifies that conscious attention 'indicates that activity is not proceeding smoothly; the heart is engaged in 'checking' or "monitoring" and thus no longer "empty" (Ibid.) Similarly, Billeter explains that in the *Zhuangzi* humans' intentional and conscious action is the source of error, failure, exhaustion, and death, while the fulsome, necessary, and spontaneous activity of animals and superior persons 'gives rise to efficacy, life, and replenishment' (Billeter 2010, 53, my translation). Leading interpreters, philosophers, and translators, whom Fraser and Billeter represent, theorize expert skilled and virtuous performance, particularly at the highest level, as subpersonal and in terms of automatized skills to a large extent. This is unsurprising, since as detailed in essay 7, there *is* forgetting and integration of skills. Acknowledging this does not mean we should jump into a subpersonally automatized bandwagon.

In this way, Fraser's discerning reading of the *Zhuangzi* highlights another facet aligned with holistic and enactive achievement: the need to make room for experts' spontaneous and productive engagements, which needs a measure of control, attentional focus, and *awareness*. Aware of the need for keen focus and attention, Fraser describes a master carpenter forgetting limbs and body, 'his skill concentrated and outside distractions having drained away,' who 'is *able to discern* wood of exceptional quality and match his unadulterated powers with the natural grain of the wood' (2014, 206, my emphasis). Fraser realizes that mindless coping is not fully adequate, yet the aforementioned tension between the subpersonal level, attention, and awareness is clear when he writes, 'Our intuitions and skills continue to guide action, albeit *unconsciously* and with a heightened sensitivity to novel, creative paths. [...] Zhuangist emptiness (xu) is *not wholesale psychological nothingness*, but a state similar to that of a jazz player improvising a solo, both taking cues and inciting responses from the other musicians' (2014, 210, my emphasis). This tension is clearest when he specifies that, 'To find an effective course, the empty, mirroring heart must respond in ways that stem partially from an awareness of the self and its relation to the environment, even if this *awareness* is unconscious' (Ibid., my emphasis). Here and elsewhere, he duly tries to preserve ecological breadth and some role for our agency by accounting for a broad environment that goes beyond the performer's inward processes, as his jazz player exemplifies. Nonetheless, it is problematic to advance both subpersonal and automatic processes alongside an agency, attention, and awareness that somehow are receptive to spontaneity and creative intuitions. There is more to expertise, particularly formidable one as has been argued extensively throughout *Skillful Striving*.

DISCLOSURE STATEMENT

No potential conflict of interest was reported by the author.

NOTES

1. Chuang Tzu and Watson (1968, 58), my emphasis.
2. As mentioned earlier, translation of ancient Chinese texts is extremely challenging. Relying on various translations partially redresses this. Presently, I use the 2014 Chinese/English Side-by-Side edition of the *Zhuangzi* (2014). The original text for this passage is also accessible online; the pertinent section cited above is available at the Chinese Text Project (Sturgeon 2014) at: http://ctext.org/zhuangzi/man-in-the-world-associated-with. I have correlated the original texts as per the *Zhuangzi Yinde (A Concordance to Chuang Tzu)*, Harvard-Yenching Institute Sinological Index Series, Supplement no. 20 (Cambridge MA: Harvard University Press, 1956) [洪業主編《莊子引得》, 哈佛燕京學社引得特刊第20號, 哈佛燕京學社引得編纂處], and the *A Concordance to the Zhuangzi* (莊子逐字索引), ed. D.C. Lau, Ho Che Wah and Chen Fong Ching. ICS series (Hong Kong: Commercial Press, 2000) [何志華, 劉殿爵, 陳方正 '莊子逐字索引' (香港: 商務印書館, 2000]. Locations of the textual references can also be determined using the Chinese Text Project website. When referencing the concordance, the letters and numerals correspond to the version, then book, page, and line, respectively. For example, ICS Zhuangzi (4/10/2) corresponds to the ICS version and concordance of the *Zhuangzi* and book 4, page 10,

line 2. The original concordance for the cited passage in the Harvard-Yenching *Zhuangzi Yinde* comprises from 9/4/26 to 9/4/28; in the ICS Zhuangzi it goes from 4/10/1 to 4/10/3.

3. For translations of this passage that are not referenced in the main text presently, see Höchsmann, Guorong and Zhuangzi (2007, 103), Legge (1891), available online at http://nothingistic.org/library/chuangtzu/. See also Zhuangzi and Legge 2014.

4. All literal translations for all three characters and other Chinese characters, unless otherwise noted, are from The Concise English-Chinese and Chinese-English Dictionary (2004), edited by Martin H. Manser. These are also correlated with the online Chinese Dictionary, http://www.chinese-dictionary.org.

5. This consummate individual is also referred to as 至人, *zhìrén*, (from 'most' as an emphatic superlative in this context) (see Fraser 2014, 203). The *Zhuangzi's* Chapter 5, which centers on the consummate individual, uses 真人, *zhēnrén* nine times. See Harvard-Yenching Zhuangzi Yinde: 15/6/4; ICS Zhuangzi 6/15/32 for the first time the term is used in said chapter. As Chuang-Tzu and Watson points out in a footnote (1968, 79), there is quite a bit of controversy as to the interpretation of 'true man' in the *Zhuangzi*, and the particular attributes associated with him in this chapter, some of which seem to be an addition by a Legalist philosopher (who would endow it with Confucian virtues rather than Daoist). Given the broader scope taken in essay 5, *Zhuangzi—Playful Wanderer*, and that presently *zhēnrén* is engaged as a referent for a holistic and enactive expert, these issues do not affect our account.

6. Billeter writes that this true person (*homme vrai*): 'is the person who is not embarrassed by any conventions, who is not lessened, who is a totality, and is directed to the whole person' (*c'est l'homme qu'aucune convention n'embarrasse ni se diminue, qui est entier et qui s'adresse à l'homme entier*) (1994, 317, my translation).

7. Since this passage is rather straightforward, one source suffices. This hits close to home personally. Not even close to Hui Shi's talents as debater or otherwise, this perennial running around in pursuit of … what? does capture this author's temperament and peripatetically hectic ways.

8. See also Ilundáin-Agurruza (2008).

9. Legge (1891) is the one exception, who translates it as 'freedom.' His decidedly Christian outlook influences his choice if words, at times instilling them with foreign connotations to the original Daoist context.

10. The original text, which uses 無, *wu*, is :三十輻，共一轂，當其無，有車之用。埏埴以為器，當其無，有器之用。鑿戶牖以為室，當其無，有室之用。故有之以為利，無之以為用。 Available at http://ctext.org/dao-de-jing Accessed 20 December 2014 (my emphasis).

11. See *The Online Liddell-Scott-Jones Greek-English Lexicon* (2009).

12. See http://ctext.org/dictionary.pl?if=en&char=虛 Accessed 18 December 2014.

13. Fraser's penetrating chapter (2014) was unavailable until after essay 5, *Zhuangzi—Playful Wanderer*, had already been submitted, unfortunately too late to duly incorporate it. His main concern is to interpret the *Zhuangzi* in relation to Foucault's ethics of self-cultivation. Nonetheless, there is a remarkable and congratulatory affinity between Fraser's interpretation and this project's understanding of the *Zhuangzi* and overall holistic framework.

14. Billeter's very description belies the fact that riding a bicycle in the way he characterizes it is not how an expert would do it. Expert cyclists do not use the handlebars to stay upright or even turn; as speeds increase and there is momentum, they lean, handlebars straight, into the turn as a unit with the bicycle.

REFERENCES

BILLETER, J.F. 1994. Étude sur Sept Dialogues du Zhuangzi [Study of seven dialogues of Zhuangzi]. *Études Chinoises* [Chinese Studies] XIII (1–2): 295–343.

———. 2010. *Leçons sur Tchouang-tseu* [Lessons on Zhuangzi]. Paris: Éditions Allia.

CHOZAN, N. 2006. *The demon sermon of the martial arts*. Translated by W.S. Wilson. Tokyo: Kodansa International.

CHUANG-TZŬ and A.C. GRAHAM. 1981. *Chuang-Tzŭ: The seven inner chapters and other writings from the book Chuang-Tzŭ*. London: Allen & Unwin.

CHUANG-TZŬ and B. WATSON. 1968. *The complete works of Chuang Tzu*. New York, NY: Columbia University Press.

FRASER, C. 2014. Heart-fasting, forgetting, and using the heart like a mirror. In *Nothingness in Asian Philosophy*, edited by J. Liu and D. Berger. London: Routledge: 197–212.

HARVARD-YENCHING INSTITUTE. 1956. *Zhuangzi Yinde* [A concordance to Chuang Tzu]. Harvard-Yenching Institute Sinological Index Series, Supplement no. 20. Cambridge, MA: Harvard University Press.

HOBERMAN, J. 1986. *The Olympic crisis: Sports, politics, and the moral order*. New Rochelle, NY: A.D. Caratzas.

HÖCHSMANN, H., Y. GUORONG, and ZHUANGZI. 2007. *Zhuangzi*. New York, NY: Pearson Longman.

ILUNDÁIN-AGURRUZA, J. 2008. Athletic bodies and the bodies of athletes: A critique of the sporting build. *Proteus: A Journal of Ideas* 25 (2): 15–22.

———. 2011. Weaving the magic: Philosophy, sports and literature. In *Philosophy of sport: International perspectives*, edited by A. Hardman and C. Jones. Newcastle upon Tyne: Cambridge Scholars Publishing: 50–71.

———. 2012. Go tell the Spartans: Honor, courage, and excellence. In *The Olympics and philosophy*, edited by H. Reid and M. Austin. Lexington, KY: Kentucky University Press: 68–85.

KAAG, J. 2012. Paddling in the stream of consciousness: describing the movement of Jamesian Inquiry. In *Pragmatism and the philosophy of sport*, edited by R. Lally, D. Anderson, and J. Kaag. London: Lexington Books: 47–61.

KRUMMEL, J.W.M. 2014. Anontology of the issue of being and nothing in Kitarō Nishida. In *Nothingness in Asian Philosophy*, edited by J. Liu and D. Berger. London: Routledge: 263–83.

LAO TZU. 1996. *Taoteching*. Translated by Red Pine (Bill Porter). San Francisco, CA: Mercury House.

———. 2012. *Tao Te Ching: An all new translation*. Translated by W. Scott Wilson. Boston, MA: Shambhala.

LAU, D.C., H.C. Wah, and C.F. Ching, eds. 2000. *A concordance to the Zhuangzi*. ICS Series. Hong Kong: Commercial Press.

LEGGE, J. 1891. The writings of Chuang Tzu. In *The sacred books of the east*. Available at http://nothingistic.org/library/chuangtzu/ (accessed 1 December 2014).

LIU, X. 2014. The notion of Wu or nonbeing as the root of the universe and a guide for life. In *Nothingness in Asian philosophy*, edited by J. Liu and D. Berger. London: Routledge: 151–65.

MAIR, V.H. 1994. Introduction and notes for a complete translation of the Chuang Tzu. *Sino-Platonic Papers* 48: 1–147.

MANSER, M.H., ed. 2004. *Concise English-Chinese and Chinese-English Dictionary*. 3rd ed. Oxford: Oxford University Press & The Commercial Press.

HOLISM AND THE CULTIVATION OF EXCELLENCE IN SPORTS AND PERFORMANCE

MARÍAS, J. 2008. Fallen from the sky. In *The global game: Writers on Soccer*, edited by J. Turnbull, J. Satterlee, and L. Raab. Lincoln, NE: University of Nebraska Press: 72–3.

ORTEGA Y GASSET, J. 1961. *History as a system and other essays toward a philosophy of history*. New York, NY: Norton.

———. 2004a. Carta a Un Jóven Argentino que Estudia Filosofía [Letter to a young Argentine philosophy student]. *Obras Completas* Vol. II. Madrid: Taurus: 467–71.

———. 2004b. El Origen Deportivo del Estado [The Sportive Origin of the State]. *Obras Completas* Vol. II. Madrid: Taurus: 707–19.

PREGADIO, F., ed. 2011. *The Routledge encyclopedia of Taoism*. Vols. 1 and 2. London: Routledge.

STURGEON, D., ed. 2014. Zhuangzi. *Chinese Text Project*. Available at http://ctext.org (accessed 12 September 2014).

SUITS, B. 1990. *The grasshopper: Game, life, and Utopia*. Boston, MA: David R. Godine.

THE ONLINE LIDDELL-SCOTT-JONES GREEK-ENGLISH LEXICON. 2009. Available at http://www.tlg.uci.edu (accessed 27 December 2014).

VARELA, F. 1999. *Ethical know-how: Action, wisdom, and cognition*. Stanford, CA: Stanford University Press.

YU, T.-D. 2014. The inside/out connectivity of Taichiquan and the body without organs. Unpublished manuscript.

ZHUANGZI and J. LEGGE. 2014. *Zhuangzi - Bilingual Edition Chinese/English Side-by-Side*. Public Domain Book. NP: Lionshare Media.

ZHUANGZI and B. ZIPORYN. 2009. *Zhuangzi: Essential writings with selections from traditional commentaries*. Indianapolis, IN: Hackett.

Index

acting intuition 250–251, 256
Action in Perception 139
Aggerholm, Kenneth 183
aikidō 234, 242
ai nuke and *ai uchi* 258
aletheia 77
Alexander, F. M. 50, 55
Alexander Technique (AT) method 50
Ames, Roger 99
amplitudinal quality 160
animate wisdom 2
Anquetil, Jacques 224
Aristotle 3, 22–23, 105
Armstrong, Lance 76–77
Art as Experience 53
articulating experience 325–328
The Art of Fielding (Harbach) 6, 105, 199, 208
asceticism, Jamesian analysis of 38
athletes: *dao* and 95–96; disabilities and 115
AT method *see* Alexander Technique method
attendance, kenosis and 310–315
attitude, lusory 107–108
authority 3
automatization 248, 254, 257
autopoietic enactivism 138, 144

Barbery, Muriel 327
Beall, E.B. 128
Bendix, Erik 162
Bennett, M.R. 129
Bergman, Dave 153–154
Best, David 15, 159–160
Billeter, Jean Francois 100, 102, 104; on deliberate and conscious movement 105
bodhisattva 292
bodymind 19; Dewey, John 51–52, 58–60; in Eastern–Western comparative framework 290; Japanese *see* Japanese integrative bodymind
bodymind integration, Ortega y Gasset, José 79–87
Bohr, Niels 93

Boklov, Jan 115
Brahman, dao and 95
brain dualism 128, 132
Breivik, Gunnar 14, 18, 72, 74, 183
Buddhism 286
bunbu ryodō 233, 246
bushido 6
bushidō 233, 245, 259
Butler, Gerard 207

calligraphy 104
Callois, Roger 67
Carlsen, Magnus 124
'carnal soul' 80
Carter, Dustin 115
central pattern generator (CPG) 186
ceteris paribus 11
Chabacanería 75–76
chance, sports, and role of 111
Chariots of Fire 296
Chemero, A. 128
Chinese Buddhism 94
choking (in sports): competition 207–210; consciousness 200, 203–207; distraction theory 201; Dreyfusian experts 203–207; environmental conditions 212–213; fitness and exertion 213–214; learning from failure 222–225; mindless coping 203–207; moderate control 200; motivation 202; phenomenological model 215–218; self-monitoring theory 201, 202; semantic analysis 200; slumps 218–219; sports specificity 211–212; team choking 219–221; training 207–210
Chuang-Tzu *see* Zhuangzi
cognition model: computation 124–127; reductionism 127–132; representation 132–136
Cognitive Neuroscience of Action, The 133
cognitivism 123, 125, 126; computational 126; theory of automatization and 125
communities and norms 319–325

INDEX

competition 207–210
'comprehensive reflection' 297
computational automatization 126;
 sports and 126
computational conundrums 124–127
computationalism 124–127
Confucianism 94, 286
consciousness 127, 200, 203–207, 216;
 fringe of 42–43, 58; Jamesian analysis of 45;
 reflective 45n4
Contraria sunt complementa 93
control, spontaneity and 105
CPG *see* central pattern generator
Crandell, M. 108, 113; on sports 113
Crease, Robert 17
Critique of Judgment 14
cultivated spontaneity 107

Dannenberg, E. 113–114
Danto, Arthur 104
dao 94–99; athletes and 95–96; *Brahman*
 and 95; described 95; Laozi on 94; performers
 and 95–96; spontaneous movement and 105
Daodejing 94
Daoism 4, 94–99, 286; doping policy and 97;
 harmony and 110–111; life and 109; radical
 sport thinking and 97
Daoist *phronesis* 98
de 95
Deep Blue victory 124
deliberate and conscious movement,
 spontaneous movement and 105
deliberative process 286
Democracy and Education 54–55
de Sales, Frances 70
Deshimaru Taishen 110, 263, 266
Dewey, J. 3, 4
Dewey, John 18, 49, 127, 130, 131; body-mind
 58–60; on habit and experience 49–55;
 philosophy of mind 58–60; self-cultivation
 and perfectionism 55–58
Dick, Philip K. 128
Dietrich, Anne 44
Dietrich, Arne 127
disability 112; as fullness of power 111–116;
 sports and 114–116; technological
 advancements and 115
distraction theories (DTs) 201
dō see Japanese *dō*
doping policy: Daoist solution 97; sports and 97
Downes, Stephen 13
Dreyfus, Hubert 3, 125, 203–205
Dreyfusian model 203–207
DTs *see* distraction theories
dualism 4–5

Duque, Orlando 235
dying, fear of 109–110
dynamic systems theory 105

Eastern account, of performance, normativity,
 and cognition 286–294
EC *see* embodied cognition
ecological facet, of holism 20
egoism 110
Eichberg, Henning 27
Eiger, Unroped 110
embodied cognition (EC) 123, 136–138
emotional process 40
emptiness 354–357
enactive wisdom 1, 2
enactivism 138–146
energy: flow 100; Western concept of 100
Engstrom, David 93
epistemological intelligence 2
epoché 155
Ericsson, Anders 257, 258
Eriksen, Jørgen 206
*Ethical Know-how: Action, Wisdom, and
 Cognition* 284
Euclid's theorem 82
excellence 23–26, 29, 30
exemplary skills: meaningful movement,
 varieties of 174–179; thick holism 172, 173;
 virtues 172–173
existential soteriology 2
Experience and Nature 52
explicit awareness 123, 125
extended cognition 137

'fasting of the mind' 98
fasting, *xin* and 103
Fernández Anaya, Iván 178
Firestein, Richard 124–125
fitness and exertion 213–214
Flynn, Erin 304–305
'folk talk' 123
Foucault, Michel 111
Frankfurt, Henry 76
freediving 59–60
free will 106; Gallagher on 106
fringe of consciousness, James,
 William 20, 42–43
functionalism 123

Gallagher, Shaun 3, 80–81, 84, 106, 126–128,
 159, 163, 164, 167, 169
Gibson, J.J. 126
gnostic truths 2
gnostic wisdom 2
Go Rin No Sho (Book of Five Rings) 243

INDEX

Guttmann, Allen 69
Gwin, Peter 109

Hadot, Pierre 17
Harbach, Chad 6, 105
harmony, Daoism and 110–111
Harrison, Victoria 110
Hay, J. 100
Heidegger, M. 3
Heinrich, Bernd 206
Hemmestad, Liv 101
Henry Skrimshander 199, 266
History as a System 73
history, situatedness and 315–319
Hodskins, Zach 115
holistic and enactive ethics, of spontaneous
    and superior performance 282–286
Hopsicker, Pete 46n7
Howe, Leslie 78
Huizi 93
Human Nature and Conduct 49
Humphreys, Joe 66
Husserl, E. 3
Husserl, Edmund 216, 217
Hutto, Dan 139–146, 162, 305

idea of self 101
imitation 105
imitative spontaneity 105
Induráin, Miguel 10
'the inner chapters' 94
An Inquiry into the Good (1990) 250
instrumental rationality 307
interpretive process 157
Issai Chozansi 246

James, William 3, 37, 216, 250; fringe of
    consciousness 20, 42–43; habit, character
    building 37–40; psychology and philosophy
    of mind 41–45
Japanese Arts of Self-Cultivation, The 245
Japanese *dō*: Aristotelian framework 246, 248;
    automatization 248; *bushidō* 245; *dōjō* 242;
    keikō 249; *mumonkan* 242; normativity of
    245; self-awareness 249; *shugyo* 242–245, 249
Japanese integrative bodymind: *karada* 235,
    236; *ki (qi)* 241; *kokoro* 237; *mi* and *mi bun*
    237–238; "right presence of mind" 241;
    seishin 235; *shinshin* 236; *shinshin ichinyo*
    236, 240; *shintai* 235, 240; stages of 240;
    taxonomy 235
Jeannerod, Marc 133–135, 140
Johnson, Mark 41, 46n5, 163
Jones, Dakota 309–310
Jornet Burgada, Kilian 306

Kaag, John 45
Kahanamoku, Duke 282
Kalokagathia 177, 178
Kalon 5, 177, 178
karada 235, 236
Kasparov, Garry 124
kata 295–296
keiken 250, 253, 327
keikō 249
Kelso, J. Scott 93, 128
kendō 258, 265, 267
kendōka 237, 246
kenjutsu 6, 259
kenosis 310–315
kinesthesia 158, 159, 325–328
kinetic signature, skillful fluency 187, 188
kokoro 237, 239
Kōng 356
Kono Yoshinori 238
Kretchmar, S. 21, 113, 116
Kuang-Ming Wu 94
kyudō 241, 271

Lally, Richard 39
Laozi 94–96, 108, 110
Larsen, Nepper 158
Lasaga Medina, José 64
Levy, David 124
Libet, Benjamin 106
Lie Yukou 109
Liezi *see* Lie Yukou
linear quality 160
Liu Xiang 223
Loland, Sigmund 18–19, 95
Longfellow, H.W. 1
Long, Lutz 314
Lowe, M.J. 128
Luria, Aleksandr 108, 182–183
lusory attitude 107–108; meditation and 108

MaCarthur, Ellen 240
MacAskill, Danny 264, 288
Machado, Antonio 30–31
Mangan, Bruce 37, 42–44
Maraldo, John 251, 252
Markman, Art 43
martial artists, disabilities and 115
martial arts, as social practice 97
Martínková, Irena 155
McDougall, Christopher 306
McEnroe, John 198, 222
McFee, Graham 15
McNamara, Garrett 53
McNamee, Mike 13, 30, 73, 78, 307, 319, 324
means/ends relations 306–310

INDEX

meditation, lusory attitude and 108
Meditations on Hunting 65
Meditations on Quixote 72
Menard, Pierre 16
Merckx, Eddie 224
Merleau-Ponty, M. 3
mi and *mi bun* 237–238
Michener, James 75
Minamoto Ryoen, 295–297
mindless coping 203–207
Moe, Vegard 125
mono no aware 239
Motoori Norinaga 239
motor representation 134
mu concept 252
Musashi Miyamoto 180, 243
mushin 104, 352; automatization 255,
    257, 258; consciousness 256; deliberation
    258, 264; effortless attention 255;
    "everyday mind" 256; *kendō* 258; *kenjutsu*
    259; mindful awareness 260; operative
    awareness 260; performers in 261;
    spontaneity of 264; unconsciousness 255;
    visualization 265
Myin, Eric 139–146, 305
'Mysterious Function' 301

Naess, Arne 95
National Geographic 122
naturalism 1
neurophenomenology 170
neuroscience, sports and 125
Nie Que 98–99
ningen 324
Nishida Kitaro 6
Nishida Kitarō (unity in difference): absolute
    nothingness 252; acting intuition 250–251;
    keiken and *taiken* 250, 253; *mu* concept 252;
    ordinary experience 254
Ni Tsan 104
normative 'gnoseology' 2
nothingness 355

Oakley, Annie 291, 294
O'Bannon, Allen 265
Origin of the Work of Art, The 333
Ortega 100, 111; on sports 113
Ortega y Gasset, José 3, 4, 24–25; bodymind
    integration 79–87; environment role 82–87;
    overview of 63–64; philosophical landscape
    64–65; philosophical perfectionism 70–79;
    philosophy of life 65–66; sportive activity
    67–69
O'Shea, Michael 157
Oshima, Harold 99–100, 111
Owens, Jesse 314

Paladins 57–58
Paralympics 114
Parry, Jim 155
Parviainen, Jaana 115
perfected person 99, 111
perfectionism 23–25
performance-centered pursuits 25
performative endeavors 10–18
performers: *dao* and 95–96;
    disabilities and 115
performer's perspective 10–18
performing arts, as social practice 97
Perrin, Nöel 317, 318
personal perfection 24
perspectivism 111; Zhuangzi 116
phenomenological descriptions 127
'philosophical dark horses' 4
philosophical landscape, Ortega y Gasset,
    José 64–65
philosophical perfectionism 70–79
philosophy of life, Ortega y Gasset, José 65–66
philosophy of mind: Dewey, John 58–60;
    James, William 41–45
phronesis 2, 98; Daoist 98
physico-chemical interactions 59
Piccinini, Gualtiero 124
Pistorius, Oscar 115
pneuma 100; *vs. qi* 100
pole-vaulter 44
Potter, Dean 109
Poulidor, Raymond 224
preservation, of skill 96
principle of parsimony 42
Principles of Psychology 37, 41
private language argument 328–333
proficient skill 26, 28
projectional quality 160
proprioception 158, 159

qi 100, 104, 352–353; *vs. pneuma* 100
qualia 327
Quammen, David 321
Quixote, Don 75, 76

radical enactive cognition (REC) 141–143
radical enactivism 5, 123
rational intuition 298–299
REC *see* radical enactive cognition
recortadores de toros 110
reductionism 127–132
reductive retreat 127–132
reflection 286
reflective consciousness 106
reflective intuition 294–306
'reflex' movements 106
"regimes or stages of activity" 102

INDEX

Reid, Heather 28, 71–72, 79
representation: human mind and 123; in neuroscience 123
representationalism 132–136
Revolt of the Masses, The 73
Riding the Wind 301
risk 110
'risky perfectionism' 77
Rodríguez Huéscar, Antonio 65
Rohrer, Finlo 124

Sainz, Carlos 206
Samurai Tsunetomo Yamamoto 223
Sansone, David 69
Scheler, Max 56, 57
Searle, J. 125, 128
seisan kata 297
seishin 235, 244
self-awareness 249, 251
self-control 107
self-cultivation 40; Dewey, John 55–58
self-focus theories (SFTs) 201, 202
sensei 103
sensorimotor process 161
Seok, Bongrae 286
SFTs *see* self-focus theories
Sheehan, George 12, 54
Sheets-Johnstone, Maxine 3, 12, 78, 108, 110, 158, 173–175
shen 100, 103
Shi Dejian 109–110
shinshin (shinshin ichinyo) 236, 240, 251
shintai 235, 236, 240
Shorter Oxford English Dictionary on Historical Principles, The (1964) 311
shugyo 6, 242–245, 249
Shu, Savvy 113
situated approach 315–319
situated cognition 137
skill development 102
skillful fluency 180–188
skillful performance 153–155; animation 163–165; expert performance 165–172; movement and skill dynamics 156–163; phenomenology 155–156
Slater, Kelly 152, 180, 289
Slingerland, Edward 101, 107–108
slumps 218–219
Socrates 98
spectator sports 15
Spectator, The 72
spontaneity 103; control and 105; cultivated 107; unbidden 107–108
spontaneous movement: deliberate and conscious movement and 105; sports and 107
sportive activity 67–69

sports: computational automatization and 126; Crandell on 113; disability and 114–116; doping policy and 97; neuroscience and 125; Ortega on 113; philosophy 123; role of chance in 111; as social practice 97; spontaneous movement and 107
sports face-off 266–271
sport skill 25–27
sports specificity 211–212
Standal, Oyvind 101
Stoll, Oliver 44, 127
Striving, as skillful, 245, 266, 292, 293, 304–5
sui generis 80
summum bonum 295
śūnyatā 356
sustained attention 211

tàijíquán 352
taiken 250, 253, 327
Takuan Soho 256, 261
Taylor, Charles 99
Taylor, Kim 248
team choking 219–221
Tengu Geijutsuron 246
tensional quality 160
Thagard, Paul 123
The Concept of Mind 17
thick holism 1, 2, 4, 18–22, 99, 288; exemplary skills and skillful fluency 172, 173; radical enactive cognition 143
Thomen, Carl 182
Thomson, Garrett 153–155, 306
Tokitsu, Kenji 326
Torres, Cesar 179
Torrey, Theodore 131
training, choke prevention 207–210
Tureztky, Philip 153–155

Ueshiba Morihei 242
unbidden spontaneity 107–108
unity in difference *see* Nishida Kitarō (unity in difference)
utilitarian attitude 66

Varela, Francisco 136, 182, 284–286
virtue ethics 282
VO2 Max 170

Wallace, James 24–26
Wang Ni 98–99
Weber, Max 66
wei 95
weiwuwei 95
Wertz, Spencer 156, 157, 163, 266, 267
White, Shaun 153
Will, Frederick 322

INDEX

William James-Pragmatic Pioneer 4
wu 95
Wuren, Bohun 109
wushu 109
wuwei 95–96, 98, 101, 107, 114

xin: described 99; fasting and 103; Oshima on 99–100; Zhuangzi 100
xing 100

Yagyū Munenori 260
Yamamoto Tsunetomo 242
yang 95
yin 95

zanshin 267
Zeami Motoyiko 104
Zen Buddhism 6
zhēnrén 351–352
Zhuangzi 3–4; on disability 112; 'fasting of the mind' 98; idea of self 101; on importance of flexibility in routine 98; introduction 93–94; on perfected person 99, 111; perspectivism 116; view on life 111; *xin* 100
Zhuangzi 94, 99, 108
zìrán 352